Research Anthology on Virtual Environments and Building the Metaverse

Information Resources Management Association
USA

Volume I

IGI Global
PUBLISHER of TIMELY KNOWLEDGE

Published in the United States of America by
    IGI Global
    Engineering Science Reference (an imprint of IGI Global)
    701 E. Chocolate Avenue
    Hershey PA, USA 17033
    Tel: 717-533-8845
    Fax: 717-533-8661
    E-mail: cust@igi-global.com
    Web site: http://www.igi-global.com

Library of Congress Cataloging-in-Publication Data

Names: Information Resources Management Association, editor.
Title: Research anthology on virtual environments and building the
   metaverse / Information Resources Management Association, editor.
Description: Hershey, PA : Engineering Science Reference, [2023] | Includes
   bibliographical references and index. | Summary: "With the advent of
   virtual environments and communities, the metaverse has been rapidly
   expanding in recent years as businesses and industries have begun to see
   the value and opportunities this technology provides. In order to ensure
   this technology is utilized to its full potential, further study on the
   best practices, challenges, and future directions is required. The
   Research Anthology on Virtual Environments and Building the Metaverse
   considers the latest research regarding the metaverse and discusses
   potential issues and benefits of the technology. The book also examines
   strategies and tactics businesses and companies can use when
   implementing the metaverse into their operations. Covering key topics
   such as immersion, augmented reality, and virtual worlds, this major
   reference work is ideal for computer scientists, business owners,
   managers, industry professionals, researchers, scholars, academicians,
   practitioners, instructors, and students"-- Provided by publisher.
Identifiers: LCCN 2022040864 (print) | LCCN 2022040865 (ebook) | ISBN
   9781668475973 (h/c) | ISBN 9781668475980 (eISBN)
Subjects: LCSH: Metaverse.
Classification: LCC QA76.9.M47 R47 2023 (print) | LCC QA76.9.M47 (ebook)
   | DDC 005.4/35--dc23/eng/20221110
LC record available at https://lccn.loc.gov/2022040864
LC ebook record available at https://lccn.loc.gov/2022040865

British Cataloguing in Publication Data
A Cataloguing in Publication record for this book is available from the British Library.

The views expressed in this book are those of the authors, but not necessarily of the publisher.

For electronic access to this publication, please contact: eresources@igi-global.com.

List of Contributors

Table of Contents

Volume I

Section 1
Applications in Business, Education, and Healthcare

Volume II

**Section 3
Designs and Frameworks**

Preface

With the advent of virtual environments and communities, the metaverse has been rapidly expanding in recent years as businesses and industries have begun to see the value and opportunities this technology provides. In order to ensure this technology is utilized to its full potential, further study on the best practices, challenges, and future directions is required.

Thus, the *Research Anthology on Virtual Environments and Building the Metaverse* seeks to fill the void for an all-encompassing and comprehensive reference book covering the latest and most emerging research, concepts, and theories for those working with virtual environments and the metaverse. This two-volume reference collection of reprinted IGI Global book chapters and journal articles that have been handpicked by the editor and editorial team of this research anthology on this topic will empower computer scientists, business owners, managers, industry professionals, researchers, scholars, academicians, practitioners, instructors, and students with an advanced understanding of critical issues and advancements of virtual environments and the metaverse.

The *Research Anthology on Virtual Environments and Building the Metaverse* is organized into three sections that provide comprehensive coverage of important topics. The sections are:

1.   Applications in Business, Education, and Healthcare;
2.   Avatars, Virtual Identities, and Virtual Communities; and
3.   Designs and Frameworks.

The following paragraphs provide a summary of what to expect from this invaluable reference tool.

Section 1, "Applications in Business, Education, and Healthcare," examines the diverse applications of virtual environments and the metaverse across industries and fields. The first chapter in this section, "The Financial Digital Assets Frontier: The Bridge Between the Past and the Future," by Prof. Andrei Dragos Popescu from the University of Craiova, Singapore, assesses the frontier of financial digital assets, which has emerged and developed the perfect infrastructure for scalability, efficiency, and transparency. The next chapter, "The Internet of Things and Blockchain Technologies Adaptive Trade Systems in the Virtual World: By Creating Virtual Accomplices Worldwide," by Prof. Vardan Mkrttchian from HHH University, Australia, presents artificial and natural intelligence technologies and considers their impact on the efficiency of electronic commerce and entrepreneurship. Another opening chapter, "Being a Post-Learner With Virtual Worlds," by Profs. Ferhan Şahin and Ezgi Doğan from Anadolu University, Turkey, evaluates virtual worlds in the transhumanism age by using anime series and film samples. The following chapter, "Virtual Worlds for Developing Intercultural Competence," by Profs. Lisiane Machado and Eliane Schlemmer from the Unisinos University, Brazil; Prof. Angilberto

Freitas from the Universidade do Grande Rio (Unigranrio), Brazil; and Prof. Cristiane Drebes Pedron of the Universidade Nove de Julho (Uninove), Brazil, presents a framework for developing intercultural competence (IC) and uses tridimensional digital virtual worlds (3DVW) as environments for developing IC. An additional chapter, "From Visual Culture in the Immersive Metaverse to Visual Cognition in Education," by Prof. Hsiao-Cheng 'Sandrine' Han from The University of British Columbia, Canada, discusses visual culture in the immersive metaverse through the visual cognition lens. The next chapter, "A Literature Review on the Use of Three-Dimensional Virtual Worlds in Higher Education," by Prof. Reza Ghanbarzadeh from the School of Business and Tourism, Southern Cross University, Australia and Prof. Amir Hossein Ghapanchi of College of Engineering and Science, Victoria University, Australia, conducts a literature review of the published research relevant to the application of three-dimensional virtual worlds in higher education. Another chapter, "Factors Affecting Learner Collaboration in 3D Virtual Worlds," by Prof. Iryna Kozlova from the University of Pennsylvania, USA, explores factors affecting learner collaboration by observing the performance of eight English as a foreign language (EFL) learners collaborating on tasks in a 3D virtual world (3D VW) over a period of six weeks. The following chapter, "Engaging Students in a Computer Diversity Course Through Virtual Worlds," by Profs. Yvonne Pigatt and James Braman from Community College of Baltimore County, USA, presents a brief literature review of the educational use of virtual worlds. An additional chapter in this section, "Stepping Out of the Classroom: Anticipated User Experiences of Web-based Mirror World Like Virtual Campus," by Prof. Minna Pakanen from Socio-Technical Design, Department of Engineering, Aarhus University, Denmark and Profs. Paula Alavesa, Leena Arhippainen, and Timo Ojala of the University of Oulu, Finland, investigates the use of geographically accurate mirror-world-like virtual campus models as an interactive learning environment. The next chapter, "Minecraft Our City, an Erasmus Project in Virtual World: Building Competences Using a Virtual World," by Prof. Annalisa A. B. Boniello from the University of Camerino, Italy and Prof. Alessandra A. C. Conti of IC Nettuno 1, Italy, reports experiences carried out to investigate the effectiveness of virtual worlds in education. A closing chapter, "The Use of Network-Based Virtual Worlds in Second Language Education: A Research Review," by Profs. Mark Peterson and Qiao Wang from Kyoto University, Japan and Dr. Maryam Sadat Mirzaei from RIKEN, Japan, reviews 28 learner-based studies on the use of network-based social virtual worlds in second language learning published during the period 2007-2017. The next chapter, "The Case for Qualitative Research Into Language Learning in Virtual Worlds," by Prof. Luisa Panichi from the University of Pisa, Italy reviews some of the most common research approaches used in investigating language learning and teaching in virtual worlds. Another chapter, "Vocabulary Acquisition From a Virtual Street-View Context," by Prof. Ya-Chun Shih from National Dong Hwa University, Taiwan, incorporates Google Street View into a 3D virtual environment, known as VECAR, in which EFL learners controlled their avatars to learn vocabulary in a context of New York City. The following chapter, "Video Game-Based L2 Learning: Virtual Worlds as Texts, Affinity Spaces, and Semiotic Ecologies," by Prof. Karim Hesham Shaker Ibrahim from Gulf University for Science and Technology, Kuwait, draws on interdisciplinary research on digital gaming from literacy studies, games' studies, and narratology to account for the L2 learning potentials of digital games, conceptualizes digital games as dynamic texts, affinity spaces, and semiotic ecologies, and discusses the implications of each conceptualization for game-based L2 learning and teaching. The next chapter, "Sustainable Engagement in Open and Distance Learning With Play and Games in Virtual Reality: Playful and Gameful Distance Education in VR," by Prof. Stylianos Mystakidis from the University of Patras, Greece, presents practical examples of virtual reality applications and recommendations for practitioners. The closing chapter in this section, "Role of Immersive (XR) Technologies in Improving Healthcare Competencies: A Review," by Prof. Anitha S. Pillai from Hindustan Institute of Technology and Science, India and Prof. Prabha Susy Mathew of Bishop Cottons Women's Christian College, India, focuses on uses, benefits, and adoption challenges of immersive technologies with specific reference to healthcare training.

Section 2, "Avatars, Virtual Identities, and Virtual Communities," discusses the impact and challenges of virtual identities and communities. The first chapter in this section, "Pioneering in the Virtual World Frontier," by Prof. Cynthia Calongne from Colorado Technical University, USA, explores the phenomenon of selfhood and society integral to the development of a vibrant educational community. The next chapter, "Participating on More Equal Terms? Power, Gender, and Participation in a Virtual World Learning Scenario," by Prof. Anders Steinvall from Umeå University, Sweden; Prof. Mats Deutschmann of Örebro University, Sweden; and Prof. Airong Wang from Xi'an Jiaotong-Liverpool University, China, investigates the potential effects of unequal power relations on participation in a group of student teachers and invited professionals in two collaborative workshops in Second Life. Another opening chapter, "Revisiting Musings on Co-Designing Identity-Aware Realities in Virtual Learning: The Shared Experiences," by Prof. Francisca Yonekura from the University of Central Florida, USA, expands on the exploratory journey looking into the identity of the collective self, the shared experiences of those co-creating the moment, and the potential for a community of practice to emerge while learning in virtual environments. The next chapter, "The Digital Cultural Identity on the Space Drawed in Virtual Games and Representative," by Profs. Hülya Semiz Türkoğlu and Süleyman Türkoğlu from Istanbul University, Turkey, analyzes the use and perceptions of virtual users in the virtual world by focusing on the construct that creates different virtual cultural experiences. An additional chapter, "My Becoming in a World of Virtual Learning Communities," by Prof. Karen Joy Koopman from the University of the Western Cape, South Africa, chronicles the author's becoming in a world of virtual learning communities (VLCs) and spaces. Another chapter, "Non-Verbal Communication Language in Virtual Worlds," by Dr. Ivonne Citarella from National Research Council, Italy, analyzes the animations present in Second Life trying to trace a socio-psychological picture of the non-verbal communication process in a virtual environment. A closing chapter, "Using Social Image Sets to Explore Virtual Embodiment in Second Life® as Indicators of Formal, Nonformal, and Informal Learning," by Prof. Shalin Hai-Jew from Kansas State University, USA, involves a review of the literature and then a light and iterated analysis of 1,550 randomly batch-downloaded screenshots from SL (including stills from machinima) to explore the potential of social image analysis to make inferences about human learning in SL in the present. The next chapter, "The Avatar as a Self-Representation Model for Expressive and Intelligent Driven Visualizations in Immersive Virtual Worlds: A Background to Understand Online Identity Formation, Selfhood, and Virtual Interactions," by Mses. Colina Demirdjian and Hripsime Demirdjian from Double Trouble Creatives, Australia, creates a backdrop for understanding the avatar in the connected modalities of the real and virtual state of environments. Another chapter, "Avatars for Clinical Assessment: Digital Renditions of the Self as Innovative Tools for Assessment in Mental Health Treatment," by Profs. Stefano Triberti, Valeria Sebri, Lucrezia Savioni, Alessandra Gorini, and Gabriella Pravettoni from the University of Milan, Italy, explores the possibility to use customized avatars within psychological assessment, as adjunctive assessment tools useful to get information on patients' self-representation(s) and communicative intentions. The closing chapter, "Avatar Teaching and Learning: Examining Language Teaching and Learning Practices in Virtual Reality Environments," by Profs. Geoff Lawrence and Farhana Ahmed from York University, Canada, examines the pedagogical potential of immersive social virtual worlds (SVWs) in language teaching and learning.

Section 3, "Designs and Frameworks," considers how virtual environments and the metaverse are designed and utilized. The first chapter, "Prosumers Building the Virtual World: How a Proactive Use of Virtual Worlds Can Be an Effective Method for Educational Purposes," by Drs. Mario Fontanella and Claudio Pacchiega from Edu3d, Italy, discusses how the teaching of "digital creativity" can take advantage of the fact that young people and adults are particularly attracted to these fields, which they perceive akin to their playful activities and which are normally used in an often sterile and useless way in their free time. The following chapter, "Framework for 3D Task Design: An Immersive Approach," by Prof. Iryna Kozlova from the University of Pennsylvania, USA, introduces a framework for 3D task design and proposes that the process of designing language learning tasks for 3D immersive simulated environments also be immersive. Another opening chapter, "POV in XR: How We Experience, Discuss, and Create the Virtual World," by Ms. Eve Weston from Exelauno, USA, introduces and explains the applications of a taxonomy for discussing point of view (POV) in XR. The next chapter, "INSIDE: Using a Cubic Multisensory Controller for Interaction With a Mixed Reality Environment," by Profs. Dimitrios G. Margounakis and Ioannis Giannios from Hellenic Open University, Greece, explores the field of mixed reality through the use of physical computing for the development of the electronic game Inside. Another chapter, "The Effects of Using On-Screen and Paper Maps on Navigation Efficiency in 3D Multi-User Virtual Environments," by Prof. Dilek Doğan from Ankara University, Turkey and Prof. Hakan Tüzün of Hacettepe University, Turkey, aims to analyze the effects of using on-screen and paper maps on navigation efficiency in 3D MUVEs. The following chapter, "The Effect of List-Liner-Based Interaction Technique in a 3D Interactive Virtual Biological Learning Environment," by Profs. Numan Ali, Sehat Ullah, and Zuhra Musa from the University of Malakand, Pakistan, investigates a simple list-liner-based interface for gaining access to different modules within a 3D interactive Virtual Learning Environment (VLE). An additional chapter, "3D Virtual Learning Environment for Acquisition of Cultural Competence: Experiences of Instructional Designers," by Profs. Stephen Petrina and Jennifer Jing Zhao from the University of British Columbia, Canada, addresses the experiences of instructional designers in a 3D virtual learning environment designed for the development of cultural competence. The next chapter, "Instructional Design Applied to TCN5 Virtual World," by Profs. Roseclea Duarte Medina, Andressa Falcade, and Vania Cristina Bordin Freitas from the Federal University of Santa Maria, Brazil and Prof. Aliane Loureiro Krassmann from Federal Institute Farroupilha, Brazil & The Federal University of Rio Grande do Sul, Brazil, presents the development and implementation of an instructional design (ID) for computer networks learning within a three-dimensional (3D) virtual world (VW) that considers characteristics of cognitive style and level of expertise of the student, titled TCN5. The following chapter, "Comparing Two Teacher Training Courses for 3D Game-Based Learning: Feedback From Trainee Teachers," by Prof. Michael Thomas from Liverpool John Moores University, UK and Prof. Letizia Cinganotto of INDIRE, Università Telematica degli Studi, Italy, explores data from two online language teacher training courses aimed at providing participants with the skills to create and use games in 3D immersive environments. The closing chapter in this section, "Design Process of Three-Dimensional Multi-User Virtual Environments (3D MUVEs) for Teaching Tree Species," by Prof. Dilek Doğan from Ankara University, Turkey and Profs. Hakan Tüzün, Gamze Mercan, and Pınar Köseoğlu of Hacettepe University, Turkey, aims to realize the concept of biodiversity with a 3D virtual worlds platform and provide awareness of the species in the immediate surroundings.

Although the primary organization of the contents in this work is based on its three sections offering a progression of coverage of the important concepts, methodologies, technologies, applications, social issues, and emerging trends, the reader can also identify specific contents by utilizing the extensive indexing system listed at the end. As a comprehensive collection of research on the latest findings related to virtual environments and the metaverse, the *Research Anthology on Virtual Environments and Building the Metaverse* provides computer scientists, business owners, managers, industry professionals, researchers, scholars, academicians, practitioners, instructors, students, and all audiences with a complete understanding of the challenges that face those working with virtual environments and the metaverse. Given the need for a better understating of how virtual environments can be utilized across industries and fields, this extensive book presents the latest research and best practices to address these challenges and provide further opportunities for improvement.

Section 1
Applications in Business, Education, and Healthcare

Chapter 1
The Financial Digital Assets Frontier:
The Bridge Between the Past and the Future

Andrei Dragos Popescu
https://orcid.org/0000-0002-9048-3055
University of Craiova, Singapore

ABSTRACT

The COVID-19 pandemic has disrupted the value chains for all major business sectors, with a great impact on the way we interact, socialize, transact, and trust the systems that we use on a daily basis. The magnitude of this major health crisis imposed a new level of digitalization, to which everyone needed to adapt, with great costs in terms of social, psychological, political, and economic transformation. In order to adapt in a new digital environment, imposed by the pandemic, we witnessed the adoption of decentralized ecosystems and technologies. One of the technologies that stood as foundation for this decentralization movement is blockchain. The first adaptations for blockchain technology happened within the financial services, with the introduction of the financial digital assets or crypto assets. This created the base for concepts like decentralized finance (DeFi), Web 3.0, and the metaverse. This chapter will assess the frontier of financial digital assets, which has emerged and developed the perfect infrastructure for scalability, efficiency, and transparency.

INTRODUCTION

Clearly, the COVID-19 pandemic has had a significant impact on all the value chains, and the global economy. In this regard, corporate sales have plummeted, industrial production has been reduced, consumer behaviors have changed, supply chains have been disrupted, businesses have faced serious financial hardships, and global unemployment rates have grown dramatically. In addition, as the number of positive coronavirus cases has grown exponentially, the COVID-19 pandemic has caused fear and the

DOI: 10.4018/978-1-6684-7597-3.ch001

temporary shutdown of industries, business sectors and enterprises in most nations all over the globe (Okorie D.I. and Lin B., 2021).

A direct consequence of all these effects was reflected in the global economy which shrank by 4.3% in 2020 (World Bank, 2021), as the health crisis and subsequent lockdowns halted travel, slowed or even closed companies, disrupted supply lines, and put millions of people out of work all over the world (International Labour Organization, 2021). A new worldwide recession was predicted and according to the World Bank, is "the deepest since 1945–1946, and more than twice as deep as the recession associated with the 2007–2009 global financial crisis." (Kose A. and Sugara N., 2021).

Based on the latest report from World Bank (2021) for the year of 2020, the Eurozone had a 7.4% decrease of the GPD, along with the United Stated who registered a fall of 3.5%. Japan, followed the trend, with a 5.3% contraction, in the same economic context with the rest of the Asean countries.

A circuit breaker strategy was adopted by Singapore and this was responsible for 2.2% of Singapore's GDP decrease in 2020, the worst reported contraction since their independence in 1965. These metrics are important to show the great impact of the pandemic effects on the global socio-economic environment.

In many respects, the COVID-19 world health crisis has put countries' competence and political will to the test. They have had to deal with an unprecedented public health catastrophe while also dealing with the complicated economic and social consequences, all while preserving public support and compliance.

During March 2020, the Dow Jones and S&P500 indexes had lost up to 30% of their value (Iqbal et al., 2021). Other stock markets, such as those in Europe, the United Kingdom, Australia, and Asia, have also experienced comparable declines (Zhang et al., 2020).

The COVID-19 pandemic has pushed the digitalization of services to a new level. Many industries have been fully disrupted and many sectors had to restructure their whole workflows, processes and procedures.

The financial industry is also going through a paradigm shift, based on a disruption model, which was accelerated by the COVID-19 pandemic, as FinTech innovations have been optimizing the accessibility, liquidity and transparency of the services.

Within the realm of FinTech, it is important to acknowledge Blockchain and Distributed Ledger Technology (DLT) as an innovative frontrunning architecture. An important property which is worth mentioning is that we should treat these novel technologies as a data enabling innovative architecture and not like a Financial Technology per se.

Given the novel and emergent status of financial digital assets, understanding the properties and the relationship between smart contracts, financial instruments, and all the participants, is providing new perspectives for financial services within a decentralized ecosystem.

Smart contracts are programmable contracts that are automatically executed when predefined conditions are met. The adoption of smart contracts will lead to reduced risks, lower administration and service costs and more efficient business processes across all major sectors of the financial services.

The potential of smart contract within the financial services industry is bridging new frontiers with regards to optimizing and creating new financial instruments that can help increase financial inclusion and integration.

The impact of modern technology with regards to the evolution of the contemporary world cannot be denied. Knowledge gained via technological improvements contributed greatly to the advancement of societies, diverse markets inception, and, of course, medicine. This is the main reason why technological advancements are considered to have the greatest influence and impact in humanity's future, with great developments and implementations in a full range of sectors.

As our research is an approach from an evolutionary model, we need to identify the necessary steps of disruption patterns by means of technology convergence.

The lifecycle of technology adoption is a very complex sociological model that outlines the adoption of a new product or innovation based on the demographic and psychological features of certain adopting groups. The adoption patterns were formed by Geoffrey Moore, and after 40 years, they were remodeled by Everett Rogers, who developed the idea of spread of innovations or "diffusion innovation". When introducing new technology, this approach considers that we have five categories of receivers or adopters, each having different requirements and expectations. In this model there were identified the following types of recipients: Innovators, Early Adopters, Early Majority, Late Majority, and Laggards.

Surprisingly, implementing breakthrough technologies is difficult and fraught with challenges. It is because businesses do not take into account the many types of adopters among their potential consumers and users. One major flaw is that by treating everyone the same, a direct consequence leads to resistance, subpar performance, and as a result, low return on investment. The second layer of risks comes from the technological implementation along with the idiosyncratic challenges.

It is critical to understand diverse groups of people in order to design a strategy that will encourage users to seek for innovation, as early as possible, in order for new technologies to be effective.

Figure 1. Crossing the Chasm
Source: Geoffrey A. Moore, (1999). Crossing the charm: Marketing and selling high-tech products to mainstream consumers

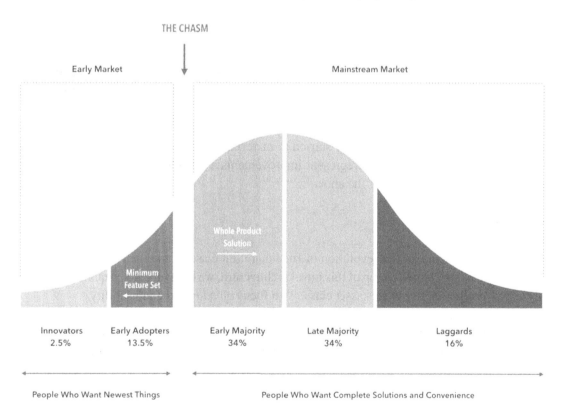

What makes it so crucial? The answer is that you must persuade each of the five user categories to adopt new technology every time it is implemented. When an invention has been accepted by Enthusiasts but not yet by Pragmatists, it is said to be "crossing the chasm". We agree that this is the most crucial stage in any adoption process. It is a difficult process as proven by major technological implementations from the first car, the lift-off of the first plane and the introduction of the internet. The trick is to fulfill the pragmatic majority's wants and expectations at the proper level and right time. This implies that the vision and ideas related to the main product must be presented flawlessly and most of the features need to function correctly.

We are addressing here the adoption of the blockchain technology, which stands as a cornerstone to the evolution of most financial digital assets and the technology convergence that followed.

Our study's approach comes from the perspective of understanding financial digital assets, the technology that powers them and the evolution of the concepts surrounding it. The pandemic context pushed digitalization and digitization in all business sectors, along with the redefinition of the way we interact, socialize and transfer value. The COVID-19 pandemic has driven and pushed the emerging digital markets and the financial digital assets to a new high in terms of acknowledgement and adoption. Novel concepts surrounding financial digital assets have taken the headlines during this challenging period of time, while paradigm shifts emerged in various business sectors. This pivoting in the face of traditional business models has been achieved by acknowledging the powerful tools and innovative features offered by blockchain technology (Popescu AD., 2021b). The applicability of such technology has been directly proportional with the discovery curve of novel business concepts involving tokens and processes of tokenization.

In this regards we can clearly state that 2019 was the year of DeFi innovation and basic concepts; 2020 followed with exceptional acknowledgement and new participants; 2021 spurred having DeFi as foundation, with the novel concept of Non-Fungible Tokens (NFTs) and adaptations in a decentralized environment; 2022 will clearly build on top of these concept with new emerging concepts of Web3.0 and Metaverse.

The years which had as main star Decentralized Finance, created the infrastructure on which new theories of trust, scalability and efficiency started to materialize, and we are seeing a great interest for the Web3.0 and the Metaverse, which represent improvements and implementations of the visions and systems we have the basis for. All of the above

Research Methodology

In order to properly understand the evolution of financial digital assets and their important role in how new concepts are being created on top of this novel architecture, we have engaged a qualitative approach to analyze and vet the frontier of this asset class, with focus on adoption and usability.

The goal of this chapter is to investigate and comprehend the link between financial digital assets, and the COVID-19 health catastrophe, along with their evolution, pre, during and post-pandemic. The intricacy and ambiguity of crypto assets' market dynamics, as compared to other traditional financial assets, motivates such analysis as we believe the novel concepts attached to this new emerging asset class will bring efficiency and stability to the investment landscape, as the frontier of the financial digital assets will radically disrupt old-school ways of the financial services sector.

We are addressing the financial services part, as this represents the underpinning for any new digital economies, and creates the framework for new visionary concepts to empower users and bring efficiency to the other industry sectors.

Based on the model of "Crossing the Chasm", we will take a look on how COVID-19 pandemic has impacted and influenced the usability of financial digital assets, with the intention of offering an overview of the new digital industries which spurred and gained acknowledgement.

LITERATURE REVIEW

Many academics have been studying the impact of the COVID-19 health crisis on stock market behavior and also the dynamics of the digital markets in the same context. On this topic, Al-Awadhi et al. (2020) indicate that daily increases in total confirmed cases and deaths owing to the COVID-19 pandemic have a negative and significant impact on the Chinese companies stock returns.

Financial digital assets markets, as an alternative investment, are likely to be affected by such unexpected movements in stock markets and economies throughout the world. In this regard, Johnson (2020) wonders if the COVID-19 health crisis would lead to an increase in Bitcoin acceptance, considering that Bitcoin is not subject to government regulation. In order to mitigate the negative impacts of the COVID-19 crisis on financial markets, Bitcoin and Ethereum are being employed as alternative investments, and they appear to outperform other assets (Iqbal et al., 2021).

According to Goodell and Goutte (2020), among others, the pandemic repercussions have a beneficial impact on different crypto assets prices, more specifically in the case of Bitcoin. Due to its independence, Huynh et al. (2020) argue that Bitcoin might be regarded a superior hedge than other tokens and cryptocurrencies. The research performed by Mariana et al. (2020), investigates if Ethereum and Bitcoin may serve as stock safe-havens amid the COVID-19 effects. Their findings show a holistic view over the crypto assets returns, which are not fully correlated with the S&P500 results. They also show that Ethereum and Bitcoin are suitable as short-term safe-havens, in this type of events which impact traditional financial markets. We agree and share these opinions as the asset classes have a very correlated behavior, due to the recent influx of institutional investors that use the same models in crisis situations, but the performance of these volatile assets are not fully associated.

Bitcoin has been a significant addition to an investor's portfolio in terms of risk mitigation since its beginnings. In this regard, investors, particularly during tumultuous moments, want additional information on whether they should invest only in traditional or financial digital assets, or combine the two (Mokni and Ajmi, 2021).

A common reaction due to the uncertainties of the socio-economic landscape, have determined investors to liquidate in a panic sale, and as a consequence of their anxieties (Le et al., 2021), the results translated in several big declines for various stocks and emerging markets (Shehzad et al., 2020).

Many academics are naturally interested in determining which assets outperform during volatile periods (Ji et al., 2020) or develop better risk management opportunities over a given market stress. In this regard, our research has important implications from a portfolio risk management perspective, since it demonstrates the role of hedging with financial digital assets in an increasing needed diversification process, that provides advantages and mitigate risks during and post COVID-19 pandemic.

Despite the pandemic effects, financial digital assets have grown to more than $2.2 trillion in market value (Coinmarketcap, 2022), which, like user adoption, roughly tracks the technology sector's market cap in early 1999. On the other hand, crypto assets today are only approximatively 3% of the global stock market value, versus roughly 14% for the technology sector in Q1 1999 (Grayscale, 2022). As we conceive an overview of this picture, financial digital assets are even earlier in their market valuation cycle than the internet was in the late 1990s. To emphasize on how COVID-19 pandemic has driven the acceptance of financial digital assets, we just need to recognize that crypto assets started being considered and allocated to new modern portfolios for institutional investors only in 2020.

Institutional investors now have the ability to use crypto assets as a new instrument for portfolio construction in an unprecedented macro environment for traditional assets. In this new paradigm, not taking risks is one of the biggest risks.

DECENTRALIZED FINANCE (DEFI) 2.0

We should deep dive in the first movement, powered by financial digital assets, which started to gain traction in 2018, and created the basis for the next digital generation shifts. Decentralized Finance or DeFi, put in motion an ecosystem of peer-to-peer value transactions, which expanded rapidly and created the first decentralized playground for digital wealth creation, storage and distribution. The first iteration of this concept, required time to grow and mature, but this organic progression received a dynamic push by the COVID-19 effects, which forced everyone to research, test and implement new models in this new environment.

Decentralized Finance is a category of blockchain-based solutions that attempts to tackle conventional finance's problems of centralization and control over an individual's financial assets. DeFi protocols are continually evolving and iterating upon established models of financial-based instruments, fueled by their inherent benefits of permissionless composability and open-source development culture. The DeFi ecosystem has grown exponentially over a surge of liquidity-focused protocols, and from these DeFi initiatives has ushered in a new generation of DeFi innovation known as DeFi 2.0.

The initial "Money Legos" in the Decentralized Finance (DeFi) ecosystem, such as the utility tokens and decentralized stablecoins, laid the groundwork for future DeFi improvements.

DeFi 2.0 is a relatively recent phrase in the ecosystem, referring to a subset of emergent protocols that build on top of the initial money legos, to progress the present DeFi landscape, particularly in the form of liquidity provisioning and incentivization.

This terminology upgrade in the blockchain world, refers to a subset of DeFi protocols that expand on prior DeFi breakthroughs like yield farming, lending, borrowing, and other decentralized financial services.

The entire DeFi economy is gradually becoming more user-friendly, safe, and accessible with the addition of these new financial primitives.

Because we are discussing the evolution of DeFi, it's important to note that the first generation of DeFi instruments addressed a wide range of financial services, including decentralized exchanges (DEXs), yield farming or liquidity provision, governance of decentralized autonomous organizations (DAOs), lending platforms, and payment gateways.

DeFi 2.0 is the second generation of DeFi protocols, and it tries to mitigate the friction points identified by addressing the issues that dominated the earlier manifestation.

The majority of new introduced technologies follow a similar adoption curve and progress through comparable phases of development. The first issue is the danger of embracing new technologies that comes with the development of every new disruption model.

A lot of issues have been identified with DeFi 1.0, as the concept of decentralization is still in early phases of experimentation.

Individual cryptocurrency volatility has repercussions in DeFi, since price movements might result in a temporary loss for Liquidity Providers (LP).

Because no single person is held responsible for security breaches on decentralized platforms, there is nothing you can do if the crypto assets are stolen or the smart contracts are exploited and hacked. Many of the users in this decentralized ecosystem put their assets into smart contracts without comprehending the possibility of their failing or the idiosyncratic risks associated.

Because crypto assets exist on multiple blockchains, less popular platforms suffer from low or inconsistent liquidity, and their related native digital assets are not always freely traded. To trade assets with limited liquidity, a user may need to use numerous platforms or suffer losses due to the slippage that is incurred.

Clearly we have gone a long way, as now, we have impermanent loss insurance, which can be used to compensate for a temporary loss. Smart contracts, likewise, can be covered by smart contract insurance, which can mitigate technical risks. Security audits conducted by open-source communities or insurance companies assist and guarantee that smart contracts do not have serious weaknesses or exploitable backdoors, while insurance reimburses participants who have lost assets.

Cross-chain bridges were introduced in this environment with a bang, as this new concept connects blockchains through layers of smart contracts and liquidity pools. It can also compensate for low liquidity by allowing users access to assets that are not native to the blockchain they have been using. If an asset does not have enough liquidity on one chain, they can trade it across adequate pools on other networks for the desired outcome.

DeFi 2.0 may mitigate, both DeFi 1.0 and traditional finance's risks and concerns, giving it a true decentralized financial sense unlike anything seen before in these digital markets.

Loans in DeFi 1.0, for example, are similar to traditional lending procedures, but on a peer-to-peer basis and with technical aspects which translate in collateralization of financial digital assets. Users borrow money from other users at a high interest rate, generally in exchange for a large quantity of collateral.

Within the DeFi 2.0, loans have been introduced to another property, which is that they can be reimbursed by themselves and this is considered an important improvement. To pay off the loan debt, self-repaying loans employ collateral for yield farming (liquidity provision that reinvests yield). The borrower's original collateral is returned after the whole sum has been repaid by what is basically a passive income stream, and they have effectively paid nothing out of the pocket.

Another key friction point, comes from the fact that each new technology implementation faces an accessibility obstacle.

While everyone now has access to the internet, only a few individuals had access to the computers required to use it at first. The adoption of financial digital assets and DeFi 1.0 ran into the same issue, as only the selected few had the skills and courage to experiment with the tools, interfaces and wallets provided.

For a decade, any crypto asset and bitcoin related business was a niche environment dominated by people who used a specific technical language that was not easily comprehended by everyone. Buzzwords like "Distributed Ledger Technology (DLT)", "Smart Contracts", "Decentralized Autonomous Organization (DAO)", "Sharding", "Non-Fungible Tokens (NFTs)", and the "Byzantine Generals Problem" might impress other crypto aficionados while making it absolutely boring to the general public who are not keen to deep dive in the ecosystem.

DeFi 1.0 is also suffering by the same self-inflicted condition, as the environment is a set of tools developed by developers for developers.

Niche platforms that need a high level of technical knowledge are frequent and not unusual. It was, and still is, a learning curve for all its participants, as excessively detailed wording makes it difficult to participate in an informal conversation.

To make matters worse, most individuals are uninformed of the existence of DeFi platforms and how to utilize them correctly, because DeFi marketing proposition has yet to evolve to the stage where it knows how to appeal to a non-technical and novice audience. Users from this unique sphere are understandably concerned about inconsistency and dangerous payouts percentages which are promoted.

By updating its story over time, the crypto environment figured out how to make itself accessible to the average person, and it's now a common issue well covered in tutorials, conferences and workshops.

DeFi 2.0 is based on this approach, and it aims to make DeFi accessible to everyone through two primary initiatives: education and interaction with established financial systems.

The most successful DeFi 2.0 initiatives are those that have streamlined front-end functionality and generated resources to teach new users about their platform and usability.

When it comes to DeFi, which is fundamentally decentralized, integration with centralized traditional banking networks is a contentious topic. This is not because of a utopian revolution, but because it just happen to create and evolve a system that is based on a trust concept performed by smart computing code, much more efficient and reliable than the existent infrastructure, which suffered from a rejection from the traditional finance environment as it projected itself like a high-tech contender.

On this note, the interconnectivity is available for the traditional financial institutions, as they can integrate DeFi 2.0 protocols into their platforms via APIs, DAOs, Smart Contracts and Oracles. This philosophy is at the core of what blockchain technology promotes, in terms of accessibility and inclusivity, therefore DeFi 2.0 can become easier and more approachable.

Users will be able to employ decentralized financial protocols from within centralized TradFi (Traditional Finance) applications and web interfaces once the integration is complete.

Usability suffers in the early phases of every new technology, much like accessibility. Throughout DeFi's history, cluttered and perplexing interfaces have been the norm, as it defined itself a collection of primitives designed by and for developers.

DeFi 2.0, on the other hand, introduces layer-2 and even layer-3 platforms that enable decentralized financial services like lending, yield farming, and asset management services, accessible to a large range of users who do not have the necessary skills or technical knowledge.

The second iteration corrects a flaw in DeFi 1.0 by guiding new users through the setup procedure quickly and easily. In this sense, the upgrade adds a degree of complexity to DeFi's use cases while simplifying the front-end procedure. This means you can do more with your money with less effort than before.

One of the main goals of major DeFi 2.0 systems is to circumvent the liquidity constraints that many on-chain transactions suffer.

If you want to benefit in this decentralized environment, seek for DeFi protocols that you can trust and that provide the characteristics and requirements you need. Most of the platforms, protocols and applications built in this ecosystem are often referred to as decentralized apps or dApps.

Figure 2. From DeFi 1.0 to DeFi 2.0

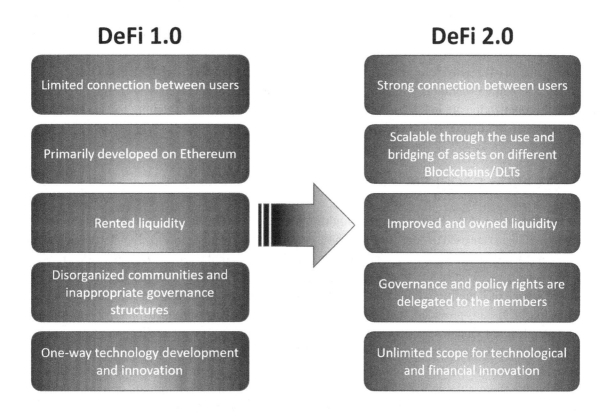

Some of the services and protocols evolving in this decentralized ecosystem are as follows:

Yield farming – Has become a catch-all word for any DeFi operation that can earn returns or yield, on a sort of model that is based on digital assets collateral placement, generally in the form of an Annual Percentage Yield (APY). Reinvesting returns is usually regarded as an important aspect of "farming" in each yield farming activity, while it is not necessarily required. For this reason, each investor should consider their objectives as well as their risk tolerance in any concept they want to engage.

Lending is a way for users to contribute to the liquidity required by providing loans in exchange for interest payments. Self-repaying loans provide both the borrower and the lender additional peace of mind.

Liquidity mining or *Liquidity Provision* (LP) – Represents another form to generate yield, and in this concept users provide crypto assets to liquidity pools for other users to trade against, in exchange for fees. In the case of major events, like the COVID-19 pandemic, if the markets flip, impermanent loss insurance can help limit losses.

Staking – Is a method of earning block rewards by becoming a validator for a proof-of-stake blockchain by locking the chain's validator token or native asset.

DAO participation – You can buy and sell these governance tokens, that can offer voting rights and other utilities within the structure of the DAO. The advantages of joining a DAO should be considered based on the organization's mission.

Trading via Decentralized Exchanges (DEXs) allow users to trade crypto assets without having to rely on a centralized third party that oversees each transaction. They usually charge lower costs than centralized exchanges and they started to provide more complex services like margin trading. DeFi crypto margin trading refers to the practice of using borrowed funds from a broker to trade a financial digital asset, which forms the collateral for the loan from the broker. Usually, a broker in DeFi it is represented by Autonomous Market Makers (AMM) (DeFi Prime, 2022).

The regulatory framework for this type of concepts vary from jurisdiction to jurisdiction.

Gaming – While decentralized gaming is a separate business, it intersects with DeFi 2.0 wherever models of monetization are involved. As the area grows, a concept worth watching for, are the play-to-earn and ownership models based on DeFi 2.0.

THE LIQUIDITY PROBLEM

Since the beginning of the DeFi economy, liquidity has been a cause of difficulty for many new DeFi enterprises. Tokens are used to bootstrap the whole ecosystem, allowing teams to align participant incentives, receive benefits from user fees, and become composable with the wider DeFi network. However, DeFi developers required access to a big pool of crypto assets in order to allocate its consumers with a reliable source of liquidity to trade their tokens on AMM (Autonomous Market Makers) protocols.

Third-party liquidity providers on AMM protocols provided a partial solution to this problem, allowing any independent individual with sufficient crypto assets to offer liquidity for a token pair. Rather of supplying liquidity themselves, teams might theoretically obtain adequate liquidity from others. End-users, on the other hand, have limited incentives to bootstrap liquidity for a new asset because doing so, would entail exposing themselves to the risk of temporary loss in exchange for minimal fee revenue through swaps. There was needed a compelling financial rationale for this risk balancing issue.

This resulted in a chicken-and-egg situation. The slippage caused by swaps discourages users from engaging in a DeFi protocol's environment if there is not enough liquidity. There is not enough fee volume created without consumers participating in token transactions to motivate third-party actors to pool their tokens and offer liquidity.

DeFi 2.0 refers to a few developing DeFi projects that aim to revolutionize the prevalent challenges related with liquidity provisioning and incentivization in the context of liquidity. They give alternatives and additions to the yield farming paradigm, allowing projects to obtain long-term financing.

This multi-faceted strategy aids in the realignment of incentives between on-chain protocols and third-party liquidity providers. Protocols are better positioned than a third-party liquidity source to be exposed to temporary loss. While third-party liquidity providers face the same opportunity costs as every other liquidity pool and yield farming protocol on the market, protocols have an extra incentive to keep liquidity because it helps secure low-slippage swaps for users transacting with their native token, lowering the cost of entry into their ecosystem.

Another subgroup of DeFi 2.0 protocols aims to create new financial instruments by building on top of past yield-generating processes and assets.

Alchemix (2022), a self-repaying loan platform with a "no liquidation" architecture, is a good representation of this. The protocol issues representative tokens that are backed by the collateralized asset 1:1. Users can, for example, borrow 50% of the amount as alDAI by posting the DAI stablecoin as collateral. The underlying collateral is then put into yield-generating processes in order for it to grow gradually.

Alchemix can provide a liquidation-free lending platform by combining representative tokens with yield-generating collateral, allowing users to spend and save at the same time as the collateral generates income.

Another DeFi 2.0 protocol, Abracadabra (2022), uses a similar technique, but with a framework that is similar to MakerDAO (2022). Users may deposit yield-bearing collateral and get the MIM stablecoin in exchange, allowing them to keep their exposure to the collateral while still gaining yield and unlocking liquidity.

DEXs and LP tokens are two of the most well-known lego models in the blockchain sector, allowing for large-scale token exchange and yield farming. Through rigorous overcollateralization methods and risk reduction, the first generation of decentralized stablecoins paved the way for newer stablecoin designs and decentralized lending platforms. None of these DeFi legos should be viewed in isolation; instead, they should be viewed as part of a larger ecosystem that supports, links, and amplifies other building blocks to open up new possibilities.

A new generation of DeFi legos is being built on top of its predecessor with DeFi 2.0, making the decentralized financial environment more efficient, user-friendly, and valuable for its members. The decentralized legos keep piling up, and with each new brick, the DeFi ecosystem gains new value and opportunities.

WEB 3.0

Financial digital assets blend the dynamics of investing in emerging markets, the technology sector and venture capital to provide exposure to the next wave of the internet. They enable investors and users to have direct ownership and control over internet economies.

Web3 has lately sprung into the popular awareness, with industry experts, from both the traditional IT sector and the blockchain environment, offering a variety of viewpoints on the internet's past and future. This is a direct consequence of the COVID-19 pandemic, as a lot of research and development was allocated towards a more inclusive internet.

The key characteristic of the first iteration of the internet, which was defined as Web1, was simple static websites. You could easily look at web pages and browse around, but the missing propriety in this scenario, was the interaction between websites and the users. As time went on, servers were upgraded, developers learned new skills, and eventually Web2 or Web2.0, emerged.

Web2 represents the second development stage of the world wide web or the internet. The difference between the simple static websites of Web1 and Web2, is the ability for the internet users to create their own content in the form of blogs, comments, reviews and social media. With the second iteration of the internet, websites became more dynamic and responsive, like the ability to do a Google search or to create directions for roadmaps. Web2 is the stage of internet where interoperability was achieved, where different websites and applications could connect and interact with each other. It's important to note that there is no formal date, roadmap or specific marker that delineated when Web1.0 morphed into Web2.0, and we believe the same will apply with the transition to Web3.0.

Web3.0 is the term used to refer to the third currently emerging developmental stage of the internet. The main difference between Web3 and the previous iterations is that the internet will operate on decentralized technologies and will be fueled by financial digital assets.

Figure 3. From Web1 to Web2 and Web3

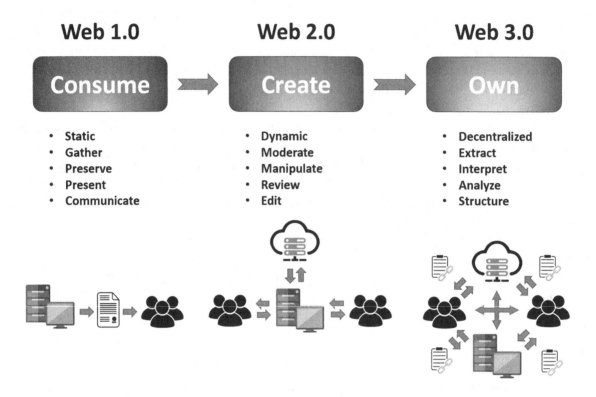

Another defining characteristic of the Web3.0 is the application of artificial intelligence, so we will see faster and more robust development, along with more inclusion of users. This version of the internet is believed to be the one who will detach itself from market cycles, as the algorithms of data will adapt. This theory is based on the fact that with Web3, everything will go through of stage of tokenization, which will give more power to the users, in the sense of how their data is used, transacted and monetized.

A new concept that will be representative for the Web3, will be in the form of new digital global economies. The underlying foundation of the current global economies use the global banking system to transact, as each of them have their own monetary, fiscal and taxation policies in place, which everyone needs to abide. With the decentralized, open, accessible and ever-advancing technology implications of Web3, we will start to see digital economies forming on the blockchain, that we can all interact with, regardless of the physical location, culture, religion, race or financial status of the users. In this scenario, people can choose which economies they would like to be a part of, and within these ecosystems, they will get to decide how the economic output is distributed.

Basically, with both, a shortage of physical and traditional assets, along with the limitations of accessing them, depending on where you live or if they are affordable, digital assets will establish themselves as the norm, which fortifies the prediction of the development of digital global economies.

As per its design and features, Web3 will help rebuild and transform the concept of class mobility. Socio-economic class mobility describes the ease with which a person can upgrade its status from a lower class into a higher class. Web3 technology is giving us a glimmer of hope that the way we distribute value, within future digital economies, can be more fair, inclusive and give everyone the opportunity to move from lower to higher classes.

HTTP pioneer Tim Berners-Lee used the phrase "Web 3.0" during the dotcom era to describe an integrated communication architecture in which internet data is machine-readable across many applications and systems; a notion he dubbed as the Semantic Web.

Ethereum Co-founder Gavin Wood recycled Berners Lee's statement in his 2014 blog post "DApps: What Web 3.0 Looks Like", referring to the power of blockchain technology to create a "fundamentally new paradigm for the interactions between parties" based on "a zero-trust interaction system."

Wood's approach is focused more on the consensus and cryptography with a decentralized vision for protocols and technology.

Web3's key propositions and protocols, as well as their implications for future trust models, are now the topic of intense discussion, with both today's IT giants and the vanguard of the blockchain sector continuing to deal with them.

It was not until the introduction of smart contracts that a genuinely decentralized internet paradigm emerged.

Web3, a redesigned web, was defined by Gavin Wood as a "Secure Social Operating System."

Simply said, Web3 is a Decentralized Internet concept that wants to develop an altogether new contracting system and revolutionize the way individuals and organizations reach agreements. Web3 combines the rich, interactive experience of Web 2.0 web applications like social media platforms with the decentralized architecture of Web 1.0, the first version of the internet, which was replete with user-hosted blogs and RSS feeds, to provide a digital ecosystem where data is user-owned and transactions are backed by cryptographic guarantees. Users may rely on deterministic software logic to implement agreements exactly as planned, rather than needing to trust brand-based paper commitments.

Web3's foundational elements are based on: Blockchain (architecture) and Financial Digital Assets (infrastructure).

An increasing stack of decentralized technologies, like blockchains, smart contracts, oracles, crypto wallets, and storage networks, are powering the Web3 architecture.

A blockchain is a highly secure and decentralized network that allows users to store data, trade currency, and record transaction activity in a shared ledger that is not centralized. Web3's backbone is comprised of blockchain networks, which provide safe execution environments for the production, distribution, and trading of financial digital assets, as well as the development of programmable smart contracts. Web3's settlement layer is comprised of blockchains and distributed ledgers.

Crypto assets are digital tokens that make use of blockchain networks' decentralized and tamper-proof ecosystems to enable extremely secure transactions. They are the native currencies of Web3 decentralized apps (dApps), and they may be used to pay for Web3 services as well as participate in Web3 governance.

Tokens granted to Web3 content providers are likewise units of value, but these units of value are digital, programmable, and have uses other than trade. A token in Web3 can be used to invest in a protocol, project, or blockchain. It could be useful for that project or protocol – for example, for paying for or insuring a service. It might also open the door to involvement in the protocol's or project's governance.

Smart contracts are tamper-proof blockchain programs that automate transactions using conditional software logic like "if x is true, then execute y." Decentralized apps, or dApps, are the cryptoeconomic protocols that bring Web3 to life and put it in the hands of consumers, thanks to programmable smart contracts.

Because they are not maintained by a single individual or organization, dApps vary from the Web 2.0 applications and the static HTML pages of the Web 1.0 era, because they are supported by the decentralized architecture of blockchain networks. These decentralized programs may be used to build complicated, automated systems like peer-to-peer financial services, data-driven insurance products, play-to-earn online games, and more.

Smart contracts must be able to access and interact with data and systems outside of blockchain networks in order to reach their full potential. Oracles are the entities that link blockchains to real-world data and current systems, as well as providing key infrastructure for the creation of a uniform, interoperable Web3 environment.

Oracles have risen to prominence as a broad layer of the Web3 stack, delivering off-chain data and services to support smart contract innovation, as well as cross-chain interoperability to provide smooth interaction across multiple on-chain settings.

Individuals may design and participate in financial protocols that give unparalleled access, security, and transparency thanks to the technology that make up Web3.

NFTs, GAMING AND THE METAVERSE

We must also consider the development of the Metaverse and ever-increasing valuations of certain NFTs marketplace, all during a time where COVID showed how fragile our physical supply chain processes can be, which greatly affected and continues to affect distribution of physical assets.

The Web3 ecosystem is now forming around NFTs, blockchain games, and the Metaverse. NFTs provide verified ownership of digital assets, allowing digital commodities to have the same level of functional uniqueness as physical things. With NFTs, one digital item may now be distinguished from another even though they appear identical, much like two copies of the same book can be distinguished by their distinct marks and signs of particular wear and tear.

Digital art, metaverse apps, and video games all stand to benefit greatly from this. Blockchains, which serve as the underlying settlement layer, NFT smart contracts, which enable verifiable ownership of digital items, and decentralized oracles, which provide key services such as verifiable randomness, smart contract automation, off-chain data, and more, are at the heart of this fundamental transformation.

The metaverse has reached the mainstream public consciousness, thanks to the recent proliferation of non-fungible tokens (NFTs) in the blockchain ecosystem and Facebook's head-turning rebranding to "Meta".

Though the notion may appear to be novel and cutting-edge, the metaverse has long been a part of popular culture. In his science fiction novel Snow Crash in 1992, Neal Stephenson invented the word to describe an all-encompassing 3D virtual environment that replicates, augments, enriches, and integrates with actual reality.

Simply described, the metaverse is a digital realm that lives in parallel to the real one. Because of its emergent nature, many various perspectives of how the metaverse will present themselves exist, and there are even disagreements over whether the metaverse exists today.

In its most idealized form, the metaverse is a virtual environment that provides parallel experiences to the actual world while also allowing for improved powers, similar to The Matrix's robot-manufactured universe. In more realistic depictions, metaverse visitors physically engage in a virtual environment, where they take the shape of virtual avatars, play games, and live pseudo-anonymous lives, using advanced motion-tracking technology and virtual reality headsets. The existence of user-owned digital commodities with historically real-world traits of scarcity, worth, and history is sometimes cited as proof that the metaverse has arrived. Some say that the metaverse exists in the human connections, sentiments, and experiences that make up our digital lives on social media, video games, and other platforms.

Despite these divergent perspectives, the metaverse's essential premise is evident. Telepresence, which is described as an immersive condition in which a person feels present in a virtual place, is critical for supporting metaverse experiences. The metaverse emerges from our ability to create virtual spaces that make us feel present – perhaps even tangible – in a digital environment, whether through a combination of immersive AR (Augmented Reality) and VR (Virtual Reality) technologies, user-owned digital goods powered by blockchains, or simply through an addictive Massively Multiplayer Online Role-Playing Game (MMORPG).

In a very real sense, the metaverse is all around us. Early trials in MMORPGs like Second Life and World of Warcraft introduced the notion of gamified social platforms, which engrossed players to the point that digital commodities, like as weaponry and apparel, carried enormous real-world value. Existing social networking services like Facebook, Instagram, and Twitter have enabled users to create pseudo-anonymous internet avatar identities and interactive virtual rooms where they may share news, discuss topics, and communicate with friends.

People are no strangers to total digital immersion through an external screen, whether it's in a Twitter Spaces hangout, a Zoom conversation with coworkers, or multiplayer gaming. Emerging technologies, on the other hand, have the potential to give the digital world additional relevance, permanency, and presence.

Our capacity to reproduce the human experience will play a big role in enabling the enhanced telepresence that will enable metaverse growth. Virtual reality (VR) headsets and movement-tracking technologies, with more accurate depictions that produce a feeling of total sensory immersion, can play a key part in this. SuperHot (2022), a Matrix-style game where time runs only as fast as the player, and VR Chat, a social network where participants construct 3D avatars, are two instances of early developments.

While Virtual Reality (VR) aspires to create an immersive virtual world separate from physical settings, Augmented Reality (AR) incorporates virtual displays into real-world environments. Microsoft's Hololens, an AR headset that tracks both what we are looking at and our body movements to superimpose virtual images and icons, allowing for compelling use cases that can help us navigate, identify objects, and interact with the physical world in a virtual manner, is one such example that exists right now.

Imagine a world where you can put on AR glasses to see which virtual shoes someone wore that day, or where you can play games on an entirely virtual screen that resides on your desk. AR glasses might provide information and enhance everyday experiences by updating in real time depending on sensors. AR's objective is to create a seamless merger of the virtual and actual worlds that will make everyday living more fascinating, useful, and authentic.

AR and VR are inspiring technologies that are helping to shape the experiences that will characterize the metaverse's future vision. However, interactive and immersive experiences are just part of the picture; the metaverse will need a value layer powered by decentralized infrastructure like blockchains to empower users as much as platform enablers in the metaverse's development. Finally, this will aid metaverse users in defining the metaverse's structure, providing the digital universe greater solidity through verified digital goods and allowing users to sense substance in a digital realm.

RESULTS

As we have analyzed some of the newest trends and concepts, that have as basis financial digital assets, let's visualize the frontier of "crossing the chasm" for these innovative technology implementations.

Figure 4. Crossing the Charm – Total Value Locked in DeFi
Source: DeFi Pulse (2022). TVL Chart taken from DeFi Pulse. Retrieved from www.defipulse.com

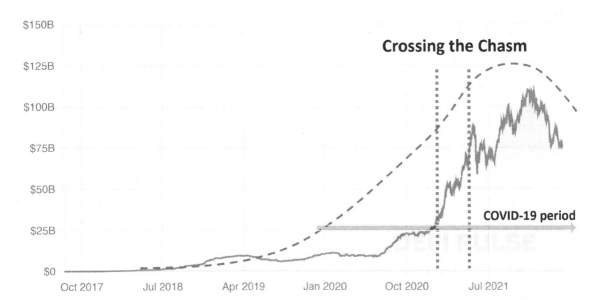

We can easily assess how the COVID-19 pandemic impacted the adoption of financial digital assets and how they rapidly evolved, enforcing the potential of blockchain technology along with the visionary concepts that we elaborated above.

Based on the data extracted from DeFi Pulse (2022), a top of $110 billion USD was reached for the Total Value Locked (TVL) of financial digital assets in DeFi projects. This represents the total balance of Ether (ETH) and ERC-20 tokens held by these smart contracts and TVL is calculated by taking these balances and multiplying them by their average price in USD.

To support our theory in the adoption and usability process for the financial digital assets, a comparison timeline provided by Grayscale Research department (2022), shows how the past trend for internet users for the 1995-1999 period, is very similar with the crypto users for the 2017- 2021 period.

During the 90's period, everyone believed that the internet will change the world, and the hyped created around every project led to the well-known tech dot-com bubble. The current situation in the financial digital assets sector, is different, as most of the bubble effect hype is generated in a tight developers' environment. This being said, most of the dApps that need to reach the end-users have not been deployed to the stage of mass adoption, and are still in a process of acknowledgement and upgrade.

To extrapolate the frontier of financial digital assets, in a post-pandemic era, we are witnessing and capturing the very beginning of a value shift from the legacy technology sector.

Figure 5. Internet Users vs Crypto Users
Source: Grayscale – The postmodern Portfolio (2022)

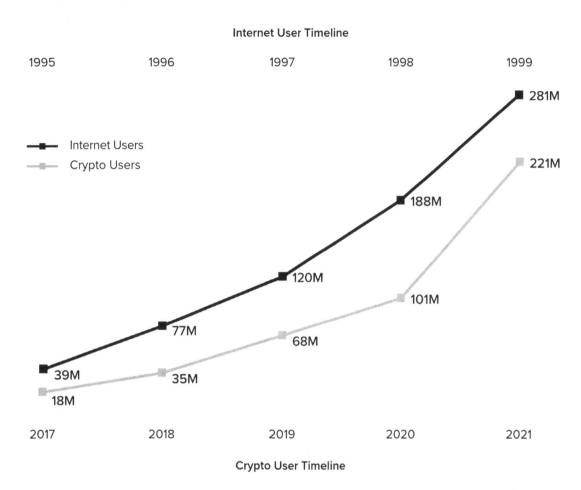

CONCLUSION

We are living in early days of a massive paradigm shift. We are accelerating into a digitized and decentralized future. What we are experiencing in these times is the largest wealth creating event in the history of the world. Never, at any point in time, have we had the freedom of financial mobility that we have been engaging with blockchain and DeFi instruments.

The paradigm shift is encompassed by a new philosophy which empowers people with a technology for a new world, where users control and hold their own data as they get to run their own financial services. This is the power of decentralization and DeFi, and based on this, the new emerging concepts which are built on top of this novel infrastructure make sense. Decentralization matters, as all the new implementations and adaptations, have proved that we are still tied to the centralized banking system in a way that is unnecessary.

One major obstacle in the proliferation of this environment is that the crypto sector, which still captures all the attention, is largely unregulated. A perfect definition of what is happening now is basically a full-service shadow banking with nobody in charge. But the vision and mission are greater than just banking and financial services, as we are seeing a technological revolution unfold right between our eyes.

Lending, borrowing, stock exchanges, currency exchanges, derivatives and insurance models, all of these have their facsimiles in the digital realm, which had been created with code rather than with brick-and-mortar institutions. This is the landscape that we are thinking of, when we say the word DeFi, which can be easily translated in an equation of: (Technology * Crypto) + Finance = DeFi.

There are two premises of DeFi on which greater things can be built on: the first one is the idea of financial inclusion, where people who do not have access to financial services can be easily integrated (Popescu, 2022); and the second one addresses the people that already had access to financial services, which are switching from snail mail to email.

It is exciting and unknown what emergent properties will come from this architecture, when you can transact much faster and in a much more trustworthy way.

The decentralized financial system is creating a disruptive model based on technology, that is eventually going to replace, or upgrade, large sections of the financial and monetary system as we know it. The potential for it to really disrupt finance and the banking system, is still very much a vision of some crypto communities, but we can clearly assess its enormous potential applicability.

This space is moving with a compounding exponential speed for innovation, as it is driven by the openness of the community, both from a software perspective and also from a genuine desire to improve and add to innovations.

It seemed very natural to unify this set of emerging decentralized technologies, from blockchain, to crypto assets and protocols, and call them Web3.

With Web1, for the first time we had access to information; as with Web2, we saw a big consolidation of this information within centralized environments, like Facebook, Google and Amazon.

Web3 is a world where the users are creating value, but also capturing the value, which is something that was lost with Web2. In the concept of Web3, the people and the users have the power and are able to create much more value with the amalgamation of these different decentralized technologies.

Web3 is based on a reinvented internet experience powered by decentralized technologies. It is already changing how we interact online, from how we invest and exchange to how we play and express ourselves creatively. Zero-trust interactions and cryptographically-backed agreements are becoming increasingly popular among people and organizations throughout the world. While Web3 is still in its early stages, it has the potential to meet the internet's original objectives of inbuilt openness, dependability, and expediency.

Besides all the opportunities and possibilities that are emerging from the financial digital market frontier, we need to address also the risks associated with them. The crypto sector today is largely unregulated, as a regulatory framework is still in research phases for many governments around the world. The lack of regulatory clarity, puts more pressure on the end users who want to participate in this ecosystem, as they need to perform some very complicated due diligence tasks. It is hard to know if a particular DeFi app is going to work as promised, or whether it was created by reputable people, unless you go through this due diligence process. The obvious risk, as of now, is that if anything goes wrong within this space, there is no counterparty to rely upon and there is no recourse. It is important to acknowledge that by removing the prime brokers, the facilitators and intermediaries, we are also removing a safety buffer.

The real value of a regulatory framework is that it gives people confidence. This relays in the sense that regardless of the activity they want to participate in, there is always someone who will make sure that everyone does what is promised and there are no victims of fraud or manipulation in the process.

In order to go mainstream, clearly some centralized aspects need to be invited within this vision, till a new technological advancement will help mitigate some of the risks.

Similar to how web and internet technology brought democracy and democratization to informational access, we are seeing technologists, developers and entrepreneurs taking the path for democratization of global finance. This mission should not be discarded or seen from a negative perspective, just because it's a young technology with no proven records, it should we encouraged as it builds on a trust foundation with iterations of everything that is good from the actual financial system. Besides the financial element, this methodology should to be treated as a cornerstone for various sectors, as the applicability extends further than the financial markets.

It's a 0 to 1 innovation, with a disruptive mindset for greater good.

The approach for this chapter comes from an angle of understanding how the frontier of the financial digital assets evolved and laid the foundation for the perfect infrastructure in order for a novel concept as DeFi to thrive. Interactions between blockchains, protocols and dApps, defined the stages of DeFi as new bridges were consolidated. This new infrastructure started to grow dynamically and the exploration of usability for different business sectors was rapidly implemented. The pivoting point for such a framework was determined only when the main properties and features, such as interoperability, connectivity, efficiency, immutability and trust, were acknowledged. A major component in the dynamics of adoption came from the COVID-19 health crisis, which forced processes and procedures to be redefined, restructured and implemented in a secure and digital environment. Institutional investors have put a lot of focus on the development of this infrastructure and deep dived into the potential opportunities that this space had to offered. Even though everyone was engaged into the topics and the interest surrounding financial digital assets and DeFi, a missing regulatory framework for this decentralized space still keeps the most important players away. The vision of the future of internet and the way we interact with people and money has been assess and vetted on the basis of this decentralized environment. The Metaverse and Web3 will be clearly be constructed on the layers of blockchain and DeFi, having financial digital assets as fuel for the operations within. This vision is very important as we need to align the expectations on solid values and concepts.

While the pandemic's impacts have been negatively presented worldwide, from the perspective of financial digital assets we can state that it was a period of acknowledgement, redefinition and implementation of various visionary concepts. As with every world disrupting event, new opportunities have risen. COVID-19 pandemic has forced the humanity to a new level of digital adaptation, and it seems the financial digital assets frontier is establishing itself as the new norm.

REFERENCES

Abracadabra. (2022). *Abracadabra.money is a spell book*. Available at https://abracadabra.money

Al-Awadhi, A. M., Alsaifi, K., Al-Awadhi, A., & Alhammadi, S. (2020). Death and contagious infectious diseases: Impact of the COVID-19 virus on stock market returns. *Journal of Behavioral and Experimental Finance, 27*, 1–5. doi:10.1016/j.jbef.2020.100326 PMID:32292707

Alchemix. (2022). *Alchemix – Self-repaying loans, spend and save at the same time*. Available at https://alchemix.fi/

Coinmarketcap. (2022). *Cryptocurrency prices, charts and market capitalization*. Retrieved from https://coinmarketcap.com/

DeFi Pulse. (2022). *Total Value Locked*. Retrieved from https://www.defipulse.com/

Goodell, J., & Goutte, S. (2021). Co-movement of COVID-19 and Bitcoin: Evidence from wavelet coherence analysis. *Finance Research Letters, 38*, 1–6. doi:10.1016/j.frl.2020.101625

Grider, D., Maximo, M., & Zhao, M. (2022). Grayscale Research – The Postmodern Portfolio. *Crypto Allocation Thesis*. Retrieved from https://grayscale.com/

Huynh, T. L. D., Nasir, M. A., Vo, V. X., & Nguyen, T. T. (2020). Small things matter most: The spillover effects in the cryptocurrency market and gold as a silver bullet. *The North American Journal of Economics and Finance, 54*, 101–277. doi:10.1016/j.najef.2020.101277

International Labour Organization. (2021). *ILO Monitor: COVID-19 and the World of Work. Seventh Edition*. ILO.

Iqbal, N., Fareed, Z., Wan, G., & Shahzad, F. (2021). Asymmetric nexus between COVID-19 outbreak in the world and cryptocurrency market. *International Review of Financial Analysis, 73*, 101–613. doi:10.1016/j.irfa.2020.101613

Ji, Q., Zhang, D., Zhao, Y., (2020). *Searching for safe-haven assets during the COVID-19 pandemic*. doi:10.1016/j.irfa.2020.101526

JohnsonJ. (2020). *The Impact of COVID-19 on Bitcoin Trading Activity: A Preliminary Assessment*. doi:10.2139/ssrn.3583162

Kose, A., & Sugawara, N. (2021). *Understanding the Depth of the 2020 Global Recession in 5 Charts*. World Bank Blogs.

Le, T. H., Do, H. X., Nguyen, D. K., & Sensoy, A. (2021). COVID-19 pandemic and tail-dependency networks of financial assets. *Finance Research Letters, 38*, 1–9. doi:10.1016/j.frl.2020.101800 PMID:33100926

MakerD. A. O. (2022). Available at https://makerdao.com/en/

Mariana, C. D., Ekaputra, I. A., & Husodo, Z. A. (2020). Are Bitcoin and Ethereum safe-havens for stocks during the COVID-19 pandemic? *Finance Research Letters*, 1–6. doi:10.1016/j.frl.2020.101798 PMID:33100925

Mokni, K., & Ajmi, A. N. (2021). Cryptocurrencies vs. US dollar: Evidence from causality in quantiles analysis. *Economic Analysis and Policy, 69*, 238–252. doi:10.1016/j.eap.2020.12.011

Moore, G. A. (1991). *Crossing the chasm: Marketing and selling technology products to mainstream customers*. HarperBusiness.

Okorie, D. I., & Lin, B. (2021). Stock markets and the COVID-19 fractal contagion effects. *Finance Research Letters, 38*, 1–8. doi:10.1016/j.frl.2020.101640 PMID:32837366

Popescu, A. D. (2020a). Alternative Investments confidence amid COVID-19 pandemic, *Scientific Bulletin - Economic Series*, *19*, 103-110. http://economic.upit.ro/RePEc/pdf/2020_3_13.pdf

Popescu, A. D. (2020b). Decentralized Finance (DeFi) – The Lego of Finance. *Social Sciences and Education Research Review*, *7*(1), 321-349. https://sserr.ro/wp-content/uploads/2020/07/SSERR_2020_7_1_321_349.pdf

Popescu, A. D. (2020c). Financial Technology (FinTech) as a Driver for Financial Digital Assets. *"Ovidius" University Annals, 20*(2), 1055-1059. https://stec.univ-ovidius.ro/html/anale/RO/wp-content/uploads/2021/03/Section%205/36.pdf

Popescu, A. D. (2020d). Transforming Capital Markets by means of Financial Digital Assets. *Revista de Științe Politice (Revue des Sciences Politiques), 68*, 108-119. https://cis01.ucv.ro/revistadestiintepolitice/files/numarul68_2020/11.pdf

Popescu, A. D. (2020e). Transitions and concepts within Decentralized Finance (Defi) Space, Research Terminals in the Social Sciences. *The Proceedings of CIL 2020: Ninth Edition of International Conference of Humanities and Social Sciences - Creativity, Imaginary, Language*, 40-61. https://www.cilconference.ro/wp-content/uploads/2020/09/cil_2020_research_terminals.pdf#page=40

Popescu, A. D. (2021a). Central Banks Digital Currency - Opportunities and Innovation. *"Ovidius" University Annals, 21*(1), 813-822. https://stec.univ-ovidius.ro/html/anale/RO/2021/Section%205/18.pdf

Popescu, A. D. (2021b). Non-Fungible Tokens (NFT) – Innovation beyond the craze, Revues et Méthodes sur le Management et le Commerce International. *Proceedings of Engineering & Technology – PET, 66*, 26-30. http://ipco-co.com/PET_Journal/IBEM-Proceedings/IBEM%20PROCEEDINGS.pdf#page=31

Popescu, A. D. (2022). *Understanding FinTech and Decentralized Finance (DeFi) for Financial Inclusion. In FinTech Development for Financial Inclusiveness*. IGI Global.

Shehzad, K., Xiaoxing, L., & Kazouz, H. (2020). COVID-19's disasters are perilous than Global Financial Crisis: A rumor or fact? *Finance Research Letters*, *36*, 1–6. doi:10.1016/j.frl.2020.101669 PMID:32837374

Stephenson, N. (1992). *Snow crash*. Bantan Books Publisher.

SuperHot. (2022). *SuperHot Game – Time only moves when you do*. Available at https://superhotgame.com/

World Bank. (2021). Global Economy to Expand by 4% in 2021. In *Vaccine Deployment and Investment Key to Sustaining the Recovery*. Author.

Zhang, D., Hu, M., & Ji, Q. (2020). Financial markets under the global pandemic of COVID-19. *Finance Research Letters*, *36*, 101–528. doi:10.1016/j.frl.2020.101528 PMID:32837360

This research was previously published in the Handbook of Research on Global Networking Post COVID-19; pages 189-209, copyright year 2022 by Business Science Reference (an imprint of IGI Global).

Chapter 2
The Internet of Things and Blockchain Technologies Adaptive Trade Systems in the Virtual World:
By Creating Virtual Accomplices Worldwide

Vardan Mkrttchian

https://orcid.org/0000-0003-4871-5956

HHH University, Australia

ABSTRACT

This chapter presents artificial and natural intelligence technologies. As part of the digital economy of the virtual world program, it is envisaged to increase the efficiency of electronic commerce and entrepreneurship; a similar task has been set by the leadership of the People's Republic of China. At present, thinking in the virtual world and China is radically transforming, along with methodological approaches to the development of trade policy and its tools in the digital economy. It is these circumstances that determine the relevance of the study, the results of which are presented in this chapter. Development of the fundamental foundations for improving the efficiency of electronic commerce and entrepreneurship in virtual world and China based on the virtual exchange of intellectual knowledge using blockchain technology and implementation multi-chain open source platform is the goal. An acceleration of scientific and technological progress in all areas of knowledge raises the task for ensuring the continuous growth of professional skills throughout the whole life.

DOI: 10.4018/978-1-6684-7597-3.ch002

INTRODUCTION IN VIRTUAL WORD AND TRADITIONAL TRADING PROCESS

This chapter is presented author idea use Artificial and Natural Intelligence Technologies. As part of the Digital Economy of the Virtual World program, it is envisaged to increase the efficiency of electronic commerce and entrepreneurship; a similar task has been set by the leadership of the People's Republic of China. At present, thinking in the Virtual World and China is radically transforming, methodological approaches to the development of trade policy and its tools in the digital economy. It is these circumstances that determine the relevance of the study, the results of which are presented in this chapter. Goal research: development of the fundamental foundations for improving the efficiency of electronic commerce and entrepreneurship in Virtual World and China based on the virtual exchange of intellectual knowledge using Blockchain technology and Implementation Multi chain Open Source Platform.

An acceleration of scientific and technological progress in all areas of knowledge raises the task for ensuring the continuous growth of professional skills throughout the whole life. In the traditional trading process, there are several more steps from concluding a contract to delivering an importer. It is difficult, the relevant institutions must carry out a large amount of data exchange, and this work should be. Banking business days, accompanied by a large number of manual reviews and paper documents, as a result of which Efficiency and security are reduced, and there are risks such as letter of credit fraud and soft conditions of the letter of credit. This has led to a gradual reduction in the use of letters of credit. A smart contract is a kind of goal for distribution and testing in an information way.

Over the past few years, information technologies have been able to create a unique environment that can provide resources for the development of global digital commerce, which allows for remote communication with the population on trade issues. This phenomenon has become especially relevant in conditions of forced self-isolation of citizens. Confirmation of this fact is the effect of the corona virus COVID-19. In terms of COVID-19, the population had the greatest demand for products and system solutions for organizing assistance providing video broadcasting, storage and data transfer.

Modern information technologies have allowed the seller and the buyer to quickly interact together at a remote distance from each other in real time. E-mail, instant messengers, Wi-Fi and software and hardware for the development of popular trading applications and technologies have become a significant leader in the market for popular services.

Among the main factors that will ensure positive dynamics in the development of global digital commerce, experts note the proliferation of wearable electronics for commercial use and virtual reality technologies.

This chapter discusses the prospects of Blockchain technology to facilitate the analysis and collection of Big Data using AI and IoT devices used by the People's Republic of China in the modern world by creating Virtual Accomplices' worldwide.

Object of Study

Virtual reality (VR) is a promising tool that can create complex events in the real world (past and present), provoked by traumatic stimuli and controlled by specialists.

VR technology has come a long way from the first experiments in the 50s of the XX century to the modern helmets of virtual reality in the 20s of the XXI century. Two main approaches to the formation of VR systems are known: a virtual room and wearable devices. Wearable VR devices include head-mounted indicators and virtual reality goggles. Currently, the market for virtual devices is formed by the following players by manufacturers: Epson BT-200, Google Glass, Oculus Rift, HTC Vive, Microsoft Hololens, Lumus dk-32, Samsung GearVR, Facebook, Sony, Nokia, etc. Publication and patent the activity of these companies allows us to distinguish four groups of manufacturers, characterized as centers of growth of new knowledge in the field of VR, sustainable research centers, dynamically developing R&D divisions and research engineers. The leading countries in this field are researchers from the USA (46% of the intellectual property market), China (34% of the intellectual property market), Japan (19% of the intellectual property market) and South Korea (13% of the intellectual property market). The market of virtual technologies and simulators in the field of global virtual trade as a whole is widely represented.

Smart contracts allow the absence of third parties. Conduct a trusted transaction. These transactions are track able and irreversible. Thanks to the smart contract technology, the credit intermediary function of the traditional bank is transferred to the smart contract for execution through the smart contract. The verification function, using a computer program to quickly judge the terms of the trading contract, and the next step is to monitor the trading process. As in a typical smart contract trading process between an importer and an exporter Creating a commercial contract based on smart contracts in a blockchain network, importers to financial institutions By providing a deposit, a financial institution registers a guarantee payment in real time to the blockchain network. After the deposit is paid, the exporter will send goods, and the conveyor will send the goods. Downloaded to the blockchain network when a smart contract, transport document and commercial sale are reached. Subject to the same conditions of payment, a financial instruction is issued to the financial institution, and the financial institution may calculate the payment for the importer. Using, thanks to effective blockchain technology, eliminates labor efficiency and low latency, can achieve high-frequency trading around the clock, through smart contracts to eliminate the human factor.

Subject of Study

The People's Republic of China in the modern world by creating Virtual Accomplices' worldwide the blockchain form is mainly divided into a public blockchain alliance. The blockchain consortium is a completely private blockchain (fully private) three, a public blockchain refers to any person in the world, anyone can read it. Anyone can send a transaction, and the transaction can be confirmed, anyone can participate in it. A blockchain process, an alliance blockchain means that its coordinated process is controlled by pre-selected nodes. Blockchain, a completely private blockchain, refers to a zone whose write rights are only in the Joint chapter hands of the Blockchain organization. Among them, the choice of alliance chain technologies is more suitable for creating information technologies for belt and road trade. For the needs of the exhibition, alliance chain nodes are pre-selected, and the pre-selection method can be effective. Eliminate bad, untrusted nodes to protect the blockchain from things like 51% Impact of point attack. In addition, the chain of alliances is not fully decentralized, and its consensus model. To control the alliance, this will contribute to the modernization and expansion of the consensus mechanism in the future. It also facilitates control of the system by the lead organization.

BACKGROUND IN VIRTUAL WORD AND TRADITIONAL TRADING PROCESS

In an environment where technology is a catalyst for new financial ideas, blockchain technology can be integrated into an existing financial system without cost. Currently, the Internet of things and artificial intelligence have become the main form of modern Internet finance, so the future blockchain will certainly develop in the direction of "blockchain + IoT blockchain + artificial intelligence". As the IoT grows geometrically, the cost of computing resources, storage and broadband for centralized services will become inaccessible to operating companies, and blockchain technology can provide direct data transfer for the IoT without the need to create and manage IoT. Secondly, it is necessary to solve the problem of protecting the privacy of the Internet of things. Because the centralized IoT service architecture stores and transmits all information and signals through the central processing unit, excessive data concentration leads to large-scale privacy leaks after information theft. According to blockchain technology, while client data is not controlled by one cloud Service Company, no one can steal data by encrypting the data transfer process, which makes client privacy more secure. Thirdly, it is creating a new business model for the Internet of things. In accordance with the current IoT architecture, clients cannot perform network transactions using another IoT and can conduct financial transactions on only one network or on a trusted network. This limitation significantly reduces the commercial value of the Internet of things. Blockchain technology eliminates trust transactions for direct transactions, for example, a system of "autonomous centralized remote control between centers" jointly developed by IBM and Samsung. The system uses a distributed network to ensure that IoT devices accessing the system can directly communicate and implement complex business logic.

With the continuous improvement of artificial intelligence technology, its application in the financial sector is becoming more and more extensive, including such important activities as account opening, analysis and trading. Therefore, the safety and reliability of artificial intelligence is attracting more attention. Blockchain can be artificially friendly through the following aspects: Firstly, blockchain technology can improve the reputation of artificial intelligence. Blockchain technology can rely on smart contract forms to ensure that during the transaction process, the system automatically creates electronic contracts and leaves irreparable traces. Secondly, the blockchain sharing mechanism will make artificial intelligence more friendly. Any transaction is carried out on the blockchain and must be confirmed by both sides of the transaction, so only two intelligent machines can confirm the transaction at a time. If a party cannot confirm for any reason, the transaction will be automatically canceled. Thirdly, blockchain technology will provide more accurate information for artificial intelligence. The blockchain system can use its own voting mechanism for the scientific classification of information on the Internet: the first level is spam, the second level is informational recommendations, and the third level is informational consent. The blockchain only sends consistent information to artificial intelligence through a rating system to evaluate and improve its accuracy. Fourth, blockchain technology will improve the security mechanism of artificial intelligence. For example, devices can register in a blockchain, perform various hierarchical evaluations using device registration information, provide different functions for different devices, and prevent smart devices from being misused to better exercise common ownership and device usage rights (Wenbin, 2015). The progress of human society and the development of the economy have benefited from the use and creation of tools since ancient times, and various tools have been continuously created. The initial driving force is undeniable from science and technology. In a market economy there will be a periodic cyclical overabundance, and even people's way of life. And the fundamental changes brought about by ideology are the result of large-scale industrial applications of science and technology. " Since the beginning of the 21st century, it has been based on the rapid development and maturity of information technologies such as the Internet and mobile Internet and cloud computing big data, which Ali, Tencent, JD, Baidu, Amazon, Facebook, Apple, Microsoft and Huawei created. A large number of great world-class enterprises have reached many well-known successful entrepreneurs, significantly increasing the efficiency and viability of socio-economic operations. However, the development of science and technology will never stop. Various new technologies are currently undergoing explosive birth and development. The business logic of applying scientific and technical industrialization is also undergoing fundamental changes, that is, from centralized information interaction. If you combine new technologies, such as artificial intelligence, the Internet of things, big data, cloud computing and block-chain, all together in one innovative project form the most effective form of economic activity. In the future, we will enter the era of the true digital economy, and the realization of the digital economy is the result of the merger of these new technologies. Social structural changes will at least completely change the behavior of business people. I think that I am afraid that these new technologies will be "organized and integrated" in various business scenarios. There is an opinion on the market that even "a predictable future = (artificial intelligence + Internet of things + big data) × blockchain". This formula shows that the three main technologies in brackets are "data", that is, deep data mining, massive data collection and transmission in real time and data mining, while a "block chain" provides data protection and trust him. The mechanisms and means of repaying value transactions allow you to safely use the value data required by the three technologies in brackets in the business environment. The right side of this formula actually expresses the product of "Blockchain Technology" and "Virtual Market".

MAIN FOCUS OF THE ARTICLE

Issues, Controversies, Problems

On the right side of the above formula, artificial intelligence is at the forefront because technology essentially embodies a kind of "ability", that is, an ability that allows intelligent machines (computer intelligent systems) to learn and model human thinking. At the same time, the results of the training model of the engine and the working model can be stored on the blockchain, which ensures that the model is not hacked, and the risk of malicious attacks by the commercial applications is further reduced (Li & Ren, 2016). Artificial intelligence technology can provide a glimpse of the future with massive historical data and real-time observations, while the Internet of Things will provide a large amount of real-time data as well as big data to provide sufficient and efficient "fuel" for artificial intelligence.

The data generated by various system sensors will naturally have some real-time data owners, but some data is temporarily unnecessary, so the data owner can desensitize this part of the temporarily unwanted data. Take it and share it with other data developers or developers, so that it can solve the problem of data loss and generate significant income, to offset the cost of the data creation process, and will also generate partial wins. For project founders, having enough data to train AI or ML models will be an endless challenge. Objectively, only large centralized technology companies with a large number of users will be able to get large data sets. However, in decentralized mode, it's very convenient to add more datasets to the artificial intelligence community, which means that IoT devices will make the data sets needed to teach artificial intelligence a big role in real-world business scenarios. Currently, there are many excellent technical research groups involved in collecting training data and the most practical research algorithms and applying these algorithms to the blockchain. Another question: how can we use a large number of unoccupied computing powers distributed in the market to launch AI or ML computing models? The answer is that blockchain technology can make the data market more equitable and efficient. The biggest injustice in the current market environment is that people tend to ignore the minority, but the most necessary thing in machine learning is the minority. Data, data belonging to a minority, will become more valuable, as I wrote in my previous article entitled "Mathematics is the cornerstone of blockchain + AI technology, and mathematics can interpret the value of all business practice." It is mentioned that if you want to increase the accuracy of the machine learning model from 90% to 99%, then you need not the data that has already been studied, but the data that several people should have that are different from the previous ones. For example, the commercial and technical logic, followed by the Ketai Structural Hole Technology Intelligent Eco-Network Investment and Structural Tunnel Financing System, is "(Artificial Intelligence + Internet of Things + Big Data) × Blockchain, which will be artificial intelligence (Such technologies like cognitive computing, intelligent management (IoT), big data and blockchain are combined with the participation of people in the division of labor on connected devices, jointly generated by management data and the operations that these devices can perform to create the first Innovative Intelligent System that "thinks" and is used for commercial purposes in the venture capital market We strongly believe that multicenter, de-mediation, self-organization and data exchange and network synergy are reliable The "intelligent ecosystem system" will be reconstructed from the existing traditional industry in accordance with this new business and technical logic. And this is what the future era of the digital economy needs (Li & Ren, 2016).

Solutions and Recommendations

1. Consensus Mechanism and Performance

A consensus protocol is used to achieve accessibility and consistency in distributed systems. This is a key technology in the blockchain, the main indicators of which include: Typical agreements include BFT consensus presented by PBFT, Nakamoto consensus presented by PoW / PoS, and the new hybrid consensus. Currently, the biggest challenge in consensus agreements is how to strike a balance between safety and efficiency.

Based on the premise of security, there are four ways to increase productivity:

1. Improving the hardware and computing capabilities, from CPU, GPU, FPGA to ASIC, mining equipment is constantly updated, and the general level of computer processing power is also rapidly developing. According to OpenAl analysis, since 2012, the task of teaching artificial intelligence, the computing power used is growing exponentially, and its current speed doubles every 3.5 months (compared with Moore's law, which doubles every 18 months). If computing power goes beyond a certain critical point, the blockchain performance issue may no longer be a problem;
2. The improvement of the consensus agreement system has not changed. Representative methods include reducing the generation interval of blocks, increasing the size of a block, adopting a two-layer chain structure, introducing a lightning-fast network, changing the basic structure of a block + chain, and reducing blocks.
3. Data, a advanced algorithms
4. New data structures, such as the use of directed acyclic graph (DAG) data structures, typical projects have 10TA and ByteBall;
5. New consistent protocols, such as the Thunder Ella algorithm for the PoW mechanism proposed by the researchers, the Algorand protocol and the Ouroboros algorithm for the PoS mechanism, PoS consensus based on the Sleepy model and Proof of Space.

2. Cross Chain

Currently, there are various chains: public, alliance and private. A public chain serves the public, an alliance chain is limited to one alliance, and a private chain serves only one private organization. From a private chain, an alliance chain to a public chain is a decentralization process, and from a public chain an alliance chain to a private chain, this is a centralization process.

During these transformations, various blockchain products will appear for private networks, alliance networks, and government networks. Then, when business interactions between different organizations, how to interact between different chains and chains becomes a big problem. There are currently three cross-chain technologies:

Notary Schemes Side Chains / Relays Hash Lock Technology

Cross-chain technology is the center of the next technological development of the blockchain. In addition, the current private network has a problem with the game, which is who, joins, and each other wants them to join their own blockchain system. Although BaaS (Backend as a Service) can reuse the underlying technology platform, the key is the exchange of data between different business systems and users, as well as collaboration between business systems. If there is no connection between the various systems, it is not possible to reuse core resources such as customers, assets and data.

There a two possible ways to solve this problem:

1.   The government or standardization organizations promote the standardization and standardization of blockchain technology and improve the interaction between different systems;
2.   The government is creating a public service platform. For example, the HKTFP supported by the Hong Kong Monetary Authority is typical. The advantage of this model is that a platform built on the basis of public interests can better resolve disputes between the subject of construction and the management mechanism, as well as open users and scenarios. And public services to achieve the integration of resources, but also easy for government regulation, improve regulatory efficiency.

3. Control Mechanisms

Since the blockchain itself is a natural voting system that contains all the logic necessary to change the validation assembly or update its own rules, and the voting results can be automated, the chain voting mechanism naturally becomes a blockchain ecosystem. The preferred control mechanism currently has a number of chain voting mechanisms, such as EOS, NEO, Lisk, and other systems in the Proof of Equity (DPOS) mechanism, through chain voting to determine who controls the super node that the network is running on or by agreement. Options are voted to determine Essence gas restriction or vote on protocol updates such as Toes.

Disadvantages of the current voting mechanism in the chain:

1.   Low participation in the vote, which leads to two problems. Firstly, the results of the vote reflect only a small number of people's opinions and it is difficult to obtain universal recognition, and secondly, an attacker can vote at low cost.

2. There may be a chapbook-style minority chain management that is detrimental to the interests of ordinary users.

In addition, relying entirely on chain management, he still cannot solve the problem of the main agent of the blockchain ecosystem, and also needs the support of chain supervision, such as legal oversight and a reputation mechanism.

Governments have now begun to take action. For example, the National Network Bureau recently announced the "Regulation on the Management of Information Services of the Blockchain (draft for comments)" and publicly sought public opinion. Of course, this is building a system level. From a technical point of view, how to improve the chain management mechanism is the next step in the study of blockchain technology.

4. Identity Management

Blockchain makes self-sovereign identity possible. By itself, it can be used as a decentralized public key infrastructure (PKI) to make public key authorities more useful and secure. Blockchain can be thought of as a decentralized certification authority that maps support for authentication to a public key.

Smart contracts can also add complex logic, implement cancellation and recovery, and reduce the burden on key management for end users. These technologies push identity ownership from centralized services to end-to-end services between people and make identity itself manageable. This is called autonomy. This approach distracts the data and calculations and transfers them to each individual, which is less economical for hackers because it takes a lot of effort to attack many people one by one.

In the alliance chain, different nodes must be assigned different permissions and they satisfy a certain control. To do this, it is necessary to create a safe and effective mechanism for authentication and identity management.

An authentication mechanism based on biometrics technology or an effective combination of biometrics and cryptography can be used;

An efficient and practical password scheme based on identifiers / attributes can also be used to achieve detailed access control / rights management for nodes / users.

5. Privacy Protection

In a public chain, it is necessary to protect confidential information, such as transaction data, address, identity, etc., and at the same time allow the accounting node to verify the legality of the transaction, and for the alliance chain, when building a privacy protection scheme, it is necessary to take into account the control / tracking of authorization.

Protection of transaction identification and content confidentiality can be achieved with cryptographic primitives and schemes, such as effective knowledge with zero knowledge, commitment and indistinguishable evidence. For example: Zkash uses zk-SNARK to implement a privacy mechanism.

A privacy mechanism based on a cryptographic scheme such as a ring signature, a group signature, and a privacy protection mechanism based on a hierarchical certificate mechanism is also optional. For example:

Montero uses a ring signature scheme to implement privacy protection mechanisms. Hyper ledger Fabric uses a hierarchical certificate mechanism to implement privacy protection mechanisms.

Protecting the confidentiality of transactional contents can also be achieved with an efficient holomorphic encryption scheme or a secure multi-part computing scheme. For example:

Ripple introduces privacy protection for trading channels, introducing a secure multi-user computing solution.

A simple coin protection mechanism can also be used to provide simple privacy protection.

6. Digital Wallet

Currently, digital wallets are trying to move from pure wallet services to environmental portals of digital assets, hoping to gain more market share and develop richer asset management services, mainly in the areas of asset management, asset trading, information aggregation, DApp distribution, etc. .

Asset management can be divided into production of value added, value added management, asset management, asset collection, etc. Asset transactions mainly include a decentralized exchange of digital assets and the exchange of legal currencies, information aggregation - this is mainly information exchange and aggregation of project information, DApp distribution is similar. In a small software store.

Although the entry points and development paths of different wallets are different, and each has its own strengths, the functions of different value-added wallets slightly overlap, because the long-term goals of each other are gradually converging. With the continuous development of the digital asset industry and the continuous improvement of the environment, the digital wallet scene function will become more and more important.

There a three aspects to its future development:

1. ensure the security, openness and convenience of the wallet;
2. Creation of a digital asset management platform based on the demand for added value of assets, providing users with rich financial products and increasing the conversion rate of users;
3. The third is to open the connection between digital assets and the real world, enrich the scenarios of digital assets and create ecology of digital assets.

Security is fundamental. Software technologies can use keyless cryptographic algorithms (a standard white box scheme or create new white box cryptographic algorithms) and code obfuscation methods to allow an adversary to extract basic cryptographic algorithms and key information, or use passwords, an authentication factor encryption algorithm such as personality and biometrics, encrypts and stores the key.

The hardware aspect can be based on the TEE (Trusted Execution Environment) or SE (Security Environment) security module and a technical solution that helps to configure the terminal device, which is one of the important additional directions for protecting a digital wallet.

7. Smart Contracts and Self-organizing Business Models

Smart contracts have the advantages of transparency, reliability, automatic execution and mandatory compliance. Once it is deployed in the blockchain, the code and data of the program are open and transparent, cannot be faked and must be executed in accordance with predefined logic to obtain the expected results, and the execution of the contract will be recorded.

It should be said that blockchain technology and its commercial application mutually reinforce each other. Self-organizing business applications built on smart contracts can help add value to blockchain technology and expand the scope of the encryption economics model.

Although from a technical point of view, a smart contract is just part of the code, it essentially carries a lot of business logic, and even a smart contract is a business model with unlimited imagination. Conversely, the implementation of a self-organizing business model also requires the delicate development of smart contracts, and also requires the support of technical measures, such as improving productivity, increasing security and protecting privacy. In other words, this is both the creation of a business model, and the development of a technical system.

The security of smart contracts is crucial. Due to the openness of smart contracts, their code and content can be obtained using open methods that allow hackers to analyze contracts and attack vulnerabilities. Once the attack is successful, this will result in significant losses. Consequently, there is an urgent need for sophisticated smart contract detection technology to detect, detect, and eliminate vulnerabilities before the contract is chained.

There were many smart contract detection tools or online testing sites, but these tests are still based on experience and there is nothing to be done about unknown contract vulnerabilities.

The formal check method is a possible solution for determining exactly whether a program can work in accordance with the developer's expectations by creating an appropriate model. However, formal verification of smart contracts is difficult, and no suitable solution has been found at this time, and further research is needed.

When applying smart contracts, on the one hand, it is necessary to clarify the possibility of using smart contracts from the legal level, on the other hand, since smart contracts have natural certainty and do not have the flexibility and selectivity of ordinary contracts, therefore, in specific scenarios, in order to establish an intervention mechanism that allows code to pause or stop execution.

FUTURE RESEARCH DIRECTIONS

- **Integration with other technologies:** It is often said that cloud computing, big data, artificial intelligence, blockchain technology, etc. In essence, they are the embodiment of "algorithm + data", and there are no other priorities. Since the essence is the same, mutual integration is inevitable.

For example, an asset securitization scenario requires ongoing disclosure of information from multiple business systems, and also requires a large-scale distributed file storage.

Blockchain technology can ensure the consistency of distributed ledgers on all sides of a transaction by signing a transaction, a consistent algorithm and cross-chain technology to ensure that a transaction is executed in real time and automatically complete real-time information disclosure to ensure accounting. Accounting and accounting are consistent, which greatly improves credit rating of traded products and significantly reduces the cost, which allows information users to receive global information ju about the activities of the enterprise in real time and through it, and receiving global information means information. Mass growth, the best way to store and retrieve the value of information, is becoming the key to the chain.

Therefore, the integration of blockchain technology with distributed file systems, big data analysis, cloud computing, artificial intelligence and other technologies is an important direction for future development.

CONCLUSION

In the presented chapter, the following tasks were solved: the analysis of goods and services of Russia and China was carried out; outline the main policy guidelines and its impact on globalization and regional integration; disclosing the prospects for the development of blockchain technologies in international trade and its impact on the global financial industry; the role of blockchain technology in the development of the global economy is substantiated.

The following research areas were disclosed:

1. The development of international cooperation based on innovative intelligent technologies
   a. Prerequisites for international cooperation on the example of "Belts and Roads". The historical need of the project "One belt – one way"
   b. China's banking industry indicators in the belt and road
   c. Blockchain Technology - the strongest push in international multilateral financial and trade cooperation
   d. Cross-border capital flows: transactional efficiency, risk management, checking the creditworthiness of counterparties
2. Creating conditions for mutually beneficial trade relations in the process of digitalization of national economic systems
   a. Application of blockchain technology in international trade in the context of the "Belt and Road" initiative
   b. Vision of the Alliance Belt and Road Blockchain
   c. Blockchain technology can be combined with more technical means
3. Development of reflective adaptive software for applying Blockchain technology, big data analysis and virtual exchange of intellectual knowledge.

Were disclosed the future direction of blockchain technology: consensus mechanism and performance, cross chain, control mechanism, identity management, privacy protection, digital wallet, smart contracts and self-organizing business models.

REFERENCES

Li, Z., & Ren, X. (2016). Analysis of the impact of blockchain on the Internet finance and its prospects. *Technical Economics and Management Studies*, *10*, 75–78.

Technology illuminates the future - when blockchain technology and adaptive security technology enter social management and economic life. (n.d.). Retrieved October 02, 2019, from http://blog.sina.com.cn/s/blog_67804b9a0102z2gn.html

The fusion of artificial intelligence and blockchain technology represents the future of the digital economy. (n.d.). Retrieved May 14, 2019, from http://www.sohu.com/a/313838766_99985608?qq-pf-to=pcqq.c2c

Wenbin, U. (2015). Principles, models and proposals of banking trading blockchain. *Hebei University Journal, 6,* 159–160.

ADDITIONAL READING

Alguliyev, R. M., Aliguliyev, R. M., & Sukhostat, L. V. (2020). Efficient algorithm for big data clustering on single machine. *CAAI Trans Intell Technol, 5*(1), 9–14. doi:10.1049/trit.2019.0048

Antonopoulos, A. M. (2014). *Mastering bitcoin: unlocking digital crypto-currencies.* O'Reilly Media Inc.

Ash, J. S., Berg, M., & Coiera, E. (2004). Some unintended consequences of information technology in health care: The nature of patient care information system-related errors. *Journal of the American Medical Informatics Association, 11*(2), 104–112. doi:10.1197/jamia.M1471 PMID:14633936

Chang, X., & Han, F. (2016). *Block chain: From digital currency to credit society.* China Citic Press.

Conoscenti, M., Vetr, A., & Martin, J. C. D. (2016) Blockchain for the internet of things: a systematic literature review. In: *Proceedings of the IEEE/ACS 13th international conference of computer systems and applications (AICCSA)*, IEEE, Agadir, Morocco 10.1109/AICCSA.2016.7945805

Devi, D., Namasudra, S., & Kadry, S. (2020). A boosting-aided adaptive cluster-based undersampling approach for treatment of class imbalance problem. *International Journal of Data Warehousing and Mining, 16*(3), 60–86. doi:10.4018/IJDWM.2020070104

Haber, S., & Stornetta, W. S. (1991). How to time-stamp a digital document. *Journal of Cryptology, 3*(2), 99–111. doi:10.1007/BF00196791

Ho, D. C. K., Au, K. F., & Newton, E. (2002). Empirical research on supply chain management: A critical review and recommendations. *International Journal of Production Research, 40*(17), 4415–4430. doi:10.1080/00207540210157204

Huang, G. Q., Lau, J. S. K., & Mak, K. L. (2003). The impacts of sharing production information on supply chain dynamics: A review of the literature. *International Journal of Production Research, 41*(7), 1483–1517. doi:10.1080/0020754031000069625

Hwang, J., Choi, M., Lee, T., Jeon, S., Kim, S., Park, S., & Park, S. (2017). Energy prosumer business model using blockchain system to ensure transparency and safety. *Energy Procedia, 141,* 194–198. doi:10.1016/j.egypro.2017.11.037

Kshetri, N. (2017). Cybersecurity in India: Regulations, governance, institutional capacity and market mechanisms. *Asian Research Policy, 8*(1), 64–76.

Li, S., Wang, G., & Yang, J. (2019). Survey on cloud model based similarity measure of uncertain concepts. *CAAI Trans Intell Technol, 4*(4), 223–230. doi:10.1049/trit.2019.0021

Lin, Q., Yan, H., Huang, Z., Chen, W., Shen, J., & Tang, Y. (2018). An ID-based linearly homomorphic signature scheme and its application in Blockchain. *IEEE Access: Practical Innovations, Open Solutions*, *6*, 20632–20640. doi:10.1109/ACCESS.2018.2809426

Ming, Z., Jun, C., Yuqing, W., Yuanfei, L., Yongqi, Y., & Jinyue, D. (2017). The primarily research for multi module cooperative autonomous mode of energy internet under blockchain framework. *Zhongguo Dianji Gongcheng Xuebao*, *37*(13), 3672–3681.

Namasudra, S. (2017). *An improved attribute-based encryption technique towards the data security in cloud computing*. Concurr Comput Pract Exer., doi:10.1002/cpe.4364

Namasudra, S. (2018). Taxonomy of DNA-based security models. In S. Namasudra & G. C. Deka (Eds.), *Advances of dna computing in cryptography* (pp. 53–68). Springer. doi:10.1201/9781351011419-3

Namasudra, S. (2018). Cloud computing: A new era. *J Fundam Appl Sci*, *10*(2), 113–135.

Namasudra, S., Chakraborty, R., Majumder, A., & Moparthi, N. R. (2020). *Securing multimedia by using DNA based encryption in the cloud computing environment*. ACM T Multi Comput Commun Appl.

Namasudra, S., & Deka, G. C. (2018). *Advances of DNA computing in cryptography*. Taylor & Francis. doi:10.1201/9781351011419

Namasudra, S., & Deka, G. C. (2018). Introduction of DNA computing in cryptography. In S. Namasudra & D. C. Deka (Eds.), *Advances of dna computing in cryptography* (pp. 27–34). Springer. doi:10.1201/9781351011419-1

Namasudra, S., Deka, G. C., & Bali, R. (2018). Applications and future trends of DNA computing. In S. Namasudra & G. C. Deka (Eds.), *Advances of DNA computing in cryptography* (pp. 181–192). Taylor & Francis. doi:10.1201/9781351011419-9

Namasudra, S., Devi, D., Choudhary, S., Patan, R., & Kallam, S. (2018). Security, privacy, trust, and anonymity. In S. Namasudra & G. C. Deka (Eds.), *Advances of DNA computing in cryptography* (pp. 153–166). Taylor & Francis. doi:10.1201/9781351011419-7

Namasudra, S., Devi, D., Kadry, S., Sundarasekar, R., & Shanthini, A. (2020). Towards DNA based data security in the cloud computing environment. *Computer Communications*, *151*, 539–547. doi:10.1016/j.comcom.2019.12.041

Namasudra, S., & Roy, P. (2016). Secure and efficient data access control in cloud computing environment: A survey. *Multiagent Grid Sys Int J*, *12*(2), 69–90. doi:10.3233/MGS-160244

Namasudra, S., & Roy, P. (2017). Time saving protocol for data accessing in cloud computing. *IET Communications*, *11*(10), 1558–1565. doi:10.1049/iet-com.2016.0777

Namasudra, S., & Roy, P. (2018). PpBAC: Popularity based access control model for cloud computing. *Journal of Organizational and End User Computing*, *30*(4), 14–31. doi:10.4018/JOEUC.2018100102

Namasudra, S., Roy, P., Vijayakumar, P., Audithan, S., & Balusamy, B. (2017). Time efficient secure DNA based access control model for cloud computing environment. *Future Generation Computer Systems*, *73*, 90–105. doi:10.1016/j.future.2017.01.017

Sarkar, M., Saha, K., Namasudra, S., & Roy, P. (2015). An efficient and time saving web service based android application. *SSRG Int J Comput Sci Eng*, 2(8), 18–21.

Swan, M. (2015). *Blockchain: blueprint for a new economy*. O'Reilly Media.

Williams, A. (2016). *IBM to open first blockchain innovation centre in Singapore, to create applications and grow new markets in finance and trade*. The Straits Times Singapore Press Holdings Ltsd. Co.

Wood, G. (2014). *Ethereum: a secure decentralised generalised transaction ledger*. Ethereum Project Yellow Paper.

Xia, Q. I., Sifah, E. B., Asamoah, K. O., Gao, J., Du, X., & Guizani, M. (2017). MeDShare: Trust-less medical data sharing among cloud service providers via blockchain. *IEEE Access: Practical Innovations, Open Solutions*, 5, 14757–14767. doi:10.1109/ACCESS.2017.2730843

Xue, T., Hongbin, S., & Qinglai, G. (2016). Electricity transactions and congestion management based on blockchain in energy internet. *Power Syst Technol*, 40(12), 3630–3638.

Zhao, X., Li, R., & Zuo, X. (2019). Advances on QoS-aware web service selection and composition with nature-inspired computing. *CAAI Trans Intell Technol*, 4(3), 159–174. doi:10.1049/trit.2019.0018

Zheng, Z., Xie, S., Dai, H. N., & Wang, H. (2016). Blockchain challenges and opportunities: A survey. *International Journal of Web and Grid Services*, 14(4), 314–335.

KEY TERMS AND DEFINITIONS

Blockchain: A continuous sequential chain of blocks (linked list) containing information built according to certain rules.

Digital Economy: Is an economic activity focused on digital and electronic technologies. This includes electronic business and commerce, as well as the goods and services they produce. This definition covers all business, cultural, economic, and social operations performed on the Internet and using digital communication technologies.

EDI (Electronic Data Interchange): A series of standards and conventions for the transfer of structured digital information between organizations, based on certain regulations and formats of transmitted messages.

Electronic Commerce: Financial transactions and transactions carried out through the Internet and private communication networks, during which purchases and sales of goods and services are made, as well as money transfers.

Intellectual Capital: Knowledge, skills and production experience of specific people and intangible assets, including patents, databases, software, trademarks, etc. that are productively used to maximize profits and other economic and technical results.

This research was previously published in Multidisciplinary Functions of Blockchain Technology in AI and IoT Applications; pages 118-136, copyright year 2021 by Engineering Science Reference (an imprint of IGI Global).

Chapter 3
Being a Post–Learner With Virtual Worlds

Ferhan Şahin
Anadolu University, Turkey

Ezgi Doğan
Anadolu University, Turkey

ABSTRACT

Transhumanism, which emerges as a movement of thought, stands out with the developments such as artificial organs, brain-to-brain knowledge and learning transfer and smart robots in the 21st century. One of these technologies, where we see early applications with the goal of reaching the post-human, is the virtual worlds. Some features of the post-humans, which can now be experienced through 3 dimensional immersive virtual worlds in a certain scale, also reveal the fact that the existing virtual worlds are a limited simulation of a transhumanist future. While the virtual worlds and transhumanism perspective is expected to be effective in various areas of human life, it will be inevitable for these effects to manifest themselves in learning processes. In this sense, evaluation of surrounding learning by virtual worlds is the main objective of this chapter. For this purpose, virtual worlds in transhumanism age were tried to be evaluated under learning context by using anime series and film samples which are yet considered as sci-fi.

INTRODUCTION

Nowadays, thought movements and technologies that will change and transform current learning conception and learning environments and perhaps move those beyond what we know are becoming an important topic. Prominent couple as predecessor and complementary of each other among these thought movements and technologies can be considered as transhumanism and 3 dimensional virtual worlds. Principles presented by transhumanism as a thought movement and impacts of 3 dimensional virtual worlds as a developing technology will create important transformation in all aspects of human life including learning activities. To understand and imagine how this transformation will occur and what the effects will be, it is beneficial to explain and evaluate these two concepts.

DOI: 10.4018/978-1-6684-7597-3.ch003

3 Dimensional Virtual Worlds

Virtual worlds are defined as feeling of users to be in another environment other than his/her real environment and environment created by computer to enable user to interact with this environment (Schroeder, 1996). User in a virtual world creates an "avatar" which is a character that represents the user in simulated environment and user moves in virtual world with this avatar and interacts with other avatars and objects in virtual world (Baker, Wentz, and Woods, 2009). Effectiveness of being there illusion created by virtual world can be evaluated as at what level do users feel they are in virtual world and what caused this feeling (Heeter, 1992). It can be said that most important factor emphasized in definition of virtual world that could impact learning environment is feeling of "being there". At this point, 3 dimensional immersive virtual worlds supported with virtual reality technologies are discussed.

In line with definition of virtual worlds, 3 dimensional immersive virtual worlds can be explained as follows (Dalgarno & Lee, 2010):

A computer-based, simulated environment in which users are able to immerse themselves, and within which they are able to, through their avatars (computer-based representations of themselves or alternative selves), experience, manipulate, interact with and/or create virtual objects and places that are graphically depicted in three dimensions.

There are two important key concepts that are related and emphasized in this definition. These could be given as immersion and 3 dimensional environments. It can be said that for a virtual world to be immersive, this world should be experienced by user in personal, social and environment manner in 3 dimensional environments. This experience can be provided by virtual reality technologies (Heeter, 1992). Technologies that completely involve perspective of user in virtual environments in terms of positioning of user in simulated virtual world in his/her unique way and exploring this virtual world with various sensory ways and interacting with this world can be called as immersive virtual reality (Osuagwu, Ihedigbo and Ndigwe, 2015; Psotka, 2015). With these technologies, users can experience i.e. experience being there feeling in virtual world with natural moves in real life and without any mediator between himself/herself and environment. User can fully commit to role of avatar in virtual world, take the steps necessitated by this role, feel the environment and have the feeling that s/he is doing all these in real world. Such role, under certain circumstances, can either be similar to human roles in real world or transhuman experiences in a fantastic world. At this point, where transhuman concept is reflected, transhumanism is discussed as another concept and a movement of thought.

Transhumanism

Transhumanism has been a movement of thought that expanded and developed in last decades (Bostrom et al., 1999; Bostrom, 2003). With this development and expansion, different definitions have emerged for transhumanism based on different perspectives of philosophical sense. However, before considering transhumanism as expression of different contexts, it is important to analyze "transhumanism" term from starting point to comprehend current condition of this philosophy and understand basis of this concept.

Throughout the history, there are expressions that uses transhumanism term which are relatively far from current meaning and there are expressions that explain similar concepts without using transhumanism term. Reade (1910) stated that humanity will act with a belief and passion to work together to eliminate disease and sin, perfect prodigy and love, find immortality, discover infinity, and divine cause of conquering creation. Although this discourse fits transhumanism perspective, transhumanism term was absent. Huxley (1957) expressed that humans can go beyond their self, transcend self as an individual within unity, and if this belief reaches sufficient number of humans, humanity will be at the edge of a new existence to realize destiny in conscious manner and used transhumanism term for this expression. Esfandiary (1972) wrote a book chapter by using transhumanism term and continued to develop transhumanist thoughts that expresses transhumanism as a transition from human to transhuman state. However, "transhumanism" was never used as a title of his definition. Transhumanism term was consciously used in an article called "Transhumanism: Towards s Futurist Philosophy" for the first time to define transhumanist philosophy (More, 1990). Accordingly, when evaluated under different expressions and interpretations context, it can be stated that it is possible to explain main themes, values and views of transhumanism (More, 2013).

World Transhumanism Association (WTA, 2018) defined transhumanism as "a philosophy that argues to set technology to work to transcend our biologic limits and transform human structure". Accelerated development of technology resulted in revolutionary situations such as transhuman artificial intelligence and molecular nanotechnology. Results of these developments may contain biochemically development or redesign of our pleasure centers; enjoy richer emotions, life-long happiness and exciting experience; eliminate aging; eliminate diseases and maybe, synthetically developing human body and gradually changing with computers.

In another definition, transhumanism was explained as a life philosophy driven by principles and values that encourage life and that desires continuation and acceleration of smart life forms with science and technological and beyond human life and human limitations (More, 1990). In addition to this definition, de Mul (2010) expressed transhumanism as adding strong belief of intelligence, science and technology will lead to social, physical and intellectual development to humanism. Transhumanism can be interpreted as philosophical and cultural movement with explanatory and normative components. In terms of descriptive perspective, transhumanism is not only strengthening of current and future technologies with previous capacities but also adding new different skills that will enable radical change for our world and humans. In normative terms, it is expressed as doing our best to accelerate uncovering of technological developments for improvement/development and realizing a post-human future possibility (Verdoux, 2009).

According to Bostrom (2005), transhumanism presents an interdisciplinary approach to understand and evaluate opportunities to develop human organism that is possible with rapid technological developments. It also draws attention to current technologies, such as information technologies and genetic engineering, as well as future technologies such as molecular nanotechnology and artificial intelligence. Among improvement options, it is possible to see significant increase in human lifetime, elimination of certain diseases, decreasing unnecessary pain and increasing intellectual, physical and emotional capacities of humans. According to this perspective, transhumanism creates an opportunity to live longer and healthier lives, to develop our memory and other intellectual skills, to improve our emotional experiences, to increase our subjective wellbeing emotion and to achieve better control level over our lives (Bostrom, 2005).

Analysis and interpretation of different definitions of transhumanism showed that these definitions harbour basic common values in general. In accessibility of such basic values, existence of certain conditions and creating ideal environment to realize foresights of transhumanism is important. At this point, basic conditions to realize transhumanist thought are stated as;

1. Global security,
2. Technological progress and
3. Wide access (Bostrom, 2005).

In first one of these basic conditions, global security, a scenario that should be avoided under all conditions is considered. This scenario can be stated as risk of existence. Accordingly, it is stated that size of risk consisting of existential risks are extremely important (Leslie, 1996; Bostrom, 2002; Rees, 2003). Existential risks show that when it comes to extinction of human race or permanently destroying further development capacity, transhumanist basic values cannot be reached, and humans will fail (Bostrom, 2005). In this sense, it is appropriate to say that global security is one of the top-ranking conditions to realize transhumanism thought.

Second one among these preconditions, technological progress, forms one of the basic cornerstones. This condition emphasizes challenges to overcome our incompetency in biologic sense (aging, disease, poor memory and intelligence level, limited emotional capacity and capacitive level for regular well-being) and we need high level tools to overcome successfully. Other points include that development of such tools would require a great struggle in terms of collective problem solving capacities of our species. Another important point emphasized was that technological advancement is closely linked with economic development and economic growth or increased production in another sense can serve as proxy to technological advancement under certain conditions (Bostrom, 2005). Based on these information, it is appropriate to comment that technological advancement has vital role to realize transhumanist ideals in various ways.

Another condition to realize transhumanist dream is stated as wide access. In transhumanist philosophy, it is emphasized that complete realization of basic values depend ideally on everyone becoming post-human. Reasons that show necessities of supporting wide access are given as decreasing inequality to achieve a just order, to show respect and solidarity between humans, to obtain help for transhumanism, to increase chance of humans to become post-human and to alleviate suffering of humans at a wider scale (Bostrom, 2005). At this point, to have a future where transhumanism is realized, importance of abovementioned conditions can clearly be seen. It emerged that to achieve positive transformation in humanity as predicted by transhumanism and to achieve determined objectives, humanity must undertake certain basic duties in responsible manner and in this sense, complete these duties. Concordantly, it can be commented that if related conditions are not met, it is highly impossible for transhumanism philosophy to invigorate in real world.

Another perspective that should be emphasized under transhumanism and concept that emerged from this perspective is singularity. In terms of this concept, first name that comes into mind is one of the largest and most important figures of transhumanism, Ray Kurzweil (Dahlin, 2012). Kurzweil (2005) defined singularity concept in his book (The Singularity is Near) as a period in the future where technological change will have higher speed, this change will cause deep impacts and human life will experience irrevocable transformation. Fundamental idea behind "The Singularity is Near" is expressed as extreme increase of development speed of technology created by humanity and expansion of powers in fast and big tempo. It is predicted that such expansion and change will start in almost incomprehensible way and explode in unexpected manner (Kurzweil, 2005).

In terms of singularity context, emphasis of information-based technologies will cover all information and competencies of humans and as a result power to define schemes, problem solving skills, emotional and ethical intelligence of human brain (Kurzweil, 2005) is in line with transhumanism philosophy. At this point, although human brain is impressive in multiple aspects, there are serious limitations. It is stated that brain uses unprecedented parallel structure (trillions of intraneuronal connection) to rapidly recognize models that are ambiguous, however, human thinking system is relatively slow and physiologic band spectrum to process new information is highly limited compared to exponential expansion of human knowledge database (Kurzweil, 2005). In line with this, if current predictions regarding increasing speed of processing capacity are correct, in not a faraway future, we would need neural implants to completely benefit from super speed computers that will exist in the future (Kurzweil, 2000). Based on this information, it can clearly be seen that basis of singularity expectation fits with transhumanism movement. This means conditions predicted under singularity context are at the point that is desired to be achieved with transhumanism perspective. It can be commented that hopes in optimistic structure of transhumanism philosophy towards future will be near to turn into reality with singularity.

As seen from these explanations, transhumanism generates certain ideas to take humanity to next level with technological and scientific developments and forms the intellectual basis to transform into post-human. At this point, post-human concept that can be experienced via virtual worlds actually reflects that current virtual worlds are only limited simulations of transhumanist future.

Transhumanism and Virtual Worlds

When statements regarding transhumanism are evaluated, this thought movement pledged a "transcending human" stated with post-human, super-human, overhuman and these pledges emerged certain concepts (Şişman-Uğur, 2018). It can be seen that these concepts are considered under increasing life quality, slowing aging, infinite life, emotion-free human, artificial organs, brain that surpasses biologic limits, order instead of chaos, human-machine integration, robot/cyborg/android, artificial reality/virtual reality, nanotechnology, artificial intelligence, divine technology, omega point, cloud information/techno-system for humans, common consciousness and singularity (Şişman-Uğur, 2018). Versatility of all these concepts led subjects related with transhumanism to have wide range of area and led a multidisciplinary area including philosophers, futurists, scientists, lawyers, sociologists, doctors, health scientists, engineers, artists, men of literature, psychologists, pharmacologists, genetic scientists, technology research institutions and even bureaucrats to evaluate this field.

When fields related with transhumanism movement are considered, in addition to predominant disciplines like nanotechnology or genetic engineering, there are some other fields that are less visible. In this sense, virtual worlds (video games etc.) are emphasized. Since high number of transhumanists appreciate this freedom and power at basis of this digital environments and realizing that these environments can support transhumanism thought (Geraci, 2012) shows the value of virtual worlds for this perspective.

It is emphasized that virtual worlds play a significant role in innovative transhumanism. In this sense, it can be said that technologic fantasies that looked borrowed from 20th century has become one of the focal points of transhumanism expectations. In this sense, it is stated that some transhumanists hope to restructure the reality in line with the vision in video games which is the fantastic world of imagination. (Geraci, 2012). Virtual worlds develop transhumanism idea with designs, options they offer and impact level they have and enable transcend human biology. In this term, it can be commented that video games and virtual worlds play a key role in transhumanism (Geraci, 2012).

By nature, technology is about crossing the lines, however, in terms of virtual worlds, these worlds work better than other technologies as an illustration of our post-human potential. Additionally, in general sense, when it is considered that inhabitants of virtual worlds live in a magical space with meaning and power, it is possible to state that almost all virtual world offers an opportunity to exceed our limits (Geraci, 2012). In line with these, it is believed to be effective to clearly understand importance of these environments under user experience and thoughts by considering video games and virtual worlds based on transhumanism context. Researchers showed that video game and virtual world users (such as World of Warcraft and Second Life etc.) would prefer to live in a virtual world if they were given the chance (Castronova, 2008). Additionally, as a realistic form of immortality, there were findings showing that they would consider living like characters in the game (Bainbridge, 2010) and it is interesting and impressive to live like that. In addition to these, another important finding is that other than players that support transhumanism, some of the players who do not share transhumanist perspective reflected that it is attractive to live in a virtual game world (Bainbridge, 2010). Based on the fact that by combination of science and science fiction preserving expansion of transhumanism in most of the 20th century (Geraci, 2011), it is stated that transhumanism has critical importance regarding belief to upload our minds to virtual worlds or to even environments such as World of Warcraft and Second Life (Geraci, 2012). Hence, in literature, it is expressed that basically including our mind and personal identity, everything is information within different schemes and in principle, there are no barriers to transfer personal memories and identity to computer (Kurzweil, 2005). Based on this information, importance of relationship of virtual worlds with transhumanism and information provided to coherently evaluate expectations towards future can clearly be seen. While it is expected that virtual worlds and transhumanist thought will be effective in various aspects of human life, it is inevitable that these effects will be visible in learning processes and environments. In this sense, it is necessary to understand and discuss what type of transformation will these two concepts cause in learning processes.

Learning Under Effect of Transhumanism and Virtual Worlds

Studies in the literature states that in following periods, education and learning activities will change for transhumans (Rikowski, 2002) and it is an important necessity to structure new learning processes and being prepared for change (Şişman-Uğur, 2018). At this point, there is a distinction between future of education under transhumanism context and future in education. First, it is about how schools and education will process and organised in the future, and second one is about considering future studies and future visions as topic content in current schools (Hicks, 2008). It is emphasized that transhumanism is valid for both and for the future, commons effects of brain science and information technologies on education practice are emphasized (Dahlin, 2012). Which path will education and learning will follow for future generations and how education system will be organized will be the main focus of this study. In addition, the moral and ethical dimensions of transhumanism in the context of individuals, society and religion are excluded from the scope of this study.

It is stated that connection with human brain with external intervention was tried and successful results were obtained as well as there were successful studies to control exploration and learning of brain and developing learning and memorizing skills of brain (HRL, 2016). Additionally, it is stated that recreation of the consciousness of individuals on computer environment and studies to back-up consciousness will be carried one step forward by transferring back-up consciousness to individuals in future steps (Now This Future, 2018; Regalado, 2018) In this sense, development in technologies like existence of virtual brains, enhanced reality, direct integration of virtual reality environment and brain and event hologram memory are predicted. To be able to evaluate the effects of transhumanist philosophy with human and technology, and to investigate its effects on learning, requires knowledge and experience related to many disciplines in the context of education and technology. (Şişman-Uğur, 2018). Effective and efficient realization of these necessities has key properties to obtain coherent predictions regarding how learning will become in transhumanism era for new generations and to generate ideas about could be done by using different disciplines.

When we consider that virtual worlds of today are preview of transhumanism future, it can be commented that considering and evaluating these virtual worlds under learning context can provide guidance to have a learning map for future generations. Even those 3 dimensional immersive virtual worlds produced with current technologies can provide unprecedented support in terms of learning as these worlds create feeling of being there and enable obtaining real life experiences. In a future where transhumanism objectives are realized, this support could be a capacity to move learning to another dimension.

MAIN FOCUS OF THE CHAPTER

Virtual worlds, transhumanism and current relationship of these two concepts on learning are analyzed above. In this study, on contrary to current situation, the purpose is to go one step forward and predict and imagine possible changes in the future. Various productions presented as science fiction in fact can be messengers of changes in the future and it is appropriate to analyze these productions to achieve abovementioned objectives. In this sense, properties expected from virtual worlds that will be used in learning environments in transhumanism age and evaluation of surrounding learning by these virtual worlds is the main objective of this chapter. For this purpose, document analysis was conducted and virtual worlds in transhumanism age were tried to be evaluated under learning context by using anime series and film samples which are yet considered as sci-fi. Certain criteria were considered to determine productions evaluated in this study. Based on these criteria, properties of productions can be listed as having a theme that caused permanent change in human mind and body, containing virtual world and artificial intelligence component. Based on these criteria, productions included in this study are Chappie, Sword Art Online, Source Code, The Upgrade, Elysium, Knights of Sidonia, Ready Player One and Automata. Considering essential body and mind system developments are possible by using biotechnology and rapidly developing genetic engineering technologies (Kurzweil, 2005), results obtained from analyzed productions and possible changes that these results can make on learning were evaluated under mind and body enhancement themes.

DISCUSSION

Virtual World Themed Productions

Sword Art Online

First season of Sword Art Online was aired in 2012 and this is an anime series in action, adventure, and science fiction genre. The first season of this anime explains that in 2022, thousands of people are trapped inside a new massive multiplayer online role playing game (MMORPG) and what they experience to get freed of this virtual world. Most basic and important feature of Sword Art Online game that is expected by thousands of gamers is that with a special headgear called Nerve Gear, gamers can link into massive virtual world. With the technology of this special headgear, gamers can connect to their characters in virtual world via their brains and can have all the interaction within the game only by thinking. The adventure starts when Kirito, the lead character of anime series, notices on the first day when the game is opened to access of gamers that there is no menu to exit the game. As game creator and game master Kayaba Akihiko announced that he removed all exit options from the game and only way to exit the game and return to real world was to beat last boss on top of 100-floored tower called Aincrad and game experience takes a new path for gamers. Additionally, other feature of this virtual world and Nerve Gear technology is that when gamers die in this virtual world, they would also die in real world by shocking users' brain with this special headgear turns these lives in the virtual world into life and death battle. Dying in Sword Art Online virtual world means dying in real world is the prominent theme of this anime. Although the death of players in this virtual world causes them to die in real life, a scene in the anime takes it a step further. An echo of Kayaba Akihiko's consciousness that continues to exist in the game server even after his death is an interesting example in the context of transhunamism.

Ready Player One

Directed by Steven Spielberg, Read Player One movie is a sci-fi, action and adventure themed movie adapted from the novel of Ernest Cline with the same name. Screenplay of this movie was written by Zak Penn and Ernest Cline. Storyline is in year 2045 and described the world as harsh environment with low living standards for most of the people. Storyline of this movie focused on experiences of lead character Wade Watts (Tye Sheridan) in a massive virtual world called OASIS. OASIS is a virtual world limited only by imagination where you can do everything, go everywhere or become the one thing you want to be and where most part of humanity spend almost all their time. In this movie, after the death of creator of OASIS, James Halliday (Mark Rylence), adventure of lead character Watts and his friends who wants to win a three-staged competition designed to select the heir to leave the all his wealth and full control of OASIS are explained in this fantastic virtual universe. It can be said that one of the things that should be emphasized in terms of technology is the technology products that are designed as wearable cloths and glasses and enable direct digital connection to OASIS where humans can interact with virtual world and their movements in real life are translated to virtual world. Another point to be emphasized is with this direct connection and translating exact motions in real world, humans are actually living in OASIS. Such that having real correspondence of money and goods in OASIS in real life and finding buyers at high price is an important indicator that this virtual world is more important than real world.

As seen in productions analyzed under virtual world theme, with brain-machine interaction, humans can completely feel themselves in virtual world in physical and cognitive way and even biologic events like death can occur in these environments. In this sense, there are both invasive and non-invasive studies at certain levels regarding these technologies. At this point, it can be stated that especially developments in nanorobot technology use can be one of the leading technologies in terms of virtual worlds and games. This technology emphasizes that humans will completely experience virtual reality in convincing manner. At this point, it is emphasized that not needing any physical contact with neurons and existing technology to bilaterally contact with neurons can be the basis for immersive virtual reality experience. For such technologies, "neuron transistors" that can detect when a nearby neuron is ignited or alternatively that can enable or disable ignition of neuron can be given as example (Weis and Fromherz, 1997). Additionally, there are studies in the literature stating that quantum dots have the feature to enable bilateral communication between neurons and electronic devices (Winter, Liu, Korgel and Schmidt, 2001). It can be stated that this virtual reality experience that can exactly be stated as immersive can process based on individual will on the basis of bilateral communication between nanorobots and neurons. In case of individual's desire to stay in reality of real world, related nanorobots will stay fixed inside capillary vessels without any functions, and these nanorobots will suppress all input data from sense organs and change these data with signals appropriate for virtual environment in case of individual's desire to enter virtual reality (Freitas, 1999). Core of this virtual reality sense provided by nanorobots with this bilateral communication is based on the fact that human body does not directly perceive brain and accordingly, these signals will be perceived as if they are coming from physical body or brain (Kurzweil, 2005). As it can be seen, in terms of theme in the production, there are researches to reach situations that are seen as utopic under current conditions. It can be stated that if such brain-machinery communication occurs and users are completely integrated within virtual world, there could be radical changes in learning context. In such scenario, learners can obtain context-special and real experiences completely independent of time and space. This way, dangerous and high cost experiences can be realized in more affordable and safe manner. At the same time, since students will see virtual world as a game, there could be positive outputs in terms of motivation. This means, learners can obtain necessary learning outputs within game scenario without noticing such process.

Body and Mind Enhancement Themed Productions

Source Code

Directed by Duncan Jones and written by Ben Ripley, Source Code is a mystery, sci-fi movie screened in 2011. This movie is about a soldier who wakes up in a different body, is assigned to find the bomber in the train as a part of experimental state program and only has 8 minutes to do that task. This experimental program was achieved by transferring human consciousness to another human body, however, this operation can only work for 8 minutes and it should be reapplied again after this time. In this movie, consciousness of Captain Colter Stevens is transferred to body of a teacher in that passenger train attacked by bomb in the morning and he is assigned to identify the bomber. Stevens, who is surprised about this cannot make sense why he is there, and he is confused about what he experiences since he doesn't know what he is doing. Managers of this experimental program explain him the situation and ask him to determine the location of the bomb and identify the bomber. At this point, the main emphasis is although an event occurred in the past, past cannot be changed and only information can be collected.

The basis of the Source Code technology in the movie is based on the fact that the brain's electromagnetic field is active for a short period of time even after death, and short-term memory allows access to the section that covers the 8-minute memory segment just before the person's death. It is possible to say that Source Code technology, which is the basis of the film, is focused on re-arranging time and providing access to a parallel reality through the memory of a dead person rather than transferring the consciousness of a human to another human being offers an interesting perspective in the context of transhumanism.

The Upgrade

Written and directed by Leigh Whannell, The Upgrade is an action, thriller and sci-fi movie. Setting of this film is near future where technology is extremely widespread and almost controls all aspects of life.

This film is about events that took place after lead character Grey Trace (Logan Marshall-Green) gets paralyzed after a traffic accident where his wife dies. Grey, who is weary of life, is treated by implanting an experimental computer chip and gets back up again and notices that his computer chip has a will of itself. In terms of technology in this film, key elements are human enhancement, nanotechnology and artificial intelligence. Mechanical or electronic enhancement of human organs (to turn into weapons), storing and operating nanorobots in human body with nanotechnology (enhancement for weapons and war), developing super capacity computer chips, transplanting these chips to humans as implant, making these chips a part of problematic area of humans that need treatment and chip having a will is the main subjects of this film. Although there are many examples in the context of the enhancement of the human body by using implants in the movie, establishing the connection between the brain and limbs of Gray who is in a quadriplegic state by means of using a computer chip (Stem) is an important part of the film. The scene where the main character begins to use all his limbs in seconds after the surgery can be expressed as a relevant example, which can be evaluated especially from the perspective of transhumanism.

Elysium

Written and directed by Neill Blomkamp, Elysium that was first screened in 2013 is in drama, action, and sci-fi genre. Timeline of this movie is in 2154 and a world with extremely rich and extremely poor people are shown. While rich people live in a space station called Elysium with various technologies, poor people are forced to live in overcrowded and ruined Earth. However, this would not stop humans on Earth to try to go to Elysium to live in better conditions or get treatment. However, strict precautions and anti-immigration laws of the state prevents these initiatives and an army of robots is used as security force both on Earth and in Elysium. In this movie, one of the poor people who tries to survive on Earth, Max (Matt Damon), has a work accident and exposed to deadly radiation and because of no treatment available other than Elysium, it focuses on the task that he started to enter Elysium. To increase his successful rate in this process, a mechanical exoskeleton to enhance physical power of skeleton system and electronic tool and interface connected to brain are implanted. In terms of technology, other key points in the movie are directly transferring and storing digital information to brain, advanced gene technology and repair and readjustment at cellular or atomic level. In this context, a small girl with an advanced disease (Acute lymphoblastic leukemia) that cannot be treated on earth, can be treated with re-atomizing method in a matter of seconds (such as the re-creation of diseased areas rather than a treatment) by using a medical technology specific to Elysium, is a striking example.

Knights of Sidonia

Created by Yuichi Matsushita and Tatsuya Shishikira, Knights of Sidonia is an anime series in action, adventure and sci-fi genre consisting of 24 episodes where first episode was aired in 2014. This series is directed by Koubun Shizonu and written by Sadayuki Murai and Shigeru Murakoshi. In this anime, after alien (Gauna) invasion that occurred thousands of years ago and humanity was at the verge of extinction, humans are escaping with giant space ships and scatter around different corners of space to find a habitable new planet. Anime focuses of one of these spaceships, Sidonia, and certain part of the journey. In storyline, we can see Nagate Tanikaza who surfaces from depth of Sidonia to find food in the year of 3394 without any knowledge of this event and situation of humankind, and his survival struggle and other problems. In this anime, key points are fight with Gauna, giant robots developed with special technologies to protect the ship and humans inside the ship, and specially trained pilots. Additionally, in terms of technology, another important point can be stated as insufficient resources for survival of crew and human population inside the ship and development of appropriate spaces to provide new resources is a genetic solution for insufficient sources of the ship. With this gene technology, humans in new generation have decreased eating need once a week and obtain most of the necessary energy from photosynthesis by using solar energy. Additionally, with gene technology, new generation is born without genders and after certain age, they can select and transform based on their partners or population. In addition, the exact cloning of people (the cloning of the individual's memory and experience can be done in a manner that can be transferred to the clone) and using this method as a backup system for important individuals has been achieved. In line with these technological developments, regeneration of human cells and self-treatment prevented aging and certain level of immortality is reached (this is not public information and only a high-level governor group have access to this feature).

In productions analyzed under body and mind enhancement theme, it can be seen that a post-human concept can exist with various technologies. Current studies and development activities show that steps are taken to build this future. When these activities are analyzed, it is important to emphasize research and development activities especially in nanotechnology field. Nanotechnology is considered as science and engineering activities at atomic and molecular level. In nanotechnology basis, this design approach consists of nanorobotics technology. Nanorobotics is defined as machinery or robot production technology at nanometer scale or similar scale. Nanorobots that work in design and production of nanotechnology engineering are defined as tools that consist of nanoscale or molecular components ranging between 01-10 micrometer (Kad, Hodgar and Thorat, 2018). One of the fields with highest potential for using nanorobots is given as biomedical nanorobots (nanomedicine). Recent developments in design, production and operation of nanorobots emphasize that power, function and versatility of these nanorobots are largely increasing. It is stated that these micro machineries have a large potential for wide range of biomedical applications (Li, Esteban-Fernández de Ávila, Gao, Zhang and Wang, 2017). Nanorobots that represent all types of smart structures with nanoscale moving, detection, signaling, information processing, intelligence, manipulation and crawling behavior (Bagade et.al., 2013) are considered as powerful tools to enhance human biological systems (Kad et al., 2018). In this sense, under reverse engineering basis, human blood studies that include redesign can be give as suitable examples. Redesign (Rob Freitas) of red blood cells that inefficiently transfer oxygen to cells in circulation system which is regarded as a system that does not work with full-efficiency can be given as example (Kurzweil, 2005). It is stated that robotic red blood cells (reciprocates) that can be created with redesign may enable humans to function for hours without oxygen (Freitas, 1999; 2003), and with newly designed robotic blood cells, we can have the capacity to store and carry hundred times more oxygen. Additionally, to develop immune system of humans, designs related with white blood cells (microbivore) (Freitas, 1999) are other approaches considered under current technologies. Microbivore are nanorobots known as nanorobotic phagocyte that act as artificial white blood cells. These microbivores capture pathogens in blood circulation and divides these pathogens to smaller molecules. Main function of microbivores that consist of four main components is absorbing pathogens in blood circulation with phagocyte process and digest these pathogens (Wilner, 2009). After neutralizing pathogens, microbivores are discarded from body via kidneys and urine. As a result of phagocytosis cycle that is completed in thirty seconds, bacterial compounds are digested and turned into non-antigenic molecules and it is emphasized that there is no sepsis or septic shock risk (Freitas, 1998). Studies showed that microbivores are 1000 times faster than phagocytes in blood circulation and did not cause pathogens to show multiple drug resistance. Additionally, in the literature, it is stated that microbivores are used in bacterial infections as well as cleaning infections in urine and synovial fluids (Kad et al., 2018). Preventing aging, minimizing biological needs with different technologies in Knights of Sidonia example can be considered as future versions of abovementioned nanorobots.

In terms of human body, by adopting current technologies, nerve tips of people without arms, hands or legs are intervened and these people were able to control robotic organs (Şişman-Uğur, 2018). This can be considered as reflection under current conditions with integrated exoskeleton and linking this exoskeleton with brain in Elysium movie.

Additionally, different techniques that would act as a communication bridge between biologic data processing and digital technologies are developed. In this sense, tools to bilaterally communicate with neurons (neuron transistors) are developed (Zeck and Fromberz, 2001) and movement of a live leach was controlled with computer. Under the scope of technological tools developed with current means can also include implants based on "neuromorphic" model (reverse engineering in human brain and nervous system) developed for certain parts of brain (Brumfiel, 2002). Among these implants, implants that directly communicate with left ventricular and subthalami nucleus of brain to reverse devastating symptoms of Parkinson's diseases and neural implants that can replace damaged retinas can be given as examples (Kurzweil, 2005). As in The Upgrade movie, this situation provides clues regarding treatment of damaged parts of body with various implants and even eliminating limitations like disease or injuries.

Another field of technology that can serve as basis for humanistic expectations is genetic engineering. In this field, human somatic-cell engineering is emphasized as a promising research field. This method includes an approach that uses stem cells called transdifferentiation. In this method, human DNA is used to transform a cell to another type of cell and creating new tissues (Collas and Hâkelien, 2003). Studies in this field successfully reprogrammed liver cells to pancreatic cells, and human skin cells to immune system and neural system cells (Horb, Shen, Tosh and Slack, 2003). Additionally, since all self-regenerating and all somatic cell types have differentiation potential, important improvements were achieved in studies conducted with human pluripotent stem cells that has great value in cellular treatment approaches (Zhou et al., 2016). To reprogram human somatic cells and transform pluripotent stem cells, on a polydopamine mediator surface specially developed for this purpose, cells obtained from human urine and navel string stem cells were reprogrammed and long-term regeneration was successfully achieved (Zhou et al., 2016). In this sense, with various methods in genetic engineering that has high potential, it is known that any organ that is compatible with human genetic properties can be developed, a complete young organ can be achieved once telomers of this new developed organ reached original youth capacity (Lanza et.al., 2000), i.e. an organ can be replaced by younger and healthier version without any operation or any immune system reactions. By applying this method to any organ or tissue of human body in certain periods, it is stated that humans can gradually be younger (Kurzweil, 2005). This method, which is currently being explored and developed with exciting expectations, is also a precursor to the utopian technologies in the Elysium and Knights of Sidonia.

Analysis of production under body and mind enhancement theme in terms of developing technologies have focused on body enhancement until this point. However, it can be seen that there are various properties to be analyzed under mind enhancement. In this sense, it is beneficial to analyze current mind enhancement applications. Firstly, direct information transfer to brain, information transfer between brains, information storing in brain, learning facilitation, and neurologic control of brain and machine interfaces (BMI) can be given as examples. There are successful experimental results in studies in this direction regarding external intervention to brain and transferring experiences by connecting with brain.

Additionally, successful results were obtained in transcranial direct current stimulation (tDCS) researches that were conducted to strengthen learning and memory (HRL, 2016). Based on increased coherence of learned skills to realize cognitive and real-world tasks with tDCS, it can be stated that transcranial direct current stimulation has an effect on gaining skills (Choe, Coffman, Bergstedt, Ziegler and Phillips, 2016). As in Elysium, direct transfer of digital information to human brain can be considered as one of the results of such studies.

In studies regarding brain to brain interface (BTBI), there are results showing that EEG was used to transfer information on brains of a human to another human brain with transcranial magnetic stimulation (TMS). As a result, it is stated that two humans jointly completed a task by direct BTBI as communication channel. In this study, it is stated that to reach the objective in a computer game, brains of two people cooperated with communication and completed a visual task (Rao et al., 2014). In another study, sensorimotor information that has behaviorally significant structure was transferred in real-time between brains of two rats. In this study, rat that showed the behavior acted as coder and the results showed that information obtained from brain of coded rat were transferred to another rat that acted as decoder (intracortical microstimulation - ICMS). As a result of these findings, it is stated that brains are merged, and a complex system is formed with technology. It is stated that BTBI can activate brain networks for bilateral transfer, processing and storing in animals and this could form the basis for new social interaction type studies and biologic information processing tool studies (Pais-Vieira, Lebedev, Kunicki, Wang and Nicolelis, 2013). In Source Code and The Upgrade examples, science fiction elements such as transferring human mind to another body and this mind having its own will describes an achievable future if abovementioned studies are developed further.

Artificial Intelligence Themed Productions

Chappie

Directed by Neill Blomkamp and written by Neill Blomkamp and Terri Tatchell, Chappie is a 2015 action, drama and crime movie. Timeline of this movie is near future and public order is preserved by mechanical police force. This movie tells the story of a robot (Chappie) that was stolen and reprogrammed after being damaged and discarded. With this new programming, our lead character robot is the first droid with thinking and feeling ability and this is the main theme of the movie. In general sense, in this movie, one of the basis for storyline is decreasing and controlling high crime rates in Johannesburg with robots of private company (Tetravaal Company). In the movie, the designer of the robots (Deon Wilson) develops a new artificial intelligence but the company will not let him to use it. His efforts trying to make this technology into a reality is another theme of the movie. After various unexpected events, by loading artificial intelligence to a discarded robot, turning this robot into a machine that has the ability to think and feel and need of this robot to learn and grow like child is a key point. Other than that, probably the most important theme of this movie is with extreme learning speed, Chappie discovers that memories and consciousness can be stored and transferred into mechanic vessels (like droids) and finally manage to achieve this. From this point of view, it is an important point in the scope of transhumanism that Chappie saves Deon by transferring his consciousness to a robot, and in a way enables him to continue to exist by just replacing his vessel.

Automata

Directed by Gabe Ibáñez and written by Gabe Ibáñez, Igor Legarreta and Javier Sánchez, Automata was screened in 2014. Automata is an action, thriller and sci-fi movie that occurs in 2044 in dystopian world. This movie is based on Automata Pilgrim 7000 robots designed and manufactured by ROC company to instigate Earth after catastrophic sun storms that annihilated 99.7% of humanity and only 21 million people survived. Key point of this movie is the security protocols of these robots. These protocols are defined as "a robot cannot harm a human and cannot make any adjustment, repair or change on itself or other robots". This movie starts when a police officer shoots a robot and the claim that this robot repaired itself. After that, ROC company agent Jacq Vacuan (Antonio Banderas) who is assigned to investigate discovers unimaginable discoveries about Automata Pilgrim 7000 robots. One of the most important discovery is that while the agent is investigating and thinking that there is someone who is illegally modifying robots, and then he finds out that another robot was making changes and turning these robots into beings that can think like them. In terms of technology, maybe the biggest plot twist is that these modified robots can create a new type of robot with higher thinking and feeling capacity as well as consciousness, and this new type of robot has the character of a child that needs learning and care and have the ability breath air. Considering these features, this child robot's characteristics and the process of its creation by other robots is an interesting example from the perspective of transhumanism.

Productions that are analyzed under virtual world and mind-body enhancement themes showed insights to develop post-human with technological developments. However, in the Chappie and Automata movies, robots that are equipped with artificial intelligence who can behave like a human with their will, mind and body are the subjects rather than effects of the abovementioned technological developments on humans. The point that needs to be considered here is that the robots are in a similar situation to people who have been enhanced as body and mind with non-biological parts. Based on this information, it can be concluded that the future robots, which may have similar characteristics in terms of thinking and feeling, like the people who have transcend into post-human with the support of their non-biological parts and the artificial intelligence these will provide.

CONCLUSION

Transhumanism based themes of productions analyzed until now are evaluated with current research and development studies under body and mind enhancement categories. It is seen that technologies in these science fiction productions have become successful at certain degrees in current studies or there are theoretical basis, design work and these studies are moving towards creating a product. In this sense, it can be predicted that such technologies or technologies with similar functions that look like products of imagination may become a part of our lives in the near future. Based on these insights, it is clearly seen that advanced technologies will create radical changes on learning and teaching and these changes should be adapted to use opportunities provided by these technologies in the best way possible for humanity. Under these necessities, it is important to evaluate development and changes in teaching and learning in terms of technological areas and methods considered under body and mind enhancement.

Today, it can be said that we have tools that can replace many organs of human body (arms, legs, hips, chin, veins, knee, elbow) and systems that can replace complex organs at certain levels. Accordingly, among technologies that may lead development and change in teaching and learning processes, it is important to consider implants that has high potential to improve and develop biologic systems of individuals in physical sense. Among these implants, usage of artificial organs to support learners in teaching and learning processes has high potential. Using artificial organs when students lack appropriate function of an organ, has missing organ or experience similar conditions is wide and effective usage area of such artificial organs. It can be stated that support of this technology will be great to increase learning process quality of learners or involve these learners within these processes without any barriers. With the support of these technological organs, it is predicted that students can experience learning activities without social and psychological damage as well as without physical challenges. This way, it is possible to achieve well-skilled, self-confident and successful individuals who can become a member of society.

Other than replacing parts of skeleton and muscle systems, another usage area of using implants to enable students to participate in learning activities or to increase quality of these activities can be seen as replacing and renewing organs or systems with mechanical parts. In this sense, correcting or improving vision sense of individuals with vision problems or vision loss with implants can be given as example. It is possible to treat and strengthen vision by replacing area of vision loss or damage with implants (replacing damaged retina with implants). At this point, it is possible that digitally replaced eye can provide opportunities to surpass limitations of biologic eyes and enable advanced properties (zoom features, augmented reality etc.) as well as undertaking vision function. Additionally, when neurons that provide vision has no function, programmable nanorobots may be used to complete various functions including moving, detection, signaling, information processing, intelligence and manipulation to enable bilateral communication between neurons and brain. Complete lack of vision or losing an eye permanently, replacing the organ with digital version as a whole can be expressed as another method that can be used for providing vision. Also, in terms of example that considers eye loss and losing eye or vision completely, somatic cell engineering can provide a solution by reprogramming cells with own DNA of the individual. With this method, it is possible to produce new tissues or organs and replace damaged ones. It is possible to state that having opportunities to improve this and other sense organs that has vital importance of education and teaching can greatly contribute to learners.

Similarly, various implants placed inside brains of individuals with physical disabilities, it is possible to achieve a scenario where virtual world created for learning can be presented without barriers, experiences can be achieved in full-immersion environment with currently developing technologies.

It is possible to say that technologies that fit transhumanism perspective in analyzed productions have different potentials in terms of human mind and these potentials can provide opportunities in education and teaching field.

With increasing internet access in line with technologic developments, educations services with low cost and wide access for different education levels are realized globally. In this sense, it can be stated that web-based education as a virtual environment has become one of the key points within education system and based on this fact, virtual worlds may have the greatest part in education of future.

Teachers working with teaching system that has flexible structure based on needs has great contribution for education quality and raise students in desired way. Popularity of virtual environments among learners and using these worlds as a part of education is another important point that should be supported by both researchers and learners. Accordingly, incremental increase to interest towards virtual worlds that has unlimited potential and ultimate and incomparable usage area indicates that education structure of the future will develop under the basis of virtual worlds. Besides, it is clear that we are unable to present an effective 3 dimensional virtual world in current technologies and virtual environments and we fail to provide being there feeling to learners with full-immersion. Currently, success of education over virtual environments is in fact a small part of results that can be provided by virtual worlds. Providing an easily accessible experience and authentic learning activities by a virtual world education environment that provides full immersion and being there feeling to learners has a key role to reach these results. In this sense, virtual worlds have unique value as these worlds enable learners to learn by doing in different fields, experience these via real world problems, and providing these experiences in an individualistic structure that has high artificial intelligence potential and offering a chance to transfer to different problems. Additionally, by succeeding in integrating of individuals with their non-biological intelligence can enable individuals to enter any virtual reality using their own will and they will be able to download and use information and skills directly. Considering these, it can be predicted that such phenomena as education and learning will undergo profound transformations and move to a new dimension.

REFERENCES

Bagade, O. M., Dhole, S. N., Kahane, S. K., Bhosale, D. R., Bhargude, D. N., & Kad, D. R. (2013). Appraisal on preparation and characterization of nanoparticles for parenteral and ophthalmic administration. *International Journal of Research in Pharmaceutical Sciences*, *4*(4), 490–503.

Bainbridge, W. S. (2010). When virtual worlds expand. In W. S. Bainbridge (Ed.), *Online worlds: Convergence of the real and the virtual* (pp. 237–251). London: Springer. doi:10.1007/978-1-84882-825-4_19

Baker, S. C., Wentz, R. K., & Woods, M. M. (2009). Using virtual worlds in education: Second Life® as an educational tool. *Teaching of Psychology*, *36*(1), 59–64. doi:10.1080/00986280802529079

Bostrom, N. (2002). Existential risks: Analyzing human extinction scenarios and related hazards. *Journal of Evolution and Technology / WTA*, *9*.

Bostrom, N. (2005). A history of transhumanist thought. *Journal of Evolution and Technology / WTA*, *14*(1), 1–25.

Bostrom, N. (2005). Transhumanist values. *Journal of Philosophical Research*, *30*(9999), 3–14. doi:10.5840/jpr_2005_26

Brumfiel, G. (2002). Futurists predict body swaps for planet hops. *Nature International Journal of Science*, *418*, 359. PMID:12140527

Castronova, E. (2008). *Exodus to the virtual world: How online fun is changing reality*. New York: Palgrave Macmillan.

Choe, J., Coffman, B. A., Bergstedt, D. T., Ziegler, M. D., & Phillips, M. E. (2016). Transcranial direct current stimulation modulates neuronal activity and learning in pilot training. *Frontiers in Human Neuroscience*, *10*, 34. doi:10.3389/fnhum.2016.00034 PMID:26903841

Collas, P., & Håkelien, A. M. (2003). Teaching cells new tricks. *Trends in Biotechnology*, *21*(8), 354–361. doi:10.1016/S0167-7799(03)00147-1 PMID:12902172

Dahlin, B. (2012). Our posthuman futures and education: Homo Zappiens, Cyborgs, and the New Adam. *Futures*, *44*(1), 55–63. doi:10.1016/j.futures.2011.08.007

Dalgarno, B., & Lee, M. J. (2010). What are the learning affordances of 3-D virtual environments? *British Journal of Educational Technology*, *41*(1), 10–32. doi:10.1111/j.1467-8535.2009.01038.x

de Mul, J. (2010b). Transhumanism: The Convergence of Evolution, Humanism, and Information Technology. In *Cyberspace Odyssey: Towards a Virtual Ontology and Anthropology* (pp. 243–262). Newcastle upon Tyne, UK: Cambridge Scholars Publishing.

Esfandiary, F. M., & FM-2030. (1989). *Are You a Transhuman? Monitoring and Stimulating Your Personal Rate of Growth in a Rapidly Changing World.* Clayton, Australia: Warner Books.

Freitas, R. A. (1998). Exploratory design in medical nanotechnology: A mechanical artificial red cell. *Artificial Cells, Blood Substitutes, and Biotechnology*, *26*(4), 411–430. doi:10.3109/10731199809117682 PMID:9663339

Freitas, R. A. (1999). *Basic capabilities.* Georgetown, TX: Landes Bioscience.

Freitas, R. A. (2003). *Nanomedicine volume IIA: Biocompatibility.* Austin, TX: CRC Press. doi:10.1201/9781498712576

Geraci, R. M. (2011). There and back again: Transhumanist evangelism in science fiction and popular science. *Implicit Religion*, *14*(2), 141–172. doi:10.1558/imre.v14i2.141

Geraci, R. M. (2012). Video games and the transhuman inclination. *Zygon*, *47*(4), 735–756. doi:10.1111/j.1467-9744.2012.01292.x

Heeter, C. (1992). Being there: The subjective experience of presence. *Presence (Cambridge, Mass.)*, *1*(2), 262–271. doi:10.1162/pres.1992.1.2.262

Horb, M. E., Shen, C. N., Tosh, D., & Slack, J. M. (2003). Experimental conversion of liver to pancreas. *Current Biology*, *13*(2), 105–115. doi:10.1016/S0960-9822(02)01434-3 PMID:12546783

HRL. (2016). *HRL demonstrates the potential to enhance the human intellect's existing capacity to learn new skills.* Retrieved from http://www.hrl.com/news/2016/02/10/hrl-demonstrates-the-potentialto-enhance-the-human-intellects-existing-capacity-to-learn-new-skills

Huxley, J. (1957). *New bottles for new wine: Essays.* London: Chatto & Windus.

Kad, D., & Thorat, S. H. K. (2018). Nanorobotics: Medicine of the future. *World Journal of Pharmacy and Pharmaceutical Sciences*, *7*(8), 1393–1416.

Kurzweil, R. (2000). *The age of spiritual machines: When computers exceed human intelligence.* New York: Penguin.

Kurzweil, R. (2005). *The singularity is near.* New York: Penguin Group.

Lanza, R. P., Cibelli, J. B., Blackwell, C., Cristofalo, V. J., Francis, M. K., Baerlocher, G. M., ... Lansdorp, P. M. (2000). Extension of cell life-span and telomere length in animals cloned from senescent somatic cells. *Science*, *288*(5466), 665–669. doi:10.1126cience.288.5466.665 PMID:10784448

Leslie, J. (1996). *The end of the world: The ethics and science of human extinction.* London: Routledge.

Li, J., de Ávila, B. E. F., Gao, W., Zhang, L., & Wang, J. (2017). Micro/nanorobots for biomedicine: Delivery, surgery, sensing, and detoxification. *Science Robotics*, *2*(4), 1–9. doi:10.1126cirobotics.aam6431

More, M. (1990). Transhumanism: Towards a futurist philosophy. *Extropy*, (6), 6-12.

More, M. (2013). The philosophy of transhumanism. In M. More & N. Vita-More (Eds.), *The transhumanist reader: Classical and contemporary essays on the science, technology, and philosophy of the human future* (pp. 3–17). Malden, MA: John Wiley & Sons. doi:10.1002/9781118555927.ch1

Now This Future. (2018). *This Start-Up Wants to Upload Your Brain to a Computer*. Retrieved from https://www.facebook.com/NowThisFuture/videos/2008861865821650/

Osuagwu, O. E., & Ihedigbo, C. E., & Ndigwe, C. (2015). Integrating Virtual Reality (VR) into traditional instructional design. *West African Journal of Industrial and Academic Research*, *15*(1), 68–77.

Pais-Vieira, M., Lebedev, M., Kunicki, C., Wang, J., & Nicolelis, M. A. (2013). A brain-to-brain interface for real-time sharing of sensorimotor information. *Scientific Reports*, *3*(3), 1319. doi:10.1038rep01319 PMID:23448946

Psotka, J. (1995). Immersive training systems: Virtual reality and education and training. *Instructional Science*, *23*(5-6), 405–431. doi:10.1007/BF00896880

Rao, R. P., Stocco, A., Bryan, M., Sarma, D., Youngquist, T. M., Wu, J., & Prat, C. S. (2014). A direct brain-to-brain interface in humans. *PLoS One*, *9*(11), 1–12. doi:10.1371/journal.pone.0111332 PMID:25372285

Reade, W. W. (1910). *The martyrdom of man*. London: Kegan Paul.

Rees, M. (2003). *Our final hour*. New York: Basic Books.

Regalado, A. (2018). *A startup is pitching a mind-uploading service that is "100 percent fatal"*. Retrieved from https://www.technologyreview.com/s/610456/a-startup-is-pitching-a-mind-uploadingservice-that-is-100-percent-fatal/

Rikowski, G. (2002). Education, capital and the transhuman. In D. Hill, P. McLaren, M. Cole, & G. Rikowski (Eds.), *Marxism against postmodernism in educational theory* (pp. 111–143). Lanham, MD: Lexington Books.

Schroeder, R. (1996). *Possible worlds: the social dynamic of virtual reality technology*. Boulder, CO: Westview Press, Inc.

Uğur, S. (2018). Transhumanizm ve öğrenmedeki değişim. *Açıköğretim Uygulamaları ve Araştırmaları Dergisi*, *4*(3), 58–74.

Verdoux, P. (2009). Transhumanism, progress and the future. *Journal of Evolution and Technology / WTA*, *20*(2), 49–69.

Weis, R., & Fromherz, P. (1997). Frequency dependent signal transfer in neuron transistors. *Physical Review. E*, *55*(1), 877–889. doi:10.1103/PhysRevE.55.877

Winter, J. O., Liu, T. Y., Korgel, B. A., & Schmidt, C. E. (2001). Recognition molecule directed interfacing between semiconductor quantum dots and nerve cells. *Advanced Materials, 13*(22), 1673–1677. doi:10.1002/1521-4095(200111)13:22<1673::AID-ADMA1673>3.0.CO;2-6

WTA. (2018). *The Transhumanist FAQ: What is transhumanism?* Retrieved from http://humanityplus. org/philosophy/transhumanist-faq/

Zeck, G., & Fromherz, P. (2001). Noninvasive neuroelectronic interfacing with synaptically connected snail neurons immobilized on a semiconductor chip. *Proceedings of the National Academy of Sciences of the United States of America, 98*(18), 10457–10462. doi:10.1073/pnas.181348698 PMID:11526244

Zhou, P., Wu, F., Zhou, T., Cai, X., Zhang, S., Zhang, X., ... Lan, F. (2016). Simple and versatile synthetic polydopamine-based surface supports reprogramming of human somatic cells and long-term self-renewal of human pluripotent stem cells under defined conditions. *Biomaterials, 87*, 1–17. doi:10.1016/j.biomaterials.2016.02.012 PMID:26897536

ADDITIONAL READING

Bainbridge, W. S. (2013). Transavatars. In M. More & N. Vita-More (Eds.), *The transhumanist reader: Classical and contemporary essays on the science, technology, and philosophy of the human future* (pp. 3–17). Malden, MA: John Wiley & Sons. doi:10.1002/9781118555927.ch9

Bowman, D. A., & McMahan, R. P. (2007). Virtual reality: How much immersion is enough? *Computer, 40*(7), 36–43. doi:10.1109/MC.2007.257

Bricken, M. (1991). Virtual worlds: No interface to design. In M. Benedikt (Ed.), *Cyberspace: First steps.* Cambridge, MA: MIT Press.

Hansell, G. R., & Grassie, W. (2011). *H+/-: Transhumanism and its critics.* Philadelphia, PA: Metanexus Institute.

Kurzweil, R., & Grossman, T. (2004). *Fantastic voyage: live long enough to live forever.* Emmaus, PA: Rodale.

Milgram, P., ve Kishino, F. (1994). A taxonomy of mixed reality visual displays. *IEICE Transactions on Information and Systems, 77*(12), 1321–1329.

Sorgner, S. L. (2009). Nietzsche, the overhuman, and transhumanism. *Journal of Evolution and Technology / WTA, 20*(1), 29–42.

Winn, W. (1993). *A conceptual basis for educational applications of virtual reality. Technical Publication R-93-9, Human Interface Technology Laboratory of the Washington Technology Center.* Seattle: University of Washington.

KEY TERMS AND DEFINITIONS

Artificial Intelligence: A branch of computer science that aims to produce intelligent machines that have the characteristics of a human like learning, perception, recognition, planning, problem solving and reasoning.

Human Enhancement: To improve humanity and the quality of human life through methods such as treating disability and illness, improving current skills of humanity and developing new ones by means of technological developments.

Immersion: The objective measure of how realistic a user experiences the virtual world sensually.

Nano Robot: A programmable micro-sized robot for various tasks that made up of nanoscale components using nanotechnology methods and tools.

Post-Human: The human of the future who will surpass the capacity of the present humans with the profound technological modifications in body and brain systems.

Singularity: It is a period in which the speed of technological developments will increase rapidly and as a result, there will be fundamental changes in humanity.

Three-Dimensional Virtual World: A 3D virtual environment simulated by a computer, where users can interact with each other, objects and the environment.

This research was previously published in the Handbook of Research on Learning in the Age of Transhumanism; pages 185-204, copyright year 2019 by Information Science Reference (an imprint of IGI Global).

Chapter 4
Virtual Worlds for Developing Intercultural Competence

Lisiane Machado
Unisinos University, Brazil

Angilberto Freitas
Universidade do Grande Rio (Unigranrio), Brazil

Eliane Schlemmer
Unisinos University, Brazil

Cristiane Drebes Pedron
Universidade Nove de Julho (Uninove), Brazil

ABSTRACT

The authors present a framework for developing intercultural competence (IC) and use tridimensional digital virtual worlds (3DVW) as environments for developing IC. They developed an artifact, via design research, constituted by an educational method using the 3DVW Second Life® as the place for a virtual exchange program between 92 Brazilian and Portuguese master students. The results of the study indicate that the 3DVW can be used for the development of IC because it allows rich experiential and relational/conversational learning opportunities, especially due to the affordances of immersion/sense of presence, social interaction, content production, and knowledge sharing. The students involved in the virtual exchange inside Second Life® had to practice a set of attitudes and skills such as communication skills; culture-specific knowledge; understanding others' worldviews; skills to analyze, evaluate, and relate; skills to listen, observe, and interpret; respect, openness; tolerance for ambiguity, among other, that are all attributes of IC.

DOI: 10.4018/978-1-6684-7597-3.ch004

INTRODUCTION

Intercultural Competence (IC) can be understood as an individual's capacity to effectively and appropriately act and communicate in intercultural situations based on intercultural knowledge, skills and attitudes (Deardorff, 2006, 2008).

The latest advances on Information and Communication Technologies (ICT) and the use of digital Three-Dimensional Virtual Worlds (3DVW) in business processes, games and education (Schultze & Orlikowski, 2010), can provide rich three-dimensional graphic spaces with audio, video, animation, and interactivity, in which individuals can live experiences via an avatar (Schultze & Orlikowski, 2010). These environments can allow people from different cultures to develop common projects and activities at low cost, with no need for physical transportation. We live in a global world where information and communication technology is changing the manner in which businesses create and capture value, how and where we work, and how we interact and communicate, for example (Cascio & Montealegre, 2016).

Thanks to their great potential, 3DVW gained legitimacy in business and educational settings for their use in activities such as multimedia meetings and training, virtual teamwork, distributed collaboration and real-time simulation (Schultze & Orlikowski, 2010). They also provide an interesting environment for innovation and experimentation among educators, scientists and software teams (Bainbridge 2007, Schultze et al., 2008).

Educators and educational institutions point the potential of the use of virtual environments for teaching and learning, as they provide the possibility of learner engagement, together with the ability to explore, construct and manipulate virtual objects, structures and metaphorical representations of ideas (Dalgarno & Lee, 2010). Dickey (2003; 2005) found that a Virtual World can support a constructivist learning environment for geographically distant learners. Communication features such as the possibility of establishing a unique identity (through the use of an avatar) and several tools for conversation provide opportunities for collaborative and cooperative learning. These opportunities are demonstrated in the studies of Hanewald (2013) and Cho & Lim (2015), for example.

Therefore, we propose the research question: *How can a 3DVW be used as an environment for the development of intercultural competence?* We propose a theoretical framework based on IC and virtual worlds, considering a relational and conversational view of experiential learning (Kolb, 1984; Kolb & Kolb, 2005; Ramsey, 2005; Baker, 2005). Based on this framework, we developed and tested an artifact, via Design Research, constituted by an educational method using a 3DVW (Second Life® - www.secondlife.com) as the environment for a virtual exchange program between 92 Brazilian and Portuguese master students. Different educational affordances of 3DVW (Warburton, 2009) and the dynamics of experiential and conversational learning of IC were explored during the empirical application of the artifact.

The next section will present a literature review on experiential learning theory, a relational-conversational perspective of experiential learning, three-dimensional virtual worlds and affordances, and intercultural competence. This will be followed by the research methodology, and finally the results, conclusions and references of this research will be presented.

THEORETICAL FOUNDATIONS

Working in intercultural contexts requires the individual ability to learn from new and different experiences. It is aligned with the concept of experiential learning, which can be defined as "the process whereby knowledge is created through the transformation of experience" (Kolb, 1984, p. 41). By transformation of experience Kolb means that experiential learning is a process of constructing knowledge that involves a creative tension among four learning modes - experiencing, reflecting, thinking, and acting - that is responsive to contextual demands. This process can be depicted as a learning cycle or spiral where the learner touches all the learning modes in a recursive process that is responsive to the learning situation and what is being learned (Kolb, 1984).

Experiential Learning Theory

In the experiential learning model proposed by Kolb (1984), learning is conceived as a four-stage cycle in which immediate concrete experience is the basis for individual observation and reflection, followed by the development of abstract concepts and generalizations from these experiences, which form "theories" that will be tested in new situations, to make decisions and solve problems. As Kolb (1981) states, learning is a process involving the resolution of dialectical conflicts between opposing modes of dealing with the world - action and reflection, concreteness and abstraction.

The Experiential Learning Theory (ELT) has been applied in a variety of learning contexts with distinct objectives (see for instance: Friar & Eddleston, 2007; Pittaway & Cope, 2007; Cook & Olson, 2006; Hardless, 2005; Hoover et al, 2010). However, despite the acceptance of ELT, it tends to be problematic from a relational point of view (Shotter, 1993), since Kolb's cycle emphasizes individual, cognitive understanding and adaptation to a real world.

A Relational-Conversational Perspective of Experiential Learning

Considering Kolb's cycle limitations, Ramsey (2005) proposes a learning cycle that is more consciously communal and centered on narrative and action. In her framework, the focus moves away from adapting action to match a given "real" world, towards a *collectively produced activity*. Also using principles of the ELT, but following a conversational perspective, Baker (2005) argues that conversation is a meaning-making process whereby understanding is achieved through the interplay of opposites and contradictions, encompassing the relational aspects of social, experiential learning, as people strive to increase understanding together.

Therefore, we consider experiential learning as a process that is relational, the individuals are not alone, they interact, negotiate and create common understanding of reality.

Three-Dimensional Virtual Worlds (3DVW) and Affordances

To Bainbridge (2007, p. 472), virtual worlds are "an electronic environment that visually mimics complex physical spaces, where people can interact with each other and with virtual objects, and where people are represented by animated characters". These environments have rich graphical three-dimensional spaces (3D) that provide an immersive, simulated, persistent, and dynamic setting in which individuals, groups, and even organizations can interact in nonphysical spaces.

Schultze e Orlikowski (2010, p. 810) claim that "initially dismissed as environments of play, virtual worlds have gained legitimacy in business and educational settings for their application in globally distributed work, project management, online learning, and real-time simulation". Virtual worlds are an effective tool for stimulating and engaging students and confirmed the need for further study in this area. New technologies used in education must be carefully chosen and applied in order to help students not only enjoy the aesthetic aspect but also to learn while playing (Wrzesien & Raya (2010).

In this sense, we have the assumption that 3DVW can provide a space for conversational, interactional experiential learning, because they are immersive digital environments, with rich 3D graphics, high- fidelity audio and animation, in which individuals can interact with each other with a strong sense of presence. In 3DVW, users can create a digital identity in the form of an avatar, which allows them to express themselves, to move, talk, socialize and perform actions (Schultze & Orlikowski, 2010). 3DVW have a set of affordances, which are defined as properties of action between an artifact and an actor (Andreas et al., 2010). Warburton (2009), Warburton and Perez-Garcia (2009) and Baker et al. (2009) summarize these affordances:

- **Immersion and Sense of Presence:** By incorporating a virtual digital persona in the form of an avatar.
- **Interaction:** Among individuals and communities, subject-object, and between objects.
- **Community Presence:** A sense of belonging and common goals among groups and subcultures inside the 3DVW.
- **Exposure:** To authentic content and culture such as artwork, and access to cultural and linguistic diversity (local, national, international).
- Identity and the role of representation/interpretation of roles in the environment context, content production, ownership of the learning environment and internal objects.
- **Visualization and Contextualization:** Allowing the production and reproduction of different types of content and artifacts.
- **Simulation:** To simulate the existence of contexts that may be too expensive or hazardous to produce in the real world; physical limitations can be overcome.

Considering these affordances, in our research we chose Second Life as the 3DVW to be applied, since previous literature indicates it as an adequate space for learning (Burgess et al., 2010). SL has also already been used in collaborative projects, for example, for language learning, between students from Japan and New Zealand (Corder & U., 2010). SL, how a multi-user virtual environment, potentially provides effective intercultural experiential learning opportunities to develop IC by challenging personal beliefs and assumptions underpinning cultural frameworks and identity. For example, the study that evaluates SL as one of the approaches used to develop IC in a first year IC module in a New Zealand university based on data from two case studies (Corder & U-Mackey (2015). Therefore we supposed that it could be applied to develop the competence targeted in our study, that is, the IC.

Intercultural Competence

Competences involves inter-related knowledge, skills and attitudes applied to successfully reach goals in a specific context (Zabala & Arnau, 2010). The development of competences demands individual situated action (Boterf, 2003). Therefore, competence needs to be demonstrated in a concrete situation, indicating the individual capacity to solve real problems (Zabala & Arnau, 2010; Perrenoud, 1999; Boterf, 2003; Zarifian, 2011).

Deardorff (2006, 2008) conceptualizes intercultural competence (IC) as an individual's ability to effectively and appropriately act and communicate in intercultural situations based on intercultural knowledge, skills and attitudes. Fantini (2007, 2009) states that IC is a set of capabilities that are needed to effectively and appropriately interact with others who are linguistically and culturally different. Trompenaars and Woolliams (2009) describe it as the ability to successfully communicate and engage in effective collaboration with people from other cultures through recognition (awareness) of differences and respecting other points of view. Byram (2000) claims that someone with some degree of IC is able to see relationships between different cultures and interpret them. IC also indicates a critical or analytical understanding of (parts of) an individual's own culture and the culture of others.

Given the complexity of the concept of IC, based on Deardorff (2006, 2008, 2009), Fantini (2009) and Trompenaars and Woolliams (2009), we define IC as *a set of integrated knowledge, skills and attitudes that allows an individual to interact and effectively collaborate with members of other cultures, having the ability to assimilate new knowledge and exhibiting open and flexible behavior.* We considered a set of 15 attributes to assess IC (Deardorff, 2006, 2008, 2009): respect for other cultures and for cultural diversity; openness to intercultural learning and to people from other cultures; tolerance for ambiguity; flexibility; curiosity; withholding judgment; cultural self-awareness / understanding; understanding others' worldviews; culture-specific knowledge (context, roles, etc.); awareness of using other languages in social contexts; listening, observation, and interpretation skills; analysis, evaluation, and relational skills; empathy; adaptability; and communication skills. It is important to recognize that IC goes beyond language and beyond knowledge about other cultures — and to recognize that skills and attitudes are equally important to the development of IC (Deardorff, 2015).

Using principles of the ELT and following a conversational and interactional perspective, we propose a conceptual framework (Figure 1) to evaluate how a 3DVW can be a context for developing IC. We assume that the affordances of a 3DVW can enhance the feeling of experiencing life like situations, providing opportunity for experiential learning (Hew & Cheung, 2010; Twining, 2009). We draw upon the premise that the affordances of 3DVW can provide an appropriate learning environment in which intercultural experiences can occur. We consider a relational/conversational view of experiential learning since the affordances provided by 3DVW allow for immersion, interaction, collaboration and the feeling of community presence. We consider that previous intercultural knowledge, experiences and competence of learners are the foundation for every educational activity aiming at further developing IC through new intercultural concrete experiences inside a 3DVW. These experiences need to be based on interactive and collaborative work between people from different cultures. Through these activities, by exploring the affordances of a 3DVW, learners can act, exercise observation, abstraction and conversation in a dialectical process. For instance, a virtual exchange program involving students from different cultures who need to work and solve problems together inside a 3DVW can be appropriate for the development of IC. By living this type of experience, observing, reflecting and talking about it with others, each individual can derive abstract concepts and generalizations, new ideas, improving his/her IC. Deardorff (2015) claims that IC development is an ongoing process and thus it becomes important for individuals to be provided with opportunities to reflect upon and assess the development of their own IC over time. We tested the main assumptions of this framework via empirical research.

Figure 1. Conceptual framework
Source: Created by the researchers based on Kolb (1976), Baker (2005), Ramsey (2005), Warburton (2009), Warburton and Perez-Garcia (2009), Baker et al. (2009), Deardorff (2006, 2008, 2009)

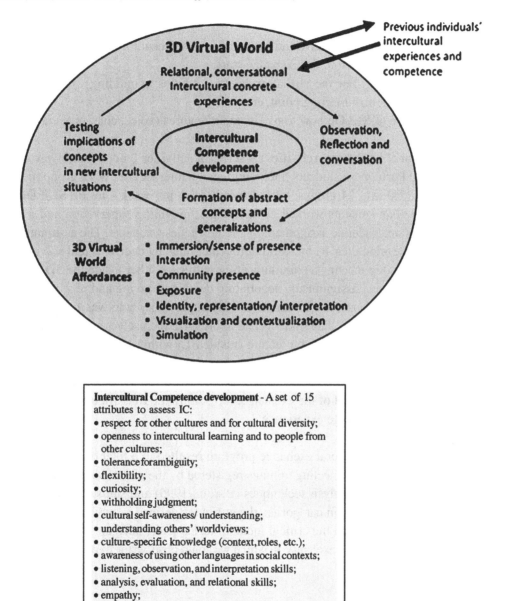

Intercultural Competence development - A set of 15 attributes to assess IC:
• respect for other cultures and for cultural diversity;
• openness to intercultural learning and to people from other cultures;
• tolerance for ambiguity;
• flexibility;
• curiosity;
• withholding judgment;
• cultural self-awareness/ understanding;
• understanding others' worldviews;
• culture-specific knowledge (context, roles, etc.);
• awareness of using other languages in social contexts;
• listening, observation, and interpretation skills;
• analysis, evaluation, and relational skills;
• empathy;
• adaptability; and
• communication skills.

METHOD

We adopted the Design Research method (Takeda et al., 1990; Vaishnavi & Kuechler, 2004; Manson, 2006). An artifact was created and applied, an educational method for the development of IC in a 3DVW, consisting of an intercultural virtual exchange in Second Life (SL), which was tested with 92

Master students (22 Brazilian students from University of Vale do Rio dos Sinos – UNISINOS - and 70 Portuguese students from the Instituto Superior de Economia e Gestão - ISEG). The artifact (virtual exchange) was composed of 5 elements:

1. **Diagnostic Assessment:** A qualitative and quantitative instrument for self-assessment of students' previous IC levels, applied before the exchange start.
2. **3D Environments in SL:** For the virtual exchange activities: a building with working spaces, panels, a conference room, a meeting point, etc.
3. **Training for the Use of SL:** On how to use its main features (voice, chat, notes, avatar features, teleporting, etc.).
4. **Virtual Intercultural Exchange Activities:** A series of activities for collaborative work between the Brazilians and Portuguese students, including: an opening lecture, work group meetings (the students were divided into 14 groups, with 4 meetings -1 per week - inside SL). During these meetings, the Brazilian students worked as facilitators, providing supervision and assistance in the development of an academic assignment by the Portuguese students. The assumption was that the students could develop their IC by working together, making decisions and solving problems, such as scheduling group meetings, communicating with each other inside the 3DVW, assigning responsibilities, delivering assignments, negotiating deadlines, giving and receiving advice, etc.. The groups were autonomous; the researchers' only supervisory role was for solving technical problems regarding the 3DVW. The students had to organize themselves and the way they worked together. The activities also included a lecture (inside SL) with a Brazilian executive, a closing meeting and a party for celebration and fun.
5. **Final Assessment:** A qualitative and quantitative instrument for self-assessment of students' IC levels was applied after the end of the exchange, replicating the first evaluation applied before it, and also evaluating the exchange experience.

In summary, the virtual intercultural exchange program resulted in a total of 55:07 hours of video recorded inside SL, plus 53 files of meeting minutes registered by the participants themselves. To analyze these data, we used content analysis techniques (Bardin, 1995) and statistics. The categorization of qualitative data considered as main categories, the attributes defined in the literature about IC, and affordances of 3DVW. We also used the critical incident technique (Flanagan, 1954) to select critical events or situations during the virtual exchange in which we could observe the experiential learning of IC.

RESULTS

Before the beginning of the exchange activities we applied a quantitative/qualitative instrument to understand the student's profile and previous intercultural experiences, the student's own perceptions about IC and their self-assessment of personal IC level of development, as well as their expectations about the exchange. This gave us elements to plan the activities.

In parallel, the exchange facilities were constructed in 3D inside SL, with a building of 6 floors. At the lobby of this building there was a meeting space for social interaction. In the other floors there were 14 meeting rooms (one for each group), each one contained tables and chairs, laptop with internet access from inside the SL, panel with direct access for editing in GoogleDocs®, a panel with communication resources (Skype®), and a panel for teleporting. There were also an auditorium equipped with projection boards (for Power Point presentations and video projections inside SL) and a party room.

The training on how to use SL happened before the beginning of the virtual exchange activities; also videos and tutorials were provided. After this, the opening meeting was held with all participants, presenting the exchange program and its objectives, the way it should work and the goals to be accomplished.

Following the opening meeting, the 14 working groups were defined. They had up to 4 or 6 Portuguese students each, with the guidance of one or two Brazilian students. Since Portuguese students were enrolled in a master course of Information Systems or Marketing, their proposed exchange activity was an academic assignment on Customer Relationship Management (CRM). Brazilian students were enrolled in a course on Management Education Methods, and worked as facilitators, so they had to put in practice their teaching skills, giving support for their Portuguese peers. Each group should hold four meetings in SL (one per week).

The 59 working group meetings occurred according to the plan. However, it is important to mention that, despite the good technological infrastructure in Portugal regarding internet access and computers, some technical constraints were faced for the use of the 3DVW. At ISEG the internal network did not allow for the use of voice over IP within SL. So, most of the time the groups had to use written chats to communicate during the meetings. In Brazil, this constraint did not happen because 3DVW had been used in research and educational activities for more than a decade at UNISINOS, so the IT department provided full access to the SL resources, including voice.

Another problem faced by ISEG students was that at the university facilities they did not have access to an individual computer. Therefore sometimes only one student entered SL with his/her avatar and the other members of the group followed the meeting only by watching what was going on inside the 3DVW. Some Portuguese students accessing SL from home also did not have all the proper resources (computer with a powerful graphics processing unit and headphones). Most of Brazilian students had their own notebook and few of them had problems to access SL, although some of them had also poor resources (ex.: lack of broadband access). As we can see later on in the data analysis, these constraints generated different perceptions about the exchange experience between Portuguese and Brazilian students.

Besides these drawbacks, during the first week of the exchange, the SL was undergoing a system upgrade at Linden Labs (the enterprise responsible for the creation and development of Second Life® and its hosting) and the voice over IP was frequently unavailable. Thus, the chat was the main tool used for communication. Another difficulty experienced by the working groups was due to time zone differences between Brazil and Portugal. Initially, the gap was +3 hours in Portugal. After the beginning of daylight time in Portugal, it increased to +4 hours, which caused difficulties in organizing the meetings.

In addition to the working groups meetings, a lecture about CRM, by a Brazilian executive, was held in the auditorium in SL with 56 students attending it. Lasting 55 minutes, it was evaluated as a very good event by the participants.

The closing meeting of the exchange was divided in two parts: a debate between all participants, assessing the experience and pointing the main lessons learned, lasting about 30 minutes, and after, a party, scheduled to last 30 minutes, which actually lasted one hour. That was a very relaxed moment of the exchange, with the avatars dancing and chatting about various subjects.

The final step was the assessment of the virtual intercultural exchange by the participants. The same scale for self-assessment of IC applied before the exchange was applied after it. The intention was to provoke the students' reflections about what they had learnt from the whole experience. A total of 82 students (60 Portuguese and 22 Brazilians) were considered as valid respondents, since only them answered the assessments before and after the exchange.

These self-assessments of individual IC attributes at the end of the exchange were very positive (Table 1). It was found that only one of the IC attributes had a significant difference between Brazilians and Portuguese: the *Culture-specific knowledge*. Portuguese students, that in general declared (in the self-assessment before the exchange) to have more previous knowledge and contact with the Brazilian culture, expanded their knowledge about it, but the contrary did not occur.

Comparing the results of the final self-assessment with the initial one (diagnostic), we identified that there were some changes in the individual's perceptions about their level of development of IC: some attributes were evaluated as higher and others as lower in the development scale, to the same respondent. Possible explanations are: students may have noticed that the exchange contributed to the development of their attributes of IC; or students may have changed their perceptions about the attributes of IC assessed; or they may have realized that some attributes that they considered as already fulfilled needed further development.

The data also shows that the students realized some of the affordances of the 3DVW as a space for interaction, content production and knowledge sharing. However, other affordances such as immersion, simulation and presence were perceived by most of the Brazilian students but not by the Portuguese students. Only 36.6% of Portuguese students were satisfied with the use of SL as a platform for the exchange, whereas 86,4% of Brazilian students indicated their satisfaction with it (Table 2). These different results between the two groups can be explained by the fact that (as already mentioned) many Portuguese students had no direct access to SL during the working groups meetings.

We asked the participants to indicate the way they perceived the contributions of the exchange for the development of their IC. Table 3 shows that Brazilian students gave more emphasis on what they learnt from the exchange than the Portuguese students.

We also used the critical incidents technique (Flanagan, 1954), selecting from videos recorded during data collection events, actions or situations in which it was possible to identify evidences of the process of development of IC among the participants, analyzing their interactional and conversational experiences during the virtual exchange. In total, 86 situations were selected showing evidences of the attributes of IC applied in action, as pointed by Deardorff (2006, 2008, 2009). Due to space limitations, we show one of them in Table 4. Most of these evidences are related to situations when the students had to cope with some type of adversity, unexpected events, different points of view. They had to expose themselves, defend their ideas, tolerate ambiguity, practice the skills to interpret, evaluate and relate with others.

As proposed in our conceptual framework, in these situations they had to exercise a concrete-abstract dialectic process through interaction and conversation, which collaborated to heighten students' awareness of themselves and their environment, promoting opportunity for developing action in the light of others' narratives, towards a collectively produced activity (Ramsey, 2005) that enable them to develop their IC.

We also noticed that informal learning episodes were important in these experiences. As informal, we define those moments of interactions either outside the meeting rooms or outside the ¨official¨, scheduled time of work meetings. For instance, these include interactions happening in the lobby of the exchange building, before the beginning of a meeting or event, and even during the closing party. These unstructured events or moments of interactions were important to provide a more ¨loose¨ personal interaction that allowed students to get closer to each other.

Finally, Table 5 shows students' suggestions for future improvements of the educational method (artifact) applied.

Table 1. Students' self-assessment after the exchange

Attributes of Intercultural competence (by descending order of development)	Mean	Mode	Mean per country		Mode per country		Significant Differences
			Portugal	Brazil	Portugal	Brazil	
Respect	4.35	5	4.40	4.23	5	4	No
Openness	4.28	4	4.28	4.27	5	4	No
Curiosity	4.23	5	4.25	4.18	5	4	No
Skills to listen, observe and interpret	4.06	4	4.10	3.96	4	4	No
Skills to analyze, evaluate, and relate	4.01	4	4.02	4.00	4	4	No
Tolerance for ambiguity	4.00	4	4.08	3.77	4	4	No
Withholding judgment	3.99	4	3.98	4.00	4	4	No
Adaptability	3.98	4	3.97	4.00	4	4	No
Understanding others' worldviews	3.95	4	3.92	4.05	4	4	No
Flexibility	3.93	4	3.92	3.96	4	4	No
Sociolinguistic awareness	3.93	4	4.03	3.64	4	4	No
Empathy	3.93	4	3.88	4.05	4	4	No
Cultural self-awareness/understanding	3.92	4	3.90	3.96	4	4	No
Culture-specific knowledge	3.82	4	3.92	3.55	4	3	Yes*
Communication skills	3.78	4	3.80	3.73	4	4	No

Notes:

* In a five point Likert scale of 1 (competence not developed) to 5 (competence developed)

** Significant results according to Student's t test, with p values <0.05

Table 2. Students' perceptions about the 3DVW affordances

Questions *	% of Portuguese Students who agree or strongly agree with the statement	% of Brazilian Students who agree or strongly agree with the statement
During the exchange activities in Second Life there were opportunities for social interaction among the working group members and the facilitators.	64.9%	77%
During the exchange activities in Second Life there were opportunities for content production among the working group members and the facilitators.	70%	77%
During the exchange activities in Second Life there were opportunities for knowledge sharing between the working group members and the facilitators.	73.4%	95.4%
I realized the simulation or reproduction of contexts and life like situations in the virtual world, allowing for interaction with people from another culture and environments.	55%	86.4%
I experienced the sensation of immersion and presence in the virtual world, through the use of my avatar.	40%	77.3%
Overall, I was satisfied with the use of the virtual world Second Life for the intercultural exchange.	36.6%	86.4%

* Percentage of students who agree or strongly agree with the statement

Table 3. Contribution of the exchange for the development of personal intercultural competence

Main contributions of the exchange	Freq. Portugal	% Portugal	Freq. Brazil	% Brazil
Teaching, learning and academic experience	20	33.3%	13	59.1%
Interaction, contact and interaction with people of other culture	19	31.7%	13	59.1%
Awareness and new perceptions about other culture	16	26.7%	8	36.4%
Intercultural openness (for learning and for interaction with other)	10	16.7%	8	36.4%
Application of intercultural practices	7	11.7%	6	27.3%
Curiosity about other culture	6	10.0%	2	9.1%
Use of technology as a means of contact with another culture	6	10.0%	5	22.7%
Intercultural adaptation	5	8.3%	5	22.7%

Table 4. Critical incident

Critical incident	*Delay x waiting*	
Key Attributes of Intercultural Competence in evidence:	*Group # 2 – Meeting # 4*	
Culture-specific knowledge; cultural self-awareness/understanding; skills to listen, observe and interpret; withholding judgment; Empathy; flexibility.		
What happened?		
In this meeting, some Portuguese students arrived late. The Portuguese group was formed by five students, but only one arrived at the meeting on time and started a conversation with the Brazilian facilitator. Considering the delay of his peers, this student wanted to start the meeting without the presence of the others, because he was keen to accomplish the tasks. Meanwhile, the Brazilian facilitator agreed to wait a while for the arrival of rest of the group. The Portuguese student made an important revelation saying: "we Portuguese are always late." To make more comfortable with the situation, the Brazilian facilitator made the following comment: "(..) here [in Brazil] is it is the same, we are always late [laughing]." They had a very friendly and relaxed conversation about their home towns. They also agreed, later on, with the other group members, that the Portuguese and the Brazilian people are also used to procrastinating (delivering assignments at the last minute of the deadlines).		

Table 5. Students' suggestions to improve the artifact

Students´ suggestions	Freq. Portugal	% Portugal	Freq. Brazil	% Brazil	Total Freq.	% Total
Improvements to solve the technical problems	16	26.7%	7	31.8%	23	28.1%
Increasing the number of meetings/interaction time	5	8.3%	7	31.8%	12	14.6%
Interaction by subject/related areas of interest	8	13.3%	2	9.1%	10	12.2%
The method was adequate	7	11.7%	3	13.6%	10	12.2%
More time to explore the resources of the virtual world	6	10.0%	2	9.1%	8	9.8%
Improvements regarding scheduling dates and times of virtual activities	7	11.7%	1	4.6%	8	9.8%
Suggestions to use other technologies for interaction	6	10.0%	1	4.6%	7	8.5%
Time to explore other places in Second Life, beyond the UNISINOS Island	2	3.3%	2	9.1%	4	4.9%
Do not agree that a virtual exchange can be considered as an intercultural experience	3	5.0%	0	0.0%	3	3.7%
Promote more interaction among participants	2	3.3%	0	0.0%	2	2.4%
Other suggestions	5	8.3%	4	18.2%	9	11.0%
No answer	9	15.0%	0	0.0%	9	11.0%

CONCLUSION

Following the tenets of ELT, as Kolb and Kolb (2005) argue, it is important to create a learning space beneficial for learning and to value learners' previous experiences, because people construct new knowledge and understanding from what they already know and believe.

In our study, we started by mapping and understanding the previous intercultural experiences and competence according to the students' perceptions. We then proposed a concrete intercultural experience in the 3DVW that demanded interaction, conversation and collaboration to the accomplishment of common goals.

According to Kolb and Kolb (2005), learning requires facing and embracing differences; whether be them differences in skills and life experiences, different ideas or beliefs. It is important to have a learning space that encourages the expression of differences with the psychological safety to support the learners that face these challenges, and to allow the flow of spontaneous conversation and interactions among learners.

In the artifact proposed, we could see that the affordances of the 3DVW allowed a rich environment for the interaction among learners, including emotional expressions. These affordances created an environment that provided a space for a conversational, interactional learning experience. This type of experience offers a relational perspective that privileges multiple narratives which led learners toward constructing new meanings and transforming their collective experiences into knowledge (Ramsey, 2005).

We perceived that the students experienced many times uncertain and ambiguous situations, and with the occurrence of mistakes or small conflicts, they had to have patience, empathy and engage in a dialogue with their peers. Events occurred that demonstrated differences in attitudes and behaviors among the participants, demanding tolerance and judgment avoidance between them. About communication skills, in some situations it was necessary to clarify and reinforce the exchange's goals. Tolerance and flexibility in front of new, uncertain, or doubtful situations and curiosity is seen as fundamental to the acquisition of knowledge and skills to the development of IC. The attempt to communicate and have a proper behavior, are attitudes that reinforce the cycle of continuous development of individual IC (Byram, 2000; Fantini, 2007; Deardorff, 2008).

An issue that emerged in our experience was the importance of informal and incidental learning opportunities. In the same token, the unpredicted, unplanned events or conflicts were the richest opportunities to reveal cultural differences and the way students tried to solve the situations and keep working together. These events are aligned with the concept of informal and incidental learning (Marsick & Watkins, 2001). While formal learning is classroom-based and highly structured, informal learning (that includes incidental learning), may occur in institutions, but is unstructured. Incidental learning is a byproduct of some other activity, such as task accomplishments, interpersonal interactions, and trial-and-error experimentation. It takes place even when the learners are not conscious of it. Informal learning is integrated with daily routines, and can be triggered by an internal or external jolt, influenced by chance. It is also an inductive process of reflection and action strongly linked to learning of others. This is an issue for future research: to understand how can we promote informal learning inside a 3DVW.

According to the method created, all the activities were planned in advance; however, we reinforce that we realized, in practice, that uncertain and unstructured situations are more adequate to reveal the cultural differences among the participants. It can be a limitation for the use of 3DVW for developing IC, since 3D objects and facilities have to be designed and implemented in advance. In summary, considering the tenets of experiential learning in a relational and conversational perspective, and the affordances of the 3DVW, we created an artifact - an educational method - for the development of intercultural competences using Second Life. Through the application of this method we observed the affordances of interaction, social presence, content production and knowledge sharing allowed for the 3DVW. The activities performed in this learning environment demanded from the participants a set of attitudes and skills such as communication skills; culture-specific knowledge; understanding others' worldviews; skills to analyze, evaluate, and relate; skills to listen, observe and interpret; respect, openness; tolerance for ambiguity, among others, that are components of the intercultural competence.

Since competence involves effective actions in a specific context, the method offered to students the opportunity to engage in a virtual exchange program in which they had to work and collaborate, to know each other, to organize their own time schedule, deliverables and group dynamics. The high level of autonomy of students in the proposed activities was key to stimulate the application of their skills in real actions.

This work has several implications. Theoretically, it contributes to understand the affordances of 3DVW for the development of competences in general, as well as for intercultural competence. It also contributes with a framework linking experiential learning to 3DVW as learning environments. For practice, the method created can be applied in different cultural environments, providing the opportunities for other sorts of virtual exchange programs in educational institutions in different places, allowing students to have intercultural experiences and develop their IC without the need for commuting and with a low cost.

Finally as a suggestion for future studies it would be useful to also consider how the development of IC might relate to curriculum, learning and teaching in management education.

REFERENCES

Andreas, K., Tsiatsos, T., Terzidou, T., & Pomportsis, A. (2010). Fostering collaborative learning in Second Life: Metaphors and affordances. *Computers & Education*, *55*(2), 603–615. doi:10.1016/j. compedu.2010.02.021

Bainbridge, W. (2007). The Scientific Research Potential of Virtual Worlds. *Science*, *317*(5837), 472–476. doi:10.1126cience.1146930 PMID:17656715

Baker, A. C., Jensen, P. J., & Kolb, D. A. (2005). Conversation as Experiential Learning. *Management Learning*, *36*(4), 411–427. doi:10.1177/1350507605058130

Baker, S. C., Wentz, R. K., & Woods, M. M. (2009). Using virtual worlds in education: Second Life as an educational tool. *Teaching of Psychology*, *36*(1), 59–64. doi:10.1080/00986280802529079

Bardin, L. (1995). *Análise de Conteúdo*. Lisboa: Persona.

Boterf, G. (2003). *Desenvolvendo a Competência dos Profissionais*. Porto Alegre: Artmed.

Burgess, M. L., Slate, J. R., Rojas-Lebouef, A., & Laprairie, K. (2010). Teaching and learning in Second Life. *The Internet and Higher Education*, *13*(1/2), 84–88. doi:10.1016/j.iheduc.2009.12.003

Byram, M. (2000). Assessing Intercultural Competence in Language Teaching. *Sprogforum*, *6*(18), 8–13.

Cascio, W. F., & Montealegre, R. (2016). How technology is changing work and organizations. *Annual Review of Organizational Psychology and Organizational Behavior, 3*(1), 349–375. doi:10.1146/annurev-orgpsych-041015-062352

Cho, Y. H., Yim, S. Y., & Paik, S. (2015). Physical and social presence in 3D virtual role-play for pre-service teachers. *Internet and Higher Education, 25,* 70–77. doi:10.1016/j.iheduc.2015.01.002

Cook, L. S., & Olson, J. (2006). The Sky's the Limit: An Activity for Teaching Project Management. *Journal of Management Education, 30*(3), 404–420. doi:10.1177/1052562905279220

Corder, D., & U, A. (2010). Integrating Second Life to enhance global intercultural collaboration projects. *ACM Inroads, 3*(1), 43–50. doi:10.1145/1835428.1835442

Corder, D., & U-Mackey, A. (2015). Encountering and dealing with difference: Second Life and intercultural competence. *Intercultural Education, 26*(5), 409–424. doi:10.1080/14675986.2015.1091213

Dalgarno, B., & Lee, M. J. W. (2010). What are the learning affordances of 3-D virtual environments? *British Journal of Educational Technology, 41*(1), 10–32. doi:10.1111/j.1467-8535.2009.01038.x

Deardorff, D. K. (2006). Identification and Assessment of Intercultural Competence as a Student Outcome of Internationalization. *Journal of Studies in International Education, 10*(3), 241–266. doi:10.1177/1028315306287002

Deardorff, D. K. (2008). Intercultural Competence: a definition, model and implications for education abroad. In V. Savicki (Ed.), *Developing intercultural competence and transformation: theory, research, and application in international education* (pp. 32–52). Sterling, VA: Stylus Publishing.

Deardorff, D. K. (2009). Implementing intercultural competence assessment. In D. K. Deardorff (Ed.), *The SAGE handbook of intercultural competence* (pp. 477–491). Thousand Oaks, CA: SAGE Publications.

Deardorff, D. K. (2015). A 21st century imperative: Integrating intercultural competence in Tuning. *Tuning Journal for Higher Education, 3*(1), 137–147. doi:10.18543/tjhe-3(1)-2015pp137-147

Dickey, M. D. (2003). Teaching in 3D: Pedagogical affordances and constraints of 3D virtual worlds for synchronous distance learning. *Distance Education, 24*(1), 105–121. doi:10.1080/01587910303047

Dickey, M. D. (2005). Three-dimensional virtual worlds and distance learning: two case studies of Active Worlds as a medium for distance education. *British Journal of Educational Technology, 36*(3), 439–451. doi:10.1111/j.1467-8535.2005.00477.x

Fantini, A. (2007). Exploring and Assessing Intercultural Competence. Brattleboro, VT: Federation of the Experiment in International Living.

Fantini, A. (2009). Assessing Intercultural Competence: issues and tools. In D. K. Deardorff (Ed.), *The SAGE handbook of intercultural competence* (pp. 456–476). Thousand Oaks, CA: SAGE Publications.

Flanagan, J. C. (1954). The critical incident technique. *Psychological Bulletin, 51*(4), 327–358. doi:10.1037/h0061470 PMID:13177800

Friar, J. H., & Eddleston, K. A. (2007). Making connections for success: A networking exercise. *Journal of Management Education, 31*(1), 104–127. doi:10.1177/1052562906286860

Hanewald, R. (2013). Learners and collaborative learning in virtual worlds: A review of the literature. *Turkish Online Journal of Distance Education*, *14*(2), 233–247.

Hardless, C., Nilsson, M., & Nuldén, U. (2005). "Copernicus": Experiencing a Failing Project for Reflection and Learning. *Management Learning*, *36*(2), 181–217. doi:10.1177/1350507605052557

Hew, K. F., & Cheung, W. S. (2010). Use of three-dimensional (3-D) immersive virtual worlds in K-12 and higher education settings: A review of the research. *British Journal of Educational Technology*, *41*(1), 33–55. doi:10.1111/j.1467-8535.2008.00900.x

Hoover, J. D., Giambatista, R. C., Sorenson, R. L., & Bommer, W. H. (2010). Assessing the Effectiveness of Whole Person Learning Pedagogy in Skill Acquisition. *Academy of Management Learning & Education*, *9*(2), 192–203.

Kolb, A., & Kolb, D. (2005). Learning Styles and Learning Spaces: Enhancing Experiential Learning in Higher Education. *Academy of Management Learning & Education*, *4*(2), 193–212. doi:10.5465/amle.2005.17268566

Kolb, D. A. (1976). Management and the Learning Process. *California Management Review*, *XVIII*(3), 21–31. doi:10.2307/41164649

Kolb, D. A. (1981). Experiential Learning Theory and The Learning Style Inventory: A Reply to Freedman and Stumpf. *Academy of Management Review*, *6*(2), 289–296. doi:10.5465/amr.1981.4287844

Kolb, D. A. (1984). *Experiential learning: Experience as the source of learning and development*. Prentice-Hall.

Manson, N. J. (2006). Is operations research really research? *Operations Research Society of South Africa*, *22*(2), 155–180.

Marsick, V. J., & Watkins, K. E. (2001). Informal and Incidental Learning. *New Directions for Adult and Continuing Education*, *2001*(89), 89. doi:10.1002/ace.5

Perrenoud, P. (1999). *Construir as Competências desde a Escola*. Porto Alegre: Artes Médicas.

Pittaway, L., & Cope, J. (2007). Simulating Entrepreneurial Learning. Integration Experiential and Collaborative Approaches to Learning. *Management Learning*, *38*(2), 211–233. doi:10.1177/1350507607075776

Ramsey, C. (2005). Narrative: From Learning in Reflection to Learning in Performance. *Management Learning*, *36*(2), 219–235. doi:10.1177/1350507605052558

Schultze, U., Hiltz, R., Nardi, B., Rennecker, J., & Stucky, S. (2008). Synthetic worlds in work and learning. *Communications of the Association for Information Systems*, *22*(19), 351–370.

Schultze, U., & Orlikowski, W. J. (2010). Virtual Worlds: A Performative Perspective On Globally Distributed, Immersive Work. *Information Systems Research*, *21*(4), 1–12. doi:10.1287/isre.1100.0321

Shotter, J. (1993). *Conversational Realities*. London: Sage.

Takeda, H., Veerkamp, P., Tomiyama, T., & Yoshikawa, H. (1990). Modeling design processes. *Artificial Intelligence Magazine*, *11*(4), 38–45.

Trompenaars, F., & Woolliams, P. (2009). Research Application: toward a general framework of competence for Today's Global Village. In D. Deardorff (Ed.), *The SAGE handbook of intercultural competence* (pp. 438–455). SAGE Publications.

Twining, P. (2009). Exploring the educational potential of virtual worlds - Some reflections from the SPP. *British Journal of Educational Technology, 40*(3), 496–514. doi:10.1111/j.1467-8535.2009.00963.x

Vaishnavi, V., & Kuechler, W. (2004). *Design Research in Information Systems*. Association for Information Systems. Retrieved October, 10, 2010, from http://desrist.org/design-research-in-information-systems/

Warburton, S. (2009). Second Life in higher education: Assessing the potential for and the barriers to deploying virtual worlds in learning and teaching. *British Journal of Educational Technology, 40*(3), 414–426. doi:10.1111/j.1467-8535.2009.00952.x

Warburton, S., & Perez-Garcia, M. (2009). 3D Design and collaboration in massively multi-user virtual environments. In D. Russel (Ed.), *Cases on collaboration in virtual learning environments: process and interactions*. Hershey, PA: IGI Global.

Zabala, A., & Arnau, L. (2010). *Como Aprender e Ensinar Competências*. Porto Alegre: Artmed.

Zarifian, P. (2001). *Objetivo Competência: por uma nova lógica*. São Paulo: Atlas.

Chapter 5
From Visual Culture in the Immersive Metaverse to Visual Cognition in Education

Hsiao-Cheng 'Sandrine' Han
 https://orcid.org/0000-0001-9827-068X
The University of British Columbia, Canada

ABSTRACT

This chapter discusses visual culture in the immersive metaverse through the visual cognition lens. Visual cognition pertains to how we learn through visual means. As educators, we should be aware of how our students learn consciously and unconsciously through the visual sense so that we can help them navigate the immersive metaverse they encounter. Culture and visual culture are discussed. Visual perception, specifically schema and Gestalt, are explained. Learning in the immersive metaverse is as concrete as in the physical world; therefore, teaching students to decode images, perceive the metaverse, and think about images from multiple cultural backgrounds becomes an issue of special importance when education occurs in the visualized immersive metaverse.

INTRODUCTION

If we compare visual and linguistic cognition, then visual cognition seems easier to understand. When we are reading, if a paper is written in a language that we do not know, then we are unable to understand it. However, when we are observing images, we do not wonder if we can understand them but simply decode them through our personal experiences and cultural backgrounds. Today, in the world of connectivity, we see images daily from different parts of the world in the metaverse; however, if our cognition can help us understand or misunderstand the images we see, then, especially in the immersive metaverse, the images are to be questioned. Further, as educators, how we should help our students navigate the visual culture in the metaverse is discussed in this chapter.

DOI: 10.4018/978-1-6684-7597-3.ch005

Cognitive psychology mainly discusses the internal and internal-external (Hoffmann, 2007, p. 187) processes that influence how we make decisions. Repeated experiences form our internalization (Efland, 2002; Hoffmann, 2007; Hutchins, 1995), and we apply "dependent cognitive ability to a corresponding abstract and implicit knowledge" (Hutchins, 1995, p. 270). Representations, such as sounds, words, and images, become important cognitive tools. When representations repeatedly present a concept, these experiences strengthen the concept and help us form internal cognition. According to Parsons' theory of cognitive development, we are not born with the ability to understand complex issues, but we acquire it from our experiences (as cited in Efland, 2002). When we face a new environment or a new situation, we utilize our past experiences to instruct us regarding where to go and what to do; this is an example of the internal-external cognitive process (Agre & Horswill, 1997). As we gain more experience or knowledge, we develop faster cognitive processes.

According to cognitive psychology, we can only understand visual images based on the information we have stored previously. As Freedman (2003) notes "Even our unconscious eye movements are detected by the search for information that will help to make sense of the stimulus based on our previous knowledge" (p67). Even images we have unconsciously perceived, if viewed repeatedly, are stored in our long-term memory and influence how we will perceive similar images in the future (Barry, 1997; Hoffmann, 2007; Kellogg, 1995). According to cognitive psychology, through visual experience we learn the repeated images around us (Hoffmann, 2007). As Hoffmann (2007) states, cognitive systems are semiotic systems: "systems mediated and constituted by signs and representations" (p. 202). Freedman (2003) notes that when we are viewing, we access knowledge from the hidden unit of our neural system to find the corresponding memory or knowledge to develop the connection between the object we are viewing and ourselves. Krampen (1990) additionally posits that images we are viewing convey "second hand information" (p. 81). Viewers utilize previous experiences to make connections with the image they are viewing; however, when image producers make images, they employ their past experiences to create new images and attempt to connect their experience to the viewers' experience. When viewers see an image they have not seen before, they are establishing a new experience initiated by the image creator's construct and understanding it based on their own personal and cultural experiences.

Images are generated through physical eyes and the cognitive process. Visual cognition, as Williams (2006) states, "operates on preconscious levels to process visual information into knowledge that motivates behavior before the conscious processes of the neocortex receive or understand the information" (p. 35). When we are processing images in our brains, visual perception allows us to gather information; through the visual perception processes, we utilize cognition to lend meaning to the image we see (Bogdan, 2002). Below, I introduce the visual culture phenomena in the immersive metaverse to develop the foundation before returning to cognitive psychology in the immersive metaverse.

IMMERSIVE METAVERSE

Immersive metaverse is networked environments connected with multiple computers, multiple users, and multiple sets of data (Aukstakalnis, 1991). However, immersive metaverse does not include the entire cyber environment that is connected through the internet. Immersive metaverse is visually presented in a three dimensional realm where social interaction and communication are of primary importance. Users of the virtual world present their virtual selves through customized avatars. In an immersive metaverse, residents can also express their creativity by building 3D animated objects and designing 3D environments (Stephen, 2007; Sturken & Cartwright, 2004).

Immersive metaverse has been adapted as educational environments, including High Fidelity Open Source VR, Engage VR, Minecraft, and Cloud Party, Open Simulator, but the most renowned immersive metaverse for education is Second Life (2019). Second Life is owned by Linden Lab (LL), and users are able to purchase virtual land from LL. However, all data are owned and controlled by LL, and users must pay to upload textures, sounds, and animations. In Second Life there are real world institutions as well as institutions that only exist in the virtual world.

Open Simulator (OS) is another immersive metaverse widely used by educators (OpenSimulator, 2019). OS has the same immersive metaverse environment as Second Life. It is open source software, so any user of OS can install an immersive metaverse on their own computer server. All the OS data are owned and controlled by the server administrator. Because OS can be owned by individuals and depends on the management of the server, users can upload textures, sounds, animations, and even create their own virtual lands for free. Moreover, the adult content, violence, and money transfers found in Second Life can be prevented in OS by the administrator.

Education in Immersive Metaverse: Introduction and Examples

Immersive metaverse is full of educational possibilities. According to Dickey (2005), "educational MOOs (Multiple User Domains Object Oriented) promote an interactive style of learning, collaboration opportunities, and meaningful engagement across time and space" (p. 440). Another powerful effect of the immersive metaverse is visual stimulation. The visually animated immersive metaverse captures the interest of students who are already digital natives, making them willing to spend more time in it (Carpenter, 2009; Sweeny, 2009). Everything students do in the immersive metaverse can be a learning experience, and learning by doing or learning by seeing fosters self-directed learning (Garris, Ahlers, & Driskell, 2002; Dewey, 1934).

In the immersive metaverse users can see all cultures represented in one place. Users may be able to also find these cultures in the real world, in fairy tales, in mythology, or in dreams. Some places in the immersive metaverse students may never otherwise have the chance to see or even imagine. Immersive metaverse users could build and interact with the virtual objects. In the immersive metaverse educators are able to join and explore the possibilities of using the metaverse for their class.

Visual Culture in the Immersive Metaverse

Culture is based on people's experiences and backgrounds; therefore, cultures in the immersive metaverse—in which users originate from around the globe—may be more complicated than real-world cultures (Han, 2015; Han, 2013a; Han, 2013b). Miller and Burton (1994) state "Reality is constructed from what we sense based on our experience, emotional condition, beliefs, and so forth" (p. 66). However, in the immersive metaverse, users encounter not only their own cultures, but also many other cultures that are created and curated by other users or companies.

High Fidelity, which is one example of an immersive metaverse, was created by its users from around the globe, and users can see, interact with, and experience it. The immersive metaverse springs from imagination, and there is almost no limit on creating a new environment or imaginative objects. It is not only a new world to live in and travel through, but it is also a place for people to create their own visual environments and culture (Han, 2010).

According to Heidegger (1977), "a world picture . . . does not mean a picture of the world but the world conceived and grasped as a picture" (p. 129). When applying Heidegger's theory to the immersive metaverse, people must be aware that the immersive metaverse propagates ideas through images, and users must also be aware of unconsciously adapting and accepting everything that is transferred through the images. Images are not innocent (Mirzoeff, 2005), and as Barry (1994) notes, approximately 80% of human perception is through vision. If a person's ways of seeing are not precise, they may not notice the full meaning of everything they see. When people see an image, they may attempt to relate their knowledge and experience to the image to make meaning of it (Freedman, 2003). As Freedman states, "an expressive object, regardless of the meaning of the production for the artist, does not have inherent meaning; the experience of an audience with visual culture makes it meaningful" (p. 69).

Culture

Culture concerns who we are and how we live our lives; therefore, culture is diverse, and each person has more than one cultural identity (Wang, 2001). "Cultural identities emerge in everyday discourse and in social practices, as well as by rituals, norms, and myths that are handed down to new members" (p. 516). Human biological differences form different cultures of gender, race, and age; human psychological differences form different cultures of career, hobby, and religion. Differences in the natural environment influence different cultural lifestyles. As McFee and Degge (1977) note, "culture is a pattern of behaviors, ideas, and values shared by a group" (p. 272). "Each culture has its own individuality and has a pattern that binds its parts together" (Dewey, 1934, p. 349). In other words, people in the same culture share a similar way of thinking, feeling, and acting (Wang; Samovar, Porter, McDaniel, & Roy, 2015).

Some scholars believe that culture is homogenizing, while others believe that cultures shift. While the macro-cultural system influences individuals, individuals also bring their unique subcultures into the community (Shifman, 2013); therefore, culture is not stable (Anyanwu, 1998). Lemke (1993) contends that "autonomous cultural dynamics" (p. 3) are present in human social systems and are interdependent with the system of material processes. "Cultural practices are . . . material processes; they construe meaning and assign valuation, but they also participate in eco-physical couplings . . . and co-evolve over time as parts of a larger unitary eco-social system" (p. 3). Culture is the "result of complex interactions among images, producers, cultural products, and readers/consumers. The meaning of images emerges through these processes of interpretation, engagement, and negotiation" (p. 69). Cultural ideas and values are maintained by visual images because images can communicate, teach, and transmit the behavior, ideas, and values of a culture (McFee & Degge, 1977).

Culture in the Immersive Metaverse

As McFee and Degge (1977) state, the more culture we study, the clearer understanding of our own cultural background we develop. The immersive metaverse is a place for collecting different kinds of cultural memory:

It is popular culture, it is narratives created by its inhabitants that remind us who we are, it is life as lived and reproduced in pixels and virtual texts. It is sacred and profane, it is workspace and leisure space, it is a battleground and a nirvana, it is real and it is virtual, it is ontological and phenomenological. (Fernback, 1997, p. 37)

In immersive metaverses, users arrive from around the world with different backgrounds. Yaple and Korzenny (1989) stress that because of the significant cultural influence from immersive metaverses, fragile cultures could be changed or eliminated by cultures that have more power in the metaverse. McPhail (2002) adds that "electronic colonialism theory posits that foreign produced, created, or manufactured cultural products have the ability to influence, or possibly displace, indigenous cultural productions, artifacts, and media to the detriment of receiving nations" (p. 243). Furthermore, "the processes of immigration and globalization lead to new 'third' identities that represent complex and shifting hybridizations of earlier cultural patterns" (Ess & Sudweeks, 2006, p. 181). Cultures in the metaverse are not only flowing across the globe, but they are also creating unique virtual cultures (Han, 2013b).

Visual Culture in the Immersive Metaverse

Vision is one of the most important senses because humans are so readily attracted by images. Immersive metaverse users seek realistic appearances regardless of whether it is a simulated environment or an imaginary world (Han, 2010). In immersive metaverses, "instead of losing sight of the real, the real is being transformed into signs and images. Instead of images colonizing reality, reality is transformed" (Duncum, 1999, p. 306). However, because we are surrounded by visual stimuli in the immersive metaverse, the importance of understanding visual culture in immersive metaverses becomes serious (Mirzoeff, 2005). When users spend time in immersive metaverses, they begin to view the immersive metaverse as reality. Because of the influence from the metaverse, many scholars (Duncum, 1999; Sturken, & Cartwright, 2004; Woolley, 1992; Mitchell, 2005; Geoffrey, 1994) have begun to consider what is real and what is virtual.

Culture is easily transmitted through technology, especially in the metaverse (Smith-Shank, 2007). However, users in the metaverse come from different countries and cultural backgrounds and have different understandings and experiences regarding the same image (Machin & Leeuwen, 2007). Images in the immersive metaverse gain their value from their "accessibility, malleability, and information status" (Sturken, & Cartwright, 2004, p. 139). Images with different meanings coexist in the metaverse, and the relationship between images and users in the metaverse is not simply direct or transparent (Burnett, 2004, p. xiiii). Users in the metaverse learn unconsciously from the images they see, and how they understand images may not follow the original meaning intended by the image creator (Han, 2010). However, regardless of what users see in the metaverse or what they think the images mean, these images influence how they will see and think about images in the future (Burnett, 2004).

COGNITIVE PSYCHOLOGY IN IMMERSIVE METAVERSES

When we perceive images, we integrate our experiences and knowledge with cognitive processes and understand what we are viewing (Williams, 2006), in both the metaverse and the physical world. Because knowledge is based on our experiences, the predominantly important factor in the cognitive process is our personal experience (Efland, 2002), the majority of which emerge from our cultural or sociocultural backgrounds (Brown, 2001). As Chandler (2008) states, sociocultural perception may be different over time or by culture.

Wiley (2003) posits that when multiple images surround us, they may lead us to poorer understanding and distract us from deciphering the central message. In the immersive metaverse, we are surrounded by images, and while all images contain certain messages, we may not understand what we are observing, and our visual cognition may consciously or unconsciously ignore images. Stephen (2007) also states that "the online interaction is a real experience" (p. 1104). According to Stephen, the physical world experience is maya—an illusion; therefore, our experiences in immersive metaverses are as real as the physical world experience.

Postmodern consciousness is a condition because we are bombarded with a substantial number of images that we have trouble comprehending (Metros, 1999). Because of the immersive environment the metaverse provides, the line between immersive metaverses and reality may become "perceptually nonexistent" (Barry, 1997, p. 61). Lanier states that the experiences in the immersive metaverse may influence our perceptions in both virtual and physical worlds (as cited in Barry). He explains that when users return from immersive metaverses to the physical world, the immersive metaverses become hyper-real, and the physical world experience resumes. Lanier believes that immersive metaverse experience provides an opportunity for people to sensitize their perceptions. He states that "with a virtual reality system you don't see the computer anymore—it's gone. All that's there is you" (as cited in Barry, 1997, p. 60). In the immersive metaverse, our visual representations are different from our real bodies. However, when we look at other avatars in immersive metaverses, our visual cognition may not inform us that the avatars are different from the real people.

Visual Perception

Perception concerns the relationship between the perceiver and the media (Jamieson, 2007), and visual perception could be considered to be the first perception within all senses (Bogdan, 2002). Visual perception involves how people perceive the element of visual media from their eyes to their brains, which mixes with their psychological feelings and sociocultural dimensions until reaching the reflection point (Bogdan). However, the majority of visual perception is processed unconsciously (Hatfield, 2002).

When we utilize our sense of vision, we immediately sense light, color, distance, space, and movement. Through the cognitive process, perceivers comprehend light and color separately (Alhazen, 1989). Different lighting changes the colors of objects and creates different atmospheres. Additionally, light allows people to recognize texture (Hatfield, 2002), and how people understand space and distance also depends on light (Hatfield). Human vision rapidly and unconsciously compares these visual impulses (Chandler, 2008). When the light of the moving object moves through our eyes to our cortical cells in the brain, we recognize that the object is moving. As Chandler (2009) notes, "retinal stabilization and motion detection" provide us the ability to perceive moving things even when we are moving.

After our eyes physically process images in our brains, the visual perception processes begin (Costall, 1990; Landwehr, 1990). As Jansz (2005) states, the first process of visual perception is emotion, and its brevity causes it to go unnoticed. The emotion reflects how people recognize the image and influences what they do next (Efland, 2002). The second phase is "context evaluation" (p. 228). In this period, people reflect on the emotional feeling and begin to appraise how to interact with the image. Therefore, when we encounter media in our daily lives, we emotionally interact with it unconsciously (Barry, 1997). Visual perceptual processes also allow us to understand and discover figures and ground, angle and depth, order and variety, similarities and dissimilarities, nearness or distance, and shapes or lines (Barry, 1997; McFee & Degge, 1977; Pettersson, 1993).

Because our experiences influence how we perceive new things, what we have seen before influences how we will visually perceive in the future (Groom, Dewart, Esgate, Gurney, Kemp, & Towell, 1999; Orde, 1997; Guenther, 1998). As Landwehr (1990) states, "visual perception is essentially based on the sequential registering of pictures" (p. 3); it is constantly adjusted and repatterned (Jamieson, 2007). It must engage with social and arbitrary signs; therefore, sometimes how we perceive is changed by our previous experiences. In other words, our previous experiences can reform our mental frameworks (Eisner, 1997; Groom, et al; Jamieson). Differences in cultural experience also play an important role in how our experiences influence our visual perception (Guenther; Chandler, 2008). Eisner (1997) states that visual perception becomes increasingly complex and refined as people extend their life experiences. "Perceptual set," as Murch (1973, as cited in Chandler, 2008) states, is "a predisposition to perceive something in relation to prior perceptual experiences. Perceptual set is broader than situational context, since it may involve either long-term (for instance, cultural) prior experience or . . . short-term or situational factors." Everything we have ever visually experienced before becomes an element of our future visual perception.

Memory, as experience, also influences how we perceive images. "We become familiar with our environment when we begin to recognize certain regularities in our experience" (Efland, 2002, p. 24). When we repeat our experiences properly, the experience may move to our short-term memory or even to our long-term memory (Kellogg, 1995). Kellogg's three stores model of human memory (Kellogg, 1995, p. 34) explains how our brains process our experiences into memory.

Figure 1. Three stores model of human memory
(Adapted from Kellogg, 1995)

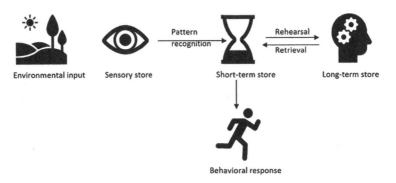

The environmental input in Kellogg's graphic can also be explained as media input, or in this case, the immersive metaverse. When media repeat the same image or idea, our brains transfer the image or idea from short-term memory to long-term memory (Barry, 1997). In other words, we do not need to have direct experience to form a long-term memory; our visual perception can transfer images into memories even without our awareness.

Helmholtz states that "visual perception is mediated by unconscious inferences" (as cited in Hatfield, 2002, p. 116). Therefore, when we are seeing, looking, or observing the visual environment, whether in the physical world or the immersive metaverse, we are unconsciously perceiving and attempting to understand all visual images (Kellogg, 1995). We selectively see the environment and also categorize all visual images that come to our eyes.

When we visually perceive, our sight is limited by our eyes because they are not multi-directional, which means that a direction of vision must be consciously chosen (Jamieson, 2007). In addition to the physiological limits, the motivation of viewing is affected by our cognitive selection. We manage and select the minimal visual data when we perceive; therefore, we do not need much data to recognize visual images (Chandler, 2008). Chandler also states that "selective perception is based on what seems to 'stand out.' Much of this 'standing out' is related to our purposes, interests, expectations, past experiences and the current demands of the situation."

When we selectively see, we are also categorizing what we are seeing. We assimilate details into one; we utilize our expectations, interests, and emotions to influence how we perceive; and we categorize what we see into verbal categories (Chandler, 2008). When we categorize our visual perception, we make complexity manageable, expedite recognition, reduce effort, make events predictable, support systemization, bond sociocultural behavior, and make the world more meaningful (Chandler).

Schema

In visual perception, schema is as important as seeing. "Seeing only occurs when shaped by the selective screen of schemata, which finally reveal that the world is available only in terms of representation" (Iser, 2006, p. 47). Schema is similar to a mental template that we employ for making sense of what we perceive (Chandler, 2008; Efland, 2002); it is developed from our personal and cultural experiences (Groom, Dewart, Esgate, Gurney, Kemp, & Towell, 1999), and it includes "a huge variety of sensory patterns and concepts" (p. 6). "The schema approach has much in common with the old saying 'beauty lies in the eye of the beholder'. . . . the more general requirements of schema theory [suggest] that 'perception lies in the eye (and brain) of the perceiver'" (Groom, Dewart, Esgate, Gurney, Kemp, & Towell, 1999, p. 7).

Schema allows us to understand the new visual images from our past visual experiences; in other words, schema fills in the gaps of what we have not seen in our experience. We also make an assumption about what we will see from our schema. When we perceive a new visual impulse, we are also modifying our old schema or forming a new schema structure. Furthermore, schema theory suggests that "our perception and subsequent memory of an input may be changed and distorted to fit our existing schemas" (Groom, Dewart, Esgate, Gurney, Kemp, & Towell, 1999, p. 7); it also implies that people perceive the same image in different ways, depending on their own personal and cultural experiences. As Freedman (2003) states, "An expressive object, regardless of the meaning of the production for the artist, does not have inherent meaning; the experience of an audience with visual culture makes it meaningful" (p. 69). In other words, schema directly forms the structure of knowledge (Kellogg, 1995, p. 18).

Figure 2, adapted from Kellogg's "Cycle of Perception" (1995), explains our exploration of the environment as connected to our inner schema.

The schema structure enables us "to build models of the physical world" (Kellogg, 1995, p. 18) and allows us to perceive, think, remember, imagine, and reflect different situations. We are not aware of preconscious visual processing; however, "it provides a tremendous amount of information to our conscious mind" (p. 43). According to Kellogg (1995), "Imagery works especially well for familiar, concrete objects that can readily be visualized. Forming images clearly elaborates the words or story events and links them with other images in long-term memory" (p. 135). Because of the preconscious process, as with schema, we may not need to consciously "think" about the images we see.

Figure 2. Cycle of perception
(Adapted from Kellogg, 1995)

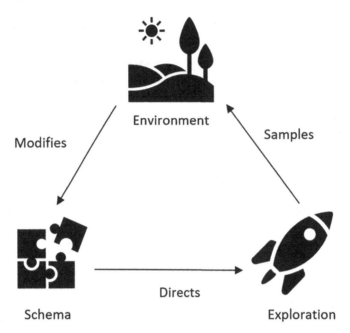

When the schema structure works in the immersive metaverse, users are attempting to build a new understanding of the world based on their previous personal and cultural schema structures. The new understanding they establish is based on the creation made by users who may not be from the same cultural background. Therefore, they are able to understand the meaning of the image that was intentionally created and curated by the creators who are unknown.

Gestalt

In addition to schema, Gestalt allows us to understand the meaning of images that we perceive (Bogdan, 2002). The difference between schema and Gestalt is this: schema enables us to understand images from parts, but Gestalt permits us to understand the meaning of the whole picture of the image.

In Gestalt theory, two and two do not equal four; the whole is greater than the sum of its parts (Kanizsa, 1979). We do not view an image alone; our eyes consistently add other images or texts to the main image in our perception, or we even add our mental images to the image we are viewing (Groom, Dewart, Esgate, Gurney, Kemp, & Towell, 1999). Further, when we see the same image with a different color or at a different time, the meaning of the image may be totally different. When we see two images combined, the meaning of the whole image may be different. As Kanizsa states, "everything depends on everything else" (p.63). According to Kohler, we "unconsciously and erroneously ascribe certain common characteristics of the visual field to a currently present stimulus constellation because they seem to belong there" (as cited in Katz, 1950, p 19). When we see, we do not see images independently; we see the relationship between the images (Eisner, 1997).

According to Gestalt theory, we interpret images mainly based on our cultural backgrounds. In other words, we learn to understand images based on our cultural experiences (Chandler, 2008; Metros, 1999).

According to Chandler, "The Gestalt principles can be seen as reinforcing the notion that the world is not simply and objectively 'out there' but is constructed in the process of perception." Gestalts synthesize and integrate both visual and mental images (Barry, 1997), facilitate our visual experience to future visual perception, and finally enable us to structure knowledge (Kellogg, 1995).

We are learning from images unconsciously, as Arnheim (2004) argues. According to Gestalt development theory, people with more visual impulses can better employ Gestalt development (as cited in Eisner, 1997). According to Frascara (2004):

Every layout conveys meaning; every meaning presupposes an organization; every organization is based on principles of integration and segregation; principles of integration and segregation are based on the Gestalt principles of similarity, proximity, and good form. Every visual message involves form and meaning. The meaning of a message requires a process of interpretation; and every message is produced to generate an action of some kind. (p. 68)

Therefore, the more images people see, the quicker and better Gestalt development allows them to further perceive the visualized world. However, as noted above, the Gestalt is constructed based on our cultural backgrounds. In the immersive metaverse, it is not clear whether our Gestalt development empowers us to conceptualize the metaverse we are situated in.

COGNITIVE PSYCHOLOGY AND EDUCATION

Because of the important relationship between cognitive psychology and knowledge (Jamieson, 2007), cognitive psychology holds a serious position in education. Eisner and Vallance add a "cognitive process approach" (as cited in Pinar, Reynolds, Slattery, & Taubman, 2002, p. 29) to curriculum orientation and stress the importance of cognitive psychology in education. Hasemann and Reber state that developing cognitive ability is the precondition for knowledge development (as cited in Hoffmann, 2007).

Efland (2002) provides three cognitive orientations in learning: "symbol-processing and sociocultural perspectives, and the view that individuals construct their own views of reality" (p.53). The symbol-processing view is based on the hypothesis that "there is an objective reality that exists independent of the knower, and that it is represented in symbols formed and manipulated by the mind, located in the head" (p. 53). Our mind constructs and creates symbols to represent the world. However, sociocultural cognitive theory assumes that

Reality is socially constructed, that it emerges in and through the communicative transactions individuals have with one another. The mind is thus not in the head, but emerges in the social interactions of individuals, and it is through these that knowledge of cultural norms and practices is both constructed and acquired. . . . Knowledge as cultural content also consists of symbolic tools (language) that enable social interaction to take place. . . . Learning is a process of construction but it is also enculturation through which growing individuals become initiated into their society. (p. 53)

In short, knowledge is constructed not only in each individual's mind, but also by the sociocultural background. Therefore, learning is based on our sociocultural backgrounds. According to both symbol-processing and sociocultural theories, knowledge is not passively received but is constructed by the learner (p. 72).

The third constructive theory states that "reality is a construction of one's own making, that individuals construct their views of reality guided by their own knowledge-seeking purposes. Emphasis is placed on human agency where meaning making is guided by personal interest and effort" (p. 53). This theory combines with the others (symbol-processing and sociocultural) in that not only are we utilizing our minds to construct our knowledge, but this knowledge is also influenced by the sociocultural background.

Piaget and Vygotsky are educational psychologists who apply cognitive psychology to education. For Piaget, "cognitive development is not a passive process but proceeds as a result of actions put forth by the learner" (as cited in Efland, 2002, p. 27). In Piaget's view, the social environment influences students to interact with others and affects the students' cognitive development. Students "construct representations of the social environment, which take the form of personal constructions or schemata" (p. 33).

For Vygotsky, "psychology is an instrumental, cultural and historical psychology" (Efland, 2002, p. 31). Culture is the most important factor for Vygotsky because it determines form and content. Only when cultural influences are internalized may higher forms of mental life begin (Efland). For Vygotsky, repeated experience develops internalization; therefore, we depend on cognitive ability to understand abstract knowledge.

Vygotsky uses the terms instruments and tools to refer to ways that human acquire knowledge that mediates their higher mental processes by modifying the stimuli they encounter, using them to both control surrounding conditions and regulate their own behavior. . . . Vygotsky tried to establish how people, with the help of instruments and signs, direct their attention and organize conscious memorization to regulate their conduct. (p. 32)

Human society is made by signs; therefore, conduct is determined by the signs attached to objects. We attach meanings to objects or images and react to those meanings we have attached. In short, we constantly internalize signs that we have restructured.

Vygotsky's cognitive notion has two main implications in the visual world. First, study of the visual should not be isolated but should be seen as connected to social context. Second, cultural symbols advance human development and create human culture through the usage of symbols (Efland, 2002). Because learning is bound by culture, how instructors teach in the immersive metaverse should also follow the culture that students are familiar with.

Education in Immersive Metaverses

When educators utilize immersive metaverses as an educational environment, what students learn from the images becomes a serious issue. Students may travel in the immersive metaverse as if they were visiting a school campus in the physical world. However, the culture in the immersive metaverse is not the same as the culture in the physical world (Mirzoeff, 2003). Therefore, how students understand, adapt, and apply virtual culture becomes a critical challenge to educators. Because students may arrive from different nations with different cultural backgrounds, intercultural interactions in the immersive metaverse become another challenge (Ess & Sudweeks, 2006). "Culture affects the individual's response to computer-related system[s]" (Wang, 2001, p. 516); how students collaborate and even communicate in the immersive metaverse without a shared cultural understanding becomes a critical question.

CONCLUSION

"When interactivity is combined with automaticity and the five-hundred-year-old perspective method, the result is one account of mediation that millions of viewers today find compelling" (Bolter & Grusin, 2000, p. 30). Our visual cognition helps us in both the immersive metaverse and the physical world. However, the speed of the cognition process is impossible to manage; we should be aware that we are constantly influenced by all the images we see and attempt to recognize what those images are really telling us before we are unconsciously influenced by them.

Consideration of visual culture in immersive metaverses that are utilized as learning environments should not only focus on the visual aspect of culture, but should also depict, criticize, and sustain the contradictions of different cultures and even include a capacity for culture building in the immersive metaverse (Burnett, 2002; Efland, 2002). However, when immersive metaverse users can build, change, and reform the visual culture in the immersive metaverse, the sources of the visual clues they are learning from are unknown. If educators are not attentive to the diverse visual cultures in the immersive metaverse learning environment, then students may consciously or unconsciously accept the cultural representations or misrepresentations they find (Freedman, 2000; Marciano, 2002). Therefore, teaching visual culture within the learning environment of the immersive metaverse is important.

Learning visual culture in the immersive metaverse allows students and instructors to understand the context of the immersive metaverse. Students are increasingly learning from visual sources (Freedman, 2000; Han, 2015); however, they struggle to understand the broad and deep meanings of the images (Semali, 2002). Visual culture can enable students to understand the issues of "gender, race, ethnicity, sexual orientation, spatial ability, and other body identities and cultures; socioeconomics, political conditions, communities, and natural and humanly-made environments, including virtual environments" (Freedman, 2000, p. 314). Visual culture involves social statements, in a social context, from a social perspective. Learning in the immersive metaverse is as concrete as in the physical world; therefore, teaching students to decode images, perceive images, and consider images from multiple cultural backgrounds becomes an issue of special importance when education occurs in the visualized immersive metaverse.

REFERENCES

Agre, P., & Horswill, I. (1997). Lifeworld Analysis. *Journal of Artificial Intelligence Research*, 6, 111–145. doi:10.1613/jair.342

Alhazen, I. (1989). *Book of optics*. London: University of London.

Anyanwu, C. J. (1998). Virtual world and virtual reality. *Journal of Australian Studies*, 22(58), 154–161. doi:10.1080/14443059809387412

Arnheim, R. (2004). *Art and visual perception: a psychology of the creative eye*. University of California Press.

Aukstakalnis, S. (1991). *Silicon mirage: The art and science of virtual reality*. Berkeley, CA: Peachpit press.

Barry, A. (1997). *Visual intelligence: Perception, image, and manipulation in visual communication.* Albany, NY: State University of New York Press.

Barry, A. M. S. (1994). Perceptual aesthetic and visual language. In D. M. Moore & F. M. Dwyer, (Eds.), Visual literacy: A spectrum of visual learning (pp. 113-132). Englewood Cliffs, NJ: Educational Technology Publications.

Bogdan, C. (2002). *The semiotics of visual languages.* Columbia University Press.

Bolter, J. D., & Grusin, R. (2000). *Remediation: Understanding new media.* The MIT Press.

Brown, N. C. (2001). The meaning of transfer in the practices of arts education. *Studies in Art Education, 43*(1), 83–102. doi:10.2307/1320994

Burnett, R. (2004). *How images think.* Cambridge, MA: The MIT Press. doi:10.7551/mit-press/3580.001.0001

Carpenter, B. S. II. (2009). Virtual Worlds as Educational Experience: Living and Learning in Interesting Times. *Journal of Virtual Worlds Research, 2*(1). doi:10.4101/jvwr.v2i1.625

Chandler, D. (2008). *Visual Perception.* Retrieved November 2008, from Reading the Visual: https://www.aber.ac.uk/media/Modules/MC10220/lectures.html

Costall, A. (1990). Introduction: Picture perception as "indirect" perception. In K. Landwehr (Ed.), *Ecological perception research visual communication and aesthetics* (pp. 1–11). Berlin: Springer-Verlag. doi:10.1007/978-3-642-84106-4_2

Dewey, J. (1934). *Art as experience.* New York: Penguin.

Dickey, M. (2005). Three-dimensional virtual worlds and distance learning: Two case studies of Active Worlds as a medium for distance education. *British Journal of Educational Technology, 36*(3), 439–451. doi:10.1111/j.1467-8535.2005.00477.x

Duncum, P. (1997). Art education for new times. *Studies in Art Education, 38*(2), 69–79. doi:10.2307/1320584

Duncum, P. (1999). A case for an art education of everyday aesthetic experiences. *Studies in Art Education, 40*(4), 295–311. doi:10.2307/1320551

Efland, A. (2002). *Art and cognition: Integrating the visual arts in the curriculum.* Teachers college press.

Eisner, E. W. (1997). *Educating artistic vision.* Reston, VA: NAEA.

Ess, C., & Sudweeks, F. (2006). Culture and computer-mediated communication: Toward new understandings. *Journal of Computer-Mediated Communication, 11*(1), 179–191. doi:10.1111/j.1083-6101.2006.tb00309.x

Fernback, J. (1997). The individual within the collective: Virtual ideology and the realization of collective principles. In S. G. Jones (Ed.), *Virtual culture: Identity and communication in cybersociety* (pp. 36–53). Sage.

Frascara, J. (2004). *Communication design: Principles, methods, and practice.* New York, NY: Alloworth Press.

Freedman, K. (2000). Social perspectives on art education in the U. S.: Teaching visual culture in a democracy. *Studies in Art Education, 41*(4), 314–329. doi:10.2307/1320676

Freedman, K. (2003). *Teaching visual culture.* Teachers College Press.

Garris, R., Ahlers, R., & Driskell, J. E. (2002). Games, motivation, and learning: A research and practice model. *Simulation & Gaming, 33*(4), 441–467. doi:10.1177/1046878102238607

Geoffrey, R. (1994). Media Theory: A framework for interdisciplinary conversations. Paper presented at the Annual Meeting of the Association for Education in Journalism and Mass Communication, Atlanta, GA.

Groom, D., Dewart, H., Esgate, A., Gurney, K., Kemp, R., & Towell, N. (1999). *An introduction to cognitive psychology.* Hove, UK: Psychology Press.

Guenther, R. K. (1998). *Human Cognition.* Academic Press.

Han, H. C. (2010). Revealing the didactic character of imagery in a 3d animated virtual world. *Journal of Virtual Studies, 1*(1), 19–24. http://ejournal.urockcliffe.com/index.php/JOVS/article/viewFile/2/1

Han, H. C. (2013a). *Teaching visual learning through virtual world viewing, creating, and teaching experiences: Why we need a virtual world for education? IPTEL conference.* UBC.

Han, H. C. (2013b). The Third Culture: Virtual world visual culture in education. *The International Journal of Arts Education, 11*(2), 37–58.

Hatfield, G. (2002). Perception as unconscious inference. In R. Mausfeld & D. Heyer (Eds.), Perception and the physical world: Psychological and philosophical issue in perception (pp. 115-143). John Wiley & Sons. doi:10.1002/0470013427.ch5

Hoffmann, M. (2007). Learning from people, things, and signs. *Study Philosophy Education*, 185-204.

Hutchins, E. (1995). *Cognition in the wild.* Cambridge, MA: MIT Press.

Iser, W. (2006). *How to do theory.* Malden, MA: Blackwell.

Jamieson, H. (2007). *Visual communication: More than meets the eye.* Chicago, IL: University of Chicago press.

Jansz, J. (2005). The emotional appeal of violent vdeo games for adolescent males. *Communication Theory, 15*(3), 219–241. doi:10.1111/j.1468-2885.2005.tb00334.x

Kang, J. (2000). Cyber-race. *Harvard Law Review*, 1130-1208.

Kanizsa, G. (1979). *Organization in vision: Essays on Gestalt perception.* New York, NY: Praeger.

Katz, D. (1950). *Gestalt psychology: Its nature and significance.* New York, NY: Ronald.

Kellogg, R. T. (1995). *Cognitive psychology.* Thousand Oaks, CA: SAGE.

Krampen, M. (1990). Functional versus dysfunctional aspects of information surfaces. In K. Landwehr (Ed.), *Ecological perception research, visual communication, and aesthetics* (pp. 81–87). Berlin: Springer-Verlag. doi:10.1007/978-3-642-84106-4_8

Landwehr, K. (1990). *Ecological perception research, visual communication, and aesthetics.* Berlin: Springer-Verlag. doi:10.1007/978-3-642-84106-4

Landwehr, K. (1990). *Introduction: The ecological optics of information surfaces Ecological perception research visual communication and aesthetics.* Berlin: Springer-Verlag. doi:10.1007/978-3-642-84106-4

Lemke, J. (1993). Education, cyberspace, and chagne. *Electronic Journal on Virtual Culture, 1*(1), 1–17.

Machin, D., & Leeuwen, T. V. (2007). *Global media: A critical introduction.* New York: Routledge.

Marciano, D. (2002). Teaching styles as evidenced in classrooms: A semiotic look at picture books. In L. M. Semali (Ed.), *Transmediation in the classroom: A semiotics-based media literacy framework* (pp. 63–70). New York: Peter Lang.

McFee, J. K., & Degge, R. M. (1977). *Art, culture, and environment: A catalyst for teaching.* Belmont, CA: Wadsworth.

McPhail, T. (2002). *Global communication: Theories, stakeholders, and trends.* Boston, MA: Allyn & Bacon.

Metros, S. (1999). Making connections: A model for on-Line interaction. *Leonardo, 32*(4), 281–291. doi:10.1162/002409499553433

Miller, H. B., & Burton, J. K. (1994). Images and imagery theory. In D. M. Moore & F. M. Dwyer (Eds.), *Visual literacy: A spectrum of visual learning* (pp. 65–83). Englewood Cliffs, NJ: Educational Technology Pubns.

Mirzoeff, N. (2005). *The visual culture reader.* New York: Routledge.

Mitchell, W. J. (2005). *What do pictures want: The lives and loves of images.* Chicago, IL: The University of Chicago Press. doi:10.7208/chicago/9780226245904.001.0001

OpenSimulator. (n.d.). Accessed December 12, 2019. http://opensimulator.org/wiki/Main_Page

Orde, B. (1997). Drawing as visual-perceptual and spatial avility training. *Association for educational communications and technology,* 271-278.

Pettersson, R. (1993). Visual information. Englewood Cliffs, NJ: Educational Technology Publications.

Pinar, W. F., Reynolds, W. M., Slattery, P., & Taubman, P. M. (2002). *Understanding curriculum: An introduction to the study of historical and contemporary curriculum discourses.* New York, NY: Peter Lang.

Samovar, L., Porter, R., McDaniel, E., & Roy, C. (2015). *Communication between cultures.* Toronto: Nelson Education.

Second Life. (n.d.). Accessed December 12, 2019. https://secondlife.com/

Semali, L. M. (2002). *Transmediation in the classroom: A semiotics-based media literacy framework.* New York: Peter Lang.

Shifman, L. (2013). Memes in a digital world: Reconciling with a conceptual troublemaker. *Journal of Computer-Mediated Communication, 18*(3), 362–377. doi:10.1111/jcc4.12013

Smith-Shank, D. (2007). Reflections on semiotics, visual culture, and pedagogy. *Semiotica, 164*(164), 223–234. doi:10.1515/SEM.2007.027

Stephen, J. (2007). Virtually sacred: The performance of asynchronous cyber-rituals in online spaces. *Journal of Computer-Mediated Communication,* 1103–1121.

Sturken, M., & Cartwright, L. (2004). *Practices of looking: An introduction to visual culture.* Oxford: Oxford University Press.

Sweeny, R. W. (2009). Lines of sight in the "Network Society": Simulation, art education, and a digital visual culture. In K. Freedman (Eds.), Looking Back: Editors' Selections from 50 Years of Studies in Art Education (pp. 219-231). NAEA.

(1977). The age of the world picture. InHeidegger, M. (Ed.), *The Question Concerning Technology and Other Essays*W. Lovitt, Trans.). New York: Garland Publishing, Inc. doi:10.1007/978-1-349-25249-7_3

Wang, C. Y. J. (2001). Handshakes in cyberspace: Bridging the cultural differences through effective intercultural communication and collaboration. *Annual Proceedings of Selected Research and Development [and] Practice Papers Presented at the National Convention of the Association for Educational Communications and Technology.*

Wiley, F. (2003). Cognitive and educational implications of visually rich media: Images and imagination. In M. E. Hocks & M. R. Kendrick (Eds.), *Eloquent images: word and image in the age of new media* (pp. 201–215). Cambridge, MA: The MIT Press.

Williams, R. (2006). Theorizing visual intelligence: practices, development, and methodologies for visual communication. In D. S. Hope (Ed.), *Visual communication: Perception, rhetoric, and technology* (pp. 32–42). Cresskill, NJ: Hampton Press.

Woolley, B. (1992). *Virtual worlds.* New York: Penguin.

Yaple, P., & Korzenny, F. (1989). Electronic mass media effects across cultures. In M. Asante & W. Gudykunst (Eds.), *Handbook of international and intercultural communication* (pp. 295–317). New Delhi, India: Sage.

ADDITIONAL READING

Balcetis, E., & Lassiter, G. D. (Eds.). (2010). *Social psychology of visual perception.* Psychology Press. doi:10.4324/9780203848043

Berg, G. A. (2000). Cognitive development through narrative: Computer interface design for educational purposes. *Journal of Educational Multimedia and Hypermedia, 9*(1), 3–17.

Collins, J. A., & Olson, I. R. (2014). Knowledge is power: How conceptual knowledge transforms visual cognition. *Psychonomic Bulletin & Review*, *21*(4), 843–860. doi:10.375813423-013-0564-3 PMID:24402731

Gooding, D. (2004). Cognition, construction and culture: Visual theories in the sciences. *Journal of Cognition and Culture*, *4*(3-4), 551–593. doi:10.1163/1568537042484896

Gooding, D. C. (2006). Visual cognition: Where cognition and culture meet. *Philosophy of Science*, *73*(5), 688–698. doi:10.1086/518523

Han, H.-C. (2016). The Third Culture: The Globalized Virtual World Visual Culture. *The International Journal of Arts Education*, *14*(1), 43–62.

Han, H.-C. (2017). The third culture: The transforming (visual) culture in globalized virtual worlds. In S. R. Shin (Ed.), *Convergence of Contemporary Art Education, Visual Culture, and Global Civic Engagement* (pp. 318–330). Hershey, PA: IGI Global. doi:10.4018/978-1-5225-1665-1.ch018

Han, H.-C. (2018). From cultural tolerance to mutual culture respect: An Asian artist's perspective on virtual world culture appropriation. *Journal of Cultural Research in Art Education*, *35*, 93–112.

Han, H.-C. (2019). Semiotic stream of communication in the era of prosumer culture. *Cultural Anthropology and Ethnosemiotics*, *5*(1), 39–43.

Jacobs, A. M., & Ziegler, J. C. (2015), Visual Word Recognition, Neurocognitive Psychology of, In J. D. Wright, Elsevier, (Eds) International Encyclopedia of the Social & Behavioral Sciences (Second Edition), Oxford, pp. 214-219

Kozbelt, A. (2001). Artists as experts in visual cognition. *Visual Cognition*, *8*(6), 705–723. doi:10.1080/13506280042000090

Mayer, R. E. (2014). Cognitive theory of multimedia learning. The Cambridge handbook of multimedia learning, 43.

Nakamura, L. (2008). Digitizing Race: Visual Cultures of the Internet. University of Minnesota Press. Retrieved from http://www.jstor.org/stable/10.5749/j.ctttswwb

Norenzayan, A., Choi, I., & Peng, K. (2007). Perception and cognition. In S. Kitayama & D. Cohen (Eds.), *Handbook of cultural psychology* (pp. 569–594). New York: Guilford Press.

Wright, T. (2008). *Visual Impact: Culture and the Meaning of Images*. Oxford: Berg.

KEY TERMS AND DEFINITIONS

Culture: Culture concerns who we are and how we live our lives. Culture is diverse; it is not stable but is a fluid process.

Gestalt: Gestalt allows us to understand the meaning of the whole picture of the image. It instructs us so that when we see, we see the relationship between things.

Immersive Metaverse: The metaverse includes all the virtual spaces that people can access through digital technology. The immersive metaverse specifically involves the metaverse that provides users with immersive experience. It currently includes both virtual and augmented reality.

Schema: Schema permits us to understand images from parts. Schema is developed from our personal and cultural experiences; it is similar to a mental template that we utilize to make sense of what we perceive.

Visual Cognition: Visual cognition explains how people make sense of the world from their visual sense. It discusses the internal and internal-external processes.

Visual Culture: Visual culture is an interdisciplinary area that includes but is not limited to media studies, cultural studies, art history, and anthropology.

Visual Perception: Visual perception is how people perceive the element of visual media from their eyes to their brains, which mixes with their psychological feelings and sociocultural dimensions and finally reaches the reflection point.

This research was previously published in Cognitive and Affective Perspectives on Immersive Technology in Education; pages 67-84, copyright year 2020 by Information Science Reference (an imprint of IGI Global).

Chapter 6
A Literature Review on the Use of Three–Dimensional Virtual Worlds in Higher Education

Reza Ghanbarzadeh
ⓘ https://orcid.org/0000-0001-9073-1576
School of Business and Tourism, Southern Cross University, Australia

Amir Hossein Ghapanchi
College of Engineering and Science, Victoria University, Australia

ABSTRACT

Three-dimensional virtual worlds (3DVW) have been substantially adopted in teaching and learning worldwide. The current study conducted a literature review of the published research relevant to the application of 3DVWs in higher education. A literature search was performed on nine scientific databases, and following scrutiny according to inclusion criteria, 176 papers were selected for review. The literature review process was summarized, reviews undertaken by the authors, and results about the applicability of 3DVWs in higher education were extracted. A wide variety of application areas for 3DVWs in higher education were found and classified into five main categories. Various 3DVW platforms and virtual environments used for educational goals were also identified. This study found that a wide range of virtual environments and tools have been implemented by 3DVW technology and applied for teaching and learning in higher education.

INTRODUCTION

A Three-Dimensional Virtual World (3DVW) is a computer-based, simulated and graphical environment, usually accessible on the World Wide Web, that is intended for users to inhabit and interact using personalized graphical and animated self-representations, known as avatars (Boulos et al., 2007). Virtual worlds are online spaces where individuals can interact with three-dimensional representations of physical locations or phenomena. The simulated environment could appear similar to the real world

DOI: 10.4018/978-1-6684-7597-3.ch006

(with real rules, real-time actions, interactions and communications) or depict a fantasy virtual world. Recently, Internet-based 3DVW have thrived and hold promise to significantly impact the way people communicate and interact with each other.

Inside 3DVWs, people can manipulate elements and experience telepresence. Increasingly, researchers, organizations and educational communities are recognizing these environments as legitimate communication media which can be used as an effective media in teaching and learning. Users of these environments not only have the opportunity to interact with each other in a sociocultural and delightful activities but also can follow virtual wealth through activities such as selling and buying lands as well as creating and trading virtual goods using virtual currencies (Ba et al., 2010).

The purpose of this chapter is to 1) identify the main activities in the application of 3DVWs in higher education, 2) highlight various 3D virtual world platforms that researchers have used in learning and teaching, 3) categorize various virtual environments designed for educational purposes. Therefore, the current chapter attempts to answer the following three research questions:

1. For what purposes have 3DVWs been used in higher education?
2. What types of 3DVW platforms have been used by researchers in higher education?
3. What kinds of virtual environments have been created for educational activities using 3DVWs?

BACKGROUND

3DVWs have been broadly adopted to favor socialization and education. These virtual worlds offer the possibility of simulating the real world or designing unique fantasy worlds. By interacting with these platforms, people can actively experience simulated realities, which can aid in understanding various concepts and in supporting independent viewpoints for users as they accomplish specific tasks. Users can easily share the virtual environment for performing highly synchronous collaborative tasks, manipulating the same virtual objects (De Lucia et al., 2009).

Numerous advances in information technology are transfiguring teaching and learning styles, especially in higher education. During the past decade, educators from a variety of backgrounds have started using the online virtual environments to support their teaching and learning activities. 3DVWs support a higher level of interactivity and richness for interaction, collaboration and communication than traditional media. They also have the potential to create engaging and meaningful experiences for students and learners. In recent years, there has been remarkable growth in the application of these environments for distance education and e-learning. These immersive platforms offer various tools to create sophisticated and highly interactive simulations using in-world programming, modeling and scripting tools. 3DVWs support teaching and learning in an educational context and they offer the functionality and capability to manage the various aspects of education such as lecturing, presentation, administration and assessment of coursework.

A wide variety of organizations, educational groups, and government agencies currently provide regular events, seminars, and workshops in virtual worlds. Furthermore, many educational institutions and organizations are creating virtual learning environments to deliver courses (face-to-face and online) and events that include 3DVW presentations, discussions, simulations and role-playing. Not only do 3DVWs amplify learning beyond the capabilities afforded by teleconferencing and online web presentation tools, they also create opportunities for field trips that go far beyond the traditional learning spaces (Linden Research, 2011).

Many studies have been conducted on the application of 3DVWs in learning and teaching. For example, Hew and Cheung (2013) discussed evidence-based educational approaches related to the application of Web 2.0 technologies in both K-12 and higher education settings. In their study, Saleeb and Dafoulas (2010b) analytically derived advantageous and disadvantageous categories and sub-categories of applying 3DVWs for conducting e-learning. Hew and Cheung (2010) reviewed past empirical research studies on the application of 3DVWs in educational settings such as K-12 and higher education and found that virtual worlds may be applied for the communication spaces, simulation of space, and experiential spaces.

RESEARCH METHOD

A literature review was conducted on the application of 3DVWs in higher education. The current literature review follows the steps used in a variety of previous studies e.g. the reviews conducted by Ghanbarzadeh et al., (2015) and Ghanbarzadeh et al., (2014). In this section, the steps in the literature review process will be described, including the procedure for deciding upon the inclusion and exclusion of pertinent literature, and data extraction and analysis during the search process will be discussed in detail.

Search Criteria, Databases, and Keywords

To start the literature review process, inclusion and exclusion criteria were established:

- Both empirical and technical studies were included.
- Studies related to education settings other than higher education were excluded.
- Studies in languages other than English were excluded.

Nine relevant scientific databases were used in the search of the keywords: ScienceDirect, ProQuest Computing, Scopus, IEEE Xplore, Association for Information Systems Electronic Library (AISel), Web of Science (via Thomson Reuters), Inspec (via Thomson Reuters), ERIC (Via ProQuest) and PsycAR-TICLES (via Ovid). The databases were selected based on their comprehensiveness in locating pertinent articles, chapters, presentations, papers; these nine databases cover thousands of sources.

Based on various search patterns proposed by each search engine, the advanced search option provided by each database was used for the search operations. 48 search keywords were selected and categorized into three main categories: three-dimensional, virtual world, and higher education. By using the selected search terms, title, abstract and keywords of the articles were searched in accordance with the various search patterns offered by each search engine. The key words that were used in the search are shown in Table 1.

The process of searching for and selecting relevant literature for the current study was completed in six different stages. Figure 1 shows this process.

In the first stage, nine scientific databases were selected. In Stage 2, by using the keywords demonstrated in Table 1, search on the databases were carried out. In Stages 3, 4 and 5, papers were excluded based on their titles, abstracts, and full text, respectively. Finally, after exclusions, at the end of the procedure, the total number of relevant papers was 176, which was a reasonable number for generating an appropriate conclusion. Therefore, the search process stopped at the end of Stage 6.

Table 1. Key words used in the search

("3D" OR "3 D" OR "3-D" OR "3_D" OR "three-dimensional" OR "three dimensional" OR "3 dimensional" OR "three D" OR "three-D") *AND* *("virtual world" OR "virtual life" OR "virtual space" OR "virtual environment" OR "virtual reality" OR "virtual community" OR "virtual inhabited world" OR "inhabited space" OR "second life" OR "active world" OR "avatar" OR "virtual immersive world" OR "Multi user virtual environment" OR "MUVE")* *AND* *("educate" OR "education" OR "educational" OR "educating" OR "distance education" OR "distance learning" OR "train" OR "training" OR "lecture" OR "lecturing" OR "pedagogy" OR "pedagogical" OR "learn" OR "learning" OR "teach" OR "teaching" OR "instruct" OR "instruction" OR "instructing" OR "edutainment" OR "university" OR "universities" OR "higher education" OR "tertiary sector" OR "tertiary education")*

Figure 1. Stages in the procedure of searching for and selecting studies

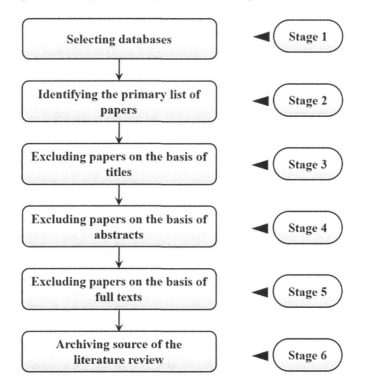

To select papers for the literature review, we considered the following inclusion and exclusion criteria:

1. As we investigated various perspectives of utilization of 3DVWs in higher education, we reviewed both the empirical evidence and design guidelines. Therefore, we targeted both the empirical and technical studies in the current literature review.

2. We examined only peer-reviewed publications (e.g. journals, conference papers, book chapters) that were found in electronic databases. All non-peer-reviewed publications were excluded.
3. Studies focusing on applications of 3DVWs in K–12 education or in non-academic organizations were excluded.
4. Studies in languages other than English were excluded.

Table 2 indicates the number of related papers which were selected from each scientific database.

Table 2. Number of related papers selected from each scientific database

Scientific Data Bases	Related Studies
IEEE Xplore	62
ERIC (Via ProQuest)	38
ScienceDirect	28
Inspec (via Thomson Reuters)	19
AISeL	12
Scopus	11
ProQuest	5
Web of Science (via Thomson Reuters)	1
PsycARTICLES (via Ovid)	0
Total number of related papers	176

Data Extraction and Analysis

The data extracted from each of the selected 176 papers includes:

*   Performed activities by using 3DVWs for learning and teaching in higher education
*   Utilized 3DVW platform
*   Created 3D virtual educational environments for the study

To perform a data analysis, full text of all extracted papers were read in their entirety in order to identify all information related to each of the mentioned research questions; then each paper was classified and labeled according to its main area of research and application area of 3DVWs. To make a better classification, the categorizing operation was performed two times. First, each paper was reviewed by one of the authors and an appropriate category code allocated, therefore, all papers were classified in various categories. To clarify the classification, the process was repeated for the second time by the other author. The results were discussed in a meeting with professionals in the same research field. During the meeting, all categories were discussed and revised, and some of them were merged. Finally, all papers were classified into five major research categories based on the main activity and application areas of 3DWVs: virtual lecturing, discussion, field trip, simulation, and gaming. After this, some demographic information extracted from each paper, then investigated and finalized. Figure 2 shows the procedure undertaken in the data analysis process.

Figure 2. The procedure of data analysis

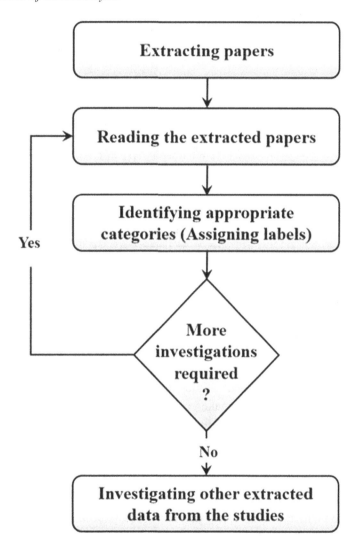

RESULTS

The purpose of this study, as stated in the introduction section, was to conduct a literature review on the application areas of 3DVWs in learning and teaching in higher education, in order to answer three research questions in relation to the technology and higher education. In this section a discussion of findings will be presented for each of the research questions.

Applications for 3DVWs in Higher Education

The results of the current literature review revealed that 3DVWs have been adopted and applied in a wide range of areas in higher education for teaching and learning. According to the nature of educational activities performed, articles were sorted into five main categories: virtual lecturing, discussion, field trip, simulation, and gaming. Some of the studies implemented two or more activities simultaneously. Figure 3 depicts the major categories of application areas of 3DVWs in the higher education settings.

Figure 3. The major categories of application areas of 3DVWs in the higher education setting

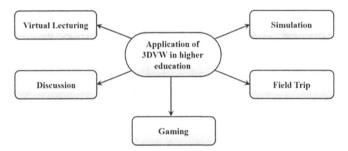

Virtual Lecturing

In this application, by using 3DVWs, a virtual replica of a classroom setting, or a laboratory as commonly used for presentations and lectures, is designed. The instructor could use two or more screens for presenting slides, videos, pictures, web resources, and even an online-desktop when a part of the desktop needs to be shared with the students. Students usually attend the virtual classroom using their own avatars and there are possibilities to make contact between the instructor and the students using two mechanisms, text chat and online voice. For voice chat, instructor and students need to have microphones and headsets hooked up to their computers. 49% of the investigated studies in the literature have content relevant to virtual lecturing, and they have mainly established a virtual lecturing activity to deliver a course to the students.

For instance, in order to understand the reaction and perception of students when using Second Life in a blended learning session with the involvement of the instructors, Zulkanain, Rahim, and Azizan (2016) conducted an exploratory study. Kawulich and D'Alba (2019) used Second Life for teaching research methods to a doctoral-level qualitative research class. In a quantitative research, Al-Hatem et al. (2018) examined impacts of second life on student nurses' confidence and motivation in developing their self-regulated learning performance. In the study of Lorenzo-Alvarez et al. (2019), attitudes and perceptions of 3rd-year medical students, as well as family physicians, toward a radiographic interpretation course in Second Life was evaluated. In another study, second life was used to enhance Mandarin essay writing by learners of Chinese as a second language in Singapore (Lan et al., 2019). Gazave and Hatcher (2017) used a 3D virtual world to implement Team-based learning (TBL) in an online undergraduate anatomy course. In a qualitative study, Linganisa et al. (2018) investigated the perception of fourth-year information systems and technology (IST) students on the usefulness of Second Life as a learning platform. Chen et al. (2010) assessed the relative effectiveness of a 3DVW-based learning environment and traditional face-to-face learning environment, and by performing a quantitative research, they found that when an interactive instructional strategy is applied in education, there is no remarkable difference for perceived learning and satisfaction between the two environments. Pereira et al. (2019) used Second Life to teach the first semester veterinary students the clinical reasoning process, and compared the results with the traditional classroom setting. Barry et al. (2013), Callaghan et al. (2009), Dafoulas et al. (2012), Dreher et al. (2009), Mendonça et al. (2011), Sharma et al. (2013), and Yalcinalp et al. (2012) carried out studies related to this category.

Discussion

Discussion boards and online meetings are other application in the 3DVW-related virtual learning programs. During the distance discussions or meetings, students engage in several social activities, such as discussing a subject matter, sharing their perspective(s), presenting students' projects, consultation, asking questions, etc. Voice, video and text-based communication are used for discussions. For example, by using text chat, students or educators could send private and public messages or post text messages in discussion forums inside the 3DVWs. For voice and live video chat, users need to have microphones, cameras and headsets hooked up to their computers. Additionally, there is the possibility of automatic recording of entire sessions as reviewable logs.

Approximately, 32% of studies have used virtual worlds as a tool for discussions and meetings in higher education. For instance, Lorenzo et al. (2012) found that 3DWV platforms can provide better capabilities for removing barriers between students and between instructors and students. The problematic issue in this application was technical difficulties in establishing video, voice and/or text communications. For example, there could be glitches in sending and receiving video, voice and text, especially when the number of simultaneous participants was high. Balcikanli (2012) used Second Life® to create an interactive discussion environment for two groups of language learners and found that it played a crucial role in encouraging them to apply the authentic language. Studies of Nikolaou and Tsolakidis (2012), Loureiro and Bettencourt (2011), Di Blas and Poggi (2007), Prasolova-Forland (2004), and Zhao et al. (2010) are classified into this category as they involve virtual meeting or discussion room for various educational purposes.

Field Trip

Field trips are mainly used as an application for self-learning. A virtual representation of a specific place such as a museum, a gallery, a hotel, a hospital, and a scientific site is designed to create visitor awareness about the place and provide information that students need. Students are able to navigate their avatars into the designed environment to visit the virtual site. Students usually perform a virtual trip to a virtual place, visit the site, read the provided information, and observe some activities inside the site.

Almost 14% of studies in the literature used 3DVWs for conducting field trip programs. For example, Aydogan et al. (2010) have built a hydroelectric power plant in Second Life® with all its important parts to teach how to produce electricity. Using avatars, students walked around and flew towards the power plant to figure out how it worked. In another study, access to a number of digital 3D models of European theatre designs was provided and participants visited the Theatre of Epidaurus during a virtual field trip; participants also explored Shakespeare's Globe Theatre (Nicholls & Philip, 2012). Huang et al. (2013)

used 3DVW for tourism education, and the majority of the hypotheses in their research model identify the factors impacting student learning experience within a 3DVW. For example, they examined the association between students' perceptions of autonomy and positive emotions, which was supported ($\beta = 0.487$, $p < 0.05$) suggesting that the perceptions of autonomy in a 3DVW predicts students' feelings of positive emotion.

Simulation

Other studies in the current review applied 3DVWs for simulation purposes in higher education. Simulation is the act of imitation of a real-world system's or process's operation over time. By definition, it is the emulation of a real-world system, an activity or a process operation over a time period. It is a powerful action that is used for teaching and learning processes that generally are impossible or very hard to practice in the real world. It is a powerful tool that is commonly used to teach processes that are generally difficult to practice in the real world (Wang & Zhu, 2009). By using virtual worlds' designing and programming tools, as well as simulation techniques, the virtual clones of a specific place or an environment is modelled and designed for training purposes. By working with simulated environments, students get familiar with various concepts which are usually inaccessible in the real world.

Twenty-eight percent of studies used 3DVWs for simulation-related teaching and learning. For example, Aydogan and Aras (2019) designed, simulated and virtually implemented a new basic programmable logic controllers (PLC) laboratory on Second Life for the purpose of online PLC training. In a study conducted by Grenfell (2013), students were working to simulate the development of a virtual art exhibition space. In another study, researchers simulated an on-line garment store in Second Life with static objects, such as buildings, sofas, costumes, advertising boards, direction boards, etc. (Dong et al., 2010). They found that to provide a successful educational service in 3DVWs, more attention should be paid to the ease of use during the whole service lifetime. Molka-Danielsen and Chabada (2010) simulated an emergency evacuation within Second Life®. Irwin et al. (2019) utilized a created nursing environment in Second Life® for three nursing courses in order to develop nursing skills among undergraduate students. In another study, a collaborative simulation was applied to educate students on construction safety (Le & Park, 2012). Brown et al. (2012) presented a simulation of handing over the 24-hour care requirements of patients in intensive care during the first hour of a shift. According to (Cheng & Wang, 2011), the simulation experience with a 3DVW for marketing was very important and irreplaceable in comparison with other ICT-based pedagogy. To achieve a higher level of simulation potential, improvements in visual effects and realism of the virtual platforms are required. Winkelmann et al. (2019) used Second Life to implement a virtual laboratory experiment for students enrolled in a General Chemistry 2 course.

Gaming

One of the significant effects of IT-based technologies on students is that they are interested in playing computer games. Computer games are useful and educationally effective approaches to teach various educational concepts. For many years, electronic games have supported entertainment-based learning. Computer games are effective approaches to teach various educational concepts. Students who play computer games tend to learn the intended concepts, and in most of the cases, they find it a relatively enjoyable experience of learning (Wang & Zhu, 2009).

About 11% of the studies in the review have used virtual worlds for gaming and machinima to improve teaching and learning in the higher education setting. For example, to determine whether and how a 3DVW enhanced software engineering education, researchers designed a Second Life-based game for computer science students (Ye et al., 2007). Arango-López et al. (2019) created a platform, CREANDO, that allows the creation and edition of pervasive gaming experiences in closed spaces on university campuses, in order to increase the motivation of higher education students in educational processes. In another study, authors designed a 3D virtual quest game to enhance English vocabulary acquisition through interaction, negotiation of meaning and observation (Kastoudi, 2011). Wang and Zhu (2009) developed a game within Second Life® for software engineering education. Students, by playing the game, were able to realize the process of developing a software. Merchant et al. (2012), in their quantitative study, designed a game in Second Life® to enable students to see molecules from multiple perspectives. They found 3D virtual reality-based instruction effective in enhancing students' chemistry achievement.

3DVWs Platforms Used in Teaching and Learning

Since the advent of the first generation of 3DVWs, various companies have developed their own virtual world platform, and currently, there are a wide variety of 3DVW platforms. Individuals and numerous companies and organizations around the world are using various samples of these platforms for their own purposes. There are a wide variety of active 3DVW platforms at the moment, however, this literature review sought to identify the platforms most widely used by researchers in their educational programs.

Figure 4 presents percentages of various 3DWV platforms found in the review of 176 studies. Second Life was the most frequently discussed 3DVW platform used for learning and teaching purposes in higher education; Second Life was discussed in 61% of studies. Fourteen percent of the studies used their own, self-developed 3DVW platform mainly using a designed single-purpose virtual world for extending educational activities. Open Simulator was discussed in 7% of the studies, as a platform utilized for learning and teaching in higher education. Five percent of the papers discussed using other platforms such as Vacademia, Zora 3-D, Croquet and AliveX3D. Active World and AET Zone are the other platforms which were discussed respectively in 3% and 2% of studies. In 8% of the studies, authors did not specify the type of 3DVW that they have applied, therefore, the used platforms considered as unknown. Table 3 indicates all 3DWV platforms used in the literature, and the exact number of studies which used each one.

Gamage, Tretiakov, and Crump (2011) investigated educators' perceptions of Second Life® affordances for learning by conducting in-depth semi-structured interviews with 22 educators. Chen et al. (2009) assessed the efficacy of two instruction strategies in Second Life®, and their effects on interactivity, social presence, and perceived learning. Garcia-Zubia et al. (2010) described the implementation of a new remote lab that allowed students to control a micro robot from Second Life®. Stiubiener et al. (2011) in their study presented two tools developed to facilitate the use and to automate the process of using Open Simulator for educational purposes. Dickey (2005) presented two exploratory case studies of different, but exemplary educational activities using Active Worlds for formal and informal education. In another study, Bronack et al. (2008) used the AET Zone platform for their teaching and learning purposes.

Table 3. Number of studies for each 3DVW platform

3D Virtual World Platform	Number of Studies
Second Life ®	107
Self-Developed	24
Open Simulator	12
Active World	5
AET Zone	3
Unknown	14
Vacademia	2
Barnsborough(AWEDU)	1
Croquet	1
GEARS	1
QA (Quest Atlantis)	1
Virtools Dev	1
Virtual Incubator World (VIW)	1
WonderLands/TEAL	1
Zora 3-D	1
AliveX3D	1

Figure 4. Percentage of applied 3DVW platforms in higher education

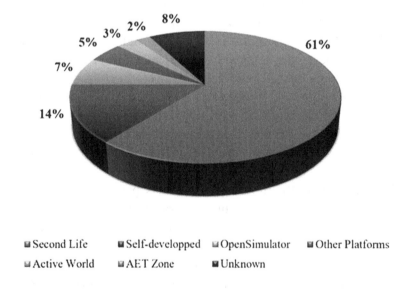

Categorization of Learning Environments for Educational Purposes

3DVW technology provides the ability for users to design and create different kinds of virtual and 3D environments for various purposes. In all of the studies in the current literature review, researchers designed and developed specific spaces inside the virtual worlds in relation to their educational activities.

The created virtual environments were categorized and 17 categories were identified. The majority of the studies created two or more categories of environments simultaneously. Table 4 shows the list of all virtual environments in higher education as well as the number of papers in each category in the literature.

Table 4. Virtual environments used in higher education and the number of related studies

Virtual Environments	Number of Studies
Virtual classroom	69
Simulated place	34
Meeting area	22
Other environments	21
Virtual campus	15
Virtual laboratory	15
Gaming environment	11
Virtual library	9
Replica of known place	9
Virtual messaging environment	8
Board room	4
Sandbox area	4
Video room	3
Quiz environment	3
Poster room	1
Outdoor environment	1
Staff room	1

As it can be noted in Table 4, in 69 studies, researchers designed virtual classroom environments for their programs. These environments resemble actual classrooms or lecture theaters (having a number of seats, a lectern for instructor, a presentation display and video display), where students' and instructors' avatars can attend and communicate with each other using voice or text chat tools. Students can see the presentation slides and educational videos and they can even see the instructor's face in an online and real-time video. For Example, Gao et al. (2009), Loureiro and Bettencourt (2011), Marcelino et al. (2012), and Yalcinalp et al. (2012) designed various virtual classroom environments inside the 3DVW platforms.

In 34 of the reviewed studies, researchers used simulated places for teaching and learning. In most cases, a specific place has been modeled, simulated and created; therefore, students can learn different things by visiting, interacting with and going around these places. For example, Cheng and Wang (2011) designed a 3D virtual supermarket to help business students transform abstract class theory into the concrete application ability in the real world. Brown et al. (2012) developed a simulated 3D ICU (Intensive Care Unit) for students to practice key steps in handing over the 24/7 care requirements of intensive care patients during the first hour of a shift. In another study, authors designed a virtual hydroelectric power plant in Second Life to teach students how to produce electricity (Aydogan et al., 2010). Students can also observe the detail of the power plant's structure, which cannot be shown even in a technical trip due to the plant being in-service.

Virtual meeting areas have been designed and used in 22 studies. These areas are mainly furnished by seats and chairs, and they contain presentations and video displays. The avatars can get together in the place and they can use microphones/speakers (voice chat) or text chat tools for sending public or private messages to each other. The main purpose of these places is to hold across-distance meetings with students, instructors or staff. For example, Bronack et al. (2008), Nikolaou and Tsolakidis (2012), and Andreas and Tsiatsos (2008) developed a virtual meeting area to hold educational meetings.

Fifteen studies discussed the development of a university campus for their activities. They designed various parts of a real campus and students could enter the campus using their avatars and visit different sections inside. In some cases, a replica of a real-world university campus is designed so the virtual campus exactly resembles the real one. In other cases, researchers designed different buildings and views for the campus and they only inserted the parts, buildings or rooms that students needed to attend or visit. For example, Bers and Chau (2010), Nishide (2011), and Nishide and Ueshima (2004) developed a campus using 3DVWs for their teaching and learning programs in higher education.

Virtual laboratories are the other virtual environments which have been created and developed by researchers for higher education in 15 studies. These laboratories are simulated environments that present the ability to perform most of the activities of the real laboratories in a virtual manner. For instance, Winkelmann et al. (2019) implemented a virtual laboratory for General Chemistry 2 course within Second Life®. Muller et al. (2012) designed a virtual mechatronics lab in Open Simulator, developed for mechatronics training, which combines immersive 3D worlds and real lab equipment. Zhong and Liu (2012) created a virtual chemistry laboratory to discuss the technical difficulties that users face when developing 3D virtual worlds. A physics laboratory was designed by dos Santos, Guetl et al. (2010) in order to support students understanding of physics concepts.

Eleven studies implemented gaming environments and activities within 3DVW. For example, in the study of Arango-López et al. (2019) a platform was created that allows students to create and edit pervasive gaming experiences.

In nine papers, virtual libraries were implemented, and in nine other studies, researchers developed a replica of a known place or a popular attraction in the world to help students get familiar with the place and atmosphere. These virtual clones are mainly used for field trips and similar activities. For example, Hsu (2012) created a virtual island of France for tourism education. In two other studies, researchers used Second Life to simulate a Saami tent and a Kalasha valley and dwellings for archaeology students (Edirisingha et al., 2009; Salmon et al., 2010).

Virtual messaging environments have also been created and used in educational settings for communication purposes. In these environments, users of virtual worlds can interact with each other using voice or text chat tools. For example, Traphagan et al. (2010) used a text chat tool for students to complete all course activities collaboratively with group members. Wigham and Chanier (2013) offer a classification of verbal and nonverbal communication acts in Second Life and outline relationships between the different types of acts by using a voice forum.

In addition to the environments mentioned, other virtual spaces have been designed for different educational purposes. Some of the other virtual environments are video rooms, virtual libraries, board rooms, poster rooms, outdoor environments, staff rooms, sandbox areas, and other miscellaneous environments.

DISCUSSION AND FUTURE DIRECTION FOR RESEACH AND PRACTICE

The principal objective of the present review was to characterize the various application areas of 3DVWs in conjunction with higher education. Following, we will take a deeper look at the aims of this study and discuss the lessons we have learned. The 176 articles retained for review demonstrate the breadth of research foci in this topic. To gain a general understanding of virtual world research in higher education, according to the application areas of this technology, we classified these research studies into 5 main categories. Figure 5 illustrates the frequency of studies included in each of these categories of activities and shows that most of the papers contained more than one activity in the context and were included in more than one category.

Figure 5. Percentage of studies included in each category of activities

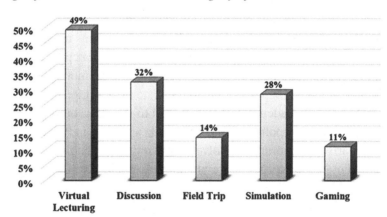

The virtual lecturing category contains the largest percentage of papers (49%). This indicates the capability of 3DVW technologies to facilitate online lectures and distance learning. The possibility of presenting lectures and classroom activities through voice, video, slide, animation and other online facilities provided by 3DVWs as well as the feeling of presence in a real classroom by students and instructors has made this technology as a mature tool to be used in higher education. Discussion and meeting (32%) and simulation (28%) are the next most common applications of 3DVWs in higher education. The great potential of this technology enabled educational systems to hold online and real-time meetings and seminars. Most 3DVW platforms provide the feasibility of simulating and modelling real-world activities through in-world programming and building tools. As shown in Figure 5, these technologies have been utilized for field trips activities in 14% of the reviewed studies. Despite the great potential of 3DVWs in gaming, studies paid less attention to this category with total of 11% of all studies.

A total of 7% of all studies, 13 out of 176, only conducted reviews, surveys and investigation of the impact of using these technologies on education. For example, Fırat (2010) evaluated the pedagogical capabilities of 3DVWs and determined the educational application of these technologies in Turkey. Hew and Cheung (2013) presented a literature review to investigate the impact of applying technologies based on Web 2.0 on K–12 and higher education students' learning performance. Boulos et al. (2007) presented the educational potential of 3DVWs for educators as well as medical and health librarians. Wang and Lockee (2010) provided a content analysis for investigating studies on the application of 3DVWs in distance education. Hew and Cheung (2010) reviewed previous empirical studies on the application of 3DVWs in education settings. Another study explored Second Life's potential and the problems 3D virtual environments present to instructors and educators (Warburton, 2009). Pricer (2011) presented a 'Webliography' which provides resources discussing the application of various forms of computer simulations such as 3DVWs for immersive education. To assess the impact of 3DVWs on education, Eschenbrenner et al. (2008) conducted a literature review to identify applications, benefits, opportunities and issues. Saleeb and Dafoulas (2010b) analytically derived the advantageous and disadvantageous themes and sub-concepts of using 3DVWs for e-learning. They also investigated the impact of architectural features of educational virtual buildings and classrooms within 3DVWs on the comfort of higher education students and staff, and they presented design preferences and propositions to enhance virtual campus learning spaces, internally and externally (Saleeb & Dafoulas, 2010a).

One of the principle goals of this research was to classify various application areas of 3DVWs in the field of education. Therefore, based on the literature, the authors provide five meaningful categories of applications in higher education (virtual lecturing, discussion, field trip, simulation, and gaming). Hence, future research can explore additional applications of these environments in the education sector. They can identify various criteria to evaluate value-added activities and strategies for effective integration of this technology into a curriculum. Future research also needs to be more creative to figure out new effective ways of teaching and learning rather than to replicate the traditional methods of education. In spite of the considerable level of academic research related to the educational application of 3DVWs, research pertaining to the practical applications of such tools are seemingly inadequate, particularly as opportunities continue to arise and continue to evolve in utilizing this technology in the field of education.

The investigated studies tended to pay more attention to qualitative data collection and analysis approaches than quantitative ones. Among the studies, approximately 11% employed a quantitative approach, and most studies used only qualitative research methods to collect educators' and students' feedback. Although some studies used multiple methods, the emphasis of the data collection was on qualitative data. The data resources mainly included interviews, participatory observation, platform log files, screen captured images, environment videos, notes, class logs and chat logs. Future research may employ quantitative data methods as well as mixed method approaches to get results that can be better generalized.

The current literature review and the results provide various implications for a wide range of organizations, universities, educational communities, schools, academic staff, educators, instructors and individuals which are able to use this study to consider all the capabilities and derived experiences that are associated with the application of 3DVWs in the professional and pedagogical objectives they want to achieve. This study also identifies any gaps that were apparent in the published research. Despite the fact that researchers paid more attention to educational benefits of 3DVWs, some gaps still exist in the literature and future research should be conducted to explore improvements to previous studies. The mentioned implications as well as existing gaps in conjunction with the topic will be discussed as following:

Collaborative Learning

According to the findings, the focus of previous studies was mainly on the possibilities of using 3DVWs for delivering distance courses, and the students' learning outcomes in the investigated studies were mostly positive for distance education. Nevertheless, as these technologies provide effective opportunities for students in respect to collaborative learning, teamwork and self-directed learning, future studies may best contribute by investigating the impacts of such technologies on individual and group student outcomes and experiences. By using various communication tools provided by 3DVWs (e.g. text chat, voice chat, online video conferencing), students can interact with each other and their educators at the same time. Moreover, 3DVWs provide synchronous communication regardless of the students' location. These environments can be designed to be a social hub, places for people to meet and a place for various events. Educators and instructors can take advantage of this technology for collaboration purposes among students. On the other hand, students with social disorders, especially those who have difficulty communicating with others for various reasons, could benefit from this technology and improve their learning and social interactive behavior. Learning as construction or co-construction can be performed easily within these environments which provide facilities for creating, mixing, and mashing up objects and content. Therefore, 3DVWs can be seen as a great collaborative tool with which multiple users can experiment with each other. Edirisingha et al. (2009) found that in spite of the fact that the creation of participants' real identity through an avatar is complex in virtual words, their experience of socialization gave them positive feelings. Ellison and Matthews (2010) found that using 3DVWs for a 3D construction-based project had various positive effects on learners.

Gaming and Machinima

Gaming and machinima aspect of 3DVWs has also received little attention in the higher education field. Machinima, in definition, is the "art of making animated movies in a 3D virtual environment in real time" (Marino, 2004). Entertainment environments and leisure activities, as well as using computers and video games, have been identified as significant educational resources. Games help impart knowledge, develop course-related skills and reinforce positive habits in students of all ages, in the form of play. Future studies are expected to put more attention to this capability of 3DVWs in teaching and learning programs. For example, the findings of Terzidou, Tsiatsos, Dae, Samaras, & Chasanidou, (2012) revealed that there is a positive attitude toward adoption of 3DVWs used from game-based learning techniques. The main problems in the 3DVW gaming applications in education are a lack of appropriate hardware performance; having low visual, acoustic and graphics specifications in comparison with different gaming consoles (which reduces the attractiveness of the environment); and the need for greater Internet speed. Another consideration of 3DVW-based games is that there is no winner and loser, which reduces some students' interest in playing.

Geographical Context

According to findings of the current study, the majority of studies in the literature in this field were conducted in North America and Europe, and there are only a limited number of studies from other countries of the world. A comparative research within various cultural and social environments is recommended in order to more effectively comprehend the influence of geographical contexts on the use of 3DVWs in higher education.

3DVW-based vs. Traditional Classroom

One of the significant questions about the applicability of 3DVWs in higher education is whether these technologies can provide comparable learning outcomes for trainees attending real-world classrooms.

In the current literature review, the researchers found a wide range of studies that covered this research topic and, according to students' and educators' feedback, they demonstrate that 3DVWs have the ability to enhance teaching and learning outcomes significantly, having a general positive impact on students' achievement and providing more options for delivering education in comparison with real-world and in-person classes. Based on the reported results, the majority of studies in the literature have come up with the same results and even better results of real-world lectures. For instance, Okutsu et al. (2013) investigated the learning outcomes of a 3DVW-based course on students. They did not find a significant difference between the exam scores of the 3DVW group and the real-world group. According to Zhao et al. (2011), 3DVWs can create a more colourful learning environment than traditional teaching, and students can recognise the experience of immersion, flexibility and interactivity.

Distance Learning Opportunities

The findings show that the focus of previous studies was mainly on the possibilities of using 3DVWs to deliver distance courses, and the students' learning outcomes based on those studies were mostly positive. Due to Internet-based characteristics, 3DVWs, provide effective opportunities to conduct distance learning and e-learning programs for students using this technology. Lectures, seminars, laboratories and workshops can be held easily using this technology, and students and educators can attend courses in the virtual venue using their own avatar from various locations all around the world.

Simulation and Modeling

Modeling is "the act of representing a system or subsystem formally" (Davis II et al., 1999). According to the promising potential of 3DVWs for modeling and simulation purposes, research or practice that may not have been practical or feasible in real life can be created through simulations in 3D virtual environments (Eschenbrenner et al., 2008), and virtual simulations using these kinds of technologies are an acceptable strategy to deliver scenarios that focus on practical skills. By using the simulation techniques, instructors, educators and trainers are able to collaborate with learners and solve problem-based scenarios in a team. Simulation also allows them to construct technical skills actively through interaction in a 3D virtual environment without having the hazard of risks or danger of making mistakes in a specific activity. Organizations such as universities, manufacturers and educational communities can model and simulate various systems, laboratories, product lines and activities, with virtual instruments and equipment that simulate real-world operations at a very low cost for education. Particularly, utilizing 3DVWs seems to be a proper method to learn design-based and visually-intensive courses like object modelling and computer graphics. Using 3DVWs seems to be particularly appropriate for learning design-based and visually intensive courses like object modelling and computer graphics. For example, Molka-Danielsen and Chabada, (2010) used Second Life® to simulate evacuation and training exercises, and they found that, despite the differences of human behaviors within virtual worlds, using a simulated environment for education has real value and experiential learning takes place.

Virtual Field Trips

By using 3DVWs, there is a possibility of holding virtual field trips inside virtual environments for educational purposes. It is a guided and narrated tour of a virtual simulation of a real place or an imaginary location inside a 3DVW that can be selected by educators and arranged so that students can visit, follow the instructions and perform an exploration with just moving around the virtual space. By traveling to virtual locations, students can get familiar with various spectacular, historical and travel points all around the world. To illustrate, by developing a virtual field trip for university students in a virtual world, Mathews et al. (2012) found that this kind of learning method is an innovative learning opportunity.

Hardware and Software Integration

A 3DVW gives developers the ability to connect and control other hardware and software to add more facilities to virtual learning and teaching environments. For example, developers can control various types of hardware from their virtual land, by adding programs and scripts to their objects within the virtual environment. Developers are also able to connect other educational applications such as Blackboard to some of the virtual worlds like Second Life to take more advantages of those applications inside the virtual learning environment. For instance, Second Life supports a programming language, Linden Scripting Language (LSL), which is a capable tool allowing control of in-world objects as well as integration and connection with other applications and hardware. Since virtual worlds support 3D shape functions, inside these environments students are able to create and sculpt shapes and showcase their individual works to others for peer review; the application of this technology is related to learning as construction or co-construction (Hew & Cheung, 2013). These environments provide facilities for reusing, remixing, and mashing up user-created objects and content; therefore, they can be seen as an effective collaborative tool with which multiple users can experiment with each other.

Virtual Campus

By creating a virtual campus, universities and colleges can provide attractive virtual environments to extend their educational programs. A virtual campus provides a specific place as a framework for learning activities as well as a set of virtual tools to benefit educational process (Clark & Maher, 2001). Various activities can be done inside the virtual lands of 3DVWs beside the educational programs such as open day programs, orientation programs, public ceremonies or any other extracurricular activities. A virtual campus can also be accessed from any Internet-connected personal computer from remote locations providing a more effective learning environment for all its students giving them the opportunity to access the learning materials and resources from own place.

Development

The current review revealed a lack of attention to the development aspect of 3DVWs. Most of the virtual worlds provide building tools and programming languages to fill in the gaps left by the platform engine. Programmers and developers can add new functionalities to objects, design new objects with new actions and even integrate other applications or hardware with their virtual environment. According to the findings of this study, few studies covered this functionality of 3DVWs; therefore, the powerful ability of 3DVWs in integrating these tools with other e-learning applications to improve their functionality could be investigated in depth. The most significant difficulty regarding development within these worlds is that students need to learn the fundamental concepts of computer graphics design as well as programming languages.

Teaching Material

Studies in the literature paid less attention to a potential of 3DVW technology in providing facilities for teaching material and resources. The technology can help educators and educational organizations to develop a rich resource of course materials through the ability of 3DVWs to store, present, play, upload and download various file formats (e.g. images, videos, voices, animations, textures, slides, other documents), as well as to connect the virtual environments to the Internet to open dynamic and static web pages. It is also possible to add visual and animated effects in order to ease access to the material and make the materials more appealing. The technology is very mature and rich for this purpose, which can make self-training and distance learning applicable. The main concern is the need for higher Internet speed and higher performance hardware to access the resources easily. Another issue can be the cost of uploading documents, videos, sounds and other files to the virtual environment, as most of the virtual world platforms charge for each file upload.

Massive Open Online Courses

Massive Open Online Courses (MOOCs) as a new method in education can also benefit from 3DVWs. MOOCs are free online courses aimed at large-scale participation and open access on the web. Many academics across the world recently have become interested in using MOOCs for delivering education around the globe on an unprecedented scale. In accordance with their basic specifications, 3DVWs can add more value to MOOCs in the educational system. 3DVWs as online infrastructures are open on a global scale; they support a massive number of residents and users, and various kinds of courses can take place within these platforms either synchronously or asynchronously. More research and practice is needed to understand the implications of this technology on MOOCs and to assess opportunities and challenges for incorporating 3DVWs into MOOCs units at the higher education and university level.

Sense of Presence

One of the main reasons for the success of 3DVW in the education field, specifically in lecturing and presenting courses, is its tremendous ability to provide users with a virtual presence within an immersive virtual environment. By using an avatar, everyone can experience a virtual presence in the virtual classroom or a laboratory area. Students can touch everything and see everything by using the visual effects.

Barriers and Issues

In the current study, some challenges related to the use of 3DWVs in higher education were identified. There is also a need for more research into the issues and barriers of using this technology, as the current studies tend to deal with only the advantages and positive aspects of the use of 3DVWs in higher education. The problems and barriers of these environments, such as complexity, speed, compatibility, behaviour, health, safety, security, cost, user adoption, and so on need to be considered, as well as factors associated with adoption and students' intention to use 3DVWs in educational activities. In order to make this technology more accessible and user-friendly, and to reduce the complexity for educators and trainees, especially those who are unfamiliar with designing and programming techniques, further studies and research are required.

The most important issues which could affect the efficiency of 3DVWs in this application area were lower hardware performance, limited Internet speed and technical problems. Furthermore, in most experiences, there is no possibility to limit students' behaviours within the virtual classroom and the type and appearance of their avatar. The lack of a personal computer or smart device as well as limited access to the Internet also could be a significant problem for a student.

Limitations

Our attempts to perform the present literature review have highlighted a number of limitations, most of which can influence future research. We believe that the research methods in the current study were thorough and exhaustive, and we aimed for a comprehensive coverage of the literature in this field, but there is a possibility of omitted relevant research during the filtering process. Therefore, we do not guarantee that we have taken all of the application areas of this technology in higher education into account as a massive number of studies relevant to this topic have been published, and some studies might have been missed. As the quality of results of a literature review study is extremely dependent on the quality of the identified papers in that study, an evaluation of the quality of the results in this study is not possible. Generally, any literature review is limited to its search terms, and the current review is not an exception in this regard. As there are only a limited percentage of the studies in the literature from countries other than the United States and in Europe, we cannot present a global conclusion regarding to the application areas of 3DVWs in the higher education sector. A further limitation of the present study is that it included only published research.

CONCLUSION

To provide a big picture of application areas of 3DVWs in the higher education sector, a literature review was conducted on the available body of knowledge. Consequently, five main categories of curricular activities were developed for which 3DVWs have been used to date: virtual lecturing, discussion, field trip, simulation and gaming. The authors also identified the most applied 3DVWs platforms in higher education. Additionally, the 3D virtual environments created for educational purposes have been identified and classified into seventeen main categories. Virtual classroom, virtual laboratory, virtual meeting area, simulated places and replicas of popular places are the most common 3D virtual environments in the literature that are used for educational pedagogical activities in higher education. The findings offer researchers, educators and educational institutions some informed directions for utilizing these technologies to achieve specific learning outcomes. They can use this technology as a creative, powerful and efficient tool to develop new and effective ways of teaching and learning. In order to close the gap between academic research and practical applications some suggestions can be made: First, educational applications should be widespread, in accordance with the proposals obtained from the researchers conducting studies in this field. Second, universities and other educational communities and organizations should lead the use of 3DVWs for their educational purposes in the future.

REFERENCES

Al-Hatem, A. I., Masood, M., & Al-Samarraie, H. (2018). Fostering student nurses' self-regulated learning with the Second Life environment: An empirical study. *Journal of Information Technology Education*, *17*, 285–307. doi:10.28945/4110

Andreas, K., & Tsiatsos, T. (2008, March). Selecting a networked virtual environment platform and the design of a collaborative e-learning environment. In *22nd International Conference on Advanced Information Networking and Applications-Workshops (aina workshops 2008)* (pp. 44-49). IEEE.

Arango-López, J., Valdivieso, C. C. C., Collazos, C. A., Vela, F. L. G., & Moreira, F. (2019). CREANDO: Tool for creating pervasive games to increase the learning motivation in higher education students. *Telematics and Informatics*, *38*, 62–73. doi:10.1016/j.tele.2018.08.005

Aydogan, H., & Aras, F. (2019). Design, simulation and virtual implementation of a novel fundamental programmable logic controllers laboratory in a 3D virtual world. *International Journal of Electrical Engineering Education*. Advance online publication. doi:10.1177/0020720919856249

Aydoğan, H., Aras, F., & Karakas, E. (2010, June). An assessment on distance education in a 3D virtual environment: How to produce electricity in a hydroelectric power plant. In *2010 2nd International Conference on Education Technology and Computer* (Vol. 1, pp. V1-346). IEEE.

Ba, S., Ke, D., Stallaert, J., & Zhang, Z. (2010). Why give away something for nothing? Investigating virtual goods pricing and permission strategies. *ACM Transactions on Management Information Systems*, *1*(1), 1–22. doi:10.1145/1877725.1877729

Balcikanli, C. (2012). Language learning in Second Life: American and Turkish Students' Experiences. *Turkish Online Journal of Distance Education*, *13*(2), 131–146.

Barry, D. M., Kanematsu, H., Fukumura, Y., Kobayashi, T., Ogawa, N., & Nagai, H. (2013). US Students Carry out Nuclear Safety Project in a Virtual Environment. *Procedia Computer Science*, *22*, 1354–1360. doi:10.1016/j.procs.2013.09.224

Bers, M., & Chau, C. (2010). The virtual campus of the future: Stimulating and simulating civic actions in a virtual world. *Journal of Computing in Higher Education*, *22*(1), 1–23. doi:10.100712528-009-9026-3

Boulos, M. N. K., Hetherington, L., & Wheeler, S. (2007). Second Life: An overview of the potential of 3-D virtual worlds in medical and health education. *Health Information and Libraries Journal*, *24*(4), 233–245. doi:10.1111/j.1471-1842.2007.00733.x PMID:18005298

Bronack, S., Sanders, R., Cheney, A., Riedl, R., Tashner, J., & Matzen, N. (2008). Presence Pedagogy: Teaching and Learning in a 3D Virtual Immersive World. *International Journal on Teaching and Learning in Higher Education*, *20*(1), 59–69.

Brown, R., Rasmussen, R., Baldwin, I., & Wyeth, P. (2012). Design and implementation of a virtual world training simulation of ICU first hour handover processes. *Australian Critical Care*, *25*(3), 178–187. doi:10.1016/j.aucc.2012.02.005 PMID:22436543

Callaghan, M. J., McCusker, K., Losada, J. L., Harkin, J. G., & Wilson, S. (2009, August). *Integrating virtual worlds & virtual learning environments for online education. In 2009 International IEEE Consumer Electronics Society's Games Innovations Conference*. IEEE.

Chen, X., Siau, K., & Nah, F. F.-H. (2009). 3-D virtual worlds: Education and learning. *Proceedings of the Eighth Annual Workshop on HCI Research in MIS (SIGHCI 2009)*.

Chen, X., Siau, K., & Nah, F. F.-H. (2010). 3-D Virtual World Education: An Empirical Comparison With Face-To-Face Classroom. *Thirty First International Conference on Information Systems (ICIS)*, 260.

Cheng, Y., & Wang, S.-H. (2011). Applying a 3D virtual learning environment to facilitate student's application ability–The case of marketing. *Computers in Human Behavior*, *27*(1), 576–584. doi:10.1016/j.chb.2010.10.008

Clark, S., & Maher, M. L. (2001). The role of place in designing a learner centred virtual learning environment. In *Computer Aided Architectural Design Futures 2001* (pp. 187–200). Springer. doi:10.1007/978-94-010-0868-6_15

Dafoulas, G., Saleeb, N., & Loomes, M. (2012, June). The impact of 3D virtual environments on communication patterns. In *2012 International Conference on Information Technology Based Higher Education and Training (ITHET)* (pp. 1-5). IEEE. 10.1109/ITHET.2012.6246065

Davis, I. I. J., Goel, M., Hylands, C., Kienhuis, B., Lee, E. A., Liu, J., Liu, X., Muliadi, L., Neuendorffer, S., Reekie, J., Smyth, N., Tsay, J., & Xiong, Y. (1999). *Overview of the Ptolemy project* (Vol. 99). ERL Technical Report UCB/ERL No. M99/37, Dept. EECS, University of California, Berkeley, CA.

De Lucia, A., Francese, R., Passero, I., & Tortora, G. (2009). Development and evaluation of a virtual campus on Second Life: The case of SecondDMI. *Computers & Education*, *52*(1), 220–233. doi:10.1016/j.compedu.2008.08.001

Di Blas, N., & Poggi, C. (2007). European virtual classrooms: Building effective "virtual" educational experiences. *Virtual Reality (Waltham Cross)*, *11*(2-3), 129–143. doi:10.100710055-006-0060-4

Dickey, M. D. (2005). Three-dimensional virtual worlds and distance learning: Two case studies of Active Worlds as a medium for distance education. *British Journal of Educational Technology*, *36*(3), 439–451. doi:10.1111/j.1467-8535.2005.00477.x

Dong, P., Ma, B., & Wang, F. (2010, May). Development and evaluation of an experiential learning service in 3D virtual world. In *2010 International Conference on Service Sciences* (pp. 374-378). IEEE. 10.1109/ICSS.2010.37

dos Santos, F. R., Guetl, C., Bailey, P. H., & Harward, V. J. (2010, April). Dynamic virtual environment for multiple physics experiments in higher education. In *IEEE EDUCON 2010 Conference* (pp. 731-736). IEEE. 10.1109/EDUCON.2010.5492507

Dreher, C., Reiners, T., Dreher, N., & Dreher, H. (2009, June). 3D virtual worlds as collaborative communities enriching human endeavours: Innovative applications in e-Learning. In *2009 3rd IEEE International Conference on Digital Ecosystems and Technologies* (pp. 151-156). IEEE.

Edirisingha, P., Nie, M., Pluciennik, M., & Young, R. (2009). Socialisation for learning at a distance in a 3-D multi-user virtual environment. *British Journal of Educational Technology*, *40*(3), 458–479. doi:10.1111/j.1467-8535.2009.00962.x

Ellison, K., & Matthews, C. (2010). Virtual history: A socially networked pedagogy of Enlightenment. *Educational Research*, *52*(3), 297–307. doi:10.1080/00131881.2010.504065

Eschenbrenner, B., Nah, F. F.-H., & Siau, K. (2008). 3-D virtual worlds in education: Applications, benefits, issues, and opportunities. *Journal of Database Management*, *19*(4), 91–110. doi:10.4018/jdm.2008100106

Fırat, M. (2010). Learning in 3D virtual worlds and current situation in Turkey. *Procedia: Social and Behavioral Sciences*, *9*, 249–254. doi:10.1016/j.sbspro.2010.12.145

Gamage, V., Tretiakov, A., & Crump, B. (2011). Teacher perceptions of learning affordances of multi-user virtual environments. *Computers & Education*, *57*(4), 2406–2413. doi:10.1016/j.compedu.2011.06.015

Gao, F., Noh, J. J., & Koehler, M. J. (2009). Comparing role-playing activities in Second Life and face-to-face environments. *Journal of Interactive Learning Research*, *20*(4), 423–443.

Garcia-Zubia, J., Irurzun, J., Angulo, I., Hernandez, U., Castro, M., Sancristobal, E., Orduna, P., & Ruiz-de Garibay, J. (2010, April). SecondLab: A remote laboratory under Second Life. In *IEEE EDUCON 2010 Conference* (pp. 351-356). IEEE.

Gazave, C. M., & Hatcher, A. R. (2017). Evaluating the use of Second Life™ for virtual team-based learning in an online undergraduate anatomy course. *Medical Science Educator*, *27*(2), 217–227. doi:10.100740670-017-0374-8

Ghanbarzadeh, R., Ghapanchi, A. H., & Blumenstein, M. (2015, May). Characteristics of research on the application of three-dimensional immersive virtual worlds in health. In *International Conference on Health Information Science* (pp. 213-224). Springer. 10.1007/978-3-319-19156-0_22

Ghanbarzadeh, R., Ghapanchi, A. H., Blumenstein, M., & Talaei-Khoei, A. (2014). A Decade of Research on the Use of Three-Dimensional Virtual Worlds in Health Care: A Systematic Literature Review. *Journal of Medical Internet Research*, *16*(2), e47. doi:10.2196/jmir.3097 PMID:24550130

Grenfell, J. (2013). Immersive interfaces for art education teaching and learning in virtual and real world learning environments. *Procedia: Social and Behavioral Sciences*, *93*, 1198–1211. doi:10.1016/j.sbspro.2013.10.016

Hew, K. F., & Cheung, W. S. (2010). Use of three-dimensional (3-D) immersive virtual worlds in K-12 and higher education settings: A review of the research. *British Journal of Educational Technology*, *41*(1), 33–55. doi:10.1111/j.1467-8535.2008.00900.x

Hew, K. F., & Cheung, W. S. (2013). Use of Web 2.0 technologies in K-12 and higher education: The search for evidence-based practice. *Educational Research Review*, *9*, 47–64. doi:10.1016/j.edurev.2012.08.001

Hsu, L. (2012). Web 3D simulation-based application in tourism education: A case study with Second Life. *Journal of Hospitality, Leisure, Sport and Tourism Education*, *11*(2), 113–124. doi:10.1016/j.jhlste.2012.02.013

Huang, Y.-C., Backman, S. J., Chang, L.-L., Backman, K. F., & McGuire, F. A. (2013). Experiencing student learning and tourism training in a 3D virtual world: An exploratory study. *Journal of Hospitality, Leisure, Sport and Tourism Education*, *13*, 190–201. doi:10.1016/j.jhlste.2013.09.007

Irwin, P., Coutts, R., & Graham, I. (2019, September). Looking Good Sister! The Use of a Virtual World to Develop Nursing Skills. In *Australasian Simulation Congress* (pp. 33-45). Springer. 10.1007/978-981-32-9582-7_3

Kastoudi, D. (2011). *Using a Quest in a 3D Virtual Environment for Student Interaction and Vocabulary Acquisition in Foreign Language Learning. In European Association for Computer-Assisted Language Learning*. EUROCALL.

Kawulich, B. B., & D'Alba, A. (2019). Teaching qualitative research methods with Second Life, a 3-dimensional online virtual environment. *Virtual Reality (Waltham Cross)*, *23*(4), 375–384. doi:10.100710055-018-0353-4

Lan, Y. J., Lyu, B. N., & Chin, C. K. (2019). Does 3D immersive experience enhance Mandarin writing by CSL students? *Language Learning & Technology*, *23*(2), 125–144.

Le, Q. T., & Park, C. S. (2012, August). Construction safety education model based on second life. In *Proceedings of IEEE International Conference on Teaching, Assessment, and Learning for Engineering (TALE) 2012* (pp. H2C-1). IEEE. 10.1109/TALE.2012.6360336

Linden Research. (2011). *Second Life education: The virtual learning advantage*. Retrieved from http://lecs-static-secondlife-com.s3.amazonaws.com/work/SL-Edu-Brochure-010411.pdf

Linganisa, A., Ako-Nai, A., & Ajayi, N. (2018, December). The Potential of Second Life as a Platform for Learning: Student's Perspective. In *2018 International Conference on Intelligent and Innovative Computing Applications (ICONIC)* (pp. 1-5). IEEE. 10.1109/ICONIC.2018.8601201

Lorenzo, C.-M., Ángel Sicilia, M., & Sánchez, S. (2012). Studying the effectiveness of multi-user immersive environments for collaborative evaluation tasks. *Computers & Education*, *59*(4), 1361–1376. doi:10.1016/j.compedu.2012.06.002

Lorenzo-Alvarez, R., Ruiz-Gomez, M. J., & Sendra-Portero, F. (2019). Medical students' and family physicians' attitudes and perceptions toward radiology learning in the Second Life virtual world. *AJR. American Journal of Roentgenology*, *212*(6), 1295–1302. doi:10.2214/AJR.18.20381 PMID:30860900

Loureiro, A., & Bettencourt, T. (2011). The Extended Classroom: Meeting students' needs using a virtual environment. *Procedia: Social and Behavioral Sciences*, *15*, 2667–2672. doi:10.1016/j.sbspro.2011.04.167

Marcelino, R., Silva, J. B., Gruber, V., & Bilessimo, M. S. (2012, July). 3D virtual worlds using open source platform and integrated remote experimentation. In *2012 9th International Conference on Remote Engineering and Virtual Instrumentation (REV)* (pp. 1-2). IEEE.

Marino, P. (2004). *The art of machinima: 3D game-based filmmaking*. ParaglyphPress.

Mathews, S., Andrews, L., & Luck, E. (2012). Developing a Second Life virtual field trip for university students: An action research approach. *Educational Research*, *54*(1), 17–38. doi:10.1080/00131881.2012.658197

Mendonça, R. F., Carreira, S. M., & Sampaio, P. N. (2011, April). VirtualLabs@ UMa: A customizable 3D learning platform for experimental activities. In *2011 International Conference on Multimedia Computing and Systems* (pp. 1-6). IEEE. 10.1109/ICMCS.2011.5945594

Merchant, Z., Goetz, E. T., Keeney-Kennicutt, W., Kwok, O. M., Cifuentes, L., & Davis, T. J. (2012). The learner characteristics, features of desktop 3D virtual reality environments, and college chemistry instruction: A structural equation modeling analysis. *Computers & Education*, *59*(2), 551–568. doi:10.1016/j.compedu.2012.02.004

Molka-Danielsen, J., & Chabada, M. (2010, January). Application of the 3D multi user virtual environment of second life to emergency evacuation simulation. In *2010 43rd Hawaii international conference on system sciences* (pp. 1-9). IEEE.

Müller, D., Chilliischi, A., & Langer, S. (2012, July). Integrating immersive 3D worlds and real lab equipment for teaching mechatronics. In *2012 9th International Conference on Remote Engineering and Virtual Instrumentation (REV)* (pp. 1-6). IEEE.

Nicholls, J., & Philip, R. (2012). Solo life to Second Life: The design of physical and virtual learning spaces inspired by the drama classroom. *Research in Drama Education*, *17*(4), 583–602. doi:10.1080/13569783.2012.727628

Nikolaou, A., & Tsolakidis, C. (2012, September). The role of three dimensional virtual environments in the development of Personal Learning Networks. In *2012 15th International Conference on Interactive Collaborative Learning (ICL)* (pp. 1-7). IEEE. 10.1109/ICL.2012.6402114

Nishide, R. (2011). Prospects for digital campus with extensive applications of virtual collaborative space. *Journal of Interactive Learning Research*, *22*(3), 421–443.

Nishide, R., & Ueshima, S. (2004, January). Digital campus project: A" dream university" over the Internet Web. *Proceedings. Second International Conference on Creating, Connecting and Collaborating through Computing*, *2004*, 122–129.

Okutsu, M., DeLaurentis, D., Brophy, S., & Lambert, J. (2013). Teaching an aerospace engineering design course via virtual worlds: A comparative assessment of learning outcomes. *Computers & Education*, *60*(1), 288–298. doi:10.1016/j.compedu.2012.07.012

Pereira, M. M., Artemiou, E., McGonigle, D., Köster, L., Conan, A., & Sithole, F. (2019). Second Life and Classroom Environments: Comparing Small Group Teaching and Learning in Developing Clinical Reasoning Process Skills. *Medical Science Educator*, *29*(2), 431–437. doi:10.100740670-019-00706-4

Prasolova-Forland, E. (2004, November). Supporting social awareness among university students in 3D CVEs: Benefits and limitations. In *2004 International Conference on Cyberworlds* (pp. 127-134). IEEE. 10.1109/CW.2004.59

Pricer, W. F. (2011). At issue: Immersive Education, an Annotated Webliography. *Community College Enterprise*, *17*(1), 41–50.

Saleeb, N., & Dafoulas, G. (2010a, June). Architectural propositions for enhancement of learning spaces within 3D virtual learning environments. In *2010 International Conference on Information Society* (pp. 410-415). IEEE. 10.1109/i-Society16502.2010.6018738

Saleeb, N., & Dafoulas, G. (2010b, June). Pedagogical immigration to 3D virtual worlds: A critical review of underlying themes and their concepts. In *2010 International Conference on Information Society* (pp. 401-409). IEEE. 10.1109/i-Society16502.2010.6018737

Salmon, G., Nie, M., & Edirisingha, P. (2010). Developing a five-stage model of learning in Second Life. *Educational Research*, *52*(2), 169–182. doi:10.1080/00131881.2010.482744

Sharma, S., Agada, R., & Ruffin, J. (2013, April). *Virtual reality classroom as an constructivist approach. In 2013 Proceedings of IEEE Southeastcon*. IEEE.

Stiubiener, I., Barbosa, W., Kamienski, C. A., & Schweitzer, C. M. (2011, October). Using Virtual Worlds in distance learning environments. In 2011 Frontiers in Education Conference (FIE) (pp. F3C-1). IEEE. doi:10.1109/FIE.2011.6142822

Terzidou, T., Tsiatsos, T., Dae, A., Samaras, O., & Chasanidou, A. (2012, July). Utilizing virtual worlds for game based learning: Grafica, a 3D educational game in second life. In *2012 IEEE 12th International Conference on Advanced Learning Technologies* (pp. 624-628). IEEE.

Traphagan, T. W., Chiang, Y.-V., Chang, H. M., Wattanawaha, B., Lee, H., Mayrath, M. C., Woo, J., Yoon, H.-J., Jee, M. J., & Resta, P. E. (2010). Cognitive, social and teaching presence in a virtual world and a text chat. *Computers & Education*, *55*(3), 923–936. doi:10.1016/j.compedu.2010.04.003

Wang, F., & Lockee, B. B. (2010). Virtual Worlds in Distance Education: A Content Analysis Study. *Quarterly Review of Distance Education*, *11*(3), 183–186.

Wang, T., & Zhu, Q. (2009, March). A software engineering education game in a 3-D online virtual environment. In *2009 First International Workshop on Education Technology and Computer Science* (Vol. 2, pp. 708-710). IEEE. 10.1109/ETCS.2009.418

Warburton, S. (2009). Second Life in higher education: Assessing the potential for and the barriers to deploying virtual worlds in learning and teaching. *British Journal of Educational Technology*, *40*(3), 414–426. doi:10.1111/j.1467-8535.2009.00952.x

Wigham, C. R., & Chanier, T. (2013). A study of verbal and nonverbal communication in Second Life–the ARCHI21 experience. *ReCALL*, *25*(01), 63–84. doi:10.1017/S0958344012000250

Winkelmann, K., Keeney-Kennicutt, W., Fowler, D., Lazo Macik, M., Perez Guarda, P., & Ahlborn, C. J. (2019). Learning gains and attitudes of students performing chemistry experiments in an immersive virtual world. *Interactive Learning Environments*, 1–15.

Yalcinalp, S., Sen, N., Kocer, G., & Koroglu, F. (2012). Higher education student's behaviors as avatars in a web based course in Second Life. *Procedia: Social and Behavioral Sciences*, *46*, 4534–4538. doi:10.1016/j.sbspro.2012.06.291

Ye, E., Liu, C., & Polack-Wahl, J. A. (2007). *Enhancing software engineering education using teaching aids in 3-D online virtual worlds. Frontiers in Education*.

Zhao, H., Sun, B., Wu, H., & Hu, X. (2010, November). Study on building a 3D interactive virtual learning environment based on OpenSim platform. In *2010 International Conference on Audio, Language and Image Processing* (pp. 1407-1411). IEEE. 10.1109/ICALIP.2010.5684986

Zhao, W., Sun, K., & Li, X. J. (2011, May). Investigation on Situational Networked Learning Environment in Virtual Campus. In *2011 3rd International Workshop on Intelligent Systems and Applications* (pp. 1-5). IEEE. 10.1109/ISA.2011.5873408

Zhong, Y., & Liu, C. (2012, June). User evaluation of a domain-oriented end-user design environment for building 3D virtual chemistry experiments. In *2012 First International Workshop on User Evaluation for Software Engineering Researchers (USER)* (pp. 5-8). IEEE. 10.1109/USER.2012.6226585

Zulkanain, N. A., Rahim, E. E. A., & Azizan, F. F. (2016, August). Exploratory study on the relationship of students' perceptions towards the instructors' involvement in Second Life. In *2016 4th International Conference on User Science and Engineering (i-USEr)* (pp. 100-104). IEEE.

KEY TERMS AND DEFINITIONS

Avatar: A computer user's digital, graphical, and animated self-representation which is completely manipulated by its owner.

Blackboard: A virtual learning environment and course management system developed by Blackboard Inc.

E-Learning: A kind of learning which is conducted by using information and communication technologies and electronic media.

Higher Education: Education provided by colleges, universities, or similar educational establishments.

Linden Scripting Language: A scripting programming language that gives behavior to Second Life's primitives, objects, and avatars.

Machinima: Use of video game and computer graphics to create animated cinematic production.

Open Simulator: An open source multi-platform and multi-user 3D application server.

Second Life: A 3D virtual world platform developed by Linden Lab Inc. in 2003.

Simulation: The act of imitation of a real-world system's or process's operation over time.

Three-Dimensional Virtual World (3DVW): A computer-based 3D graphical and simulated environment in which users can interact via their own avatars.

Virtual Lecturing: The act of delivering of lectures by utilizing the Internet, Web, and virtual world technologies.

This research was previously published in Current and Prospective Applications of Virtual Reality in Higher Education; pages 21-47, copyright year 2021 by Information Science Reference (an imprint of IGI Global).

Chapter 7
Factors Affecting Learner Collaboration in 3D Virtual Worlds

Iryna Kozlova
University of Pennsylvania, USA

ABSTRACT

This chapter explores factors affecting learner collaboration by observing the performance of eight English as a foreign language (EFL) learners collaborating on tasks in a 3D virtual world (3D VW) over a period of six weeks. Students used an audio channel to interact with their peers and a text-based channel to make notes on a collaboration board. Their performance was recorded using Camtasia Relay, a screen-capture software, and then transcribed. Data analysis revealed that students' collaboration skills improved over time. The factors that facilitated collaboration included (1) learners and instructors' familiarity with 3D VWs, (2) learners' familiarity with the format of the learning activity, (3) learners' experience with the spontaneous use of the second language (L2), and (4) instructors' use of pedagogical techniques that facilitated collaboration. These results suggest that for students to benefit from collaborative learning, both learners and instructors need to be prepared for this type of instruction.

INTRODUCTION

Designed for collaboration, 3D virtual worlds (3D VWs) have been gaining popularity because of their resemblance to real-world contexts, which may inspire learners to interact as they would in real life (Cooke-Plagwirz, 2008, p. 549). 3D VWs, such as Second Life, are multi-modal immersive web-conferencing environments that provide users with a simulation of real-life experiences by embodying the user in graphical form, referred to as an avatar (Gerhard, Moore, & Hobbs, 2004), and immersing them in worlds resembling real-life locations (Peterson, 2011). These environments are conceptually different from face-to-face and other web-conferencing contexts in that they take learners outside of traditional learning spaces and immerse them in a simulated real-life context (Author & Priven, 2015). In 3D VWs "people experience others as being there with them and where they interact with them"

DOI: 10.4018/978-1-6684-7597-3.ch007

(Schroeder, 2008, p. 2); thus, such environments can engage learners in learning experiences different from those they may have other learning contexts. Because learners can experience 3D worlds alongside other learners utilizing audio- and text-based communication channels, they can learn through "experiential problem solving and complex and spatially distributed forms of collaboration" (Cornille, Thorne, & Desmet, 2012, p. 245).

Learner collaboration in 3D VWs has been the main focus of many of the studies examining these types of environments (e.g., Dalton & Devitt, 2016; Jauregi, Canto, de Graaff, & Moonen, 2010; Lan, 2014; Lan, Kan, Sung, & Chan, 2016; Peterson, 2006, 2010; Toyoda & Harrison, 2002). In particular, studies that explore the relationship between task type and learner collaboration have found that reasoning-gap, problem-solving, and decision-making tasks provide learners with more opportunities for collaborative learning than information-gap and jig-saw tasks (Lan, 2014; Lan, Kan, Sung, & Chung, 2016; Peterson, 2006). Learner collaboration is also facilitated by the incorporation of environment exploration into task design, which encourages learners to explore the environment and share their observations with other group members (Jauregi, Canto, de Graaff, & Moonen, 2010; Kozola, 2018; ; Lan, Kan, Sung, & Chung, 2016).

Jauregi et al. (2010) found that learners' interactional patterns in tasks with an environment exploration component were different from those than in tasks with information and opinion exchange components. When exploring the environment, participants usually do not talk, and so the interactional patterns were characterized by long stretches of silence. In information and opinion exchange tasks, however, Jauregi et al. found that the interactional patterns featured "a dynamic verbal turn-taking exchange among participants, with almost no space for silences" (p. 86). Another study, Peterson (2010), similarly investigated learners' participation patterns in collaborative interaction during open-ended, opinion-exchange, and giving-presentation tasks. Peterson reported a high level of task-focused student interaction in all three of the tasks, attributing these results to the task type as well as to the "highly learner centered nature of the interaction" (p. 289).

Deutschmann, Panichi, and Molka-Danielsen (2009) likewise showed that learner participation in the role-play tasks increased over the course of the study; however, they also discovered factors that negatively affected learner participation in these tasks. These factors included: (1) instructors' assumptions that role-play tasks would work in the same way in the 3D context as they do in face-to-face contexts; (2) learner unfamiliarity with the affordances of 3D VWs and the nature of interaction in this type of environment; (3) the authenticity of the task; (4) instructors' behavior, and; (5) learners' attitudes towards the environment.

Although 3D VWs are multimodal environments with audio- and text-based communication channels available for collaboration, studies conducted in 3D worlds largely employ only one communication channel. In Lan (2014), Lan et al. (2016), Jauregi et al. (2010), and Deutschmann et al. (2009), participants collaborate via audio-based chat; in Peterson (2006, 2010) and Toyoda and Harrison (2002), learners use text-based chat for collaboration. Research that examines learner collaboration and factors affecting collaboration through more than one modality is scarce. The present study bridges this gap by exploring learner collaboration in two modalities: learners can use the audio channel while also taking notes on collaboration boards located in the environment. By observing eight EFL learners collaborating on six tasks in the 3D VW, this study explores factors affecting their collaboration and monitors whether their collaboration skills improve over a period of six weeks.

BACKGROUND

Learners' development of collaboration skills has important implications for their language learning: when working together towards achieving a common goal–e.g., solving a problem or making a decision– learners use language to mutually construct new knowledge by sharing their own ideas and accepting contributions from other participants (Donato, 2004). Collaborative learning is based on the assumption that knowledge is socially owned, and learning, or the internalization of socially distributed knowledge, occurs when learners interact with others using language, which mediates cognitive processes (Lantolf, 2000). Thus, learning is "anchored in social activity" (Lantolf, 2000, p. 13). Initially, others can mediate the activity in which learners are engaged, but over time, learners develop the regulatory means to control their learning processes independently. Collaboration is especially important for language learning because over the course of collaboration, language is used as both a learning object and a tool that mediates language learning (Swain, 2000). In other words, when working together, learners use language to learn it.

Collaboration and Language Learning

Within the field of second language acquisition (SLA), the focus of research on collaborative language learning has been on collaborative scaffolding (e.g., Donato, 2004), instructional conversation when learners achieve their learning goal with the assistance of more knowledgeable interlocutors (Tharp & Gallimore, 1991), and language-related episodes (LREs; e.g., Dobao, 2012; Swain & Lapkin, 1998; Swain, 2000; Storch & Aldosari, 2012). LREs are defined as the parts of learners' dialogue "where the students talk about the language they are producing, question their language use, or correct themselves or others" (Swain & Lapkin, 1998, p, 326). Language production, or output, plays a pivotal role in language learning because learners "need to create linguistic form and meaning, and in so doing, discover what they can and cannot do" (Swain, 2000, p. 99). Another important role of language production is promoting noticing of salient language features, gaps between the target form and the form learners produce, and how to express the intended meaning (Swain, 2000). What output and collaborative activity have in common is that they both involve a cognitive activity and its product (Swain, 2000). Thus, "when learners collaborate to solve linguistic problems, they engage in language-mediated cognitive activities that serve to build linguistic knowledge" (Dobao, 2012, p. 229).

Collaboration and Fluency Development

Collaboration not only engages cognitive processes that lead to language learning but also provides opportunities for spontaneous language use, which helps learners become more fluent language users (Di Silvio, Diao, & Donovan, 2016; Huensch & Tracy-Ventura, 2017). Fluency is a multifaceted concept associated with various features of speech and can be defined in a broad and narrow sense (Lennon, 1990). In a broad sense, fluency is associated with overall use of language, accurate grammar, a large vocabulary, and native-like pronunciation (Bosker, Pinget, Quené, Sanders, & de Jong, 2012). In a narrow sense, it correlates with speech characteristics such as speech rate, frequency, length, and location of pauses, length of fluent runs between pauses (as summarized in Wood, 2001), and, possibly, frequency of repair (Bosker, Pinget, Quené, Sanders, & de Jong, 2012).

Some evidence that learners' use of spontaneous speech improves their fluency, especially in regards to speech rate and the length of talk between pauses (DiSilvio, Diao, & Donovan, 2016; Huensch & Tracy-Ventura, 2017), comes from study-abroad research. DeKeyser (2007) explains that fluency can be developed through practice or specific activities that intentionally and methodically engage learners in the production of the target language to develop target language skills. When developing certain skills, DeKeyser notes that learners are often first presented with information in the form of rules. This information contributes to learners' declarative knowledge, or knowledge about the language and how it works. With practice, declarative knowledge becomes procedural knowledge, which also contains specific rules, but the application of these rules occurs faster and with fewer errors. Procedural knowledge can become automatized, or altered "from initial presentation of the rule in declarative format to the final stage of fully spontaneous, effortless, fast, and errorless use of that rule, often without being aware of it anymore" (DeKeyser, 2007, p. 3). When learning a language in a second language context, learners have plenty of opportunities to practice their target language; in foreign language contexts the opportunities to practice spontaneous language use are significantly more limited. Engaging learners in collaborative tasks could be one of the ways of creating a learning context where learners can practice the spontaneous use of the target language in order to develop fluency.

Collaboration and Development of Interactional Skills

In addition to assisting in the development of fluency as well as accuracy in the production of meaning and form, collaboration promotes the development of interactional skills. In order to collaborate, learners are required to engage in dialogic or multi-party discourse and perform various interactional functions such as realizing various speech acts and managing interactions. Since the purpose of collaboration is to achieve the common goals, collaborative discourse involves a specific type of interaction, which Johnson and Johnson (2004) characterize as *promotive interaction*, i.e., interaction that "occurs as individuals encourage and facilitate each other's efforts to reach the group's goals (such as maximizing each member's learning)" (p. 790). Johnson and Johnson (2004) identify eight interactional patterns of collaborative discourse, which Nor, Hamat, and Embi (2012) organize into three larger categories that reflect the general interactional behaviors of collaborative work: (1) contributing; (2) seeking input, and; (3) monitoring (p. 244). Contributing includes the actions of assisting other group members—specifically, responding to questions and requests, providing feedback, exchanging resources and information, sharing knowledge, challenging the contributions of other team members, and supporting learners' own positions. Seeking input incorporates requesting help from other members, asking for feedback, and inviting other members' contributions. Monitoring involves commenting on the process of collaboration and managing collaboration. Although these interactional patterns are analyzed in the instructional setting, they also occur outside of the classroom; so, while participating in collaborative activities, learners are practicing and developing interactional skills applicable to the real-life context.

Multimodal Technology-Supported Collaboration

Technology-supported collaboration occurs when instructional technology is used by groups of learners in order to work together on a certain task (Johnson & Johnson, 2004). While there are studies comparing collaboration in different modalities (e.g., Loewen & Wolff, 2016; Rouhshad & Storch, 2016), research on collaboration through multiple communication channels, e.g., voice- and text-based chat, is rather scant. Kozlova (2013), for example, studied how tasks with a problem-solving component mediated language learning in a multimodal web-conferencing environment (MWCE). She found that a MWCE "allows students at different developmental levels and with different learning styles to participate in the co-construction of the task via the communication channel of their preference" (p. 61). Another benefit of MWCEs is that they can engage multiple learners at the same time through several modes of communication (Kozlova, 2014; Kozlova & Zundel, 2013). Learners can respond via the audio-based channel and/or use the chat tool or the whiteboard to post text-based responses. MWCEs are especially supportive for lower level learners because learners have the option of collaborating via a text-based channel if they have difficulties negotiating meaning in the oral mode (Kozlova, 2014). Text-based messages also give learners more time to process the information and incorporate it in their new utterances.

One type of technology-supported collaboration occurs when learners' activity is organized around a computer screen in a face-to-face context (Meskill, 2005) or a collaboration board in a virtual environment. Drawing on Wood, Bruner, and Ross' (1976) definition of scaffolding–which includes such properties as focusing learners' attention, constraining degrees of freedom to make tasks more manageable, sustaining learners' focus on the problem-solving activity, and highlighting important features (p. 99)–Meskill (2005) maintained that the computer screen has the same properties as scaffolding. When learners focus their attention on the computer screen, the information that appears on the screen constrains learners' choices and makes the task more manageable, it keeps students focused on the problem-solving activity, and it illuminates important linguistic and non-linguistic features, making them more noticeable to students. These features may prompt interactional routines that are "so central to the language learning process" (Meskill, 2005, p. 48).

Dooly (2018) showed that organizing learner collaboration around a single computer screen (i.e., group members sit together and look at the same computer screen) impacts learners' collaborative practice. Learners who were not sharing their computer screen with other group members were instructed to collaborate on the assignment, but they did not do so; instead, they found alternative ways to complete the assignment without collaboration. Some students, for example, typed their individual answers in an online document, while others found answers on the Internet and then copied and pasted them in the document. In contrast, Dooly noted that when a student in one of the groups was absent from class, the two other group members contacted her via WhatsApp, a mobile messaging application, and all three students continued actively collaborating on the activity. Since the two present students were using one cell phone, they composed responses to the absent student and read and discussed their peer's suggestions together. It was concluded that students who focus their attention on one single screen, whether a cell phone or a computer screen, collaborate better than students who do not.

Taking into consideration the importance of collaboration for language learning and development and the importance of creating contexts that promote collaboration, this study focuses on the type of collaboration that occurs when EFL learners' activities are organized around collaboration boards. Learners use both an audio channel for interaction, as well as collaboration boards for note taking. By observing learners' interaction, this study seeks answers to the following research questions:

1. What factors influence learners' multimodal collaboration in 3D VWs?
2. Do students' collaboration skills improve over the six weeks of study?

METHODS

This study was conducted in the context of an international project administered jointly by a Canadian college and a Turkish university's English Language School that prepares students for admission to the university where the language of instruction is English. The minimum English language requirement for students to be considered for university admission is at least intermediate-high proficiency on the American Council on Teaching of Foreign Languages (ACTFL) scale. Since the students at the English Language School learn English as a foreign language, the School was looking for opportunities for their students to improve their speaking skills by working with native English speakers.

Participants

The volunteer participants included eight EFL students enrolled in upper-intermediate English courses at the English Language School in Turkey and six teacher-trainees (henceforth referred to as teachers) enrolled in the Teaching English as a Second/Foreign Language Certification Program in the Canadian college. Of the eight EFL students, six were female—Ayleen, Dilara, Miss Jane, and Princess—and two were male—Daniel and Onur. All were 18 years old at the time of the study. The teacher group included five female teachers and one male, all between 31 and 53 years old. The female teachers—Diane, Gerri, Joan, Lynn, and Simone—were native English speakers, whereas the male teacher, Jack, was a native speaker of Korean and a near-native speaker of English. All of the participants were computer literate and used computers on daily basis to meet their personal needs and educational requirements, but none had previous experience teaching and learning in 3D VWs. At the beginning of the project, the participants had a one-hour session with a 3D technology consultant, who showed them how to use the environment and provided a navigation guide to the environment and its tools.

3D Virtual Worlds

Two immersive 3D environments, Algonquin College Campus and Tipontia Island, were developed on the cloud-based platform AvayaLive™ Engage for use in the study. Both environments have real-life collaboration and web-conferencing tools. Algonquin College Campus is a virtual reproduction of the real college campus with several office buildings, a study hall, and two amphitheaters. Tipontia Island is a massive virtual island covered with trees and mountains. It also has a lake, a river with waterfalls, beaches, and several landmarks including a lighthouse, tree houses, a campfire, and a gigantic piano (Figure 1). Upon logging in to the environment, participants are embodied in form of personalized avatars that can walk, run, jump, and perform some gestures, e.g., clapping, nodding, pointing, raising their hands. The environments used are multimodal, meaning participants can interact through audio- and text-based chat. Both environments have many collaboration boards located inside and outside of the virtual buildings (Figure 2). Some of the boards can be used as computers for surfing the Internet and for collaborative real-time note taking.

Figure 1. Tree houses on Tipontia Island

Figure 2. Students collaborating on a collaboration board

Instructional Design of Collaborative Tasks

Task-based language teaching (TBLT) was chosen as the instructional approach to help students partici-pating in this study improve their speaking skills. Since speaking involves the accurate expression of an intended meaning, fluent use of language, and interaction with other learners, collaborative tasks were deemed ideal for this study, as they engage students in dialogic/multi-participant interaction. When col-laborating on tasks with the purpose of achieving task outcomes, learners use language spontaneously, employ their language resources to process language in order to produce meaningful output, and employ interactional skills to communicate with peer-collaborators (Ellis, 2003).

Since the Turkish students were improving their speaking skills for further study at the university, the tasks were designed so that students could also develop academic skills, such as doing research/ gathering information, generating and presenting ideas, and taking notes. Another reason for including note taking in the task design was previous research that found that text-based language production positively impacts learners' oral fluency development (Blake, 2009; Razagifard, 2013). Using Levelt's (1989) Model of Speech Production, Blake (2009) argues that the production of oral and text-based messages involves the same cognitive processes but engages different muscles in the body. According to Blake, production of both oral and text-based messages begins with the conceptualization of ideas to be expressed in the intended messages. Then, these pre-verbal messages are transferred into internal speech, or a phonetic plan, which assists speakers in formulating the messages through grammatical and phonological encoding. Then the messages are articulated, or converted from internal to overt speech, either with the muscles in the jaw and oral cavity in oral speech or with the muscles in the hands and fingers in text-based messaging.

Blake (2009) goes on to argue the benefits of written language production—namely, that learners have more time for the production and revision of written messages, and can see the language produced by themselves and others. These factors "have the cumulative effect of providing the learners with more time to focus on language structure, which, in turn, may lead to more efficient and fluent use of the language over time" (Blake, 2009, p. 238). Thus, the note taking component was included in the task design in order to allow students to process and articulate their messages twice: once when they produce them orally to share with their group, and again when they write them on the collaboration board. Likewise, in order to write down what they heard, learners might need to reformulate the oral messages. This dual processing and articulation of the same idea in different ways may positively affect fluency development and the development of speaking skills in general.

Six language-learning tasks were developed by the teachers participating in the study. Informed by research on task-based pedagogy (Ellis, 2003; Pica, Kanagy, & Falodun, 1993), each teacher was responsible for developing and teaching just one task, though they collaborated on task development (for further details see Author & Priven, 2015). When task development was complete, teachers tested the tasks, made necessary changes, and then used them to teach the EFL learners.

All six tasks were designed with a similar structure consisting of four stages: (1) brainstorming; (2) researching/exploring the environment; (3) preparing for a presentation, and; (4) presenting. The four-stage structure was intended to involve learners in *procedural task repetition*, or repetition of the same procedures with different task content (Kim & Tracy-Ventura, 2013). Repetition of the same task procedure favorably affects the development of both oral and written fluency (Amiryousefi, 2016; Kim & Tracy-Ventura, 2013; Lynch & Maclean, 2000). Repetition draws learners' attention to the use of vocabulary and pronunciation and was found to reduce the frequency of grammar-related errors, increase information density, lexical density, and accuracy (Kim & Tracy-Ventura, 2013), and improve expression of meaning (Lynch & Maclean, 2000). While learners may not necessarily improve their speech rate as a result of procedural task repetition, they more frequently perform LREs and confirmation checks and improve their interactional competence (Kim & Tracy-Ventura, 2013). Likewise, procedural task repetition may help learners improve their collaboration skills because repeating the same procedure several times may help learners routinize collaboration practices.

The EFL learners' collaboration was organized around collaboration boards positioned around the environment. The collaboration boards were used similarly to how computer screens were used in Meskill's (2005) study; they facilitated collaborative learning by focusing learners' attention on given problem-solving and decision-making activities, and drawing learners' attention to the meaning they wanted to express and the forms they wanted to use.

Data Collection

All class sessions were recorded using screen-capture software (Camtasia Relay). Because learners were working in groups in several locations, e.g., different offices or landmarks, the researcher was not able to be in several places at the same time, and so a teacher who was not engaged in the task delivery helped with the recording. The recorded data were transcribed using transcription conventions adapted from Jefferson (1984). Since students used spoken and text-based modalities to collaborate, the transcript included both modalities in the same transcript. This was intended to demonstrate the complexity of learner interaction.

Data Analysis

This study operationalized collaboration as a multimodal interactional activity during which students not only participate in LREs but also used language to share their ideas, provide feedback, and monitor their collaborative activities using both audio- and text-based channels. Learners' collaborative skills were measured not by the number of LREs produced, but by the variety of the interactional patterns performed by the learners. To code the data, Nor, et al.'s (2012) scheme with the interactional patterns from Johnson and Johnson (2004) was adapted according to the patterns that emerged in the data (see Table 1).

Coding participants' contributions in terms of interactional intentions, e.g., asking for and providing feedback, allowed the researcher to observe learner collaboration through the lens of *adjacency pairs,* or "paired utterances such that on production of the first part of the pair (e.g., question) the second part of the pair (e.g., answer) becomes *conditionally relevant*" (Seedhouse, 2004, p. 17, italics in original). Analyzing learner collaboration from this perspective was important because collaborative discourse is characterized by participants' reactions to other members' contributions (Donato, 2004). If participants do not respond to or at least acknowledge other members' contributions, then collaboration does not take place.

Table 1. Coding scheme

Categories	Interactional Pattern Codes
Contributing	• Sharing knowledge • Providing feedback • Backchannelling • Accepting contributions • Challenging others' contributions • Supporting learner's own position • Expressing opinions • Editing other members' contributions
Seeking input	• Requesting help from others • Asking for feedback • Negotiating meaning • Negotiating form • Engaging in a discussion and negotiating ideas
Monitoring	• Commenting on collaboration process • Urging to accept contribution or take notes

Adapted from Nor, Hamat, and Embi (2012, p. 245)

Since the EFL learners participated in the 3D VW tasks through multiple modalities, i.e., jointly used voice- and text-based tools to produce language, this study took into consideration adjacency pairs in which the first and the second parts were performed in one or both modalities and sometimes in different languages, as shown in the following example (see Appendix for transcription conventions):

Q 6 Dilara: how do I write it? ((in Turkish))
A 7 Ayleen: dropbox ((pronounces slowly))
Acc 8 Dilara: *drop[loks*

This example shows two adjacency pairs. Ayleen's answer (line 7) to Dilara's question (line 6) is the second part of a Question-Answer adjacency pair and simultaneously the first part of an Answer-Acceptance adjacency pair (lines 7 and 8). In the first adjacency pair, the question is asked in Turkish, but the answer is provided in English. While both parts of the Question-Answer adjacency pair are performed orally, the second part of the Answer-Acceptance adjacency pair is realized in text-based form.

STUDY RESULTS

Analysis of learners' interactions during the collaboration segments of the tasks in the 3D VWs revealed four factors that facilitated their collaboration: (1) learners and instructors' familiarity with 3D VWs; (2) learners' familiarity with the format of the learning activity; (3) learners' experience with the spontaneous use of the L2, and; (4) instructors' use of pedagogical techniques that facilitated collaboration. The results showed that over the period of six weeks, learners' collaboration skills improved. While in Week 1, some learners did not collaborate at all and some only typed a few words in silence, after the teachers' introduction of several collaboration techniques, learners employed a variety of interactional patterns, as summarized in Table 2.

The next sections address each of the four factors influencing learner collaboration and discuss how particular collaborative skills developed over the period of six weeks.

Learners and Instructors' Familiarity With 3D VWs

One of the factors that affected learners' collaboration was learners and instructors' experience with 3D WVs. For example, when developing tasks, the teachers discovered that collaboration boards, which could be used as personal computers to browse the Internet, did not allow for opening more than one window or tab at a time. In order for students to browse the Internet and access MoPad, an open source editor that allows for collaboration in real time, teachers thus prepared two boards, each in a different room. Students conducted Internet searches in one room, while collaborating in another room. While at the time this seemed to be a good solution to the problem, in practice, having boards in separate rooms was inconvenient and counter productive.

Although the tools available in the environment were explored and tested during the task development stage, the first weeks of teaching revealed several more technology-related problems. Some students were not able to use the Internet on the collaboration boards, for example. Gerri, who taught Week 1, suggested that students do research outside of the environment, on their own computers. Students collected information and took notes in this way, but they did so in silence and did not share or discuss their findings with their peers. Another problem was that some students could not type on the boards directly from the environment. Jack, who taught Week 2, provided instructions on how to access MoPad from students' personal computers. After teachers and students became aware of these problems and found ways to avoid them, collaboration went smoother and with fewer interruptions.

Table 2. Interactional patterns used over the period of six weeks

Category	Interactional Patterns	Week					
		1	2	3	4	5	6
Contributing	Sharing knowledge	V	V	V	V	V	V
	Providing feedback		V	V	V	V	V
	Backchannelling		V	V	V	V	V
	Accepting contributions		V	V	V	V	V
	Challenging others' contributions		V	V	V	V	V
	Supporting learner's own position		V	V	V	V	V
	Expressing opinions		V	V	V	V	V
	Editing other s' contributions					V	
Seeking input	Requesting help from others			V	V	V	V
	Inviting other members' contributions			V	V	V	V
	Asking for feedback		V	V	V	V	
	Negotiating for meaning		V	V			
	Negotiating for form		V	V			V
	Engaging in a discussion and negotiating ideas		V		V	V	V
Monitoring	Commenting on collaboration				V	V	V
	Urging to accept peer contributions			V			

Learners' Familiarity With the Format of the Learning Activity

Another factor that influenced collaboration was learners' familiarity with the format of the learning activity. In Week 1, students were to complete a decision-making task in which they were playing role of curators—specifically, members of a (fictional) Canadian Culture Committee. As curators, they were to select one piece of art each from among those posted on the boards in the exhibition hall and create a special Canadian art exhibition that would take place at the famous Istanbul Modern Museum of Art. Once the paintings were selected, the student-curators were required to find information about the selected paintings and their artists on the Internet, and then develop an argument to convince the President of the committee to include the paintings in the exhibition. Students were divided into two groups of four, but due to a poor Internet connection, three students had to leave the environment. In the end, one group had only two students and the other group had three.

Although Gerri explained the task, and the students confirmed that they understood the task, some students were not sure what to do after they got into their groups. Examples 1, 2, and 3 demonstrate how two students, Princess and Onur, tried to figure out their task.

(1) 1 Princess: Onur, what are we going to do? I don't understand xxx
      2 Onur: ye-ah I think we should write that Robert Harries was a-
      3 was Welsh-born Canadian painter.
      4 Princess: There must me a presentation ((students switch to Turkish))
      5 ((Onur leaves the room; Diane enters the room))

After Onur left the room, Princess double-checked what they were required to do with the teacher, Diane, who had just entered the room (Example 2).

(2) 1 Princess: Diane, excuse me.
      2 Diane: yes, Princess
      3 Princess: Uhhhh, uh, we do not understand we.. uhhh we do a
      4 presentation about uhhm this picture and painter
      5 Diane: yes
      6 Princess: the both, the both
      7 Diane: [yeah
      8 Princess: [okay
      9 Diane: uh-[huh
      10 Princess: [uhh and we can write the sentences on the other
      11 room?
      12 Diane: Yes, you go to the other public pad, you write sentences,
      13 [something you like about it, something you learned
      14 Princess: [ah-hah

While Princess was talking to Diane, Onur went to the office where the other group was working and asked Gerri what to do (Example 3).

(3) 1 Onur: Gerri?
      2 Gerri: yes
      3 Onur: Are we presenting the picture or the artist?
      4 Gerri: Both because what you need to do is to convince which of
      5 the- your paintings should be in the exhibition in Istanbul
      6 Modern Museum. So you have to present the author and the
      7 painting. So, that's why you need to do a little bit of
      8 research, okay?

After Gerri and Diane explained the task to Princess and Onur, the students still struggled with it. Gerri, who was floating between the offices where students were collaborating, noticed that Onur and Princess were standing in front of the Internet board in silence and asked about their progress on the task. The students explained that they did not have experience with this type of activity (Example 4).

(4) 1 Gerri: How is it going? Princess? Onur? Are you finding
      2 information about this painting?
      3 Onur: yeah [((unintelligible))

4 Princess: [It's hard hah hah ha

5 Gerri: yes (.) what- what are you having difficulty with?

6 Princess: it's new [because difficult, because we can't do its-

7 Gerri: [yes

8 Princess: we can't do it someth- something like that before

9 like that before, and we can't use it hah hah right now

Meanwhile, three other students—Maria, Daniel, and Dilara—seemed to understand the task and typed some information about the painting "Dieppe" by James Wilson Morris on the collaboration board. However, their work can hardly be considered collaborative, as the students shared information by typing on the board, but did so in silence and without acknowledging each other's contributions (Example 5).

(5) 1 Maria: *Mystery of Dieppe*

2 *James Wilson*

3 Daniel: *Was born in Montreal*

4 Maria: *James Wilson he is Canadian is known as*

5 *battle of Dieppe*

6 Dilara: *This picture made in 1906*

7 *It is famous for crafts ma*

Instructors and learners' experience with 3D VWs and learners' familiarity with collaborative task-based learning were not the only factors that impacted learners' collaboration during Week 1. The next section addresses language-related issues that also emerged at that time.

Learners' Inexperience With Spontaneous L2 Use

A third factor that prevented learners' collaboration during the first session related to their inexperience with the spontaneous use of English. While researching their selected painting, Princess and Onur stood in front of the board, reading the information from Wikipedia that one of the teachers had accessed for them. They were not talking, and so Gerri thought they were having problems using Google. Onur explained that in fact they were having difficulties because it was unusual for them to speak English with their peers. Gerri asked all of the students if this was their experience, too. Princess and Daniel agreed with Onur (Example 6, lines 9–11, 13, 14).

(6) 3 Gerri: Some of you, one of you said that it was difficult to

4 speak to your classmates

5 [in a– yeah

6 Onur: [I said

7 Gerri: So, how it was talking English with them, do you think

8 you are talking English with them in class more?

9 Onur: I think it was strange because the people you are

10 knowing and while you are speaking Turkish, when

11 here you need to speak English with your native people

12 Gerri: yes

13 Daniel: I agree with Onur

14 Princess: Me too

In Week 1, two of the three groups did not collaborate in ways that were expected. For example, students looked for information about their paintings, but did not discuss the information they found with each other. Although both groups presented their findings, in one group, students presented pieces of information that each had found separately; in the other group, only Onur presented his findings. Onur and Princess chose the painting "A Meeting of the School Trustees" by Robert Harris. When presenting, Onur stated that he did not know the meaning of the word 'trustee'. Although Princess had negotiated the meaning of this word with Diane during the task, she did not add anything to his presentation. So, teachers' goal for the following weeks was to encourage pedagogical techniques that would encourage learners' to interact.

Pedagogical Techniques that Facilitated Collaboration

In Week 2, students were asked to offer ideas to a smartphone company about apps they would like to have on their smartphones that would help them with schoolwork. Students were to do Internet research on existing apps, make a list of their favourite apps, and then select the three most useful apps from the list.

To facilitate learner collaboration, Jack used three pedagogical techniques: (1) asking students to talk to each other when making lists; (2) asking one student to take notes and the rest of the group to contribute verbally (an idea first brought up by Lynn at the task development stage), and; (3) having students work with the same input by accessing the same Internet sites. A fourth technique, scaffolding students' responses, was utilized by all of the teachers to mediate students' collaboration.

Asking Students to Talk to Each Other

Asking students to talk to each other prompted collaboration, as illustrated in Example 7. When Daniel and Onur began to verbally share their ideas, they used a variety of interactional patterns from two categories, contributing and seeking input.

(7) 21 Daniel: how about TOEFL? |TOEFL preparation maybe

22 |enlg|lish

23 Onur: |TOEFL? [hm

24 Daniel: [because it's useful

25 |for us

26 |dicti|onary

27 Onur: |right, right

28 [easy-to-share notes

29 Daniel: [to ((deletes to))

30 Onur: I say easy-to-share notes=

31 Daniel: =yes

32 Onur: like [in the- ((to share in class)) like xxx database

33 Daniel: [yeah, yeah, yeah

34 why about- |what about Colornote xxx

35 |*colornote*
36 Onur: What's that?
37 Daniel: We can we can write something in Colornote
38 Onur: Um! [it is taking notes
39 Daniel: [yes, it's it reminds [me
40 Onur: [um! Colornote
41 harmony you said
42 Daniel: yes

The students' collaboration is observed through adjacency pairs, which indicates that Onur and Daniel not only shared their knowledge but also attended to each other's contributions. For example, Daniel suggested including a TOEFL app (line 21), but Onur challenged his contribution with a skeptical comment (line 22). Daniel further justified his proposition (lines 24, 25), which Onur accepted (line 27). The pattern from the seeking input category is observed in lines 34–38, where students were negotiating the meaning of the word *Colornote*.

This example also demonstrates that students were speaking and writing on the board, thus engaging two language skills at the same time. While talking about TOEFL (lines 21, 24, 25), Daniel typed *English dictionary* on the board (lines 22, 26); he also orally suggested *Colornote* and typed the word on the board at the same time (lines 34, 35). This example of collaboration in two modalities, spoken and written, shows complex language processing, as in the message articulation stage of Levelt's (1989) model. For example, in lines 21 and 22, 24–26, and in 34–35, Daniel articulates two different messages simultaneously, one orally and one in written form. Dual message processing is observed in lines 28 and 30 when Onur first types the message and then reformulates it verbally. Since collaboration in two modalities makes learners process and articulate the same messages twice, this experience provides learners with more opportunities to practice language, which, according to DeKeyser (2007), assists in developing automaticity and, consequently, fluency.

Using One Student as a Scribe

The technique of having one student take notes while others contribute verbally was intended to draw students' attention to form. In Example 8, Dilara was taking notes on the board while Ayleen contributed verbally. This excerpt provides evidence of students' employment of interactional patterns from the seeking input category—specifically, asking for help and negotiating form. Dilara did not know the spelling of the word *Dropbox*, and so she asked Ayleen for assistance.

(8)   (Translation from Turkish by Nuket Nowlan)
      Dilara types on the board: *google translate, radio, youtube, enlgish-enlgish*
      dictionary
      5 Ayleen: you can write dropbox (.) maybe
      6 Dilara: how do I write it? ((in Turkish))
      7 Ayleen: dro::pbox
      8 Dilara: *drop||loks*
      9 Ayleen: |((says something in Turkish))
      10 Dilara: ((deletes *loks*))

11 how? ((in Turkish))
12 Ayleen: dro::pbox
13 Dilara: hah?
14 *dropdocks*
15 Ayleen: ((says in Turkish that the word is misspelled))
16 Dilara: |what?
17 |((deletes *docks*))
18 hah-hah
19 *box*

In line 5, Ayleen suggested an app, *Dropbox*, but Dilara did not seem to know the word or understand what Ayleen said and asked her how to spell it. Ayleen slowly repeated the word (line 7), but Dilara misspelled it again (line 8). Ayleen said something in Turkish that was not intelligible in the recording. It is likely that she corrected Dilara because the misspelled part of the word (-*loks*) was clearly heard in the recording (line 9). In response, Dilara deleted -*loks* (line 10) and asked in Turkish how to spell that part (line 11). Ayleen repeated "dro::pbox" (line 12), but Dilara misspelled the word again (line 14). Ayleen then used Turkish to point out the mistake, which Dilara then corrected (line 19). This excerpt exemplifies that having one student take notes on the collaboration board while the other one contributes orally makes linguistic features and errors more noticeable to students, helps them process input better (Meskill, 2005), and prompts negotiation of form.

Accessing the Same Input

To facilitate students' collaboration, Jack suggested that students work with the same input by accessing the same web page from their computers (since opening several tabs on collaboration boards in the environment was impossible). When Maria, Miss Jane, and Princess accessed the page listing various apps, they read the information and discussed the apps they found useful. The excerpt in Example 9 starts after Miss Jane suggested an app, *SimpleMind*, used for organizing and generating ideas, but Maria did not agree with her (line 49).

(9)   49 Miss Jane: but it's a calendar
       50 Princess: it's not a real calendar, it says if you need a subject um a
       51 grammar etcetera um this application reminds you- this
       52 application give you um this um lack of lesson. I can't- I
       53 can't tell [hah
       54 Miss Jane: [um
       55 ((students talk at the same time))
       56 Miss Jane: why um is the name myHomework? It's only about
       57 homework, it's not the way to do lessons
       58 Princess: yes
       59 Maria: I think its individual
       60 Miss Jane: yeah both I think- if we use SimpleMind um, it can
       61 create (xxx) homework
       62 Princess: um maybe, but it's not all- its not about the homework,

63 the SimpleMind, it's about the representation its

64 [umm

65 Miss Jane: [but representations its kind of homework

66 Princess: Yes [I know [but it's not just um, you know

67 Miss Jane: [he heh

68 [((Maria leaves the environment))

69 Princess: its not a paper its not question one and bla bla bla

70 question two bla bla bla its not um this like its not like

71 that

72 Miss Jane: hah-hah

73 Princess: and both SimpleMind and myHomework it's complete

74 each other [umm my homework its xxx

75 Miss Jane: [he heh

76 We should mix Simpleminds and myHomework

77 Princess: Absolutely! Absolutely! We should mix it and its- will be

78 perfect application in the world

Princess' suggestion of the app *myHomework* to generate ideas engaged the students in a discussion and negotiation of ideas. Miss Jane challenged Princess' suggestion by saying that *myHomework* looks like a calendar (line 49). Princess tried to explain that it is not (lines 50–53), but her linguistic repertoire did not allow her to fully express her thoughts. Miss Jane expressed an opinion that this app does not help to prepare homework (lines 56–57), whereas *SimpleMind* helps to "create homework" (lines 56, 57). Princess argued that *SimpleMind* helps to create representations, but not homework (lines 62, 63). Miss Jane then made the point that creating representations, or mapping ideas, is related to homework (line 65). Princess still disagreed with her (lines 66, 69–71), but then stated that the two applications complement each other, although she used the wrong word ("complete"; lines 73, 74). Miss Jane agreed and suggested that these two applications should be combined to make one app. Finally, the students came to the agreement that combining *SimpleMind* and *myHomework* would make a perfect application (lines 77, 78).

In the above example, Princess, Miss Jane, and Maria not only expressed their ideas but also discussed and negotiated them. They responded to each other's contributions by employing the interaction patterns of giving feedback, challenging each other's contributions, and supporting their positions to reach a compromise. While discussing the apps, the students were reading the same information from the web page and trying to understand the text by rephrasing the input in their own words, thus employing interactional routines that facilitate language learning (Meskill, 2005).

Scaffolding Students' Responses

After making a list of ten apps, students were asked to choose the three most useful ones. The way some of the groups approached the selection of these three apps cannot be considered collaborative. For example, Daniel and Onur made the initial list of ten apps together, but when Gerri asked them to select the top three apps, they each simply typed the numbers 1, 2, and 3 next to the apps they thought were best. Ayleen and Dilara did not discuss their top three choices, either. To encourage collaborative behavior,

Joan scaffolded Ayleen and Dilara's explanation of their choices after they made their individual list of apps (Example 10, lines 1–3).

(10) 1 Dilara: *Newspapers*
    2 Ayleen: *Youtube*
    3 *Wikipedia*
    4–15 …
    16 Joan: so why do you think those would make good apps?
    17 Ayleen: because learn (xxx) we learn something um we
    18 learn new words maybe. And that's why it's a good
    19 application for learn English
    20 Joan: uh-huh
    21 Dilara: YouTube- we can learn some information or a
    22 video we can watch, (also) Wikipedia- we can search
    23 something

The introduction of scaffolding and other teaching techniques that facilitated students' collaboration in Week 2 had a great impact on learner collaboration. While in Week 2, teachers mediated learners' activities by using techniques that encouraged collaboration, over the next four weeks (see Table 2) students adopted the mediation means offered by the teachers and even expanded their repertoire of collaborative patterns, as sociocultural theory proposes (Lantolf, 2000).

Collaboration Patterns After Week 2

Two interactional patterns emerged in Week 3, namely, inviting other members' participation (seeking input category) and urging peers to accept their contributions (monitoring category). Students seemed to be more comfortable collaborating as well as managing their collaboration. At times, they did not even welcome their teachers' attempts to assist in managing collaboration. The task in Week 3 was administered on Tipontia Island. According to the task scenario, there was a nuclear accident at the power reactor on the mainland and people were being evacuated to the island for safety. The students were asked to explore the island and determine how island resources could be used for the evacuees.

While brainstorming about the resources they would need on the island (Example 11), Princess and Onur invited Maria's participation, as she was not contributing to their discussion. In line 36, Princess asked Maria what she was thinking, but Maria, who was apparently browsing the Internet, responded that she could not find anything. In line 55, Onur addressed her again, but Maria only chuckled in response, saying "o-oh" (lines 52, 53).

(11) 32 Onur: |management of people
    33 |organization and |management of people
    34 Princess |uh-huh
    35 (5)
    36 Princess: Maria, what are you thinking?
    37 Maria: umm I can't find h. hah (.) um
    38–55 …

55 Maria, I'm waiting ideas from you
52 Maria: ((chuckles))
53 Onur: um
54 Maria o:oh

The teacher, Joan, attempted to manage the students' interaction and help Maria by initiating a specific topic, "Maria, where do you think people would sleep when they come to the island?" (Example 12, line 56). Onur did not welcome Joan's help, pointing out that this question had already been discussed and added to the list as part of the topic "Management of people". Joan, however, insisted on her question and repeated it (lines 62–63). Maria did not respond, and so Onur managed a six-minute pause (line 65) by adding something. Princess then managed a three-second pause (line 67) by offering a new idea, "greenhouses" (line 68). She began elaborating on her idea, "people make um um make yeah", at which point Maria finally contributed an idea, finishing Princess' utterance with a new idea, "people make a house" (line 70). She provided an example (line 72), but what she said was not clear in the recording. Princess enthusiastically accepted Maria's idea (lines 71, 73), but Onur did not, and so Maria urged him to write her idea on the board (lines 75, 77).

(12) 56 Joan: So Maria, where do you think people would
      57 sleep when they come to the island?
      58 Maria: [Sorry?
      59 Onur: That's the organization of people
      60 Joan: [Where
      61 Maria: [yeah
      62 Joan: Maria, where do you think people would sleep (.)
      63 when they come to the island?
      64 Maria: hm
      65 (6)
      66 Onur: xxxx
      67 (3)
      68 Princess greenhouse (2) um people make um um make yeah
      69 [um
      70 Maria [people make a house
      71 Princess: yeah
      72 Maria: um for example (threads) 73 Princess: oh yes!
      74 (6)
      75 Maria: Onur!
      76 Onur: hm?
      77 Maria: hah hah [Write please! (smiley voice)

As students became more familiar with the format of the activity, they became better able to manage collaboration themselves, and sometimes were even reluctant to allow their teachers to manage collaboration for them. Likewise, students began to pay attention to silent participants and invite their contributions to the task.

Commenting on Collaboration

A pattern from the monitoring category—commenting on the collaboration process—emerged in Week 4. In that week, students were tasked with creating a plan to help twenty twelve-year-old disadvantaged children to become healthy, learn to trust, gain self-confidence, and have fun during their holiday on Tipontia Island. Example 13 shows an exchange between Princess and Miss Jane about how their group's list of suggested activities all relate to the goal of having fun, but do not address the three other goals.

(13) 32 Princess: um we can discuss two um other topics like exercise, body
        33 and mind, and making self-confidence, making trusts. And
        34 this all about fun, we can discuss three other topics.
        35 Miss Jane: Hm
        36 Princess: what do you think about exercise, or self-confidence, or
        37 making trusts?

This interactional pattern of commenting on collaboration was also observed in the fifth and sixth weeks of the project, which shows that students became more independent collaborators over time, becoming more able to focus on the activity at hand and stay on track.

Editing Each Other's Contributions

Recollect, Jack suggested that in order to facilitate collaboration, one student take notes and the rest of the group members contribute verbally. In the first four weeks, some groups employed this technique, but others had several students taking notes and participating in the discussion at the same time. In the latter case, when several students took notes, they edited only their own contributions. Week 5 revealed a new interactional pattern—editing their peers' text-based contributions. This was an important change in students' collaborative practice because it showed that the group began taking shared ownership of their jointly constructed product, thus showing greater involvement with the task and a higher degree of collaboration.

The following example is from Week 5 when students' task was to create a time capsule to represent their school/city. The capsule would be opened in 100 years by future students. Dilara, Miss Jane, and Princess discussed and added ideas to the collaboration board. Miss Jane shared the thought that they cannot put real flowers, fruits, or vegetables into the time capsule, but only pictures or plant extracts, although she used the wrong word ("abstracts") and asked Dilara for feedback (Example 14, lines 37–39).

(14) 37 Miss Jane: you have special flowers, fruit and vegetables, maybe we
        38 can't put in real, but we can put their pictures or um
        39 or their abstracts. Dilara, what do you think?
        40 Princess: *picture of flowers and vegetables*
        41–44 ((unintelligible))
        45 Miss Jane: seeds
        46 ((typing sound))
        47 they are seeds
        48 l*or seed* ((edits Princess's line *picture **or seed** of flowers*

49 *and vegetables*))
50 Princess: |yes
51 Miss Jane: seeds, English name
52 Princess: [*information about our university*
53 Miss Jane: [**which they are endemic** ((adds to the line *picture **or***
54 *seed of flowers and vegetables* **which they are endemic**))

After Princess wrote down *picture of flowers and vegetables* (line 40), the students start talking, though it was unclear from the recording whether they were speaking English or Turkish (lines 41–44). It is likely that some of them did not know the English word for "seeds" because Miss Jane repeated the word several times: "seeds", "they are seeds", "seeds, English name" (lines 45, 47, 51). She also edited Princess' contribution (lines 48, 53, 54; edits in bolded italics). Princess, however, continued typing a new idea at the same time as Miss Jane edited her previous contribution.

DISCUSSION

The analysis revealed four factors that influenced learner collaboration in 3D VWs. The first factor was instructors and students' familiarity with the environment and its tools. This finding supports Deutschmann et al.'s (2009) assertion that knowing how to use the technology is crucial for computer-based task completion. For example, some students' inability to type on the collaboration boards in the environment and teachers' unawareness of how to solve problems that arose with the technology prevented some of the groups from collaborative note taking in the first week.

The second factor that affected collaboration was learners' familiarity with the format of the learning activity. Existing research has identified that learner collaboration can be influenced by learners' orientation to the activity, language proficiency, and group relationships (Dobao, 2012; Storch, 2002; Storch & Aldosari, 2012, but learners' familiarity with the activity format has not yet been addressed in the literature. Collaboration in this study required students to use an audio channel to interact and a text-based channel to take notes; although multimodal communication is not a new interactional format and also occurs in the face-to-face classroom, students' use of familiar note taking tools—pens, pencils, or computer key boards—does not require an additional cognitive effort. Being complex online environments (Kozlova & Priven, 2015), 3D VWs are more cognitively and technologically demanding, as they require learners to coordinate speech production with the use of technology such as a keyboard and a mouse to control an avatar, in addition to a microphone and a key board to interact with other avatars, plus collaboration boards to take notes. Not being familiar with this type of activity and not having mastered all these skills, students were unable to collaborate fully at the beginning of the project.

The third finding brings a new perspective on learners' spontaneous use of the second language. Simply put, this study found that learners may not use their second language for collaboration not because they lack the linguistic knowledge, but because it is unnatural for them to speak in their second language to those who share their first language.

The fourth factor that was found to influence learner collaboration was instructors' use of pedagogical techniques to facilitate learner collaboration. In Meskill's (2005) study, the teacher directed students' work around the computer by drawing their attention to the information on the computer screen. Dooly (2018), however, demonstrated that students were able to manage their collaborative work around a cell phone without instructor's help. Since students in the present study were expected to carry out their tasks independently, incorporating several pedagogical techniques to encourage and enhance collaboration allowed teachers to familiarize students with both the format of the activity and help them to control the collaboration process without the teacher's assistance.

In sum, these four findings suggest that collaboration practices could be improved as a result of procedural task repetition. Similar to the participants in Kim and Tracy-Ventura's (2013) study who were extensively engaged in interaction and produced a variety of confirmation checks and LREs, the students in this study were able to employ a variety of interactional patterns over the study period of six weeks. As students became more familiar with the task routines and more comfortable with the use of the technology, they demonstrated an improved ability to monitor their own work.

SOLUTIONS AND RECOMMENDATIONS

The results of the study suggest that for students to benefit from collaborative learning, both learners and instructors need to be prepared for this type of instruction by familiarizing themselves with the environment and its tools. However, simply knowing how to use the tools is not enough for collaboration; unfamiliarity with the format of the activity may prevent students' participation, as well. In other words, in order to collaborate, students need to know what collaboration entails. For example, in the context of this study, collaboration required both spoken interaction and note taking on collaboration boards. Before students understood how to collaborate in these ways, they were unable to carry out the task as expected. While students employed a variety of interactional patterns by the end, interactional patterns from the monitoring category emerged later. It appears that students began to monitor the collaborative process only once they became more comfortable with the format of the activity and could participate without the teachers' assistance. This suggests that teachers may need to: (1) show students how to use the tools, and then; (2) introduce techniques, like Jack did, in order to engage them in collaborative learning.

Although the interactional patterns of negotiating for meaning, form, and ideas emerged early in the study (Week 2), they were not employed in all of the tasks (see Table 2). Students' use of these interactional patterns seemed to depend on several factors, including the type of input students received. When interacting with input from the Internet in Week 2, students encountered vocabulary they did not know and messages they may not have understood. This prompted a negotiation of meaning of the unknown items. In Week 3, when students interacted with park workers to collect information about the island's resources, they negotiated the meaning of unfamiliar vocabulary with the workers instead of with their peers. Likewise, in Week 5, students did a jigsaw reading task prior to their collaboration where they learned new words before they began to collaborate on the board. In Weeks 4 and 6, students generated the input themselves, and so they may not have used vocabulary unfamiliar to others.

Negotiation of form depended on students' output, specifically, whether the student producing output requested help or not, or whether inaccuracies in spelling or grammar were salient enough to be noticed. Negotiation of ideas was contingent on whether all students agreed with their peers' ideas. Only when students had different thoughts or opinions did they enter into a negotiation process. These findings suggest that task design impacts students' use of interactional patterns, and so if teachers want learners to negotiate for meaning, form, and ideas, they need to take into consideration whether input includes new language. Teachers should also consider when in the task sequence the input is introduced, how to make learners' output more salient to learners, and whether the task topics may invite different opinions or interpretation of concepts.

LIMITATIONS OF THE STUDY

Although the collaborative tasks were developed to assist learners in developing their speaking skills and included elements that drew students' attention to meaning and form and facilitated the development of fluency and interactional skills, the study mainly focused on learners' use of interactional patterns that characterize collaborative discourse and not whether their speaking improved on the measures of accuracy and fluency. Since this study used data from a larger project, measuring fluency was not included in the study design.

FUTURE RESEARCH DIRECTIONS

The findings of this study call researchers and educators to further explore the capabilities of 3D VWs for engaging learners in complex multimodal interaction in order to advance their language learning experience. As shown in this study, collaboration in spoken and written modalities engages both cognitive (e.g., negotiating meaning and form) and social processes (interaction), and since 3D VWs support multimodal interaction, the field would benefit from studies that further explore how multimodal features of immersive environments could be incorporated into task design to promote learner collaboration.

Learner collaboration in 3D VWs enhances students' opportunities for practicing their spontaneous language use in a real-life-like context, which facilitates fluency improvement. It would be worth exploring whether learners' fluency improves as a result of collaboration in multiple modalities.

CONCLUSION

This research project is among several studies that have examined opportunities for students to collaborate through multiple modalities in 3D VWs. The findings of this study demonstrate that organizing learners' work around collaboration boards engages them in interaction and prompts their use of a variety of interactional patterns. However, there are still factors that need to be considered when administering collaborative tasks. Showing students how to use collaboration tools and familiarizing them with the format of the activity are the first steps to collaboration. Another factor is helping students to become comfortable with the use of the target language for communicating with peers. Showing students what exactly collaboration involves by equipping them with techniques to improve their collaboration is also critical for developing successful collaborative practices. Collaboration in 3D VWs is not an easy and self-explanatory learning behavior, but rather a complex activity that integrates cognitive, linguistic, interactional, and digital skills without which collaboration may not be possible.

REFERENCES

Amiryousefi, M. (2016). The differential effects of two types of task repetition on the complexity, accuracy, and fluency in computer-mediated L2 written production: A focus on computer anxiety. *Computer Assisted Language Learning, 29*(5), 1052–1068. doi:10.1080/09588221.2016.1170040

Blake, C. (2009). Potential of text-based Internet chats for improving oral fluency in a second language. *Modern Language Journal, 93*(2), 227–240. doi:10.1111/j.1540-4781.2009.00858.x

Bosker, H. R., Pinget, A.-F., Quené, H., Sanders, T., & de Jong, N. H. (2012). What makes speech sound fluent? The contributions of pauses, speed and repairs. *Language Testing, 30*(2), 159–175. doi:10.1177/0265532212455394

Cooke-Plagwitz, J. (2008). New directions in CALL: An objective introduction to Second Life. *CALICO Journal, 25*(3), 547–557. doi:10.1558/cj.v25i3.547-557

Cornille, F., Thorne, S. L., & Desmet, P. (2012). Digital games for language learning: From hype to insight? Editorial for ReCALL special issue: Digital games for language learning: Challenges and opportunities. *ReCALL, 24*(3), 243–356. doi:10.1017/S0958344012000134

Dalton, G., & Devitt, A. (2016). Irish in a 3D world: Engaging primary school children. *Language Learning & Technology, 20*(1), 21–33.

DeKeyser, R. (2007). *Practice in a second language perspectives from applied linguistics and cognitive psychology.* Cambridge, UK: Cambridge University Press. doi:10.1017/CBO9780511667275

Deutschmann, M., Panichi, L., & Molka-Danielsen, J. (2009). Designing oral participation in Second Life: A comparative study of two language proficiency courses. *ReCALL, 21*(2), 206–226. doi:10.1017/S0958344009000196

DiSilvio, F., Diao, W., & Donovan, A. (2016). The development of L2 fluency during study abroad: A cross-language study. *Modern Language Journal, 100*(3), 610–624. doi:10.1111/modl.12343

Dobao, A. F. (2012). Collaborative dialogue in learner-learner and learner-native speaker interaction. *Applied Linguistics, 22*(3), 229–256. doi:10.1093/applin/ams002

Donato, R. (2004). Aspects of collaboration in pedagogical discourse. *Annual Review of Applied Linguistics, 24*, 284–302. doi:10.1017/S026719050400011X

Dooly, M. (2018). "I do which the question": Students' innovative use of technology resources in the language classroom. *Language Learning & Technology, 22*(1), 184–217.

Ellis, R. (2003). *Task-based language learning and teaching.* Oxford, UK: Oxford University Press.

Gerhard, M., Moore, D., & Hobbs, D. (2004). Embodiment and copresence in collaborative interfaces. *Human-Computer Studies, 61*(4), 453–480. doi:10.1016/j.ijhcs.2003.12.014

Huensch, A., & Tracy-Ventura, N. (2017). L2 Utterance fluency development before, during, and after residence abroad: A multidimensional investigation. *Modern Language Journal, 101*(2), 275–293. doi:10.1111/modl.12395

Jauregi, K., Canto, S., de Graaff, R., & Moonen, M. (2010). Vernal interaction in Second Life: Towards a pedagogic framework for task design. *Computer Assisted Language Learning*, *24*(1), 77–101. doi:10.1080/09588221.2010.538699

Jefferson, G. (1984). Transcript notation. In J. M. Atkinson & J. Heritage (Eds.), *Structures of social action: Studies in conversation analysis* (pp. ix–xvi). Cambridge, UK: Cambridge University Press.

Johnson, D. W., & Johnson, R. T. (2004). Cooperation and the use of technology. In D. H. Jonassen (Ed.), *Handbook of research on educational communications and technology* (2nd ed.; pp. 785–812). Mahwah, NJ: Lawrence Erlbaum.

Kim, Y., & Tracy-Ventura, N. (2013). The role of task repetition in L2 performance development: What needs to be repeated during task-based interaction? *System*, *41*(3), 829–840. doi:10.1016/j.system.2013.08.005

Kozlova, I. (2013). Online pedagogy: Development of the communicative skills in Russian online courses. *OLBI Working Papers*, *5*, 53-70.

Kozlova, I. (2014). Collaborative tasks for beginner-level language learners: Issues and implications. *Refereed Proceedings of TESL Ontario Research Symposium*, *40*(2), 101–127.

Kozlova, I. (2018). Task-based language learning and learner autonomy in 3D virtual worlds. In Y. Qian (Ed.), *Integrating multi-user virtual environments in modern classrooms* (pp. 50–73). Hershey, PA: IGI Global. doi:10.4018/978-1-5225-3719-9.ch003

Kozlova, I., & Priven, D. (2015). ESL teacher training in 3D virtual worlds. *Language Learning & Technology*, *19*(1), 83–101.

Kozlova, I., & Zundel, E. (2013). Synchronous online language teaching: Strategies to support language development. In C. Meskill (Ed.), *Online teaching and learning* (pp. 99–116). London: Bloomsbury Academic.

Lan, Y. J. (2014). Does Second Life improve Mandarin learning by overseas Chinese students? *Language Learning & Technology*, *18*(2), 36–56.

Lan, Y. J., Kan, Y. H., Sung, Y. T., & Chung, K. E. (2016). Oral performance language tasks for CSL beginners in Second Life. *Language Learning & Technology*, *20*(3), 60–79.

Lantolf, J. P. (2000). Introducing sociocultural theory. In J. P. Lantolf (Ed.), *Sociocultural theory and second language learning* (pp. 1–26). Oxford University Press.

Lennon, P. (1990). Investigating fluency in EFL: A quantitative approach. *Language Learning*, *40*(3), 387–417. doi:10.1111/j.1467-1770.1990.tb00669.x

Levelt, W. J. M. (1989). *Speaking: From intention to articulation*. Cambridge, MA: MIT Press.

Loewen, S., & Wolff, D. (2016). Peer interaction in F2F and CMC contexts. In S. Masatoshi & S. Ballinger (Eds.), *Peer interaction and second language learning: Pedagogical potential and research agenda* (pp. 163–184). Amsterdam: John Benjamins. doi:10.1075/lllt.45.07loe

Lynch, T., & Maclean, J. (2000). Exploring the benefits of task repetition and recycling for classroom language learning. *Language Teaching Research, 4*(3), 221–250. doi:10.1177/136216880000400303

Meskill, C. (2005). Triadic scaffolds: Tools for teaching English language learners with computers. *Language Learning & Technology, 9*(1), 46–59.

Nor, N. F. M., Hamat, A., & Embi, A. M. (2012). Patterns of discourse in online interaction: Seeking evidence of the collaborative learning process. *Computer Assisted Language Learning, 25*(3), 237–256. doi:10.1080/09588221.2012.655748

Peterson, M. (2006). Learner interaction management in an avatar and chat-based virtual world. *Computer Assisted Language Learning, 19*(1), 79–103. doi:10.1080/09588220600804087

Peterson, M. (2010). Learner participation patterns and strategy use in Second Life: An exploratory case study. *ReCALL, 22*(3), 273–292. doi:10.1017/S0958344010000169

Peterson, M. (2011). Towards a research agenda for the use of three-dimensional virtual worlds in language learning. *CALICO Journal, 29*(1), 67–80. doi:10.11139/cj.29.1.67-80

Pica, T., Kanagy, R., & Falodun, J. (1993). Choosing and using communication tasks for second language instruction and research. In C. G. Crookes & S. M. Gass (Eds.), *Tasks and language learning: Integrating theory and practice* (pp. 9–34). Bristol, UK: Multilingual Matters.

Razagifard, P. (2013). The impact of text-based CMC on improving L2 oral fluency. *Journal of Computer Assisted Learning, 29*(3), 270–279. doi:10.1111/jcal.12000

Rouhshad, A., & Storch, N. (2016). A focus on mode: Patterns of interaction in face-to-face and computer-mediated contexts. In S. Masatoshi & S. Ballinger (Eds.), *Peer interaction and second language learning: Pedagogical potential and research agenda* (pp. 163–184). Amsterdam: John Benjamins. doi:10.1075/lllt.45.11rou

Schroeder, R. (2008). Social interaction in virtual environments: Key issues, common themes, and a framework for research. In R. Schroeder (Ed.), *The social life of avatars: Presence and interaction in shared virtual environments* (p. 118). London: Springer-Verlag.

Seedhouse, P. (2004). The interactional architecture of the language classroom: A conversation analysis perspective. *Language Learning Monograph Series, 54*(1), 1–54.

Storch, N. (2002). Patterns of interaction in ESL pair work. *Language Learning, 52*(1), 119–158. doi:10.1111/1467-9922.00179

Storch, N., & Aldosari, A. (2012). Pairing learners in pair work activity. *Language Teaching Research, 17*(1), 31–48. doi:10.1177/1362168812457530

Swain, M. (2000). The output hypothesis and beyond: Mediating acquisition through collaborative dialogue. In J. P. Lantolf (Ed.), *Sociocultural theory and second language learning* (pp. 97–114). Oxford University Press.

Swain, M., & Lapkin, S. (1998). Interaction and second language learning: Two adolescent French immersion students working together. *Modern Language Journal*, *82*(3), 320–337. doi:10.1111/j.1540-4781.1998. tb01209.x

Tharp, R. G., & Galliomore, R. (1991). *The instructional conversation: Teaching and learning in social activity*. Santa Cruz, CA: National Center for Research on Cultural Diversity and Second Language Learning.

Toyoda, E., & Harrison, R. (2002). Categorization of text chat communication between learners and native speakers of Japanese. *Language Learning & Technology*, *6*(1), 82–99.

Wood, D. (2001). In search of fluency: What is it and how can we teach it? *Canadian Modern Language Review*, *57*(4), 573–689. doi:10.3138/cmlr.57.4.573

Wood, D., Bruner, J., & Ross, G. (1976). The role of tutoring in problem solving. *Journal of Child Psychology and Psychiatry, and Allied Disciplines*, *17*(2), 89–100. doi:10.1111/j.1469-7610.1976. tb00381.x PMID:932126

KEY TERMS AND DEFINITIONS

Collaboration: A multimodal interactional activity during which students not only participate in LREs, but also use language to share their ideas, provide feedback, and monitor their collaborative activities using both audio- and text-based channels.

Fluency: A concept associated with the overall use of language, accurate grammar and vocabulary, pronunciation, and features of speech, such as its rate, quality of pauses, and length of speech between pauses.

Interactional Pattern: An interactional move made with a certain intention (e.g., to ask a question or to challenge someone's opinion).

Negotiation of Form: A conversation with the purpose of requesting or providing corrective feedback on inaccurate language use.

Negotiation of Meaning: A conversation with the purpose of clarifying the meaning of a word or an utterance.

This research was previously published in Assessing the Effectiveness of Virtual Technologies in Foreign and Second Language Instruction; pages 26-60, copyright year 2019 by Information Science Reference (an imprint of IGI Global).

APPENDIX

Princess: Voice-based utterances are typed in regular font

Tree-house: Utterances types on collaboration boards are in *italics*

or seed: **Bold italics** indicates the text portions edited not by the text author but by another student

[yes: Square brackets indicate the onset of overlapping

[where: utterances performed in the same mode, oral or written

|management: straight lines indicate the onset of overlapping

|*organization*: utterances performed in different modes

(we have a question): Utterances in parentheses indicate transcriber best guess

((runs to the lake)): Utterances in double parentheses indicate transcriber's comments

xxx: Signs of x's are used to indicate unintelligible utterances. Each "x" corresponds to one audible syllable

all water-: dash indicates an interrupted utterance

(4): A four-second pause

(.): A pause shorter than one second

h. hah: Dot indicates aspiration inserted in the speech

o:oh: dash indicates a prolonged sound

notes=: =equal signs indicate latching utterances =yes

Chapter 8
Engaging Students in a Computer Diversity Course Through Virtual Worlds

Yvonne Pigatt

Community College of Baltimore County, USA

James Braman

ⓘ https://orcid.org/0000-0001-6080-3903

Community College of Baltimore County, USA

ABSTRACT

Virtual world technology allows for an immersive 3D experience with rich content and interactive potential for students. Through this richness and interactivity, educators have abundant creative power to design and facilitate meaningful learning experiences and collaboration opportunities. In this chapter, the authors discuss one such initiative using Second Life as an educational space for a community college course activity to enhance student engagement. A brief literature review of the educational use of virtual worlds will be presented, which underpin our pedagogical methodology for the project framework. Focusing on a specific community college course titled "Diversity in a Technological Society," the course goals and project requirements will be discussed. The chapter concludes with a detailed description of the proposed methodology for the next phase, recommendations, and future work.

INTRODUCTION

Student engagement is one key component in the process of learning and often coincides with attaining learning outcomes (Carini et al., 2006). There are many techniques to engage students and to spark additional interest in course topics. Some methods are aimed at classroom activities, while others are more aligned as homework or outside activities for practice and discovery. Student engagement can be achieved through the gamification of activities (Domíngues et al., 2013), flipped classrooms (Roehl et al., 2013), augmented reality (Dunleavy et al., 2009), virtual reality (Putman & Id-Deen, 2019) and

DOI: 10.4018/978-1-6684-7597-3.ch008

mobile applications (Arnone et al., 2011), which are just a few methods using technology to engage students through active learning. Selecting the technology that best supports student learning depends on the instructional content and core learning outcomes. Certain course topics demand extra focus on specific skill sets and skill levels, while others are designed to sharpen skills in a more general sense. Technology in these courses can greatly enhance an educator's ability to reach students and provide them with unique learning opportunities.

Within the community college environment, teaching a general education course can be challenging due to the diverse set of student skill levels, varied technology literacy, and course workload balance. This is compounded by differences in age and enrollment statuses compared to students enrolled in more traditional four-year institutions (Cohen & Brawer, 2003). Adding to this complexity are the many challenges faced when dealing with underprepared (Gabriel & Flake, 2008) or at-risk learners (Zheng et al., 2014). Reaching all students and keeping them engaged in the content and context of the class becomes increasingly complex and dynamic. Therefore, instructors need to be resourceful and open to change as new challenges arise. This also applies to the need to be resourceful and knowledgeable with and about technology.

With the many available technologies and web 2.0 sites available today, educators have a wide array of tools to use in the classroom. Social media for instance now permeates many facets of everyday life and social interaction. Society has grown accustomed to everyday reliance on many forms of digital information (Pew, 2009; Lenhart et al., 2010). However, some technologies do not work or fit well in some contexts, nor are they always appropriate for education. Using technology in the classroom poses its own set of problems and challenges. Instructors may not have knowledge about a particular technology, or even have the resources available. Computing resources, space and internet connectivity all pose potential problems. In some cases, students may be apprehensive of learning with a new technology or may have limited use of a particular resource outside of a school setting. While some schools may have open labs or computing resources available through the library, these can be a challenge to maintain or monitor since they are often outside of the instructor's domain of control.

Despite these challenges for this project, the virtual world of Second Life® (SL) was selected as the virtual world technology of choice. SL is a 3-dimensional (3D) virtual world created by Linden Lab that can be accessed through the Internet via a downloadable client application. Users are represented in this world through an *avatar*, where one can interact with other users, content, and explore their surroundings. This online world has seen a large influx of users over the last several years, with an estimated number of "residents" reaching over 57 million accounts worldwide (Linden Lab, 2018). It also estimated that there have been over 482,000 years of time spent in-world collectively. This immense amount of time has contributed to SL's richness in content and unique user experiences. There are many categories of virtual worlds other than SL, each can be classified by their technology, graphics, goals or specific design. Some worlds are designed to be very open-ended and creative, while other worlds are designed to be more game-like or specific for a particular age group. SL should not be generalized as a game in the traditional sense, but instead as an open collaborative space that lends itself to much potential.

Students are accustomed to working with interactive media for learning and using educational games. While SL itself is not a game, it does have several game-like qualities that work well in teaching certain types of content or topics. As students are often attracted by games and other forms of interactive media, SL is an intriguing medium to use. Some studies have shown that many users of games also enjoyed being immersed in a simulated environment (Yee, 2006). Following Csikszentmihalyi's research on flow (1990) and applying this into areas of virtual environments to create an engaging and immersive space for learning is a useful goal. Using this approach for assignments can create engaging educational material for students. Additionally, virtual environments can provide students with a sense of presence, which some researchers have noted as a key benefit of using the technology (Holmberg & Huvila, 2008; Salmon, 2009).

Many other 3D virtual environments are available, such as IMVU, Twinity, Active Worlds and Minecraft (just to name a few). While these other technologies are competitors, SL still has a strong user base and strong attraction for new users looking to create and share content, with some attributing its popularity to the large amount of varying in-world activities (Wagner, 2008). There have also been a growing number of available 3D environments that are intended for more targeted users and age groups (Kzero, 2014). Minecraft, in particular, has seen an increase in use for the gamification of material for younger students (Gallagher, 2014) or for project-based learning (Callaghan, 2016).

Virtual worlds and other 3D spaces have been used for an array of educational purposes over the last several years (Kapp & O'Driscoll, 2010; Vincenti & Braman, 2011; Dudley & Braman, 2015); including use in general education curriculum in some schools as a vehicle for research and social exploration (Braman et al., 2013). As virtual worlds continue to grow in popularity, so too will the possibilities of their use. Virtual worlds have also been used in wider areas, such as in theater, art, geography, science and English courses, and many more (Vincenti & Braman, 2011; Vincenti & Braman, 2010; Braman & Yancy, 2017). Second Life® has been used in more specific domains, such as computer science and in computer ethics (Wang et al., 2009). The perception of use of Second Life in computing courses has generally been positive (Braman et al., 2011; Braman & Yancy, 2017).

SL was best suited for the pilot study discussed in this chapter due to the authors' experience, the diversity of in-world users, the capabilities of the platform, and the potential for dynamic interactivity through built-in scripting language. In addition, it is possible to link Second Life to external programs and applications to extend its capabilities. Finally, one of the authors has extensive experience conducting workshops and training on Second Life® which helped to facilitate the project. The purpose of using SL in the diversity course discussed in this chapter was twofold: 1) To increase student engagement in the context of the course by increasing participation, student enthusiasm and assignment quality and 2) To teach a new emerging technology. This chapter will begin with background discussion of virtual worlds and creating and using a virtual educational space. Secondly, a pilot study completed at a community college will be described, including the difficulties experienced inside and outside the classroom. A third section will discuss the pilot study and recommendations. Lastly, future research directions and conclusions will be provided.

BACKGROUND

Virtual worlds can be defined as "an electronic environment that visually mimics complex physical spaces, where people can interact with each other and with virtual objects, and where people are represented by animated characters" (Bainbridge, 2007, p. 472). The realism of virtual worlds and the "animated characters" or Avatars, have increased over the years as hardware and video capabilities have improved. The origins of virtual worlds are rooted in online text-based "worlds", referred to as Multi-User Dungeons or Multi-Users Dimension (MUDs) (Bartle, 2003). As technologies have improved, so too have their capabilities, features and representations, which have evolved into the many environments and games seen today. There are other terms that can be used to refer to virtual worlds such as Multi-User

Virtual Environments (MUVEs) which can encompass many online worlds, and more specifically, in the context of education, Virtual Learning Environments (VLEs). Typically, VLEs are web-based, are less open-ended compared to MUVEs, and are more focused on learning, communication and include assessment tools (Britain & Liber, 2004). VLEs can be used in a broader sense to include virtual worlds that are focused on education. Common tools are supported in most virtual environments which include capabilities for communication, voice interaction, building tools, polygon mesh, and other 3D support. Adding to realism of virtual worlds is the increase in support for platforms such as the Oculus Rift, making for a very immersive experience. The Oculus Rift is a virtual reality head mounted display device that can be used to create realistic immersive experiences for the wearer. With the increase in realism, the potential for new ways of interaction may become more commonplace. There has also been work to enhance the social interaction between users through emotive avatars that capture real expressions, as in the virtual world High Fidelity (High Fidelity, 2015). Through the use technologies like Google Cardboard (Google VR, 2019), virtual reality can be brought into the classroom where Oculus Rift would not be possible due to costs or other constraints.

While the use of simulations, video and other computerized tools in education are not new, the use of virtual 3D worlds is still experimental. 3D worlds have potential as an educational tool due to the creative nature and capabilities. 3D worlds do present some design challenges in term of creating an educational resource or "space" for the students to work. Unlike the traditional classroom, the virtual classroom has fewer restrictions on time, space and movement. In the next section we examine the creation and use of virtual educational space.

Creating and Using a Virtual Educational Environment

What does it mean to have an education space in a virtual world? What does it look like? In a virtual world, educators are not bound by many of the same physical limitations inherent in the traditional physical classroom. Educators are also not bound by the same limitations of websites or Content Management Systems (CMS) such as Blackboard or Moodle. As John Lester pointed out during his Keynote Talk at the e-LEOT 2014 conference, there is a tendency among educators "to use new tools like old tools" (Lester, 2014). While educators have the power of virtual worlds, which can be used to create new imaginary environments the tendency is to recreate a 3D replica of a traditional classroom. A replica of a classroom in virtual worlds certainly does not guarantee that learning will take place. A virtual world activity for a class needs deliberate planning, testing and integration with specific content to be successful. Unlike some virtual environments where everything is pre-created by the creating company, Second Life relies on the content creation of its residents (users). Content creation in Second Life is more difficult compared to virtual worlds with environments created by software developers, such as World of Warcraft (McArthur et al., 2010). Since many educators may lack the time needed to successfully build all the components needed for their online virtual environment, other options are possible such - as purchasing premade content from other users (via in-world stores or the Second Life Marketplace) or even hiring someone to create the space for a fee. Before designing a space, it is recommended that one spends time in-a virtual world in order to get a sense of the possibilities, and what other educators have designed. Educational spaces can consist of open areas of land which can contain replicas and models of particular systems. These spaces may include interactive kiosks, or somewhat more traditional areas that include meeting spaces like offices with desks. More often, these spaces are more open, creative and unique.

Students benefit from learning new technological platforms such as Second Life®. 3D platforms and games are increasingly commonplace, thus having knowledge of how to operate one can be useful in learning to operate another. Having an avatar can be useful in the operation of various multiuser applications. As noted by Bélisle and Bodur (2010), with the increasing use of consumers today having avatars, it is important to understand how avatars are being used to improve marketing. Many researchers agree that Second Life® can provide an engaging learning environment for students compared to current education platforms, including an "around the clock" accessible meeting place (Bradshaw, 2009; The Schome Community, 2007; Wang & Braman, 2009). Engaging students is also enhanced when instructors maintain additional office hours in-world or include additional training material in a 3D format. This has been observed broadly when teaching in an all online format while engaging and interacting with students using video conferencing tools such as Zoom (Pigatt & Braman, 2018). A search on video sites, such as www.youtube.com, yield many choices of videos showcasing educational designs. Students may be more willing to interact with an interactive training kiosk in Second Life in addition to lecture notes from class or the required text, rather than just reading the textbook alone. As discussed by Antonacci et al. (2008), there are three major educational benefits from using virtual worlds:

1. Virtual worlds give users the ability to carry out tasks that could be difficult for them in the "real world" due to constraints, including cost, scheduling or location;
2. Virtual worlds' persistence allows for continuing and growing social interactions, which can serve as a basis for collaborative education;
3. Virtual worlds can adapt and grow to meet user needs.

These three benefits, particularly for some topics, provide the dynamic flexibility needed to complete projects that would be difficult to complete in the normal time frame of a class.

Duncan et al. (2012) reviewed virtual world educational literature and summarized several advantages of using virtual worlds in an educational setting.

1. The use of SL provides an intuitive modern approach for distance teaching in terms of the use of avatars.
2. Collaboration is greatly facilitated when conducting educational activities in-world.
3. Experimental and constructive learning can be achieved in SL.
4. Higher order thinking, such as analyzing, evaluating and creating can be achieved in virtual worlds as well as lower order thinking, such as remembering, understanding and applying (Falloon, 2010).
5. As geographical boundaries are broken down in SL, there is a large diverse background among participants.

As noted previously, the flexibility of the environment to be changed and adapted to the dynamics of student needs or to the content of a particular course is quite useful. This is dependent however on the instructor and available resources in the classroom. Successful lesson plans using a virtual world needs to be carefully planned, often more so than a traditional lecture. These characteristics are indeed important for integration of a virtual environment into any classroom. As engagement through visual and interactive components can promote active learning, attention needs to be placed carefully on this element. Once students are acclimated to the software, teachers can serve as a guide of the lesson plan to facilitate collaboration between students, assist with challenges and problem solving, and keep the class on task. Instructors can also lead classes on virtual fields trips and create immersive content to enhance and reinforce class topics.

USING SECOND LIFE®: A PILOT PROJECT – CASE 1

A computing course titled "Diversity in a Technological Society" was selected for the Second Life® Pilot Project. The official course catalogue description reads:

Explores the influences of technology on human diversity. Students are introduced to basic human relationship factors, international cultures, technologies, people with disabilities, human and data communications, artificial intelligence, computer security, and various individuals who have influenced technology.

This course is a popular general education course offered by the Computer Science / Information Technology Department and is offered each semester including winter and summer semesters. This course was selected due to the nature and flexibility of the course, and due to the instructor's schedule to carry out the pilot project. In this course the instructor discusses a variety of diversity-related topics, as seen in the real-world. For example, personal and social barriers to success, teamwork, and leadership. The use of computer technology topics helps the learner realize and appreciate the value of technology and how it supports and improves the quality of life, and the role it plays in the success of people working together around the world. For example, topics discussed are global social media, the global digital divide, collaboration software and emerging technologies. An essential outcome for the course is to raise the diversity consciousness of the learner and to teach students to work with people of all ages, races, ethnicities, religions, cultures, and other isms by using technology as the means for communication and collaboration. The instructor in the course has taken a constructivist approach to teach this course. Constructivism focuses on learning how to think and understand. Constructivism gives students ownership of what they learn since learning is based on students' questions and explorations. Constructivism promotes social and communication skills by creating a classroom environment that emphasizes collaboration and the exchange of ideas (Laureate Education, 2014).

In the course for a final semester project, students were assigned a topic from their normal class textbook which served as a basis for a group project. In semesters prior to the Pilot Study, students were to work in a small group of three or four people to construct a detailed written report on a given course related topic. Once the report was complete, students were to present the topic to the class using Microsoft PowerPoint (or similar presentation tool). The report topics included: Artificial Intelligence, virtual reality, military applications of technology, electronic health records, medical information systems, etc., and several other emerging technology trends. Based on assigned topics, through their own research, and from the information in the textbook chapter, students were required to write a summarizing report and presentation (both were graded). This assignment was typical for the course, and was a normal activity assigned at the end of each semester. Students are normally required to attend the presentations of other groups, take notes and ask questions. However, for the pilot study, the "traditional" assignment for the course was altered for use in Second Life.

Introducing Second Life® to Students

In class, students were assigned groups and group topics for the report they would be completing as a course assignment, the same procedure as used pre-pilot study. Groups consisted of three to four students. Students were also asked to create a SL account. Next, the class was introduced to SL in two ways: 1) A homework assignment was administered where students had to watch a documentary on SL and virtual worlds, titled Life 2.0. As part of this homework assignment students were asked to create an avatar; and 2). Students were introduced to SL by means of an in-class lecture and a training session including the in-world navigation controls. Based on our experience, when students spend some time learning about virtual worlds and navigation elements before an actual SL graded project, students are better acclimated to the requirements of the assignment and there is less stress related to learning new software.

The initial in-class practice assignment using SL reviewed the main features and controls, such as chatting, basic avatar control, flying and teleportation. In the exercise, all of these features were included, and students were asked to explore various aspects of the "grid" while paying extra attention to the layout and design of buildings, stores and general places they visited. Students were asked to make notes of their observations. Students were also introduced to aspects of the economy and how to purchase items if needed. In the last 15 - 20 minutes of class, a brief building tutorial was conducted to give students a very basic understanding on how to build and shape objects. This overview was a beneficial method of showing to the class how much time other users put into creating virtual items and buildings.

After students completed these initial practice assignments, the changed aspect of the group project (compared to past semesters) was revealed. Students were instructed that the presentation for the given topic would not be conducted in the "traditional sense" but instead would be presented to the class through Second Life® using their new skills. In addition, each group was asked to upload their final presentations slides into SL, and also to create an interactive kiosk area as an alternative presentation medium for their given topic. For example, if the group's topic was on artificial intelligence, they were asked to create an inviting space to capture their audience's attention, provide a seating area, presentation area and also include decorative items and/or posters or pictures to emphasize their topic. This required some creativity from the students and an understanding of the topic. The group kiosk areas also needed to include several interactive components which could be accessed by the class. The interactive components could include objects that linked to external websites and dispensed other objects or virtual notecards with additional information. An instructor led discussion on the topics, through the Second Life based learning kiosks, served as a content source for the class while immersed in-world. In order to complete the assignment, students needed prior experience in SL to control and manipulate their avatars, understand the interface, and communicate effectively with other students (as avatars). To facilitate this experience, students were exposed to several deliberate exercises within Second Life to learn the controls. Students needed basic building knowledge and, in some cases, basic scripting knowledge in order to create the interactive kiosks. Thus, an outline was developed for the approach that would be used to teach students how to use SL for completion of a report presentation assignment.

Assignment (Version 1)

Outline for Integrating Second Life® into an Assignment

1. Introduce students to Second Life® through homework assignments:
   a. Search for basic information online about SL and similar virtual worlds
   b. Create a free basic SL account by going to http://www.secondlife.com
   c. Watch a video on SL and virtual worlds titled: Life 2.0: https://www.imdb.com/title/tt1518809/
2. Class 1 (Lecture / Discussion):
   a. Lecture topic on virtual worlds, SL (in general) and the SL culture. Emphasis on how SL can be used for education, collaboration, business and for entertainment.
   b. Class discussion questions related to virtual worlds
   c. Textbook assignment: "Real Self vs. Virtual Self"
3. Class 2 (Applied Learning):
   a. Using SL / Create an avatar
   b. Learn navigation controls / Flying / Teleporting
   c. Learn Communication / Search /Editing Appearance / Inventory System
   d. In-world Exploration Assignment
   e. Getting started with groups and coordination of Projects
4. Class 3 (Applied Learning):
   a. Assign groups to in-world spaces
   b. Groups work on designs and upload presentation files in-world
   c. Group Assignment:
      i. Read textbook chapter, complete presentation with interactive kiosk area in SL that discusses an emerging technology topic and group research
5. Class 4 (Applied Learning):
   a. Class exploration and group topic presentations in SL and real life
   b. Class feedback and conclusions

Students were given in-class time to work on their project and to collaborate with their groups to complete the project. Extra time outside of class was also needed, as most groups needed extra study time on the topics and also time to complete the presentation files. In Second Life®, an area was purchased in the main grid by the instructors, specifically in the Goodnight region. This area was 16,384 square meters and was sufficient for several class sections to work. The virtual space was divided into multiple sections and separated by fences. The space was also sufficient in size to have enough space in between each group area for additional separation. Each group was assigned a specific area to build and to contain their design. It is important to let students know that there is a specific number of virtual objects (or "prims", short for primitive objects) that are housed in an area to avoid an excessive number of unneeded objects in their design. It is also important to remind students not to build in other student areas or disrupt other groups. When students are using the in-world chat feature, other conversations can be "heard" by other groups if they are too close.

Figure 1. Beginning of group kiosk building within fenced in areas

By the last in-class building session, student groups had managed to complete most of the assignment. Some groups struggled to build kiosk areas that were related to their topic and some had problems getting their presentation slides uploaded without help. On the last day of the project, each of the groups presented the research completed on their assigned topic. The presentations took place in-world and in real life simultaneously. In real life, the presenting group stood in front of the class at the instructor station. One group member was logged into SL at the instructor station with Second Life projected on the overhead screen. The other members of the group were also at the front of the room to discuss their section of the presentation. These students were logged in at their desk computers, but physically located at the front of the classroom. The remainder of the class was able to watch and listen to the presentation though Second Life® (by being logged into SL as their avatar) and in Real Life at the same time. Being in-world and in the real-life class had the advantage of allowing students multiple ways to interact with the content and at the same time provide a real life overlay of the presentation in which they were more accustomed. The class did experience a few technical difficulties during two presentations, which included the platform crashing for one group, and another group had their presentation slides inadvertently reset. Having the real-life aspect of the presentation, allowed the group to continue presenting during the challenges. At the conclusion of each presentation, students asked questions to the presenting group via SL through the chat window where each presenting group responded through SL and in person to the class. Several of the presenting groups also posed their own created quiz questions to the class virtually, creating a multi-layered discussion. Figure 2 illustrates a group of students, represented by avatars, in a virtual presentation area.

At the conclusion of the project, the instructors had open discussions with the class to elicit feedback on their experiences with Second Life® and the alternate form of presenting. The instructors also wanted to gain key insights into what parts of the project were useful, difficult or lacking in order to make improvements for the future. As mentioned previously, this was a preliminary pilot study in the early testing phase where more in-depth analysis will occur in the future. Feedback was elicited through class discussion and was not explicitly recorded. Student feedback after the project was generally positive on this mixed reality mode of presenting. Many expressed surprise in presenting in this format, as it was something very new that they had never experienced before. During the presentations there were very minimal technical problems or complications and by this time in the project, students were much more comfortable being able to navigate and control the avatars for the presentation without help. There were some challenges encouraged in and out of the classroom, beyond those of a technical nature.

Figure 2. Students in-world listening to a group presentation

USING SECOND LIFE®: A PILOT PROJECT – CASE 2

Following the pilot study as outlined above in Case 1, the same course and general design of the project was repeated in the Fall 2019 semester. Like the previous final project, students worked in groups of 3 to 4 students to research and write a report on a specific topic and to present their findings to the class. This time however, the topics were not emerging technologies but instead were related to virtual worlds. As the course relates to diversity and the impacts of technology, we adjusted the topics and approach compared to Case 1. The topics included conducting research on: subcultures in virtual worlds, virtual relationships, 3D technologies, future of virtual worlds, security and privacy in virtual worlds, impacts of virtual world and gaming addiction, identity in virtual worlds, discrimination in virtual worlds, etc. As there was only a brief mention of virtual worlds in the course textbook, the instructor recommended some additional readings to align with course activity objectivities. In alignment with the constructivist approach to teaching, this assignment required additional creative thinking and deeper research and analysis than what was required compared to Case 1 due to the nature of the research topics. Students were asked to use scholarly sources for their research but were allowed to intertwine a few recent news articles if it would enhance their report and presentation. As the topics were not as simple as reporting on an issue directly, they had to piece together evidence to support their overall group topic to build a case. For instance, the group that was focusing on discrimination in virtual words was quite surprised and intrigued by what they discovered in the literature about how avatars were treated differently based on appearance. In addition to their research, the group decided to carry out their own in-world experiment by exploring populated places in SL and observing how they were treated. Specifically, they were surprised at some of the rude comments directed at them for looking like a "noob" or new user to the world and how little effort they had put into their appearance. They expressed feelings of overall rejection and were unsettled about some additional harsh comments that some residents made about their appearance and lack of knowledge about in-world norms. Students learned firsthand about micro-aggressions, discrimination and social barriers to success. Of particular interest was the lesson on discrimination faced by students who felt that they had never been judged by their differences. For the research on virtual world topics, students were not limited to only SL, but many concentrated on that world due to their familiarity from class and the literature.

Changes to the Assignment

Although we followed the overall structure outlined for Case 1, there were some adjustments made to the overall class activity Due to limited class time during the semester and the desire to adjust the research topics. As before, students were asked to create free SL accounts at home for a homework assignment. Groups and topics were assigned in class for the project. Students were introduced in a similar way through an in-class lecture and discussion about virtual world technology, their impact and usage. During the second pilot study, we only had one in-world training session as an introduction to SL which covered basic needed skills of how to control one's avatar. A primary change to the assignment was the removal of the presentation requirement from within SL. While this was desired, we removed this requirement due to limited time and had students present in a traditional format within class. This also removed the additional time needed for students to build a space in the world and the need for additional training sessions on building. However, due to the more complex nature of the topics, more time was needed for researching and assisting in the writing process of the report which included significant time outside of class and homework time.

Assignment (Version 2)

Outline for Integrating Second Life® Into an Assignment

1. Introduce students to Second Life through homework assignments:
   a. Search for basic information online about SL and similar virtual worlds
   b. Create a free basic SL account by going to http://www.secondlife.com
   c. Assigned to Watch a video on SL and virtual worlds titled: Life 2.0: https://www.imdb.com/title/tt1518809/
2. Class 1 (Lecture / Discussion):
   a. Lecture topic on virtual worlds, SL (in general) and the SL culture. Emphasis on how SL can be used for education, collaboration, business and for entertainment.
   b. Class discussion questions related to virtual worlds
   c. Brief in-class research assignment on examples of how virtual words are being used.
   d. Find and briefly summarize a scholarly article on virtual worlds (with suggestions to the class such as looking at the Journal of Virtual Worlds Research).

3. Class 2 (Applied Learning):
    a. Create an avatar in SL
    b. Learn navigation controls / Flying / Teleporting
    c. Learn Communication / Search /Editing Appearance / Inventory System
    d. In-world Exploration Assignment
    e. Getting started with groups and coordination of Projects
4. Class 4 (Presentations):
    a. During the following week all groups presented to the class
    b. Class feedback and conclusions

CHALLENGES IN AND OUT OF THE CLASSROOM

This section highlights some issues that were encountered during both Pilot Projects, both inside the classroom and for at home assignments.

Inside the Classroom

The real-life classroom was a typical computer lab setting with twenty-four computers. The computers were positioned around the perimeter of the room, so that the instructor could easily assist students that were having problems and keep students on task. This also helped with the collaboration component of the project, as other students could easily maneuver around the class to help other group members. The computers used for the first pilot study were 3.2 Ghz with i5 processors with 4GB of RAM, all running the Windows 7 operating system. During the second study, the same classroom was used but the computers were running Windows 10 with 3.2 Ghz with i5 processors with 4GB of RAM. The instructors were pleasantly surprised with the low number of technical difficulties encountered in the classroom. There were issues during the second pilot with student computers that resulted from the campus wireless network signal being weak in the classroom. Several students that wanted to use their own laptop, had to use a computer in the classroom instead.

To make installation and access less problematic, the instructors were able to obtain a large set of 2 gigabyte USB flash drives. These flash drives were generously donated by the college to assist in the first pilot project. A copy of SL was installed on each flash drive. The intention was to have flash drives readily available with a SL install so that students could use it in class, on another computer on campus, or off-campus. Providing a flash drive, with SL installed was a support system so students could keep working without needing to worry about installing additional software. There were a few issues with defective flash drives, and in those cases the students temporarily installed SL on the lab computer as needed. At the end of the activity, the flash drives were collected back from students who expressed that they would not need the drive or would not use SL in the future. During the second pilot, we purchased a new set of flash drives and preloaded SL for the students. Software security in the labs had changed, and no software could be added to the system, so this was the only option to run the program in class. Again, these were collected back after the class period.

Additionally, the class did not encounter many problems with the video cards or graphics capabilities during class. Most installations of the SL software defaulted to the highest video settings (which later needed to be adjusted in some instances). During the first project pilot about 10-15% of the computers experienced periodic crashes, causing SL to need restarting. Lowering the graphic settings one to two levels below maximum seemed to limit the number of crashes. Crashing often occurred when users were moving between regions or teleporting, or when students were located within graphically rich areas. Being close to large bodies of water in SL also seemed to cause problem with some of the graphics cards. The instructors made sure to notify students of these issues as they became known. This was not the case during the second pilot, as only one computer needed to be restarted.

Outside the Classroom

A first challenge outside for the classroom pertained to documentary Life 2.0 by Jason Spingarn-Koff that students were asked to watch. While the instructors considered this to be a useful documentary that revealed several motivations of why some people use or are attracted to SL, student feedback, was mixed. The class had a discussion about the video, along with several related instructor led questions about how students felt about the video. It is important to note that this discussion was held prior to the students experience within the virtual world of SL. One perception that was communicated during the discussion was that many students had the impression that users of SL were addicted to the environment, led unfulfilled lives and that SL was not a useful space for "normal" people. Other students had opinions that were different and observed that indeed SL has very useful purposes in many contexts and could be an interesting collaborative and social space. Overall, students' first impressions of SL were more negative than positive. In the future an alternative video that provides more focus on SL content or several shorter introductory videos on virtual worlds will be used.

A second challenge that occurred was related to those students that did not complete the avatar creation assignment prior to class. Students that failed to complete this homework assignment had difficulties creating their accounts while on campus. After a few students created their account, additional students were blocked from registering because the Internet Protocol (IP) address for the campus location that was temporarily blocked from creating additional accounts. As of the time of this writing, this is still a problem, and additional accounts cannot be created on campus. The remaining students were able to complete the registration process by using their internet connection on their phone (using their own data plan and different IP address). In future semesters, the need to complete the registration process prior to the class will be stressed in order to alleviate this challenge in the future.

DISCUSSION AND RECOMMENDATIONS

Overall, the Pilot Project using SL in a "Diversity in a Technological Society" course was successful. We gained key insights for increasing student engagement from the project, and additionally identified improvements. The original instructor for the course noted improvement in enthusiasm and detail in submitted projects compared to non-SL usage. Anecdotal evidence from the experience suggests that using a virtual world can have a positive impact on student perception of the project and it can increase enthusiasm for some assignments. Some students did report seeing a positive benefit pertaining to gaining knowledge about virtual worlds for future use. After participating in the assignment, most students that previously had a negative view of SL, had changed their viewpoints. This initial negative opinion may be due to the novelty of the software, but additional research is needed in order to understand preconceived negative perceptions. Understanding these perceptions would be helpful as they could be addressed in the beginning of the assignment.

In future incarnations of this project there are several elements that the instructors wish to change and improve. To assist in streamlining the assignment in the future, the instructors plan on creating additional videos on virtual worlds, in addition to video tutorials on how to create objects, upload the presentation files and purchase items in-world. The assignment instructions themselves will also be enhanced to include more detail. Video recorded training sessions will provide additional context for the students of the importance of knowing about virtual world software. It is our wish that other educators can gain insight on how similar projects for their classes may be adapted and used for other diverse content. By placing several of the training videos online, other educators could make use of the information in their classes.

Adjusting the topics from emerging technologies to virtual world related topics infused with the course topics were beneficial and were well received by the class as interesting and important. It also reinforced research and writing skills. The topics also seemed to capture the attention of the class during the presentations as the topics were very new to the students and related to current events and class topics. Groups presenting also had to ask the class two discussion questions related to the topic which sparked some very interesting and lively debates and discussions. As we continue to make improvements to the assignment, the new adjusted research topics may be used as a replacement to the emerging technology topics for this activity.

RECOMMENDATIONS

Following is a list of recommendations for integrating the virtual world of SL into a college course using an approach similar to the Pilot Projects discussed in this chapter. With each recommendation is a discussion of how the authors plan to implement the changes in future courses.

1. **Include at least two smaller training sessions for students to increase awareness of virtual worlds.**

Overall, the initial lectures and discussion sessions about SL, combined with several training sessions on the use of SL were helpful for students based on their general comments in class and observations during the project. These training sessions (which included controls, communication, building etc.) were instrumental for student success in using SL to complete the assignment. As students became conformable with the SL technology and understood its application in a wider scope, communication and collaboration expectations were established. Students were able to communicate effectively with their group in-world to complete assigned tasks. Anecdotal evidence, gathered through the author's observations, suggests that training (even at a basic level) greatly improves overall outcomes when using SL for an educational purpose. There are several orientation areas (e.g., Orientation Island) premade and maintained within SL that can be used by students when instructors do not have a readily available class module for orientation.

2.   **Require students to complete virtual world activities outside of the classroom.**

It is beneficial for both the students and instructors to conduct some preliminary research about virtual worlds outside of the classroom. This allows students to pursue topics related to virtual worlds that may be interesting to them. It would be useful to provide a set of guiding questions, depending on the context of a particular course and how virtual worlds could be useful in that domain. For example, in a business course, an instructor could assign specific readings on the value of virtual goods, or articles on virtual world marketing. In the case of this project students were asked to watch a video related to SL. There are many other such videos available that are more general that may be appropriate. Based on student feedback, an alternate video (yet to be determined) will be selected for future semesters. An additional benefit of having students do a portion of the investigation outside of class time is that more time can be focused on the technology and on the collaboration component. A flipped classroom approach for the individual group project topics is useful.

3.   **Evaluate the available resources and technology.**

Having backup plans for technical problems will allow for a much smoother class activity. It is important to test the equipment available in the labs especially that of the video card and internet speed. Since SL relies on both components, problems with the video card or internet speeds can easily derail an activity, and frustrate students. Furthermore, be sure to check for any scheduled updates for SL, as it may pose some complications if there are any glitches. One major problem that many may face is the lack of ability to install the SL client application on lab computers. Without administrator rights, installation can be difficult or impossible. Also needed updates to the platform that occur periodically can cause problems if instructors lack administrator rights to perform the updates. In this pilot we used flash drives with pre-installed copies of SL which cut down many problems in the classroom. Even though we did have the ability to install software as needed, computers are reset each day which would have required the reinstallation of the program. Be aware however, that the downside of the flash drive approach is the amount of time needed to install the software on each drive. This should be completed well in advance to the actual class activity.

4.   **Provide students with sufficient use of context for the use of Second Life.**

It is important that students understand the importance of virtual worlds and that it is a technology that is increasingly being used in education, business settings and for social interactions. Having an understanding of the technology and its impacts can be advantageous. To help students become more fluent and comfortable with the technology in a general sense (not just with SL), then sufficient knowledge of virtual worlds is helpful. If students can use a virtual world throughout the semester, and not just for one project, then additional skills may develop. Students can learn more advanced features and skills that can be used in outer areas. If a course does not lend itself to using a virtual world platform all semester, then be sure to provide students with enough context information about how the technology can be used and examples of its current use. For example, show the class how businesses are using the technology to reinforce that it's not just a "game" but a serious place to conduct work. One could also show the class how it could be used in the medical field by describing its usage in medical education for simulation and information display (Meskó, 2008). There are numerous examples of how educators and researchers are using the platforms in many areas.

5. Aim to reduce costs of conducting an in-class project.

The cost of conducting and implementing SL into a course, especially if there are many students or a large land requirement, can be rather expensive. One needs to purchase an area of land, and then in addition to that expense, a monthly land rental fee is assessed. For example, a smaller 2,048 square meter parcel costs $15.00 USD or a 32,768 square meter parcel costs $125.00 USD as a repeating monthly fee. A full link to the Mainland Pricing and fees can be found at: https://secondlife.com/land/pricing.php. It is important to access the particular needs for implementation prior to purchasing space to avoid incurring unneeded costs. There are alternative worlds available, some of which are free that can be hosted locally and customized, such as OpenSim. As an added benefit of using a locally hosted world to that institution, security and control of the space can be better maintained.

An additional cost that was incurred as part of this Pilot Project was the purchase cost for each group's PowerPoint presentation boards. In order for the students to present their slides on the topic, they needed a presentation object to do so (discussed more in the next section). For the duration of the Pilot Project each group was given a limited amount of virtual currency (Linden dollars) so that they could purchase a presentation viewer to display their presentation slides. Any additional money that remained could be used by the group to purchase additional decorative items for their space if needed. The students were encouraged to use as many freely available items and content as possible. Students did quickly discover how to obtain and search for free items in the SL marketplace: https://marketplace.secondlife.com. Students did learn valuable knowledge on how to make real purchases and how to work with alternate virtual currencies for the project, as well as how to buy from the web, items for their avatar and how to un-package items. There is a large amount of content available in the marketplace and within Second Life for the needs of most projects.

In the second pilot (Case 2) the removal of the requirement of building a static presentation space helped to reduce the cost of in-world building. As a class we briefly experimented with building in a free open zone, but we did not need to keep these objects or need a dedicated area. Instead we only visited popular free areas which reduced the cost significantly. We also did not need to purchase the presentation boards as we did previously.

6. Use a created display board instead of a purchased display board for the activity.

Part of the Pilot Project required that students upload their final version of their presentation files to SL as image files (either in .jpg or .png format) to be integrated into an in-world presenter object. These presenter objects act as an interactive display board, where a presenter can show a slide and then advance to the next one while speaking. It is similar to using the instructor station in a classroom to go through a set of PowerPoint slides.. Initially, to save time and to allow students a chance to actually purchase goods in SL, the instructors requested that students visit the SL Marketplace to purchase a specific item for the assignment. In order for this to work, each group needed approximately $500L (500 Linden dollars) which was supplied by the instructors. This amount of virtual currency is approximate equivalent to $1.89 USD, but the exchange rate of the virtual current changes daily and is controlled by

Linden Lab (Bray & Konsynski, 2008). While this is not a substantial amount of money, it could become problematic if there are a large number of groups across many sections. In the future it is planned to create a specific presentation object for the activity that can be copied and modified by each group for no cost. If time allows, students could be given instructions to create this presentation object on their own (given adequate time and directions). This would be a more advanced exercise. As previously noted in the second pilot this requirement was removed and we had presentations in the classroom and not in Second Life which removed the need of a purchased display board and removed the time needed to setup the presentations. Groups were instructed to use presentation software such as Prezi, Google Slides or Microsoft PowerPoint.

7. Train instructors to be fluent with Second Life® and acclimated to the platform.

It is also strongly recommended that educators stay current in topics related to virtual worlds so that they can provide relevance to students about why they are using the technology and how it can be useful in their future as a technology tool. Providing relevance to using virtual worlds in class can strengthen the relationship of its importance as a learning activity. This can often be accomplished by adding additional readings or discussions that highlight high profile uses of the platform in the business world, educational institutions, government, and in medicine.

Additionally, due to the technical nature of the software and the many changing features, it is helpful for students to have an instructor that is able to help if, and when problems occur during use. Students can face an array of challenges and raise many questions during the activity. As some students are hesitant about using the software or quickly overwhelmed by it, having a background in the features often helps to calm student fears if something happens. It is also helpful as an educator to be familiar with many of the advanced features and how to use many of the building tools as one can then create much more inviting and engaging learning spaces. This advanced ability could lend itself to being able to link the learning space to outside resources such as websites or to create very engaging self-directed learning tools for outside class time learning.

8. Decide on a design for the virtual world space.

As the nature of the virtual learning space is very fluid, the environment can take on many forms. The authors recommend analyzing the needs of a particular project to help determine the form of the virtual space early. The size of the area, the amount of avatars for the class that need to be supported, the need for a sandbox area, and the need for certain tools are all main elements to consider. Visiting public educational areas in SL, to get a sense of what is possible and to see what tools are available in-world (such as display areas, simulations, posters, lecture areas, or video screens, etc.), is recommended. It can be a daunting task to figure out how one's educational space should appear, balancing both functionally and having an interesting and inviting landscape. Often virtual learning environments are designed very differently depending on the subject matter of a course and discipline. Virtual environments can range from being a recreation of a scene from a science fiction novel or a play, which could be used by an English course, or an area that is visually simpler such as a lecture style amphitheater for class presentations. Alternatively, the environment could be a replica of a full scale campus. Simulations through Second Life have great potential (Teoh, 2012).

FUTURE RESEARCH DIRECTIONS

In this section, future goals for the Pilot Project are discussed, specifically addressing improvements needed. A first goal is to integrate SL further into the curriculum and also compare retention and learning outcomes in courses integrating SL and those that do not. Although specific measurable feedback from students or grade outcomes from the assignment were not measured at this time, the instructors observed that this Pilot Project, was extremely beneficial in increasing student confidence for using SL in the future and enthusiasm for the assignment. A more detailed and integrated approach using SL earlier in the course, and in multiple assignments would be advantageous. However, further experimentation on selecting specific assignments and best practices are needed.

A second goal is to seek feedback from students using Second Life for class activities. Student feedback is essential for making improvements in the assignment and for understanding strategies that were helpful. Hepplestone et al. (2011) discusses the importance of student feedback regarding technology used within courses and particularly use that encourages engagement. While the teaching methods and features may be quite different with technology providing a 3D environment compared to more traditional technology, student involvement and feedback is equally essential. Instructors using any virtual world or classroom assignment based on SL should continually seek student comments. These environments change often, and content and directions will need to be updated and checked regularly. Using additional student feedback will be useful in implementing changes noted earlier in the chapter.

A third goal, is to use varied quantitative and qualitative methods for collecting detailed feedback from students through discussions, assignments and also through surveys using a more detailed research methodology. Using a more solid project framework that measures student skills and knowledge as well as perceptions about engagement and perceptions would be greatly beneficial. The authors plan to adopt a similar set of survey questions following Wang and Braman (2009) and Braman et al. (2011) with additional questions aimed at engagement and student perception of virtual worlds. A fourth goal is to create and maintain a more permanent space within Second Life that could be used for additional projects, virtual office hours and display of student and faculty projects. Having a fixed space to serve as a location online where students can meet virtually could help improve the project's visibility and encourage more collaboration. As the cost of maintaining a permanent space can be difficult, we intend to explore OpenSimulator as a solution. A space here can be maintained with more control and no cost due to the open source and multi-platform nature (OpenSimulator, 2019).

While these future directions pertaining to the Pilot Projects provides ideas for those who are interested in the next steps for the authors, there is a need to make specific directions for use of SL in higher education courses in general. To date, use of SL in higher education has been limited compared to other technology adoption. For those readers who have not yet implemented a virtual world tool, following are future directions suggested as an extension of this chapter.

1. Identify colleagues that are interested in identifying tools to engage students in active learning and begin the processing of exploring SL (or other virtual worlds), such as those described in this chapter, for the purpose of increasing instructor knowledge, skills, and self-efficacy with virtual world technology.
2. Meet regularly to share what has been learned individually; use journal articles and book chapters that describe the use of SL in college courses; develop a reference list. The list at the end of this chapter could be an initial resource.

3. Stay current in educational trends related to virtual worlds and aim to tailor 3D content to be relevant to the course using the technology.

4. Seek continuous student and faculty feedback from those involved in using virtual worlds in a course to enhance content and interaction. Including students in the process is helpful in increasing engagement and for making improvements.

CONCLUSION

In this chapter, the authors have discussed a Pilot Project using Second Life® in a diversity course to help foster interest and increase student engagement. The original pilot study as well as a secondary version was presented. As discussed in this chapter, there have been many changes in this technology over the years including how it can be used in an educational context. By using tools such as SL to increase student engagement, educators can improve their courses and teach materials in new ways. In this chapter we have provided key background on virtual worlds including how they can be used in higher education. Following, a discussion on a pilot project using SL in a diversity course at a community college where the goal was to increase student engagement and teach a new technology tool. This discussion included the project outline and key activities and student feedback. A discussion about difficulties, both in and out of the classroom was presented as well as a set of recommendations for educators interested in incorporating SL into their own classes. A set of future research goals were also presented as the authors move forward into more detailed research questions and collection of student feedback.

It is a sincere hope that more educators decide to use virtual worlds or similar platforms for educational purposes. SL can be an effective tool to excite and engage students in new ways and extend the capabilities of the traditional classroom setting. With the growing set of features and affordances of virtual worlds, they can become even more commonplace where educators are encouraged to experiment more. While much research is still needed to determine best practices, the literature suggests many positive aspects and potential learning outcomes using virtual worlds as a teaching resource for student engagement, critical thinking, verbal and written communication skill improvement

REFERENCES

Antonacci, D., DiBartolo, S., Edwards, N., Fritch, K., McMullen, B., & Murch-Shafer, R. (2008). *The power of virtual worlds in education: A second primer and resource for exploring the potential of virtual worlds to impact teaching and learning. ANGEL Learning ISLE Steering Committee.* Retrieved December 15, 2014, from http://www.angellearning.com/products/secondlife/downloads/The%20Power%20of%20Virtual%20Worlds%20in%20Education_0708.pdf

Arnone, M., Small, R., Chauncey, S., & McKenna, H. (2011). Curiosity, interest and engagement in technology-pervasive learning environments: A new research agenda. *Educational Technology Research and Development*, *59*(2), 181–198. doi:10.100711423-011-9190-9

Bainbridge, W. (2007). The scientific research potential of virtual worlds. *Science*, *317*(5837), 472–476. doi:10.1126cience.1146930 PMID:17656715

Bartle, R. (2003). *Designing virtual worlds*. New Riders Publishing.

Bélisle, J., & Bodur, H. (2010). Avatars as information: Perception of consumers based on their avatars in virtual worlds. *Psychology and Marketing*, *27*(8), 741–765. doi:10.1002/mar.20354

Bradshaw, D. (2009). *New practices in flexible learning: virtual worlds – real learning! Pedagogical Reflections*. Retrieved Jan. 30, 2009, from http://virtualworlds.flexiblelearning.net.au/reports/VWRL_pedagog_reflect.pdf

Braman, J., Dudley, A., Colt, K., Vincenti, V., & Wang, Y. (2011). Gaining insight into the application of second life in a computer course: Student's perspectives. *Proceedings of the 14th HCI International Conference on Online Communities and Social Computing*. 10.1007/978-3-642-21796-8_3

Braman, J., Meiselwitz, G., & Vincenti, G. (2013). Virtual worlds in the general education curriculum. *Proceedings of the Society for Information Technology & Teacher Education International Conference*, *2013*(1), 2692-2697.

Braman, J., & Yancy, B. (2017). Infusing Writing and Research in Technology Courses through Multi-User Virtual Environments. *Proceedings of the 11th International Multi-Conference on Society, Cybernetics and Informatics (IMSCI 2017)*.

Bray, D. A., & Konsynski, B. (2008). Virtual worlds, virtual economies, virtual institutions. *Proceedings of Virtual Worlds and New Realities Conference*.

Britain, S., & Liber, O. (2004). A framework for pedagogical evaluation of virtual learning environments. *JISC Technology Applications Program*, (41). Retrieved from https://hal.archives-ouvertes.fr/hal-00696234/document

Callaghan, N. (2016). Investigating the role of Minecraft in educational learning environments. *Educational Media International*, *53*(4), 244–260. doi:10.1080/09523987.2016.1254877

Carini, R., Kuh, G., & Klein, S. (2006). Student engagement and student learning: Testing the linkages. *Research in Higher Education*, *47*(1), 1–32. doi:10.100711162-005-8150-9

Cohen, A., & Brawer, F. (2003). *The American community college* (4th ed.). Jossey-Bass Publishing.

Csikszentmihalyi, M. (1990). *Flow: The psychology of optimal experience*. Harper Perennial Modern Classics.

De Freitas, S. (2008). *Serious virtual worlds: A scoping study*. Joint Information Systems Committee. Retrieved February 28th, 2020 from https://www.jisc.ac.uk/media/documents/publications/seriousvirtualworldsv1.pdf

Domínguez, A., Saenz-de-Navarrete, J., de-Marcos, L., Fernández-Sanz, L., Pagés, C., & Martínez-Herráiz, J. (2013). Gamifying learning experiences: Practical Implications and Outcomes. *Computer Education*, *63*, 380–392. doi:10.1016/j.compedu.2012.12.020

Dudley, A., & Braman, J. (2015). Using virtual worlds in ethical case studies: Evaluating computer students' perceptions. Proceedings from the 19th World Multi-conference on Systemics, Cybernetics and Informatics.

Duncan, I., Miller, A., & Jiang, S. (2012). A taxonomy of virtual world usage in education. *British Journal of Educational Technology, 43*(6). DOI: 10:1111/j.1467-8535.2011.01263.x

Dunleavy, M., Dede, C., & Mitchell, R. (2009). Affordances and limitations of immersive participatory augmented reality simulations for teaching and learning. *Journal of Science Education., 18*, 7–22.

Falloon, G. (2010). Using avatars and virtual and virtual environments in learning: What do they have to offer? *British Journal of Educational Technology, 41*(1), 108–122. doi:10.1111/j.1467-8535.2009.00991.x

Gabriel, K., & Flake, S. (2008). *Teaching unprepared students: strategies for promoting success and retention in higher education.* Stylus Publishing.

Gallagher, C. (2014). *Minecraft in the classroom: Ideas, inspiration, and student projects for teachers.* Peachpit Press.

Google, V. R. (2019). *Google Cardboard.* Retrieved https://arvr.google.com/cardboard/

Hepplestone, S., Holden, G., Irwin, B., Parkin, H., & Thorpe, L. (2011). Using technology to encourage student engagement with feedback: A literature review. *Research in Learning Technology, 19*(2), 117–127. doi:10.3402/rlt.v19i2.10347

High Fidelity. (2015). *High Fidelity Inc.* Retrieved May 1, 2015 from: https://highfidelity.com/

Holmberg, K., & Huvila, I. (2008). Learning together apart: Distance education in a virtual world. *First Monday, 13*(10). Advance online publication. doi:10.5210/fm.v13i10.2178

Kapp, K., & O'Driscoll, T. (2010). *Learning in 3D: adding a new dimension to enterprise learning and collaboration.* Pfeiffer.

KZero. (2014). *KZero Reports – Universe Charts.* Retrieved May1, 2015 from http:// kzero.co.uk/

Laureate Education (Producer). (2014). Anatomy of eLearning: Conceptual framework [interactive media]. Baltimore, MD: Author.

Lenhart, A., Purcell, K., Smith, A., & Zickuhr, K. (2010). *Social media & mobile internet use among teens and young adults.* Pew Research Center. Retrieved November 20 2014 http://67.192.40.213/~/media/Files/Reports/2010/PIP_Social_Media_and_Young_Adults_Report_Final_with_toplines.pdf

Lester, J. (2014). *Augmented mind- The evolution of learning tools from language to immersive reality.* Keynote speech presented at the 1st International Conference on e-Learning e-Education and Online Training, Bethesda, MD.

Linden Lab. (2015). *Mainland Pricing and Fees.* Retrieved July 10, 2015 from https://secondlife.com/land/pricing.php

Linden Lab. (2018). *Infographic - 15 Years of Second Life.* Retrieved December 10, 2019 from https://community.secondlife.com/blogs/entry/2349-celebrating-15-years-second-life-infographic-town-hall-video/

McArthur, V., Teather, R., & Stuerzlinger, W. (2010). Comparing 3D content creation interfaces in two virtual worlds: World of Warcraft and second life. *Journal of Gaming & Virtual Worlds., 2*(3), 239–258. doi:10.1386/jgvw.2.3.239_1

Meskó, B. (2008, August 17). Unique medical simulation in second life! *Science Roll Blog*. https://scienceroll.com/2008/08/17/unique-medical-simulation-in-second-life/

OpenSimulator. (2019). *What is Open Simulator?* Retrieved from http://opensimulator.org/wiki/Main_Page

Pew Internet. (2009). *Internet, broadband, and cell phone statistics*. Retrieved September 18, 2011 http://www.distributedworkplace.com/DW/Research/Internet%20broadband%20and%20cell%20phone%20statistics%20-%20Pew%20Internet%20Report%20Jan%202010.pdf

Pigatt, V., & Braman, J. (2018). *Promoting success and engagement in online programming courses.* Poster presented at the League of Innovations Conference, National Harbor, MD.

Putman, S., & Id-Deen, L. (2019). "I Can See It!" Math understanding through virtual reality. *Educational Leadership, 76*(5), 36.

Roehl, A., Reddy, S., & Shannon, G. (2013). The flipped classroom: An opportunity to engage millennial students through active learning strategies. *Journal of Family and Consumer Sciences, 105*(2), 44–49. doi:10.14307/JFCS105.2.12

Salmon, G. (2009). The future for (second) life and learning. *British Journal of Educational Technology, 40*(3), 526–538. doi:10.1111/j.1467-8535.2009.00967.x

Teoh, J. (2012). Pre-service teachers in second life: Potential of simulations. *Journal of Educational Technology Systems, 40*(4), 415–441. doi:10.2190/ET.40.4.g

The Schome Community. (2007). *The schome-NAGTY teen second life pilot final report: a summary of key findings and lessons learnt.* http://kn.open.ac.uk/public/getfile.cfm?documentfileid-11344

Vincenti, G., & Braman, J. (2010). *Teaching through multi-user virtual environments: Applying dynamic elements to the modern classroom.* Information Science Reference.

Vincenti, G., & Braman, J. (2011). *Multi-User virtual environments for the classroom: Practical approaches to teaching in virtual worlds.* IGI Global. doi:10.4018/978-1-60960-545-2

Wagner, M. (2008). Second life's popularity rests on breadth of activities. *Information Week*. https://www.informationweek.com/news/personal_tech/virtualworlds/showArticle.jhtml?articleID=210602197

Wang, Y., & Braman, J. (2009). Extending the classroom through second life. *Journal of Information Systems, 20*(2). 235-247.

Wang, Y., Dudley, A., Braman, J., & Vincenti, G. (2009). Simulating ethical dilemmas: Teaching ethics through immersive virtual environments. *Proceedings of the 12th IASTED International Conference on Computers and Advanced Technology in Education.*

Yee, N. (2006). The demographics, motivations, and derived experiences of users of massively multi-user online graphical environments. *Presence (Cambridge, Mass.), 15*(3), 309–329. doi:10.1162/pres.15.3.309

Zheng, B., Warschauer, M., Hwang, J. K., & Collins, P. (2014). Laptop use, interactive science software, and science learning among at-Risk students. *Journal of Science Education and Technology, 1*(5), 591–603. doi:10.100710956-014-9489-5

ADDITIONAL READING

Aldrich, C. (2009). *Learning online with games, simulations, and virtual worlds: strategies for online instruction*. John Wiley & Sons.

Balkin, J., & Noveck, S. (2006). *The state of play: law, games, and virtual worlds*. New York University Press.

Bartle, R. A. (2004). *Designing virtual worlds*. New Riders.

Boellstorff, T., Nardi, B., Pearce, C., & Taylor, T. L. (2012). *Ethnography and virtual worlds: A handbook of method*. Princeton University Press. doi:10.2307/j.cttq9s20

Castronova, E. (2007). *Exodus to the virtual world: how online fun is changing reality*. Palgrave Macmillan.

Corneliussen, H., & Rettberg, W. (2008). Digital culture, play, and identity: a world of warcraft reader. The MIT Press. Cambridge, Massachusetts. London, England.

Duncan, I., Miller, A., & Jiang, S. (2012). A taxonomy of virtual world usage in education. *British Journal of Educational Technology*, *43*(6), 949–964. doi:10.1111/j.1467-8535.2011.01263.x

Gregory, S., Lee, M. J., Dalgarno, B., & Tynan, B. (Eds.). (2016). *Learning in virtual worlds: Research and applications*. Athabasca University Press. doi:10.15215/aupress/9781771991339.01

Hai-Jew, S. (2010). Virtual immersive and 3D learning spaces: Emerging technologies and trends. *IGI Publishing, ISBN-10*, 1616928255.

Heaton, J. (2007). *Scripting recipes for second life*. Heaton Research Inc.

Hinrichs, R., & Wankel, C. (2012). *Engaging the avatar: new frontiers in immersive education*. Information Age Publishing.

Hodge, E., Collins, S., & Giordana, T. (2011). *The virtual worlds handbook: how to use second life and other 3D virtual environments*. Jones and Bartlett Publishers.

Jerald, J. (2015). *The VR book: Human-centered design for virtual reality*. Morgan & Claypool. doi:10.1145/2792790

Kapp, K., & O'Driscoll, T. (2010). *Learning in 3D: adding a new dimension to enterprise learning and collaboration*. Pfeiffer.

Lakkaraju, K., Sukthankar, G., & Wigand, R. T. (Eds.). (2018). *Social Interactions in Virtual Worlds: An Interdisciplinary Perspective*. Cambridge University Press. doi:10.1017/9781316422823

Martinelli, R. J., Waddell, J. M., & Rahschulte, T. J. (2017). *Projects without boundaries: Successfully leading teams and managing projects in a virtual world*. John Wiley & Sons.

Nelson, B., & Erlandson, B. (2012). *Design for learning in virtual worlds: Interdisciplinary Approaches to Educational Technology*. Routledge. doi:10.4324/9780203836378

Turkle, S. (1995). *Life on the screen: identity in the age of the internet*. Simon & Schuster Paperbacks.

Vincenti, G., & Braman, J. (2010). *Teaching through multi-user virtual environments: applying dynamic elements to the modern classroom.* Information Science Reference.

Vincenti, G., & Braman, J. (2011). *Multi-user virtual environments for the classroom: practical approaches to teaching in virtual worlds.* IGI Global., doi:10.4018/978-1-60960-545-2

Wankel, C., & Kingsley, J. (2009). *Higher education in virtual worlds: teaching and learning in second life. International Perspectives on Education and Society.* Emerald Group Publishing.

Wankel, C., & Malleck, S. (2009). *Emerging ethical issues of life in virtual worlds.* Information Age Publishing.

KEY TERMS AND DEFINITIONS

Active Worlds: Is an online 3D world and social space initially released in 1995. Similar to other online worlds, user can create and view 3D content, chat and explore. The main website is https://www.activeworlds.com/.

Avatar: A 3D representation of a user within a virtual world. Avatars can take many shapes and forms such as a humanoid representation, animal, shape, or other figure which allows the use to interact within the world and with other users.

Educational Game: A game in which the main goal is a specific learning outcome. Educational games are often used to increase student engagement.

Educational Space: A web-based, 3D or virtual representation of a classroom or learning area. In relation to virtual worlds, an educational space is often related to the 3D area used for learning which can be represented in a myriad of ways.

IMVU: Founded in 2004, IMVU is an online 3D virtual world and social networking platform. In 2014 there were an estimated four million active users. The main website is https://secure.imvu.com/.

Minecraft: Is a 3D "blocks" based world that can be used as a game, a creative space or in a multi-player mode with other users. The program can be run on multiple device types offline, or setup to run on a server for other users to connect.

Multi-User Virtual Environment: Also known as a MUVE. This term can be used to describe a virtual world that can be used for a collaborative purpose where users can interact in real-time.

OpenSimulator: An open source 3D virtual world available on many platforms which is similar to the Second Life virtual world.

Second Life®: A popular internet-based 3D world created by Linden Labs.

Script: A set of instructions or a small program designed to carry out a specific function or task. In Second Life the Linden Scripting Language is used (LSL) to make objects interactive.

Social Networking Site (SNS): A website that is aimed at social interaction that often includes a public profile, ability to post user generated content and also to connect to other users.

Student Engagement: Increasing student interest, focus and, or motivation for a particular learning activity.

Twinity: Is an online 3D virtual world and social platform originally released in 2008 and considered by some to be a mirror world. The main website is http://www.twinity.com.

Virtual Reality: A term that can refer to a virtual representation of a scene or reality simulation in 3D. Virtual Reality can be viewed on a traditional display or using immersive VR goggles.

Virtual World: A virtual world often refers to an internet-based 3D or 2 ½ D environment where users can interact within the world or with other users through an avatar. Often virtual worlds are persistent environments where a large number of users can participate.

This research was previously published in Current and Prospective Applications of Virtual Reality in Higher Education; pages 170-193, copyright year 2021 by Information Science Reference (an imprint of IGI Global).

Chapter 9

Stepping Out of the Classroom:
Anticipated User Experiences of Web-based Mirror World Like Virtual Campus

Minna Pakanen

Socio-Technical Design, Department of Engineering, Aarhus University, Aarhus, Denmark

Paula Alavesa

Center for Ubiquitous Computing, University of Oulu, Oulu, Finland

Leena Arhippainen

Interact Research Group, University of Oulu, Oulu, Finland

Timo Ojala

Center for Ubiquitous Computing, University of Oulu, Oulu, Finland

ABSTRACT

While three-dimensional virtual learning environments have attracted plenty of research interest, mirror-world-like virtual campuses have been used mainly for virtual tours, promotions, or for simulation purposes. In this article, the authors investigate the use of geographically accurate mirror-world-like virtual campus models as an interactive learning environment. The initial prototype of the virtual campus covers about 2,300 m^2 of a university campus and contains basic pedagogical, communicational, and content creation functionalities. A qualitative study with 14 participants explored their anticipated user experiences as well as their needs for the services and functionalities of the virtual campus. The findings suggest that a more profound link of reality and virtuality than just mirroring physical spaces in the virtual realm is needed. A hybrid reality approach is required to foster social community building and collaboration, 3D space design, and service integration. Finally, stepping out of the classroom introduces privacy issues that should be considered carefully.

DOI: 10.4018/978-1-6684-7597-3.ch009

INTRODUCTION

The boom of e-learning and especially 3D Virtual Learning Environments (3DVLEs) began with the digital age. It coincided with the technological advances that revolutionized other fields of human living in past decades. As networked computers and their capabilities have shaped the basic modalities and affordances of writing and passing knowledge, their influence on education has been unavoidable (Beetham & Sharpe, 2013). During the past two decades, the rise of 3DVLEs has been witnessed. Ubiquitous high-speed networking, powerful personal computers, and 3D web technologies have made 3DVLEs more accessible, as they can be used with web browsers on low-cost personal computers (Chittaro & Ranon, 2007). 3DVLEs are also of interest to educators and educational institutions as they afford rich learner engagement by allowing the exploration, construction, and manipulation of virtual objects, structures, and metaphorical or abstract depictions of ideas (Dalgarno & Lee, 2010). Another important property of 3DVLEs is their ability to convey the feeling of being there (Heeter, 1992); the stronger this feeling of presence is, the more meaningful experiences are gained (De Lucia, Francese, Passero, & Tortora, 2009). The full potential created by the interplay between the physical reality and the affordances of the virtual realm has not been realized in existing 3DVLEs. While a substantial amount of studies has been conducted with 3DVLEs in the context of small class rooms and group work, there is still lack of understanding of for what purposes such virtual spaces are designed for (Minocha & Reeves, 2010; Reisoğlu, Topu, R. Yılmaz, T.K. Yılmaz, & Göktaş, 2017). Further, prior research has not addressed the design of 3DVLEs as mirror worlds of corresponding large real-word indoor spaces. Also, the hybrid reality (De Souza e Silva & Delacruz, 2006) type of linking of services in university level 3DVLEs has not been thoroughly investigated. To fill this knowledge gap, an anticipated user experience (AUX) study with an initial virtual campus model built as an accurate mirror world of the main campus of the University of Oulu (Figure 1) is conducted. In virtual campus an existing commercial 3DVLE, the Finpeda Virtual Space (FVS) (Finpeda, n.d.), is used for providing pedagogical content, communication means, and avatars. FVS was chosen because it is a commercial product that has been used and evaluated in different pedagogical contexts, such as in primary school (Arhippainen, Pakanen, Hickey, & Mattila 2011) and vocational education (Mattila, Krajnak, Arhippainen, & Brauer, 2012). The purpose of this study was to guide the subsequent design of the virtual campus by answering to two research questions:

1. How do users experience the initial web-based mirror world like hybrid reality linking the virtual campus?
2. What are the needs of students, teachers, researchers and staff members for the design, services and functionalities of the hybrid reality linking the virtual campus?

This paper is organized as follows. First, related work on 3DVLEs and the authors' perspective on them serving as mirror worlds are described. Next, the creation of the initial version of the virtual campus used in the study and the commercial 3DVLE platform are presented. Then, the AUX study with 14 participants and its qualitative findings are reported. Finally, the findings are discussed with conclusions.

Figure 1. AUX study in progress in Virtual Campus model of University of Oulu

BACKGROUND

Collaborative virtual environments (CVEs) have been subject to extensive research since the 1990s (Benford et al., 1997). CVEs have six features that are common in all of them: shared space, graphical user interface, immediacy, interactivity, persistence, and socialization/community (Chen, Huang, & Lin, 2009). A subcategory of CVEs, relevant to this study, is 3D virtual learning environments (3DVLEs) (Zuiker, 2012) that have also been named Computer Supported Collaborative Learning (CSCL) environments (Sutcliffe & Alrayes, 2012). The latter solution already has intrinsic functionality for social construction, yet these solutions have been found somewhat unsuitable for educational context (Sutcliffe & Alrayes, 2012). 3DVLEs have been successfully used for teaching several subjects at university level ranging from under graduate business computing to object modelling courses (Dickey, 2005) as well as graduate interdisciplinary communication course (Jarmon, Traphagan, Mayrath, & Trivedi, 2009).

3D VIRTUAL LEARNING ENVIRONMENTS

3DVLEs have been built both on top of existing game engines (Finpeda, n.d.) and collaborative virtual environments (Maiberg, 2016). One of the most popular, large-scale fictional social virtual worlds is Second Life (SL) (Linden Research Inc., n.d.) with approximately 600,000 monthly users in May 2017 (Lee, 2016). Though SL was originally designed for social interaction, it has been further used as an educational platform for several reasons: it is an existing multi-user platform, as well as easy, and cost-effective solution for setting up a collaborative learning environment (De Lucia et al., 2009). Possibly because of that, SL has been used in most (99/167) of prior 3DVLE studies (Reisoğlu et al., 2017). Next most popular, even though substantially less so (21/167) is Active Worlds (AW) (Reisoğlu et al., 2017).

It contains a sub-world titled *A world for learning* (n.d.) that is dedicated solely for learning purposes. AW have been used for experiential spatially distant learning and found as an effective medium as it provides user-extensible world building (e.g., allows learner to create, make decisions, solve problems, and reflect) that fosters a sense of place, presence, and community as well as enhance student engagement and learning (Dickey 2005). Both SL and AW are perceived to support learning and pedagogic needs and therefore they are more interesting for educational purposes (Dalgarno & Lee, 2010). Other platforms used at least in more than one study include Open-Sim, Open wonderland, and World of Warcraft (Reisoğlu et al., 2017).

According to Jarmon et al. (2009) SL has been used in wide range of educational activities offering core content in subjects such as cultural anthropology, Spanish, English, Japanese culture, history, literature, library science, professional development, music, educational informatics, algebra, human reproduction, ecology, genetics, toxicology, and training for emergency personnel. SL has been found suitable for experiential learning as it allows students to work on a project while exploring and communicating across geographic boundaries (Jarmon et al., 2009). Even though SL has features supporting its use for educational purposes, prior research has also indicated limitations. For example, Sutcliffe and Alrayes (2012) noted that SL is not a virtual world tailored for CSCL purposes, but a generic collaborative technology platform. Therefore, they recommended that considerable design and configuration should be done to adapt it for educational purposes (Sutcliffe & Alrayes, 2012). Further, Petrakou (2010) pointed out that a virtual world is not an adequate learning environment on its own as it is not possible to add course information within the 3D environments without interrupting its graphically and socially rich context. Therefore, additional information spaces are needed for displaying course information (Petrakou, 2010). SL is also perceived by students as more of a gaming platform than a learning environment (Sutcliffe & Alrayes, 2012).

Also, more pedagogically driven 3DVLEs have been developed, for example, a Collaborative Learning Environment with Virtual Reality (CLEV-R) (Monahan, McArdle, & Bertolotto, 2008), Designing Digitally Inc. (n.d.), and FVS (Finpeda, n.d.). All environments have been developed from a pedagogical point of view with grounding in pedagogical practices. They have built-in support for collaboration and communication between the students in forms of chat, sharing, and linking documents inside the 3DVLE which supports collaborative and cooperative learning (Dickey, 2005). These can also be extended with educational simulations and serious games. As suggested by Fokides (2017) game-like features are essential in 3DVLEs, as they allow constructivist learning (e.g., to learn by doing) (Dickey, 2015). However, many of these environments are small-scale and designed for simple group work scenarios, such as CLEV-R (Monahan et al., 2008), FVS (Finpeda, n.d.), and Designing Digitally Inc. (n.d.). As Prasolova-Førland (2008) pointed out, these 3DVLEs are designed for supporting established groups rather than fluid communities more common in university campuses. Further, current trends in building and repurposing campuses support designing multipurpose environments, where the needs of not just groups but individual learners can be met in regards of privacy and functionality (Mattila & Silander, 2015; O'Neill, 2013). In addition, due to their closed commercial nature, any additional functionalities need to be acquired from the companies.

DESIGN OF 3DVLES

According to Wahlstedt, Pekkola, and Niemelä (2008) when a space becomes meaningful for people through social interaction and familiarity with the space, it becomes a place where people are more likely to learn. In addition, if this learning space is social, it can attract more users (Krejns, 2004). Therefore, the design of e-learning environments should be a combination of technologies, tools, and media for social purposes (Wahlstedt et al., 2008). The design of current 3DVLEs can vary from imaginary fantasy worlds (Arhippainen et al., 2011) to replication of a real university (Designing Digitally Inc., 2011). Minocha and Reeves (2010) suggested considering visual realism in the design of a 3DVLE, because it provides familiarity and comfort to users new to 3DVLEs. Also, aesthetical design of a virtual space can make the space more engaging for students (Minocha & Reeves, 2010). According to Prasolova-Førland (2008), the important building blocks of 3DVLEs are those that rise from the real-environment related metaphors (e.g., the social, aesthetic, and semantic qualities of the real-world). However, she does not present any conclusive results on what the most significant metaphors for 3DVLEs should be. Prior research suggests that similar private and public spaces as well as objects in physical learning environments should also appear in 3DVLE as they give familiarity to the pupils (Arhippainen et al., 2011). In addition to learning purposes, realistic virtual campuses are used for giving virtual tours to promote universities to students and guests (Designing Digitally Inc., n.d. & 2011). 3DVLEs can also be used for simulations (Sun, Wan, & Yu, 2016) where the visual quality of the 3D model becomes more important. Prior research has shown that the design and evaluation of 3DVLEs is not yet rigorously understood (Minocha & Reeves, 2010). Also, Reisoğlu et al. (2017) point out that there are only a few studies exploring why 3D learning environments are designed in the first place. According to the authors' knowledge, prior AUX studies have not been conducted to inform the design of web-based 3DVLE virtual campuses as a mirror world of the corresponding physical campus.

3D VIRTUAL ENVIRONMENT AS MIRROR WORLD

A realistic looking, detailed, and immersive large-scale 3D virtual space can be regarded as a mirror world of the corresponding real-world physical space (Gelernter, 1991). In order to be able to create a realistic mirror world, all real-world structures should be presented in it with as high geographical accuracy as possible (Roush, 2007).

Mirror worlds are not just realistic virtual models of real places viewed and used for data collection purposes, but they are supposed to facilitate collaboration by bringing people together (Leigh & Brown, 2008). However, in their most basic form mirror worlds have no direct interaction with the real-world counterpart after which they are modeled. Various approaches portray the coupling between real environments (reality) and virtual worlds (virtuality). For example, De Souza e Silva & Delacruz (2006) define hybrid reality as the space that is created when one or more realities are blended by the social interaction and communication across those realities. In turn, Lifton et al. (2009) defined dual reality as something: "where both real and virtual worlds are complete unto themselves, but also enhanced by the ability to mutually reflect, influence, and merge by means of sensor/actuator networks deeply embedded in everyday environments." Further, Hoshi, Pesola, Waterworth, and Waterworth (2009) defined blended reality as an interactive mixed-reality environment where the physical and the virtual are combined in the service of interaction goals and communication environment. Hybrid reality logic by De Souza e Silva and Delacruz (2006) describes the complexity of the interplay between realities in a holistic manner. The hybrid reality simply is and can be described and observed through real-world environment and virtual world and two-way interactions that shape and combine these realities (De Souza e Silva & Delacruz, 2006).

Well-known examples of mirror worlds are Google Earth and Microsoft Visual Earth that have proven very useful for a wide range of applications (Roush, 2007). They have enabled developing mirror worlds of university campuses such as Northeastern University (Mellen, 2010) to different use purposes. For example, a 3D mirror world of the university campuses has been created for a building escape training simulation purposes (Sun et al., 2016; Mattila & Silander, 2015). In Tallinn University of Technology, Estonia, a part of a large campus has been modelled specifically for the purpose of serving as a platform for virtual reality experimentations (Kose, Petlenkov, Tepljakov, & Vassiljeva, 2017). It is quite obvious that mirror world like virtual campuses are useful for simulations and guidance applications, but their exploitation as 3DVLEs is still an open question. 3DVLE specific theories tend to emphasize the learning component, therefore the related metaphors and resulting affordances (Prasolova-Førland, 2008) designed into the 3DVLEs can be too concise to be adapted to 3DVLEs that expand outside the classroom.

The Virtual Campus

The overarching goal for building a mirror world version of the real-world campus is to have a platform for visualizations and applications. A virtual campus is developed atop an open source platform so that it encourages practitioners from all fields to developing contents in it. The special interest of a virtual campus lies in the unique characteristics of the very wide indoor space, which allows developing specific applications in education, emergency simulation/training, orientation, and research. The aim is to combine it to be part of the larger outdoor area, Virtual City of Oulu, Finland, to be able to study hybrid reality linking of services in both indoor and outdoor contexts.

3D Model Creation of the Real University Campus

In this study, the 3D model of the main lobby area of the campus (Figure 2) is used. It corresponds to about 9 percent of the currently modelled area (2300 m^2) along the 1.1 kilometers long main corridor (Figures 2 & 3), which in turn is a fraction of the full floor area of the campus. The main lobby is a social and educational hotspot with two cafes, a paper shop, group workspaces and entrances to the four largest lecture halls on campus. Due to the initial nature of the virtual campus model, it does not contain all the interior design details, such as furniture, plants, paintings, etc. In addition, large corridor doors that do not exist in the physical campus, were modeled in it to prevent user study participants from seeing or wandering to the unfinished parts of the model. The 3D model is built on top of blueprints with 3DS Max and Blender. The virtual campus prototype is published on the web at (Adminotech, n.d.; Alavesa et al., 2017; Pakanen et al., 2018) using Meshmoon Web Rocket (n.d.) a commercial version of the realXtend open source platform for building collaborative 3D virtual spaces (Alatalo, 2011).

Figure 2. Entrance to lecture hall 3: (a) a photograph of the physical campus; (b) a screenshot from the virtual campus

(A)   (B)

Figure 3. The main lobby (b) used in this study is approximately 9 percent of the virtual campus (a)

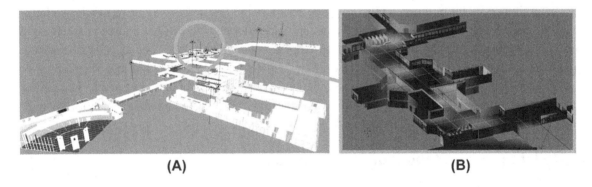

(A)   (B)

Pedagogical Platform

The virtual campus model was furnished with a commercial pedagogical platform, to provide interaction, communication, and content creation functionalities. The commercial realXtend (Alatalo, 2011) based Finpeda Virtual Space (Finpeda, n.d.) platform was selected, because it provides avatars, pedagogical content, and communication functions (Figure 1). For instance, FVS contains male and female avatar that can walk and fly, and are controlled with arrow and WASD keys. The avatar can also sit on a chair and has a laser pointer for showing to other users where they should focus their attention to. FVS also provides basic communication functionalities in form of text chat, voice, and video call. Users can create virtual (sub)spaces and content, such as documents, photos, furnishings, links, and text into them. Any user created content is visible and editable to all users of the space. (Finpeda, n.d.)

AUX STUDY

Anticipated User Experience (AUX) is a particular temporal dimension of the user experience. Prior research has acknowledged that user can have experiences also before the actual use situation (ISO 9241-210, 2010; Roto, Law, Vermeeren, & Hoonhout, 2011; Pakanen, 2015). According to Roto et al. (2011) AUX can happen before the first use, during and after the use, and over time, as a person may imagine using the product during all before mentioned time spans. McCarthy and Wright (2004) describe anticipation to happen all the time and it suggests something before the actual experience takes place. According to Pakanen (2015), AUX means "experiences, needs, and wishes that result from anticipated interaction with the concept of a product before the actual product exists." Pakanen (2015) suggest that it is easier for non-professional participants to imagine their futures with a technology with a visual representation of the final solution. Therefore, authors decided to conduct an AUX study with a initial version of the virtual campus model and with functionalities provided by the FVS platform, to obtain rich feedback before committing a plenty of resources and time into a full-blown implementation of the complete virtual campus. The aim of the AUX study was 1) to investigate user experiences of initial web-based mirror world like hybrid reality linking in the virtual campus of University of Oulu and 2) to investigate the needs of the users regarding the design, services and functionalities of the virtual campus.

Evaluation Setting

To gather as rich qualitative data as possible, the AUX evaluation was conducted in seven pairs in semi-controlled condition. In contrast to individual evaluation, pair evaluation can provide more rich feedback as the participants can explore and discuss the features together as well as it allows testing real social interaction in the virtual campus model. Due to the hybrid reality focus of the study a hybrid reality evaluation (HRE) setting was designed for the study, where participants actions were observed both in the physical evaluation room and the virtual campus (Figure 4). Facilitator (position 1) interviewed participants and joined them in the virtual campus in task 3 with her avatar (position 2). Two observers in evaluation room concentrated each on one participant's behavior and took notes. In addition, a third observer was in the virtual campus model observing the behavior of the participants' avatars. Her avatar was not visible to participants so that she could observe their avatars' behavior in an unobtrusive manner. Evaluation was video recorded both in reality and in the virtual campus. Video camera in the physical evaluation room was located between the participants, recording both laptop screens as well as all the activities of the participants (Figure 5). Both participants were given 15-inch Asus G501J game laptop equipped with a wired mouse. Participants were encouraged to talk aloud while conducting tasks and a semi-structured interview supplemented with video and audio recordings captured were the main data collection means. Evaluation sessions lasted from 57 to 91 minutes, with a mean duration being 74 minutes. Each participant was rewarded with a cinema ticket worth approximately 10 euros (Figure 4).

Figure 4. Hybrid reality evaluation setting

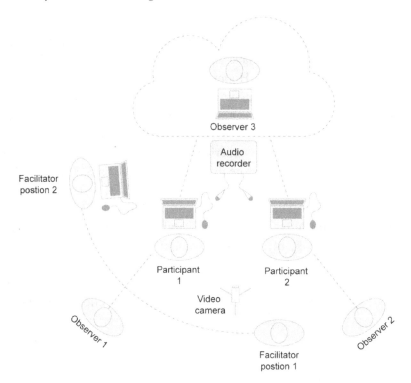

Figure 5. Participants constructing their design in self-expression task while on computer screen their (offline) avatars are still in the virtual campus after the earlier task

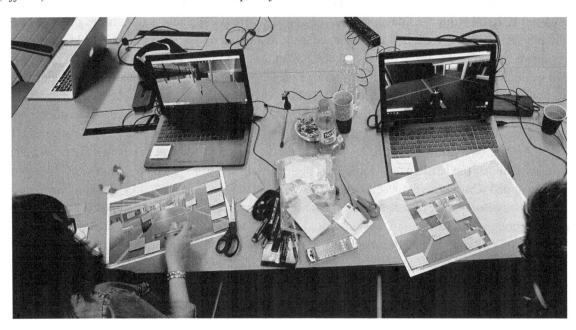

Procedure

The study contained three tasks: familiarization and use of the initial virtual campus (T1), a self-expression task (T2), and a walkthrough of the visually richer virtual campus (T3).

T1: Familiarization and use of the initial virtual campus. Participants were given laptop computers and instructed to sign in with predefined email accounts with given credentials. Participants found an email form their mailbox which contained the URL of the virtual campus model. When both participants were in the virtual campus, facilitator asked participants to comment on their first perceptions of it. Then they were asked to start exploring the virtual campus. If necessary, they were instructed how to move around in the model with keys (WASD or arrow keys). The facilitator interviewed participants while they were moving around in the virtual campus.

T2: Self-expression task. Participants were asked to prompt their needs and ideas for the virtual campus on given Self-Expression Templates (SET) (Arhippainen & Pakanen, 2013). The template was an A3-sized printout of an existing 3D scene from the virtual campus model (Figure 5). In addition, participants were given various materials such as post-it notes, colored pens, and cutouts of avatar figures to construct their idea on the template. Participants were asked to explain their designs after they were finished.

T3: Virtual walkthrough of the visually richer virtual campus. The initial version of the virtual campus lacked all the interior design details. Therefore, researcher created a visually richer version of the virtual campus that contained furnishings, paintings, example of virtual evaluation of café interior design, virtual lecture adds, and video screens (Figure 1). The participants were then asked to enter this second version of the virtual campus with the facilitator in this case being there with them. Facilitator walked with her avatar in certain predefined locations and asked the participants to join her avatar to these locations (e.g., cafeteria, in front of campus shop, janitors' desk, lecture hall) and she then interviewed participants about the contents (e.g., timetables, advertisements, videos, furniture, Google documents) in those locations.

Participants

Braun and Clarke (2013) suggest that for a medium sized research project the number of interviews can be set between 10-20, therefore, 14 participants were requited through convenience sampling from the University of Oulu. As the aim was to get participants from teaching/research staff and campus mainte-nance staff as well as current and earlier students, the best possible representative sample (e.g. all user groups represented with equal distribution of staff members and students), participants were recruited through personnel and student mailing lists as well as PATIO online community (Haukipuro, 2019). The participants' ages varied from 22 to 55 with a mean of 35. Nine of the participants were male. Seven of the participants were research or teaching staff with research and teaching fields of Information Possessing Science, Computer Science, and Industrial Engineering and Management. Six of the participants were students from the following study majors: Information Research, Architecture, Economics, and Computer Science. One participant was a staff member. Most of the participants (10/14) had prior experience of 3D movies and games. Eight participants further had experience with some 3D modeling software and Oculus Rift (Facebook Technologies LLC, n.d.). Virtual worlds were familiar to five participants. The user study pairs did not know each other in advance.

Data Analysis

The study resulted in total of 435 minutes of video and audio recordings from the physical evaluation room of which approximately 2/3 contained interview responses of the participants. The video and audio data were transcribed. Data analysis was initiated by watching videos from which important moments in interaction were marked down for closed analysis. Important moments were when a participant did some unexpected interaction with her/his avatar (e.g., back and forth movement, standing for long time in one position, testing interactive contents) or when a participant started to comment something in more detail (e.g., interaction issues, mismatch with reality and virtuality, interaction with another user's avatar). The data analysis followed general qualitative coding principles where the idea of the coding is to identify topics for sorting and synthesizing the research material for writing the results (Charmaz, 2008). The transcribed data was first read and then annotated by using categorization of the content under emerging themes: social interaction, services, 3D space design, wayfinding, privacy, and FVS related issues: usability/ UX, avatar appearance and interaction, and functions. Participants' SET collages were analyzed by collecting participants needs for services, 3D spaces, and functionalities. These identified topics were then used for categorizing the data until saturation was reached, (e.g., no new themes rose from the data). The final four main themes were identified as: virtual campus as a hybrid reality social community, the virtual campus as a hybrid reality service platform, the virtual campus 3D spaces to support hybrid reality linking, and Privacy Issues with the virtual campus. Corresponding results are reported in the following sections.

RESULTS

Virtual Campus as a Hybrid Reality Social Community

At the time of the study, the University had three separate physical campuses dispersed around the city. The main campus is very large, sprawling along the 1.1 kilometer main hallway. The three separate campuses and the large main campus were seen as the cause for people mostly meeting only students from the same faculty. Therefore, the participants wished that the virtual campus could unite people better and serve as a link between different campuses and faculties. As one participant stated: "[It could bring] all faculties under the same roof" (P8/M, Student). Participants thought that the virtual campus would provide a nice place for meeting their friends and colleagues, but more importantly and not surprisingly, it would enable meeting people easier than in reality, because the threshold for initiating chat with unfamiliar people in virtual environment was perceived to be lower than in reality. As one participant stated: "This is primarily a social community, you can see other people here and get to know new people through this…as university is so shattered…this could try to bring people together, especially people with same interests." (P7/F, Student).

The participants also wanted to link reality with virtuality to enhance social communication. They aspired being able to see in the virtual campus where their friends, colleagues, and bosses are moving currently in reality. As one participant stated: "It would be cool if you could see your boss [in] here, you could then escape him [in reality]…ha ha" (P3/M, Researcher/ Teacher). Another stated: "Could it be showed in here where your friends are in reality…with a shadow or something like that" (P14/M, Researcher/ Teacher). For allowing more communication means within the virtual campus, participants wanted to integrate university emails, and their private social media and communication services, such as Facebook and Skype in it.

All participants notified that there were not any other users except their evaluation pair in the virtual campus during the evaluation. As one participant stated: "It is clear, but it is missing humanity as a real-world campus is a hectic place with all the people…after all it's people who makes this place" (P4/F, Staff member). Another participant was even so excited to see her pair's avatar approaching and yelled: "Yeah, one person is approaching me!" (P7/F, Student). All participants wished that there would be more users at the virtual campus. To attract more people, participants suggested that place should contain collective memories from the real-world campus. As one participant suggested: "People spend here five to six years of their life in [campus] of which a lot of memories and stories will be cumulated which could be collected [in here] …otherwise those will be lost forever…you could attach old photos and stories of the places where we used to sit…which could contain also links to people or their Facebook profiles" (P3/M, Researcher/ Teacher).

Avatar Appearance

The number of avatars in an initial version of the virtual campus was limited to two, a female and a male. Unsurprisingly, this was perceived to be too few, because two female participants had to use the same avatar. In addition, in this kind of realistic representation of an authentic physical space it is important to have realistic looking or identifiable representations of students and staff members. For example, one participant explained her SET illustration: "I would prefer more like Facebook kind of way to identify people, using real names, at least it would make it easier to connect with people you already know" (P7/F, Student). Another participant stated: "If you could make the avatar to represent yourself…It would be somehow more intriguing and would make this more real…now this is more like just playing around here." (P6/M, Researcher/ Teacher). For some participants, it was essential to have also real images [profile pictures] from the internal mail service: "…when you are in the virtual lecture, if it [avatar] looks like the person [user], then you can be sure that it is really him/her and not just some research assistant." (P5/F, Researcher/ Teacher).

Interaction and Usability Issues with Avatars

The perceived utility of the virtual campus was questioned because of its large size and perceived shortcomings in the interaction. One participant explained: "Would I really want to start moving here back and forth because it is so clumsy and takes so much time" (P11/F, Researcher/ Teacher). Another participant was not familiar with 3D VEs and was not able to move even by walking, although she had been instructed at the beginning. The problem was that she did not press continuously the arrow key, so her avatar was bouncing slowly forward. She also stood long times in same position. After the use, she stated: "By now, I would have taken care of my business many times by running in the real-world campus...ha ha" (P4/F, Staff member). Not surprisingly, walking was perceived to be too slow for moving in such a large indoor place, as described by one participant: "If you do not want to walk around searching for things in reality, then why would you want to do it in virtual campus?" (P10/M, Student). Also, other FVS avatar actions (e.g., flying, sitting down, and laser pointers) were perceived to be childish, funny, gamified, and relate more to Sims or Habbo Hotel (Sulake Corporation Oy, n.d.) than serious mirror world like virtual campus. As one participant stated when trying flying: "Ha ha… you can be a superhero!...but seriously, how you can take this system into more serious context...is it a bit wrong if all the students in virtual lectures would start flying around" (P7/F, Student). Even though the flying action was perceived to be a fast way to move from place to another, in indoors it did not work that well, because participants were constantly flying through the walls and roofs. Instead of flying, participants suggested teleportation through search engine or a 2D minimap based user interface for travelling across the 3D campus, because it would be faster, better, and more usable choice. As one participant stated: "Shortcuts for your places... and if you click your friends face [profile picture], it teleports to him" (P6/M, Researcher/ Teacher). Also, as in the physical campus janitors are using kick scooters, participants suggested that those would be more context depended choices for faster movement.

Participants also wished that their avatar could indicate to other users what the person is currently doing, as in the current version an avatar is just standing idle when the user is for example adding or editing a document. As one participant suggested: "It could give some kind of visual indication above the avatar, indicating what the user is doing" (P6/M, Researcher/ Teacher).

Virtual Campus as a Hybrid Reality Service Platform

Participants suggested that it would nice to combine all the services and systems into one comprehensive platform such as the virtual campus. As one participant expressed: "Only one world, where all the services are integrated, now you need to Google things separately." (P7/F, Student). The participants perceived that the mirror world 3D space would ease finding documents. For example, instead of using a lot of time in finding study related forms from the hierarchical layers of webpage or Google them, participants could just go to the same location in virtual campus as student services is situated in reality and initiate a chat with person working there or use some search engine for finding the right form. The interaction with services was expected to be smooth and launch automatically when the user is in proximity. For example, one participant described: "When an event is about to begin or is taking place, an information sign [of an event] could pop-up when a user [an avatar] is approaching the event location" (P10/M, Student). In addition, UI design should allow customizing needed services on UI layer atop of 3D VE on which the user can select services, apps, and features that she/he needs (see Figure 5). Also, it was notified that the system should allow storing these personal UI layouts.

Virtual lectures were seen as the most important education related service that participants would like to have in the virtual campus. Students perceived virtual lectures as positive, as they would be accessible from remote locations and allow them to take part in different lectures: "MIT technical university has all the lectures in the internet, similarly University of Oulu could provide this virtual learning space where people could come to browse and taking lectures" (P10/M, Student). However, teachers were concerned about how much more complicated and time consuming would it be to create lectures in the 3D space and how well university's current learning systems would support virtual lectures.

The participants commented that 3D virtual space would be a good place for creating group assignment documents as people were perceived to be more physically present, as one participants stated: "This is more personal and presence of other people can be sensed better than in, for example, Google Docs, where people do editing whenever they will, in here people would gather to edit document together" (P1/M, Student).

Virtual Campus as a Platform for Guiding and Virtual Tours

Unsurprisingly, participants wanted to use the virtual campus as a navigation platform for finding locations in the complex multilayered real-world campus. The mirror world aspect of the campus model was perceived to be extremely handy for this: "This realism eases navigation when you have been in the physical campus…as things are located in familiar places" (P9/M, Student). The participants wanted also to check the route from virtual campus before walking there in real-life or check from it when they got lost. As one participant stated: "Quite often you imagine that you know where the place is, and you just go there, and then it is not there, then you could use this to check where it is then" (P11/F, Researcher/ Teacher).

The participants suggested presenting navigation routes as visual footprints on floors (Figure 6) or as videos. One participant had an idea for video guidance: "If you type the room number here, the guy [avatar] would walk the path there and would guide you how to get there before you go wandering in there in reality" (P11/F, Researcher/ Teacher). One participant also reflected that no artificial service can substitute real human contact: "We have tried to guide people to places with signs and other information, but people do not read them, somehow human is the most essential in guiding…this guy [avatar] then could guide… to the desired place and help in navigation problems" (P4/F, Staff member). Janitors were seen important in helping wayfinding and general source of information, therefore it was suggested that there should be a live chat connection with them in janitors' desk.

Figure 6. Participant's (P14/M, Researcher/ Teacher) illustration on how footprints could be used for wayfinding

The participants suggested that the virtual campus could be used also for promotion and planning. For example, when new students apply to the university, they could go to the virtual campus to check places in advance (e.g., virtual tours). "It would be good if high school students could use this for getting to know the place and deciding whether they would be interested in coming to study here" (P7/F, Student). Also, as the University hosts special events such as employment fairs and exhibitions comprising of a large number of booths, the virtual campus model could be used for planning which booths to visit during the actual event.

Virtual Campus 3D Spaces to Support Hybrid Reality Linking

In general, the mirror world version of a physical campus was perceived to be nicely modeled and as accurate: "This has been created realistically driven...quite precisely done, nothing spots in to my eye" (P10/M). However, some missing details caught peoples' attention and the initial version of the virtual campus space was perceived to be sterile, empty, dead, and plain. As one participant commented: "Just like after renovation...It is stripped out of all the experiences, people, sunlight, and temporal phenomenon" (ID7/F, Student). The participants suggested that authentic feeling could be created with small things such as, jackets in coat racks, signs, notice boards, furniture, plants, and flowers to make it more verdant and cozier. However, this should not be overdone, as one participant stated: "This is so plain... definitely clear though, [as it] should not contain too much information" (P4/F, Staff member). The visually richer virtual campus version was perceived to be visually more pleasing as it contained some of the aforementioned things.

Figure 7. Avatar observed standing and staring in virtual environment as user has noticed difference between (A) virtuality and (B) reality

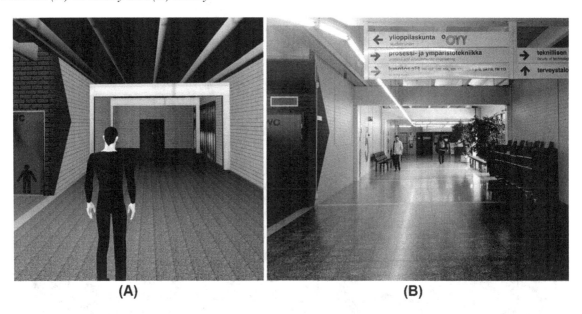

(A)   (B)

Figure 8. User trying out adding furniture and 3D texts

The initial virtual campus model had doors that do not exist in the physical campus, to prevent participants from seeing the unfinished parts of the campus. The participants paused for a long time to watch whenever there was this type of inconsistency between the physical and virtual spaces. As one participant stated when he stopped in front of this kind of door: "This corridor ends here even though in reality it would go on" (P9/M, Student) (Figure 7). In fact, it was observed in the virtual campus that three participants left their avatars to this spot when they paused to do activities such as self-expression task in reality. Another participant went to look for his office and he noticed that there was a door that is not actually there in reality and stated: "This reminds [to me], that this is not the same...I lost the idea that I am here in the university" (P14/M, Researcher/ Teacher). These observations highlight that the architectural consistency of a mirror world like virtual campus is important. The expectations of similarity between the parallel realms is so great that there is an element of surprise when the interior of the virtual building does not match the reality. However, it was also notified that not all the spaces need to be exactly the same, if it causes usability problems, as one participant stated: "You should not create mazes just because it is existing [spaces in reality]" (P10/M, Student). The participants also questioned whether all physical spaces are needed in the virtual campus, such as one participant stated: "Why there are restrooms...you cannot do any activities there?" (P12/M, Researcher/ Teacher). However, this did not apply to all spaces, as the participants came up different things that could be purchased from the virtual campus shop and cafeterias: electric versions of course learning materials, load money for lunch passes, and order caterings. From the janitors' desk people wanted to book spaces for lectures and meetings.

Needs for 3D Spaces

The participants wanted to create their own private spaces, for chatting and meetings with friends and colleagues as well as classrooms and smaller group workspaces for studies, lectures, and guild meetings. In addition, they wanted to have semi-private spaces for group work or guild meetings. Here the creator of the space would be responsible for inviting people: "I could create a virtual classroom for my group, where I could invite certain people at a certain time." (P13/F, Researcher/ Teacher).

The possibility to add furniture and customize the space was generally perceived as useful and bringing a lot of use potential for the platform (Figure 8). The virtual campus was suggested to serve as a co-design platform for the collaborative development of the physical campus: "This could be a world, where you could start creating this environment...anyone as a user could do changes... and if people like them, it [physical campus] would probably change towards it." (P7/F, Student). In addition, smaller scale design explorations were suggested, as one participant stated: "You could use this for designing your new office space, such as testing how big table you could have in it." (P11/F, Researcher/ Teacher).

The participants also suggested that there could be a separate subspace or area for user generated art content, an art hall, or a possibility for filtering user created content to prevent the actual campus model from becoming too messy if people would create art on it.

Needs for Hybrid Reality Linking

The participants also wanted to have a hybrid reality, where the virtual campus would be linked with the physical campus. For example, they proposed "peepholes" to reality and vice versa, through which people could see real-time imagery of the food and pastries served in the cafeterias and items available in the campus shop. Additionally, real-time information of queues in restaurants was requested: "You could see queue information visualized by showing realistic number of avatars standing in the line...so you could easily check when it is best time to go for lunch" (P14/M). The participants wanted to connect reality and virtuality also through public displays located in the campus, as one participant explained: "Public screen would be a window to virtual campus from real campus...and in the 3D world it would be a window to reality." (P11/F). Also, hybrid reality linking of user created art was suggested: "It would be nice to draw on the walls...or put some photos on them and share those to other users...there could be a projector in physical campus which could project on the wall the things that people create in virtual campus" (P14/M, Researcher/ Teacher).

The participants suggested multiple ways for linking reality and virtuality such as visualization of outdoor weather, real-time bus timetable, clock, and a calendar of topical events at the University. Additionally, checking meeting and lecture hall spaces before booking the space was perceived as nice features. As one participants stated: "It would show 3D model of the lecture hall, and what you have there... (e.g., number of seats, teaching equipment)...temperature and route to this lecture hall" (P11/F, Researcher/ Teacher). This would ease the life of the teacher, as this remote service would not require a kilometer walk to check those things before lecture, in addition it would allow adjusting the space climate beforehand. One participant (P4/F, Staff member) suggested that there could be interactive virtual garden in the virtual campus, where people could learn about plants that are growing in the University's botanical garden and take part in nurturing them. In addition, the University's library services, such as e-library or virtual library were of interest to the participants. They wanted to use them for reading e-library materials and finding books, (e.g., navigating to the right bookshelf in reality).

Privacy Issues with Virtual Campus

The participants were concerned about who can access the virtual campus. They suggested that there could be different kinds of access levels or accounts for different people. Visitors could access only public areas, such as lobbies, main hallway, cafes, and libraries, as they can do that also in reality. Student or staff accounts would have access to files such as lectures, and would be able to add and edit items in the virtual campus based on study field or faculty of the user.

The participants also raised concerns about who can see the content they have created, (e.g., documents, chat conversations, and open voice and video conference calls). As FVS was designed to be used as a virtual classroom shared by a limited number of users knowing each other in advance, it does not provide any access control mechanisms, but the virtual classroom is open for everyone. This design issue raised a lot of discussion during the study. For example, one participant created a laptop containing a link to certain webpage and thought that the laptop would follow him, he stated: "It will not follow me… is it said somewhere that I created it or own it? Can you take it…see what is inside of it? [asks from his pair]... my initial idea was that I can specify who I share it with." (P12/M, Researcher/ Teacher). Another participant commented on the visibility of a video chat: "…I would not like to share my photo [face on video] to all, so it would be nice, if I could be able to define who could see it" (P3/M, Researcher/ Teacher). One participant suggested: "Guild, personal, or Faculty level information that would show only to those who are belonging into that group…group leader would be the moderator and responsible on the content shared in that group" (P6/M, Researcher/ Teacher).

DISCUSSION

Prior research indicates that the design of 3DVLEs is not yet thoroughly understood (Minocha & Reeves, 2010) and why they are designed in the first place (Reisoğlu et al., 2017). In addition, mirror world like campuses have been used mainly for giving virtual tours to promote university to students and guests (Designing Digitally Inc., n.d., 2011) or simulation purposes (Sun et al., 2016). The findings of this study suggest that a mirror world like virtual campus calls for a more profound linking of reality and virtuality than just mirroring physical spaces in the virtual realm to reveal their full potential as both virtual communities and virtual learning environments.

Prior research suggests that physical and virtual realities can be blended together by the social interaction and communication across those realities (De Souza e Silva & Delacruz, 2006) and the service of interaction goals and communication environment (Hoshi et al., 2009). The findings of this study suggest that there are possibilities in blending realities while designing 3DVLEs other than just embedding digitalized contents, such as presentation slides or videos, into the virtual space. These possibilities are rooted into the cultural practices and metaphors housed in the campus space and the people dwelling there. Our study indicated that student and staff needs for the virtual campus were not so focused on learning, but on hybrid-reality type of linking of social community building, comprehensive service integration, and spaces. This may be because the campus is a community in addition to being a school, therefore

3DVLEs developed for learning purpose (Designing Digitally Inc., n.d.; Finpeda, n.d.; Monahan et al., 2008) may not be ideal for a context where their benefits and pedagogical accuracy are not always needed. More importantly, this study indicated that people would like to have hybrid reality connection through the multiplicity of interplay between reality and virtuality, to make the virtual campus an inviting place for people to meet, co-live memories, and hang out with their peers and colleagues.

In the following subsections, the design considerations for a mirror world like the virtual campus are presented. What are the metaphors for creating a virtual community for higher education at campus scale and what does it mean to step out of the classroom? Although Prasolova-Førland (2008) did not offer the most significant metaphors for 3DVLEs, she suggested that the social, aesthetic, and semantic qualities of the real-world are important building blocks for them. It is apparent that learning environment related metaphors are not adequate, as they focus on actions directly linked with learning outcomes. Persistent 3DVLEs accessible anywhere anytime may need to provide users with additional complexity of interactions that correspond to the real-life environment. This study recognized four candidate metaphors for combining the two realms at the scale of a virtual campus: Community, Services, Space, and Privacy.

Hybrid-Reality Community

The findings of this study agree with prior research in that if learning space is social, it is more attractive to the users (Kose et al., 2017; Prasolova-Førland, 2008) and that people are an important factor for place making (Krejns, 2004; De Lucia et al., 2009). However, findings suggest also that not only social interaction is important, but the community with shared memories of studying and working together needs to be considered when creating mirror world virtual campuses. The hybrid-reality virtual campus should allow storing shared memories from peoples' real-life experiences in spatially accurate locations and allow memorizing and co-living those moments again virtually. In addition, different kinds of collective projects, such as collective art, co-design of the spaces as well as virtual garden nurturing, could be used to create or deepen hybrid-reality connection between people.

To make the virtual campus more alive, a real-world phenomenon could be brought in, such as by showing people walking in the physical campus as shadows moving in the virtual campus. Another proposal for bringing social connection between realities involved peepholes through cameras and public displays located in the reality. The aforementioned ideas describe how people need complexity in interactions, and in surprisingly imaginative ways. But more importantly, as described by Farman (2013), they expected the pleasure of virtuality embedded in the experience of the interplay between virtual and real-world environments. As more the 3DVLEs are able to convey the feeling of 'being there' (Heeter, 1992); and the stronger this feeling is, the more meaningful experiences are gained (De Lucia et al., 2009).

Spatial Similarities and Ambiguities

To support hybrid-reality community building, a visual realism of a virtual environment is important. It has proven to provide familiarity and comfort to the users of 3DVLEs (Minocha & Reeves, 2010). When the campus model represents real space as a mirror world, visual consistency is even more important in architecture and in certain details. The inconsistency of the virtual environment with the reality was easily noticed by the participants of this study and it can even create a feeling of out of place, which can cause a loss of flow and break the illusion of "being there" (Heeter, 1992). Prasolova-Førland (2008) reported similar results when studying place metaphors for 3DVLEs. She did not report on related user experience but stated that there were irrelevant connections and ambiguities noted in the contents of the environment, such as content banner floating in the air, when there was no such banner in the real-world environment (Prasolova-Førland, 2008). It is interesting that although participants of this study found architectural accuracy important, interior design was much less important. This might be explained by the fact that interior design is strongly affected by user created content that is perceived to add liveliness and make the place nicer for the users. Also, as is pointed out in prior research, aesthetical design of a virtual space can make the space more engaging for students (Minocha & Reeves, 2010). In addition, participants notified that not all real-world spaces are needed in a virtual campus, if they are not usable in the virtual environment, such as bathrooms. However, if virtual campus pursues an authentic mirror world like coupling (Lifton et al., 2009; De Souza e Silva & Delacruz, 2006), such spaces could be utilized for maintenance purposes such as checking the need for cleaning or adding necessities.

Hybrid-Reality Service Platform

Prior research has suggested that e-learning environments should be a composition of technologies, tools, and media combined for social purposes (Wahlstedt et al., 2008). The findings of this study confirm and supplement these prior results with the importance of linking reality with virtuality in a mirror world like virtual campus to make it into a platform combining all campus services. This means integrating all the documents, and services, but more importantly, a real-time information of places and their utilities, such as sold items in the cafes and shops, and an ability to control facilities, such as temperature in facilities before going in there in reality.

However, the perceived utility of the virtual campus was questioned because of the large area and perceived shortcomings in interaction. Therefore, the interaction with the virtual campus and its services needs to be smooth, so that users are not forced to use more time on conducting the same task as with regular webpages or in physical campus. As prior research has suggested already a decade ago, interaction design of 3D VEs should not mimic reality, but should support fast movement within the VE (Shneiderman, 2003) such as teleports to different locations and to people. The findings of this study suggest in addition that service discovery could be simplified by integrating services into similar places in a virtual campus as in reality and automatic avatar location or proximity-based triggering and execution of these services would make interaction smooth and easy. One candidate design solution for this is proposed in prior research (Kukka, Pakanen, Badri, & Ojala, 2017). While navigation and wayfinding in virtual campuses are well covered by prior research (e.g., Designing Digitally Inc., n.d., 2011), the findings of this study suggest that to serve as hybrid-reality navigation aid more visual means are needed, such as video or footprints on the floor of the virtual campus. In addition, real-time chat conversations with important service providers, such as janitors and student office personnel are needed to ease complex navigation problems as well as issues that cannot be solved by own. However, janitors and student office personnel cannot personally reply 24/7 to all questions especially when they have to take care their tasks in physical campus, therefore chatbots could help them to reply users' frequently asked questions.

Privacy

FVS was originally designed to be used in a classroom context with a small and private user group hence FVS does not provide any access control or privacy mechanisms. In contrast, the virtual campus is large, partly public and open community, therefore FVS's original privacy design is not sufficient. As pointed out in prior research, commercial 3DVLEs are designed for supporting established groups rather than fluid communities more common in university campuses (Prasolova-Førland, 2008). The findings of this study support this, but also extend on privacy concerns raised by the participants. A virtual campus should be a semi-private space where there are both public and private areas, as proposed by prior research in a primary school context (Arhippainen et al., 2011). The access rights could be given through university account enabling user to enter classes, documents, and systems as well as give them possibility to create and modify contents on the virtual campus. In addition, users should be able to define who can see and take part in the discussions between avatars or see and modify created content.

Limitations and Future Work

We acknowledge that our study was conducted with a limited portion of the virtual campus and that using of commercial FVS for learning components and interaction can have affected the results. However, as this was an AUX study trying to provide information for the design of such virtual campuses, it gave an impression to the participants that they still have a possibility to change the final virtual campus model and its functionalities. This allowed us to collect many suggestions for improvements as well as give design considerations to other virtual campus designers.

Due the nature of our study we were not able to study some of the important things that will arise with actual use of this kind of vast indoor VLE with services and possible hundreds or thousands of simultaneous users. Future studies should focus in more detail on privacy and security issues that can rise from the use of virtual campus and its hybrid reality linking services. Another important research stream is the scalability of a virtual campus when there are hundreds or even thousands of users occupying a virtual campus environment simultaneously as this can increase network traffic and make the space unusable.

After this study, the design and implementation of stronger hybrid reality linking in the virtual campus has proceeded. One study explored campus dwellers creating with HTC Vive 3D paintings that were shown almost in real-time on public screens on the campus and on the virtual hallways of the virtual campus (Pakanen et al., 2017). Another study investigated a game where janitor's kick scooter was driven along the main hallway of the campus (Alavesa et al., 2018). But most importantly, the authors are looking at possibilities to link people from reality to virtuality with augmented and virtual reality headsets (Koskela et al., 2018). Future plans include also converting highly detailed 3D scans of humans into personal avatars roaming the virtual campus.

CONCLUSION

Mirror world like virtual campuses exists, but their full potential as hybrid-reality platforms has not been investigated thoroughly in prior research. In addition, prior research has focused on smaller classroom sized groups rather than large multidisciplinary university communities, therefore it is not well understood how these kinds of virtual spaces and services should be designed. To contribute to the design of mirror world like virtual campuses, an AUX study was conducted with 14 participants to understand students', researchers'/ teachers', and facility maintenance personnel's needs for a mirror world like the virtual campus. Our findings indicate that the design of a mirror world like campus calls for a more intense association between reality and virtuality than just mirroring real-world spaces in the virtual realm. When designing and creating a mirror world like the virtual campus, our study suggests four main themes to be used as the hybrid reality linking metaphors: Community, Services, Space, and Privacy. These should be taken into consideration to allow the users to have an inviting place for social community building and connecting current and past memories. The 3D mirror world of the real-world campus needs to be architecturally accurate, but it should be customizable by users so that they can personalize the place and the experience. More importantly, the participants wished that they could have extensive linking between reality and virtuality, which would allow combining all services into one virtual campus platform. Finally, stepping out of a classroom introduces privacy issues that should be considered in the design of any constantly changing virtual campus.

ACKNOWLEDGMENT

We thank all the user study participants of your valuable insights. We thank also the anonymous reviewers who helped to improve this paper. This research was supported by the COMBAT project [293389] funded by the Strategic Research Council at the Academy of Finland, the Open Innovation Platform of Six City Strategy project [A70202] funded by the ERDF and the City of Oulu, the Academy of Finland 6Genesis Flagship [318927], as well as it was partly supported by the Reboot Finland IoT Factory [33/31/2018] funded by the Business Finland.

REFERENCES

Adminotech. (n.d.). *University of Oulu - Virtual Campus*. Retrieved from https://campusoulu.meshmoon. com

Alatalo, T. (2011). An Entity-Component Model for Extensible Virtual Worlds. *IEEE Internet Computing*, *15*(5), 30–37. doi:10.1109/MIC.2011.82

Alavesa, P., Korhonen, O., Sepponen, J., Martinviita, M., Abrabado, M., Pakanen, M., . . . Pouke, M. (2017). Janitor Run: Studying the Effect of Realistic Mirror World like Game Scenes on Game Experience. In *Proceedings of the 9th International Conference on Virtual Worlds and Games for Serious Applications (VS-Games'17)* (pp. 179-180). 10.1109/VS-GAMES.2017.8056595

Arhippainen, L., Pakanen, M., Hickey, S., & Mattila, P. (2011). User experiences of 3D virtual learning environment. In *Proceedings of the 15th International Academic MindTrek Conference: Envisioning Future Media Environments (MindTrek'11)* (pp. 222-227). 10.1145/2181037.2181075

Arhippainen, L., & Pakanen, M. (2013). Utilizing Self-Expression Template Method in User Interface Design - Three Design Cases. In *Proceedings of the 17th Academic MindTrek (MindTrek'13)* (pp. 80-86). 10.1145/2523429.2523477

A World for Learning. (n.d.). *Welcome future of learning*. Retrieved from http://www.aw3du.com

Beetham, H., & Sharpe, R. (2013). *Rethinking pedagogy for a digital age: Designing for 21st century learning*. New York, NY: Routledge.

Benford, S., Greenhalgh, C., & Lloyd, D. (1997). Crowded collaborative virtual environments. In *Proceedings of the ACM SIGCHI Conference on Human factors in computing systems (CHI'97)* (pp. 59-66). 10.1145/258549.258588

Braun, V., & Clarke, V. (2013). *Successful qualitative research: A practical guide for beginners*. London, UK: Sage.

Charmaz, K. (2008). Grounded theory as an emergent method. In P. Leavy and S. N. Hesse-Bider (Eds.), Handbook of emergent methods (pp. 155-170). New York, NY: Guilford Press.

Chen, B., Huang, F., & Lin, H. (2009). Using virtual world technology to construct immersive 3D virtual university. In *Proceedings of the 17th International Conference on Geoinformatics, (Geoinformatics'09)*.

Chittaro, L., & Ranon, R. (2007). Web3D technologies in learning, education and training: Motivations, issues, opportunities. *Web3D Technologies in Learning, Education + Training, 49*(1), 3–18.

Dalgarno, B., & Lee, M. J. W. (2010). What are the learning affordances of 3-D virtual environments? *British Journal of Educational Technology, 4*(11), 10–32. doi:10.1111/j.1467-8535.2009.01038.x

Designing Digitally Inc. (n.d.). Educate Engage Entertain. Retrieved from http://www.designingdigitally. com/#axzz4f3GnHfr8

Designing Digitally Inc. (2011). 3D Virtual Campus Tours - Virtual Campus Tour - Real Virtual Admissions Tour [YouTube video]. Retrieved from https://www.youtube.com/watch?v=9Ehj9QVP_L8

Dickey, M. D. (2005). Three-dimensional virtual worlds and distance learning: Two case studies of Active Worlds as a medium for distance education. *British Journal of Educational Technology, 36*(3), 439–451. doi:10.1111/j.1467-8535.2005.00477.x

Dickey, M. D. (2015). Brave New (Interactive) Worlds: A Review of the Design Affordances and Constraints of Two 3D Virtual Worlds as Interactive Learning Environments. *Interactive Learning Environments, 13*(1-2), 121–137. doi:10.1080/10494820500173714

Facebook Technologies L. L. C. (n.d.). Oculus Rift. Retrieved from https://www.oculus.com

Farman, J. (2013). *Mobile interface theory: Embodied space and locative media*. New York: Routledge. doi:10.4324/9780203847664

Finpeda. (n.d.). Finpeda Virtual Space (FVS). Retrieved from http://www.finpeda.fi/services/finpeda-virtual-space/

Fokides, E. (2017). A model for explaining primary school students' learning outcomes when they use multi-user virtual environments. *Journal of Computers in Education, 4*(3), 225–250. doi:10.100740692-017-0080-y

Gelernter, D. (1991). *Mirror Worlds: The day software puts the universe in a shoebox... how it will happen and what it will mean?* Oxford: Oxford University Press.

Haukipuro, L. (2019) *User-centric product and service development in a multi-context living lab environment: case OULLabs and PATIO* [Doctoral dissertation].

Heeter, C. (1992). Being there: The subjective experience of presence. *Presence (Cambridge, Mass.)*, *1*(2), 262–271. doi:10.1162/pres.1992.1.2.262

Hoshi, K., Pesola, U.-M., Waterworth, E. L., & Waterworth, J. (2009). Tools, perspectives and avatars in blended reality space. *Annual Review of Cybertherapy and Telemedicine*, *7*, 91–95.

ISO. (2010). ISO 9241-210 Ergonomics of human-system interaction - Part 210: Human-centred design for interactive systems. Geneva: International Standardization Organization (ISO).

Jarmon, L., Traphagan, T., Mayrath, M., & Trivedi, A. (2009). Virtual world teaching, experiential learning, and assessment: An interdisciplinary communication course in Second Life. *Computers & Education*, *53*(1), 169–182. doi:10.1016/j.compedu.2009.01.010

Kose, A., Petlenkov, E., Tepljakov, A., & Vassiljeva, K. (2017). Virtual Reality Meets Intelligence in Large Scale Architecture. In *Proceedings of 4th International Conference Augmented Reality, Virtual Reality, and Computer Graphics (AVR 2017)* (Part II, pp. 297-309). 10.1007/978-3-319-60928-7_26

Koskela, T., Mazouzi, M., Alavesa, P., Pakanen, M., Minyaev, I., & Paavola, E. (2018). AVATAREX – Telexistence System based on Virtual Avatars. In *Proceedings of the 9th Augmented Human International Conference (AH'18)*. 10.1145/3174910.3174926 ·

Krejns, K. (2004). *Sociable CSCL environments. Social affordances, sociability, and social presence* [Doctoral dissertation].

Kukka, H., Pakanen, M., Badri, M., & Ojala, T. (2017). Immersive Street-level Social Media in the 3D Virtual City: Anticipated User Experience and Conceptual Development. In *Proceedings of the 2017 ACM Conference on Computer Supported Cooperative Work and Social Computing (CSCW'17)* (pp. 2422-2435). 10.1145/2998181.2998341

Lee, C. (2016). Who still hangs out on Second Life? More than half a million people. *The Globe and Mail*. Retrieved from https://www.theglobeandmail.com/life/relationships/who-still-hangs-out-on-second-life-more-than-half-a-million-people/article35019213/

Leigh, J., & Brown, M. D. (2008). Cybercommons: Merging real and virtual worlds. *Communications of the ACM*, *51*(1), 82–85. doi:10.1145/1327452.1327488

Lifton, J., Laibowitz, M., Harry, D., Gong, N.-W., Mittal, M., & Paradiso, J. J. A. (2009). Metaphor and manifestation: Cross-reality with ubiquitous sensor/actuator networks. *IEEE Pervasive Computing*, *3*(3), 24–33. doi:10.1109/MPRV.2009.49

Linden Research, Inc. (n.d.). *Second Life. Connect with the global community*.

De Lucia, A., Francese, R., Passero, I., & Tortora, G. (2009). Development and evaluation of a virtual campus on Second Life: The case of SecondDMI. *Computers & Education*, *52*(1), 220–233. doi:10.1016/j.compedu.2008.08.001

Maiberg, E. (2016). Why Is 'Second Life' Still a Thing? *Vice*. Retrieved from https://motherboard.vice.com/en_us/article/why-is-second-life-still-a-thing-gaming-virtual-reality

Mattila, P., Krajnak, J., Arhippainen, L., & Brauer, S. (2012). Education in 3D virtual learning environment - Case Virtual-Mustiala. In *Proceedings of the 2nd European Immersive Education Summit*, Paris, France (pp. 134-145).

Mattila, P., & Silander, P. (2015). *How to create the school of the future: Revolutionary thinking and design from Finland*. Oulu, Finland: Multiprint.

McCarthy, J., & Wright, P. (2004). *Technology as experience*. Cambridge, MA: MIT Press.

Mellen, M. (2010). 3D virtual campus at northeastern university. Retrieved from http://www.gearthblog.com/blog/archives/2010/12/3d_virtual_campus_at_northeastern_u.html

Meshmoon. (n.d.). *Create 3D space*. Retrieved from https://meshmoon.com/

Minocha, S., & Reeves, A. J. (2010). Design of learning spaces in 3D virtual worlds: An empirical investigation of Second Life. *Learning, Media and Technology, 35*(2), 111–137. doi:10.1080/17439884.2010.494419

Monahan, T., McArdle, G., & Bertolotto, M. (2008). Virtual reality for collaborative e-learning. *Computers & Education, 50*(4), 1339–1353. doi:10.1016/j.compedu.2006.12.008

O'Neill, M. (2013). Limitless learning: Creating adaptable environments to support a changing campus. *Planning for Higher Education, 42*(1), 11.

Pakanen, M. (2015) *Visual design examples in the evaluation of anticipated user experience at the early phases of research and development* [Doctoral dissertation].

Pakanen, M., Alavesa, P., Kukka, H., Nuottajärvi, P., Hellberg, S., & Orjala, L.-M. ... Ojala, T. (2017). Hybrid Campus Art: Bridging Two Realities through 3D Art. In *Proceedings of the 16th International Conference on Mobile and Ubiquitous Multimedia (MUM'17)* (pp. 393-399).

Petrakou, A. (2010). Interacting through avatars: Virtual worlds as a context for online education. *Computers & Education, 54*(4), 1020–1027. doi:10.1016/j.compedu.2009.10.007

Prasolova-Førland, E. (2008). Analyzing place metaphors in 3D educational collaborative virtual environments. *Computers in Human Behavior, 24*(2), 185–204. doi:10.1016/j.chb.2007.01.009

Reisoğlu, I., Topu, B., Yılmaz, R., Yılmaz, T. K., & Göktaş, Y. (2017). 3D virtual learning environments in education: A meta-review. *Asia Pacific Education Review, 18*(1), 81–100. doi:10.100712564-016-9467-0

Roto, V., Law, E., Vermeeren, A., & Hoonhout, J. (Eds.). (2011). UX white paper. *AllaboutUX*. Retrieved from http://www.allaboutux.org/uxwhitepaper

Roush, W. (2007). *Second earth. The World Wide Web will soon be absorbed into the World Wide Sim: An environment combining elements of second life and Google Earth*. Retrieved from http://www.technologyreview.com/Infotech/18911/?a=f"/>

Shneiderman, B. (2003). Why not make interfaces better than 3D reality? *IEEE Computer Graphics and Applications, 23*(6), 12–15. doi:10.1109/MCG.2003.1242376

Sun, O., Wan, W., & Yu, X. (2016). The simulation of building escape system based on Unity3D. In *Proceedings of International Conference on Audio, Language and Image Processing (ICALIP)* (pp. 156-160). 10.1109/ICALIP.2016.7846656

De Souza e Silva, A., & Delacruz, G. C. (2006). Hybrid Reality Games Reframed: Potential Uses in Educational Contexts. *Games and Culture*, *1*(3), 231–251. doi:10.1177/1555412006290443

Sulake Corporation Oy. (2012). *Habbo Hotel*. Retrieved from https://www.habbo.fi

Sutcliffe, A., & Alrayes, A. (2012). Investigating user experience in Second Life for collaborative learning. *International Journal of Human-Computer Studies*, *70*(7), 508–525. doi:10.1016/j.ijhcs.2012.01.005

Wahlstedt, A., Pekkola, S., & Niemelä, M. (2008). From e-learning space to e-learning place. *British Journal of Educational Technology*, *39*(6), 1020–1030. doi:10.1111/j.1467-8535.2008.00821_1.x

Zuiker, S. J. (2012). Educational virtual environments as a lens for understanding both precise repeatability and specific variation in learning ecologies. *British Journal of Educational Technology*, *43*(6), 981–992. doi:10.1111/j.1467-8535.2011.01266.x

This research was previously published in the International Journal of Virtual and Personal Learning Environments (IJVPLE), 10(1); pages 1-23, copyright year 2020 by IGI Publishing (an imprint of IGI Global).

Chapter 10
Minecraft Our City, an Erasmus Project in Virtual World:
Building Competences Using a Virtual World

Annalisa A. B. Boniello
University of Camerino, Italy

Alessandra A. C. Conti
IC Nettuno 1, Italy

ABSTRACT

Virtual worlds (VWs) offer alternative learning environments for geoscience education and give students a feeling of "being there." In fact, VWs are also immersive environments that enable situated learning and constructivist learning in accordance with the Vygotsky theory, because the learner is inside an "imaginary" world context. In this environment, many activities and experiences can take place as scaffolding, cooperative learning, peer-to-peer and peer evaluation, coaching, scientific inquiry. Therefore, VWs can be a new technology to motivate students and provide the educational opportunities to learn in a socially interactive learning community. In the literature already, some studies report experiences carried out to investigate the effectiveness of virtual worlds in education. In the world, there are virtual worlds used for education such as Opensim and Samsara. Minecraft (https://www.minecraft.net/en-us/) is a virtual world used by new generations specially.

INTRODUCTION

Nettuno 1 Comprehensive Public School - https://icnettuno1.edu.it - has been taking part in the Erasmus plus Project with Greece, the school leader, France and Spain from 2018 to 2020. The project is called 'OUR CITY' that involves primary and secondary school grades and is part of a search action path led by a group of teachers skilled in Virtual Worlds based learning: Open sim, Minecraft etc.

DOI: 10.4018/978-1-6684-7597-3.ch010

Our City Project started from the cooperation of four European countries: France, Greece, Italy and Spain.

Teachers focus their attention on European culture and cooperation using the rebuilding of their cities in different ways.

This activity is based on the largest tangible pieces of the nations' cultural heritage, France, Greece, Italy and Spain, for instance.

In this project students recreated their cities and monuments of their cities in Italy, Greece, Spain and France using different tools. The Italian team chose MINECRAFT. A groups of teachers used this tool to recreate monuments in Rome, Nettuno and Italian cities. This project promotes collaborative inclusion among the participants of the project through Minecraft. Constructivism is the educational philosophy that involves students in a world in which everything is created with their imagination and creativity. This environment improves the students' skills such as problem solving, creativity, language and socialization.

In this environment immersive education and learning is possible through lessons that improve the 21st century skills, creative problem solving and digital citizenship. It is possible to use Minecraf Education Edition as a support of education in a world of tutorial and best practices.

Minecraft can be used on personal computer, notebook, tablet and smartphone. This is a potential aspect of this educational world.

In this environment it is possible to carry out exploration, storytelling, digital learning and game based learning. All these aspects are involved in this project.

The Project has been following different phases. Project 'OUR CITY' was planned in three years and three stages. During the first year every country contributed to the design activities. The Italian team made up of Alessandra Conti, Maria Simona Lambiase, Raffaela Di Palma, Loredana Rocchetti, Raffaella Verbeni and other teachers created activities in their classrooms on Minecraft and chose the monuments of the city of Rome and the seatown of Nettuno in order to create a 3-D construction outline. Every classroom chose a monument and recreated it in the virtual world.

In the first part of the first year students and teachers were in a training phase. Teachers learnt to use Minecraft attending a course held by an expert in Minecraft Marco Vigelini.

In the same period students learnt how to use different tools on Minecraft and worked on Minecraft design and construction.

Every classroom was divided into small groups of 3-4 students under the supervision of a coordinator. They worked in different environments and created monuments to share with students from France, Greece and Spain. At the end of first year (2018-19) students created different videos, shared them on YouTube and explained their work and environments. In the second year, in May 2019, students travelled to Greece to show their work to Spanish, French and Greek students. This collaborative work and the sharing of skills were fundamental for this project. Twelve students and six teachers worked in the Hill School in Athens and the other 49 members with the Spanish students from Barcelona, French students from Paris and Greek students from Athens. In October 2019 the Greek students arrived in Italy in the seatown of Nettuno near Rome and stayed a week to gain and have knowledge of the real Italian monuments that they visited in the virtual world of Minecraft. They managed to do sightseeing of the Colosseum and the monuments of Nettuno such as Borgo, Torre Astura, Forte Sangallo etc. During this meeting Italian students became the tutors of the Greek students and peer tutoring was used for the activities during the Italian week's exchange.

From 2020 to 2021 there is the last part of the project with a final journey to Spain in the city of Barcelona in the school of Saint Gervasi. In this project the Ecole Alsacienne of Paris took part, too.

Figure 1. Students at work

The project participants are all students aged from 10 to 12 years old attending the last year of the primary school and the first year of the secondary school.

All students worked in cooperation using different languages, digital devices and social media to exchange their cultural heritage and cultural knowledge.

Background

There are only few examples in the literature presenting the use of virtual worlds for education and for game design (Slator et al., 1999). Other words as 'cyberspace' (from the science fiction's books of Gibson, 1984) and 'metaverse' (from Snow Crash of Neal Stephenson, 1993) are often used to describe a virtual world. They give the idea of a space, particularly a 3D space, in which we can move, act, work, interact with others as in the real world. The virtual worlds were born especially as role play worlds (Castronova, 2008), firstly, in 1980s, as textual worlds called MUD (Multi User Dungeon or Multi User Dimension), then, in the 1990s, they became three dimensional worlds, known as MMORPG (Massive Multiplayer Online Role Playing Game).

Figure 2. Building of work

Figure 3. Avatar of Minecraft

Seymour Papert (1980) understood the importance of computer simulation for learning, introducing the concept of 'microworld' defined as 'subset of reality or a constructed reality whose structure matches that of a given cognitive mechanism so as to provide an environment where the latter can operate effectively. The concept leads to the project of inventing microworlds so structured as to allow a human learner to exercise particular powerful ideas or intellectual skills'.

Meanwhile researchers explored the use of virtual worlds according to the pedagogical principles of social - constructivism . This theory defines knowledge as the product of an active construction of the subject, it has a "located character ", anchored to a concrete context, taking place through special forms of collaboration and social negotiation. In this sense the student must be an 'active learner' that controls his learning. The focus point is the student (learner - centred) and his learning mode or style. Constructivism introduces also the concept of 'learning environment' that Wilson defines as "a 'setting' or a 'space' in which a learner acts, uses tools and resources, researches and interprets information by interacting with others (Wilson, 1996). It is 'a learner centered process', because it defines knowledge as complex strategy that meets his/her needs, involving and motivating learners.

This project born from these experiences and it is based on use of new technologies to rebuild important cities of Europe: Barcelona, Paris, Athens, Rome and Nettuno (near Rome).

MAIN FOCUS OF THE CHAPTER

Issues, Controversies, Problems

This research was aimed at a new approach in education using a Multi User Virtual environment (Muve), defined Virtual World. Virtual Worlds (VWs) offer alternative learning environments for education and give students a feeling of "being there" (Slater, 2009). In fact, VWs are immersive environments that enable situated learning and constructivist learning in according to the Vygotsky theory (Vygotsky, 1978), because the learner is inside an "imaginary" world context. In this environment many activities and experiences can take place as scaffolding, cooperative learning, peer to peer and peer evaluation, coaching, scientific inquiry (Nelson & Ketelhut, 2007). Therefore, VWs can be a new technology to motivate students and provide the educational opportunities to learn in a socially interactive learning community.

In the literature already some studies report experiences carried out to investigate the effectiveness of virtual worlds in science education, as ecology or biology (Dede 2009, 2014; Dickey, 2003, 2005a, 2005b) but there are no studies, up to now, about using virtual worlds for geoscience education (e.g. geo-game design, development a scientific literacy and best practices for geoscience education).

The starting point of this research arises from the possibility of exploring the applications of VWs in education. The research focused on investigating the effectiveness of virtual worlds in the teaching/learning for students of middle (11years old). Two are the research questions investigated:

- Can a virtual world be effective to improve skills in education topics?
- Can an immersive experience in virtual worlds be a resource to motivate students in education?

To answer the research questions, the following issues have been examined:

- Use of virtual worlds (knowledge and skill on virtual worlds)

- Student perception of the virtual path before and after the experience.

The starting point of this research is based on problem to address: the poor motivation in the study of in schools to learn cultural and history of our cities which carries away the students from these topics

About motivation of students, two problems have become essential for teachers in the last years: first, trying to increase student motivation for cultural issues, by "keeping students motivated enough to stick with the learning process to the end of anything in classroom" (Prensky, 2002).

In more recent years, the learning environment in education has diversified using virtual environments and new technologies At the same time this has produced different training methods in relation to students' different learning styles (Gardner, 2011). In fact Gardner introduces the concept of multiples intelligences and for every type of intelligence there is a different learning style and a different training method (Kolb, 1986, 2005).

Virtual worlds can improve intelligence multiple using immersive virtual environment that are built like reality, so student has impression to be in reality.

In this context, immersive 3D environments have proved to be meaningful in offering an effective approach to support situated learning (Dede, 2014), learner- centered education and increasing new generation students' motivation. Prensky defines this new generation of students as "digital native" suggesting that they need to be motivated in different ways (Prensky, 2001), closer to their interests and attitudes, such as the game-play (Prensky, 2002) and immersive environments (Clarke et al., 2006).

A new technology that includes situated learning, learner - centered education, game based education can be the Virtual Worlds (VWs). These worlds like Minecraft use Game based approach, and it is easy for students and teachers 'live' in a game based environment using them. A virtual world can be considered a technology suitable to motivate students and provide educational opportunities to learn in a socially interactive learning community (Dede, 2010).

Applications of the use of Virtual Worlds can be seen in the works of Dede (1995) and Dodds (2013). Dede uses the inquiry in two virtual world scenario called River City and Ecomuve, in which students as little scientist can explore and look for data on the biology of a river or of a lake. Dodds has experienced an experimental activity in Second Life using a sample of participants between the ages of 18 and 65. They were recruited from educator mailing lists and Second Life and divided in a control and an experimental group. Participants have learned data on genetics using an environment in Second Life (Genome Island) and at end of experimentation they filled a final test to detected acquired information.

Table 1. Educational Uses of MUVEs (Dieterle & Clarke, 2007) (rielaborated)

Uses in education of MUVEs
creating online communities for pre-service teacher training and in-service professional development
engaging science-based activities while promoting socially responsive behavior
helping students understand and experience history by immersing them emotionally and politically in a historical context
promoting social and moral development via cultures of enrichment
providing an environment for programming and collaboration
creatively exploring new mathematical concepts
engaging in scientific inquiry

Dalgarno (2011) define, analyzing the subjects using 3D immersive virtual worlds, that only 19% of virtual worlds is on education and 5% on science. Dieterle and Clarke (2007) suggest several educational uses of virtual worlds, as reported in table 1.

In the virtual worlds an avatar, a virtual representation of an user, can be called a "knowledge worker" (Bredl et al 2012) and he lives an alternative experience to reality,

where the value he attaches to his presence may influence the effectiveness of such environments in education and teaching (Fedeli, 2014). These environments have, therefore, a socio - constructivist aspect in which the learning is 'situated' and develops through learning by doing. Here an authentic assessment can take place by simulating real contexts. This feature allows multiple educational activities. Duncan, Miller and Jiang (2012) have elaborated the following taxonomy of virtual worlds use in education: 'Problem Based Learning (PBL), Enquiry Based Learning (EBL), Game Based Learning (GBL), Role Playing (RP), Virtual Quests, Collaborative Simulations (learn by simulation), Collaborative Construction (building activities), Design Courses (Game, Fashion, Architectural), Language Teaching and Learning, Virtual Laboratories, Virtual Field Works, Attending lectures or classes.'

Moreover Dede lists in his work the insights about learning and knowledge representation using virtual worlds, as reported in the table 2. His idea is very interesting because underline the effectiveness of virtual worlds to increase motivation in the students.

Table 2. Insights about learning and knowledge representation using virtual worlds (Dede, 1996)

Insights about learning and knowledge representation using virtual worlds
'Multisensory cues can engage learners, direct their attention to important behaviors and relationships, help students better understand different sensory perspectives, prevent interaction errors through feedback cues, and enhance perceived ease of use.'
'The introduction of new representations and perspectives can help students gain insights for remediating misconceptions formed through traditional instruction (e.g., many representations used by physicists are misleading for learners), as well as aiding learners in developing correct mental models. Our research indicates that qualitative representations (e.g., shadows showing kinetic energy in NewtonWorld, colors showing the magnitude of a force or energy in MaxwellWorld) increase saliency for crucial features of both phenomena and traditional representations.'
'Allowing multimodal interaction (voice commands, gestures, menus, virtual controls, and physical controls) facilitates usability and seems to enhance learning. Multimodal commands offer flexibility to individuals, allowing them to adapt the interaction to their own interaction preferences and to distribute attention when performing learning activities. For example, some learners prefer to use voice commands so that they need not redirect their attention from the phenomena of interest to a menu system. (However, if virtual worlds are designed for collaborative learning, voice may be a less desirable alternative.)'
'Initial experiences in working with students and teachers in Maxwell-World suggest collaborative learning may be achievable by having two or more students working together and taking turns "guiding the interaction," "recording observations," and "experiencing activities" in the virtual reality. Extending this to collaboration among multiple learners co- located in a shared synthetic environment may further augment learning outcomes.'
'In general, usability of the virtual environment appears to enhance learning. However, optimizing the interface for usability does not necessarily optimize for learning. We have found instances in which changes to make the user interface more usable may actually impede learning. For example, in NewtonWorld to use size as an indication of a ball's mass is facile for learners, but would reinforce a misconception that mass correlates with volume.'

The virtual reality interface has the potential to complement existing approaches to science instruction through creating immersive inquiry environments for learners' knowledge construction (Dede et al, 1996). All these works describe the reasons why participants might become engaged in a VWs because they promote: 1) intrinsic motivation, 2) intrapersonal factors such as challenge, 3) control, 4) fantasy, and 5) curiosity as well as interpersonal factors, such as 6) competition, 7) cooperation, and 8) recognition (Bartle, 2004).

Moreover, a learning scenario on the screen can be the simulation of a scientific context even an imaginary context in which the feeling of immersion occurs with:1) The use of inputs (graphics, sound, visual perceptions of the passage through the environment);2) The customization of the avatar;3) The abilityto touch objects;4) The maps for geo-location;5) The possibility of communication through chat, instant messaging (IM) and voice (Boniello, 2010);6) The freedom of choice and autonomy in running the environment;7) The ability to design and build aspects of the environment;8) The presence of feedback mechanisms that help students to visualize their progress in the environment (Dede, 2012);9) The possibility of containing role play and serious game elements (Boniello and Paris, 2014).Students aren't only observers, but they are active in the metaverse, develop new skills, can acquire new knowledge and behaviors, learn the consequences or impact of their actions in a protected environment (Joyce and Weil, 1996 cit in Ranieri 2005). These activities can have effects and outcomes in the real life. Bartle (2003) states that "Virtual Worlds offer automated rules that enable users to change the world they live in. Students can live a virtual learning experience similar to real experience and this is possible through the use of simulation to recreate, in a safety mode, an event, a context or a problem

Dede, 1996)and chemistry (Trindade, J., and C. Fiolhais., 1999 and Lang & Brandly, 2009). Some examples of educational uses of virtual worlds have been recently presented by many University and school educators in three conferences: Immersive Education Summit (IeD), Opensimulator online conference (OOC) and Virtual Worlds Best Practice in Education conference (VWBPE).There aren't in these conferences and in the international framework many researches on virtual worlds on geoscience education although in these learning environments, scientific skills can be improved (National Research Council, 2011). Some examples of virtual worlds presented in the international conferences and dedicated to the sciences are: Vibe, Fleepgrid, River City and EcoMuve (an Harvard university project in particular on biology and ecology). Especially Harvard University is working on the MUVEs for learning scientific inquiry and 21st century skills with the projects River city and Ecomuve since 2002 to present.Edward Dieterle and Jody Clarkeof Harvard University suggest that this approach is changing teaching and learning strategies.

Dieterle and Clarke underline the importance of these environments as mentioned by the following quotation: 'such as River City, is their ability to leverage aspects of authentic learning conditions that are hard to cultivate in traditional classroom settings (Griffin, 1995). In addition to creating experiences that take advantage of the situated and distributed nature of cognition, MUVE also allows for the design of situations that are not possible or practical in the real world. Through the affordances of a MUVE, researchers and designers can create scenarios with real-world verisimilitude that are safe, cost effective, and directly target learning goals.'Indeed the experimentation on the geoscience educationis not many represented. There are only some examples as the World Wide Web Instructional Committee (WWWIC) at North Dakota State University (Borchert & alt., 2001), 3D virtual geology field trips of Daden (2013) or on geology explorer (Slatoret al., 1999).In particular for disaster management and to improve best practice in civil protection there are not experiences or works published. Unfortunately in the international scenario and especially in Italy there are not a lot of quantitative or qualitative research on geoscience education to promote best practices for civil protection using virtual worlds.In addition, there are no information of application about this topic in the Italian school system. Therefore, this study represents an experimentation carried out to investigate the outcomes of an innovative strategy in italian context to improve the teaching and learning geoscience and to obtain information on the effectiveness of the method in geoscience education to improve best practices in civil protection. Unfortunately in the international scenario and especially in Italy there are not a lot of quantitative or qualitative research on geoscience education to promote best practices for civil protection using virtual worlds. In Italian framework we can see some examples of educational virtual world based on Opensim. A first examples is EdMondo, a project of INDIRE (National Institutefor Documentation, Innovation and Educational Research, to promote the use of virtual worlds in education and create a community of educators that use the virtual worlds for teaching. A second Examples is Craft a general purpose worlds that organizes educational activities on differents topic as mathematics, history and art. An interesting experience is developed by prof. Michelina Occhioni that created a group of a dozen thematic islands dedicated to mathematics, chemistry, biology and earth science. Student target is K6-K8 grade. She is a science and math teacher in a middle school of south of Italy. The goal is to integrate different learning setting in order to increase the quality of teaching and to motivate students

Instructional design for a educational virtual world like this project is based on a background of experiences.

In the international framework, there are different examples and models to build an educational virtual environment (Dede, 2010). In this research, the model of instructional design to develop and create the virtual environment take start from another experience (https://d7.unicam.it/unicamearthisland/) called Unicam Earth Island project (Boniello et others, 2009, 2010, 2011, 2013, 2014, 2015, 2016) has been done according to the ADDIE model. This model is the most used for 3D educational virtual environment (Soto, 2013). The ADDIE model is divided in the following cyclic phases: Analyze, design, develop, implement, evaluate. To create paths, for every step of the cycle the following activities has been applied:

The Analyze phase consisted in the analysis of learners, the learning context, the time of implementation. The Design phase dealt with the learning theory and goals of learning. In the Develop phase, the island and the geoscience paths were built. In the

Implement phase tutorials and guide sheets were created, to work in the virtual learning environment. The last phase, the Evaluation, was applied before the experimentation (with pilot groups of science teachers) and during the experimentation.

Other aspects considered in Implementation of this project are those about the computer-mediated communication (CMC) such as the principles described by Mayer (2009).

Others principles used in the implementation of learning paths are Merrill principles. They are key principles for instructional design for Merrill (2002), they are described in the following table 3.

Table 3. Principles for CMC – Merrill

PRINCIPLES OF MERRILL (2002)
Engage in a task-centered instructional strategy (Task-centered).
Activate prior knowledge or experience (Activation).
Observe a demonstration (Demonstration).
Integrate their new knowledge into their everyday world (Integration).
Apply the new knowledge (Application).

The task-centered principle puts students in the center of strategy, activation principle underlines that must be activate prior knowledge or experience, demonstration defines that student must observe a demonstration of a theory, integration defines that new knowledge of students must be integrated with their everyday world, last principle is application, students must apply new knowledges.

Since its creation and up to the moment of the writing of this chapter, the implementation of environments in Minecraft has been a work in progress because in every experimentation the users (students and teachers) interact with the environment, adding their contents or objects. The project has been a community of practice on education and a laboratory in which there are always new paths or projects in progress. An example is the final project of the online interaction between Greece and Italy in the Minecraft world, created by Italian students themselves.

This virtual world have been built according to the educational theory of constructivism, such as a constructivist environment, where teachers and students have experienced learning paths and activities on cultural aims. Situated learning and learning by doing activities have been applied in order to improve knowledge and skills on geosciences and engaging students in a virtual learning environment based on geoscience experiences.

The classification learning paths created for the research, I have used an elaboration of the classification of educational materials in virtual worlds of the Salamander project (Richter, 2007). According to this guide the engagement types of the learning paths can be: demonstrative, experiential, diagnostic, role play, constructive and collaborative. I suggest also other categories, which I used in this research: cooperative, serious game, informative and explorative. In the table 4 there is an elaboration of Richter's table (2007) on engagement types.

Table 4. Engagement types, modified from Richter (2007)

Engagement Types	
demonstration	Learners engage with learning objects through observation and demonstration most closely aligned with real-life traditional educational experiences
experiential	Differs from a demonstration in the degree to which the student is immersed in the Learning Materials. Learner is enveloped or immersed using multiple modes of input (sound, color, texture, etc.).
diagnostic	Learners interact with a simulated environment designed to promote inquiry, analysis, and identification with formative or summative assessment tools
role play	Learners on personas enabling them to learn and engage through interaction with a story or narrative aligned with a specific character. critical and or historical inquiry the self-personified in situated contexts community / relationships / situations
constructive	learners access to information through hands-on experimentation, discovery, and creative building and problem solving
collaborative	Learners collaborate to produce knowledge or make activities and develop skills
cooperative	Learners, each one of them for a single part, cooperate to build something all together
serious game (or challenge)	Learners are engaged in a game with a challenge or a mission and to complete it they learn and develop skills
informative	Learners can read a text, click on a object to get information with pictures, sounds or models
explorative	Learners walk and explore an area such as a volcanic landscape or a seismograph and observe how this one works.

To make use of the virtual words listed above, educators have experienced different learning designs and different technologies. The project on the best learning designs or the best technology for virtual worlds is quite recent because there are several possibilities to create a learning environment in the VWs. In fact, a variety of educational methodologies and approach have been applied and experienced in virtual worlds. Some experiences are on EBL (Dodds, 2013) or on IBSE24 (Ketelhut, D. J., Nelson, B. C., Clarke, J., & Dede, 2010; Boniello, 2009a, 2009b, Boniello & Gallitelli, 2013a, 2013b, 2013c), on PBL (Bignell & Parson, 2010), on Role Play (de Freitas, 2008). Only in the field of game design there are a lot of publications, which can help educators working on virtual worlds design (Dondlinger M. J., 2007).

A simplification comes out from the work of Aldrich (2009), who suggests that virtual worlds, games, and simulations are in the same sphere of interest. He defines them all 'highly interactive virtual environments (Hives)'. The idea of effectiveness of a game in the learning process was born with the book 'Homo Ludens' of Huizinga (1973) while, in the following years, Marc Prensky (2005) suggests the effectiveness of digital games in learning for the new generation so called digital native. In the virtual environment can be used a structured level of inquiry in which students as scientists acquire scientific skills such as: 1.Characterize scientific matters 2.Give a scientific explanation of the phenomena 3.Using evidence based on scientific data. Analyzing data, students formulate responses so they can go to the next step click on an object in the virtual world.

The word 'serious game' was born in the last years to mark the games with educational purpose. de Freitas defines 'serious' the virtual worlds with educational aims.

Only in 2008 Sara de Freitas gives a classification on the use of virtual worlds in education. She suggests a classification of virtual worlds. They can be divided into: role play worlds as World of Warcraft or Everquest, social worlds as Second life, Active world, Whyville, Kitely, working worlds as IBM Metaverse, training worlds(as military simulation) and mirror worlds as Google Earth. The educational features of a Virtual World are: sharing, collaboration, user control, persistence, preservation and duration, immersion and interactivity (De Freitas, 2006).Today the word 'MUVE' (Multi user Virtual environment) describes better a virtualworld according to the social aspect of this environment. In these metaverses it is possible to recreate educational activities and experiences in a multi user mode.Muves can be created with different technologies. In fact in the international frameworkmany types of technologies are used to create virtual worlds as Unreal Engine, Unity, Minecraft, World of Warcraft, Opensim, Second life., but many educators use virtual worlds based on the Opensimtechnology because this technology is an open source and easy to use both for teachers and students.

Educational simulations use rigorously structured scenarios with a highly refined set of rules, challenges, and strategies which are carefully designed to develop specific competencies that can be directly transferred into the real world.

Games are fun engaging activities usually used purely for entertainment, but they may also allow people to gain exposure to a particular set of tools, motions, or ideas. All games are played in a synthetic (or virtual) world structured by specific rules, feedback mechanisms, and requisite tools to support them – although these are not as defined as in simulations.

Virtual worlds are multiplayer (and often massively multiplayer) 3D persistent social environments, but without the focus on a particular goal, such as advancing to the next level or successfully navigating the scenario. (from games in education: serious game)purpose as well. A serious virtual world can include games and simulations and in it students can learn according to the model of experiential learning cycle of Kolb (1984).

They suggest to follow the principles of Paul Gee (2003, 2005) that defines the most important features for an effective game based learning. Six of thirty-six principles are described in Table 5 and they represent an examples of how we can create a serious game path.

Table 5. Six of Principles of Paul Gee (2003)

Six of Principles of Paul Gee on game based learning	
Active, Critical Learning Principle	All aspects of the the learning environment (including ways in which the semiotic domain is designed and presented) are set up to encourage active and critical, not passive, learning
Design Principle	Learning about and coming to appreciate design and design principles is core to the learning experience
Semiotic Principle	Learning about and coming to appreciate interrelations within and across multiple sign systems (images, words, actions, symbols, artifacts, etc.) as a complex system is core to the learning experience
Committed Learning Principle	Learners participate in an extended engagement (lots of effort and practice) as an extension of their real-world identities in relation to a virtual identity to which they feel some commitment and a virtual world that they find compelling
Practice Principle	Learners get lots and lots of practice in a context where the practice is not boring (i.e. in a virtual world that is compelling to learners on their own terms and where the learners experience ongoing success). They spend lots of time on task.
Probing Principle	Learning is a cycle of probing the world (doing something); reflecting in and on this action and, on this basis, forming a hypothesis; reprobing the world to test this hypothesis; and then accepting or rethinking the hypothesis

Cycle of four stages: of (1) having a concrete experience followed by (2) observation of and reflection on that experience which leads to (3) the formation of abstract concepts (analysis) and generalizations (conclusions) which are then (4) used to test hypothesis in future situations, resulting in new experiences.

These principles have been used in this research to build serious game on earth science. Practice and probing principles of a game in education have been more used in the building of Unicam Earth island serious game.

The interaction between teachers and students in a 3D learning environment was studied by Gilly Salmon (2011).

She worked on the Media Zoo27 project in Second Life and has suggested 'five stage model' to develop a course in a virtual world. In these principles, Salmon describes the role of teacher called 'e-moderator' and a model for teaching in virtual worlds (Salmon, 2010, 2013).

The principles are listed in the table 6.

Table 6. Elaborated from five stage model of Salmon (2010)

PRINCIPLES OF GILLY SALMON	
access and motivation	welcoming and encouraging
online socialization	familiarization and providing bridges between cultural social and learning environments
information exchange	Facilitating task and supporting use of learning materials
knowledge construction	Facilitating process
Development	supporting responding

The principles of Salmon are used in the interaction in virtual worlds for teachers or for students.

The principles used and listed in the tables represent the last applications of new technologies in education. Only Gilly Salmon has worked in virtual worlds for her theory. In this research other principles and theories described have been applied for the first time in virtual worlds to build educational paths.

In this research, the aim was to evaluate the effectiveness of virtual world technology using also principles of research of Santoianni in education (Santoianni, 2006 and 2010).

The principal idea in this project was to create educational paths on cities for students and teachers of middle school experimenting their effectiveness on motivation and citizenship skills.

This experience takes place in a 3D virtual island, called Minecraft, built for this research project using software of Minecraft education (www.minecraft.net). Minecraft is a virtual platform where students and teachers can study, collaborate and create activities on education.

In the world, the following paths have been designed and developed for the research project: Rebuild of Torre Astura, centre of Nettuno city, Tor Caldara (geological syte), naturalistic landscape of Nettuno with sea, Colosseum of Rome, Centre of Nettuno.

So this project is based on improving cultural, scientific and citizenship competencies.

This experience is part of a Erasmus plus project. The use of a 3D virtual world as Minecraft is an element of innovation because this world is a virtual world in use of new generation of students especially in pupils of primary school. Minecraft Education Edition is a collaborative 3D platform that teachers and educators can use to improve competences and digital skills in their students. Minecraft is a 3D virtual land where users-students can create their own worlds and experiences, using building blocks, resources discovered on the site and their own creativity The game is available on a computer, smartphone, tablet, XBox or Playstation. Students in their daily life use this environment to play, build environment and interact eachothers also in online interaction. So this tool looked much easy to use for them and much near their life. So Minecraft was, for project, the best option like tools and virtual world.

Expected impact and transferability potential were based on these starting points:

1)Minecraft is as a game with no rules. 2)It doesn't come with a set of instructions, or a stated objective – players can build and explore however they want. It's often compared to virtual Lego. 3)Users can recreate an existing fantasy world or build a new one from scratch, they can fight villains and seek adventure, and they can play alone or with friends. 4)In Minecraft, children can create their own adventures at any level of play. 5)Minecraft's focus on creatively building and exploring could help children build their problem solving, planning and organisation skills. 6) kids who play with their friends might find it improves their ability to work as a team. After these starting points there were some interesting aspects like these following: Some parents of children with autism have credited the game with improving their children's social skills and communication abilities – there is even a Minecraft server specifically for young people with autism and ADHD. This digital activity can be proposed in different context, different countries and with different children because Minecraft is growing in popularity especially among primary-aged children. Minecraft is a game, but it is a serious game in which children can learn using game based learning methodology.

Teachers works in Minecraft with students using photo, google map and collecting real data with a collaborative and cooperative learning work in little groups.

In this environment teachers are as coordinators of all groups using a student centered activity with a constructivist methodology. Teachers are like mentors to improve a significant learning with a final authentic assessment and at end of project guidelines and tutorials on this work as a best practices for other teacher have been made and spread to other countries partners.

Students in this project used Minecraft to build a scale model of their city and monuments of their cities. Minecraft has some interesting features: it is a game where you dig (mine) and build (craft) different kinds of 3D blocks within a large world of varying terrains and habitats to explore. Users-students can play by themselves (single player) or with others (multiplayer). There are two game modes to choose from - creative (where players have an unlimited number of blocks and items to build but in this game option you can't die) or survival (players must find and build everything they need to avoid death by hunger, injury or attack from hostile creatures). There are also different levels of difficulty, each with its own unique features and challenges. We have used the creative mode for this project so students made and created their cities (Rome and Nettuno) and they could walk in them as virtual avatar (a digital representation of themselves) the city to other students, also creating videos in the virtual world. They will build the virtual city using photos, google map and real data.

Each partner (France, Greece and Spain) used Minecraft to build a part of this virtual world, rebuilding their cities in Minecraft. Students of different cities

For this aim, Italian students and teachers created activities and tutorials that partners have used to learn and use Minecraft virtual world, classroom activities and lesson plans created by italian teachers team.

Students of 4-5 class of primary school (9 and 10 years old) and first class of secondary school (11 years old).

The project we involved students with special needs to improve social skills and citizenship competencies.

This Erasmus+ is a wonderful opportunity for both our pupils, staff and parents to embed a European dimension into our school ethos. We will benefit from the experience of partners who have already taken part in Erasmus+ as well as developing our own ability to work with European partners. This project wanted a sharing of ICT tools: how they teach with these tools, especially the use of the environment, so that we can develop and improve our own teaching and learning.

In this project we involved all of the school pupils from age 9 to 11, all staff and the wider community at every opportunity.

The activities and experience of school IC Nettuno 1 in the areas relevant to this project will be the creation of a digital game based learning using the software on Minecraft Education Edition

Objective wasto transfer the project into the virtual environment Minecraft: Education Edition

In addition to practical implementation there will be the development of tutorial and tools to create a Minecraft "world" called "OUR CITY" related to the construction of cities, as well as the development of examples of "worlds" based on the real experience deriving from the implementation of the project.

These activities will provide a useful tool for the dissemination of project results through the implementation of the educational project by teachers to other groups of children. It will also be useful for transmitting the educational content of the project to children in an engaging way.

Our experience will be based on ICT. It will experiment with the introduction of new educational methods (game based learning), created on the use of an interactive digital 3D environment and will facilitate the implementation of the project in many schools and the dissemination of the project results directly to children.

The final product will be as complete as possible, subject to the limitations established by the "Minecraft" software distributors.

The skills and competences of the key people involved in this project are already underway because in some of our classes we are already experimenting with the use of Minecraft to improve learning, there are teachers who are training to improve their skills and that at the time of implementation of the project will be able to achieve the goal and to be able to communicate to other partners how to use the software.

This study reports the results of the experimentation carried out on a group of classes of primary and middle school in Italy, Spain, Greece and France, comprising 50 students and 16 teachers.

Teachers have been involved as well, to investigate how and to which extent an innovative strategy could improve the teaching of in school. Both teachers and students participate to the online activities and to the evaluation of the competences. To collect the data and answer the research question, a mixed method, including both quantitative and qualitative, data has been used and are in evaluation: questionnaires, observations and interviews have been used to test the paths. The first results obtained from this research suggest that virtual worlds are potentially effective in education.

The results obtained on the student's evidence that this immersive environment 1) is motivating and involving, 2) increases the learning outcomes about knowledge and skills acquisition, 3) increases the students' interaction with peers and teachers and their appreciation for collaborative work, 4) improve their interest to study topics as culture and history of our cities. The teachers participating the research, also noted the effectiveness of this methodology on motivation and learning of students, more of a traditional mode. In particular, the teachers noted that this approach: 1) increases attention and motivation, 2) increases problem solving and development of creativity, collaboration and cooperation, 3) allows simulation of ideal city and situated learning, 4) can be an environment to create education activities, E-Activities and authentic assessment.

The intellectual outputs of the proposed project are designed with a view to facilitating its reiteration in different environments, by different schools, teachers, children, that did not participate in the original implementation. A "multichannel" approach is followed, that ranges from traditional printed material to web-based applications, including a board game and a documentary. This approach is based on the conviction that the multiplicity of ways to reach content can largely improve pedagogical effectiveness.

Our cities: Pedagogical implementation guide and open educational resources on selected subjects

Scope: A detailed guide of the educational project for application by teachers to schools/groups of children, beyond project participants and OER on subjects elaborated during the implementation of the project: technical (transport, recycling, energy, pollution …), political (democracy, representation, minority rights …), social (refugees, multiculturalism, unemployment, poverty …)

Various chapters regarding theoretical and practical aspects of the project, step-by-step guide for implementation and an Annex with appropriately designed sheets for evaluation of the results of the project's implementation. Project also include:

- theme maps of actual and imaginary cities,
- bibliographies,
- list of useful sites for educators,
- file containing material produced by each group of children during the implementation of the project (interviews, journals, questionnaires, records of meetings)

Contribution to the general objective of the project: will be essential for the dissemination of the project's results and will provide a useful basis for the implementation of the educational project by other teachers/schools/groups of children.

Innovation of project is both in design and in content and will carry the innovative capacity of the project to larger audiences.

Potential impact will enable the implementation of the project in many schools/groups of children, who are expected to benefit from its educational potential. It will also provide valuable material for other educational activities.

This project will include elaborations of guidelines and tools for developing new Minecraft "worlds" related to city-construction, as well as the development of examples of "worlds", based on the actual experience from the implementation of the project.

Contribution to the general objective of the project: will provide a useful tool for the dissemination of the project's results through the implementation of the educational project by teachers to other groups of children. It will also be useful for conveying the educational content of the project to children in an immersive way.

SOLUTIONS AND RECOMMENDATIONS

Whereas all the previous aspects have been very well received by the teachers, some problems have been also detected, like 1) the digital divide between teachers and students, 2) the still scarce access to technologies by schools, 3) the limited time to dedicate to new experiences, 4) the necessary training of teachers. Most of these issues can be resolved with solutions based on a good planning of the experience and an active involvement of the Principal and the instrumental figures in the school. On the other side, this approach contributes effectively to decrease the digital divide and effectively connect teachers and students.

These results can be used to new experimentations in the future on other virtual paths and on the development of expertise of teachers in the use of virtual worlds in education.

This research doesn't claim that virtual learning environments can replace traditional teaching but they represent an excellent integration. In this perspective virtual worlds have strong potentials to reproduce real situations into virtual environment. This is especially interesting to model a situation or a phenomenon in time or space, with good applications in education topics requires a better knowledge about the environment.

FUTURE RESEARCH DIRECTIONS

As a final remark, the results obtained in this research do not claim that virtual learning environments can replace real environment learning, but they represent an excellent integration. In this perspective virtual worlds, in the planning of the activities proposed, must also show virtual problematic situations linked to live experiences or phenomena. These results can bring to new experimentations in future on other virtual paths and on the development of the teachers' expertise in the use of virtual worlds in education.

CONCLUSION

The aim of this research was to investigate the use of virtual worlds in education and evaluate its effectiveness for learning in Minecraft in an Erasmus plus project. To carry out this experiment a virtual 3D world was built using Minecraft. In this virtual island students and teachers have experienced virtual

3D paths on topics related to monuments and their cities. This study was experimented in Italian middle and primary school, where students and teachers used paths built in a virtual world called Minecraft.

To answer the research questions the following issues have been examined:

1. Use of virtual worlds like Minecraft (knowledge and skills on virtual worlds)
2. Effectiveness of using virtual worlds in terms of acquired knowledge and skills in education topics
3. Motivation of students to use virtual worlds for learning

This research is based on the starting point that there is still little application of virtual worlds in education in the international framework and, moreover, there is no experience about education in Italy and abroad. Also, there are no attempts of experimentations or data collection on the use or effectiveness of virtual worlds on education. This project is the first (to my knowledge at August 2020) that use Minecraft for an Erasmus plus project..

The results of this research suggest that virtual worlds are potential effective in education to enhance learning outcomes in learning for students of middle school.

It emerged that science teachers can be motivated to use a virtual world for education. Results highlight that Italian teachers think that a virtual world is an innovative way to do education, different from a more traditional methodology, for the following points: 1) Increase of attention and motivation 2) increased level of problem solving and development of creativity, collaboration and cooperation 3) allow simulation of a context and situated learning 4) can be an environment to create authentic assessments.

These data are similar to data collected from the research on other topics (biology or ecology) in other countries using virtual worlds (Dede, 2010, Barab et Al., 2007 and Clark, 2009). In this study many of the teachers involved in the research noted the positive effect of this methodology on motivation and learning of students in the education.

To show the effectiveness of this methodology, in this research a online course for science teachers was organized in a world.

The results of participation and of the test show that the demand of new technologies in education is growing fast. Online collaboration between teachers increased collaboration between teachers even outside the course.

As a final remark, the results obtained in this research do not claim that virtual learning environments can replace real environment learning, but they represent an excellent integration. In this perspective virtual worlds, in the planning of the activities proposed, must also show virtual problematic situations linked to live experiences or phenomena. These results can bring to new experimentations in future on other virtual paths and on the development of the science teachers' expertise in the use of virtual worlds in education.

The research project evidenced that 3D environment is useful for education, but results highlighted some limitations. These can be regarded as cultural obstacles, for example the digital divide between teachers and students, or technical obstacles, like the access to technologies by schools, the time required for the experience, the training of teachers. All these obstacles, seen as serious limitations at first, can be solved with different solutions based on a good planning of the experience and involving the principal and the instrumental figures in the school.

A positive aspect was that for the online course is that no travel was required, so students can participate from the comfort of their own homes, encouraging them in participating also in lockdown.

This gave them more time to learning the use of virtual worlds for education and, at the end, more confidence.

Finally, regarding the digital divide between students and teachers, the initial worries of the teachers rapidly disappeared and the experience in the class with the students proved instead that the communication between them actually improved.

Confidence is based on the use of virtual worlds in education, and there are so much teachers that could and should learn and use new technologies in their classroom.

This experience ended in Covid pandemic situation. The only chance was provided by the virtual world of Minecraft in which students were able to meet each others in virtual worlds. This is a good starting point for a new project in the future.

REFERENCES

Aldrich, C. (2009). Virtual worlds, simulations, and games for education: A unifying view. *Journal of Online Education, 5*, 5.

Bartle, R. A. (2004). *Designing virtual worlds*. New Riders.

Bignell, S., & Parson, V. (2010). *Best practice in virtual worlds teaching. Collaboration with funding from the Higher Education Academy Psychology Network and Joint Information Systems Committee.* University of Derby, Aston University.

Boniello, A. (2009a). Esperienze Didattiche In Ambienti Virtuali 3d. *Proceedings of the Conference DULP 2009. Ubiquitous Learning in Liquid Learning Places: Challenging Technologies, Rethinking Pedagogy, Being Design*, 87-88.

Boniello, A. (2009b). Laboratori di scienze come ambienti di apprendimento 3d. In *Proceedings of the Conference Didamatica 2009*. University of Trento.

Boniello, A. (2010). Computer Mediated Communication (CMC) e Second Life. *Form@ re-Open Journal per la formazione in rete, 10*(72), 40-45.

Boniello, A. (2011). Serious Game in Second Life. In *Virtual World Best Practices in Education* (p. 97). E-Journal Of Virtual Studies.

Boniello, A. (2014). Earth sciences in the Muve. In *Virtual World Best Practices in Education. e-jouranl* (p. 30). E-Journal Of Virtual Studies.

Boniello, A. (2015), *A serious geosciences game: path in a volcanic area*. The Second Scientix Conference. http://files.eun.org/scientix/conference/Scientix_A5_publication_2_final.pdf

Boniello, A. (2016). *Geoscience education using virtual worlds: the Unicam Earth Island project* [Unpublished doctoral dissertation]. University of Camerino.

Boniello, A., Cuccurullo, D., & Elia, A. (2010a). E-Learning in ambienti virtuali 3D. *Proceedings of the Conference Moodlemoot 2010*.

Boniello, A., Cuccurullo, D., & Elia, A. (2010b). Nuovi scenari E-learning per la formazione docenti: integrare Moodle a Second Life … un approccio vincente*?* In *Proceeding of the Conference Moodle-Moot*. Politecnico di Bari.

Boniello, A., Elia, A., & Fedeli, L. (2010). Educational Tools e Second Life: ibridazione ed esperienze a confronto. In *Proceedings of the Conference Didamatica 2010*. Università di Roma La Sapienza.

Boniello, A., & Gallitelli, M. (2013a) IBSE in Virtual World. *Proceeding of the Conference Didamatica 2013*

Boniello, A., & Gallitelli, M. (2013b). Le scienze della terra in Virtual Worlds. *Briks online Journal*. http://bricks.maieutiche.economia.unitn.it/?p=3996

Boniello, A., & Gallitelli, M. (2013c). Inquiry Based Science Education in Virtual Worlds. In *Proceeding of International Workshop Science education and guidance in school: the way forward*. University of Florence, Scuola di Sant'Anna Pisa.

Boniello, A., Lancellotti, L., Macario, M., Realdon, G., & Stroppa, P. (2014). Didattica delle scienze della Terra: l'esperienza di Unicam Earth. *Bricks online Journal*.

Boniello, A., & Paris, E. (2013). Teaching Earth Science. In *Proceeding of the Conference IeD 2013*. King's College London.

Boniello, A., & Paris, E. (2014a). Geosciences in virtual worlds: a path in the volcanic area of the Phlegraean Fields. In *IV Scientific Day of Science and Technology* (p. 46). UNICAM.

Boniello, A., & Paris, E. (2014b). I Campi Flegrei nei Mondi Virtuali. DIDAMATICA2014, 230-233.

Boniello, A., & Paris, E. (2014c). *Engage students using a serious game in an Open Sim: a path on volcanism in Phlegraean field*. Academic Press.

Boniello, A., & Paris, E. (2015a). Knowledge Emergence in Virtual Spaces. *Journal of Virtual Studies*, *6*(2), 12–15.

Boniello, A., & Paris, E. (2015b). A teacher training on geosciences in virtual worlds. In *Conference proceeding of New perspective in science education*. International Pixel Conference, Libreriauniversitaria.it.

Boniello, A., & Paris, E. (2016). Geosciences in virtual worlds: A path in the volcanic area of the Phlegraean Fields. *Rend. Online Soc. Geol. It.*, *40*, 5–13. doi:10.3301/ROL.2016.64

Boniello. A. & Colombrita G. (2011). Utilizzo di Moodle e Sloodle per la formazione dei docenti in ambienti virtuali 3D (Second Life). In *E-learning con Moodle in Italia: una sfida tra passato, presente e futuro* [E-learning with Moodle in Italy: a challenge between past, present and future]. Proceedings of the Conference Moodlemoot 2009. Torino: Seneca.

Bredl, K., Groß, A., Hünniger, J., & Fleischer, J. (2012). The Avatar as a Knowledge worker? How immersive 3D virtual environments may foster knowledge acquisition. *Electronic Journal of Knowledge Management*, *10*(1), 15–25.

Castronova, E. (2008). *Synthetic worlds: The business and culture of online games*. University of Chicago press.

De Freitas, S. (2006). *Learning in immersive worlds: A review of game- based learning.* Joint information systems committee, Bristol, JISC e-Learning Programme.

De Freitas, S. (2008). Serious virtual worlds. A scoping guide. JISC e-Learning Programme, The Joint Information Systems Committee (JISC).

Dede, C. (1995). The evolution of constructivist learning environments: Immersion in distributed, virtual worlds. *Educational Technology, 35*(5), 46–52.

Dede, C. (2009). *Immersive interfaces for engagement and learning science.* Academic Press.

Dede, C. (2010). *Comparing frameworks for 21st century skills. 21st century skills: Rethinking how students learn.* Academic Press.

Dede, C., Nelson, B., Ketelhut, D. J., Clarke, J., & Bowman, C. (2004, June). Design- based research strategies for studying situated learning in a multi-user virtual environment. In *Proceedings of the 6th international conference on Learning sciences* (pp. 158-165). International Society of the Learning Sciences.

Dede, C., Salzman, M. C., & Loftin, R. B. (1996, March). ScienceSpace: Virtual realities for learning complex and abstract scientific concepts. *Virtual Reality Annual International Symposium, 1996. Proceedings of the IEEE, 1996,* 246–252.

Dieterle, E., & Clarke, J. (2007). Multi-user virtual environments for teaching and learning. Encyclopedia of multimedia technology and networking, 2, 1033-44.

Dodds, H. E. (2013). *Can virtual science foster real skills? A study of inquiry skills in a virtual world.* Academic Press.

Dondlinger, M. J. (2007). Educational video game design: A review of the literature. *Journal of Applied Educational Technology, 4*(1), 21–31.

Duncan, I., Miller, A., & Jiang, S. (2012). A taxonomy of virtual worlds usage in education. *British Journal of Educational Technology, 43*(6), 949–964.

Fedeli, L. (2014). *Embodiment e mondi virtuali. Implicazioni didattiche.* Franco Angeli.

Gardner, H. (2011). *The unschooled mind: How children think and how schools should teach.* Basic books.

Gee, J. P. (2003). What video games have to teach us about learning and literacy. *Computers in Entertainment, 1*(1), 20.

Gee, J. P. (2005). Good video games and good learning. In *Phi Kappa Phi Forum* (Vol. 85, No. 2, p. 33). The Honor Society of Phi Kappa Phi.

Gibson, W. (1984). *Neuromancer.* New York: Ace.

Huizinga, J. (1973). *Homo Ludens.* Einaudi.

Kolb, D. A. (1984). *Experiential learning: Experience as the Source of Learning and Development.* Prentice-Hall Inc.

Kolb, D. A. (1986). Learning styles and disciplinary differences. The modern American college, 232-255.

Kolb, D. A., & Fry, R. E. (1974). Toward an applied theory of experiential learning. MIT Alfred P. Sloan School of Management.

Kolb, A.Y., & Kolb, D.A. (2005). *The Kolb Learning Style Inventory – Version 3.1: 2005 Technical Specifications*. Haygroup: Experience Based Learning Systems Inc.

Mayer, R. E. (2009). *Multimedia learning*. Cambridge University press. doi:10.1017/CBO9780511811678

Merrill, M. D. (2002). First principles of instruction. *Educational Technology Research and Development*, *50*(3), 43–59. doi:10.1007/BF02505024

Nelson, B. C., & Ketelhut, D. J. (2007). Scientific inquiry in educational multi-user virtual environments. *Educational Psychology Review*, *19*(3), 265–283. doi:10.100710648-007-9048-1

Nelson, B., Ketelhut, D. J., Clarke-Midura, J., & Dede, C. (2006). *Designing for real-world inquiry in virtual environments*. Academic Press.

Papert, S. (1980). Computer-based microworlds as incubators for powerful ideas. In R. Taylor (Ed.), *The computer in the school: Tutor, tool, tutee* (pp. 203–210). Teacher's College Press.

Prensky, M. (2001). *Digital game-based learning*. McGraw-Hill.

Prensky, M. (2002). - The Motivation of Gameplay or, the REAL 21stcentury learning revolution. *On the Horizon*, *10*(1), 5–11. doi:10.1108/10748120210431349

Richter, J., Anderson-Inman, L., & Frisbee, M. (2007). Critical engagement of teachers in Second Life: Progress in the salamander project. *Second Life Education Workshop*, 24-26.

Salmon, G. (2004). *The five stage model*. http://www. gillysalmon. com/five-stage-model. html

Salmon, G. (2011). *E-moderating: The key to teaching and learning online* (3rd ed.). Routledge.

Salmon, G. (2013). *E-tivities: The key to active online learning* (2nd ed.). Routledge. doi:10.4324/9780203074640

Salmon, G., Nie, M., & Edirisingha, P. (2010). Developing a five-stage model of learning in Second Life. *Educational Research*, *52*(2), 169–182. doi:10.1080/00131881.2010.482744

Santoianni, F. (2006). *Educabilità cognitiva. Apprendere al singolare, insegnare al plurale*. Carocci.

Santoianni, F. (2010). *Modelli e strumenti di insegnamento. Approcci per migliorare l'esperienza didattica*. Carocci.

Scapellato, B., Paris, E., & Invernizzi, C. (2013). In-Service Teacher Training to Take Ibse Approach into Earth, Science Teaching in Italian Secondary Schools. *Intern. Conference on New perspectives in Science education*.

Slator, B. M., Saini-Eidukat, B., & Schwert, D. P. (1999). A Virtual World for Earth Science Education in Secondary and Post-Secondary Environments: The Geology Explorer. *Proceedings of International Conference on Mathematics / Science Education and Technology Association for the Advancement of Computing in Education (AACE)*, 519-525.

Slator, B. M., Saini-Eidukat, B., & Schwert, D. P. (1999). A Virtual World for Earth Science Education in Secondary and Post-Secondary Environments: The Geology Explorer. *Proceedings of International Conference on Mathematics / Science Education and Technology Association for the Advancement of Computing in Education (AACE)*.

Soto, J. (2013, September). Which instructional design models are educators using to design virtual world instruction? *Journal of Online Learning and Teaching*, *9*(3).

Stephenson, N. (1993). *Snow Crash*. Bantam-Random.

Vygotsky, L. S. (1967). Play and its role in the mental development of the child. *Social Psychology*, *5*(3), 6–18.

Wilson, B. G. (1996). Constructivist learning environments: Case studies in instructional design. *Educational Technology*.

KEY TERMS AND DEFINITIONS

Active Learning: Learning with action in active mode and not in passive mode.

Immersion: Feeling to 'be here' in an environment (also if it is virtual).

Minecraft: Virtual world and social world for game and education.

Second Life: Virtual world and social world.

Serious Game: Game in Education with education aim.

Social World: Environment where there is social interaction.

Virtual Worlds: Virtual worlds are multiplayer (and often massively multiplayer) 3D persistent social environments.

This research was previously published in the Handbook of Research on Teaching With Virtual Environments and AI; pages 293-315, copyright year 2021 by Information Science Reference (an imprint of IGI Global).

Chapter 11
The Use of Network–Based Virtual Worlds in Second Language Education:
A Research Review

Mark Peterson
https://orcid.org/0000-0002-3497-0203
Kyoto University, Japan

Qiao Wang
https://orcid.org/0000-0001-9273-7082
Kyoto University, Japan

Maryam Sadat Mirzaei
RIKEN, Japan

ABSTRACT

This chapter reviews 28 learner-based studies on the use of network-based social virtual worlds in second language learning published during the period 2007-2017. The purpose of this review is to establish how these environments have been implemented and to identify the target languages, methods used, research areas, and important findings. Analysis demonstrates that research is characterized by a preponderance of small-scale studies conducted in higher education settings. The target languages most frequently investigated were English, Spanish, and Chinese. In terms of the methodologies adopted, analysis reveals the majority of studies were qualitative in nature. It was found that the investigation of learner target language production, interaction, and affective factors represent the primary focus of research. Although positive findings relating to the above areas have been reported, the analysis draws attention to gaps in the current research base. The researchers provide suggestions for future research.

DOI: 10.4018/978-1-6684-7597-3.ch011

INTRODUCTION

The emergence of ubiquitous network-based virtual worlds (henceforth VWs) has opened up new arenas for learning. These multi-user environments offer access to persistent and highly engaging virtual reality-based simulations designed specifically to facilitate social interaction. Contemporary VWs such as the well-known *Second Life* incorporate visually appealing high-quality three-dimensional (3D) graphics, personal avatars, multimodal real time communication tools and large-scale international user communities. Researchers in the field of computer assisted language learning (CALL) have viewed the use of these environments as a positive development and interest in their use is increasing (Peterson, 2017; Sadler, 2012). In an expanding body of work, researchers are investigating the potential of VWs as a means to facilitate language learning. This context highlights the current need for a systematic review in order to provide a principled framework to guide future development in this dynamic and important area of CALL research.

The discussion in this chapter first identifies the distinguishing features of the major social VWs that have been investigated in CALL research, and moves on to examine rationales for their use in foreign language education. The researchers then describe the methods used to answer the following research questions that motivated this review: How have the current generation of social VWs been implemented in language education? What languages have been targeted in studies on the use of social VWs in CALL research?

What methodologies have been adopted by researchers investigating the use of this type of VW? What have been the main areas of research? What major findings have been reported? The researchers examine key findings and draw attention to gaps in research. The discussion concludes by identifying promising areas for investigation in future research.

BACKGROUND

As one of the most popular of the computer-mediated communication (CMC) environments that have emerged with the rapid development of computing technologies in recent decades, VWs are increasingly being utilized in language education (Deutschmann & Panichi, 2013). This phenomenon is due, in part, to the dramatic expansion in worldwide Internet usage and the emergence of accessible, low-cost and robust VWs. Researchers further note that although VWs share a number of technologies in common with other CMC environments they combine a number of features that, when taken together, offer language learners access to virtual reality-based communication environments with unique potential for language learning (Peterson, 2011; Sadler, 2012).

Features of Social VWs

The current generation of multi-user VWs such as *Second Life* and *Active Worlds* provide access to customizable theme-based virtual reality simulations rendered in high-quality 3D graphics. Unlike other CMC environments that utilize virtual reality such as multiplayer digital games, where user behavior is limited by constraints imposed by the game's programmer, social VWs are specifically designed as open environments where registered users may easily create new online content (Thorne, 2008). As a result, these environments provide access to user-created worlds that are frequently large-scale and that incorporate a wide variety of themes reflecting the interests of their users (Peterson, 2011).

A distinguishing feature of VWs noted in the literature is that these environments are designed primarily to facilitate real time communication and social interaction (Dickey, 2005). In most VWs, users may utilize voice and text chat tools such as instant messaging. The use of these network-based communication tools enables users to interact both publicly and, if required, privately in the target language (henceforth TL) with interlocutors including peers and native speakers located in diverse geographical locations. A further aspect of VWs that enhances their potential as arenas for language learning is that they incorporate a wide variety of shared software applications. Users can access web browsers, presentation tools, word processors, recording tools, note cards, whiteboards and machinima. The easy access to these tools supports the communication environment. Furthermore, the availability of these applications facilitates learner's active engagement in the process of content creation, interaction and task completion (Ganem-Gutierrez, 2014).

A noteworthy feature of VWs is that they enable individual users to create unique personal avatars that can engage in role-play and interaction with other user-controlled avatars in real time (Peterson, 2005). These avatars may also interact with preprogrammed avatars known as *bots*, that are not under the control of an individual user. Registered users of virtual worlds can utilize pseudonyms and customize their own avatar in order to create unique online personae. Avatars in contemporary VWs are capable of manipulating virtual objects within a simulation. Moreover, they can traverse virtual space in real time as users can click built-in menus to enable their avatars to walk, run or fly. Avatars are capable of moving rapidly to different worlds within a simulation a feature known as *teleporting*. They are also designed to facilitate communication with other avatars as the written output of their creators is displayed in onscreen speech bubbles. Avatars can manifest, in real time, a limited range of emotional states including happiness and sadness. They can also carry out a range of nonverbal communication cues such as gestures. These features are perceived as supporting immersion, telepresence, interaction and emotional investment (Dalgarno & Lee, 2010; Petrakou, 2010; Privas-Bréauté, 2015).

Another feature identified in the literature as facilitating learning is the presence of VW-related online communities (Peterson, 2017). Researchers note that these are frequently large-scale and function as important support venues for users (Thorne, Black, & Sykes, 2009). Online communities associated with particular VWs such as *Second Life*, frequently incorporate features such as dedicated user web sites, FAQ pages, wikis, blogs, mailing lists and news groups.

Rationales for the Use of Social Virtual Worlds

Researchers have drawn on developments in SLA research to justify the use of social VWs (Peterson, 2017). As Table 1 shows, from the perspective of psycholinguistic research, these environments offer a combination of features that are identified as providing access to many of the optimal conditions for individualized learning in CMC contexts (Doughty & Long, 2003). One important feature emphasized in the literature is that by providing access to tools that facilitate real time communication in the target language with a variety of interlocutors, VWs provide learners with exposure to rich sources of input (Peterson, 2006). Moreover, they have the potential to elicit forms of meaning-focused TL interaction involved in SLA such as the provision of feedback, modified output and the negotiation of meaning (Toyoda & Harrison, 2002). The availability of text, scrolling and data recording may facilitate reflection, noticing and the raising of metalinguistic awareness (Peterson, 2011; Schwienhorst, 2009).

In the above context, additional features of VWs are perceived as supporting learning. The theme-based nature of these environments provides a comprehensible framework for TL interaction. Provision of accessible authoring tools facilitates implementation of new forms of task-based learning that utilize the unique features of these environments in order to provide learners with opportunities to engage in purposeful TL interaction (Peterson, 2005). The presence of customizable personal avatars enhances the sense of immersion, telepresence and emotional investment experienced by learners promoting participation (Peterson, 2006). In addition, the anonymity afforded by the online nature of the interaction in virtual reality where many social context cues are either removed or greatly reduced may act to lower anxiety and the affective filter (Schwienhorst, 2002). Researchers assert that many VWs are characterized by a low-stress atmosphere, where learners display reduced inhibition, enjoyment and positive attitudes (Kuriscak & Luke, 2009). These aspects of the communication environment support the operation of factors identified as playing a key role in SLA including risk-taking, motivation, and the development of learner autonomy (Ho, 2010; Svensson, 2003).

Accounts of SLA that draw attention to the social nature of learning represent a further rationale for the use of VWs. From this perspective, the social nature of interaction in these environments represents a potentially valuable source of language learning opportunities. It is claimed in the literature that as VWs are customizable, they provide ideal venues for the application of language tasks designed to foster the social interaction that mediates the process of SLA (Ganem-Gutierrez, 2014). This aspect, and the opportunities to interact with both native speakers and peers are perceived as supporting learning as in VWs learners can engage in forms of TL dialogue involving assistance and co-construction (Sadler, 2012). In sociocultural accounts of SLA, this type of collaborative interaction is identified as supporting learning: as it facilitates the operation of intersubjectivity, enabling learners to experience zones of proximal development (ZDP) that promote the achievement of self-regulation (Lantolf & Thorne, 2006). Another feature identified as supporting learning are the online communities associated with VWs (Thorne, Black, & Sykes, 2009). Informal in nature and operating outside the confines of traditional educational settings these groups are perceived as potentially valuable as they enable learners to access communities of practice (Lawrence & Ahmed, 2018) where they can interact with more capable peers located in diverse locations facilitating the development of cross-cultural knowledge (Panichi, Deutschmann, & Molka-Danielsen, 2010) and language socialization (Thorne, Black, & Sykes, 2009).

As the prior discussion shows, from the perspective of SLA research VWs designed for social interaction offer new and potentially valuable opportunities to extend learning beyond the classroom. Further benefits of learner participation in VW-based learning are noted in the literature. The computer and network-based nature of the interaction reduces barriers to learning such as time and distance constraints. Moreover, the isolation that can inhibit learning in conventional educational environments may be reduced by participation in VW-based communities where learners can experience an authentic and dynamic context for TL interaction with a wide variety of interlocutors including native speakers and peers from diverse cultural and linguistic backgrounds (Thorne, Black, & Sykes, 2009). In addition, the accessibility of these environments holds particular appeal to the younger generation of language learners who have grown up in the digital age (Cooke-Plagwitz, 2009). Although VWs appear to offer advantages over traditional teacher-led language classrooms researchers have identified potential issues associated with their use. It is noted in the literature that the effectiveness of these environments may be influenced by factors such as the need for learner training and network infrastructure issues (Peterson, 2011; Toyoda & Harrison, 2002; Wang, 2017). Researchers further draw attention to the importance of

Table 1. Features of virtual worlds hypothesized as facilitating second language acquisition

Features	Hypothesized Advantages
Persistent theme-based virtual worlds that may be modified to incorporate new user-created virtual content.	• Themes provide a comprehensible framework for purposeful interaction. • Facilitate implementation of task-based learning.
Real time communication tools such as text and voice chat.	• Learner-centered real time TL interaction with diverse groups of interlocutors provides exposure to rich TL input. • Facilitate the provision of feedback, production of modified TL output and the negotiation of meaning. • Presence of text and the availability of scrolling supports noticing and the raising of metalinguistic awareness. • Participation in collaborative dialogue enables peer learning involving the operation of ZPDs. • Cross-cultural learning opportunities. • Anonymity and reduced social context cues may lower the affective filter. • Facilitate risk taking, autonomy and motivation.
User access to customizable personal avatars.	• Enhance immersion, telepresence, emotional investment and participation.
Online user communities.	• Provide access to communities of practice. • Facilitate language socialization.

planning (Gonzalez-Lloret & Ortega, 2015) and emphasize that successful projects involving the use of VWs require careful alignment with learner needs and curricular goals (Cooke-Plagwitz, 2008).

METHOD

The purpose of this chapter is to review learner-based research on the use of social VWs in CALL. The review was guided by the questions outlined below:

1. How have the current generation of social VWs been implemented in language education?
2. What languages have been targeted in studies on the use of social VWs in CALL research?
3. What methodologies have been adopted by researchers investigating the use of this type of VW?
4. What have been the main areas of research?
5. What major findings have been reported?

As noted at a previous stage of this discussion, work in this area is expanding and a review is now timely. A review that answers the above questions offers the prospect of identifying the strengths and weaknesses of the research base. Moreover, such an endeavor facilitates the identification of areas that are underresearched and strands of work that are worthy of further investigation. In addition, this review contributes to providing a principled basis for the conduct of future research. The remainder of this section outlines the conduct of the literature search, including the procedures used and the criteria for paper selection.

Literature Search

In order to answer the research questions that motivated this review a search of relevant journals and a database was carried out in two stages. In the first stage, the researchers each working independently performed a keyword search using the terms *virtual world*. The journals selected for investigation were identified in the literature as utilizing peer review and focused on CALL research (Smith & Lafford, 2009). The eight publications targeted in this review included the following CALL journals, *CALL-EJ, CALICO Journal, Computer Assisted Language Learning, International Journal of Computer-Assisted Language Learning & Teaching, JALT CALL Journal, ReCALL, Language Learning & Technology, System*. Although the above publications do not represent the full spectrum of journals that carry papers relevant to this review, it was considered likely they would incorporate learner-based studies relevant to research on the use of social VWs in language education. In addition to the above journals, a search was conducted using the online database Education Resources Information Clearinghouse (ERIC). This database was selected as it is large-scale and provides access to a wide range of peer reviewed publications. In searching the database, each of the researchers used the search terms *virtual world* and *language*. The use of these terms enabled the identification of papers that included the search terms in the title, abstract and keywords within a journal. In the second stage, the search functions of each publication were utilized. The researchers carried out a search using the above terms. This was restricted to the period 2007-2017. This process yielded additional relevant articles and book chapters that had not been identified in the first stage of the search. To achieve inter-coder reliability on conclusion of the above searches, the researchers discussed and resolved discrepancies in paper selection drawing on the selection criteria described in the following discussion.

Criteria for Inclusion

The search process outlined above produced a total of 228 potentially relevant publications. In order to qualify for analysis the publications were reviewed using the following criteria:

1. The study was published during the period 2007-2017.
2. The study was peer-reviewed.
3. The study utilized network-based social virtual worlds.
4. The study focused on the activities of second language learners.
5. The study provided a detailed overview of participants, data collection procedures, analysis methods, and significant outcomes.

Of the above publications, opinion pieces, commentaries, technological descriptions, book reviews or conceptual papers were disregarded, as they did not meet the criteria for inclusion. The remaining journal papers (n=26) and book chapters (n=2) were selected and are subject to investigation in this review. The distribution of the journal papers and book chapters is set out in Tables 2 and 3.

Table 2. Distribution of research in journals

Journal	Number of Articles	Study
ReCALL.	6.	• Deutschmann, Panichi, and Molka-Danielsen (2009). • Levak and Son (2016). • Melchor-Couto (2016). • Peterson (2010; 2012). • Wigham and Chanier (2013).
Computer Assisted Language Learning.	4.	• Jauregi, Canto, de Graaff, Koenraad, and Moonen (2011). • Liou (2012). • Wehner, Gump, and Downey (2011). • Wigham and Chanier (2015).
JALTCALL Journal.	3.	• DuQuette (2011). • Kruk (2013). • Wang, Deutschmann, and Steinvall (2013).
Language Learning & Technology.	3.	• Lan (2014; 2015). • Lan, Kan, Sung, and Chang (2016).
Australasian Journal Of Educational Technology.	2.	• Chen (2016a). • Henderson, Huang, Grant, and Henderson (2012).
International Journal of Computer-Assisted Language Learning & Teaching.	2.	• Kruk (2015). • Thomas (2013).
Educational Technology Research and Development.	1.	• Wang, Calandra, Hibbard, and McDowell Lefaiver (2012).
Canadian Journal of Learning and Technology.	1.	• Jee (2014).
Computers and Education.	1.	• Chen (2016b).
The Language Learning Journal.	1.	• Milton, Jonsen, Hirst, and Lindenburn (2012).
Language Learning in Higher Education	1.	• Canto & Jauregi (2017).
Language Awareness.	1.	• Deutschmann and Panichi (2009).

Table 3. Distribution of research in books

Book	Number of Chapters	Chapter
Thomas, M., Reinders, H., & Warschauer, M. (Eds.). (2013). *Contemporary Computer-Assisted Language Learning.* London: Bloomsbury.	1.	Sadler & Dooly (2013).
Gonzalez-Lloret, M., & Ortega, L. (Eds.). (2014). *Technology and tasks: Exploring technology-mediated TBLT.* Washington, DC: Georgetown University Press.	1.	Canto, deGraaff, and Jauregi (2014).

FINDINGS

Implementation of Social Virtual Worlds

In the context of answering research question one, analysis of relevant research revealed pertinent findings regarding implementation. The majority of studies (20) identified in this review investigated the use of VWs in higher education and involved either undergraduates or graduate students (Canto, de Graaff, &

Jauregi, 2014; Canto & Jauregi, 2017; Deutschmann & Panichi, 2009; Deutschmann, Panichi, & Molka-Danielsen, 2009; Henderson, Huang, Grant, & Henderson, 2012; Jauregi, Canto, de Graff, Koenraad, & Moonen, 2011; Jee, 2014; Lan, 2014; Lan, Kan, Sung, & Chang, 2016; Liou, 2012; Melchor-Couto, 2016; Milton, Jonsen, Hirst, & Lindenburn, 2012; Peterson, 2010; 2012; Thomas, 2013; Wang, Calandra, Hibbard, & McDowell Lefaiver, 2012; Wang, Deutschmann, & Steinvall, 2013; Wehner, Gump, & Downey, 2011; Wigham & Chanier, 2013; 2015). It was found that fewer studies were conducted in schools, with a total of four studies carried out in elementary (Lan, 2015; Sadler & Dooly, 2013) and high schools (Kruk, 2013; 2015). No studies were identified as being carried out in settings involving language learners enrolled in institutions of further education. Moreover, analysis further reveals that four studies incorporated into this review investigated use of VWs in informal out-of-school contexts (Chen, 2016a; 2016b; DuQuette, 2011; Levak & Son, 2016).

Languages Investigated in Research

In answer to research question two namely the languages examined in the research studies, analysis shows that a total of six target languages were identified. English was the most frequent L2 investigated with 19 studies focusing on EFL learners (Chen, 2016a; 2016b; Deutschmann, Panichi, & Molka-Danielsen, 2009; DuQuette, 2011; Jee, 2014; Kruk, 2013; 2015; Lan, 2015; Lan, Kan, Sung, & Chang, 2016; Levak & Son, 2016; Liou, 2012; Peterson, 2010; 2012; Sadler & Dooly, 2013; Thomas, 2013; Wang, Calandra, Hibbard, & McDowell Lefaiver, 2012; Wang, Deutschmann, & Steinvall, 2013; Wigham & Chanier, 2013; 2015). A further five studies involved Spanish (Canto, de Graaff, & Jauregi, 2014; Canto & Jauregi, 2017; Jauregi, Canto, de Graff, Koenraad, & Moonen, 2011; Melchor-Couto, 2016; Wehner, Gump, & Downey, 2011) and three studies focused on Chinese (Henderson, Huang, Grant, & Henderson, 2012; Lan, 2014; Lan, Kan, Sung, & Chang, 2016). The remaining research involved French (Wigham & Chanier, 2013; 2015), Hungarian (Milton, Jonsen, Hirst, & Lindenburn, 2012) and Croatian (Levak & Son, 2016). It was found that three studies identified in the data adopted a novel approach that focused on the study of two L2 languages within a single project. Research by Wigham and Chanier (2013; 2015) focused on the use of English as a foreign language and French as a foreign language. The study conducted by Levak and Son (2016) also adopted the above approach and involved the study of English and Croatian. A striking feature of the data was the lack of research involving less commonly taught languages. Only two studies (Milton, Jonsen, Hirst, & Lindenburn, 2012; Levak & Son, 2016) concerned less commonly taught languages.

Methods Employed in Virtual World Research

In the context of answering research question three it was found that qualitative and mixed methods approaches were the most frequently employed. A total of 11 qualitative papers were identified (Chen, 2016b; Deutschmann & Panichi, 2009; Deutschmann, Panichi, & Molka-Danielsen, 2009; DuQuette, 2011; Jee, 2014; Liou, 2012; Jauregi, Canto, de Graff, Koenraad, & Moonen, 2011; Peterson, 2010; 2012; Sadler & Dooly, 2013; Thomas, 2013). In addition, a further eleven studies were found to have employed mixed methods (Canto, de Graaff, & Jauregi, 2014; Canto & Jauregi, 2017; Chen, 2016a; Kruk, 2013; Lan, 2014; 2015; Levak & Son, 2016; Melchor-Couto, 2016; Wang, Calandra, Hibbard, & McDowell Lefaiver, 2012; Wang, Deutschmann, & Steinvall, 2013; Wigham & Chanier, 2013). Studies utilizing the above methods accounted for a total of twenty two of the twenty eight studies identified for inclusion in this review. Moreover, it was found that of the studies that adopted mixed methods, a qualitative approach predominated. Research designs identified in the above research included case studies (Jauregi et al., 2011; Peterson, 2010), ethnography (DuQuette, 2011; Thomas, 2013), action research (Deutschmann et al., 2009) discourse analysis (Deutschmann & Panichi, 2009; Jee, 2014; Peterson, 2012) and ecological perspectives (Liou, 2012). Moreover, six studies were identified as being explicitly experimental in nature (Canto & Jauregi, 2017; Kruk, 2013; Melchor-Couto, 2016; Peterson, 2010; Sadler & Dooly, 2013; Wang, Calandra, Hibbard, & McDowell Lefaiver, 2012).

Studies that adopted an exclusively quantitative approach to data analysis were less frequent than the above approaches and accounted for only six studies (Henderson, Huang, Grant, & Henderson, 2012; Kruk, 2015; Lan, 2014; Lan, Kan, Sung, & Chang, 2016; Milton, Jonsen, Hirst, & Lindenburn, 2012; Wehner, Gump, & Downey, 2011; Wigham & Chanier, 2015). Overall, data indicate that the majority of studies were qualitative and descriptive. A noteworthy feature of the research is the prevalence of small-scale studies that were of limited duration. Only a minority of studies utilized a statistically significant number of participants (Wang, Calandra, Hibbard, & McDowell Lefaiver, 2012; Canto & Jauregi, 2017; Jee, 2014; Henderson, Huang, Grant, & Henderson, 2012; Lan, 2015) or a control group (Wang, Calandra, Hibbard, & McDowell Lefaiver, 2012; Canto & Jauregi, 2017; Kruk, 2015; Melchor-Couto, 2016; Wehner, Gump, & Downey, 2011). Moreover, it was found that cross-sectional (Henderson, Huang, Grant, & Henderson, 2012) and longitudinal research (Chen, 2016b; Lan, 2015; Liou, 2012; Thomas, 2013) accounted for a minority of studies.

Research Areas

In answering research question four data analysis reveals that eight areas have been investigated in research. The analysis draws attention to interesting differences in the areas that have been explored in current research. Data shows that studies focusing on aspects of TL production were the most frequent with sixteen studies identified as examining these areas. Within this research area it was found that ten studies investigated oral TL output (Canto & Jauregi, 2017; Chen, 2016a; Deutschmann & Panichi, 2009; Deutschmann, Panichi, & Molka-Danielsen, 2009; Jauregi, Canto, de Graff, Koenraad, & Moonen, 2011; Jee, 2014; Lan, 2014; 2015; Lan, Kan, Sung, & Chang, 2016; Sadler & Dooly, 2013). In contrast, only two studies focused exclusively on writing (Peterson, 2010; 2012). Another four studies focused on examining both oral and written TL production (Milton, Jonsen, Hirst, & Lindenburn, 2012; Wang, Deutschmann, & Steinvall, 2013; Wigham & Chanier, 2013; 2015). It was found that the application of task-based learning represented the second most frequent area of research. Analysis shows that a total of fifteen papers were identified as involving this approach (Canto, de Graaff, & Jauregi, 2014; Canto & Jauregi, 2017; Chen, 2016a; 2016b; Deutschmann, Panichi, & Molka-Danielsen, 2009; Jauregi, Canto, de Graff, Koenraad, & Moonen, 2011; Jee, 2014; Liou, 2012; Henderson, Huang, Grant, & Henderson, 2012; Lan, 2014; Lan, Kan, Sung, & Chang, 2016; Peterson, 2010; 2012; Thomas, 2013; Wigham & Chanier, 2013).

Another subset of research concerned the investigation of affective factors. It was found that eight studies were concerned with this area. Analysis reveals that of the above research learner attitudes were the most frequently area explored accounting for six studies (Chen, 2016b; DuQuette, 2011; Henderson, Huang, Grant, & Henderson, 2012; Liou, 2012; Thomas, 2013; Wang, Calandra, Hibbard, & McDowell Lefaiver, 2012). In this context a further two studies were found to concentrate specifically on issues relating to motivation (Wehner, Gump, & Downey, 2011) and anxiety (Melchor-Couto, 2016). Analysis also shows that in addition to the above a total of five other areas were investigated in research. Areas identified include grammar (Kruk, 2013; 2015), listening (Levak & Son, 2016), and the development of intercultural competence (Canto, de Graaff, & Jauregi, 2014; Canto & Jauregi, 2017). Additional areas of interest were the integration of VW-based activities into the regular curriculum (Canto & Jauregi, 2017; Chen, 2016b; Deutschmann & Panichi, 2009; Kruk, 2013; Liou, 2012; Wigham & Chanier, 2013) and also the examination of learning in informal out-of-school contexts (Chen, 2016a; 2016b; DuQuette, 2011; Levak & Son, 2016).

Major Findings: Language Production

Analysis reveals findings that are of relevance to answering research question five and shed new light on the claims made in the rationales proposed for the use of VWs. In terms of the hypothesized benefits of interaction, the research lends limited support to the claims made in the literature. The findings reported in studies examined in this review lend credence to the assertion that sustained participation in projects involving WVs provides exposure to rich sources of TL input and facilitates learner-centered interaction (Chen, 2016b; Lan, 2015; Liou, 2012; Peterson, 2010; 2012). In addition, there is evidence reported across studies involving a variety of project configurations that participation in VWs elicits TL production and meaning-focused interaction (Canto, de Graaff, & Jauregi, 2014; Canto & Jauregi, 2017; Chen, 2016a; Deutschmann, Panichi, & Molka-Danielsen, 2009; Jauregi, Canto, de Graff, Koenraad, & Moonen, 2011; Jee 2014; Lan, 2014; Milton, Jonsen, Hirst, & Lindenburn, 2012; Peterson, 2012; Wang, Calandra, Hibbard, & McDowell Lefaiver, 2012; Wigham & Chanier, 2015). From the perspective of rationales for the use of VWs informed by the sociocultural account of SLA the findings reported by Jee (2014) and Peterson (2012) are of particular relevance in this regard. The researchers in both studies reported that learners engaged in collaborative dialogue involving peer assistance and the negotiation of unknown lexis during voice (Jee, 2014) and text-based (Peterson, 2012) interaction in *Second Life*. Research conducted from a psycholinguist perspective confirms these findings. In the small-scale study conducted by Chen (2016a) it was found that during voice-based interaction in the above environment participants negotiated meanings and successfully employed both metacognitive and discourse management strategies that were appropriate to the online nature of the communication environment. In a project involving the use of voice and text chat in *Second Life* Wigham and Chanier (2015) found that the learners utilized the latter tool in order to provide feedback in the form of recasts on errors made in the audio modality. In contrast, a project involving *Second Life* conducted by Milton et al. (2012) produced contrary findings. It was reported that over four one-hour sessions there was no evidence for vocabulary acquisition. However, the researchers claimed that the environment elicited TL output and provided potentially valuable fluency practice.

Major Findings: Affective Factors

As noted at a previous stage of this discussion, the second most frequent area of research concerns the investigation of affective factors. Analysis of the data reveals extensive evidence to support the claim made in the rationales for the use of VWs that participation frequently elicits positive learner attitudes (Chen, 2016b; DuQuette, 2011; Henderson, Huang, Grant, & Henderson, 2012; Liou, 2012; Thomas, 2013; Wang, Calandra, Hibbard, & McDowell Lefaiver, 2012; Wehner, Gump, & Downey, 2011). Positive findings regarding learner beliefs were reported in study involving *Second Life* conducted by Henderson et al. (2012). The researchers reported a statistically significant increase in learner's self-efficacy beliefs across a range of language skills. Although the research was of limited duration its findings are nonetheless important as it involved a large sample size of 81 learners. In addition, the researchers employed questionnaires and utilized pre and post-tests. The claim that participation in projects involving VWs may reduce learner anxiety has been explored in the literature. In experimental research Melchor-Couto (2016) investigated the foreign language anxiety levels of EFL learners who undertook oral interaction activities in *Second Life*. The data collected on these learners was compared to that of a control group who undertook similar activities in a conventional foreign language classroom. Results indicated that as the project unfolded anxiety levels decreased in the experimental group and were lower than the control. The researcher speculated that the anonymity afforded by the online avatar-based nature of the interaction may have contributed to these findings. Researchers have also attempted to confirm the contention that participation in CALL projects involving social VWs enhances learner motivation. In longitudinal research undertaken by Peterson (2010) questionnaire data indicated that sustained interaction in a *Second Life* world elicited high levels of motivation from the majority of participants. Wehner et al. (2011) reported on empirical research that involved a group of undergraduate learners of Spanish who undertook activities in *Second Life* and a control. Statistical analysis of results based on responses to an attitude/ motivation test battery suggest that overall the learners who participated in *Second Life*-based activities consistently reported more positive feelings with regards to motivation when compared to the control.

Major Findings: Implementation of Task-Based Learning

The suitability of VWs for the implementation of task-based learning is noted in the literature (Chen, 2016b; Ganem-Gutierrez, 2014). As a result of this context, it was anticipated that researchers would investigate this approach. This expectation was borne out to a degree, as analysis shows that a total of 16 papers were identified as involving the successful application of task-based learning. There was a noteworthy divergence in the approach adopted by the researchers in the above studies. In seven of the papers the researchers implemented language tasks utilized in traditional language classrooms (Canto & Jauregi, 2017; Chen, 2016b; Jee, 2014; Henderson, Huang, Grant, & Henderson, 2012; Lan, 2014; Lan, Kan, Sung, & Chang, 2016; Thomas, 2013). In the remaining studies, the researchers utilized tasks that were specifically designed to make use of the online affordances provided by VWs (Canto, de Graaff, & Jauregi, 2014; Chen, 2016a; Deutschmann, Panichi, & Molka-Danielsen, 2009; Jauregi, Canto, de Graff, Koenraad, & Moonen, 2011; Liou, 2012; Peterson, 2010; 2012; Sadler & Dooly, 2013; Wigham & Chanier, 2013). In examples of this approach, in research reported by Peterson (2012) participants successfully utilized an online graphing tool during an opinion exchange task held in *Second Life*. In a paper describing the results of two courses held in a purpose-built world in *Second Life* Deutschmann et al. (2009) found that in the first course role-play tasks were not successful for novice users who appeared to find the communication environment challenging. However, in the second course participation increased substantially when authentic meaning-focused tasks were implemented. The above studies lend considerable support to the contention made in the literature that VWs are viable venues for the application of task-based learning.

Major Findings: Grammar

Learner grammatical development represents an area of interest in research. In experimental work Kruk (2013) examined the use of the browser-based virtual world *Yoowalk* as a means to facilitate acquisition of the English second conditional among high school EFL learners. This research involved the use of mixed methods. Data were drawn from a grammar pre-test and two post-tests. In addition, a background questionnaire and an evaluation sheet were administered. Results showed that instruction using the virtual world assisted the participants in using the TL structure more correctly both immediately after the experiment and afterwards. Furthermore, the learners viewed the virtual world positively and claimed that it provided valuable opportunities for TL practice. In further study focusing on grammatical development, Kruk (2015) explored the effectiveness of using the VW *Active Worlds* to teach the present simple tense. This research project involved an experimental group of EFL learners who used the chat feature of *Active Worlds* during instruction and a control group who were taught in a conventional language classroom. Data were collected from a background questionnaire, grammar test and a post-study questionnaire. Findings suggest that although both groups benefitted from instruction long-term retention was superior in the treatment group.

Major Findings: Intercultural Competence

Another focus of research lies in the use of VWs as a means to enhance the development of intercultural competencies. In an example of this approach, Canto et al. (2014) reported on the results of a study that involved use of *Second Life* as a means to enhance the intercultural competence of a group of Dutch learners of Spanish. In this project, the learners worked with native speakers of Spanish and undertook language tasks designed to facilitate social interaction and the development of intercultural competence. This project utilized information gap tasks that focused on intercultural issues. Quantitative and qualitative data showed that tasks elicited instances of intercultural negotiation. Learner feedback indicated that participation enhanced the awareness of intercultural issues. Canto and Jauregi (2017) reported on mixed methods research that involved learners of Spanish who undertook task-based interaction during a language course in *Second Life*. The tasks focused on intercultural content. Data showed that the participants engaged in the negotiation of meaning. Moreover, it was found that a substantial element of this type of interaction involved the resolution of intercultural communication gaps. Analysis also indicated that the participants who undertook interaction in *Second Life* scored higher than groups that undertook video-based and face-to-face interaction involving the same tasks. Survey results showed that the learners who undertook interaction in *Second Life* claimed that their knowledge of the TL culture was enhanced.

Major Findings: Integration into the Curriculum

It was found that researchers have investigated the integration of VW-based activities into regular courses. Analysis indicates that six of the studies utilized integration to some degree (Canto & Jauregi, 2017; Chen, 2016b; Deutschmann & Panichi, 2009; Kruk, 2013; Liou, 2012; Wigham & Chanier, 2013). Deutschmann and Panichi (2009) reported on the conduct of a teacher-supported EFL oral proficiency course for doctoral students held in *Kamino Island* a *Second Life*-based virtual world. The learners undertook six 90-minute voice chat sessions. Qualitative and quantitative data showed that in the early sessions teacher-initiated turn taking predominated. However, as the project progressed it was found that the learners displayed increasing autonomy and took the initiative in managing the TL interaction. In qualitative longitudinal research held over 18 weeks Liou (2012) implemented an elective course involving EFL learners. The participants were novice users who undertook a variety of text-based activities in *Second Life*. Learner feedback indicated that network issues and the need to learn commands hampered the interaction and caused frustration among the participants. However, positive findings were also reported. Over half of the learners expressed positive attitudes. The learners commented favorably on the ability to teleport, explore and experience the environment, activities that were viewed as motivating. Learners identified additional features positively including enhanced understanding of the TL culture, and opportunities for self-expression in a low-stress environment.

Major Findings: Informal Learning

Influenced by speculation in the literature regarding the value of participation in VW-based learning in out-of-school contexts (Thorne, Black, & Sykes, 2009) researchers have investigated the use of VWs in informal non-institutional settings. It was found that four studies have examined this phenomenon (Chen, 2016a; 2016b; DuQuette, 2011; Levak & Son, 2016). In a noteworthy exemplar of this approach Chen (2016b) reported on the findings of a study involving interaction in the virtual island *VIRTLANTIS* located in *Second Life*. Volunteer EFL learners from eight countries undertook a task-based online course that was implemented over ten sessions. Data was collected from questionnaires, learner journals, a focus group interview and observation. Findings indicate that sustained interaction in *Second Life* elicited positive learner attitudes. Learners in this study claimed that the unique features of the environment made for a rewarding experience that was less stressful and more enjoyable than a conventional language class. The ability to build 3D objects fostered engagement and a sense of achievement. Participation in role-play was perceived as providing valuable opportunities to experiment while developing fluency and language skills transferable to real world contexts. Moreover, it was observed that as the project progressed the collaborative nature of the interaction and the reduction of status cues supported the development of a sense of community that enhanced confidence and intercultural understanding. DuQuette (2011) carried out small-scale qualitative research on volunteer EFL learner's attitudes towards language lessons held in an informal chat group in the simulation *Cypris Village* that forms part of *Second Life*. Data showed evidence that the participants consistently displayed autonomy. Moreover, it was found that the advanced level learners manifested high levels of motivation.

FUTURE RESEARCH DIRECTIONS

As the discussion in this review shows, research on the use of social VWs in CALL is expanding and has produced encouraging results. However, it is important to acknowledge that current research is not definitive. There are significant limitations in many of the research designs adopted by researchers. For example, none of the studies that employed discourse analysis utilized measures to ensure inter-coder reliability. In addition, the majority of studies were of limited duration, involved small groups of learners and did not employ a control. Moreover, most work focused on learner feedback collected through the use of questionnaires. However, none of studies that employed this data collection instrument highlight the well-known limitations on learner self-reporting. Overall it was found that most studies were qualitative and descriptive in nature. However, as this work in this area is a relatively recent phenomenon this finding was to be expected. Although subject to limitations, current work is nonetheless valuable as it lays the ground work for further studies that can assist in the process of systematically identifying important variables for empirical investigation in future research.

This review draws attention to a number of gaps in the literature and promising areas for future research. There is a pressing need for more empirical research, involving larger sample sizes, controls, delayed post-tests and more diverse learner groups. In addition, current research highlights the need, from a qualitative perspective, for more longitudinal studies that can provide insights into learners language development over time. The absence of replication studies in this review draws attention to the crucial importance of additional work in this area. As noted previously, present research is heavily focused on EFL learners based in higher education. Additional studies are necessary that explore other TLs and learning in informal non-institutional settings. Moreover, as current research emphasizes the potential of task-based learning further studies in this area offer the prospect of providing new insights into the value of this approach. In this context, research also highlights the need to investigate the potential of the unique mix of features provided by VWs. Although text and voice-based interaction remain the most frequently researched areas other features of these environments such as the potential of role-play and the creation of new virtual content appear promising issues for investigation in future research.

CONCLUSION

The purpose of this chapter was to review the body of research on the use of social VWs in language education. This review established how these environments have been implemented, identified the target languages, methods employed in research, areas of interest and major findings. Data show that of the 28 studies analyzed the majority (20) involved research conducted in higher education settings focusing on EFL learners. Data further show that research is predominately descriptive in nature with qualitative data collection and mixed methods the most frequently employed. It was found that only six of the studies utilized quantitative methods. Research is focused on the investigation of TL production and interaction, affective factors, implementation of task-based learning, grammar, intercultural development, integration and learning in informal contexts. Positive findings have been reported that lend limited support to the claims made in the rationales for the use of VWs proposed in the literature. Studies provide evidence that confirms the assertion that VWs elicit TL production and opportunities to engage in meaning-focused dialogue particularly in conjunction with task-based learning. Positive attitudes are reported and there is evidence to suggest that grammatical and intercultural development may be enhanced in both formal and informal settings. Although research is subject to limitations and is not conclusive overall findings have been positive. As this review shows, as research continues to expand more work is needed in order to establish the ways in which the unique potential of virtual worlds can be leveraged to the benefit of learners.

ACKNOWLEDGMENT

This research was supported by the RIKEN Center for Advanced Intelligence Project.

REFERENCES

Canto, S., de Graaff, R., & Jauregi, K. (2014). Collaborative tasks for negotiation of intercultural meaning in virtual worlds and video-web communication. In M. Gonzalez-Lloret & L. Ortega (Eds.), *Technology and tasks: Exploring technology-mediated TBLT* (pp. 183–212). Washington, DC: Georgetown University Press. doi:10.1075/tblt.6.07can

Canto, S., & Jauregi, K. (2017). Language learning effects through the integration of synchronous online communication: The case of video communication and Second Life. *Language Learning in Higher Education*, *7*(1), 21–53. doi:10.1515/cercles-2017-0004

Chen, C. (2016a). EFL learners' strategy use during task-based interaction in Second Life. *Australasian Journal of Educational Technology*, *32*(3), 1–17.

Chen, J. (2016b). The crossroads of English language learners, task-based instruction, and 3D multi-user virtual learning in Second Life. *Computers & Education*, *102*, 152–171. doi:10.1016/j.compedu.2016.08.004

Cooke-Plagwitz, J. (2008). New Directions in CALL: An objective introduction to Second Life. *CALICO Journal*, *25*(3), 547–557. doi:10.1558/cj.v25i3.547-557

Cooke-Plagwitz, J. (2009). A new language for the net generation: Why Second Life works for the net generation. In R. Oxford & J. Oxford (Eds.), Second Language Teaching and Learning in the Net Generation (pp.173-180). National Foreign Language Resource Center, University of Hawai'i.

Dalgarno, B., & Lee, M. J. W. (2010). What are the learning affordances of 3-D virtual environments? *British Journal of Educational Technology*, *41*(1), 10–32. doi:10.1111/j.1467-8535.2009.01038.x

Deutschmann, M., & Panichi, L. (2009). Talking into empty space? Signalling involvement in a virtual language classroom in Second Life. *Language Awareness*, *18*(3-4), 310–328. doi:10.1080/09658410903197306

Deutschmann, M., & Panichi, L. (2013). Towards models for designing language learning in virtual worlds. *International Journal of Virtual and Personal Learning Environments*, *4*(2), 65–84. doi:10.4018/jvple.2013040104

Deutschmann, M., Panichi, L., & Molka-Danielsen, J. (2009). Designing oral participation in Second Life: A comparative study of two language proficiency courses. *ReCALL*, *21*(2), 70–90. doi:10.1017/S0958344009000196

Dickey, M. D. (2005). Three-dimensional virtual worlds and distance learning: Two case studies of active worlds as a medium for distance education. *British Journal of Educational Technology*, *36*(3), 439–451. doi:10.1111/j.1467-8535.2005.00477.x

Doughty, C. J., & Long, M. (2003). Optimal psycholinguistic environments for distance foreign language learning. *Language Learning & Technology*, *7*(3), 50–80.

DuQuette, J. P. (2011). Buckling down: Initiating an EFL reading circle in a casual learning group. *JALTCALL Journal*, *7*(1), 79–92.

Ganem-Gutierrez, G. A. (2014). The third dimension: A sociocultural theory approach to the design and evaluation of 3D world virtual tasks. In M. González-Lloret & L. Ortega (Eds.), *Technology-mediated TBLT: Researching technology and tasks* (pp. 213–237). Amsterdam, The Netherlands: John Benjamins. doi:10.1075/tblt.6.08gan

González-Lloret, M., & Ortega, L. (2015). Staking out the territory of technology mediated TBLT. In M. Bygate (Ed.), *Domains and directions in the development of TBLT: A decade of plenaries from the international conference* (pp. 59–86). Amsterdam: John Benjamins.

Henderson, M., Huang, H., Grant, S., & Henderson, L. (2012). The impact of Chinese language lessons in a virtual world on university students' self-efficacy beliefs. *Australasian Journal of Educational Technology*, *28*(3), 400–419. doi:10.14742/ajet.842

Ho, C. M. L. (2010). What's in a question? The case of student's enactments in the Second Life virtual world. *Innovation in Language Learning and Teaching*, *4*(2), 151–176. doi:10.1080/17501221003725397

Jauregi, K., Canto, S., de Graff, R., Koenraad, T., & Moonen, M. (2011). Verbal interaction in Second Life: Towards a pedagogic framework for task design. *Computer Assisted Language Learning*, *24*(1), 77–101. doi:10.1080/09588221.2010.538699

Jee, M. J. (2014). From First Life to Second Life: Evaluating task-based language learning in a new environment. *Canadian Journal of Learning and Technology*, *40*(1), 1–15. doi:10.21432/T2F595

Kruk, M. (2013). Helping students to learn the second conditional by blending Internet resources with virtual worlds: The results of a study. *JALTCALL Journal*, *9*(3), 241–257.

Kruk, M. (2015). Practicing the English present simple tense in Active Worlds. *International Journal of Computer-Assisted Language Learning and Teaching*, *5*(4), 52–65. doi:10.4018/IJCALLT.2015100104

Kuriscak, L. M., & Luke, C. L. (2009). Language learner attitudes toward virtual worlds: An investigation of Second Life. In L. Lomicka & G. Lord (Eds.), *The next generation: Social networking and online collaboration in foreign language learning* (pp. 173–198). San Marcos, TX: CALICO Publications.

Lan, Y. J. (2014). Does second life improve mandarin learning by overseas Chinese students? *Language Learning & Technology*, *18*(2), 36–56.

Lan, Y. J. (2015). Contextual EFL learning in a 3D virtual environment. *Language Learning & Technology*, *19*(2), 16–31.

Lan, Y. J., Kan, Y. H., Sung, Y. T., & Chang, K. E. (2016). Oral-performance language tasks for CSL beginners in Second Life. *Language Learning & Technology*, *20*(3), 60–79.

Lantolf, J., & Thorne, S. L. (2006). *Sociocultural theory and the genesis of second language development*. Oxford, UK: Oxford University Press.

Lawrence, G., & Ahmed, F. (2018). Pedagogical insights into hyper-immersive virtual world language learning environments. *International Journal of Computer-Assisted Language Learning and Teaching*, *8*(1), 1–14. doi:10.4018/IJCALLT.2018010101

Levak, N., & Son, J.-B. (2016). Facilitating second language learners' listening comprehension with Second Life and Skype. *ReCALL, 29*(2), 200–218. doi:10.1017/S0958344016000215

Liou, H. C. (2012). The roles of Second Life in a college computer assisted language learning (CALL) course in Taiwan, ROC. *Computer Assisted Language Learning, 25*(4), 365–382. doi:10.1080/095882 21.2011.597766

Melchro-Couto, S. (2016). Foreign language anxiety levels in Second Life oral interaction. *ReCALL, 29*(1), 99–119. doi:10.1017/S0958344016000185

Milton, J., Jonsen, S., Hirst, S., & Lindenburn, S. (2012). Foreign language vocabulary development through activities in an online 3D environment. *Language Learning Journal, 40*(1), 99–112. doi:10.10 80/09571736.2012.658229

Panichi, L., Deutschmann, M., & Molka-Danielsen, J. (2010). Virtual worlds for language learning and intercultural exchange – Is it for real? In S. Guth & F. Helm (Eds.), *Telecollaboration 2.0: Languages, literacies and intercultural learning in the 21st century* (pp. 165–195). Bern: Peter Lang.

Peterson, M. (2005). Learning interaction in an avatar-based virtual environment: A preliminary study. *PacCALL Journal, 1*(1), 29–40.

Peterson, M. (2006). Learner interaction management in an avatar and chat-based virtual world. *Computer Assisted Language Learning, 19*(1), 79–103. doi:10.1080/09588220600804087

Peterson, M. (2010). Learner participation patterns and strategy use in Second Life: An exploratory case study. *ReCALL, 22*(3), 273–292. doi:10.1017/S0958344010000169

Peterson, M. (2011). Toward a research agenda for the use of three-dimensional virtual worlds in language learning. *CALICO Journal, 29*(1), 67–80. doi:10.11139/cj.29.1.67-80

Peterson, M. (2012). EFL learner collaborative interaction in Second Life. *ReCALL, 24*(1), 20–39. doi:10.1017/S0958344011000279

Peterson, M. (2017). Introduction. In M. Peterson (Ed.), Digital language learning and teaching: Critical and primary sources: Vol. 4. New developments in computer assisted language learning (pp. 1-18). London: Bloomsbury.

Petrakou, A. (2010). Interacting through avatars: Virtual worlds as a context for online education. *Computers & Education, 54*(4), 1020–1027. doi:10.1016/j.compedu.2009.10.007

Privas-Bréauté, V. (2015). Creating an avatar to become a "spect-actor" of one's learning of English for specific purposes. *The EUROCALL Review, 23*(2), 40–52.

Sadler, R. (2012). *Virtual worlds for language learning: From theory to practice.* Bern: Peter Lang. doi:10.3726/978-3-0351-0406-6

Sadler, R., & Dooly, M. (2013). Language learning in virtual worlds: Research and practice. In M. Thomas, H. Reinders, & M. Warschaeur (Eds.), *Contemporary Computer-Assisted Language Learning* (pp. 159–182). London: Bloomsbury.

Schwienhorst, K. (2002). The state of VR: A meta-analysis of virtual reality tools in second language acquisition. *Computer Assisted Language Learning*, *15*(3), 221–239. doi:10.1076/call.15.3.221.8186

Schwienhorst, K. (2009). Learning a second language in three dimensions: Potential benefits and the evidence so far. *Themes in Science and Technology Education*, *2*(1-2), 153–163.

Smith, B., & Lafford, B. A. (2009). The evaluation of scholarly activity in computer-assisted language learning. *Modern Language Journal*, *93*(s1), 868–883. doi:10.1111/j.1540-4781.2009.00978.x

Svensson, P. (2003). Virtual worlds as arenas for language learning. In U. Felix (Ed.), *Online language learning: Towards best practice* (pp. 123–142). Amsterdam: Swets & Zeitlinger.

Thomas, M. (2013). BLT in business English communication: An approach for evaluating Adobe Connect and Second Life in a blended language learning format. *International Journal of Computer-Assisted Language Learning and Teaching*, *3*(1), 73–89. doi:10.4018/ijcallt.2013010105

Thorne, S. L. (2008). Transcultural communication in open Internet environments and massively multiplayer online games. In S. S. Magan (Ed.), *Mediating discourse online* (pp. 305–327). Amsterdam: John Benjamins. doi:10.1075/aals.3.17tho

Thorne, S. L., Black, W., & Sykes, J. M. (2009). Second language use, socialization, and learning in Internet interest communities and online gaming. *Modern Language Journal*, *93*(1), 802–821. doi:10.1111/j.1540-4781.2009.00974.x

Toyoda, E., & Harrison, R. (2002). Categorization of text chat communication between learners and native speakers of Japanese. *Language Learning & Technology*, *6*(1), 82–99.

Wang, A. (2017). Using Second Life in an English course: How does the technology affect participation? *International Journal of Computer-Assisted Language Learning and Teaching*, *7*(1), 67–86. doi:10.4018/IJCALLT.2017010105

Wang, A., Deutschmann, M., & Steinvall, A. (2013). Towards a model for mapping participation: Exploring factors affecting participation in a telecollaborative learning scenario in Second Life. *JALT CALL Journal*, *9*(1), 3–22.

Wang, X. C., Calandra, B., Hibbard, S. T., & McDowell Lefaiver, M. L. (2012). Learning effects of an experimental EFL program in Second Life. *Educational Technology Research and Development*, *60*(5), 943–961. doi:10.100711423-012-9259-0

Wehner, A. K., Gump, A. W., & Downey, S. (2011). The effects of Second Life on the motivation of undergraduate students learning a foreign language. *Computer Assisted Language Learning*, *24*(3), 277–289. doi:10.1080/09588221.2010.551757

Wigham, C. R., & Chanier, T. (2013). A study of verbal and nonverbal communication in second life—the ARCHI21 experience. *ReCALL*, *25*(1), 63–84. doi:10.1017/S0958344012000250

Wigham, C. R., & Chanier, T. (2015). Interactions between text chat and audio modalities for L2 communication and feedback in the synthetic world of second life. *Computer Assisted Language Learning*, *28*(3), 260–280. doi:10.1080/09588221.2013.851702

ADDITIONAL READING

Aldrich, C. (2009). *Learning online with games, simulations and virtual worlds: Strategies for online instruction*. San Francisco: Jossey-Bass.

Gisbert, T., & Bullen, M. (Eds.). (2015). *Teaching and learning in digital worlds: Strategies and issues in higher education*. Tarragona, Spain: Publicacions Universitat Rovira I Virgili.

Kim, S. H., Lee, J., & Thomas, M. K. (2012). Between purpose and method: A review of educational research on 3D Virtual Worlds. *Journal of Virtual Worlds Research*, *5*(1), 1–18. doi:10.4101/jvwr.v5i1.2151

Molka-Danielsen, J., & Deutschmann, M. (Eds.). (2009). *Learning and teaching in the virtual world of Second Life*. Trondheim: Tapir Academic Press.

Nelson, B. C., & Erlandson, B. E. (Eds.). (2012). *Design for learning in virtual worlds*. New York: Routledge.

Peachey, A., Gillen, J., Livingstone, D., & Smith-Robbins, S. (Eds.). (2010). *Researching learning in virtual worlds*. London: Springer. doi:10.1007/978-1-84996-047-2

Peterson, M. (2016). Virtual worlds and language learning. In F. Farr & L. Murray (Eds.), *Routledge handbook of language learning and technology* (pp. 308–319). Oxford: Routledge.

Wankel, C., & Kingsley, J. (Eds.). (2009). *Higher education in virtual worlds*. UK: Emerald.

KEY TERMS AND DEFINITIONS

Avatar: An online graphical representation of a virtual world user.

Bot: Software-generated agent that operates within an online virtual world.

Machinima: Animations created within a 3D virtual world.

Teleport: The ability of an individual user controlled avatar to rapidly change location within a virtual world.

Telepresence: The feeling of being present in an online environment.

This research was previously published in Assessing the Effectiveness of Virtual Technologies in Foreign and Second Language Instruction; pages 1-25, copyright year 2019 by Information Science Reference (an imprint of IGI Global).

Chapter 12
The Case for Qualitative Research Into Language Learning in Virtual Worlds

Luisa Panichi

ⓘ https://orcid.org/0000-0001-9106-1607

University of Pisa, Italy

ABSTRACT

This chapter reviews some of the most common research approaches used in investigating language learning and teaching in virtual worlds. In particular, the author makes the case for qualitative research approaches to the investigation of language learning and teaching in virtual worlds. The highly representational and immersive nature of online environments such as virtual worlds demands that researchers pay specific attention to the quality of teacher and learner experience and to individual reactions to the visual and kinesthetic stimuli of the environment. The chapter discusses some of the advantages of qualitative practitioner research in relation to the specific nature of virtual world contexts for language learning.

INTRODUCTION

Virtual worlds are generally understood within the recent computer assisted language learning (CALL) literature as 3D computer renderings and have been a recognised platform for language learning and teaching for nearly 20 years, in particular within the context of synchronous computer mediated communication (CMC) often also referred to as CMCL (computer mediated communication in language learning and teaching). The main affordances for language learning and teaching are generally considered to be the use of avatars for student-teacher and student-student synchronous interactions and the rich visual environment which can be tailored to recreate infinite contexts for language learning scenarios and simulations. Without doubt, the potential for interaction with objects and educational artefacts - in addition to avatar movement within the virtual space - have made virtual worlds particularly appealing to educators and users who place value on *immersiveness* in online education. Recent technological developments in the field also include the use of virtual reality headsets such as *Google Oculus* which

DOI: 10.4018/978-1-6684-7597-3.ch012

have the potential to impact on the perception of immersiveness in ways that are yet to be investigated. Though initial in-world (i.e., in the virtual world platform) communication among teachers and learners was limited to text-based chat, the addition and adoption of voice-chat undoubtedly made virtual world platforms increasingly attractive for language education within CALL. Last but not least, while the body of virtual world research literature within CMCL generally focuses on language learning in formal educational contexts, often as part of formalized online language exchanges between two or more educational institutions, one also needs to bear in mind that virtual worlds are also used within the context of informal and incidental language learning which has been documented in particular in online 3D gaming platforms such as *World of Warcraft* and massively multiplayer online games (MMOGs) in general.

The aim of this chapter is two-fold. Firstly, it aims to provide an up-to-date overview of the virtual world research literature within CALL, in particular in terms of the research foci and the methodological approaches adopted by researchers to date. In addition, it is a first attempt to discuss the rationale for many of the research decisions that have created the predominantly qualitative research landscape that emerges from the review itself. In particular, this chapter aims to provide a discussion not only of what we have done as a virtual world research community but also of the *why*. Indeed, research decisions do not come from nowhere. Thus, this chapter is an attempt to "go behind the scenes" of virtual research within CALL in order to provide our community with greater insight and critical awareness into what has been achieved so far and why qualitative research continues to be a valid research option. In addition, this chapter is an attempt to clarify our contribution to the CALL research landscape not only in terms of our output (i.e., our research outcomes) but also in terms of our input – who we are and what we bring to the research context as researchers. In the tradition of qualitative research, this chapter is an attempt to include ourselves - the research community - as an integral part of both the research landscape and findings. Finally, this attempt at *making sense* of what we have done as a virtual world research community in CALL over the last 15 years can also be understood as a way of opening up our thinking as a community to wider scrutiny and debate in the interest of the validity of our research on the one hand, and future research decisions and directions on the other. This need to be "making sense" is also echoed in a recent review of the CALL landscape by Blin. She writes (2019):

CALL research is no longer only about searching for and studying applications of the computer in language teaching and learning. It is also about making sense of the way we inhabit digital spaces through language, about making sense of the way we construct and expose our digital identity in different languages. It is also about the way we communicate and make meaning across multiple spaces, time, and cultures. It is about understanding and critically engaging with different world views. (Blin, 2019, p. 4)

This chapter is divided into three main sections. The first section provides the backdrop against which research into language learning and teaching has generally been carried out. It offers an initial discussion of how the context and the medium impact on specific research decisions that have often determined methodological choices and approaches. The second section, provides an up-to-date overview of the research focus into *learner interaction* within the context of language learning and teaching in virtual worlds, and a discussion of the most common research approaches used by the virtual world research community within CALL and the development of these approaches over time. The third section analyses in greater detail some of the research into the most common affordances which have, over the years, attracted both researchers and teachers to this particular medium.

THE NATURE AND CONTEXT OF VIRTUAL WORLD RESEARCH

The CALL literature on virtual worlds for language learning can be generally divided into two main categories: literature which focuses mainly on the description of the affordances and potential for language education of the virtual world platforms and literature which attempts to evaluate and analyze language learning and teaching in-world within the research traditions of CALL. In addition and in line with a significant proportion of CALL research, a considerable amount of literature on virtual worlds and language learning over the years has been - and continuous to be - practitioner-researcher based where teachers and educational specialists have attempted to make sense of the learning experience for learners as they themselves came to terms over time with the potential and complexity of virtual world environments for teaching. Indeed, as a virtual world researcher-practitioner myself (Deutschmann & Panichi, 2009a; Panichi, 2015b) and as one of pioneer teacher-researchers into the platforms at the time voice-chat was being introduced, I have, over the years, experimented with different practitioner research approaches including action research, reflective practice and exploratory practice (EP), a protocol I have found particularly useful in capturing both teacher and learner concurrent "learning" within the platform.

Finally, because virtual world platforms started off as a niche educational interest within CALL and have continued to be developed within and by a considerably small community within CMCL – for a number of reasons that go beyond the scope of this chapter – one will often find that even in some of the major research studies, a considerable amount of time and space is often devoted to the description of the platforms in an attempt to provide the novice practitioner-researcher (novice in terms of their knowledge about virtual world platforms) with sufficient technical information about the CMCL research context. Furthermore, of the combined total of 30 publications recently reviewed in Peterson (2016) and Sadler (2017), all of them are small scale teacher-researcher based with limited number of participants (from under 10 to a maximum of 50 in some instances) and data collection is in general carried out only for the duration of the in-world language course. The studies make use of some of the most common qualitative research approaches such as collection of learner feedback via questionnaires, interviews, teacher observations, chat transcripts and recordings or the virtual world sessions. In some cases, the studies make use of what is defined as "mixed-methods" approaches where qualitative data collected from interviews, for example, is analyzed both qualitatively, through discourse analysis, and quantitatively via the measurement of certain instances or episodes of learner interaction in-world. In a few instances, researchers applied statistical analysis to the data collected. A small percentage of the studies are longitudinal in the sense that the data collection spanned over a period of at least one year.

In view of what has been discussed so far, i.e. that most of the virtual world research to date in CMCL is teacher-researcher based and that rich descriptions of the environment and its features are usually considered to be highly relevant in contextualizing the research itself, it comes as no surprise that most research into virtual worlds for language education, is, to date, qualitative in its general approach. Furthermore, as most research focuses on formal language teaching and learning scenarios of some sort where student numbers tend to be small both out of necessity (the environment is notoriously complex to manage with large numbers of students) and as a result of current dominant language teaching methodology such as communicative language teaching. Indeed, where verbal interaction between participants is considered a priority (and difficult to manage with large numbers of learners), the use of quantitative research that attempts to measure the behaviour of large numbers of students does not really make sense. A further and final justification for the continued use of qualitative and small-scale approaches into virtual worlds within CMCL also lies in the focus of much of the research itself. Indeed, a significant part of the research literature has focused on the theme of *interaction* and in-world participation where particular attention is paid to the detailed description of interaction episodes, both in terms of text-chat, voice-chat, avatar movement and activity, the use of the environment in supporting interaction, learner strategies, learner emotional reaction to the environments (affect), motivation, teacher intervention, task design and collaboration. In this research, the emphasis is on determining how interaction takes place in the virtual world environment, on documenting the quality of the experience both for teachers and learners and validating the teaching methodology, that is, how we are making use of the environment for language education.

In addition to the above, one also needs to bear in mind the challenges involved when carrying out virtual world research and collecting data in-world compared to other online platforms such as the ethical issues surrounding avatar identity and the recording of virtual world data. As practitioner research continued to develop, one of the research needs that was identified within the CALL community was for more systematic and theoretically framed research projects (Chapelle, 2010; Deutschmann & Panichi, 2013). And, in an attempt to go beyond the practitioner-researcher approach yet without renouncing their practitioner researcher background, several researchers and developer groups went on to devote considerable time and energy to addressing this call. Wigham (2012), for example, developed a much needed and robust multimodality framework in her work on the interplay between verbal and non-verbal activity in virtual worlds, Panichi (2015b) combined an exploratory research lens with case study research and reflexivity in providing a thorough examination of learner participation in virtual worlds while Nocchi (2017) applied activity theory to generate a detailed analysis of a 4 year language programme in a virtual world. Wang's (2017) study looked at learner participation and verbal interaction using a combination of activity theory, conversation and discourse analysis.

In a recent publication, Peterson (2016) argues for the need for more quantitative research into CMCL in virtual worlds on the grounds that a significant amount of qualitative research has already been carried out and that qualitative findings now need to be generated that will enable us, as a research community, to extend the validity of our initial findings by increasing their generalisability. While recognizing the legitimacy of Peterson's claim (generalisability is always a beneficial outcome), the aim of this chapter is, nevertheless, to make the case for ongoing qualitative research into language learning and teaching within virtual worlds not because we like it (we do!) but because, ultimately, it continues to make sense. I will attempt to do so by providing a critical appraisal of the topics explored by researchers to date and the context of their research. The thrust of my argument is that qualitative and quantitative research should not be discussed as one against the other but rather as complementary approaches which make use of different tools in support of our research questions. I would like to argue that our research questions are intimately and legitimately connected to the contexts within which we operate and to the knowledge development we perceive as priority within these contexts. I would like, thus, to shift the focus of the debate to a discussion of how we can best serve our research needs (what we need to know to move forward) rather than the needs of research.

While it is certainly true that large-scale quantitative research is lacking within the virtual world literature in CALL, this needs to be nevertheless weighed against ongoing teacher-researcher-developer needs to explore platforms as the technology develops so that we are able to provide students with state-of-the art learning environments. And, just as above I pointed out how virtual world research in CALL is predominantly practitioner based, we also need to bear in mind that many of us are often also developers, not only of the lesson and linguistic material that we provide our students with but also of the 3D environments we use for our teaching. Many practitioners within the community are indeed developers in the sense that they are *3D builders* and have, over the years, created, or rather "scripted," numerous and exquisite open-access interactive 3D environments for language learning often from scratch and for free. In particular, if one considers the impact in terms of the quality linguistic and cultural knowledge that is being made accessible and constantly validated though practitioner qualitative research, it can be argued that the need for quantitative results may be less urgent than recently suggested. Significant pedagogic development has also been carried out by fellow practitioners and researchers in-world for heritage languages, of which North Sami is just but one example (Deutschmann, Outakoski, Panichi, & Schneider, 2010; Outakoski, 2014). If one considers the importance and the urgency of providing remote communities with quality materials for the learning of heritage languages that risk disappearing, we may want to be excused for not prioritizing the generalisability of our research. Indeed, and to conclude this first section, I would argue that the exploration of new contexts should actually be considered best practice and should never be put on hold as it provides us with a constant stimulus for thinking about what we are doing. Furthermore, as we develop an understanding of what works and what doesn't work, we are also arguably contributing to the emergence of understandings about language learning and teaching in general which may have implications for the broader field of language education to which CALL research belongs (Panichi, 2012; 2015a).

Finally, in support of my stance, I would like to argue that highly representational and immersive online environments such as virtual worlds demand that researchers pay specific attention to the *quality of teacher and learner experience* and to *individual reactions* to the visual and kinesthetic stimuli of the environment. In order to do justice to the specific nature of the environment and to the affordances for language education that it provides, I propose that we are in need of research approaches that are specifically geared to capture the quality and the complexity of learner interactions at the heart of virtual world language learning contexts (Wigham, Panichi, Nocchi, & Sadler, 2018; Panichi, 2015b). In a recent call for more qualitative research within CALL itself, Levy and Moore (2018) discuss the need for research that is exploratory in nature especially when attempting to uncover emergent phenomena. In particular, they underline how in CMC environments "qualitative research provides the tools for a deep description of a process as it unfolds" (2018, p.5) where the circumstances of the interactions are fluid, unpredictable and emergent. In addition, it needs to be pointed out that the speed of developments and the time and energy involved in carrying out research as researcher-practitioners tend to lead us to carrying out small scale qualitative rather than quantitative research. And, at the end of the day, our research inevitably reflects the general conditions in which we operate.

Research Foci and Approaches

The following is a review of the CALL virtual world literature on learner interaction and includes some of the initial research carried out in 2D virtual worlds before voice-chat functions were enabled. The aim of this section is to highlight both the foci of the studies and illustrate some of the different research approaches within the general qualitative and practitioner-researcher paradigm. Some of these studies were exploratory and made use explicitly of exploratory research approaches (Peterson 2010) while others were less so (Sykes, 2005; 2009) or took a specific and focussed look at a clearly identified area or topic in relation to learner interactions. For example, Schweinhorst (2004; 2009) and Shield, Davies and Weininger (2000) examined the role of virtual worlds in relation to learner autonomy; Shield (2003) discussed the emergence of oral discourse in written format; Zheng, Young, Wagner and Brewer (2009) discussed learner Negotiation for Action within virtual world language learning tasks; Sykes (2005;

2009) discussed the relationship between the platform and learner pragmatics; Kuriscak and Luke (2009) explored learner attitudes to virtual worlds for language learning. In addition, all of these studies, with the exception of Sykes (2005; 2009), discussed learner interaction in text-based communication only, limiting the analysis of interaction to one mode of communication. Moreover, Kuriscak and Luke (2009) did not include data from the virtual world platform at all in their analysis. Peterson's work on learner participation strategies (2010) is particularly relevant to understanding learner interaction though it was also limited to data from text-based chat logs. Indeed, even though VoIP (Voice over Internet Protocols) had been available for use with virtual world platforms at least since around 2003 and integrated into some virtual world platforms themselves such *Second Life* in 2007, the bulk of research into virtual worlds available at the time within CMCL continued to focus mainly on the use of text-based chat in learner interactions.

The reasons why many researchers continued to focus on text-based learner interactions despite the availability of voice-chat can only be speculated upon. One possibility is that voice protocols add a layer of complexity to the running of educational events within virtual worlds. It may be the case that in many educational contexts, text-based interaction is easier to manage in view of the type and amount of technical support required. It can thus be argued that the researcher's focus is often limited by what is more practical to capture. However as of 2010, studies started to appear that looked at language learner interaction in virtual worlds from a multimodal perspective as well. Some studies in fact looked at the combination of student interaction in the environment both in terms of written and oral communication (Canto, Jauregi & van den Bergh, 2013; Deutschmann, Molka-Danielesen, & Panichi, 2011; Jauregi, Canto, de Graaff, Koenraad, & Moonen, 2011; Wang, Deutschmann, & Steinvall, 2013), while some continued to focus on text-chat only (Peterson 2011; 2012a; 2012b). However, none of these studies expanded on the existing research approaches in any way. They either focussed on a discussion of learner interaction within the communicative channels with which we were already acquainted such as voice and text based chat (Canto et al., 2013; Peterson 2011; 2012a; 2012b; Wang et al., 2013) or used an experimental and control approach to examining the phenomenon of learner interaction (Canto et al., 2013) which arguably did not allow for an exploration of the issues. Deutschmann et al., (2011) used an activity theory framework which, while broader in its general research approach, was focussed more on describing the technicalities of telecollaboration than exploring the notion of learner interaction and participation in any way. The most innovative research to be published at the time was the study by Wigham and Chanier (2013). In this study, the authors take a more comprehensive look at communication in the virtual world in an attempt to broaden our view of what was going on and provide, for the first time in the virtual world literature within CMCL, a discussion of *multimodality* in virtual worlds understood as a combination of both learner verbal (text-based and voice-based communication) and non-verbal communication such as through avatar appearance, proxemics (orientation in the three dimensional space) and kinesics (gaze, posture, gestures). Similarly, Panichi (2015b) provided a broader understanding of interaction and learner participation by using a qualitative case study research approach and visualisation based on direct observation and interpretation as the primary analytical tool for the visual data. According to Panichi (2015b, p. 328), learner participation in virtual worlds is to be understood as *verbal and intentional and contextualised non-verbal activity*. This is in line with Wigham's (2012) distinction between verbal and non-verbal interaction in virtual worlds where she makes use of a learner corpus of verbal and non-verbal acts achieved through a discourse analysis approach. The similarity of the reciprocal findings of Panichi (2015b) and Wigham (2012) is all the more significant as they were reached by using different methodological approaches.

A more recent study is Nocchi's (2017) systematic analysis of the affordances of virtual worlds for foreign language learning through an activity theory framework. Nocchi uses language tasks as the unit of analysis and identifies instances of task disruption. The study examines the cause of the disruptions in each episode and the actions taken by the participants to resolve them thus providing insight into the participants' role and their use of the medium with particular emphasis on its technical and social affordances. Of particular significance to the field is Hartwick's (2018) discussion of interaction in virtual worlds which draws on classroom interaction research thereby substantially enriching the theoretical framework of reference for future researchers. Finally, there are a number of recent studies that build on many of the previous work reviewed in this section both in terms of the methodology employed and their foci. For example, Palomeque and Pujolà (2018) adopt a social semiotic approach to studying communication by creating a multilayered transcription method to account for the multimodal nature of interactions in virtual worlds and to describe how different communication modes or channels are used in combination by participants to create meaning in-world. Park (2018) examines cognitive and metacognitive strategies in simulation tasks for the virtual training of military air traffic controllers in South Korea. Yamazaki (2018) combines the instructional approach of computer-assisted learning of communication (CALC) with a mixed-methods case study approach to investigate participants' natural acquisition of Japanese in a 3D virtual environment. In analysing whether foreign language virtual world interaction is beneficial for learners that present a specific personality profile, Melchor-Couto (2018) explores various facets of affective interaction in the virtual world, ranging from how the anonymity afforded by the environment interacts with the language learners' personality profile to how the perception of anonymity interacts with the learner's foreign language anxiety (FLA) profile and self-efficacy beliefs.

Research Into Affordances for Language Learning

The discussion in this section is informed mainly by literature from CMCL and, where relevant, by debate in the general virtual world literature in the fields of education and educational technology. The discussion is informed by research and studies that look at learner participation in the environment in terms of linguistic interaction on the one hand and in terms of learner activity and learner affect on the other. In addition, there are also a certain number of studies that discuss learner participation and interaction in the environment from the point of view of task design.

Panichi, Deutschmann and Molka-Danielsen (2010) discuss language learning in virtual worlds from an ecological perspective according to which the learner interacts not only through the environment but becomes part of the environment. The ecological model sees systems as open, complex and adaptive, comprising elements that are dynamic and interdependent. According to this model, all learning is situated in an environment and is as such contextualised. In this view of learning, for example, the learner is not only part of the environment but also one of the variables in determining subject matter (the target language content) and the outcome of learning and teaching. In an ecological perspective, and in line with sociocultural theory, people and the learning community are also constituent features of the environment and levels of engagement are dependent upon meaningful participation in human events involving perception, action and joint construction of meaning. Furthermore, in collaborative learning setups as in the case of the communicative language teaching approaches, communication skills are of primary importance and central to engagement. The authors suggest that, in highly complex communicative environments such as virtual worlds, learners need to be equipped not only with the technical but also the participatory communicative skills – be they social, linguistic, pragmatic and/or intercultural – so that they may engage more effectively with the specific environment. As part of this argument, the authors (2010, pp. 174-176) identify four key affordances of the virtual world of *Second Life* that may have an impact on participation and collaborative language learning. They are: "sense of place" discussed as the user's perception of the 3D environment, collaborative building features, openness of the world to other users and representation of self via an avatar. All of these virtual world characteristics offer significant language and intercultural learning opportunities to the foreign language student.

Learner Activity

Some of the literature describes learner participation in terms of activity within the virtual world (Panichi, 2015b). According to this review, learners participate in virtual world learning activities through:

- exploration
- experimenting
- experiencing
- searching for information
- belonging
- collaboration
- social interaction and communication
- being (learning that results from exploration of self and identity)
- building
- championing (i.e. promotion of real life causes such as charities)
- expressing (communicating about virtual world experiences outside of the virtual world platform)
- doing
- sharing
- acting, performing, role play and story telling
- playing and games
- problem solving

Immersiveness

Building on his previous studies, Schwienhorst (2009) discusses the contribution of virtual world environments to learner autonomy, reflection, and authentic communication concluding that the immersiveness of the 3D environment has a positive impact on learner interaction in the target language. Two key affordances of the environment according to the author (2009) are the use of avatars which allow for identity expression which can be linked to both in-world and out-of-world identity and the flexibility of the space which allows for experimentation with learning scenarios which are not possible in face-to-face educational contexts. In his 2004 study, he examines students' use of indexical language (such as the use of "here"), for example, as an indication of a heightened sense of presence and co-presence compared to non-3D environments for online learning. Schwienhorst argues (2009) thus for further research into mapping of cognitive and meta-cognitive activity triggered by this sense of presence in the environment as a result of immersiveness.

Another study that highlights the role of immersiveness and cognitive development or higher order thinking skills (HOTs) in relation to language development is Leong's (2011) study of Chinese as a mother tongue language in Singapore. In designing the tasks and to ensure deep learning, the researchers followed the *total participation technique cognitive engagement model*. According to this model, deeper learning can be supported through the creation of classroom opportunities that encourage young learners to think through the implications and the relevance of classroom activities to their own world. Their findings showed that with the use of role-play activities which build on the specific affordances of virtual worlds, students display greater higher order thinking skills than in the non-ICT control groups suggesting that the 3D environment has an impact on cognitive development. However, as the authors themselves remark, these findings are based on student and teacher feedback only and do not include all of the data collected over the entire research period and are limited to text-based interaction.

Finally, the notion of sense of presence as triggered by the immersiveness of the environment and the role-play potential it carries is also advocated by Lim (2009, p. 8) in his discussion of "learning by being" in virtual worlds. According to Lim (2009, p. 8), *learning by being* refers to the learning that one experiences as a result of explorations of self and identity in the virtual world environment as made possible by the immersive nature of the environment.

Negotiation for Action (NfA)

In their paper, Zheng et al. (2009) analyze the user chat logs and other artefacts of a virtual world, *Quest Atlantis* (QA), and propose the concept of *negotiation for action* (NfA) to explain how interaction, specifically, avatar-embodied collaboration between native and non-native speakers, provided resources for English language acquisition. This concept is developed from the notion of *negotiation for meaning* at the heart of the interaction process between second language learners. Iterative multilayered analyses revealed several affordances of QA for language acquisition at both utterance and discourse levels. Through intercultural collaboration on solving content-based problems, participants successfully reached quest goals during which emergent identity formation and meaning making took place. The study also demonstrates that it is in this intercultural interaction that pragmatics, syntax, semantics, and discourse practices arose and were enacted.

Participation, Interaction and Learner Strategies

In an exploratory study, Peterson (2010) builds on his previous work and provides a discussion of learner participation patterns and strategy use in the language learning of seven intermediate EFL (English as a foreign language) students in Japan in a virtual world platform. Discourse analysis of student chat logs revealed that the specific context appeared to elicit a high degree of participation and autonomy. Participation and autonomy were measured in terms of student turns, peer-to-peer exchanges, learner-centred interactions, limited use of the L1 (students native language) and a high degree of focus on task of the interactions. The transcripts showed the use of 5 main transactional strategies (split turns, time saving devices, addressivity, upper-case and quotation marks) and of 2 key interactional strategies (politeness and keyboard symbols). It was observed that adaptive strategies are also used by students such as transfers from both non-computer forms of interaction and other types of CMC such as email. Learners' attitudes were also taken into consideration but no causal relationship was established between positive attitudes and participation strategies. Task design and telepresence, which is understood as learners' sense of presence in the virtual world as experienced through their avatars, are listed as features which may have had an impact on the study outcomes and which require further investigation.

Non-verbal Participation

In their study, Wigham and Chanier (2013) provide a classification of verbal and non-verbal communication acts within a CLIL (content and language integrated learning) course for architecture students in *Second Life*. The study attempts to understand multimodal communication structures through learner participation and learning practices in a collaborative learning setting. The classification developed by the authors builds on studies in the second language acquisition (SLA) research literature on non-verbal and verbal communication in face-to-face contexts and a discussion of non-verbal communication in *Second Life* where a distinction is made between user-generated and computer- generated acts. The authors then proceed to subdivide these categories further based on the communication act rather than with reference to how they are encoded by the user and the synthetic world. The modalities listed by the authors (2013, pp. 66-68) are those of avatar proxemics (orientation), kinesics (gaze, posture and gestures) and appearance. The category of gestures is subdivided further to include extra-communicative acts (not defined by the authors in this paper), iconics (gestures which are a representation of an action or an object), deitics (the act of an avatar touching or manipulating an object), emblems (cultural gestures) and pantomimes (avatar animations of crying, smoking and typing, for example). Emblems are further divided into performative emblems, word emblems and meta-discursive emblems but these concepts are not expanded upon by the authors.

A comparison between learner verbal and non-verbal communication during the course led the authors to conclude that nonverbal acts contribute to communication and learning in virtual worlds and that the preference for one mode over the other was determined by the role of the learner within a given learning task. The study indicates, furthermore, that learners were able to adapt to the communicative features of the environment and to use the nonverbal communicative features to overcome ambiguity in verbal communication. In particular, the authors highlight (2013, p. 82) the importance of proxemic closeness for L2 activities which involve collaboration and building. To conclude, Wigham (2012) discusses this supportive and dynamic relationship between verbal and non-verbal activity within the context of language learning in virtual worlds in general as *interplay*.

Engagement Among Peers

In Deutschmann and Panichi (2009b), learner interaction is discussed with reference to language awareness and learner engagement in online communication. In particular, the authors compared the first and the last sessions from an online oral proficiency course aimed at doctoral students conducted in the virtual world, *Second Life*. The study attempts to identify how supportive linguistic moves made by the teacher encourage learners to engage with language, and what type of linguistic behaviour in the learners leads to engagement in others. Overall differences in terms of floor space and turn-taking patterns were compared, and an in-depth discourse analysis of parts of the sessions was conducted with a focus on supportive linguistic moves such as back-channelling and elicitors. Their research indicates that the supportive linguistic behaviour of teachers is important in increasing learner engagement. In the study the authors were also able to observe a change in student linguistic behaviour between the first and the last sessions with students becoming more active in signalling involvement as the course progressed.

Language Learner Turn Taking and Floor Space

In Deutschmann, Panichi and Molka-Danielsen (2009), two stages of an action research project involving two oral proficiency courses held in the virtual world, *Second Life*, were compared. Based on the experiences of this course, the researchers redesigned many aspects of it in order to improve student activity in terms of oral participation. The study was able to measure student participation based on floor space, turn lengths and turn-taking patterns and examine whether changes in design had contributed to more favourable outcomes in terms of learner participation. Results seem to indicate that meaning-focused task-design, which involves authenticity and collaborative elements, had a direct impact on learner participation and engagement. Furthermore, the results suggest that technical and social initiations into a complex environment such as SL are important factors to be borne in mind when designing tasks for a course in a virtual world. Recent research in the field by Wang (2017) uses a similar approach and confirms the validity of both the initial study by Deutschmann and Panichi (2009b) in the previous subsection and Deutschmann et al. (2009) mentioned in this section.

A Sense of Belonging

Molka-Danielsen, Panichi and Deutschmann (2010) reviewed reward models used in learning and teaching in virtual worlds and illustrated how reward models in language education are often irrelevant and have minimum impact in traditional face-to-face settings. The authors also refer to reward models borrowed from flow theory and self-determination theory and suggest ways of applying these to language learning activities in virtual worlds to increase motivation to participate. They make the distinction between tangible and intangible rewards. Tangible rewards include, for example, objects such as T-shirts while intangible rewards would be the awarding of a specific status within the world which would carry specific privilege. They identify key elements that need to be included in a reward model for active language learning in *Second Life* such as immersion through the use of a narrative genre, encouraging a "flow-state" with the right balance between challenges and achievements and, last but not least, space for personal constructs that foster a sense of belonging and community. The main argument of this article is that the greater the "tangibility" of the rewards afforded to the learner through the specific features of the virtual world environment, the higher is the learners' sense of belonging to and participation in the language learning community both within the virtual world and within the broader learning context.

Community

Closely related to learners' sense of belonging is the concept of community and community building. Molka-Danielsen and Panichi (2010) look at teacher and trainer strategies that are supportive of community building and relevant to learner participation in learning. Examples are taken from the Avalon Learning Project. Active learning theories such as activity theory are used to explain the importance of building community for adoption and success of a learning system. In particular, this article focuses on the role of the expert teacher in encouraging the development of a sense of a community among learners and the skills required for such task. The importance of community is also confirmed by Nocchi's (2017) activity theory-based analysis of learners of Italian within the Italian native speaker community of the virtual world, *Second Life*.

Factors Affecting Interaction in Virtual Worlds

Wang et al., (2013) examined factors that affect interaction within an online virtual world course in sociolinguistics and collected information regarding learner linguistic participation through the learner contributions to voice-chat and text-based chat within the virtual world platform. The authors suggest that future research not only needs to take into consideration these factors in relation to participation but also needs to look at how factors influence other factors in a more dynamic and complex relationship to participation. In addition, the authors proposed that virtual worlds have a stronger amplifier effect on participation compared to other CMC tools and that, as a result, greater attention needs to be paid in the literature on the medium as a factor effecting participation. More specifically, they argue that the role of virtual world platforms such as *Second Life* can be neutral, positive or negative based on the degree of intensification of impact of the medium on the factors which have been deemed to influence participation. In particular, they point to teacher intervention as a way of addressing the role played by virtual world platforms on learner interaction and participation.

In addition to the above, Molka-Danielsen, et al., (2010) argue for the need to take into consideration quality of experience in understanding factors that impact on technology supported learning, including virtual worlds. With reference to learner motivation and participation in virtual worlds they list the following variables as being relevant: clear course design, the nature of the environment; the scope of student self-determination; strong peer collaboration and appropriate technical initiation (2010, p. 46). They also explain that the degree to which a virtual environment is authentic and reflects the personal interest of its users is an important factor in quality of experience for end-users and its applicability to serve pedagogical innovation (2010, p. 49).

Designing for Participation in Virtual Worlds

This section will examine the CMCL literature on task design with a special focus on designing for participation in the context of language learning in virtual worlds from different theoretical stances and/ or methodological approaches.

Participation as Simulation

Jauregi et al. (2011) examine the development and use of interaction tasks for intercultural communication within the context of the EU funded Niflar project with the specific aim of exploiting the affordances of the environment. The activities that took place under the project made use of both text-based and voice-chat. The authors conclude that general task design principles as stated in the SLA literature need to be adapted for 3D virtual worlds so that rich oral interaction is triggered for task completion while making the most of the exploratory, functional and gaming possibilities of the virtual world platform of *Second Life*. In particular, the authors point to the need to exploit the specific realism or "life-likeness" of the environment to support more immersive simulations.

Participatory Skills in Online Gaming for Language Learning

Building on his previous research into language learner strategies in virtual worlds, Peterson (2012b) reports on an exploratory case study of student linguistic and social interaction in text-based chat in the massively multiplayer online role-playing game (MMORPG) of *Wonderland*. This study is different to the previous study by Jauregi et al. (2011) as it does not discuss task design explicitly. However, as the author points out (Peterson, 2012b), the design of the game itself structures the type of activities that are available to students. It should be noted that the aim of all activities within the game are to enhance player participation in the game itself (playing) and that language learning in this specific study is incidental to the game. This case study differs also from previous studies carried out by Peterson as it looks at student interaction with players within the game who are not part of their formal learning context thus making the development of rapport with these players an essential part of the experience. Specific linguistic and social strategies that proved important in the learners' efforts to build rapport with other players were the use of positive politeness in the form of greetings, leave-takings, informal language, small talk and humour. Significant moves by students in building rapport and for their participation in the game were also the establishment and maintenance of intersubjectivity through the creation of friendships, teams and ongoing use of continuers or utterances designed to signal attention and interest in what interlocutors are saying. In addition, requests for assistance and requests for information were also used by students throughout the experience and considered important in terms of rapport building and maintenance of relationships with other players. The second part of this study looks explicitly at learner attitudes towards participation in virtual world platforms for massively multiplayer online role-play gaming (MMORPG). Results from the post-study oral interviews indicate that, in line with previous findings discussed elsewhere (Peterson, 2011), the game provided a steep learning curve for students in terms of their becoming familiar with the objectives of the game and with the required actions. Students also commented on the limitations of the in-game help features. Students however commented more favourably on other aspects of participation in the game. In particular, students claimed that the nature of the computer-based interaction combined with the use of pseudonyms and avatars helped reduce anxiety and contributed towards risk-taking in the use of the target language. Students also appreciated the opportunity to come into contact with native or expert speakers of the target language.

Transient Spaces for Different Modes of Participation

In the previous two studies (Jauregi et al., 2011 and Peterson, 2012b), task design is discussed from the point of view of design principles, in the general language learning literature in the first case, and from the point of view of gaming in the second. In a different project, "Virtual Campus for Life Long Learning", Molka-Danielsen, Deutschmann and Panichi (2009) discuss the virtual representations, tools, context and spaces used in course activities. This project provided for the design and building of spaces for language learning within a virtual world platform. They observed that, while the virtual world of *Second Life* can replicate the dynamics of the classroom lecture, it gives further opportunities for interactive and active teaching as learning activities can take place in dispersed and diversified virtual spaces. These can be defined as transient spaces insofar as participants, activities and representations change over time (Molka-Danielsen et al. 2009, p. 22). Designing transient learning spaces raises different challenges and opportunities from designing learning in the traditional physical classroom. Challenges include, *inter alia*, enabling new users to orient themselves in these spaces and how to behave in the new environments, for example. Transient learning spaces also offer new opportunities, such as the ability to design and develop a specific space for each course. In addition to this, the nature of the 3D environment is such that it allows for change and adaptation to occur and for the stakeholders in the process (teachers, learners and institutions) to negotiate the modes of participation that are relevant to them (i.e., formal, informal settings and processes, the tailoring of the environment, etc.).

Managing Participation through Instructional Design

Deutschmann and Panichi (2009a) discuss the various phases involved in designing a course for language learning in virtual worlds from scratch in an attempt to maximise learner participation specifically during the course. The key areas of this process they have identified include:

1. Familiarisation with the environment
2. Preparation of appropriate content
3. Meaningful task design (i.e., tasks that make use of the specific affordances of the environment)
4. Giving explicit instructions
5. Technical support
6. Socialisation opportunities
7. Taking learners' prior attitudes and expectations into account
8. Teacher roles and behaviour
9. Feedback opportunities
10. Fostering learner autonomy

As far as managing participation, the authors make several recommendations based on research findings published elsewhere (Deutschmann et al., 2009; Deutschmann & Panichi, 2009b). These findings suggest that learners can "learn" to participate in the virtual world if provided with specific input and support from teachers and that this skill can be developed over time as learners become not only more proficient in the target language but in the negotiation of communication skills in the specific environment as well. One final aspect that needs monitoring and to be made explicit with learners in the interest of participation and interaction is the use of the various communication channels for multimodal communication within the specific setting.

As far as task design is concerned in relation to the specific affordances of virtual world platforms, such as *Second Life*, the authors discuss (Deutschmann & Panichi, 2009a, p. 36) three dimensions in particular. The first dimension they refer to is the social/communicative/cognitive dimension. Tasks that make use of this dimension encourage learners to share and build on their knowledge through social interaction. The second dimension the authors refer to is the affective/creative dimension. Tasks that make use of this dimension promote the exploration of identity, cultural norms, values and encourage artistic expression and representation such as performance. The third dimension of virtual worlds that can be exploited through specific task design is the spatial/physical dimension. Tasks in this dimension encourage learners to use the virtual world platform as a source of information and for the exploration of existing artefacts, as a space for navigation and movement and as a place for cross-linguistic and intercultural contact through interaction with other users.

A final consideration is made by Panichi et al., (2010) in relation to designing for the affective dimension of learners in virtual worlds. In particular they discuss how the visual nature of the environment may impact on learners. For example, they suggest learners may react differently to the environment based on their own individual beliefs about teaching and learning. Some students may find the game-like feel of the platform does not coincide with their understandings of what education "should" be. They suggest that the creation of environments which somehow replicate learners' previous experiences of learning (i.e., a space with desks or a whiteboard) may facilitate transition to and acceptance of learning in the virtual world platform. Similarly, it may be that the replication of non-virtual reality rituals such as sitting in a circle, standing up to talk to the class, facing an avatar who is talking to you and walking out of the door when you leave the room may contribute to individual perceptions of participation and control (Panichi et al., 2010, p. 183). Last but not least, the authors also suggest teachers and designers bear in mind teacher avatar appearance and the impact that it might have on learners from different backgrounds.

Combining Different Participation Needs

Deutschmann et al. (2011) use activity theory to examine how task design incorporated a variety of aspects which ultimately led to greater learner motivation and participation. Using an activity theoretical model, the case study describes the design and initial implementation of a telecollaborative learning activity between four universities in *Second Life*. The four student groups were all attending quite different programs within their own institutions. The main challenges encountered were that of accommodating the different needs taking the diverse motivational objectives of each group into account, and making use of the affordances of the tool (the virtual world of *Second Life*) in this pursuit. Examples of different learner needs in this context were:

- language proficiency levels
- institutional requirements
- timetabling and attendance options
- syllabus requirements
- learning objectives

CONCLUSION

In this final section, I would like to summarize what CALL CMCL research into virtual worlds has achieved since its outset based on the discussion in the previous three sections. In doing so, I would also like to discuss what our research says about us as a research community and what the implications of this are in terms of future research. First, if we examine the progression of the research foci discussed in both sections it is clear that the primary interest of the research community remains *learner in-world interaction* in support of language learning. This primary research focus on learner interaction has been and continues to be discussed in relation to learner verbal and non-verbal activity, learner affect, community and task-design. Indeed, this should come as no surprise as these aspects of language learning are primary concerns of the language teacher and materials developer in face-to-face, classroom-based education as well. If we were to run a validity check or some sort of quality control on this, I would argue that we have indeed been researching those aspects of CALL that are meaningful to our profession and to language acquisition in general and beyond CALL. Furthermore, it needs to be highlighted that while there are a number of limitations with regard to practitioner research outcomes in terms of external validity and generalisability, there are also several advantages. In particular, the research carried out to date has certainly benefitted from the practitioner-researcher knowledge of and ongoing learning about the environment and their ability to constantly act as intermediaries in mediating between pedagogic knowledge and knowledge of the learning context. Undoubtedly, the depth of understanding that comes from informed pioneer practitioner experience and the intuitions that spring therefrom are both important elements in the creation of collective knowledge and are arguably of great value when documented within research frameworks albeit reflective practice ones.

If we take a look at the breadth and the complexity of the research, it is clear to see how we have progressed from exploratory teacher-researcher studies to the carrying out of more methodologically grounded research. If we consider in particular the work by Wigham (2012), Panichi (2015b), Nocchi (2017) and Wang (2017) it needs to be noted that this research is the result of four PhD projects carried out independently in four different European countries (France, the UK, Ireland, and Sweden respectively) and which arguably gave the researchers the necessary time and formal institutional framework and support to carry out the broader research projects our community had explicitly called for. The contribution to the field in particular of these broader research projects lies in their applying a combination of existing theories and approaches within the SLA and CALL tradition to uncharted territory and by adapting existing qualitative research methods in ways that enabled researchers to document for the first time, instances of interaction that had previously gone undetected.

Finally, having had the privilege to work closely with many fellow researchers over the last 10 years and having been directly involved in the management and intellectual development of two major research projects on virtual worlds for language education funded by the European Union such as *Avalon* and *Euroversity* from 2007 onwards, I would like to suggest that we, as a community, have achieved what was reasonable and necessary to achieve given the constant constraints of time, funding and human resources. In other words, we must not forget the context in which virtual world research has been carried out from the outset, at least within Europe. Indeed, most practitioner-research was carried out thanks to the determination and the computer and technical skills of the pioneer researchers and was often entirely dependent upon the individual teacher-researcher's ability to instigate opportunities for in-world language exchanges through personal networks and to develop and build courses in-world for their learners. In this sense, we cannot overlook the time and the technical know-how that were constantly required of all of us as a virtual world educational community to build, run, validate and maintain virtual world environments and to keep up concurrently with the speed of new developments and changes in protocols. To sum up, the reviews in the sections above have illustrated how we have gone from small manageable research studies by individual practitioner-researcher-developers that well served our teaching and learning communities at the time as a way of validating our thinking about teaching, to providing a response to the call from our research community for broader methodological approaches in our research. The question, thus, is now: *Where do we go from here?*

Now, while recognizing Peterson's call (2016) mentioned in the introduction to this paper for quantitative research as a justified means of attempting to approach what we have done so far from a different angle, I am not, however, convinced that quantitative research in opposition to qualitative approaches is what we really need in light primarily of the medium which is at the heart of our investigations. The authors argue, for example, in Wigham et al.'s editorial (2018) on interaction in virtual world language learning with reference to virtual worlds that:

These spaces are now recognised as complex environments that need to be better understood if researchers want to tap into their educational potential, and this requires a drastic change of approach. The trend is quite clear: researchers in VWs are now showing an interest in looking at these environments through a different lens, which is able to incorporate the complexity of learning in VWs. (Boellstorff, 2015; Gregory, Lee, Dalgarno & Tynan, 2016), (Wigham et al., 2018, p. 154)

This call for research approaches that are better equipped to capture complexity is echoed in recent CALL research and with particular reference to virtual worlds in Schultze (2017). Here the author argues that complexity theoretical approaches may provide new ways of hypothesizing about and conceptualizing the complex phenomena of language use and (second) language development, and will require different data gathering and analytical methods. Schultze argues that learner interaction in CALL and virtual worlds need to be understood as complex adaptive systems (CAS) which, due to their complexity and fluidity, are not completely deterministic in the sense that causal relationships between events and their outcomes cannot always be established, in particular in view of the innumerable variables that come into play. The question, thus, for virtual world researchers, would appear to be how to proceed in capturing complexity. Could this be a much-needed opportunity for us as a research community to make the effort of going beyond the traditional and often overbearing binary distinction between qualitative and quantitative? Can we conceive of a research paradigm that is able to, on the one hand, take into account the depth of our practitioner-research knowledge and both the richness and constraints of our contexts; and, on the other, do full justice to the foci of our research, to the complexity of learner interactions in virtual worlds and, simultaneously to our need to move forward? In a call for innovation in research approaches to interaction in virtual worlds, Savin-Baden, Gourlay and Tombs (2010) argue that while established research methodologies have been successfully applied to the context of virtual worlds, the specific features of these immersive realities require new approaches that are congruent with the environment. For example, they state how capturing the concept of "immersion" which involves notions of embodiment and various types of 'presence' is an ongoing challenge for virtual world researchers within the constraints of traditional paradigms.

A final consideration that needs to be made, I would argue, is that we need ultimately to think about what we want to achieve both in the short term and the long term. In particular, when dealing with technology which is forever evolving, perhaps small scale, tentative, exploratory practitioner-led research is what we actually need. While recognizing that much has been done in terms of small scale qualitative teacher-led research already and that we do now have at our disposal more robust methodological approaches, I would like to argue that our research decisions, however, constantly need to be reviewed with reference to the contexts in which we operate and the communities we serve. In this sense, without excluding other approaches, I think we can nevertheless continue to benefit from research studies that are small and exploratory and whose results are adaptive and suggestive of what might be.

REFERENCES

Blin, F. (2019). Looking back at 30 years of ReCALL. *ReCALL*, *31*(1), 3–4. doi:10.1017/S0958344018000204

Boellstorff, T. (2015). Three real features for virtual worlds. *Journal of Virtual Worlds Research*, *8*(2), 1–5. doi:10.4101/jvwr.v8i2.7167

Canto, S., Jauregi, K., & van den Bergh, H. (2013). Integrating cross-cultural interaction through video-communication and virtual worlds in foreign language teaching programmes: Is there an added value? *ReCALL*, *25*(1), 105–121. doi:10.1017/S0958344012000274

Chapelle, C. (2010). The spread of computer assisted language learning. *Language Teaching*, *43*(1), 66–74. doi:10.1017/S0261444809005850

Deutschmann, M., Molka-Danielsen, J., & Panichi, L. (2011). Analyzing the design of telecollaboration in Second Life using activity theory. In A. Cheney & R. L. Sanders (Eds.), Teaching and learning in 3D immersive worlds: Pedagogical models and constructivist approaches (pp. 151–168). Hershey, PA: IGI Global; doi:10.4018/978-1-60960-517-9.ch009.

Deutschmann, M., Outakoski, H., Panichi, L., & Schneider, C. (2010). Virtual learning – real heritage: Benefits and challenges of virtual worlds for the learning of indigenous minority languages. Proceedings of the 3rd International Conference ICT for Language Learning (pp. 194-198). Florence, Italy: Simonelli Editore.

Deutschmann, M., & Panichi, L. (2009a). Instructional design, learner modeling, and teacher practice in Second Life. In J. Molka-Danielsen & M. Deutschmann (Eds.), *Learning and teaching in the virtual world of Second Life* (pp. 27–44). Trondheim, Norway: Tapir Academic Press.

Deutschmann, M., & Panichi, L. (2009b). Talking into empty space? Signalling involvement in a virtual language classroom in Second Life. *Language Awareness*, *18*(3-4), 310–328. doi:10.1080/09658410903197306

Deutschmann, M., & Panichi, L. (2013). Towards models for designing language learning in virtual worlds. *International Journal of Virtual and Personal Learning Environments*, *4*(2), 65–84. doi:10.4018/jvple.2013040104

Deutschmann, M., Panichi, L., & Molka-Danielsen, J. (2009). Designing oral participation in Second Life: A comparative study of two language proficiency courses. *ReCALL*, *21*(2), 70–90. doi:10.1017/S0958344009000196

Gregory, S., Lee, M. J. W., Dalgarno, B., & Tynan, B. (Eds.). (2016). Learning in virtual worlds: Research and applications: Issues in distance education. Edmonton, Canada: AU Press. doi:10.15215/aupress/9781771991339.01.

Hartwick, P. (2018). Investigating research approaches: Classroom-based interaction studies in physical and virtual contexts. *ReCALL*, *30*(2), 161–176. doi:10.1017/S0958344017000386

Jauregi, K., Canto, S., de Graaff, R., Koenraad, A., & Moonen, M. (2011). Verbal interaction in Second Life: Towards a pedagogic framework for task design. *Computer Assisted Language Learning*, *24*(1), 77–101. doi:10.1080/09588221.2010.538699

Kuriscak, L., & Luke, C. (2009). Language learner attitudes toward virtual worlds: An investigation of Second Life. In L. Lomicka, & G. Lord (Eds.), The next generation: Social networking and online collaboration in foreign language learning. CALICO Monograph Series, 8, 173-198.

Leong, T. C. (2011). Using virtual world platforms for language and critical thinking skills, learning and practice. Proceedings of the 4th International Conference ICT for Language Learning. Florence, Italy: Simonelli Editore.

Levy, M., & Moore, P. J. (2018). Qualitative research in CALL. *Language Learning & Technology*, *2*(2), 1–7.

Lim, K. (2009). A framework for designing curricular interventions in-world. JVWR, 2(1), 3–11. doi:10.4101/jvwr.v2i1.424

Melchor-Couto, S. (2018). Virtual world anonymity and foreign language oral interaction. *ReCALL*, *30*(2), 232–249. doi:10.1017/S0958344017000398

Molka-Danielsen, J., Deutschmann, M., & Panichi, L. (2009). Designing authentic communication for language learning in virtual space. *Designs for Learning Journal*, 2(9), 22–33. doi:10.16993/dfl.22

Molka-Danielsen, J., & Panichi, L. (2010). Building a language-learning community in a virtual world. In T. Fallmyr (Ed.), NOKOBIT proceedings (pp. 81-94). Trondheim, Norway: Tapir Akademisk Forlag.

Molka-Danielsen, J., Panichi, L., & Deutschmann, M. (2010). Reward models for active language learning in 3D virtual worlds. In Y. Peng, G. Kou, F. I. S. Ko, Y. Zeng, & K. D. Kwack (Eds.), Proceedings from the 3rd International conference on Information Sciences and Interaction Sciences. Chengdu, China. doi:10.1109/ICICIS.2010.5534711

Nocchi, S. (2017). *The affordances of virtual worlds for language learning* (Unpublished doctoral dissertation). Dublin City University, Ireland.

Outakoski, H. (2014). Teaching an endangered language in virtual reality. In M. C. Jones & S. Ogilvie (Eds.), *Keeping languages alive: Documentation, pedagogy, and revitalization* (pp. 128–139). Cambridge, UK: Cambridge University Press.

Palomeque, C., & Pujolà, J.-T. (2018). Managing multimodal data in virtual world research for language learning. *ReCALL*, *30*(2), 177–195. doi:10.1017/S0958344017000374

Panichi, L. (2012). Virtual worlds: An opportunity for thinking about learning. Proceedings of the International Conference Learning a Language in Virtual Worlds: A Review of Innovation and ICT in Language Teaching Methodology (pp. 25-32). Warsaw, Poland: Warsaw Academy of Computer Science Management and Administration.

Panichi, L. (2015a). A critical analysis of learner participation in virtual worlds: How can virtual worlds inform our pedagogy? In F. Helm, L. Bradley, M. Guarda, & S. Thouësny (Eds.), Critical CALL – Proceedings of the 2015 EUROCALL Conference, Padova, Italy. Dublin, Ireland: Research-publishing.net.

Panichi, L. J. (2015b). Participation in language learning in virtual worlds: An exploratory case-study of a business English course (Unpublished doctoral dissertation). University of Hull, Hull.

Panichi, L., Deutschmann, M., & Molka-Danielsen, J. (2010). Virtual worlds for language learning and intercultural exchange: Is it for real? In S. Guth & F. Helm (Eds.), *Telecollaboration 2.0: Languages, literacies, and intercultural learning in the 21st century* (pp. 165–195). Bern, Switzerland: Peter Lang.

Park, M. (2018). Innovative assessment of aviation English in a virtual world: Windows into cognitive and metacognitive strategies. *ReCALL, 30*(2), 196–213.

Peterson, M. (2010). Learner participation patterns and strategy use in Second Life: An exploratory case study. *ReCALL, 22*(3), 273–292.

Peterson, M. (2011). Towards a research agenda for the use of three-dimensional virtual worlds in language learning. *CALICO Journal, 29*(1), 67–80.

Peterson, M. (2012a). EFL learner collaborative interaction in Second Life. *ReCALL, 24*(1), 20–39. doi:10.1017/S0958344011000279

Peterson, M. (2012b). Learner interaction in a massively multiplayer online role-playing game. (MMORPG): A sociocultural discourse analysis. *ReCALL, 24*(3), 361–380.

Peterson, M. (2016). Virtual worlds and language learning. An analysis of research. In F. Farr & L. Murray (Eds.), *The Routledge handbook of language learning and technology* (pp. 308–319). London, UK: Routledge.

Sadler, R. (2017). Virtual worlds and language education. In S. L. Thorne & S. May (Eds.), Language education and technology (3rd ed., pp. 375–388). New York: Springer; doi:10.1007/978-3-319-02237-6_29.

Savin-Baden, M., Gourlay, L., & Tombs, C. (2010). Researching in immersive spaces. In C. Savin-Baden & C. H. Major (Eds.), *New approaches to qualitative research* (pp. 162–171). New York: Routledge.

Schultze, M. (2017). Complexity approaches to computer assisted language learning. In S. L. Thorne & S. May (Eds.), *Language education and technology* (3rd ed., pp. 301–312). New York: Springer.

Schwienhorst, K. (2004). Detachment and reflection: Awareness and presence in a synchronous text-based environment. In R. Satchell & N. Chenik (Eds.), *University language centres: Forging the learning environments of the future* (pp. 43–62). Paris, France: CercleS.

Schwienhorst, K. (2009). Learning a second language in three dimensions: Potential benefits and the evidence so far. *Themes in Science and Technology Education, 2*(1-2), 153–163.

Shield, L. (2003). MOO as a language learning tool. In U. Felix (Ed.), *Language learning online: Towards best practice* (pp. 97–122). Lisse, The Netherlands: Swets & Zeitlinger.

Shield, L., Davies, L. B., & Weininger, M. J. (2000). Fostering (pro)active language learning through MOO. *ReCALL, 12*(1), 35–48. doi:10.1017/S0958344000000513

Sykes, J. (2005). Synchronous CMC and pragmatic development: Effects of oral and written chat. *CALICO Journal, 22*(3), 399–431.

Sykes, J. (2009). Learner requests in Spanish: Examining the potential of multiuser virtual environments for L2 pragmatics acquisition. In L. Lomicka, & G. Lord (Eds.), The next generation: Social networking and online collaboration in foreign language learning. CALICO Monograph Series, 8, 199-234.

Wang, A. (2017). *Learning English in a multi-user virtual environment: Exploring factors affecting participation* (Unpublished doctoral dissertation). Mid Sweden University, Sweden.

Wang, A., Deutschmann, M., & Steinvall, A. (2013). Towards a model for mapping participation: Exploring factors affecting participation in a telecollaborative learning scenario in Second Life. *JALT CALL Journal*, *9*(1), 3–22.

Wigham, C. R. (2012). The interplay between non-verbal and verbal interaction in synthetic worlds which supports verbal participation and production in a foreign language (Unpublished doctoral dissertation). Université Blaise Pascal - Clermont-Ferrand II.

Wigham, C. R., & Chanier, T. (2013). A study of verbal and nonverbal communication in Second Life: The ARCHI21 experience. *ReCALL*, *25*(1), 63–84.

Wigham, C. R., Panichi, L., Nocchi, S., & Sadler, R. (2018). Editorial: Interactions in and around virtual worlds. *ReCALL*, *30*(2), 153–160.

Yamazaki, K. (2018). Computer-assisted learning of communication (CALC): A case study of Japanese learning in a 3D virtual world. *ReCALL*, *30*(2), 214–231.

Zheng, D., Young, M. F., Wagner, M. M., & Brewer, R. A. (2009). Negotiation for Action: English language learning in game-based virtual worlds. *Modern Language Journal*, *93*(4), 489–511. doi:10.1111/j.1540-4781.2009.00927.x

ADDITIONAL READING

Allwright, D., & Hanks, J. (2009). *The developing language learner*. Basingstoke: Palgrave Macmillan. doi:10.1057/9780230233690

Godwin-Jones, R. (2018). Chasing the butterfly effect: Informal language learning online as a complex system. *Language Learning & Technology*, *22*(2), 8–27.

Jabbari, N., & Eslami, Z. R. (2019). Second language learning in the context of massively multiplayer online games: A scoping review. *ReCALL*, *31*(1), 92–113. doi:10.1017/S0958344018000058

Kostoulas, A. (Ed.). (2019). *Challenging boundaries in language education*. Cham, Switzerland: Springer. doi:10.1007/978-3-030-17057-8

Kruk, M. (Ed.). (2019). *Assessing the effectiveness of virtual technologies in foreign and second language instruction*. Hershey, PA: IGI Global. doi:10.4018/978-1-5225-7286-2

Levy, M. (2016). Researching in language learning and technology. In F. Farr (Ed.), *L. Murray, The Routledge handbook of language learning and technology* (pp. 101–114). London: Routledge.

Mengmeng, W. (2018). A study of qualitative research method used in language teaching. *International Journal of Learning and Teaching*, *4*(4), 306–310. doi:10.18178/ijlt.4.4.306-310

Tojo, H., & Takagi, A. (2017). Trends in qualitative research in three major language teaching and learning journals 2006-2015. *International Journal of English Language Teaching*, *4*(1), 37–47. doi:10.5430/ijelt.v4n1p37

KEY TERMS AND DEFINITIONS

Immersive: When talking about virtual worlds in language learning, we say that the experience is "immersive" when you feel like you are part of the environment.

Interaction: In virtual world CALL research, interaction is understood as learner verbal and non-verbal activity in the platform.

In-world: This expression is used largely by users of virtual worlds to refer to the act of being in the virtual world platform through the use of an avatar. If you are in the platform you are "in-world", i.e., in the virtual world.

Participation: In virtual world CALL research, participation is a broader notion than interaction and can be understood as learner target language use and intentional and contextualised nonverbal activity in support of learning.

Practitioner Research: Research that is carried out by teachers when investigating their own practice and the context of their teaching.

Qualitative Research: Research that focuses on understanding phenomena via in-depth detailed descriptive and observational analysis. In qualitative research, the researcher recognizes herself as being an integral part of the research context.

Quantitative Research: Research that attempts to measure phenomena and that will generally include large data sets so that any statistical information that is produced can be considered predictive of phenomena in identical contexts.

Virtual Worlds: Nowadays, these are mostly three-dimensional computer simulation platforms which users can access via an avatar. These platforms may be used to interact with other people such as *Second Life*™ or for online gaming with other players such as *World of Warcraft*.

Chapter 13
Vocabulary Acquisition From a Virtual Street-View Context

Ya-Chun Shih
National Dong Hwa University, Taiwan

ABSTRACT

This study incorporated Google Street View into a 3D virtual environment, known as VECAR, in which EFL learners controlled their avatars to learn vocabulary in a context of New York City. New York City's Times Square is full of real-life materials, realia, which can be used to assist situated incidental vocabulary learning and to connect vocabulary acquisition to the real world. The case study design combining both qualitative and quantitative analysis was used mainly to investigate the program's impact on vocabulary acquisition, and to track the ongoing dynamics of the vocabulary acquisition across the four research phases, learner motivation in terms of self-efficacy and attitudes toward vocabulary learning, and strategy use across learners. The results showed that all participants involved in the study acquired the target vocabulary, increased motivation, and deepened strategy use gradually over time. The program supported both contextualized and motivated vocabulary learning processes in realistic situations.

INTRODUCTION

The underlying vocabulary knowledge, which serves as the first step towards second and foreign language (L2) acquisition, is dominant in learners' four language skills (Nation, 2001) and communicative competence (Schmitt, 2000). Vocabulary acquisition goes far beyond consulting a dictionary, memorizing word definitions and drills. Instead, a large proportion of vocabulary is acquired incidentally from or through real-world contexts in which the words are actually used. As Stahl (2005) indicated, "the knowledge of a word not only implies a definition, but also implies how that words fits into the world" (p. 95). Word meanings are context-sensitive and dynamic; in other words, word meanings are determined or defined dynamically within or by a context. Hence, vocabulary is best acquired or learned in context. However, in English as a Foreign Language (EFL) settings, the lack of a rich oral target language environment, a dearth of authentic language input and contextualized vocabulary learning in real-world situations, and repetitive, isolated vocabulary drills or study can result in learners' partial or inadequate mastering

DOI: 10.4018/978-1-6684-7597-3.ch013

of vocabulary knowledge, and can eventually lead to less effective vocabulary learning. This dilemma, commonly faced by EFL learners, highlights the importance of vocabulary acquisition in target language-rich and authentic real-world contexts.

The lack of motivation is another obstacle for EFL learners to overcome, and one that impedes successful vocabulary acquisition through written and oral contexts. Vocabulary acquisition is an incremental learning process highly associated with motivational conditions. Motivation is one of the key factors influencing the success of L2 vocabulary learning (Deng, 2010; You, 2011). Deng (2010) emphasized the specific effect of motivation, namely self-efficacy and attitude, in vocabulary learning. Tseng and Schmitt (2008) proposed a model of "motivated vocabulary learning," whereby learners' "ever-changing motivational state" (p. 360) is posited to be closely related to their vocabulary learning process.

In response to the aforementioned dilemma, we built Virtual English Classroom Augmented Reality (VECAR) to help EFL learners overcome the obstacles facing them through contextualized and motivated vocabulary learning. VECAR is a blend between virtual reality and augmented reality, which involves projections of real-world images into virtual spaces. After launching VECAR, users can arrive at various preset destinations and explore by controlling their avatars and navigating through the panoramic street-level imagery. VECAR served as a means to situate explicit vocabulary instruction and to motivate incidental vocabulary learning in context, via both language learners' reading of text and their immersion in "real-world" situations that provided "context-embedded" understanding and facilitated vocabulary learning. VECAR lets learners "spot" vocabulary words embedded in real-world contexts through having the learners tour various locations of New York, such as Yankee Stadium, the Statue of Liberty, and Times Square (see Figure 1).

Figure 1. Students participated as avatars standing in Times Square

This research asserted that a hybrid combination of virtual and real-world environments, VECAR, motivated and scaffolded EFL learners' contextual vocabulary acquisition and strategy use through their meaningful interactions with a native speaker (NS) as well as with the authentic materials (i.e., street-view images). This research seeks to investigate the influence of VECAR on the learners' vocabulary learning process, including motivation (i.e., self-efficacy and attitude toward English vocabulary learning) and strategy use, through learners' immersion in a hybrid context under the guidance of a NS as they visit popular sites in New York City. Inspired by Tseng and Schmitt's (2008) model of "motivated vocabulary learning" and Godwin-Jones' (2018) term, "contextualized vocabulary learning," this study explored the dynamics among vocabulary knowledge, motivation, and strategy use, which were assumed to be inextricably intertwined factors in the contextual vocabulary learning process. The research questions are as follows:

- Are learners able to acquire the target vocabulary in terms of vocabulary knowledge?
- Is learners' motivation, in terms of attitudes and self-efficacy, enhanced after participation in the program?
- What are learners' attitudes towards the program in contextual vocabulary acquisition?
- How does the ongoing process of contextualized vocabulary learning change over time? Specifically, how do vocabulary knowledge, motivation, and strategy use interact in the vocabulary learning process within the VECAR context?

LITERATURE REVIEW

The Nature of Vocabulary Acquisition

Vocabulary acquisition is generally defined as the process of knowing, learning or acquiring the words of a language. Due to the "complex" and "incremental" nature of vocabulary acquisition (Schmitt, 2000; Kim, Crossley, & Kyle, 2018), vocabulary acquisition is considered to be the multifaceted aspects of words (knowledge) which "are gradually learned over a period of time from numerous exposures" (p. 4). The distinct levels or types of vocabulary knowledge have been explored with a view to developing learners' vocabulary acquisition (e.g., Nation, 1990). In other words, the concepts of vocabulary acquisition, including covering different aspects of lexical knowledge, have been defined or discussed in relation to the aspects of and perspectives on knowing a word, for instance, acquisition of word meaning, written and spoken forms, grammatical behavior, collocation, register, association, frequency, and use (Nation, 1990, 2001), intentional and incidental vocabulary learning (Richards & Schmidt, 2002), and vocabulary learning strategies, such as context clues (e.g., Greenwood & Flanigan, 2007).

Previous studies suggest that vocabulary acquisition (or knowledge) is a crucial component to second or foreign language acquisition (e.g., Barcroft, 2004). However, Schmitt (2008) indicated, "the best means of achieving good vocabulary learning is still unclear, partly because it depends on a wide variety of factors" (p. 329). Despite the success of the related studies on the role of vocabulary acquisition in elucidating important issues in the area of language learning, there is still room for further investigation in the search for the optimal technique for facilitating vocabulary acquisition, especially in the high technology age, in furtherance of both pedagogical and research purposes.

In order to unveil the complexities of vocabulary learning, a hypothesized model of "motivated vocabulary learning," proposed by Tseng and Schmitt (2008), integrates three constructs (vocabulary knowledge, motivation, and strategy use) into six latent factors: "1. Initial appraisal of vocabulary learning experience; 2. Self-regulating capacity of vocabulary learning; 3. Strategic vocabulary learning involvement 4. Mastery of vocabulary learning tactics; 5. Vocabulary knowledge; 6. Post-appraisal of the effectiveness of vocabulary learning tactics" (p. 360). The model highlights the importance of the constructs, especially in terms of their interactions with each other in the vocabulary learning process. More specifically, their research mainly focuses on how the ongoing motivational state affects vocabulary learning and strategy use in terms of "frequency" and "mastery of individual strategies" to acquire vocabulary knowledge (p. 357), and investigates the relationship between strategy use and vocabulary knowledge. The model proposes a developmental and cyclical vocabulary learning process, influenced by learners' "ever-changing motivational state" (p. 360), from the initial motivational state, namely "initial appraisal of vocabulary learning experience," to the last stage, "post-appraisal of the effectiveness of vocabulary learning tactics," which in turn influences the next initial motivational state and the subsequent factors in a cycle of vocabulary learning.

Acquiring Vocabulary From Context

As mentioned previously, *context* plays a critical role in vocabulary acquisition and learning. The use of various types of context facilitates reader's vocabulary acquisition or learning (Edwards, 2009), most vocabulary is acquired or learned from context (Sternberg, 1987), and word knowledge is gained through context and user interaction (Kasper & Wagner, 2018). The definition of *context* can be approached in two ways: It can be conceptualized narrowly as *linguistic context* or more broadly as *situational context* (Gu, 2003). Traditionally, when context is defined as linguistic context, researchers (e.g., Thornbury, 2002) focus on language context and stress the importance of learning vocabulary in or from language context. Learners are allowed to observe how the word is used in sentences grammatically, in context, which promotes their vocabulary retention (Edwards, 2009), as well as word meaning, collocations and their grasp of the grammar of sentences (Thornbury, 2002). In broader terms, context is used to indicate a situational context in which learning or reading occurs (Gu, 2003), and situational context which refers to "visual" or "situative" contexts (Rapaport, 2003, p. 2). As for the learning or situational context in which learners are provided with contextualized, situated and visualized vocabulary presentation (situational context), learners also use their prior knowledge and experiences to draw inferences and guess word meanings from situational context (e.g., real-life locations, or street view in this study) in order to facilitate vocabulary learning. A hybrid approach, "multi-modal context" is proposed and defined as the situation in which learners employ a variety of context types, such as linguistic context, situational or visual context, to discover word meanings (Kohne, 2011, p. 17). The multi-modal context is significant to vocabulary development and retention.

Use of Vocabulary Learning Strategies

Vocabulary learning strategies (VLSs), a branch of language learning strategies (Nation, 2001), are used to guess the meaning of unfamiliar words, retain these words in long-term memory and recall them from it, and use them in oral or written form (Jiménez-Catalan, 2003, p. 56). Several studies have proposed taxonomies of VLSs (e.g., Schmitt, 2000). VLSs can be categorized as "shallow" strategies (e.g., repetition, note-taking, and simple memorization), or as "deeper" strategies (e.g., association), based on the depth of mental processing involved (Schmitt, 2000, p. 132). According to Schmitt (2000), "deeper" VLS strategies are more effective than "shallow" ones in improving learners' vocabulary acquisition and retention. Other studies (e.g., Cohen & Aphek, 1980) also confirm that deep and active manipulation of vocabulary-related information, such as imagery and context associations, leads to successful vocabulary learning for advanced learners.

Learners' motivation is hypothesized to have direct and indirect effects on strategy use across both quantitative and qualitative dimensions. According to Tseng and Schmitt (2008), the use of VLSs can be divided into two aspects. The first is the quantitative aspect, measured in terms of the frequency of VLS use, namely "strategic vocabulary learning involvement," as learners make attempts and discoveries through their vocabulary learning acts and experiences. The second aspect is the qualitative one (i.e., mastery), which considers "mastery of vocabulary learning tactics" as specific VLSs through which learners can acquire vocabulary knowledge (pp. 364-365). Tseng and Schmitt hypothesized that a causal relationship exists between the initial motivational state and the two aspects of strategy use.

The Roles of Motivational Constructs in Vocabulary Learning: Self-Efficacy and Attitude

Self-efficacy and attitude represent the motivational system that underlies human behavior (Kwan & Bryan, 2010) as well as the vital constructs of language-learning motivation (Kormos, Kiddle & Csize´r, 2011). These motivational components interact with one another to influence language learning behavior. Self-efficacy beliefs and attitude are important aspects of learners' motivation and behavior which influence the effects of language learning, and more specifically, vocabulary learning (e.g., Deng, 2010).

Self-efficacy refers to an individual's belief about his or her ability to perform a given activity or accomplish certain tasks successfully in specific situations (Bandura, 1995). The role of self-efficacy is a critical element for the success of vocabulary learning (Deng, 2010). Moreover, the impact of different learning or teaching approaches on self-efficacy in relation to vocabulary learning was investigated by previous researchers. For instance, the results of the longitudinal study conducted by Mizumoto (2013) revealed that the self-regulated learning approach promotes self-efficacy "which in turn may contribute to the development of vocabulary knowledge" and also implies "the importance of measuring self-efficacy as a measure of mastery in vocabulary learning" (p. 22) due to the vital role self-efficacy plays in vocabulary development.

Attitudes towards learning are regarded as a motivational construct (Gardner, 1985). According to the "tripartite model of attitudes" (Bizer, Barden, & Petty, 2003, p. 246), which includes three domains (i.e., affective, behavioral, cognitive), the affective component of attitude is defined as the "feelings, moods, and emotions" an individual holds toward an "attitude object" (p. 246). The individual learner differences in the affective domain, including motivation and attitudes toward vocabulary learning, play a role in vocabulary development (Pavičić Takač, 2008, p. 17). The relevant research findings reveal that learners develop positive attitudes toward vocabulary after exposure to CALL (e.g., Ali, Mukundan, Baki & Ayub, 2012), and positive attitudes toward English vocabulary learning with the help of technologies (e.g., Farshi & Mohammadi, 2013), and point to the positive effects of affective attitudes on learners' vocabulary learning (e.g., Deng, 2010).

It has been shown that self-efficacy and attitudes toward language learning can be promoted, for instance, through learner immersion in a 3D virtual world, namely, Quest Atlantis (QA), in which students developed their positive attitudes toward English and language learning, as well as their self-efficacy in terms of English use and e-communication (Zheng, Young, Brewer & Wagner, 2009, p. 218). In a case study involving four EFL learners in a multi-user virtual environment (MUVE), namely, "Languagelab" in Second Life, students' speaking self-efficacy, authentic target language use, vocabulary learning, and motivation to engage in self-regulated learning were enhanced (Rahayu & Jacobson, 2012).

Virtual Environment-Enhanced Vocabulary Acquisition

It has been increasingly suggested that immersive virtual environments can support language learning (Lawrence & Ahmed, 2018), and vocabulary acquisition and retention in a number of ways, e.g., interactions through virtual worlds (Godwin-Jones, 2018). One of the new possibilities involves grounding vocabulary acquisition in virtual environments, avatar-based immersions, and computer-mediated interaction (e.g., Kastoudi, 2011; Lan et al. 2015; Newgarden & Zheng, 2016; Sanchez, 2006). Researchers have attempted to create beneficial effects on vocabulary acquisition by combining virtual environments and tasks, and situating language learners in various settings.

Kastoudi (2011), for example, proposed the idea of integrating interaction, tasks and virtual environments (i.e., Pot Healer Adventure Quest in Second Life) to facilitate incidental vocabulary learning and second language acquisition. Kastoudi conducted a qualitative case study which involved four advanced adult English learners, and a native speaker. The project has yielded results in terms of increasing vocabulary acquisition through interaction. Another example of the use of virtual environments to facilitate vocabulary acquisition is Sanchez's research project (2006). Since many students struggle with vocabulary learning due to lacking mastery of prerequisite real-world knowledge, Sanchez integrated the use of a synthetic learning environment (SLE) known as Virtual Field Trip (VFT), along with real-world situations, into second grade classrooms to provide situated experiential learning, and promote vocabulary acquisition. The VFT incorporates a real-world environment, consisting of pictures and videos, into a virtual world where users can view real-world images in 360 degrees. It connects vocabulary knowledge with real-world experiences, and provides a meaningful context for situated vocabulary instruction. These studies provide a valuable reference for studying the potential of combining embodying avatars and interacting with virtual environments with real-world images for promoting vocabulary acquisition and retention.

METHODOLOGY

The present study aimed at understanding a bounded phenomenon by investigating a small number of typical instances of the phenomenon of vocabulary acquisition as an individual's incremental developmental process occurring over time in context, in an in-depth and holistic manner. Thus, a decision was made to investigate the phenomenon from a longitudinal perspective, with individual participants repeatedly exposed to the target words, and the various facets of their vocabulary learning re-evaluated several times. The qualitative case study method was used in combination with a time series analysis to probe both the receptive and productive vocabulary developmental processes involved in utilizing contextualized and visual-word association learning strategies.

Context and Participants

The study took place at the Department of Computer Science of a national university situated in a rural environment in Eastern Taiwan. The department runs several sophisticated computer laboratories, the size of which facilitate small group interactions. Four EFL students pursuing graduate studies in computer vision and specializing in divergent research areas had the opportunity to join the VECAR project. The ages of the participants ranged from 23 to 25. The participants were first screened using the General English Proficiency TEST (GEPT), a five-level (superior, advanced, high-intermediate, intermediate, elementary) criterion-referenced testing system used in Taiwan. Only EFL graduate students who had already passed the GEPT Intermediate Level, but had not passed the GEPT High-Intermediate Level were invited to participate.

In this study, we chose a context and four participants reflecting the common scenario in which university students need to improve their vocabulary learning in an EFL context. We focused, in particular, on individual students who could be described as struggling, at least to some degree, to deal with vocabulary learning problems and to enhance their vocabulary learning efficiency and retention.

Design and Implementation of the Vocabulary Program

We incorporated Google Street View with the virtual environment to render the world, known as VECAR, in a street-view panorama, in which virtual objects are combined with real scenes (Figure 1). VECAR provides 360° street-level imagery of popular locations worldwide, allowing virtual access to location-specific settings for vocabulary learning. Using virtual avatars in conjunction with real street views, language learners can explore real street-view scenes, and interact with virtual objects or other avatars.

Figure 2. Three-step vocabulary learning model

In view of the incremental and complex nature of vocabulary acquisition, we adopted diverse vocabulary instructional and learning techniques, including contextual and mnemonic approaches (i.e., strategy use), explicit instruction and incidental learning, with the intention of placing vocabulary learning squarely in "real-world" (i.e., street-view) situations by engaging learners in sightseeing tasks so that vocabulary could be learned from this multi-modal context, including both linguistic and situational contexts. The three-stage loop vocabulary learning process (Figure 2) was implemented on a weekly basis to study several dimensions of learners' acquisition of 60 target words.

Step 1. Guided Reading

The native English-speaking instructor guided students to read the "Newspaper" created using Prezi with emphasis on the form, meaning, and use of 10 target words.

Step 2. Virtual Field Trip

Students, guided by the instructor, explored places around a target site through the 360-degree, panoramic, street level imagery (i.e., realia) offered by VECAR, and were exposed to the target vocabulary in context.

Step 3. Vocabulary Consolidation

Students completed the vocabulary worksheet(s) (Table 1). Students refocused on the 10 target words, including their meanings, and memory cues, for example, street-view pictures, cartoons, synonyms, related words, antonyms and so on.

Table 1. Vocabulary worksheet: An example

Key Word	Information	Memory Cue
Example: Browse	Definition: to look through or glance at casually Use it in a sentence: I **browsed** through some magazines while I waited.	
1. junction	Definition: Use it in a sentence:	

Data Collection

The mixed-methods case study design presented in the study, by combining continuous exploratory virtual and real-world fieldwork, and time-series measurements of learners' weekly performance, investigated the incremental process of vocabulary acquisition through collecting data from different resources, i.e., vocabulary knowledge scale (VKS), observations of virtual events, questionnaires, and interviews. The operationalization of a time-series design involved four periods of data collection: Baseline Phase A (3 waves), Treatment Phase B (8 waves), Posttest Phase C (3 waves), and Delayed Posttest D (3 waves). During the Treatment Phase B, weekly VKS tests for 60 target words, as well as weekly observations of 1-hr virtual events, were collected over 8 weeks.

A modified version of the VKS (Paribakht & Wesche, 1996) was used in this study, as shown in Table 2. The first two options (A and B) evaluated learners' recognition of the word form, the third option (C) assessed their understanding of the word meaning and ability to articulate its meaning, and the fourth option (D) captured both their productive knowledge of word meanings and word usage in a sentence context. In terms of scoring, each option (A, B, C, D) chosen for each item was awarded from 0 to 3 points, respectively. The maximum possible score, therefore, was 180 for the 60 items.

Table 2. Vocabulary knowledge scale: An Example

A= I don't remember having seen this word. B= I have seen this word but I don't know what it means. C= I know what this word means, but I'm not sure how to use it. I think it means… D= I know what this word means and I can use it in a sentence. Try to use this word in a sentence in English. Note. Please mark the appropriate column (A, B, C or D) for each word.				
1. junction	A	B	C	D
I think it means (in Chinese or English): Use this word in a sentence (in English):				

Note. Adapted from "Enhancing Vocabulary Acquisition through Reading: A Hierarchy of Text-related Exercise Types," by T. S. Paribakht and M. Wesche, 1996, The Canadian Modern Language Review, 52(2).

The questionnaires used in this study were mainly based on the Motivation for Vocabulary Learning Questionnaire (MVLQ) (Deng, 2010), assessing two learner motivational constructs (i.e., attitude and self-efficacy), and were followed by in-depth interviews to allow for elaboration on respondent's initial answers in the questionnaires to further investigate students' motivation toward vocabulary learning in this context.

Data Analysis

Both qualitative and quantitative data were analyzed to validate the study. We conducted a systematic and relevant qualitative analysis of data collected from observations, and interviews through identifying and coding categories and themes (Table 3) emerging from the data and comparing the results across four learners, looking specifically at the development of their vocabulary, as well as their motivation in terms of a process with four stages and strategy use. Miles and Huberman's (1994) three main stages of qualitative data analysis, i.e., data reduction, data display and conclusion drawing, guided the process of coding data from observations and interviews. In this study, the starting point for these stages was the development of an organizing conceptual framework for the codes, followed by an analysis of the data using the framework, and conducting a member check. A thematic framework was developed based on participants' data, and initially informed by Tseng and Schmitt's (2008) framework of "motivated vocabulary learning". Our thematic framework is presented in Table 3, along with descriptions and examples for the codes. In looking at the quantitative data, we analyzed the time-series data, collected mainly from VKS, visually, and employed the C-statistic to investigate variability in data points and changes across four phases. Researchers (Gottman & Glass, 1978) have suggested that conducting both a visual analysis and a statistical analysis can improve the reliability of the former.

Additionally, we focused on the motivational constructs: perceived self-efficacy and affective perspectives of attitude, to investigate whether the learners' motivation changed. We measured this by comparing learner ratings on questions relating to these two constructs in the pre- and post-questionnaires. Each of these questions provided respondents with a five-point Likert scale as follows: 1. Strongly Disagree 2. Disagree 3. No Idea 4. Agree 5. Strongly Agree. The learner ratings, along with the results from follow-up interviews with them, were used to determine how the two constructs might be integrated into, or influence, vocabulary learning. The validity of this qualitative case study was strengthened by the analysis of the time-series data. The quantitative results were further triangulated using in-depth interviews with and observations of the four learners as they expressed their opinions regarding the given statements.

Table 3. Thematic framework used to code interviews and observations

Thematic Category	Code	Description/Example
Vocabulary Knowledge	Form	Recognize a target word
	Meaning	Understand the meaning of a target word
	Usage	Use a target word with grammatical and semantic accuracy in a sentence
Motivation	Attitudes	(the affective component of attitude in this study) Feelings, moods, and emotions toward an attitude object (e.g., VECAR program, vocabulary learning, strategy use)
	Self-Efficacy	A belief about his or her ability to perform a given activity or accomplish certain tasks successfully in specific situations
Strategy Use	Shallow	The use of "shallow" strategies (e.g., repetition, learning words out of context, using a word list, and simple memorization)
	Deep	The use of "deeper" strategies (e.g., association, guessing from contextual clues)

RESULTS AND DISCUSSION

Results of Within-Case Analysis

First, the results of each individual learner are described. Each case begins with a short background description. Following this appears information shedding light on each learner's preferences, motivation, and strategy use with regard to vocabulary learning.

Chou (S1) is a 25-year-old second-year graduate student in the Computer Science and Engineering Department, which prepares students to become programmers. He has passed the Intermediate Level of the GEPT. He has been motivated to learn English language and vocabulary since commencing senior high school. However, he uses few vocabulary learning strategies, such as repeating a new word a number of times, and uses them less effectively when it comes to vocabulary acquisition and retention. He tends to look for new vocabulary learning strategies in order to advance his career. He also appreciates the way the VECAR program gives users the options represented by the following program features: visual-word association, and contextualized vocabulary presentation and instruction, as evidenced by his expression of these features making a strong impression on him and his motivation to acquire vocabulary knowledge through virtual street-view immersion.

Kuo (S2) is a 23-year-old second-year graduate student, majoring in Computer Science and Engineering. He has passed the Intermediate Level of the GEPT. He shows interest in learning English language and vocabulary, and, in particular, is highly motivated to learn English through listening because of his self-identification as a less proficient listener. His previous vocabulary learning, relying on the method of rote learning and memorization of vocabulary words from A to Z, had been ineffective, resulting in low retention rates. The VECAR program, and the teacher's explicit instruction, which included providing clear and vivid examples of word meanings in context (i.e., written context and street-view images or scenes), as well as the use of association strategies to improve vocabulary learning and word recall were all highly valued by Kuo. After undergoing VECAR training, he reflected that he was more readily able to use new vocabulary in sentence context.

Sun (S3) is a 24-year-old first-year graduate student in the Computer Science and Engineering Department, and looks forward to becoming a programmer. He has passed the GEPT Intermediate Level, but seemed to possess little confidence in his ability to learn English. He is used to learning vocabulary through rote learning and repetition, although Sun admitted that this method has a number of limitations, citing its inefficiency and his tendency to easily forget vocabulary. However, after starting the VECAR program, he became more interested and confident in learning English, and vocabulary in particularly, as time went on, owing to the following features of VECAR: a conversational teaching style, the creation of a lively and visual teaching situation.

Wei (S4) is a 24-year-old first-year graduate student in the Computer Science and Engineering Department. His English ability is roughly equivalent to the GEPT Intermediate Level. He is better at reading and writing English than he is at listening and speaking. He expressed that he had an interest in learning English, but struggled with vocabulary learning, and was eager to find out the vocabulary building method that would work best for him. His previous experiences consisted of learning or memorizing new vocabulary by using translated Chinese (L1 equivalents), with this vocabulary often being associated with word lists. After joining the VECAR program, he became more confident in listening and speaking English, and performed better and retained vocabulary he had learned more effectively, and used VLSs, particularly deeper strategies, actively.

Vocabulary Knowledge Acquisition

There is strong evidence of the program's effectiveness in terms of the four learners' receptive and productive vocabulary knowledge, acquisition and retention. The results indicated that the four learners gradually increased and retained their vocabulary knowledge over time with regard to three aspects of the target words: (1) form, (2) meaning, and (3) use.

The baseline data has a stable, flat trend, and mean scores ranged from 30 to 52 for the four learners (S1=52, S2=49, S3=43, S4=30) (see Figure 3). Under treatment conditions, the data display an upward trend. Figure 3 shows level changes (S1=19, S2=21, S3=18, S4=27) from the baseline (Phase A) to the treatment period (Phase B) with a PND (percentage of non-overlapping data) of 100%, and a direction change (flat to accelerating). The level changes, ranked in descending order, were as follows: (1) S4, (2) S2, (3) S1, and (4) S3. Additionally, the C-statistic results (see Table 4) also suggest that in the baseline (A) + treatment (B) phase (when the treatment data are appended to baseline data), there was a statistically significant change at the .01 level for all cases.

During the treatment phase (B), a gradual accelerating trend in the direction of improvement occurred when the program was introduced. At the end of the treatment phase (week 9), all students almost reached the maximum score (S1=180, S2=174, S3=171, S4=178). Additionally, a comparison of the phases (between Phase B and C, C and D) revealed no level change or only very slight level changes. The results indicated that the levels of the students' scores were maintained, and, in other words, most target vocabulary was retained across the maintenance phases (Phase C and D).

Figure 3. Time series graph: Weekly score changes for four participants

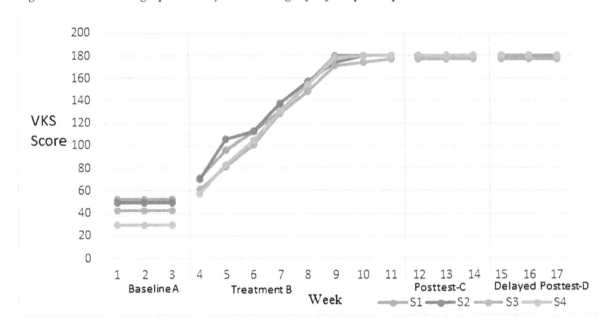

Table 4. C-statistic analysis of scores achieved in different phases

Participants	Phases	C	Sc	z
S1	A+B	0.951284	0.273861	3.473599**
S2	A+B	0.947423	0.273861	3.459499**
S3	A+B	0.954230	0.273861	3.484356**
S4	A+B	0.953279	0.273861	3.480881**

** $p < 0.01$

Motivation Toward Vocabulary Learning

The study also aimed at investigating learners' motivation, in terms of *attitudes* and *self-efficacy*, after they were exposed to the VECAR program, toward vocabulary learning and teaching methods—namely contextualized, visual-word association strategies.

Attitudes

The four students' overall reactions toward vocabulary learning via the VECAR program were positive. After participating in the VECAR program, students had positive motivational *attitudes* toward vocabulary learning (#1 "I enjoy learning new words.") (see Appendix A), and were satisfied with the program (# 2 "I enjoy learning vocabulary in this program."), with an average response of 4.25 respectively. All four learners showed an overall positive motivational/attitudinal change (+1 or +2) in the average response (see #1 in Figure 4). These results were also supported by the qualitative data recorded over the course of the VECAR program. The following qualitative evidence, for example, is associated with the previous quantitative data.

I did enjoy learning new words in this program, and feel good or happy when I figure out (a) new word(s) in or am using VECAR. (Interview #3, S1)

Figure 4. Motivational change after vocabulary learning in VECAR

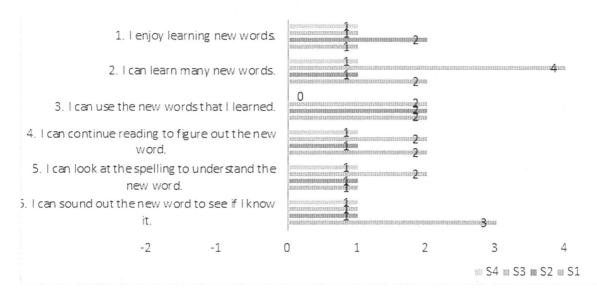

Key features of the program were highly appreciated and accepted by the users. Ranked in descending order, these are as follows (see Appendix A): Strategies and Teacher's Instruction (4.75), Worksheet (4.5), Prezi Newspaper (4.25), System (4). On a case-by-case basis, S1 scored the following statement with a 5: "I enjoy learning vocabulary in this program" and expressed that he especially appreciated reading "Prezi Newspapers". S2 responded to the same statement with a 4, and mentioned that he especially appreciated the vocabulary worksheets, the teacher's direct instruction (e.g., giving examples of vocabulary words), the experience-based, contextualized learning, and visual association strategies. He also expressed his opinions in the following way:

This is the first time I experienced this method (i.e., VECAR and visual association) and did those activities. I find it exciting to learn this way. (Interview #2, S2)

S3 responded to the same statement with a 4, and, in particular, was impressed by the visual association strategy, and the instructor's teaching style (i.e., teaching words as exemplified in jokes or based on daily experiences). S4 responded to the statement with a 4, and said he highly valued the visual association strategies, "Prezi Newspapers", and teaching materials and methods for their ability to assist his learning.

Vocabulary acquisition entails learners' active involvement and engagement in vocabulary learning tasks, as well vocabulary learning. The VECAR program provided the learners with fruitful forms of activities and contexts for vocabulary acquisition. The learners came away from it with an appreciation of the vocabulary tasks (see #3 & #4 in Appendix A) provided in the program, with an average response of 4.25 to the statement "I enjoy doing vocabulary tasks in this program," and an average response of 4 to the statement "I am relaxed while I am doing vocabulary tasks in this program". The tasks or sites were appreciated by the students. Ranked in descending order they were as follows: Broadway Theater District (4.5), Yankee Stadium (4.5), Statue of Liberty (4.5), One Times Square (4), Duffy Square TKTS (4), and Times Square (3.75). S3 described the program as follows:

Some tasks are fun and challenging... I like this learning atmosphere very much... I choose the new method (task-based learning) since I think those tasks and the new method(s) (i.e., visual association, learning in "real-life" context, VECAR, and so on) are useful. (Interview #4, S3)

Qualitative data also revealed that, from the learners' perspective, the program offered a valuable learning atmosphere, real-world context, and opportunities for task-based vocabulary learning.

Self-Efficacy

After participating in the program, learners' levels of *self-efficacy* in relation to vocabulary learning were high (see Appendix A), with an average response of 4.5 for question #5, measuring general self-efficacy for vocabulary learning, 4 for question #6, asking about *lexical usage*, 3.5 for question, #7 asking about *written form and meaning*, 4 for question #8, for *spoken form and meaning*, and 4.25 for question #9, about *guessing from context*. Their attitudes toward their guessing abilities in context, with an average response of 4 for question #10 and 4.5 for question #11, were also high. The qualitative confirmatory results from the observations and interviews helped interpret these quantitative findings. For instance, S1 indicated, "I can use the visual-word association strategies and contextual clues to guess and learn new vocabulary from context after participating in the project" (Interview #3, S1).

The students also displayed positive changes in self-efficacy as follows (see #2-6 in Figure 4): S3's change was (+4) regarding the statement "I can learn many new words," and S1's change was (+3) on the item "I can sound out the new word to see if I know it," for example. The other cases showed positive changes (+1 or +2), with the exception that S4 showed no change in his response to the given statement "I can use the new words that I learned," which might be explained by the fact that he already demonstrated a high level in general self-efficacy during the pretest. The learners' growing self-efficacy, along with their development in terms of vocabulary acquisition, were also observed in the qualitative data.

In sum, the learners' motivation ascribed to vocabulary learning was promoted through the program, especially when subjects were learning with the visual mnemonic (i.e., visual-word association) strategy, and when the native English-speaking instructor provided explicit vocabulary instruction along with the New York virtual sightseeing panoramas, especially Broadway, Yankee Stadium and the Statue of Liberty. The learners varied in terms of their preferences for specific vocabulary tasks, sites, and strategy use, reflecting their divergent interests in VECAR 's various theme-based contexts. The results clearly showed that immersion and interactions with the street-view context and real-life materials (realia) through the program, influenced learners' motivational attitudes and self-efficacy toward vocabulary learning, and strategy use.

Interaction Among Vocabulary Knowledge, Motivation, and Strategy Use Within the VECAR Context

The vocabulary learning process was highly associated with the learner's process of changing motivational states, and strategy use within the context. Based on the results from the longitudinal data, we presented a conceptual framework (Figure 5) that postulates vocabulary knowledge, motivation, and strategy use as the main focal constructs in contextualized vocabulary acquisition or learning. Our research set out to shed new light on the role of context in vocabulary learning, and to develop a conceptual framework of motivated vocabulary acquisition within the newly expounded context. The conceptual framework partly corroborated Tseng and Schmitt's (2008) model of motivated vocabulary learning, which emphasized the core elements of vocabulary knowledge and learning, motivation, and strategy use.

The results of the present study corroborated findings from Kastoudi's (2011) and Rahayu and Jacobson's (2012) case studies which suggested that the context of virtual environments can help enhance students' vocabulary acquisition and learning. Our findings also supported previous research pointing out the fact that the context of virtual environments, along with real-world situations, have the potential to enhance learner motivation (e.g., Sanchez, 2006). From a process-based point of view and in response to Chen and Li's (2010) statement, context serves as "an important consideration in the language learning process and can enhance learner learning interest and efficiency. Restated, meaningful vocabulary learning occurs only when the learning process is integrated with social, cultural and life contexts" (Chen & Li, 2010, Abstract); namely, multiple contexts. Thus, we proposed a "multi-modal context," defined as the situation in which learners used different context types, including both language context and situational context (i.e., socio-cultural and real-life context), to acquire word meanings, whether incidentally or intentionally. The above results, which exhibit an increase in learners' vocabulary knowledge and retention, correspond with Kohne's statement that "the multi-modal environment does not only help to identify word meanings (incidentally and intentionally); there is evidence that learning with multi-modal cues enhances retention" (Kohne, 2011, pp. 17-18). The importance of "multi-modal context" in vocabulary development and retention was confirmed in this study. Students' learning in real-life communicative context (i.e., street-view and virtual environment) and in linguistic context (i.e., Prezi newspaper) resulted in meaningful and effective vocabulary learning.

The learners' motivation, namely self-efficacy and attitudes, developed along with their vocabulary acquisition (Figure 3), as evidenced by both the qualitative and quantitative data (see Figure 4). All four learners demonstrated an attitude of acceptance toward the new program. They expressed a preference for and appreciation of VECAR, self-efficacy, specifically in terms of lexical usage, written and spoken forms and meaning, and guessing from context, in relation to vocabulary learning in this program. This, in turn, affected their follow-up practical pursuit of vocabulary knowledge in the street-view settings. Namely, their motivation, increased through their exposure to the vocabulary, which in turn facilitated the vocabulary learning process; results which corresponded with those of earlier studies (e.g., Tseng & Schmitt, 2008) which indicated that motivation can help vocabulary learning.

Figure 5. Conceptual framework

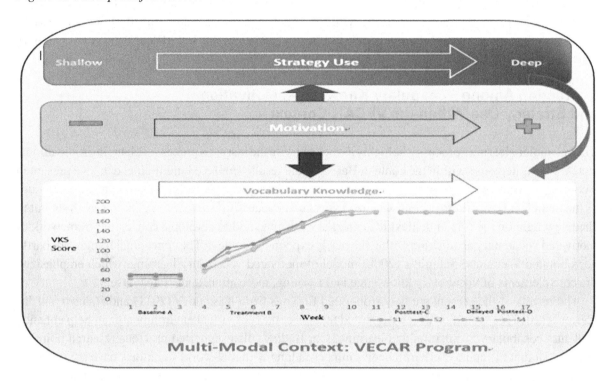

The participants' motivational attitudes and self-efficacy also facilitated their vocabulary learning-related behavior, namely vocabulary learning strategy use. This result is in line with Deng's proposition that "students' affective attitude for vocabulary learning comprises their emotion, feeling, and desire for vocabulary learning, and subsequently is likely to affect students' behavior in vocabulary learning" (2010, p. 8). Results from the qualitative data, namely interviews and observations, supported the correspondence between students' motivation in vocabulary learning and their strategy use. Specifically, an increase of students' motivation and changing types of students' VLS use were found in interviews and observations. Along with students' motivational development, they improved the quality of VLS use, namely, switched from "shallow" VLS (such as rote repetition, learning words out of context, e.g., through using a word list, and simple memorization) to "deeper" (to use Schmitt's term) VLSs, such as guessing from contextual clues and actively mastery of the visual-word association strategy. This result corresponds with Tseng and Schmitt's (2008) statement, which indicated that motivation might influence "the types of strategy use" (p. 362) (i.e., the qualitative dimension), and students' strategy use has shifted from the use of shallow VLS strategies to the use of deep VLS strategies.

The students benefited from efficiently using different types of association (e.g., context, visualization of the word, mental image) and deep VLS strategies, and consequently enhanced vocabulary learning and retention. The result is in accordance with Schmitt's, and Cohen and Aphek's propositions. Deep VLS strategies are more effective than shallow strategies in improving learners' vocabulary acquisition and retention (Schmitt, 2000), and (advanced) learners' deep and active manipulation of vocabulary-related information, such as imagery and context associations, leads to successful vocabulary learning (Cohen & Aphek, 1980).

Vocabulary, motivation, strategy use, and context were inextricably intertwined, and motivation influenced the whole process of vocabulary acquisition and learning, as well as strategy use of the EFL learners. Along with the students' development of their vocabulary knowledge and motivation, they actively used deeper vocabulary learning strategies, and therefore acquired more vocabulary knowledge in context.

CONCLUSIONS, LIMITATIONS AND IMPLICATIONS

The case study was employed to investigate this relatively unexplored research area and provided a case-by-case overview of the process of vocabulary acquisition across four stages. The current findings suggested that all four of the learners developed their vocabulary, and were motivated in multi-modal context to similar extents. Their vocabulary knowledge and retention increased in terms of form, meaning and use. Moreover, the program can work to motivate learners to enhance their attitude change, self-efficacy, and to master the deeper strategies during or after their exposure to contextualized vocabulary learning through the VECAR program. The learners developed positive attitudes toward the vocabulary tasks, sites, and strategy use in VECAR 's various theme-based contexts.

A study of vocabulary acquisition will never be complete without taking the interconnected elements-vocabulary knowledge, motivation, strategy use, and context- into consideration in a situated or situation-specific manner. This research explored a model of contextualized vocabulary acquisition (Figure 5), which incorporates these related elements. Changing motivation influenced the whole process of contextualized vocabulary acquisition and learning, as well as the EFL learners' strategy use.

This case study provides possibilities for further studies into a combination of virtual and street-view platforms designed for contextualized, motivated, and strategic vocabulary learning. The current qualitative case study is delimited by its focus on a relatively small number of EFL learners, best regarded as a community of practice, in which vocabulary learning involved participation and interaction. The results gained from the longitudinal data suggest hypotheses for future testing. Moreover, they enabled us to gain insights into a complex phenomenon-vocabulary acquisition-which involves the dynamics of contextualized and motivated vocabulary learning in this new setting. The results can serve as a springboard for further research into larger-scale research design.

This study also carries with its pedagogical implications for task design in blended-learning situations; namely, blending virtual and real worlds, explicit vocabulary instruction and incidental vocabulary learning, in context. The effectiveness of this program confirms researchers' assumption that explicit and implicit vocabulary learning can be complementary to lexical development (e.g., Feldman & Kinsella, 2005), providing support for the claim that "most vocabulary is learned from context" (Sternberg, 1987).

REFERENCES

Ali, Z., Mukundan, J., Baki, R., & Ayub, A. F. M. (2012). Second language learners' attitudes towards the methods of learning vocabulary. *English Language Teaching*, 5(4), 24–36. doi:10.5539/elt.v5n4p24

Bandura, A. (1995). *Self-efficacy in changing societies*. Cambridge University Press. doi:10.1017/CBO9780511527692

Barcroft, J. (2004). Second language vocabulary acquisition: A lexical input processing approach. *Foreign Language Annals*, *37*(2), 200–208. doi:10.1111/j.1944-9720.2004.tb02193.x

Bizer, G., Barden, J., & Petty, R. E. (2003). Attitudes. In *Encyclopedia of cognitive science* (Vol. 1, pp. 247–253). MacMillan.

Chen, C. M., & Li, Y. L. (2010). Personalized context-aware ubiquitous learning system for supporting effective English vocabulary learning. *Interactive Learning Environments*, *18*(4), 341–364. doi:10.1080/10494820802602329

Cohen, A. D., & Aphek, E. (1980). Retention of second-language vocabulary over time: Investigating the role of mnemonic associations. *System*, *8*(3), 221–235. doi:10.1016/0346-251X(80)90004-4

Deng, Q. (2010). *Motivation for vocabulary learning of college students. Theses, Student Research, and Creative Activity*. Department of Teaching, Learning and Teacher Education, University of Nebraska–Lincoln.

Edwards, L. (2009). *How to teach vocabulary*. Pearson Education.

Farshi, N., & Mohammadi, Z. (2013). Use of podcasts in effective teaching of vocabulary: Learners' attitudes, motivations and limitations. *Theory and Practice in Language Studies*, *3*(8), 1381–1386. doi:10.4304/tpls.3.8.1381-1386

Feldman, K., & Kinsella, K. (2005). *Narrowing the language gap: The case for explicit vocabulary instruction. Research Monograph*. Scholastic.

Gardner, R. C. (1985). *Social psychology and second language learning: The role of attitudes and motivation*. Edward Arnold.

Godwin-Jones, R. (2018). Contextualized vocabulary learning. *Language Learning & Technology*, *22*(3), 1–19.

Gottman, J. M., & Glass, G. (1978). Analysis of interrupted time-series experiments. In T. Kratochwill (Ed.), *Single subject research: Strategies for evaluating change* (pp. 197–234). Academic Press. doi:10.1016/B978-0-12-425850-1.50011-9

Greenwood, S. C., & Flanigan, K. (2007). Overlapping vocabulary and comprehension: Context clues complement semantic gradients. *The Reading Teacher*, *61*(3), 249–254. doi:10.1598/RT.61.3.5

Gu, P. Y. (2003). Vocabulary learning in a second language: Person, task, context and strategies. *TESL-EJ*, *7*(2), 1–31.

Catalan, R. M. J. (2003). Sex differences in L2 vocabulary learning strategies. *International Journal of Applied Linguistics*, *13*(1), 54–77. doi:10.1111/1473-4192.00037

Kasper, G., & Wagner, J. (2018). Epistemological reorientations and L2 interactional settings: A postscript to the special issue. *The Modern Language Journal, 102*(SI), 82–90.

Kastoudi, D. (2011). Using a quest in a 3D virtual environment for student interaction and vocabulary acquisition in foreign language learning. *Proceedings of the EUROCALL 2011 Conference*, *2*, 87–89.

Kim, M., Crossley, S. A., & Kyle, K. (2018). Lexical sophistication as a multidimensional phenomenon: Relations to second language lexical proficiency, development, and writing quality. *Modern Language Journal, 102*(1), 120–141. doi:10.1111/modl.12447

Kormos, J., Kiddle, T., & Csize'r, K. (2011). Systems of goals, attitudes, and self-related beliefs in second-language-learning motivation. *Applied Linguistics, 32*(5), 495–516. doi:10.1093/applin/amr019

Kwan, B. M., & Bryan, A. D. (2010). Affective response to exercise as a component of exercise motivation: Attitudes, norms, self-efficacy, and temporal stability of intentions. *Psychology of Sport and Exercise, 11*(1), 71–79. doi:10.1016/j.psychsport.2009.05.010 PMID:20161385

Lan, Y. J., Fang, S. Y., Legault, J., & Li, P. (2015). Second language acquisition of Mandarin Chinese vocabulary: Context of learning effects. *Educational Technology Research and Development, 63*(5), 671–690. doi:10.100711423-015-9380-y

Lawrence, G., & Ahmed, F. (2018). Pedagogical insights into hyper-immersive virtual world language learning environments. *International Journal of Computer-Assisted Language Learning and Teaching, 8*(1), 1–14. doi:10.4018/IJCALLT.2018010101

Miles, M. B., & Huberman, A. M. (1994). *Qualitative data analysis: An expanded sourcebook* (2nd ed.). Sage Publications.

Mizumoto, A. (2013). Enhancing self-efficacy in vocabulary learning: A self-regulated learning. *Vocabulary Learning and Instruction, 2*, 15–24.

Nation, I. S. P. (1990). *Teaching and learning vocabulary*. Heinle and Heinle Publishers.

Nation, I. S. P. (2001). *Learning vocabulary in another language*. Cambridge University Press. doi:10.1017/CBO9781139524759

Newgarden, K., & Zheng, D. (2016). Recurrent language activities in World of Warcraft: Skilled linguistic action meets the Common European Framework of Reference. *ReCALL, 28*(3), 274–304. doi:10.1017/S0958344016000112

Paribakht, T. S., & Wesche, M. (1996). Enhancing vocabulary acquisition through reading: A hierarchy of text-related exercise types. *Canadian Modern Language Review, 52*(2), 155–178. doi:10.3138/cmlr.52.2.155

Pavičić Takač, V. (2008). *Vocabulary learning strategies and foreign language acquisition*. Multilingual Matters. doi:10.21832/9781847690401

Rahayu, P., & Jacobson, M. J. (2012). Speaking self-efficacy and English as a foreign language: Learning processes in a multi-user virtual environment. In M. Piscioner (Ed.), *Effectively implementing information communication technology in higher education in the Asia-Pacific Region* (pp. 161–182). NOVA Science Publishers, Inc.

Rapaport, W. J. (2003). What is the "context" for contextual vocabulary acquisition? In P. Slezak (Ed.), *Proceedings of the 4th International Conference on Cognitive Science/7th Australasian Society for Cognitive Science Conference (ICCS/ASCS-2003)* (*Vol. 2*, pp. 547–552). Sydney, Australia: University of New South Wales.

Richards, J., & Schmidt, R. (2002). *Longman dictionary of language teaching and applied linguistics.* Pearson Education.

Sanchez, A. D. (2006). *Enhancing vocabulary acquisition through synthetic learning experiences: Implementing virtual field trips into classrooms* (Doctoral dissertation). University of Central Florida, Orlando, FL, USA.

Schmitt, N. (2000). *Vocabulary in language teaching.* Cambridge University Press.

Schmitt, N. (2008). Instructed second language vocabulary learning. *Language Teaching Research, 12*(3), 329–363. doi:10.1177/1362168808089921

Stahl, S. A. (2005). Four problems with teaching word meanings and what to do to make vocabulary an integral part of instruction. In E. H. Hiebert & M. L. Kamil (Eds.), *Teaching and learning vocabulary: Bringing research to practice* (pp. 95–114). Erlbaum.

Sternberg, R. J. (1987). Most vocabulary is learned from context. In M. G. McKeown & M. E. Curtis (Eds.), *The nature of vocabulary acquisition* (pp. 89–105). Lawrence Erlbaum Associates.

Thornbury, S. (2002). *How to teach vocabulary.* Pearson Education Limited.

Tseng, W., & Schmitt, N. (2008). Towards a model of motivated vocabulary learning: A structural equation modeling approach. *Language Learning, 58*(2), 357–400. doi:10.1111/j.1467-9922.2008.00444.x

Wesche, M., & Paribakht, T. S. (1996). Assessing second language vocabulary knowledge: Depth versus breadth. *Canadian Modern Language Review, 53*(1), 13–40. doi:10.3138/cmlr.53.1.13

You, Y. (2011). Factors in vocabulary acquisition through reading. *Indiana Teachers of English to Speakers of Other Languages Journal, 8*(1), 43–57.

Zheng, D., Young, M. F., Brewer, B., & Wagner, M. (2009). Attitude and self-efficacy change: English language learning in virtual worlds. *The Computer Assisted Language Instruction Consortium Journal, 27*(1), 205–231.

This research was previously published in the International Journal of Computer-Assisted Language Learning and Teaching (IJCALLT), 10(4); pages 14-32, copyright year 2020 by IGI Publishing (an imprint of IGI Global).

APPENDIX

Summary of the 5-Point Likert Scale Post-Questionnaire Results

Table 5.

	Statements (After participating in the program, ...)		Mean
1	I enjoy learning new words.		4.25
2	I enjoy learning vocabulary in this program.	System	4
		Prezi Newspapers	4.25
		Worksheet	4.5
		The Use of Strategies (visual association, contextualized learning, ...)	4.75
		Teacher's Instruction	4.75
		Overall	4.25
3	I enjoy doing vocabulary tasks in this program.	Times Square	3.75
		One Times Square	4
		Duffy Square TKTS	4
		Broadway Theater District	4.5
		Yankee Stadium	4.5
		Statue of Liberty	4.5
		Overall	4.25
4	I am relaxed while I am doing vocabulary tasks in this program.		4
5	I can learn many new words.		4.5
6	I can use the new words that I learned.		4
7	I can look at the spelling to understand a new word.		3.5
8	I can sound out the new word to see if I know it.		4
9	I can continue reading to figure out a new word.		4.25
10	I feel good when I figure out a new word.		4
11	I feel happy when I figure out a new word.		4.5
Overall			4.19

Chapter 14
Video Game–Based L2 Learning:
Virtual Worlds as Texts, Affinity Spaces, and Semiotic Ecologies

Karim Hesham Shaker Ibrahim

Gulf University for Science and Technology, Kuwait

ABSTRACT

Video/digital games have grown into sophisticated, realistic, and engaging problem-solving virtual worlds that have their own literacy practices, affinity spaces, and online virtual communities. As a result, various studies have examined theirs to promote L2 learning and literacy. The findings of these studies suggest that digital games can promote multilingual communication, L2 vocabulary development, and situated L2 use. However, promising these findings, to-date little is known about the specific dynamics of gameplay that can facilitate L2 learning. To address this gap in the literature, this chapter will draw on interdisciplinary research on digital gaming from literacy studies, games' studies, and narratology to account for the L2 learning potentials of digital games. To explain their L2 learning potentials, the chapter will conceptualize digital games as dynamic texts, affinity spaces, and semiotic ecologies, and discuss the implications of each conceptualization for game-based L2 learning and teaching.

INTRODUCTION

Over the past three decades recent innovations in digital technology and special effects have transformed digital gaming from a frivolous and childish form of entertainment into a sophisticated and widespread recreational activity. Video games have advanced in design to involve complex plots, compelling narratives, and immersive detail-rich 3D virtual worlds (Squire, 2002). This transformation has led to a massive expansion in the consumer-base of digital games to include different genders and age groups. For instance, 40% of all gamers today are females, and the average age of a video-gamer is 31 (Entertainment Software Association, 2014). Also, with the spread of local-area-networks (LANs) and high-speed Internet, video gaming has acquired a social dimension, especially with the rise of online multiplayer games that require players to collaborate in online gaming servers to achieve shared in-game goals (e.g.

DOI: 10.4018/978-1-6684-7597-3.ch014

kill a monster). Multiplayer gaming usually involves active communication and continuous interaction between players face-to-face or online through internet-mediated communication tools (e.g. chat) to plan gameplay and coordinate shared action. In addition, the popularity of digital games along with the rise of user-created content in Web 2.0 technologies have given rise to online virtual communities centered on digital gaming and gameplay strategies. Over time these communities have grown in size and sophistication, and they developed their own social structures, sociocultural values, and literacy practices (Steinkuehler, 2006). Some of the common practices in these communities include: (a) writing, sharing, and discussing strategy guides; (b) writing, reviewing, and editing fan fiction based on video games' narratives and characters; (c) planning and coordinating shared gameplay; (d) creating and sharing gameplay resources such as gaming mods (i.e. modified game content), cheat codes (i.e. codes that enhance a player's capabilities in a video game), and game save-files (i.e. files that save gameplay progress to grant a player access to any level in a game), and; (e) video-recording and streaming of live gameplay and game strategy tutorials (i.e. video demonstrations of gameplay strategies). Besides the dominance of language-mediated interactions and literacy practices in online gaming communities, recent research on digital game-based L2 use demonstrated that L2 gaming is a common and popular activity among a significant proportion of L2 learners (Chik, 2011), and recent studies on extramural L2 gaming suggest that digital gaming can offer an engaging and immersive environment for L2 use and practice (e.g. Jensen, 2017).

The popularity of digital gaming among L2 learners (Chik, 2011), the engagement of gameplay activities (Squire, 2002), and the centrality of language use and literacy practices in gaming communities (Alexander, 2009) have motivated various studies that explored the L2 learning potentials of digital gaming (for a thorough review see Reinders, 2012). The findings of these studies suggested that digital games can promote: (a) intercultural and multilingual communication (e.g., Newgarden & Zheng, 2016); (b) L2 vocabulary development (e.g., Jensen, 2017); (c) collaborative social interaction (e.g., Peterson, 2012); (d) L2 literacy development (e.g., Benson & Chik, 2010), and; (e) situated L2 use and socialization (e.g., Zheng, Young, Wagner, & Brewer, 2009a). However promising these findings, to-date it is not clear how digital gaming can facilitate L2 learning. In other words, the literature underlines the L2 learning potential of digital gaming, but it does not offer a clear account of the specific dynamics of gameplay that can motivate, scaffold, and/or facilitate L2 learning. For instance, many empirical studies have demonstrated that digital gaming can facilitate incidental vocabulary learning (e.g., Hitosugi, Schmidt, & Hayashi, 2014); however, to-date very little is known about how gameplay can facilitate vocabulary learning and what specific dynamics of gameplay can do so (exceptions: Butler, 2015; Bytheway, 2015). Understanding the specific dynamics of digital game-based L2 learning is necessary to inform: (a) the selection and adaptation of commercial video games for L2 learning purposes; (b) the design of educational video games for L2 instruction, and; (c) the effective integration of digital games in L2 learning and teaching contexts. To address this gap in the literature, the present study will draw on interdisciplinary research on digital games to explain the L2 learning potentials of digital games in terms of specific forms of engagement with L2 discourse in the course of gameplay. The chapter will emphasize the conceptualizations of digital games as *texts*, *affinity spaces*, and *semiotic ecologies* because each of these conceptualizations underlines peculiar qualities of game-based language use that can further our understanding of the L2 learning potentials of digital gaming.

This chapter will open with a brief review of the literature on game-based L2 learning to demonstrate the L2 learning potentials of digital games. After that, the researcher will draw on theoretical frameworks of digital gaming from literacy studies, games studies, and narratology to conceptualize digital games as *texts, affinity spaces*, and *semiotic ecologies,* and account for their potentials for L2 practice and learning. Finally, the chapter will close with a discussion of the implications of each of these conceptualizations of digital games for the pedagogical integration of digital games in L2 learning and teaching contexts.

L2 LEARNING POTENTIALS OF DIGITAL GAMING

Many empirical studies in the field of computer-assisted language learning (CALL) explored the L2 learning potential of digital gaming, and demonstrated that it can promote: (a) extramural L2 learning (Jensen, 2017; Sundqvist & Wikström, 2015; Sylvén & Sundqvist, 2012; Sundqvist & Sylvén, 2012; Kuppens, 2010; Sundqvist, 2009); (b) exposure to L2 input (e.g., Ryu, 2013; Thorne, Fischer, & Lu, 2012; Chik, 2011; Rankin, Gold, & Gooch, 2006; deHaan, 2005); (c) L2 vocabulary learning (Franciosi, Yagi, Tomoshige, & Ye, 2016; Hitosugi, Schmidt, & Hayashi, 2014; Ranalli, 2008; Miller & Hegelheimer, 2006; Yip & Kwan, 2006), and; (d) immersive cross-cultural interaction with L2 native speakers (Newgarden & Zheng, 2016; Zheng, Newgarden, & Young, 2012; Zheng, Young, Wagner, & Brewer, 2009a), and; (e) learners' self-efficacy and willingness to communicate (Zheng, Young, Wagner, & Brewer, 2009b; Reinders & Wattana, 2015; Vosburg, 2017).

A number of studies in the field found a positive correlation between the frequency of extramural gameplay and L2 learning (Jensen, 2017; Sundqvist & Wikström, 2015; Sylvén & Sundqvist, 2012; Sundqvist & Sylvén, 2012; Kuppens, 2010; Sundqvist, 2009). For example, Jensen (2017) examined the relationship between ESL vocabulary development and the frequency of extramural English gaming with 107 Danish ESL learners. Self-reported language diaries were used to collect data about participants' extramural gaming in English, and pre- and post-study tests were administered one year apart to assess vocabulary gains. Statistical analysis of the participants' scores on pre- and post- study tests' revealed a significant development in ESL vocabulary, and analysis of the correlation between test scores' and extramural gaming time revealed a strong positive correlation between ESL vocabulary development and the frequency of extramural gameplay in English. Similarly, Sundqvist and Wikström (2015) examined the relationship between extracurricular gameplay and L2 vocabulary learning with 80 Swedish ESL learners. Pre-study questionnaires and self-reported language diaries were used to collect information about the participants' gaming habits, and accordingly participants were classified into frequent gamers, moderate gamers, and non-gamers. Two post-study vocabulary tests were used to assess the participants' receptive and productive ESL vocabulary knowledge, and the participants' scores on the national English proficiency test for this year and the previous year were compared as a general measure of ESL learning. Statistical analysis of the data revealed a significant positive correlation between the participants' ESL vocabulary learning and the frequency of gameplay for male participants, but the correlation was not significant for females. In a similar vein, Sylvén and Sundqvist (2012) explored the relationship between extramural digital gaming and incidental L2 learning with 86 intermediate Swedish ESL learners. Quantitative analysis of data collected through questionnaires, language diaries, and proficiency tests revealed a significant difference in language proficiency and vocabulary knowledge between frequency gamers, average gamers, and non-gamers, where the frequency of gameplay correlated positively with L2 proficiency. Similarly, in a pilot study, Sundqvist and Sylvén (2012) examined the correlation between extramural English activities, especially video gaming, and the vocabulary knowledge of 244 Swedish ESL learners. Analysis of data collected through questionnaires, proficiency tests, and language diaries revealed a significant positive correlation between time spent in digital gaming and vocabulary production and recognition. In another study, Kuppens (2010) investigated the effects of extracurricular English activities, especially digital gaming, on the incidental development of L2 skills with 374 Dutch ESL learners. A survey was used to collect information about the participants' use of English language media, and an oral language proficiency test and a translation task were administered to assess the participants' English proficiency. Statistical analysis of the data revealed a significant positive correlation between the participants' consumption of English media, especially video games, and their oral proficiency and translation skills. Also, in a longitudinal study Sundqvist (2009) investigated the effects of extramural English activities, especially digital gaming, on the oral proficiency and vocabulary development of 80 Swedish ESL learners. Statistical analysis of data collected through interviews, questionnaires, vocabulary tests, and language diaries demonstrated that time spent on extramural English activities, especially digital gaming, correlated positively with L2 vocabulary size and oral proficiency.

Also, several studies revealed that gameplay can promote exposure to and engagement with L2 input (e.g., Chik, 2011; deHaan, 2005; Rankin, Gold, & Gooch, 2006; Ryu, 2013; Thorne, Fischer, & Lu, 2012). For example, in a multiple-cases study, Ryu (2013) examined the L2 learning potentials of participating in L2 gameplay and online gaming communities. He surveyed the perspectives of six EFL gamers of *Civilization* (Activism, 1991), who were active members of the online gaming forum *Civfanatics.com.* Framed in an ecological approach to L2 learning, data about the participants' engagement in gameplay and the gaming forum were collected through observations of their computer-mediated communications and a series of email interviews. The study found that participation in gameplay and online gaming communities offered participants opportunities to practice and learn English through exposure to in-game L2 discourse in gameplay and computer-mediated interactions in online gaming communities. Similarly, in a qualitative study, Chik (2011) investigated L2 use and learning in out-of-class gaming practices with ten Chinese ESL learners. Data about the participants' digital gaming activities were collected through group discussions, learning histories, gameplay recordings, stimulated recall sessions, interviews, and blog entries. Data analysis demonstrated that games offer three spaces for autonomous L2 use and learning: in-game texts, online discussion forums, and online gaming platforms. The data further revealed that the L2 learning potential of digital gaming is relative, and that it depends primarily on the gamers' autonomous efforts to utilize gameplay for L2 learning. Also, in an exploratory study Thorne et al. (2012) investigated the L2 learning potentials of massive-multiplayer gaming ecologies by examining the linguistic complexity of texts generated and used in the course of playing the massive multiplayer game *World of Warcraft* (Blizzard Entertainment, 2004). The researchers complied a corpus of quest texts and strategy guides used frequently by gamers based on data collected from 64 experienced gamers through questionnaires and interviews. A linguistic complexity analysis of a random sample of these texts was conducted based on 4 criteria: readability, lexical sophistication, lexical diversity, and syntactic complexity. The study found that the game exposed the participants to sophisticated L2 input, but it is also revealed that the participants did not attend to in-game texts unless they were necessary to guide gameplay. Also, in a pilot study, Rankin et al. (2006) examined the effect of participation in the massive-multiplayer game *Ever Quest II* (Sony, 2004) on L2 learning with four ESL learners. Data about the participants' L2 interactions in four gaming sessions were collected through interviews, field notes, observations, questionnaires, vocabulary test, and chat logs. The study revealed that the participants noticed and internalized new L2 discourse used by non-player-character (NPCs) in the course of gameplay; however, the data also demonstrated that low-proficiency participants experienced difficulty adapting to the game world, and were cognitively overloaded trying to attend both to gameplay and in-game FL discourse. In a similar vein, but with a focus on single-player gaming, deHaan (2005) examined the L2 learning potential of a Japanese baseball video game with an intermediate L2 learner of Japanese. Data about the participant's L2 learning were collected through gaming journals, vocabulary tests, and personal interviews. Data analysis suggested that the participant improved in kanji character recognition, reading comprehension, and listening comprehension after playing the game, but it also suggested that he was cognitively overloaded by the dual task of attending to gameplay and in-game discourse.

Also, a number of studies in the field demonstrated that gameplay can facilitate L2 vocabulary learning (Franciosi, Yagi, Tomoshige, & Ye, 2016; Hitosugi, Schmidt, & Hayashi, 2014; Miller & Hegelheimer, 2006; Ranalli, 2008; Yip & Kwan, 2006). For instance, Franciosi et al. (2016) examined the potential of simple simulation games to promote L2 vocabulary learning with 162 Japanese ESL learners. Using a quasi-experimental design, they examined L2 vocabulary learning and retention in two conditions: playing the simulation game *3rd World Farmer* in small groups besides practicing vocabulary through digital flashcard and practicing vocabulary through digital flashcards only. A pre-test, immediate post-test, and delayed post-test were administered to measure vocabulary learning gains. Statistical analysis of test scores revealed that participants in both groups retained new vocabulary, and that the learning gains were significantly higher for the gaming group on the delayed post-test. Similarly, in a mixed-methods study, Hitosugi et al. (2014) investigated the effect of playing the educational game *Food Force* (United Nations World Food Program, 2005) on vocabulary learning with 20 intermediate and advanced Japanese ESL learners. Informed by a sociocognitive approach to L2 learning, the study compared vocabulary retention in two conditions: gameplay and textbook exercises. Analysis of data collected through testing, interviews, and surveys demonstrated that participants in both groups retained new vocabulary, and that they retained significantly more vocabulary from the game than from the textbook. Also, in a quasi-experimental study Miller and Hegelheimer (2006) investigated the potential of the simulation video game *The Sims* (Maxis, 2000) to facilitate vocabulary learning with 18 intermediate ESL learners. Participants played the game and completed in-game tasks in three conditions of access to supplementary materials: mandatory supplementary materials, voluntary supplementary materials, and no supplementary materials. Statistical analysis of the data demonstrated that participants gained new vocabulary from their interaction with the game, and that vocabulary learning gains correlated positively with their degree of access to supplementary materials. In a replication of Miller and Hegelheimer (2006) 's study, using a mixed methods design, Ranalli (2008) examined the potential of *The Sims* (Maxis, 2000) to promote L2 vocabulary learning with nine intermediate ESL learners. The participants formed dyads that took turns playing the game in three levels of access to supplementary materials. Analysis of data collected through pre- and post-task tests and surveys suggested that the learners experienced significant gains in vocabulary learning that correlated positively with their level of access to supplementary materials. In another study, Yip and Kwan (2006) examined the L2 learning potential of online vocabulary games with 100 ESL learners. The participants were randomly assigned to experimental and control conditions: the experimental group practiced vocabulary in online games, while the control group practiced vocabulary in classroom activities. Pre- and post- tests were administered to measure vocabulary gains. Statistical analysis of test scores demonstrated that both groups gained new vocabulary, and that the vocabulary gains of the experimental group were significantly higher than those of the control group.

Besides examining the L2 vocabulary learning potentials of digital gaming, a few studies have investigated the dynamics and strategies of gameplay that can facilitate vocabulary learning. To illustrate, in a qualitative study, Butler (2015) examined the vocabulary learning dynamics of digital gaming in an instructional game design with 86 Japanese ESL learners (6th graders). The project involved: (a) examining various games and analyzing game design elements; (b) discussing vocabulary learning strategies and their integration in gameplay; (c) designing a vocabulary learning video game in groups, and; (d) presenting and evaluating game design plans. Data about the participants' perspectives on the vocabulary learning dynamics of gameplay were collected through video recordings of in-class interactions and discussions. The findings revealed that the participants identified a number of gameplay dynamics that can facilitate L2 vocabulary learning, including repetition and recovery, controlling own learning, using multiple modalities, and grouping similar words; also, they identified a number of game design elements that motivated engagement in gameplay such as challenge, competition, clear rules, and goals and objectives. Also, in a qualitative study, Bytheway (2015) examined the vocabulary learning strategies used by six experienced ESL gamers in the massive-multiplayer online game *World of Warcraft* (Blizzard Entertainment, 2004). Informed by methods derived from Grounded Theory (Glaser & Strauss, 1967), the researcher collected data about the participants' vocabulary learning strategies through observations, in-game texts, semi-structured interviews, and elicited email texts. The findings revealed that the participants used a variety of vocabulary learning strategies during gameplay including reading in-game texts, playing in English, recognizing knowledge gaps, looking up words in a dictionary, and guessing meaning from context.

In addition, several studies in the field reported that multiplayer online digital gaming can offer opportunities for collaborative L2 interaction (Sholz, 2017; Newgarden & Zheng, 2016; Zhao, 2016; Zheng, Newgarden, & Young, 2012; Rama, Black, van Es, & Warschauer, 2012; Zheng, Young, Wagner, & Brewer, 2009a). For example, in a qualitative study, Scholz (2017) examined the potential of gameplay trajectories to promote L2 learning in the massive-multiplayer online game *World of Warcraft* (Blizzard Entertainment, 2004) with 14 L2 learners of German. Framed in a complex adaptive systems framework (Larsen-Freeman & Cameron, 2008), the researcher gathered rigorous data about the participants' linguistic development during their interactions with native-speaker players in the game over the course of four months. Data were collected through pre-study questionnaires, transcripts of oral and written communications inside and outside the game, post-study questionnaires, and debriefing interviews. The findings revealed that the participants noticed, internalized, and produced new L2 discourse in their gameplay interactions. The study also revealed that the effectiveness of extramural digital game-based L2 learning is heavily influenced by the attitudes of learners towards digital gaming as an L2 learning context. Also, Newgarden and Zheng (2016) examined the L2 learning affordances of gameplay in the massive-multiplayer online game *World of Warcraft* (Blizzard Entertainment, 2004). Framed in distributed approaches to L2 learning, the researchers analyzed the communicative and gameplay activities used in the interactions of four ESL learners with native-speaker players in three gaming episodes. Data comprised of recordings of the participants' voice calls over Skype and gameplay trajectories' screencasts were coded and analyzed for patterns and trends. The study found that the participants used linguistic action (i.e. communicative activities) to collaborate with native-speaker players to plan and coordinate gameplay. In a similar vein, using a multiple case-study design and informed by an ecological approach to L2 learning (van Lier, 2004), Zhao (2016) examined L2 interactions of two EFL learners in the massive multiplayer online game *Guild Wars 2* (ArenaNet, 2012). The Participants were instructed to play the game at their leisure for 3-6 hours a week and attend a bi-weekly collaborative gaming session for eight weeks. Data about the participants' L2 interactions were collected through questionnaires, interviews, gaming journals, and gameplay observations. The study found that online gaming communities offered participants opportunities for L2 use and socialization, but the participants' FL-learner identity, unfamiliarity with game discourse, and novice gaming status impeded their ability to take full advantage of these opportunities. Also, Zheng et al. (2012) examined the L2 learning affordances of the distributed communicative and languaging activities involving the coaction between three ESL learners and native English speakers in a 43-minute gaming episode of *World of Warcraft* (Blizzard Entertainment, 2004) from an ecological distributed perspective. Using enhanced discourse analysis methods, the researchers identified 13 communicative activity sub-types utilized by the players to manage coaction and coordinate gameplay. Based on the findings the authors concluded that quests are key affordances for L2 learning that promote collaboration, establish a need for coordinated action and interaction, and motivate players by reward. Similarly, in a qualitative study, Rama et al. (2012) analyzed the interactions of two L2 Spanish learners in the massive-multiplayer online game *World of Warcraft* (Blizzard Entertainment, 2004) to examine the L2 learning affordances of the game. The participants were instructed to play the game at their convenience, preferably for five hours a week, for the period of seven weeks. Informed by a sociocultural framework and using discourse analysis methods, data were collected through chat logs, gaming journals, field notes and interviews. The findings demonstrated that the game provided several L2 learning affordances including: (1) a safe environment for L2 languaging; (2) emphasis on communicative competence, and; (3) goal-directed collaborative interaction between experts and novices. The researchers concluded that multiplayer online games can be useful contexts for L2 learning and socialization. Also, Zheng et al. (2009a) investigated the L2 learning potential and affordances of avatar-embodied interactions between native-speakers (NS) and non-native speakers (NNS) in the game *Quest Atlantis* (The Atlantis Remix Project, 2003). Framed in an ecological framework, the study examined the interactions of two Chinese-American NS-NNS dyads to solve content-related problems and coordinate shared activities in the game for ten weeks. Using ethnographic and discourse analysis methods, data collected from chat logs, interviews, and gameplay artifacts were analyzed. The findings indicated that NNS players engaged in meaning making and intercultural identity formation through intercultural collaborative interaction with native-speaker players to reach quest goals.

Besides facilitating collaborative L2 interaction and socialization, several studies revealed that digital gaming can promote L2 learners' self-efficacy and willingness to communicate (Vosburg, 2017; Reinders & Wattana, 2015; Zheng, Young, Wagner, & Brewer, 2009b). In a qualitative study, Vosburg (2017) examined the effects of group-play dynamics on the potential of multiplayer online games to promote willingness to communicate in extramural gaming with seven learners of German as a second language. Aided by two native-speakers of German who were recruited as language guides, the participants played the massive-multiplayer online game *World of Warcraft* (Blizzard Entertainment, 2004) for ninety-minutes twice a week for eight weeks. Data about the participants' L2 use and group dynamics were collected through gaming journals, semi-structured interviews, group interviews, and audio-recordings of in-game communications. The findings revealed that game-based interactions promoted the participants' willingness to communicate, but the lack of common interests between the group members and their diverse levels of motivation for L2 learning limited their L2 interactions. In another qualitative study, Reinders and Wattana (2015) examined the potential of digital gaming to promote willingness to communicate in a foreign language (FL) with 30 Thai EFL learners. The participants completed six quests in the video game *Ragnarok Online* (Gravity Interactive, 2002) during class time. Data about the participants' interactions and affective factors were collected through questionnaires, semi-structured interview, in-game chat transcripts, and stimulated recall interviews. The findings revealed that the participants experienced a greater sense of relaxation and confidence during their interactions, which resulted in greater language production. The researchers concluded that the engagement of gameplay lowered the affective barriers of FL use and offered a safe environment for FL practice, which promoted the participants' self-efficacy and willingness to communicate. However, one of the participants was challenged by the immediate and synchronous nature of the interactions, and suggested that she felt tense as she did not have sufficient time to formulate her responses. Also, Zheng et al. (2009b) examined the self-efficacy and attitudes of 61 Chinese ESL learners towards L2 learning in the video game *Quest Atlantis* (The Atlantis Remix Project, 2003). Using a quasi-experimental post-test design the researchers compared two groups of ESL Chinese learners; the experimental group participated in *Quest Atlantis* for 60 minutes per week for 25 weeks, and the control group used that time to work on English test preparation. Data were collected using a post-treatment survey of learners' attitudes and self-efficacy. Data analysis revealed a significant difference between the two groups in self-efficacy and attitudes in favor of the experimental group. The authors concluded that game-like virtual worlds enhance learners' self-efficacy and attitudes towards learning English by affording them opportunities for authentic L2 socialization with native speakers.

This review of the literature demonstrates that video games offer an engaging and immersive context for active L2 use and learning, and that video games constitute a rich resource for designing L2 use and learning activities. It also reveals that like any learning environment digital games are not without limitations; however, equipped with a deep understanding of the peculiar qualities of digital gaming as an L2 learning environment, educators can design engaging game-based L2 learning activities and harness the full L2 learning potential of this engaging medium.

VIDEO GAMES AS TEXT, AFFINITY SPACES, AND SEMIOTIC ECOLOGIES

Video games are dynamic, complex, and multidimensional media that can be conceived in different ways on different levels and from different perspectives. Therefore, to harness the full L2 learning potentials of digital gaming and avoid its shortcomings, educators should gain a deeper understanding of the peculiar qualities of digital gaming that render it a fruitful resource and context for L2 practice and learning. To this end, this section will conceptualize digital games on different dimensions as dynamics texts, affinity spaces, and semiotic ecologies to underline their L2 learning potentials and help educators take advantage of these potentials. On a textual dimension, modern video games can be perceived as dynamic texts in which meaning is constructed through in-game action and interaction (Apperley & Beavis, 2011). Understanding the textual dimension of digital gaming can help educators harness the potential of digital games as an authentic resource of L2 input and an embodied context for multimodal composition and literacy. On a spatial dimension, video games can be viewed as affinity spaces centered on the production and dissemination of knowledge and literacy practices that pertain to gameplay (Gee, 2004). Understanding the participatory literacy practices associated with gaming spaces is vital for utilizing these spaces as immersive and authentic environment for collaborative purposeful L2 communication and socialization. On a semiotic level, digital games can be seen as complex semiotic systems that create meaning through an intricate and interrelated network of signs (Salen & Zimmerman, 2005). Understanding the semiotic complexity of digital gaming and its role in meaning-making is necessary to guide the selection and integration of digital games in L2 learning activities that promote situated L2 practice and embodied cognition (Lave & Wenger, 1991).

Video Games as Texts

Modern video games have developed in content and design to become dynamic, multimodal texts (Apperley & Beavis, 2011) that situate gameplay in sophisticated narratives, realistic graphics, and rich linguistic content (Gee, 2008). They capitalize on embodied action in the virtual world of the game to make meaning and develop the game narrative (Carr, 2006). To elaborate, a player's actions in a video game generate meaning in the virtual world of the game, and the player's trajectory in gameplay (i.e., series of in-game actions) develops the backstory of the game (Zimmerman, 2004). That is by acting on/ manipulating the game world these actions are combined and certain events are actualized and sequenced in a chronological order, and a distinct narrative is plotted (Neitzel, 2005). This narrative that is generated in gameplay and embodied in the virtual world of the game is closely associated with linguistic discourse inside and outside the game system. Video games typically engage players with linguistic discourse in the game interface, such as notifications, descriptions, or pop-up messages, to educate players about the rules of a game and provide information about their progress in gameplay (e.g., game summary). Also, hardcore gameplay usually requires players to interact collaboratively through computer-mediated communication channels (e.g., chat) to coordinate shared action in multiplayer games (Alexander, 2009) or draw on linguistic and multimodal discourse in online gaming communities, such as strategy guides and gaming walkthroughs, as resources to guide gameplay and/or resolve complex challenges in gameplay (Chik, 2011). In that digital games utilize a player's actions in a game to create meaning that embodies his/her interpretation of linguistic and multimodal discourse that s/he engaged with in (i.e. in-game discourse) or around gameplay (i.e. linguistic interaction with other players or discourse from an online gaming community) insofar as the player draws on these discourse to inform in-game actions and choices. Therefore, similar to an orthographic text, gameplay maps linguistic and multimodal discourse to meaning (i.e. in-game action), and promotes a player's literacy in these discourse by creating associations between these discourse and their meaning in gameplay. In that sense, video games can function as intercultural dynamic texts that motivate and contextualize L2 learners' immersion in and active engagement with authentic L2 discourse (Ryu, 2013).

Video Games as Affinity Spaces

The popularity of digital gaming and the sophistication of digital game-based problem-solving activities have given rise to persistent and highly structured online gaming communities centered on social learning of gameplay. Gee (2004) uses the term *affinity spaces* to refer to these online gaming communities as social spaces characterized by the distribution and sharing of knowledge among people, mediating devices, places, sites, and modalities. In affinity spaces gamers affiliate with each other on the basis of shared activities, interests, and goals (Gee, 2004) forming communities of practice centered on social learning of gameplay through shared action and interaction with more capable peers (Steinkuehler, 2006). These affinity spaces are characterized by: (a) emphasizing common endeavors, practices, or interests; (b) equity of access; (c) use of portals (i.e. access points) as generators of content; (d) adapting to the actions and interactions of users by transforming their content; (e) facilitating and encouraging gaining and sharing of extensive and intensive knowledge; (f) accommodating individual and distributed knowledge (i.e. on sites, mediating devices, and between people), and; (g) offering multiple routes of participation (Gee, 2004). Gaming affinity spaces, including discussion forums, strategy guides, and walkthrough video hosting sites (e.g., www.twitch.tv), have grown in size and sophistication that they have developed their own identities, values, and participatory literacy practices (Steinkuehler, 2008). In addition, participation in gaming affinity spaces involves practicing a variety of new and traditional literacies, especially composition and reading. To elaborate, participation in online gaming forums involves extended reading, and writing, and collaborative social interaction. Also, searching, authoring, and/or interacting in these communities requires developing a variety of digital literacy skills, such as using computer-mediated communication platforms and screen casting software. In addition, drawing on these communities as a resource to guide gameplay involves a variety of traditional literacies, such as evaluating references and hypothesis testing (Apperley & Beavis, 2011). For instance, when a player resorts to online gaming communities as a resource to find a solution to a challenge s/he encountered in gameplay, s/he would have to: (a) search for and identity relevant and appropriate solutions; (b) assess the effectiveness, practicality, and feasibility of these solution against his/her gameplay situation (i.e. available resource, health, challenge level, reward, etc.); (c) select the most appropriate solution, and; (d) apply this solution in gameplay to test it in action. That is gaming affinity spaces are engaging and immersive social learning spaces that capitalize on the collective intelligence of its participants to promote social learning, literacy development, and collaborative problem solving. Therefore, digital gaming affinity spaces can serve as immersive, collaborative, and purposeful contexts for task-based L2 practice, socialization, and literacy development.

Video Games as Semiotic Systems

On a semiotic level, a video game is a dynamic and complex semiotic system in which signs (e.g., sounds, in-game discourse, or visual effects) are utilized to generate meaning in the virtual world of the game and inform a player of his/her progress in gameplay (Gee, 2004). These signs take meaning by virtue of their relations to the game system and to other signs in this system (Salen & Zimmerman, 2005). Generating meaning in gameplay is necessary to update the player on the status of his/her in-game character, and guide his/her actions in the game. Therefore, the explicit interactivity of the game system uses these signs to generate a discernable embodied outcome for every action the player takes in the game according to the rules of the game (Zimmerman, 2004). As a result, gameplay progresses through action-outcome cycles that embody the rules of the game allowing the player to learn the game rules experientially (Zimmerman, 2004). Thus, by acting on and manipulating the virtual world of a game, the player engages in deconstructing and reconstructing a network of semiotic signs that comprise the game system to uncover the rules of the game. And, since video games present these rules verbally through in-game discourse and most game-related discourse outside the game pertain to the game rules, it is fair to conclude that the explicit interactivity of gameplay situates the meaning of in-game and game-related discourse in the embodied virtual world of the game through various semiotic signs (Gee, 2008). Therefore, digital games as semiotic systems can be seen as highly immersive and situated contexts for engaging with of L2 discourse (to inform gameplay), and that the semiotic signs that comprise this system and embody these discourse can be utilized as semiotic resources for decoding and designing these L2 discourse (Ibrahim, 2018). These multimodal semiotic signs are accessible to L2 learners because they are encoded in a universal multimodal semiotic system (e.g., red color as a sign of warning); and thus, they transcend the limitations of any given linguistic system, and L2 learners can draw on them as meaning-making resources and compensate for their limited L2 proficiency when design and decoding unfamiliar in-game or game-related L2 discourse. This participation in gameplay can involve active engagement with L2 discourse, contextualization of in-game and game-related L2 discourse in the embodied context of gameplay, and semiotic design of unfamiliar in-game and game-related L2 discourse. Therefore, digital games can be employed as immersive and engaging semiotic ecologies for situated L2 use and learning.

L2 LEARNING POTENTIALS OF DIGITAL GAMES AS TEXTS, AFFINITY SPACES, AND SEMIOTIC SYSTEMS

Video games as dynamic texts, affinity spaces, and semiotic systems can support L2 practice and learning in different ways. As texts, video games can offer a wide variety of authentic linguistic discourse, interactive narratives, and multimodal texts. This wide range of texts can offer rich and authentic L2 texts for analysis, discussion, and practice that: (a) suit different levels of learners; (b) cover a wide range of topics, and; (c) represent a wide range of language varieties (e.g., registers, dialects, genres, modes). For instance, L2 educators can have learners play an L2 video game, decode in-game L2 discourse to inform gameplay, and discuss their gameplay strategies around gameplay in the target language. Also, teachers can have learners play an L2 video game, and complete write narrative essays that describe their play trajectories (i.e. personal narratives) in the game. Teachers can have learners play a video game in small groups and discuss their gameplay strategies in the target language. In addition, teachers can ask learners to play an L2 video games and fill in a gaming journal; the journal can ask them to note salient L2 vocabulary that they noticed in gameplay and use embodied meaning in the game to deduce their meanings. Another way video games can support L2 instruction is by being examined and analyzed as textual artifacts for qualities of textual design, such as genre and rhetorical strategies, to promote advanced literacy in L2 classes. For instance, L2 learners can play a video game in small groups and based on their gaming experience discuss the elements that comprise a narrative. Also, L2 educators can ask learners to play games from different genres (e.g., first person shooter, strategy, simulation, etc.), discuss the concept of genre and analyze the distinctive qualities of different gaming genres. In addition, L2 educators can use digital games as model of multimodal texts and have students examine and discuss the meaning-making potential of in-game modalities and its implications for multimodal and remix composition.

As affinity spaces, video gaming communities can serve both as immersive and engaging environments and resources for L2 practice and socialization. Firstly, texts generated in gaming affinity spaces, such as strategy guides and fan fiction, can serve as engaging and authentic L2 texts that educators can utilize to engage learners in intensive reading. For instance, L2 teachers can have students work in groups to develop a comprehensive strategy guide for a popular video game. In this project students would read, summarize, and cite a variety of online strategy guides and narratives to create their guide. Also, educators can assign students complex tasks in a popular video game and allow them to consult online strategy guides to complete these tasks. In this activity students would research, read, and discuss several strategy guides to identify the resources and strategies that they can use to complete their tasks in the game. In addition, L2 teachers can ask students to develop a ranking of video gaming titles in a given gaming genre based on online reviews and discussion threads (i.e. without playing these games). In this activity, learners would have to read dozens of reviews of different games, discuss the pros and cons of each game, and present their ranking list. Besides offering a resource for practicing L2 reading, affinity spaces can support L2 writing and multimodal composition. That L2 educator can utilize gaming affinity spaces as publishing platforms where learners can compose L2 texts, publish their texts to a real audience, and receive feedback on the content, mechanics, and design of their texts. For instance, teachers can ask students to play different video games, write their personal narratives in gameplay, and post them on fan-fiction sites for feedback and discussion. Learners can then discuss the feedback they received from the affinity space in class and revise their narratives. Also, educators can ask students to play different video games and write reviews for these games and posting them on gaming discussion boards. This activity would involve not only a purposeful and authentic L2 writing experience, but also a genuine L2 interaction with a real audience who might agree or disagree with the learners' reviews. This activity would probably involve dozens of discussions and interactions with many members of the audience who might react to the learners' reviews in such a massive platform (where thousands of users interact all any given moment). Besides writing traditional orthographic texts, participation in affinity spaces can involve remix and multimodal L2 composition. For instance, L2 educators can ask students to work in groups to create gaming walkthrough videos and post them online. Such a project would involve not only active L2 use to explain gameplay, but also active discussion among team members to plan the content and design of the video and active interaction with members of the gaming community who will comment on or respond to their video. Also, L2 educators can ask students to work in groups to create and publish trailers for existing video games in the target language. Such a project would offer valuable opportunities for practicing L2 use and developing multimodal composition literacies. In addition to practicing L2 reading and composition, affinity spaces offer valuable opportunities for cross-cultural interaction and L2 socialization. That is L2 educators can have learners collaborate and interact with native-speaker players in multiplayer online games, and engage in authentic and purposeful social interaction focused on strategizing and managing shared gameplay. For instance, teachers can ask students to create guilds (i.e. gaming teams) in the L2 servers of popular online multiplayer games such as *Ever Quest II* (Sony, 2004) and collaborate with native-speakers to achieve challenging quests/missions in the game. Joining the community of an online video game would offer invaluable opportunities for building social relations with native-speaker players around the common endeavor of gameplay, which could promote further social interaction and active L2 use beyond digital gaming.

As semiotic systems, video games can provide immersive and embodied contexts for L2 practice and learning. That is given that video games are semiotic system that embody in-game and game-related L2 discourse (by embodying the rules of gameplay that these discourse describe), video games can be used as immersive and contextualized L2 practice environment, where learners practice reading and listening comprehension as they draw on in-game L2 discourse to manage gameplay. For instance, L2 educators can ask learners to play an L2 video game in small groups and figure out the rules of the game collaboratively to achieve specific goals in the game. In this activity, gameplay would motivate learners to draw on in-game L2 discourse as a resource to understand the game rules and their limited L2 proficiency would require them to draw on relevant semiotic signs in the game system to deduce the meaning of in-game L2 discourse and manage gameplay. Also, educators can have students work in dyads were one student has access to the game interface only while the other has access to a strategy guide only, and in each dyad students work together to decode the L2 discourse in the strategy guide and match it to the game interface and play the game. This activity would help learners associate in-game L2 discourse with their embodied meaning in the game. And because digital gaming is a highly engaging experience, the utility of L2 discourse for managing gameplay in any activity can motivate extended and repeated exposure to L2 discourse alongside gameplay, which in turn, can facilitate form-meaning association and internalization of new L2 discourse.

PEDAGOGICAL INTEGRATION OF VIDEO GAMES IN L2 LEARNING CONTEXTS

As for integrating video games in L2 classrooms, video games can be integrated in L2 learning and teaching contexts as L2 learning: (a) prompts; (b) environments, and/or; (c) resources. As engaging activities that draw millions of L2 learners, digital games can be used as personally meaningful prompts/ topics for L2 practice activities to promote learners' active and extended participation in L2 use. For instance, teachers can have L2 learners play a video game and write a game review, create a gameplay walkthrough movie, or discuss their gameplay strategies in the target language. Using the personally meaningful and engaging experience of gameplay as a prompt/topic for L2 practice activities has the potential to transform these activities from disengaging and tedious assignments into authentic and purposeful communicative activities. Also, as linguistically mediated social activities and affinity spaces, video gaming spaces can serve as immersive and authentic environments for L2 use and practice where learners engage in active and purposeful L2 use to guide and inform gameplay. For instance, teachers can ask their students to participate in an online multiplayer video game and reach a certain level in the game to use the appeal of gameplay as a motive for cross-cultural interaction with native-speaker players to manage collaborative gameplay. And, as an affinity space and online community with distinct literacy practices (Steinkuehler, 2006), video gaming spaces can serve an L2 learning resource and authorizing platform that offers a wide range of authentic L2 texts spanning different topics, language varieties, and writing genres and provides a genuine platform for L2 composition and interaction. For instance, L2 learners can engage in intensive and extensive L2 practice by reading and writing online game reviews, strategy guides, and/or game-related fan fiction.

CONCLUSION

This chapter has explored the potentials of digital games for L2 learning and teaching in light of interdisciplinary theoretical conceptualizations of digital games as *dynamics texts, affinity spaces,* and *semiotic ecologies.* The purpose of this chapter has been to offer L2 educators a deeper understanding of the textual, spatial, and semiotic dimension of video games to deepen their understanding of the L2 learning potentials of digital games and guide their efforts to integrate them in L2 instructional contexts.

To this end, the chapter surveyed the literature on digital game-based L2 learning to offer a concise overview of the L2 learning potentials of digital gaming. The literature review demonstrated that digital gaming can provide an engaging and immersive space for L2 practice and learning, but it also revealed that like any other learning environment video games are not without limitations. To explain the L2 learning potential of digital games in specific terms of gameplay dynamics and guide L2 educators to harness the learning potential of this engaging medium, the present author drew on interdisciplinary research from literacy studies, narratology, and games' studies to conceptualize video games as *texts*, *affinity spaces*, and *semiotic systems*. Conceptualizing digital gaming on each of these dimensions served to explain the L2 learning potentials of digital games from different perspectives: (a) as dynamic texts video games offer a rich variety of authentic linguistic and multimodal L2 texts that can be decoded and analyzed for L2 practice and literacy development; (b) as affinity spaces digital games offer an immersive and engaging environment for purposeful L2 use and collaborative social interaction, and; (c) as semiotic ecologies digital games provide an engaging and embodied environment for decoding and designing L2 discourse. Finally, the chapter concluded with a brief discussion on integrating digital games into L2 learning and teaching contexts as learning prompts, environments, and resources.

REFERENCES

3rd World Farmer. (2005). [Computer software]. Retrieved from https://3rdworldfarmer.org/about.html

Alexander, J. (2009). Gaming, student literacies, and the composition classroom: Some possibilities for transformation. *College Composition and Communication*, 35–63.

Apperley, T., & Beavis, C. (2011). Literacy into action: Digital games as action and text in the English and literacy classroom. *Pedagogies*, *6*(2), 130–143. doi:10.1080/1554480X.2011.554620

Atlantis, Q. (2003). *Beta Version* [Computer software]. The Atlantis Remix Project.

Benson, P., & Chik, A. (2010). New literacies and autonomy in foreign language learning. In M. J. Luzón, M. N. Ruiz-Madrid, & M. L. Villanueva (Eds.), *Digital genres, new literacies and autonomy in language learning* (pp. 63–80). Newcastle, UK: Cambridge Scholars.

Butler, Y. G. (2015). The use of computer games as foreign language learning tasks for digital natives. *System*, *54*, 91–102. doi:10.1016/j.system.2014.10.010

Bytheway, J. (2015). A taxonomy of vocabulary learning strategies used in massively multiplayer online role-playing games. *CALICO Journal*, *32*(3), 508–527. doi:10.1558/cj.v32i3.26787

Carr, D. (2006). Games and narrative. In D. Carr, D. Buckingham, A. Burn, & G. Schott (Eds.), *Computer Games: Text, narrative and play* (pp. 30–44). Cambridge, UK: Polity.

Chik, A. (2011). Learner autonomy development through digital gameplay. *Digital Culture & Education*, *3*(1), 30–45.

Civilization. (1991). [Computer software]. Santa Monica, CA: Activism.

deHaan, J. (2005). Acquisition of Japanese as a foreign language through a baseball video game. *Foreign Language Annals*, *38*(2), 278–282. doi:10.1111/j.1944-9720.2005.tb02492.x

Entertainment Software Association. (2014). *2014 Essential facts about the computer and video game industry*. Retrieved from http://www.theesa.com/facts/pfds/ESA_Essential_Facts_2014.PDF

Ever Quest II. (2004). [Computer software]. San Diego, CA: Sony.

Food Force. (2005). [Computer software]. United Nations World Food Program.

Franciosi, S. J., Yagi, J., Tomoshige, Y., & Ye, S. (2016). The effect of a simple simulation game on long-term vocabulary retention. *CALICO Journal*, *33*(3), 355–379.

Gee, J. P. (2004). *Situated language and learning: A critique of traditional schooling*. New York, NY: Routledge.

Gee, J. P. (2008). Game-like Learning: An example of situated learning and implications for opportunity to learn. In P. Moss, D. Pullin, J. P. Gee, & E. Haertel (Eds.), *Assessment and opportunity to learn: New voices, new views*. Cambridge, UK: Cambridge University Press. doi:10.1017/CBO9780511802157.010

Glaser, B., & Strauss, A. (1967). *The discovery of grounded theory*. Chicago: Aldine.

Guild Wars 2. (2012). [Computer software]. Bellevue, WA: ArenaNet.

Hitosugi, C. I., Schmidt, M., & Hayashi, K. (2014). Digital Game-Based Learning (DGBL) in the FL classroom: The impact of the UN's off-the-shelf videogame, food force, on learner affect and vocabulary retention. *CALICO Journal, 31*(1), 19–39. doi:10.11139/cj.31.1.19-39

Ibrahim, K. (2018). Player-game interaction: Ecological analysis of L2 gaming activities. *International Journal of Game-Based Learning, 8*(1), 1–18. doi:10.4018/IJGBL.2018010101

Jensen, S. H. (2017). Gaming as an English language learning resource among young children in Denmark. *CALICO Journal, 34*(1), 1–19. doi:10.1558/cj.29519

Kuppens, A. H. (2010). Incidental foreign language acquisition from media exposure. *Learning, Media and Technology, 35*(1), 65–85. doi:10.1080/17439880903561876

Larsen-Freeman, D., & Cameron, L. (2008). *Complex systems and applied linguistics.* Oxford, UK: Oxford University Press.

Lave, J., & Wenger, E. (1991). *Situated learning: Legitimate peripheral participation.* New York: Cambridge University Press. doi:10.1017/CBO9780511815355

Miller, M., & Hegelheimer, V. (2006). The SIMs meet ESL incorporating authentic computer simulation games into the language classroom. *Interactive Technology and Smart Education, 4*(4), 311–328. doi:10.1108/17415650680000070

Neitzel, B. (2005). Narrativity in computer games. In J. Raessens & J. Goldstein (Eds.), *Handbook of computer game studies* (pp. 227–245). Cambridge, MA: The MIT Press.

Newgarden, K., & Zheng, D. (2016). Recurrent languaging activities in World of Warcraft: Skilled linguistic action meets the common European framework of reference. *ReCALL, 28*(3), 274–304. doi:10.1017/S0958344016000112

Peterson, M. (2012). Learner interaction in a massively multiplayer online role playing game (MMORPG): A sociocultural discourse analysis. *ReCALL, 24*(03), 361–380. doi:10.1017/S0958344012000195

Ragnarok Online. (2002). [Computer software]. Buena Park, CA: Gravity Interactive.

Rama, P., Black, R., van Es, E., & Warschauer, M. (2012). Affordances for second language learning in World of Warcraft. *ReCALL, 24*(3), 322–338. doi:10.1017/S0958344012000171

Ranalli, J. (2008). Learning English with the Sims: Exploiting authentic computer simulation games to FL learning. *Computer Assisted Language Learning, 21*(5), 441–455. doi:10.1080/09588220802447859

Rankin, Y. A., Gold, R., & Gooch, B. (2006). *3D role-playing games as language learning tools.* Paper presented at the EuroGraphics 2006, Vienna, Austria. Retrieved from http://www.thegooch.org/

Reinders, H. (Ed.). (2012). *Digital games in language learning and teaching.* London, UK: Palgrave Macmillan. doi:10.1057/9781137005267

Reinders, H., & Wattana, S. (2015). Affect and willingness to communicate in digital game-based learning. *ReCALL, 27*(1), 38–57. doi:10.1017/S0958344014000226

Ryu, D. (2013). Play to learn, learn to play: Language learning through gaming culture. *ReCALL*, *25*(2), 286–301. doi:10.1017/S0958344013000050

Salen, K., & Zimmerman, E. (2005). Game design and meaningful play. In J. Raessens & J. Goldstein (Eds.), *Handbook of computer game studies* (pp. 59–80). Cambridge, MA: MIT Press.

Scholz, K. (2017). Encouraging free play: Extramural digital game-based language learning as a complex adaptive system. *CALICO Journal*, *34*(1), 39–57. doi:10.1558/cj.29527

Squire, K. (2002). Cultural framing of computer/video games. *Game Studies*, *2*(1), 1–13.

Steinkuehler, C. A. (2006). Massively multiplayer online video gaming as participation in a discourse. *Mind, Culture, and Activity*, *13*(1), 38–52. doi:10.120715327884mca1301_4

Steinkuehler, C. A. (2008). Cognition and literacy in massively multiplayer online games. In J. Coiro, M. Knobel, C. Lankshear, & D. Leu (Eds.), *Handbook of research on new literacies* (pp. 611–634). Mahwah, NJ: Erlbaum.

Sundqvist, P. (2009). *Extramural English matters: Out-of-school English and its impact on Swedish ninth graders' oral proficiency and vocabulary* (Doctoral dissertation). Karlstad University Studies.

Sundqvist, P., & Sylvén, L. (2012). World of VocCraft: Computer games and Swedish learners' L2 English vocabulary. In H. Reinders (Ed.), *Digital games in language learning and teaching* (pp. 189–208). London, UK: Palgrave Macmillan. doi:10.1057/9781137005267_10

Sundqvist, P., & Wikström, P. (2015). Out-of-school digital gameplay and in-school L2 English vocabulary outcomes. *System*, *51*, 65–76. doi:10.1016/j.system.2015.04.001

Sylvén, L., & Sundqvist, P. (2012). Gaming as extramural English FL learning and FL proficiency among young learners. *ReCALL*, *24*(03), 302–321. doi:10.1017/S095834401200016X

The Sims. (2000). [Computer software]. California: Maxis.

Thorne, S. L., Fischer, I., & Lu, X. (2012). The semiotic ecology and linguistic complexity of an online game world. *ReCALL Journal*, *24*(3), 279–301. doi:10.1017/S0958344012000158

van Lier, L. (2004). *The ecology and semiotics of language learning: A sociocultural perspective*. Boston: Kluwer Academic. doi:10.1007/1-4020-7912-5

Vosburg, D. (2017). The effect of group dynamics on language learning and use in an MMOG. *CALICO Journal*, *34*(1), 58–74. doi:10.1558/cj.29524

World of Warcraft. (2004). [Computer software]. Irvine, CA: Blizzard Entertainment.

Yip, F. W., & Kwan, A. C. (2006). Online vocabulary games as a tool for teaching and learning English vocabulary. *Educational Media International*, *43*(3), 233–249. doi:10.1080/09523980600641445

Zhao, J. (2016). L2 languaging in a massively multiplayer online game: An exploration of learner variations. *International Journal of Computer-Assisted Language Learning and Teaching*, *6*(4), 1–17. doi:10.4018/IJCALLT.2016100101

Zheng, D, Newgarden, K., Young, M. (2012). Mulimodal analysis of language learning in World of Warcraft play: Languageing as values-realizing. *ReCALL, 24*, 339-360.

Zheng, D., Young, M., Wagner, M., & Brewer, R. (2009a). Negotiation for action: English language learning in game-based virtual worlds. *Modern Language Journal, 93*(4), 489–511. doi:10.1111/j.1540-4781.2009.00927.x

Zheng, D., Young, M., Wagner, M., & Brewer, R. (2009b). Attitude and self-efficacy change: English language learning in virtual worlds. *Modern Language Journal, 27*(1), 205–231.

Zimmerman, E. (2004). Narrative, interactivity, play, and games: Four naughty concepts in need of discipline. *First Person: New Media as Story, Performance, and Game*, 154-164.

This research was previously published in Assessing the Effectiveness of Virtual Technologies in Foreign and Second Language Instruction; pages 216-237, copyright year 2019 by Information Science Reference (an imprint of IGI Global).

Chapter 15

Sustainable Engagement in Open and Distance Learning With Play and Games in Virtual Reality:
Playful and Gameful Distance Education in VR

Stylianos Mystakidis
https://orcid.org/0000-0002-9162-8340
University of Patras, Greece

ABSTRACT

Open and distance learning became a global household term as it came to the forefront of education and work due to the proliferation of remote emergency teaching imposed by the pandemic's social distancing. Virtual reality (VR) is a technology that can transform distance education by overcoming the shortcomings of 2D web-based systems such as learning management systems and web-conferencing platforms. VR-powered teaching can support educators in implementing game-based methods, such as playful design, gamification, and serious games (e.g., educational escape rooms that promote intrinsic motivation towards sustainable engagement for durable, deeper learning). However, a transition from 2D to 3D teaching in the context of the Metaverse is not straightforward or intuitive as it requires a mental and paradigm shift. This chapter presents practical examples of applications and recommendations for practitioners.

DOI: 10.4018/978-1-6684-7597-3.ch015

INTRODUCTION

In the fictional two-dimensional world of Flatland in E. Abbot's mathematical novel (Abbott, 1885), citizens have the shape of 2-D geometric shapes such as triangles, squares, and circles. They live in private, pentagon houses, create families and work in regular jobs. They are certain about the reality they experience around them: the world and the universe consist of the familiar two dimensions of a flat surface. Alpha is an open-minded gentleman, a square, who is introduced to the evasive third dimension and the sense of a three-dimensional space in the eve of a new millennium. He meets a messenger in the form of a sphere who shows him the 3-D Spaceland and convinces him empirically: there is a third dimension after all. Subsequently, he sets to share the news and inform the perceptions of his fellow countrymen based on his ground-breaking and reality-altering discovery that opens new avenues for exploration and communication. Unfortunately, the regime accuses and condemns Alpha of heresy. He is imprisoned and the truth is suppressed to maintain the status quo and peace in Flatland.

This novella could be relevant to contemporary education. The recent COVID-19 pandemic disrupted physical activities and forced emergency remote teaching in all levels of education (Christopoulos & Sprangers, 2021). However, educational institutions were not prepared, and teachers were not trained and skilled to teach from a distance. As a result, remote emergency teaching faced many problems and did not manage to achieve high quality of teaching and learning (Schultz & DeMers, 2020). Students in all levels of education reported lack of interest, motivation, low levels of engagement, participation, achievement, performance. Many times, school pupils' participation was nominal, they appeared present in the virtual classrooms while not paying attention during teachers' monologues. Additionally, teachers, students, and workers reported sentiments labeled as "Zoom fatigue", an overload due to long and repetitive online meetings (Bailenson, 2021). As a result, this outbreak increased the anxiety levels of students (Wang & Zhao, 2020) and deteriorated mental health (Wheaton et al., 2021). Indeed, although there is abundant knowledge on how to organize online learning effectively, web-based solutions have their limitations due to their technological affordances. As a result, to the minds of some people, online learning, confused with improvised emergency remote teaching, becomes a synonym of monologue, boredom, a desert of closed microphones among a forest of abandoned cameras. These experiences constitute potentially a threat to how young people, teachers and parents perceive open and distance learning. The philosophy of open learning, closely associated to life-long learning is paramount is today's information age (Mystakidis & Berki, 2014). Distance education is also essential for flexible, continuous online professional development (Bragg et al., 2021). During the pandemic, notable initiatives were recorded accelerating the digital transformation of education (Ball et al., 2021). A comprehensive literature review revealed that online teaching practices need a comprehensive view of the pedagogy of online education that integrates technology to support teaching and learning (Carrillo & Flores, 2020). More specific, teaching presence depends on pedagogy, learning design, and facilitation practices; cognitive presence requires experience, action, contextualization, and conceptualization; social presence is related to interaction, participation, and belongingness. Interestingly, one study focusing on the barriers preventing the integration of educational technology into education suggested the exploration of gamification beyond primary schools also for secondary and higher education (Christopoulos & Sprangers, 2021). This trend was also observed in dental education through the adoption of serious games to improve online learning (Sipiyaruk et al., 2021).

However, there is a different way to teach and learn that is unknown to many educators; it requires stakeholders to follow Alpha square's footsteps and take a leap of evidence-informed faith towards the powerful third dimension, from web-based 2-D systems to 3-D virtual worlds. Online teaching in virtual worlds opens new pedagogical horizons for educators to challenge students cognitively while offering them enjoyable experiences where pupils are no longer passive recipients of content (Mystakidis, Berki, et al., 2021) and engage in active learning practices (Mystakidis, Mourtzis, et al., 2022). One method to reconceptualize distance teaching is using game design thinking to organize learning through playification, gamification, and serious games. All these methods can be applied both in learning management systems (LMS), 2D web-based platforms and in 3D virtual worlds. The main objective of this study is to demonstrate how learner engagement can be achieved and sustained through playful approaches to online teaching and learning using a multiple case study design. This study has wider practical implications for online education in the Metaverse featuring immersive, multiuser, networked environments (Mystakidis, 2022).

The rest of this chapter is structured as follows: in the next section the theoretical background is presented, followed by the research method, playful and gameful educational virtual reality (VR) applications, and conclusion.

BACKGROUND

Game design, mechanisms, processes, and effects are proposed foci of study for education practitioners so as to derive useful conclusions on practical ways to enhance and facilitate learning by increasing students' intrinsic motivation (Gee, 2004). An intrinsic goal orientation means that students enjoy learning for the sake of it, not as a necessary means to the achievement of external goals. Game-based learning strategies include playful design (playification), gameful design (gamification), and serious games (Patrício et al., 2018). Game-based motivation amplification strategies have been applied in education and e-learning and are at the epicenter of interdisciplinary research and business development towards motivational (Koivisto & Hamari, 2019).

These motivation amplification strategies can be projected in a continuum of complexity, holistic view, and degree of user autonomy. Playful design or playification is the simplest way to integrate the enjoyable element of fun in a 'serious', non-gaming context (Kangas, 2010). Playful learning is the simplest approach; it can be used sporadically with maximum freedom. It adds a layer of playfulness on top of the actual educational activity with minimal systemic interference where teachers and students are encouraged to exercise their creative agency (Mystakidis, Filippousis, et al., 2021). Playification can be applied in education considering four design elements: theme, actions, narrative, and auxiliary components (Mystakidis, 2021). The theme is an appropriate, common semiotic domain, e.g., science fiction, fantasy, a historic period, a cultural reference or artwork. Actions such as quests turn academic tasks into meaningful individual, group, or class challenges. Theme and actions should be part of an encompassing narrative, a story, or a hero's journey that is relevant to both students' and teachers' preferences (DePorres & Livingston, 2016). Story-based learning, narrative-based learning, storytelling, and storyfication can be considered a form of playification (McQuiggan et al., 2008; Shen et al., 2009; Wu & Chen, 2019).

Gamification in education is the application of game design principles to transform a pedagogical activity into a game (Deterding, 2011). Gamification turns a system or process into a game with a comprehensive strategy where users must achieve concrete goals following specific rules. For instance, a gamified e-learning course turns student evaluation into a multiplayer game (Mystakidis, 2020; Sheldon

& Seelow, 2017). Various gamification models have been proposed for educational settings. Game-informed learning proposes the production of compelling, immersive learning experiences through game-like teaching practices (Begg et al., 2005). Game-like learning engages students in their own quests adopting different roles, e.g., inventor, designer, innovator, and problem solver. This model is applied in the Quest to Learn public US middle and high school with an innovative game-based educational philosophy (Salen, 2017). Sheldon proposed the creation of multiplayer classrooms adopting techniques from massively multiplayer online games involving game mechanics such as avatars, points, levels, badges, and leaderboards (Sheldon, 2011). In a gamified curriculum, coursework is re-arranged as a game where students earn points as they choose and complete online and offline learning activities organized around various roles and skills (Sheldon & Seelow, 2017). As a result, quest-based learning management systems were developed to support educators in organizing and scoring both online and offline class learning activities (Haskell & Dawley, 2013). The model of meaningful gamification towards persistent behavioral change uses reflection, exposition, choice, information, play, and engagement (Nicholson, 2015). In contrast to extrinsic reward-based systems, this model aims at increasing intrinsic incentives through personal associations.

Serious games are enjoyable self-contained experiences with an educational purpose (Bellotti et al., 2011). Serious games can be considered an evolution of edutainment systems (de Freitas & Liarokapis, 2011). A serious game is a rather costly, self-contained digital entity where learning takes place while engaging in its context. Serious games can comprise the entirety of the educational experience or a part of it (Freire et al., 2014; Mystakidis et al., 2017b). In order to be effective and not sacrifice fun in the cost of learning, serious game mechanics and aesthetics need to align with intended course outcomes and learning mechanics (Arnab et al., 2015).

Virtual worlds are social spaces in virtual reality (VR), persistent computer-generated three-dimensional online spaces (Girvan, 2018). In the literature they are also called 3-D immersive environments or multiuser virtual environments. Virtual worlds can support effectively active learning paradigms such as problem-based learning and inquiry-based learning (Metcalf et al., 2018; Savin-Baden, 2014). Game-based learning in virtual worlds has been applied successfully in primary, secondary, and higher education. Most common game mechanics for gameful interventions in VR are story, realism, role-play, collaboration, movement, status, points, competition, token, levels, and game turns (Pellas et al., 2021). A systematic review has concluded that interventions in virtual worlds with certain characteristics can have positive, euergetic effects on academic performance, achievements, outcomes, and engagement (Pellas & Mystakidis, 2020). This has been observed in science, technology, engineering, and mathematics (STEM) as well as in humanities, arts, and social sciences (Hornik & Thornburg, 2010; Stokrocki & Chen, 2012; Wang et al., 2020). Engagement is the cognitive expenditure and affective investment for the active participation in a learning procedure (Lim et al., 2006). Student engagement in e-learning environments can be classified in seven levels of increasing achievement: disengagement, unsystematic engagement, frustrated engagement, structure dependent engagement, self-regulated interest, critical engagement, and literate thinking (Bangert-Drowns & Pyke, 2001). The achieved level of student engagement is associated with factors such as task complexity, attention, intrinsic goal orientation, volition, and self-directed learning (Kucirkova et al., 2014). Apart from the obvious student engagement, teacher engagement is also another vital dimension in distance education (Bragg et al., 2021). Not all educators are equally excited and passionate about teaching from a distance, especially in higher education where research is considered academics' top priority and precondition for tenure and advancement (Mills et al., 2009).

METHOD

The guiding research question was: "How can online learners' engagement enhanced sustainably in 3-D virtual worlds?" In this post-hoc study we analyze four case studies on the effects of the application of game-based learning in distance online education. The methodological frame is of qualitative underpinnings and is grounded on the evaluative case study paradigm. Case studies provide opportunities for in-depth exploration of specific learning activities. A qualitative study's analytic benefit is substantial when two or more cases are studied (Yin, 2009). For enhanced external generalizability of findings and recommendations, we adopted a multiple-case study approach and examined four cases where the author played a principal role in their design, development, and delivery. Representative cases were selected purposefully to demonstrate how playful design (playification), serious games, and gameful design (gamification) can be applied to enhance the motivation and engagement of online learners.

PLAYFUL AND GAMEFUL DISTANCE EDUCATION IN VR

Under the following headings lessons from four implementation approaches of game-based motivation enhancement methods in 3-D virtual worlds are presented that can be useful and applicable for distance remote teaching.

Playful Open Education with Colorful Massive Open Online Courses

Sometimes, the structure of an educational event is pedagogically pre-defined due to academic reasons or too rigid to change. For example, a synchronous guest lecture/webinar in the context of a massive open online course (MOOC), followed by a questions & answers session. Using 3-D meeting spaces it is possible to energize and facilitate blended e-learning, as demonstrated in a case study implemented at the University of Patras, Greece (Mystakidis et al., 2017a). One of the first MOOCs ever to feature virtual worlds was the "Open Workshop on Information Literacy" (Kostopoulos et al., 2014). The course had a total duration of 18 months spanning over five units related to information literacy skills, tailor-made for postgraduate students and doctoral candidates. The MOOC had a blended format combining flexible individual and group work as well as weekly online meetings in virtual worlds with trainers and expert guest speakers. A conscious effort has made to create variety in VR to keep online meetings interesting and aesthetically pleasing. Hence, the course made extensive use of theming, through buildings, avatar accessories, 3-D objects, and props. More specific, the term "workshop" provided the inspiration to adopt a medieval theme, organizing the main meeting space as an alchemist's lab (Figure 1). Additionally, whenever the season or the topic would be fitting, meetings were held in other temporary spaces with informal community building activities. For instance, in winter months, meetings would be organized in a virtual frozen lake. During breaks and after the end of each meeting, snowball fights would break out. Other times, attending avatars would receive a surprise virtual gift. Over 300 students experienced a pleasant, enjoyable community atmosphere that supported the sustainable engagement of participants. As a result, over 33% of participants were able to complete the course successfully in both MOOC iterations.

Figure 1. Themed MOOC meeting space in a 3-D virtual world with props

Multimodal Playful Quest-based Learning in a Virtual Museum

The design, planning, building, and customizing of 3-D learning experiences in VR is usually a complex and time- and energy-consuming venture. Once the digital assets have been built, it is a smart idea to use them for multiple purposes to accommodate personalized user needs. For instance, a story or a serious game can be experienced in different interaction modes best suited for free exploration, guided practice, or unassisted assessment (Ferguson et al., 2019; Mystakidis, Besharat, et al., 2022).

In 3-D virtual words, interactive environments can be experienced asynchronously through multiple ways, facilitating guided or autonomous explorations. The University of Washington organized from 2009 to 2014 the Virtual Worlds certificate as one of its professional and continuing education programs. The program run from a distance over a nine-month period. Participants from all over the world met weekly in a social virtual world, experienced and learned how to design, build, and program interactive virtual environments. During the final trimester of each year, one entire virtual island was created, dedicated to a timely chosen topic. The cohort of 2012-13, designed the Museum of Virtual Media inspired by a book chapter dedicated to the history of virtual reality from the dawn of humanity till today (Blascovich & Bailenson, 2011). In fact, the virtual museum was designed in consultation and with direct communication with both book authors. Other final project foci of previous years were Cybersecurity (Endicott-Popovsky et al., 2013), Maya civilization (Hill & Mystakidis, 2012), and Value Sensitive Design (Friedman et al., 2002).

The museum of virtual media featured twelve exhibits that corresponded to the major virtual reality media. Eleven of them were openly accessible: storytelling, graphics, sculpture, theater, manuscripts, movable type (typography), photography, cinematography, electricity, broadcast media, computer/internet (Figure 2). The twelfth and final exhibit dedicated to the future of immersive VR was hidden and could only be unlocked if someone completed a playful activity, a quest. The quest was one of the four modes to experience the virtual museum as illustrated in Figure 3.

Figure 2. Aerial snapshot of the Museum of Virtual Media in Second Life

Figure 3. Interaction modes in the 3-D Museum of Virtual Media

The quest was organized around the following fictional story:

"In the beginning of time there existed a book which told the tale and story of the Universe from the creation to the present, and even peered into the future. This book was revered and awed by all. The most intriguing and read chapter of the book divulged dark and secret information that one would only dare to think about. These concepts touched on the possibility of the continuation of existence after death. The winding road that led to this mystical unknown was portrayed through different virtual reality forms. Many chapters took readers on a journey of communication technology throughout time.

At the turn of the last century, the guardians took a journey across the ocean to inhabit a new land and took the esoteric book with them. A Thief, seeing how protective the humans were of the book, devised a plot to capture the book. The book had its own safety against evil and when the Thief touched the book, its golden pages flew high up in the air and were lost. As the pages fell, the story of the book was resurrected on the land into a three-dimensional exhibit, which came to be known as the Museum of Virtual Media.

As the pages fell to the ground the Thief scurried around trying to collect them in his clumsy and disorganized way. As he found one page, he lost another, and the sections have now become buried deep within the Museum of Virtual Media.

As a patron and visitor, we are in need of your assistance in collecting the 11 missing sections of the book to reveal the 12th exhibit.

Follow the path of the Thief as he tries to collect the pages of the golden book and collect them yourself. By wearing the Quest MVM HUD, upon completion, the 12th exhibit will appear and, because of your good work, you will be automatically admitted".

As reported by individuals and group visitors, the quest sparked visitors' curiosity, provided motivation for structured, prolonged, and repeated engagement in the virtual museum. Visitors returned to the museum to complete the quest by visiting each 3-D exhibit, unlock and discover the hidden exhibit.

Serious Games and Escape Rooms for Deeper Online Learning

Serious games in VR can supplement online learning and elicit engagement and deeper learning. Designing cost-effective serious games such online breakout or escape rooms can ignite active blended learning (Armellini & Padilla Rodriguez, 2021). Team games of short duration have been used in virtual worlds to supplement online lectures (Mystakidis et al., 2017b). The games featured visual and functional metaphors to convey Cybersecurity-related terms and processes.

Another popular serious game type is digital educational escape rooms. Educational escape rooms are live-adventure games where users have the challenge to complete pedagogically meaningful tasks to exit from one or more rooms. The "Room of Keys" VR escape room has been developed for Biology to help learners build mental models of the function of enzymes in chemical reactions (Christopoulos et al., 2022). The room was accessible both through desktop computers and head-mounted displays. A case study in the USA with high school pupils showed that adolescents appreciated the resource and improved significantly their academic performance by 14% (Mystakidis et al., 2019). Moreover, it increased their interest in the topic leading to a tendency to engage more with the subject.

Collaborative Problem-based Learning (PBL) for Assessment Gamification

The next level of a playful design disposition in distance education is a systematic, more complex arrangement of multiple game design elements towards a gamified experience. This approach was applied in a semester-long gamified distance postgraduate course at the University of the West of England Bristol, United Kingdom (Mystakidis, 2020). The "Artificial Intelligence, Bots and Non-Player Characters" course utilized both virtual worlds (Second Life) and the Blackboard learning management system for written assignments.

The game layer included mainly story, character categories, experience points, ranks, and quests. The story prompted students to step into the shoes of a professional practitioner and prove their abilities to be admitted into a –fictional- elite institutional unit. To reach their goal, students have climb game ranks towards becoming masters of non-player characters. A higher rank is reached though the accumulation of experience points that are earned through learning activities, namely quests. Quests were organized in three different types: solo, raid, or guild corresponding to individual, group, or class tasks respectively. Quests were also classified in three categories of characters aligned with the course's intended outcomes: monk, artisan, and bard. Monk quests dealt with reading and writing assignments, artisan quests developed programming skills, while bard quests had components of open, public performance.

In this context, it was essential to organizing group activities and case studies with tangible 3-D objects to enable theoretical knowledge application for in-depth comprehension. For this purpose, a new type of collaborative problem-solving activity was developed. The activity involves the analysis of cases or of a problem according a theoretical model using 3-D assets that learners can create, copy, and move in VR (Figure 4). A detailed guide for practitioners with has been developed in a handbook for teachers (Mystakidis, Mourtzis, et al., 2022). A study conducted revealed that gamified elements increased students' interest, motivation, and autonomy towards critical engagement (Mystakidis, 2020).

Figure 4. Collaborative problem-solving session in action in a 3D virtual world

CONCLUSION

This chapter constitutes a modest attempt to replicate Alpha square's quest to showcase and establish the engaging power of the third, spatial dimension in distance education; it advocates the introduction of fun-driven distance education in the pursuit of winning the minds and hearts of students with the help of 3-D social environments in VR. The underlying assumption is that once students are emotionally engaged, they become curious and interested in the studied domain, they are more likely to adopt an intrinsic goal orientation, engage frequently with content, and ultimately achieve a durable knowledge and competency. The assumption is corroborated by the affective context model (Shackleton-Jones, 2019). Instructional design for 3-D virtual worlds can be very different from 2-D environments borrowing elements from theater, cinematography, storytelling, and games (Kapp & O'Driscoll, 2010) in the service of creating emotionally charged learning experiences. Four application examples of progressive complexity were presented. The first stage according to the TANC model for playful learning (Mystakidis, 2021) is the playful arrangement of components of 3-D buildings such as buildings based on a suitable theme. The next level involves the planning of quests, meaningful learning activities, interwoven with a narrative, a story. These quests can be cooperative problem-solving tasks and projects in virtual worlds. The third step is to build short serious games such as escape rooms to address parts of the course and the outcomes. In the final stage, it is possible to devise a comprehensive plan to gamify the entire curriculum and assessment where students win their grade through their active engagement.

Critical success factors that practitioners should consider are the following: (i) Educators without prior experiences with game-based learning or 3-D virtual worlds should start small, experiment with playfulness, and build confidence gradually. (ii) Ask for user feedback often. Do not strive for technical perfection in the first iteration. Students tend to appreciate teachers' efforts and can be very constructive in their feedback. (iii) These experiences should help academics and teachers to construct their signature pedagogies that correspond naturally with their character, interests, and teaching style (Nørgård et al., 2017).

Teachers are receptive to the use of playful and gameful methods in their practice (Mystakidis, Papantzikos, et al., 2021). Continuous teacher professional development opportunities and educational communities of practice can accelerate the acceptance and active adoption of virtual and augmented reality in education (Mystakidis, Fragkaki, et al., 2021). These technologies are cornerstones of the tech stack of the Metaverse, the 3D iteration of the Internet. The Metaverse has profound affordances that can enhance online education (Mystakidis, 2022). The ultimate challenge is to improve the perceived quality to the point that distance education is regarded as equal as or even superior to classroom-based instruction, a critical achievement in our information-intensive, innovation-driven era (Patrício et al., 2021).

ACKNOWLEDGMENT

This research received no specific grant from any funding agency in the public, commercial, or not-for-profit sectors.

REFERENCES

Abbott, E. A. (1885). *Flatland: A Romance of Many Dimensions*. Roberts Brothers.

Armellini, A., & Padilla Rodriguez, B. C. (2021). Active Blended Learning. In B. C. P. Rodriguez & A. Armellini (Eds.), *Cases on Active Blended Learning in Higher Education* (pp. 1–22). IGI Global. doi:10.4018/978-1-7998-7856-8.ch001

Arnab, S., Lim, T., Carvalho, M. B., Bellotti, F., de Freitas, S., Louchart, S., Suttie, N., Berta, R., & De Gloria, A. (2015). Mapping learning and game mechanics for serious games analysis. *British Journal of Educational Technology*, *46*(2), 391–411. doi:10.1111/bjet.12113

Bailenson, J. N. (2021). Nonverbal overload: A theoretical argument for the causes of Zoom fatigue. *Technology, Mind, and Behavior*, *2*(1). Advance online publication. doi:10.1037/tmb0000030

Ball, C., Huang, K.-T., & Francis, J. (2021). Virtual reality adoption during the COVID-19 pandemic: A uses and gratifications perspective. *Telematics and Informatics*, *65*, 101728. doi:10.1016/j.tele.2021.101728 PMID:34887619

Bangert-Drowns, R. L., & Pyke, C. (2001). A taxonomy of student engagement with educational software: An exploration of literate thinking with electronic text. *Journal of Educational Computing Research*, *24*(3), 213–234. doi:10.2190/0CKM-FKTR-0CPF-JLGR

Begg, M., Dewhurst, D., & Macleod, H. (2005). Game informed learning: Applying computer game processes to higher education. *Innovate*, *1*(6).

Bellotti, F., Berta, R., De Gloria, A., Ott, M., Arnab, S., de Freitas, S., & Kiili, K. (2011). Designing serious games for education: from pedagogical principles to game mechanisms. *Proceedings of the 5th European Conference on Games Based Learning*, 2, 1–9.

Blascovich, J., & Bailenson, J. (2011). *Infinite Reality: Avatars, Eternal Life, New Worlds, and the Dawn of the Virtual Revolution*. Harper Collins.

Bragg, L. A., Walsh, C., & Heyeres, M. (2021). Successful design and delivery of online professional development for teachers: A systematic review of the literature. *Computers & Education*, *166*, 104158. doi:10.1016/j.compedu.2021.104158

Carrillo, C., & Flores, M. A. (2020). COVID-19 and teacher education: A literature review of online teaching and learning practices. *European Journal of Teacher Education*, *43*(4), 466–487. doi:10.1080 /02619768.2020.1821184

Christopoulos, A., Mystakidis, S., Cachafeiro, E., & Laakso, M.-J. (2022). Escaping the cell: Virtual reality escape rooms in biology education. *Behaviour & Information Technology*, 1–18. doi:10.1080/0 144929X.2022.2079560

Christopoulos, A., & Sprangers, P. (2021). Integration of educational technology during the Covid-19 pandemic: An analysis of teacher and student receptions. *Cogent Education*, *8*(1), 1964690. Advance online publication. doi:10.1080/2331186X.2021.1964690

de Freitas, S., & Liarokapis, F. (2011). Serious games: A new paradigm for education? In Serious Games and Edutainment Applications (pp. 9–23). doi:10.1007/978-1-4471-2161-9_2

DePorres, D., & Livingston, R. E. (2016). Launching new doctoral students: Embracing the Hero's journey. *Developments in Business Simulation and Experiential Learning, 43*.

Deterding, S. (2011). Situated motivational affordances of game elements: A conceptual model. *Conference on Human Factors in Computing Systems (CHI 2011)*.

Endicott-Popovsky, B., Hinrichs, R. J., & Frincke, D. (2013). Leveraging 2nd life as a communications media: An effective tool for security awareness training. *IEEE International Professional Communication 2013 Conference*, 1–7. 10.1109/IPCC.2013.6623945

Ferguson, C., van den Broek, E. L., & van Oostendorp, H. (2019). On the role of interaction mode and story structure in virtual reality serious games. *Computers & Education*. Advance online publication. doi:10.1016/j.compedu.2019.103671

Freire, M., del Blanco, A., & Fernandez-Manjon, B. (2014). Serious games as edX MOOC activities. *2014 IEEE Global Engineering Education Conference (EDUCON)*, 867–871. 10.1109/EDUCON.2014.6826198

Friedman, B., Kahn, P., & Borning, A. (2002). Value sensitive design: Theory and methods. *University of Washington Technical Report, 2–12*.

Gee, J. P. (2004). *What Video Games Have to Teach Us About Learning and Literacy*. Palgrave Macmillan.

Girvan, C. (2018). What is a virtual world? Definition and classification. *Educational Technology Research and Development*, *66*(5), 1087–1100. doi:10.100711423-018-9577-y

Haskell, C., & Dawley, L. (2013). 3D GameLab: Quest-Based Pre-Service Teacher Education. In Y. Baek & N. Whitton (Eds.), *Cases on Digital Game-Based Learning: Methods, Models and Strategies* (pp. 302–340). IGI Global. doi:10.4018/978-1-4666-2848-9.ch016

Hill, V., & Mystakidis, S. (2012). Maya Island virtual museum: A virtual learning environment, museum, and library exhibit. *2012 18th International Conference on Virtual Systems and Multimedia*, 565–568. 10.1109/VSMM.2012.6365978

Hornik, S., & Thornburg, S. (2010). Really engaging accounting: Second Life™ as a learning platform. *Issues in Accounting Education*, *25*(3), 361–378. doi:10.2308/iace.2010.25.3.361

Kapp, K. M., & O'Driscoll, T. (2010). *Learning in 3D: Adding a New Dimension to Enterprise Learning and Collaboration*. Pfeiffer.

Koivisto, J., & Hamari, J. (2019). The rise of motivational information systems: A review of gamification research. *International Journal of Information Management*, *45*, 191–210. doi:10.1016/j.ijinfomgt.2018.10.013

Kostopoulos, K. P., Giannopoulos, K., Mystakidis, S., & Chronopoulou, K. (2014). E-learning through virtual reality applications: The case of career counseling. *The International Journal of Technologies in Learning*, *21*(1), 57–68. doi:10.18848/2327-0144/CGP/v20i01/49125

Kucirkova, N., Messer, D., Sheehy, K., & Fernández Panadero, C. (2014). Children's engagement with educational iPad apps: Insights from a Spanish classroom. *Computers & Education*, *71*, 175–184. doi:10.1016/j.compedu.2013.10.003

Lim, C. P., Nonis, D., & Hedberg, J. G. (2006). Gaming in a 3D multiuser virtual environment: Engaging students in science lessons. *British Journal of Educational Technology*, *37*(2), 211–231. doi:10.1111/j.1467-8535.2006.00531.x

McQuiggan, S. W., Rowe, J. P., Lee, S., & Lester, J. C. (2008). Story-Based Learning: The Impact of Narrative on Learning Experiences and Outcomes. In B. P. Woolf, E. Aïmeur, R. Nkambou, & S. Lajoie (Eds.), *Intelligent Tutoring Systems* (pp. 530–539). Springer Berlin Heidelberg. doi:10.1007/978-3-540-69132-7_56

Metcalf, S. J., Reilly, J. M., Kamarainen, A. M., King, J., Grotzer, T. A., & Dede, C. (2018). Supports for deeper learning of inquiry-based ecosystem science in virtual environments - Comparing virtual and physical concept mapping. *Computers in Human Behavior*, *87*, 459–469. doi:10.1016/j.chb.2018.03.018

Mills, S., Yanes, M., & Casebeer, C. (2009). Perceptions of distance learning among faculty of a college of education. *Journal of Online Learning and Teaching*, *5*(1).

Mystakidis, S. (2020). Distance Education Gamification in Social Virtual Reality: A Case Study on Student Engagement. *11th International Conference on Information, Intelligence, Systems and Applications (IISA 2020)*, 1–6. 10.1109/IISA50023.2020.9284417

Mystakidis, S. (2021). Combat tanking in education - The TANC model for playful distance learning in social virtual reality. *International Journal of Gaming and Computer-Mediated Simulations*, *13*(4), 1–20. doi:10.4018/IJGCMS.291539

Mystakidis, S. (2022). Metaverse. *Encyclopedia*, 2(1), 486–497. doi:10.3390/encyclopedia2010031

Mystakidis, S., & Berki, E. (2014). Participative Design of qMOOCs with Deep Learning and 3d Virtual Immersive Environments : The case of MOOCAgora. *Can MOOCs Save Europe's Unemployed Youth? Workshop. ECTEL 2014 Conference.*

Mystakidis, S., Berki, E., & Valtanen, J.-P. (2017a). Designing and Implementing a Big Open Online Course by Using a 3d Virtual Immersive Environment – Lessons Learned. *9th Annual International Conference on Education and New Learning Technologies (EDULEARN17)*, 8070–8079. 10.21125/edulearn.2017.0487

Mystakidis, S., Berki, E., & Valtanen, J.-P. (2017b). Toward Successfully Integrating Mini Learning Games into Social Virtual Reality Environments – Recommendations for Improving Open and Distance Learning. *9th Annual International Conference on Education and New Learning Technologies (EDU-LEARN17)*, 968–977. 10.21125/edulearn.2017.1203

Mystakidis, S., Berki, E., & Valtanen, J.-P. (2021). Deep and meaningful e-learning with social virtual reality environments in higher education: A systematic literature review. *Applied Sciences (Basel, Switzerland)*, 11(5), 2412. doi:10.3390/app11052412

Mystakidis, S., Besharat, J., Papantzikos, G., Christopoulos, A., Stylios, C., Agorgianitis, S., & Tselentis, D. (2022). Design, development and evaluation of a virtual reality serious game for school fire preparedness training. *Education Sciences*, 12(4), 281. doi:10.3390/educsci12040281

Mystakidis, S., Cachafeiro, E., & Hatzilygeroudis, I. (2019). Enter the serious e-scape room: A cost-effective serious game model for deep and meaningful e-learning. *2019 10th International Conference on Information, Intelligence, Systems and Applications (IISA)*, 1–6. 10.1109/IISA.2019.8900673

Mystakidis, S., Filippousis, G., Tolis, D., & Tseregkouni, E. (2021). Playful metaphors for narrative-driven e-learning. *Applied Sciences (Basel, Switzerland)*, 11(24), 11682. doi:10.3390/app112411682

Mystakidis, S., Fragkaki, M., & Filippousis, G. (2021). Ready teacher one: Virtual and augmented reality online professional development for K-12 school teachers. *Computers*, 10(10), 134. doi:10.3390/computers10100134

Mystakidis, S., Mourtzis, P., & Tseregkouni, E. (2022). *Collaborative Problem Solving for In-Depth Conceptual Knowledge in 3D Virtual Worlds. In 100+ Ideas for Active Learning*. Active Learning Network.

Mystakidis, S., Papantzikos, G., & Stylios, C. (2021). Virtual Reality Escape Rooms for STEM Education in Industry 4.0: Greek Teachers Perspectives. *2021 6th South-East Europe Design Automation, Computer Engineering, Computer Networks and Social Media Conference (SEEDA-CECNSM)*, 1–5. 10.1109/SEEDA-CECNSM53056.2021.9566265

Nicholson, S. (2015). A RECIPE for Meaningful Gamification. In T. Reiners & L. C. Wood (Eds.), *Gamification in Education and Business* (pp. 1–20). Springer International Publishing., doi:10.1007/978-3-319-10208-5_1

Nørgård, R. T., Toft-Nielsen, C., & Whitton, N. (2017). Playful learning in higher education: Developing a signature pedagogy. *International Journal of Play*, 6(3), 272–282. doi:10.1080/21594937.2017.1382997

Patrício, R., Moreira, A. C., & Zurlo, F. (2018). Gamification approaches to the early stage of innovation. *Creativity and Innovation Management, 27*(4), 499–511. doi:10.1111/caim.12284

Patrício, R., Moreira, A. C., & Zurlo, F. (2021). Enhancing design thinking approaches to innovation through gamification. *European Journal of Innovation Management, 24*(5), 1569–1594. doi:10.1108/EJIM-06-2020-0239

Pellas, N., & Mystakidis, S. (2020). A systematic review of research about game-based learning in virtual worlds. *Journal of Universal Computer Science, 26*(8), 1017–1042. doi:10.3897/jucs.2020.054

Pellas, N., Mystakidis, S., & Christopoulos, A. (2021). A systematic literature review on the user experience design for game-based interventions via 3D virtual worlds in K-12 education. *Multimodal Technologies and Interaction, 5*(6), 28. doi:10.3390/mti5060028

Salen, K. (2017). Designing a place called school: A case study of the public school quest to learn. *She Ji: The Journal of Design, Economics, and Innovation, 3*(1), 51–64. doi:10.1016/j.sheji.2017.08.002

Savin-Baden, M. (2014). Using problem-based learning: New constellations for the 21st century. *Journal on Excellence in College Teaching, 25*(3 & 4).

Schultz, R. B., & DeMers, M. N. (2020). Transitioning from emergency remote learning to deep online learning experiences in geography education. *The Journal of Geography, 119*(5), 142–146. doi:10.1080/00221341.2020.1813791

Shackleton-Jones, N. (2019). *How People Learn: Designing Education and Training that Works to Improve Performance*. Kogan Page Publishers.

Sheldon, L. (2011). *The Multiplayer Classroom: Designing Coursework as a Game*. Cengage Learning PTR.

Sheldon, L., & Seelow, D. (2017). The multiplayer classroom: The designer and the collaboration. *International Journal on Innovations in Online Education, 1*(4). Advance online publication. doi:10.1615/IntJInnovOnlineEdu.2017024959

Shen, E. Y.-T., Lieberman, H., & Davenport, G. (2009). What's next? Emergent storytelling from video collections. *Proceedings of the SIGCHI Conference on Human Factors in Computing Systems*, 809–818. 10.1145/1518701.1518825

Sipiyaruk, K., Hatzipanagos, S., Reynolds, P. A., & Gallagher, J. E. (2021). Serious games and the COVID-19 pandemic in dental education: An integrative review of the literature. *Computers, 10*(4), 42. doi:10.3390/computers10040042

Stokrocki, M., & Chen, J. (2012). Taiwanese undergraduates' digital story quests for art treasures in Second Life. *Journal of Cultural Research in Art Education, 30*(13), 32–59.

Wang, C., Lan, Y.-J., Tseng, W.-T., Lin, Y.-T. R., & Gupta, K. C.-L. (2020). On the effects of 3D virtual worlds in language learning – a meta-analysis. *Computer Assisted Language Learning, 33*(8), 891–915. doi:10.1080/09588221.2019.1598444

Wang, C., & Zhao, H. (2020). The impact of COVID-19 on anxiety in Chinese university students. *Frontiers in Psychology*, *11*, 1168. doi:10.3389/fpsyg.2020.01168 PMID:32574244

Wheaton, M. G., Messner, G. R., & Marks, J. B. (2021). Intolerance of uncertainty as a factor linking obsessive-compulsive symptoms, health anxiety and concerns about the spread of the novel coronavirus (COVID-19) in the United States. *Journal of Obsessive-Compulsive and Related Disorders*, *28*, 100605. doi:10.1016/j.jocrd.2020.100605 PMID:33251098

Wu, J., & Chen, V. D.-T. (2019). A systematic review of educational digital storytelling. *Computers & Education*, *103786*. Advance online publication. doi:10.1016/j.compedu.2019.103786

Yin, R. K. (2009). *Case Study Research: Design and Methods* (4th ed.). SAGE Publications.

ADDITIONAL READING

Dalgarno, B., & Lee, M. J. W. (2010). What are the learning affordances of 3-D virtual environments? *British Journal of Educational Technology*, *41*(1), 10–32. doi:10.1111/j.1467-8535.2009.01038.x

Damer, B., & Hinrichs, R. (2014). *The Virtuality and Reality of Avatar Cyberspace*. Oxford University Press. doi:10.1093/oxfordhb/9780199826162.013.032

Fisher, J. A. (Ed.). (2021). *Augmented and Mixed Reality for Communities*. CRC Press. doi:10.1201/9781003052838

Freina, L., & Canessa, A. (2015). Immersive vs desktop virtual reality in game based learning. In R. Munkvold & L. Kolås (Eds.), *European Conference on Games Based Learning* (pp. 195–202). Nord-Trondelag University College Steinkjer.

Gregory, S., Lee, M., & Dalgarno, B. (Eds.). (2016). *Learning in Virtual Worlds: Research and Applications*. AU Press. doi:10.15215/aupress/9781771991339.01

Grivokostopoulou, F., Kovas, K., & Perikos, I. (2020). The effectiveness of embodied pedagogical agents and their impact on students learning in virtual worlds. *Applied Sciences (Basel, Switzerland)*, *10*(5), 1739. doi:10.3390/app10051739

Palkova, Z., & Hatzilygeroudis, I. (2019). Virtual Reality and its Applications in Vocational Education and Training. In Y. A. Zhang & D. Cristol (Eds.), *Handbook of Mobile Teaching and Learning* (pp. 1245–1274). Springer Singapore. doi:10.1007/978-981-13-2766-7_88

Savin-Baden, M., Falconer, L., Wimpenny, K., & Callaghan, M. (2017). Virtual Worlds for Learning. In E. Duval, M. Sharples, & R. Sutherland (Eds.), *Technology Enhanced Learning: Research Themes* (pp. 97–107). Springer International Publishing. doi:10.1007/978-3-319-02600-8_9

This research was previously published in the Handbook of Research on Gamification Dynamics and User Experience Design; pages 409-424, copyright year 2022 by Engineering Science Reference (an imprint of IGI Global).

KEY TERMS AND DEFINITIONS

Educational Escape Room: Live-adventure game where one or more users have to complete a mission, usually to break out of one or more rooms.

Engagement: The active involvement of students in the learning process.

Gameful Design (Gamification): The transformation of a non-gaming procedure or function into a game.

Playful Design: The application of game design elements in a non-gaming context.

Problem-Based Learning: Teaching method to organize learning around an authentic or realistic challenge.

Serious Game: Digital game with a primary epistemic, pedagogical purpose.

Virtual World: A persistent, computer-generated 3D multi-user environment where users can populate and communicate as avatars.

Chapter 16
Role of Immersive (XR) Technologies in Improving Healthcare Competencies:
A Review

Prabha Susy Mathew
Bishop Cottons Women's Christian College, India

Anitha S. Pillai
 https://orcid.org/0000-0002-3883-8234
Hindustan Institute of Technology and Science, India

ABSTRACT

Immersive technology refers to technology that enhances reality by blending the physical environment with virtual content or by completely taking the user to a virtual world far away from reality. Different immersive technologies are augmented reality (AR), virtual reality (VR), and mixed reality (MR). As immersive technology is becoming more affordable, user-friendly, pervasive, and ubiquitous, it's been adopted and embraced by several industries. Though its early adopters were from the gaming industry, now it's explored and used by many other industries such as mining, healthcare, and medicine, retail, education, automotive, manufacturing, etc. Using these technologies, medical professionals can improve their competencies, and they will be able to effectively transfer the skill acquired through simulations to the operation theatre. This chapter focuses on uses, benefits, and adoption challenges of Immersive technologies with specific reference to healthcare training.

INTRODUCTION

As a result of technological advancements industries and consumers are inundated with technology choices that they can use it to their advantage. One such technology is immersive technology or extended reality (XR) that's been recently transforming the healthcare training by reducing medical errors, improving

DOI: 10.4018/978-1-6684-7597-3.ch016

medical practitioners' competency, reducing training costs and providing immersive and interactive learning environment. Immersive technologies such as augmented reality (AR), virtual reality (VR) and mixed reality (MR) are increasingly used in Healthcare education to train medical professionals' complex procedures by simulating it, making the scenario interesting and realistic. Right from training medical doctors, it is used in treatment planning, pharmacy- specific training and in surgery. (Michael, Simon & Nicholas, 2018). These immersive technologies-based training programs focus on procedural skill thereby improving patient safety and competencies of medical practitioner. Compared to traditional tools for training, immersive learning tools can greatly improve the quality of training, reduces costs, provides deeper understanding opportunities and improves patient satisfaction through better care from healthcare professionals.

IMMERSIVE TECHNOLOGIES

Immersive technology refers to technology that provide users with an experience of immersing oneself in simulated world that users can interact with. Immersive technology or extended reality (XR) is a term used for collectively referring technologies such as AR, VR and MR each of these have some key differences. (Reality Technologies, n.d.) The AR, VR ecosystem can be largely classified in to components, Head Mounted Devices (HMD) and Applications (Goldman Sachs, 2016). The Landscape for Immersive technology is as indicated in Figure1.

Virtual reality refers to fully immersive virtual world environment which substitutes the real world. An important pieces of virtual reality kit are the VR Head-Mounted Device (HMD) which is the similar to glasses and may or may not require a PC/Smartphone/Console to power the content being produced. The tethered VR headset / HMD needs to be connected to a PC via cable for the VR experience, while untethered does not require a PC or a console to be connected as it has in-built processor, memory, battery, sensor, display etc. The Virtual learning experience is enhanced, when the VR HMD is worn along with Headphones, special gloves, tracking devices and other optional devices such as bio controller. The HMD has several sensors to aptly simulate the visual, aural and haptic senses of the user through sensory feedback integrated with the output devices. (Oluleke & Xuming, 2013). The three categories of VR based on the level of immersion they provide are: Non-immersive simulations which is the least immersive technology achieved using conventional desktop, Semi-immersive simulations give user a partial immersive experience using High performance computing systems and Fully immersive simulations give user fully immersive experience through HMD and tracking devices. Some of the VR headsets used are Occulus Rift, Occulus Go, HTC Vive, PlayStation, Google Daydream and Cardboard, Samsung Gear, Lenevo Mirage solo (Greenwald, 2018). (Bhone, 2019) in their systematic review, assessed the effectiveness of VR interventions for education of Health Professionals. They found evidence showing a small improvement in knowledge and moderate-to-large improvement in skills of learners taking part in VR interventions compared to traditional or other forms of digital learning. For VR HMD, trackers (head, motion, eye) and sensors with modern graphic processing unit (GPU) will give learners better immersive experience (Hamacher, Kim, Cho, Pardeshi. Lee, Eun & Whangbo., 2016) However they found VR has few challenges such as lack of accurate head-tracking and motion sickness experienced by users.

Figure 1. Immersive technology landscape

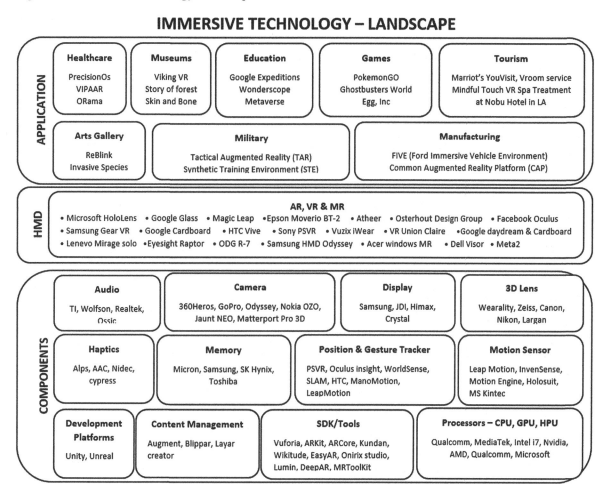

Augmented reality refers to superimposing digital/virtual content on to user's physical world thereby enhancing user's reality. Smartphones, Tablets, Smart Glasses, Tethered AR HMDS etc. to give user the immersive experience. Google Glass and Epson Smart Glasses are the most frequently used devices, newer devices, such as Hololens (Microsoft) are used in many of the recent applications. Apart from the basic devices such as glasses and tablet, it also requires components such as camera, projector, sensor, trackers. Oculus tracker uses infrared tracking systems while HTC VIVE uses a laser-based system to identify users' position in the environment, device such as Microsoft HoloLens is used for interactions which does not require additional programming as it is a part of the system itself. (Hamacher et al., 2016). Few categories of AR are: Marker based AR and Markerless AR. Marker based AR, it uses camera to recognize visual markers such as an image or a QR code. It allows users to view image from all directions in detail, while Markerless AR is a widely accepted and it uses simultaneous localization and mapping (SLAM) technology, which is an advanced AR technology that uses GPS, digital compass etc. to provide location-based data. The Smithsonian's National Museum of Natural History uses Skin & Bones App that allow their visitors to point the camera of their mobile device at one of 13 skeletons displayed and view those animal's come to life "with its skin on". Some of the animals that come to life via the app are vampire bats, a 150-pound Mississippi catfish, giant sea cows, rattlesnakes. The visitors are able to learn everything about that animal as to how it sounded, lived and preyed on other animals, its anatomy and evolution. This is made possible through advanced technologies of 3D AR and 3D tracking. ("Smithsonian", 2015) AR enhanced T-shirt can be used to learn human anatomy through a user-friendly interface. It has a printed code on it which is recognised by AR application that allows user to visualize and explore organs that look real. (Wee Sim, Benjamin, Kavit, Adrian, Ketan, & Jason, 2016) PokemonGo is an example of most popular location-based AR game. The game uses GPS technology to superimpose digital character Pokemon into user's real-world location. Users smart phone camera is used as a guide to find those creatures hidden in the real-world location. Projection based AR, projects artificial lights on real world environment or even to project 3D interactive hologram into thin air and superimposition-based AR works by either fully or partially replacing the original view of an object with the new augmented view of the same object. it provides graphical overlay-based guidance to medical professionals. (Reality Technologies, n.d.) There are a wide variety of Smart Glasses available in market such as Sony, Epson, Vuzix Blade AR, Google Glass Enterprise Edition, Eyesight Raptor, ODG R-7, Magic Leap, Microsoft HoloLens to name a few. (Steve Noble., 2019). In educational training set up AR has been used in several places such as ImmersiveTouch surgical simulation uses HMDs, patient-specific anatomy, and haptic feedback to train surgeons and educate patients. An AR based Vein viewing system, AccuVein is used to help professionals locate veins for IV placement, which is great in reducing the rate of multiple needle pricks on patient. It uses a handheld scanner that superimposes map of patient's veins over his/her skin surface in real time. Accuvein even helps the cosmetic physicians to view and avoid veins while giving Botox treatment to their patient's. A similar system Augmedix allows physicians to enter patient centric data in a hands-free way by just wearing google glass. All the information is passed through the glass to the Augmedix software and is automatically inputted into the patient's electronic health records (EHR). It reduces the physicians administrative work of entering patient details in to the system, thereby giving them more time to interact with patients. VIPAAR (Virtual Interactive Presence and Augmented Reality) is a remote mentoring system. VIPAAR is used with Smart Glass which allows a skilled surgeon in a remote location to communicate and instruct a surgeon in another location by projecting mentor's augmented "hands" into the surgeon's display. (Jasmine Sanchez, n.d.; Smith, Nelson, & Maul, 2018).

Mixed Reality on the other hand intertwines the digital as well as the real world thereby allowing interactions between the digital and the real-world objects. There are not many MR headsets available when compared to AR and VR headsets. Some of the MR headsets are Microsoft's HoloLens, Magic Leap, Samsung HMD Odyssey, Acer windows MR, Dell Visor, HP windows MR headsets, Lenovo explorer etc. (Steve Noble., 2019) Mixed reality ultrasound simulation solution with Microsoft HoloLens used by CAE healthcare team allows learners to examine the 3D anatomy inside the body of Vimedix mannequins. Learner can understand a concept better by getting a detailed view of the hologram. Even physicians will be benefitted as they can practice placing implants or other complex procedures before they perform a procedure on their real patients. (CAE Healthcare, 2017). MR applications are not just used for training the learners, it can also be used as an effective tool for preoperative communications by surgeons. With MR technology the surgeon can simulate the operation that enables patient and the caregivers clear understanding of the patient condition, surgical process and risks involved improving the doctor-patient understanding. MR surgical simulators such as MR simulator for ventriculostomy procedure and a subclavian central venous access (SCVA) can boost confidence of surgeons when dealing with a complex and unfamiliar technique as it provides real-life experience mimicking the procedures. (Hong-zhi, Xiao-bo, Zeng-wu, Mao, Song, Xing-huo & Zhe-wei, 2019)

USE CASES OF XR IN MEDICAL AND HEALTHCARE TRAINING

Medical training requires more realistic training approach. To provide such realistic training without putting the real patients at risk mannequins have been used since long. These Mannequins that were used for learning did not give options of reusability as well as initial investment was often costly. Till recent past medical students have relied on human cadavers to identify, locate and understand different organs in human anatomy. (John, 2017). In recent times technologies such as extended reality (XR) is embraced by healthcare sector and there are multitude of use cases that proves its worth in the industry. XR which also consists of AR, VR and MR is well suited to provide realistic simulation-based training to medical professionals at a reduced cost when compared to the traditional approach. XR technologies are reusable, can be reconfigured, dependence on live subjects is eliminated and improves learning curve by providing better visualization of human body.

Surgical Training

In a traditional set up, practicing a complex surgical procedure was limited as it relied majorly on the availability of cadavers. Oranges or faux skin was used to learn incision and suturing Surgical training which was a decent option, but it was not useful to simulate more complex procedures. Given the complex nature of training required in surgery some of earliest VR applications in medical training was for the surgical domain. There are several companies that provide AR/VR/MR based training option for a surgical skill practice before actual surgery. Some of the semi-immersive surgical simulators like Osso VR, Immersive touch, MIST VR, LapSim, ProMIS allow surgeons to practice a complex procedure any number of times using VR headsets and haptic technology till they perfect the skill (Scott Christian., 2018). (Kamarudin & Zary, 2019). VR and AR based surgical simulators such as Touch Surgery which is an innovative and cost-free app for mobile devices can help learners to understand surgical procedures in a more realistic and interactive way. It has been used to simulate surgical procedure for orbital floor construction (Khelemsky, Hill & Buchbinder, 2017). Touch surgery has also been identified as a serious game approach and an effective tool in teaching medical students chest tube insertion procedure and self-assess their training performance.(Haubruck, Nickel, Ober, Walker, Bergdolt, Friedrich, Müller-Stich, Forchheim, Fischer, Schmidmaier, & Tanner, 2018) some of the surgery domains that use XR as their training tools are discussed below:

a. Plastic and reconstructive surgery

AR used in plastic and reconstructive surgery, can give the patient a 3D simulation of the final facial appearance and can help the trainee in understanding technically complex aesthetic procedures and overlaying patient-specific 3D model of the desired facial reconstruction onto the operative field during surgery to reduce the risk of error. (Khelemsky et al., 2017). Crisalix Surgeon is a simulator for visualizing plastic surgery results. (Younjun, Hannah, & Yong Oock., 2017) in their paper categorized AR/VR based plastic surgery into surgical planning, navigation and training. According to their review it helped surgeons with preoperative surgical planning for more accurate prediction of outcomes, Intraoperative navigation reduced the complications improving surgical performance, 3D human anatomy provided a great learning and training platform for plastic and reconstructive surgery. Surgeons can understand their surgical plans in 3D with XR better. Surgeons trained using immersive technologies completed their procedures 29% faster and made 6 times fewer mistakes than surgeons trained traditionally made. (Armando, 2019). A marker-based AR system that used already existing devices, free software and libraries for improvements of the body surface, important for plastic surgery was devised and evaluated. (Mitsuno, Daisuke, Ueda, Koichi, Itamiya, Tomoki, Nuri, Takashi, Otsuki, & Yuki, 2017). The system used Moverio BT-200 smart glasses for visualizing the 3D image, Blender for 3D image processing, Unity app development software with an IDE. Vuforia, a free software development kit was incorporated as neither Unity nor Moverio has program for marker recognition. The 3D Image of the body surface and the bone were superimposed, onto the surgical site. Overlapping the 3D image on the Actual surgery site is essential for guided surgery on the planned position and to perform cutting procedure precisely.

b. Laparoscopic Surgery

Laparoscopic AR provides intraoperative guidance for identification of targets such as tumors, infection etc. and critical structures such as organs, nerves etc. Laparoscopic AR would help surgeon match information (mostly images) from different sources to the scene and are able to increase their spatial awareness. Minimally Invasive Surgical Trainer-Virtual Reality (MIST-VR) is a low fidelity simulator which does not support force-feedback option and also lacks stereoscopic visualization. It is used to learn basic laparoscopic skills such as suturing and tying knots. LapVR simulators uses haptic technology that lets the learners acquire the tactile laparoscopic surgical skills such as suturing, knot-tying, cutting, clipping and loop ligation. LapVR module has basic laparoscopic techniques as well as modules for gallbladder removal, laparoscopic cholecystectomy, ectopic pregnancy and bilateral tubal occlusion with alternative cases and level of difficulty. Instructor can customize case parameters to match each learner's performance (Panteleimon, Angeliki, Ioanna, Georgios, Christos, Thrasyvoulos, Georgios & Michail, 2017; CAE Healthcare, 2017) The ProMIS AR simulator (Haptica, Ireland) is used for training laparoscopic tasks including navigation, object positioning, suturing, traction, knot tying and sharp dissection (Barsom, Graafland, & Schijven, 2016) LapSim(Surgical Science, Sweden) which is a high fidelity simulator includes basic skill modules, anastomosis and suture and laparoscopic cholecystectomy scenarios, and one case is dedicated to gynecology. LAP Mentor (3D System, USA) is a high fidelity, haptic feedback-based simulator that targets both learners and experienced surgeons, teaching from basic laparoscopic skills to complete operations. The modules include basic laparoscopic skills, suturing, laparoscopic cholecystectomy, ventral hernia, gastric bypass, and gynecology cases. A relatively cheap AR simulator LTS3-e (LTS) is capable of training and assessing the technical laparoscopic skills of Fundamentals of Laparoscopy (FLS) program. It is an electronic evolution of McGill inanimate system for training and evaluation of laparoscopic skills (MISTELS) and offers a few more tasks. It provides validated exercises and scenarios that are assessed electronically with McGill metrics. (Panteleimon et al., 2017). VBLaST a laparoscopic skill training simulator is used for learning laparoscopic tasks peg transfer, pattern cutting, ligating loop and suturing. It provides automatic and immediate assessment of skill but gives learners less immersive experience. To improve surgical immersion VatsSim-XR a versatile simulator that performs multiple surgical training scenarios in different simulation modes (VR, CVR, AR, and MR) on a single device was developed for patient-specific training environment. The experiments conducted by both professional and novice thoracic surgeons show that the (cognitive virtual reality) CVR trainer shows a better result than that of the traditional VR trainer. The AR trainer can provide visuo-haptic fidelity and accuracy in training environment, while the box trainer and MR trainer both demonstrated the best 3D perception and surgical immersive performance. However, the box, VR, and

AR simulators provide less immersive experience compared to its MR counterpart which may not be perfect in operation time (T), surgical clamps track length (CL), endoscope track length (EL), surgical clamps angle accumulation (CA), endoscope angle accumulation (EA), and the numbers of block drop (ND) but provides highly realistic operating rooms for the trainers. (Zhibao, Yonghang, Chengqi., Jun, Xiaoqiao, Zaiqing, Qiong & Junsheng, 2019). Biophotonics based AR system guarantees alignment between the augmentation and laparoscopic image thereby eliminating the need for camera calibration. In laparoscopy, this technique has been used to monitor blood supply in intestinal MIS. (Bernhardt., Nicolau, Soler & Doignon, 2017).

c. Robotic Surgery

In recent past robotic surgery has become preferred choice for surgical procedures because of faster recovery, lesser complication, minimal scarring and decreased blood loss. As a result of such demand surgeons are in constant need to improve and retain their skill without compromising on patient safety. Using simulators could help surgeons in perfecting their skill and recuing error rates. The most popular use of XR technology is in robotic surgery. Some of the simulators available are Robotic surgery VR trainers (RoSS), SimSurgery Educational Platform (SEP), ProMIS, Mimic dV Trainer (MdVT), Surgical SIM RSS, RobotiX Mentor (RM) and the da Vinci Skills Simulator (dVSS). Educational impact has been there for all the simulators except for SEP (Omar M, 2019). RoSS and DV-Trainer have shown face and content validity. DV-Trainer, along with SEP Robot (SimSurgery) and da Vinci Skills Simulator, provides metrics about the trainees' performance with construct validity. RoSS™ is the only one that incorporates whole procedural tasks (Panteleimon et al., 2017), (Hertz, George, Vaccaro, & Brand, 2018) in their comparative study on 3 most commercially available VR robotic simulators provided statistically significant evidence that all the 3 demonstrated face and content validity. Although dVSS had the highest scores and is least expensive of all 3. The dVT and RM have similar cost and availability, training modules available on these models may be a differentiating feature between them.

d. Orthopedic Surgery

The ImmersiveTouch simulator is used in a variety of spine surgery procedures. ImmersiveSim and ImmersiveTouch platforms are the training and education simulators that provide high fidelity, haptic feedback along with realistic user interface. The simulator provides a realistic environment for surgeons and residents, giving them ability to feel the layers of the spinal cord while performing procedures. The system provides immediate feedback for relevant parameters in each module within the chosen surgery, enabling trainees to identify their weaknesses and evaluate their performance. Phantom haptics interface is used for spinal needle insertion. In a comparative study of VR models used for training in arthroscopy, it was found that Arthro MENTOR and ArthroSIM displayed face, content, and construct validity. ArthroS (Virtamed) has demonstrated greater face validity than Arthro MENTOR and ArthroSIM (Panteleimon et al., 2017). Osso VR, a VR surgical training platform uses handheld technology to provide immersive coaching for a robotics-assisted device. This solution offers the largest knee portfolio aided by robotics and offers the accuracy of robotics-assisted technology for bi-cruciate retaining total knee implant. It is Haptic-enabled to provide an immersive training environment. (Justin, 2019). Precision OS is an orthopaedic surgical training using immersive virtual reality. It gives detailed performance metrics to the surgeon at any step of the procedure in order to evaluate him or her on the procedure being performed. Precision OS offers three different simulation platforms: Arthroplasty Platform, Patient Specific Anatomy and Trauma Platform. The first platform allows surgeons to become familiar with patient anatomy, identify precision metrics and perform virtual surgery. The second platform allows surgeons to use advance imaging to perform surgery of a specific upcoming procedure with relevant data before the actual procedure. The third Platform focuses on fracture configuration, screw trajectory and plate position about trauma surgery. (Kristi, 2018).

e. Neurosurgical Procedures

ImmersiveTouch is AR simulation-based surgical training systems. It is a high-fidelity simulator with haptic technology that allows trainees to perfect their skills in a risk-free environment which replicates a real surgery experience for neurosurgery residents. This simulator is used in many surgical disciplines, including spine surgery, ophthalmology, ENT surgery, and neurosurgery (Panteleimon et al., 2017). (Barsom et al., 2016) mentions that an AR setup in neurosurgery that requires basic equipment such as personal computers (PC), a monitor, a camera, tracking tools and 3D image editing software. PC is used for preoperative editing of clinical images and for projection of the augmented image to the real scene. The Augmented images are displayed on Monitors for the surgical team. After evaluating the system, it was found to be a valid training method not only for thoracic pedicle screw placement (face and predictive validity) and clipping aneurysms (face validity) but also for percutaneous trigeminal rhizotomy (construct validity). Besides, it had positive effect on learning, reduced time taken to hone their skill in many neurosurgical procedures, such as ventriculostomy, bone drilling percutaneous treatment for trigeminal neuralgia, lumbar puncture, pedicle screw placement and vertebroplasty. (Wright, Ribaupierre & Eagleson, 2017).

NeuroVR is a neurosurgical training and assessment platform with complex computer-generated metrics in 13 categories. It simulates procedures such as microdissections, tumour aspiration, and hemostasis. variation of this is Neurotouch cranio a virtual reality simulator for select cranial microsurgery procedures that uses stereovision and bimanual tool handles with forced feedback. It computes real-time interactions between surgical tools and tissue, using contact algorithms and tool-specific interaction models for doing neurological procedures. (Panteleimon et al., 2017). (Wright et al., 2017) designed an easy to use and affordable endoscopic third ventriculostomy (ETV) simulator using Unity, Vuforia and the leap motion (LM) for an AR environment. The LM-based system was compared with NeuroTouch for its usability and training efficiency on two parameters task speed and accuracy. From the study it was observed that LM-based system provides a more intuitive 3D interactive experience than the stylus, experts showed higher targeting success rate than the novices and had almost similar task completion times. The PerkStation is a training platform for image-guided interventions. Trainees perform AR image overlaying while training on a phantom,. The PerkStation measures total procedure time, time inside phantom, path length, potential tissue damage, out-of-plane deviation and in-plane deviation. The procedures such as facet joint injections and lumbar puncture has been taught by using PerkStation. Studies conducted to validate the performance of perk station revealed success rate of facet joint injections was significantly higher in comparison with the control group, with significantly less tissue damage and in another study lumbar punctures carried out by Perk Station group outperformed the control group with a shorter period of needle insertion time and less tissue damage (Barsom et al., 2016). UpSim neurosurgical box is a simulator for the advanced training in neurosurgery. It is a physical scenario which interact with a mobile App for AR. With this system it is possible to replicate all the steps of a microsurgical procedure combining a physical scenario with an augmented reality simulation, from the skin incision to microsurgical manipulation of deep neuroanatomy, providing the mental and manual skills required to learn neurosurgical procedures. ("hybrid neurosurgical simulator", n.d.) Some of the other VR/AR simulators mentioned in (Panteleimon et al., 2017) are RoboSim, Vascular Intervention SimulationTrainer (VIST), EasyGuide Neuro, ANGIO Mentor, VIVENDI, Dextroscope and Anatomical Simulator for Pediatric Neurosurgery (ASPN)

f. Ocular Surgery

A study on efficacy Eyesim, a high-fidelity ophthalmic training simulator application developed for intraocular surgery training, demonstrated that it was effective in refining surgical skills of trainees on capsulorhexis of high-tension capsules. The system is more effective in improving surgical skills of the novice surgeons who have less skills. (Panteleimon et al., 2017; Anuradha, 2019). Training modules include ocular anatomy, pupil simulator, ocular motility simulator, and a visual pathway simulator. It is available on Mobile Platforms, Desktop, Ibench Mobile, and Icatcher. Instructors using the simulator can select from any number of functions and have their students perform a diagnosis, providing learners with an opportunity to practice and understand different cases (Pfandlera, Marc, Stefan, & Weigl, 2017). Some other cataract surgery simulators are PhacoVision (Melerit Medical), and MicroVisTouch (ImmersiveTouch). (Panteleimon et al., 2017).

g. Spine Surgery

(Pfandler et al., 2017) in their study identified various AR, VR and MR simulators used for training, assessment, and planning in spinal surgery. Virtual Protractor (AR) is used for Percutaneous vertebroplasty, Medtronic Surgical Technologies (MR), Immersive Touch Simulator (VR) is used for Thoracic pedicle screw placement, Percutaneous spinal needle placement, Pedicle screw placement, Sensable Phantom Premium1.5 (VR) is used for Lumbar puncture, Stealth 3D navigation unit (Medtronic) (MR) is used for Placement of lateral mass screw, PerkTutor; Sonix Touch US system in conjunction with the SonixGPS (AR) is used for facet joint injection, Torso Mannequin, Micron Tracker2 optical tracking system, PHANToM haptic device, graphical user interface (AR) is used for Spinal needle insertion, NovintFalcon (MR) is used for Vertebroplasty, PerkStation (AR) is used for Percutaneous facet joint injection, Phacon Corporation (MR) for Posterior cervical laminectomy and foraminotomy. The quality of the studies mentioned were assessed with the Medical Education Research Study Quality Instrument (MERSQI) The six domains of study quality of the MERSQI (study design, sampling, type of data, and validity of evaluation instrument, data analysis, and outcomes) were rated. From the study it was observed that the simulator-trained group(s) outperformed the non–simulator trained group proving that simulator-based training and assessment of surgical skills in spinal surgery can significantly improve the success rate with less potential tissue damage and reduces completion time of a procedure.

h. Cardiac Surgery

INSIGHT HEART is an AR and MR app for medical education. Learners can take a MR tour of heart anatomy, zoom, rotate, and scale the high-quality 3D MR holograms that floats in front of them and they are able to control the app via voice control or gestures. The 3D holograms of the heart beats in real time is reproduced through audio visual simualtion along with visual effects of artery hypertension, partial fibrillation, and myocardial infraction. The SentiAR is a Microsoft HoloLens-enabled intraprocedural 3D augmented reality platform. Other healthcare companies have been using HoloLens for holographic MR training simulations, however SentiAR differs from them by offering a real-time holographic image of the patient's actual anatomy over the patient in the operation room, allowing surgeons to see patient specific details. (Tagaytayan, Kelemen, & Sik-Lanyi, 2018). The EchoCom is an AR based echocardiography training system for neonates consisting of a 3D tracking system attached to a mannequin to identify congenital heart diseases using sonographic information. The system was tested on experts, intermediates and beginners and it has achieved Face validity and construct validity. (Barsom et al., 2016). The CAE VIMEDIX is an AR system for echocardiography training consisting of a mannequin and a transducer. It can be used to train transthoracic echocardiography or transesophageal echocardiography. It has displayed face validity. (Barsom et al., 2016; Panteleimon et al., 2017).

Other simulators are ANGIO Mentor system is used in conjunction with standard guidewires, catheters, balloons, stents, and similar devices for monitoring the patient's vital signs. It is used in many endovascular procedures, such as carotid stenting and renal, iliac, and other vascular interventions. Vascular Intervention Simulation Trainer (VIST) is like the ANGIO Mentor. Where along with endovascular procedures, it has an electrophysiology module for training in pacemaker lead placement. Nakao Cardiac Model is a VR for training in surgical palpitation of the beating heart. It supports haptic feedback. It does not provide any metric for evaluation. A VR Lobectomy Simulator includes video-assisted thoracoscopic surgery resection, lobectomy; it supports haptic feedback and has metrics tools that can evaluate surgical performance. (Panteleimon et al., 2017).

i. Dental Training and Surgery

The Voxel-Man a surgical simulator is used for training in a variety of disciplines such as ENT, Voxel-Man Tempo for ear surgery and Voxel-Man Sinus for endoscopic sinus surgery. The Voxel-Man Dental is used for dental training. This device allows the learners to use High and low speed burs with matching haptics and sound, provides virtual dental mirror and magnification of teeth, Drilling with realistic haptic feedback and additional cross-sectional images. Microtomography is used to derive high-resolution tooth models from real teeth. The software allows students to work with realistic cases like remove of caries, preparation of cavity with automatic skill assessment for immediate feedback on their performance. A surgical navigation system "3D Tooth Atlas 9", IGI (DenX Advanced Dental system) assists the dental clinicians during preoperative and intraoperative phases of dental implant surgery. During the procedure the clinician can navigate implant to precise location and depth, assisted by audio and visual feedback, thereby avoiding mistakes and performing the surgery with high level of accuracy (Bogdan, Dinca & Popovici, 2011). In an evaluation study oral surgery simulator, Forsslund system was suggested to be an effective training tool to improve dental education. Iowa Dental Surgical Simulator (IDSS) is developed by the College of Dentistry at the University of Iowa. It has a joystick and a modified handle from an explorer, a dental instrument that allows the students to explore tooth surfaces for carious lesions. It's a cost-effective system that uses force feedback to teach and assess the tactile skill of the learner. (Wee Sim et al., 2016)

Anatomy Training

Currently medical students studying anatomy can access the cadaver lab only during the specific allotted hours, getting detailed understanding and view of organs is tough. XR based clinical anatomy curriculum could be far more engaging compared to traditional method. It will help students to understand spatial concepts better and provide them access to educational resources without geographic constraints. Tools like Microsoft HoloLens enables learners to view individual organs in motion from different perspectives, see its functioning and hear heartbeat sound providing a more realistic learning experience. It provides students an opportunity to learn at their own pace, access training outside of Lab and to delve into details that further interests them (Zweifach & Triola, 2019). Several AR/VR related software used for anatomy education such as Blender, Occulus Rift, Vuforia V5, DextroBeam, Aurasma and Magicbook, ARTHRO, dVSS, MistVR, LapSim, ProMIS etc used for medical education were reviewed by (William, Brandon, Perez & Sarah, 2017) which suggests that these simulators are noninferior to standards of practice with regard to learning anatomy. However, Radiation oncology would benefit from the integration of AR/VR technologies, as it provides a cost effective, scalable solution that improves quality of patient care and individual proficiency. At Case Western Reserve, replaced their cadaver lab and 2D illustrations in medical books with HoloLens headsets. HoloAnatomy app is being used which allows medical students to rotate and virtually dissect a body to see and understand the structures, systems, and organs. (Emory & Maya, 2017; "3D Tooth Atlas 9",2018) developed by University of the Pacific's Arthur A. Dugoni School of Dentistry in collaboration with eHuman Digital Anatomy is a VR based dental training system, that will enable dentists to get in-depth understanding of the tooth structure and aliments. The VR model will give students a realistic representation of each type of tooth, how they grow and why they develop cavities and other issues. The improved version of 3D model of teeth with AR capabilities is organized into five sections: Periodontology, Anthropology, Odontogenesis, Dental Embryology and Clinical Access. The Clinical Access section includes over 550 Holographic models of teeth considering every known anatomical pathology and development. (Ta-KoHuang, Chi-HsunYang, Yu-HsinHsieh, Jen-ChyanWang & Chun-ChengHung, 2018)

Clinical Skills Training

Another application of AR/VR has been the use of virtual patients to practice clinical skills such as taking patient history, diagnosing medical condition and prescribing medicines (Scott Christian, 2018). Immersive practice with XR based Think F.A.S.T. (Face, Arms, Speech, Time) training simulation is a powerful and engaging VR simulation that puts learners in a medical emergency. Medical students use VR to educate themselves on how to recognize symptoms of a stroke using the F.A.S.T. system while interacting in real-time with a virtual patient. It uses the Qualcomm® Snapdragon™ 835 VR development kit; a standalone all-in-one mobile XR headset with a single panel AMOLED head mounted display (HMD) and an integrated Snapdragon 835 mobile platform, 3D audio tools, Unity 3D to build the training platform which is compiled to an Android package and Leap Motion for precisely tracking the hand movement (Leilani, 2017). An interactive educational program Virtual Hernia Clinic (VHC) uses virtual patient simulations model to provide learners with clinical scenarios to identify, assess, diagnose and treat patients with hernias. It provides surgeon with opportunities to practice and make the clinical judgment required to perform hernia surgery ("Virtual Health Clinic", n.d.). VR based HumanSim system enables doctors, nurses and other medical personnel to interact and engage in a training scenario with a patient or healthcare professional within a 3D environment only. It provides an immersive experience by measuring the participant's emotions with the help of sensors (Moisaka solutions, 2017). HoloPatient is a MR project undertaken through Pearson's partnership with Microsoft HoloLens. Both Texas Tech University Simulation Program and San Diego State University School of Nursing are working with Pearson. It uses Holographic Capture (HCAP) technology from Microsoft. Actors simulate the real-world scenario which is then transferred as video into Holograms placed into any environment to let students conduct patient assessments and make a diagnosis. (Emory & Maya, 2017). some of the dental simulators for improving future dentists' clinical skills are DentSim an AR based advanced dental training simulator, the system allows the students to train individually and evaluates the work, thus enhancing their clinical skills. Individual Dental Education Assistant (IDEA) simulator provides haptic feedback to the trainee while they practice. The system offers modules for Manual Dexterity, Caries Detection, Oral Med, Scaling and Root Planning. A study in ("3D Tooth Atlas 9", 2018) reported that the system provides a platform for gaining crucial clinical experience. However, they reported that scoring system and the tactile sensation needed to be improved for more realistic experience. The Simodont Dental Trainer a 3D VR based system by Moog industrial group. The training modules offer simulation for manual dexterity, cariology, crown and bridges exercises with different dental burrs. Like forsslund system, the Simodont trainer also has been incorporated to the training curriculum of Academic Centre for Dentistry in Amsterdam (ACTA) (Elby, Bakr, & Roy, 2017). PerioSim is a VR based haptic simulator aimed to improve skills in diagnosing and treatment of periodontal diseases. It is a part of dental training curriculum of University of Illinois in Chicago. Though the easy access to the system via internet and the provision through which instructor can upload a dental procedure and students can replay it at any later time are things that makes it most appropriate to be used for educational training. It was identified that the realism of the tactile feedback had some issue that needs further work. ("3d Tooth Atlas 9",2018; Bogdan, Dinca & Popovici, 2011) Preparation of primary tooth stump is an important skill for performing the dental restorations. For improvising the skills of trainees in fixed prosthetics preparation, a virtual and augmented reality technologies-based simulator (VirDenT) system can be used. Nvint Technologies and the Harvard School of Dental Medicine together developed Virtual Reality Dental Training System (VRDTS). With this system students can practice cavity preparations, work with a virtual decayed tooth, use a drill for cavity repair, fill the prepared cavity with amalgam, and carve the amalgam to match the original tooth contour. VRDTS enables the learner to feel the difference between enamel, dentin, caries, amalgam, and pulp throughout the procedure unlike how it is in the conventional plastic teeth used for training. The student's procedure can be tracked and quantified with feedback to both student and teacher. VR Haptic dental system HAP-DENT is a multi-layered virtual tooth model with different mechanical hardness that allows learners to feel tooth cutting which is like that with a real tooth. The learners can operate a stylus of the haptic device in six degrees of freedom to control dental turbine movement and to feel a tactile force. (Wee Sim et al., 2016) Oculus and Children's Hospital Los Angeles (CHLA) jointly developed a virtual reality software that is used to efficiently train residents, existing clinicians and staff in handling pediatric emergencies. The Oculus Go headset used for this simulation is portable and convenient to use. (Tagaytayan et al., 2018)

Remote Training

In many countries people living in rural areas have less or limited access to healthcare facilities. Shortage of medical practitioners, healthcare facilities, less preventive cares and longer waiting in case of emergencies are typical challenges of remote areas. AR as a Telemedicine Platform for Remote Procedural Training enables the learners or novice practitioners to perform complex medical procedures such as Point of Care Ultrasound (PoCUS) without visual interference. (Wang, Parsons, Stone-McLean, Rogers, Boyd, Hoover, Meruvia-Pastor, Gong, & Smith, 2017) Their proposed system uses the HoloLens to capture the view of a simulated remote emergency room (ER) through mixed reality capture (MRC), mentor's hand gestures are captured using a Leap Motion and virtually displayed in the AR space of the HoloLens to support remote procedural training. Comparison of the system with the full telemedicine set-up did not show any statistical difference. The results were not negative which suggests that these types of AR systems have the potential to become a helpful tool in telemedicine, just like the full telemedicine set-up, provided it is made more robust and lightweight. In several studies, HoloLens which is a MR technology has been used for medical training, training for patients with Alzheimer's disease to improve the short-term memory of patients, viewing magnetic resonance imaging (MRI) images on a HoloLens for MRI-guided neurosurgery. Implementation of E-consultation system leveraged on holographic and augmented reality systems, in a typical intensive care unit (ICU) environment, for remote consultancy services. It was found very beneficial in providing care to critically ill ICU patients and in reducing the rate of morbidity and mortality. (Sirilak, & Muneesawang, 2018). While performing a shoulder surgery using AR a local surgeon was able to interact with a remote surgeon and was able to receive live feedback. The University of Alabama, Birmingham developed Virtual Interactive Presence and Augmented Reality (VIPAAR) system that allowed the remote surgeons to parallelly view the procedure and participate in virtual interactions with the local surgeon. The local surgeon sees the virtual interaction from the remote surgeon through the Google glass. The report suggested that the surgery performed using VIPAAR resulted in no complications and provided an additional support for complex procedures and high-risk surgeries. (Herron, 2016). Use of AR shows a promising new development in telemedicine systems as it can be used by inexperienced doctors who can consult and obtain advice from specialist practitioners who is in a remote location. ORamaVR is redefining medical education through cutting edge VR techniques. With ORamaVR, trainees can improve their skills and remember complex surgical procedures in a virtual environment by collaborating with up to seven remote users and carrying out operations on virtual patients. Recently, some of the medical schools such as Stanford Medical School, the USC Keck School of Medicine, the New York University Langone Medical School and the Aristotle University Medical School participated in ORamaVR demonstration for collaborative surgical training. Surgeons and medical residents collaborated to perform a Total Hip arthroplasty operation out of which five participants were located remotely. A cooperative system like this training multiple young surgeons simultaneously within the same virtual space can reduce the time it takes to train medical students as well as the cost. Proximie, is a cloud-based AR platform used to remotely connect surgeons and students from anywhere in the world via live video feed and Augmented interaction. Economically weaker countries and conflict zones are currently using this platform to train their surgeons remotely. Proximie is being used in an educational setting to teach medical students at Yale University Medical School (New Haven, Connecticut, USA), the Royal Free Hospital, Chelsea and Westminster Hospital and St Tomas' Hospital (London, United Kingdom) giving positive feedback and encouraging results (Perkins Coie LLP, 2019).

Equipment Operation Training

(Bifulco, Narducci, Vertucci, Ambruosi, Cesarelli & Romano, 2014) in their paper presented an application prototype based on AR to train untrained users, with limited or no knowledge, to effectively interact with an ECG device and to place ECG electrodes on patient's chest which was achieved by presenting text, graphics and audio messages to the user. The system when tested, was found to be intuitive and easy to use.

Benefits and Hurdles of XR Adoption in Medical and Healthcare Training

Over the last decade healthcare sector has adopted and benefitted from the immersive technologies. In healthcare, Immersive 3D environments have been used to teach medical students, train new staff members and improve current medical professionals' clinical skills. These immersive training models have been found to be more engaging and effective compared to the traditional teaching models. However, there may be several adoption challenges faced by educational institutions which cannot be ignored.

Benefits of XR Adoption in Medical and Healthcare Training

Remote Learning and collaboration

XR technologies can bridge the distance between the trainer and trainees. Trainees can learn remotely from an expert. The immersive technologies make the whole experience of remote learning very engaging. Virtual interactive presence and augmented reality (VIPAR) simulator allows a remote surgeon to provide assistance and training by projecting their hands into the display of another surgeon wearing a headset. (Herron, 2016). A recent trend of educational meetings is to incorporate live surgery as part of the programme. "VR in OR" application enable medical students around the world to see and learn surgeries or complex procedures broadcasted live on their smartphone. (Monsky, James, & Seslar, 2019; Eran Orr., 2018).

Real Life Concepts with Greater Retention

XR tools promotes learning by doing as opposed to passive learning thereby helping the learners retain or absorb the procedure or skill learned. According to Dr. Narendra Kini, CEO at Miami's Children Health System, VR training programs offer a better retention compared to a traditional education. From his observations, trainees retain 80% of the information after one year of training, while only a 20% retention rate was observed when trained with traditional methods. (Matthew & Shailee, 2017). XR technologies can make learners job-ready through simulations before attending the real patients.

Reduced Cost and Risk

Medical training often involves investment into material or cadaver that has to be disposed after a single training. Simulators reduce this cost by allowing the trainees to practice procedure any number of times till they perfect the procedure without putting actual patients at risk. The initial investment cost will pay off after a short period of time. (William et al., 2017) The tracheal insertion training cost per employee is $3,000 at an elderly care facility in America. While the same training on VR based Next Galaxy's tracheal insertion system costs only $40 per employee, it also saves them the travel cost to other training centres and the need to depend on live subjects. The training can be done remotely and repeatedly with no additional costs (Monsky et al., 2019)

Reduced Learning Curve

Simulation allows training that is independent of place and time. One does not have to wait for the cadaver's lab or the operation room to be free to practice a procedure. It is available 24/7 and a greater number of procedures can be practiced within a limited time providing a more comfortable learning curve. Case Western medical school's dean, Pamela Davis, explained that "students have commented that a 15-minute session with HoloLens could have saved them dozens of hours in the cadaveric lab." (Monsky et al., 2019)

Significant Improvements in the Operating Room

Training with original instruments and 3D graphics makes the surgeon familiar with the devices and eases the transfer of skills from the simulator to the operating room. It has been observed that surgeons trained on a simulator take less time to complete procedures and tend to make fewer mistakes. Socpis developed MR based Holographic Navigation system, which incorporates a Microsoft HoloLens that is worn by the surgeon to enhance the spatial presentation to track pedicle screws and other surgical markings. It significantly improves their speed, precision and reduces errors. Berlin Humboldt Hospital's Spinal Surgery Clinic Chief Christian Woiciechowsky believes that "solutions such as these has the potential to make surgery more effective, safe, and precise" (Monsky et al., 2019)

HURDLES THAT HINDER XR ADOPTION IN HEALTHCARE TRAINING

Content Offering

The key challenge that healthcare sector faces now lack in quality content and its availability for engaging the user in VR applications. For this reason, the right talent in areas including skilled 3D artists, VR programmers, experienced designers and other specialists needs to be identified to craft quality and engaging content needed to bring in to make the user experience more immersive. Recent survey conducted by VR Intelligence and SuperData revealed that 52% of respondents felt that lack of content is a great barrier against the adoption of VR. (Cardiff, 2018; Peter H.,2019).

Uncomfortable Hardware

The other barrier to adoption of immersive technology is lack of good user experience design. The VR and AR HMDs available are cumbersome to use (Cardiff, 2018). For most high-quality VR experience requires the trainees to be tethered to the desktop. Operators have reported being dizzy, disoriented, or nausea like motion sickness. (Marta, 2018). Shiyao Wang et al. in their study found several problems with the HoloLens that impacted the user experience. Some of the issues mentioned by trainees about the device were that they found HoloLens to be heavy and painful to wear, nose pad was not comfortable, some participants could not find a suitable fit to their head available in the device. (Wang et al., 2017)

Technological Glitches

1. **Battery Life:** Most of the training and collaborative AR/VR apps available does not have battery life that can sustain for longer at least during the entire training session. In a system that used HoloLens for telementoring it was found that HoloLens could last for only approximately four participants or about 100 minutes before having to be charged again. (Wang et al., 2017)

2. **Latency:** VR latency is the time taken between initiating a movement and a computer-generated response. In the study of a telementoring system, it was noticed that, the latency, was the key reason for poor performance. 5G devices can reduce latency Enhancing real-time connectivity. (Wang et al., 2017)

3. **Field of View (FOV):** It is the angle of observable view from a VR headset. FOV greatly influences the user experience. In the study (Wang et al., 2017) many users felt FOV was narrow, though the HoloLens has a field of view of 120 degrees horizontally. Other high-end headsets such as ODG R-9, Magic Leap one has limited FOV, original HoloLens FOV was around 35 degrees, HoloLens 2 is around 70 degrees while meta 2 has a reasonably better FOV of 90-degree rate but require a cable attachment. (Adrienne, 2015).

4. **Vergence Accommodation Conflict:** This is a viewing problem for VR HMDs. It is the difference between the physical surface of the screen and the focal point of the simulated world the user views. Such display of 3D images in VR goggles creates conflicts that are unnatural to the eye, which can cause visual fatigue and discomfort resulting into headaches and nausea in users. A good VR user experience (UX) design can reduce or evade VAC-induced discomfort. (Adrienne, 2015).

5. **Eye-Tracking Technology:** VR head-mounted displays haven't been adequate at tracking the user's eyes for computing systems. Advances in eye tracking techniques and eye tracking hardware add-ons and software to AR/VR headsets, decreases systems demand by tracking a user's eye and rendering only in the fovea region, may soon reduce power consumption and increase responsiveness of the system. (Smith et al., 2018; Adrienne, 2015).

6. **Interoperability issue:** With more and more AR and VR systems being used, and multiple devices Connecting to form a system, there is a varying degree of compatibility issue that one needs to work on. (Eran Orr., 2018).

7. **Privacy and Security Concerns:** Perkins Coie LLP and the XR Association in their survey results show that consumer privacy (47%) and data security (42%) top the charts for legal risks concerning immersive technologies. Data confidentiality is also a major concern when recording data on to HMDs, stricter means of data protection must be devised to protect it from being hijacked. The seven principles of storing and handling must be known by all the health professional dealing with them. (Eran Orr., 2018).

Other issues are computational power, cost of immersive technologies, high-quality graphics resolution, User Interface and the ability of the system to tackle computational loads. (Smith et al., 2018)

FUTURE DIRECTIONS

In spite of advancements in technology and demand from across the industries, immersive technology still needs to evolve in order to give its users improved seamless immersive experience. Some areas which need to evolve are discussed below:

Security, Safety, Health, Hygiene and Comfort: The AR and VR HMD's constantly tracks the minute details of the user to give them personalized experience. In this process security and privacy of the user should not be compromised, so appropriate means must be implemented to ensure it. Injuries have been reported while the users were using fully immersive HMD's. As the user's real-world view is replaced with virtual or augmented view user as a result user may end up colliding with real world objects. Other possible cause of injury could be user tripping over the wire that connects the HMD to the computer. Safety of the user from such injuries should be provided. When AR and VR HMD's are used by large number of users especially in Museum's it becomes a breeding ground for infection causing organisms and often the design of HMD makes it difficult to sanitize. Some economic means must be devised to keep the device clean and hygienic. The size, weight and fit of the HMD are very important to factors to improve user experience. In past several research works have mentioned about simulator driven sickness such as nausea, headache, dizziness experienced by users. The physical discomfort can be reduced by designing HMD's that are light weight and comfortable for the users to seamlessly wear it. Perhaps use contact lenses instead of smart glass. (Guy, Gareth, Nicole, Martin, Dawn, Jonathan, Damian, Julian & Lewis, 2018).

Performance enhancement through Edge computing: Hosting the AR and VR services on mobile edge computing instead of cloud architecture can help deal with issues such as latency, processing speeds, high energy consumption affecting battery life and user experience. Edge computing keeps data closer to the user by storing it at Mobile edge computing (MEC) servers thereby increasing the processing speed and reducing latency as opposed to cloud computing where reaching data centres would take long time. Newer architecture using edge computing can tackle existing performance related issues of Mobile Augmented Reality (MAR). (ETSI, 2018; Alisha, 2019).

XR enhanced with AI and ML: Immersive (XR) and emerging technologies such as Artificial Intelligence (AI) and Machine Learning (ML) provides enhanced multidimensional and interactive AR experience. AI and ML algorithms can bring sophistication and cognitive functionality to the existing XR based systems. Already many social media applications like Snapchat, Facebook and Instagram are using AI and AR for either image enhancements or to design realistic avatars based on the image captured for fun, experimental and personalized user experiences. AI when combined with XR systems for medical education can improve training as more data facts can be included and the system will provide more interactive and personalised virtual environment for learners. (Nilima, 2019; Yitzi, 2018)

Improved connectivity through 5G: The current 4G system has limited bandwidth resulting in to AR systems that is not very effective for shared or multiuser experiences. As the concurrent users increase the efficiency of the network drops. The laggy connection often ruins the user experience and often leave the user feeling physically sick which can have detrimental effect on its adoption by user. 5G is one disruptive technology that will offer low latency, better network performance, higher bandwidth with 6Dof (Degree of freedom) which will allow users to walk through the environment. These features of 5G will provide consistent user experience and will enable real- time collaborations with a greater number of concurrent users. The HMD devices need to evolve in order to incorporate the 5G chipset to deliver the 5G benefits which are very critical for the XR applications. (Qualcomm, 2017)

Future enhancements can be in the topics mentioned but not limited to it, as there are many more areas that needs to be explored such as sensory enhancement, benefits of IoT and AR, Improving the field of view (FOV), enhanced multi-sensation rendering framework, Mobile Content for AR apps etc. that can make digital reality more powerful and immersive. (Yitzi, 2018).

CONCLUSION

Immersive technology is a boon to next-gen medical education. Simulations that immersive technology provide, transports the students into an emergency or allows students to view organs in all perspectives from close angles. It exposes medical students to real-life situations without putting patients at risk. Advancements in technology constantly up the quality of users training experience.

From the paper it can be well summarized that immersive technology provides a very strong and positive impact on its learners. The residents and surgeons can benefit as it reduces the learning curve, allows learners to practice complex procedures at their convenience any number of times till they master a skill and for surgeons' time taken to complete a procedure is reduced as they can overlay images on the patient for improved navigation during surgery. However, the challenges identified need to be addressed for adoption rates to improve. Healthcare training can leverage form the immersive technologies as in future with technological advancements, price drops and developers creating newer and richer contents -teaching modules, its use in healthcare training appears almost definite.

REFERENCES

Aboumarzouk, O. M. (2019). *Blandy's urology*. Hoboken, NJ: John Wiley & Sons; Available at https://books.google.co.in/books?isbn=1118863372

ARpost. (2018, August). *3D tooth atlas 9: The virtual reality training system for dentists of the future*. Available at https://arpost.co/2018/08/14/3d-tooth-atlas-9-the-virtual-reality-training-system-for-dentists-of-the-future/

Bamodu, O., & Xuming, Y. (2013). Virtual reality and virtual reality system components. In *Proceedings of the 2nd International Conference on Systems Engineering and Modeling (ICSEM-13)*. Paris, France: Atlantis Press.

Barad, J. (2019). *Reality training for robotics-assisted surgery*. Available at https://healthiar.com/osso-vr-creates-first-virtual-reality-training-for-robotics-assisted-surgery

Barsom, E. Z., Graafland, M., & Schijven, M. P. (2016). Systematic review on the effectiveness of augmented reality applications in medical training. *Surgical Endoscopy*, *30*, 4174. doi:10.100700464-016-4800-6

Bernhardt, S., Nicolau, S. A., Soler, L., & Doignon, C. (2017). *The status of augmented reality in laparoscopic surgery as of 2016*. Medical Image Analysis 37, 66–90. http://dx.doi.org/ 1361-8415/ doi:10.1016/j.media.2017.01.007

Bifulco, P., Narducci, F., Vertucci, R., Ambruosi, P., Cesarelli, M., & Romano, M. (2014). Telemedicine supported by Augmented Reality: An interactive guide for untrained people in performing an ECG test. *Biomedical Engineering Online, 13*(1), 153. doi:10.1186/1475-925X-13-153

Bogdan, C. M., Dinca, A. F., & Popovici, D. M. (2011). A brief survey of visuo-haptic simulators for dental procedures training. In *Proceedings of the 6th International Conference on Virtual Learning* (pp. 28-29).

CAE Healthcare announces first mixed reality ultrasound simulation solution with Microsoft HoloLens. CAE Healthcare Inc. Orlando, FL: CAE Healthcare; (2017). Available at https://www.cae.com/news-events/press-releases/cae-healthcare-announces-first-mixed-reality-ultrasound-simulation-solution/

Cardiff, E. (2018). *Response to local surgical challenges.* Available at https://eu.augmentedworldexpo.com/sessions/proximie-augmented-reality-providing-a-global-response-to-local-surgical-challenges/

Christian, S. (2018, March 22). *Using virtual, augmented, and mixed realities for medical training.* Available at http://designinteractive.net/using-virtual-augmented-mixed-realities-medical-training/

Craig, E., & Georgieva, M. (2017, Aug. 30). *VR and AR: Driving a revolution in medical education & patient care.* Available at https://er.educause.edu/.blogs/2017/8/vr-and-ar-driving-a-revolution-in-medical-education-and-patient-care

DeLeon, L. (2017, Oct. 26). *ForwardXP: XR Training for a F.A.S.T. Response.* Available at https://developer.qualcomm.com/blog/forwardxp-xr-training-fast-response

Diamandis, P. H. (2019). *5 breakthroughs coming soon in augmented and virtual reality.* Available at https://singularityhub.com/2019/05/10/5-breakthroughs-coming-soon-in-augmented-and-virtual-reality/

ETSI. (2018). *AR and VR at Glance.* Available at https://www.etsi.org/images/files/ETSITechnology-Leaflets/Augmented_VirtualReality.pdf

Greenwald, W. (2018). *The best VR headsets of 2018.* Available at https://in.pcmag.com/consumer-electronics/101251/the-best-vr-virtual-reality-headsets

Hamacher, A., Kim, S. J., Cho, S. T., Pardeshi, S., Lee, S. H., Eun, S. J., & Whangbo, T. K. (2016). Application of virtual, augmented, and mixed reality to urology. *International Neurourology Journal, 20*(3), 172.

Haubruck, P., Nickel, F., Ober, J., Walker, T., Bergdolt, C., Friedrich, M., ... Tanner, M. C. (2018). Evaluation of app-based serious gaming as a training method in teaching chest tube insertion to medical students: Randomized controlled trial. *Journal of Medical Internet Research, 20*(5), e195. doi:10.2196/jmir.9956

Herron, J. (2016). Augmented reality in medical education and training. *Journal of Electronic Resources in Medical Libraries, 13*(2), 51–55. doi:10.1080/15424065.2016.1175987

Hertz, A. M., George, E. I., Vaccaro, C. M., & Brand, T. C. (2018). Head-to-head comparison of three virtual-reality robotic surgery simulators. JSLS. *Journal of the Society of Laparoendoscopic Surgeons, 22*(1). doi:10.4293/JSLS.2017.00081

Hlova, M. (2018). *What does it take to develop a VR solution in healthcare.* Digital Health. Available at https://www.mddionline.com/what-does-it-take-develop-vr-solution-healthcare

Hu, H. Z., Feng, X. B., Shao, Z. W., Xie, M., Xu, S., Wu, X. H., & Ye, Z. W. (2019). Application and Prospect of Mixed Reality Technology in Medical Field. *Current medical science, 39*(1), 1-6. https://doi.org/ doi:10.1007/s11596-019-1992-8

Huang, T. K., Yang, C. H., Hsieh, Y. H., Wang, J. C., & Hung, C. C. (2018). Augmented reality (AR) and virtual reality (VR) applied in dentistry. *The Kaohsiung Journal of Medical Sciences, 34*(4), 243–248.

Hunter, A. (2015). *Vergence-accommodation conflict is a bitch — here's how to design around it.* Available from vrinflux-dot-com/vergence-accommodation-conflict-is-a-bitch-here-s-how-to-design-around-it.

Jin, W., Birckhead, B., Perez, B., & Hoffe, S. (2017, December). *Augmented and virtual reality: Exploring a future role in radiation oncology education and training. applied radiation oncology.* Available at https://appliedradiationoncology.com/articles/augmented-and-virtual-reality-exploring-a-future-role-in-radiation-oncology-education-and-training

Kamarudin, M. F. B., & Zary, N. (2019, April). Augmented reality, virtual reality, and mixed reality in medical education: A comparative web of science scoping review. doi:10.20944/preprints201904.0323.v1

KhannaA. (2019). *EyeSim.* Available at https://www.eonreality.com/portfolio-items/eyesim- ophthalmology/

Khelemsky, R., Hill, B., & Buchbinder, D. (2017). Validation of a novel cognitive simulator for orbital floor reconstruction. *Journal of Oral and Maxillofacial Surgery, 75*(4), 775–785.

Khor, W. S., Baker, B., Amin, K., Chan, A., Patel, K., & Wong, J. (2016). Augmented and virtual reality in surgery—the digital surgical environment: Applications, limitations and legal pitfalls. *Annals of Translational Medicine, 4*(23), 454. doi:10.21037/atm.2016.12.23

Kim, Y., Kim, H., & Kim, Y. O. (2017). Virtual reality and augmented reality in plastic surgery: a review. *Arch Plast Surg. 44*(3), 179–187. Published online. doi:10.5999/aps.2017.44.3.179

Kosowatz, J. (2017, May 1). *Mixed reality replaces cadavers as teaching tool.* Available at https://aabme.asme.org/posts/mixed-reality-replace-cadavers-as-teaching-tool

Kyaw, B. M., Saxena, N., Posadzki, P., Vseteckova, J., Nikolaou, C. K., George, P. P., ... Car, L. T. (2019). Virtual reality for health professions education: Systematic review and meta-analysis by the Digital Health Education collaboration. *Journal of Medical Internet Research, 21*(1).

Lloyd., M., Watmough, S., & Bennett, N. (2018). Simulation-based training: applications in clinical pharmacy. *The Pharmaceuticals Journal-A royal pharmaceuticals society publication.*

Mitsuno, D., Ueda, K., Itamiya, T., Nuri, T., & Otsuki, Y. (2017). Intraoperative evaluation of body surface improvement by an augmented reality system that a clinician can modify. *Plastic and Reconstructive Surgery. Global Open, 5*(8). doi:10.1097/GOX.0000000000001432

Monsky, W. L., James, R., & Seslar, S. S. (2019). Virtual and augmented reality applications in medicine and surgery-the fantastic voyage is here. *Anatomy & Physiology, 9*(1), 313.

Noble, S. (2019, March 25). *The 10 best augmented reality smartglasses in 2019.* Available at https://www.aniwaa.com/best-of/vr-ar/best-augmented-reality-smartglasses/

Onkka, K. H. (2018). *Precision OS allows surgeons to practice before taking on real surgery.* Available at https://healthiar.com/precision-os-allows-surgeons-to-practice-before-taking-on-real-surgery

Orr, E. (2018). *Virtual reality as an effective medical tool.* Available at https://www.xr.health/virtual-reality-effective-medical-tool.html/

Ortiz, A. (2019). *Welcome to extended reality: Transforming how employees work and learn.* Available at https://www.ibm.com/blogs/insights-on-business/ibmix/welcome-to-extended-reality/

Pantelidis, P., Chorti, A., Papagiouvanni, I., Paparoidamis, G., Drosos, C., Panagiotakopoulos, T., . . . Sideris, M. (2017, Dec. 20). *Virtual and augmented reality in medical education, medical and surgical education - past, present and future,* IntechOpen, doi:. Available at https://www.intechopen.com/books/medical-and-surgical-education-past-present-and-future/virtual-and-augmented-reality-in-medical-education doi:10.5772/intechopen.71963

Perkins Coie LLP. (March 2019) *Industry insights into the future of immersive technology.* Perkins Coie LLP and the XR Association VOLUME 3.

Pfandlera, M., Lazarovici, M., Stefan, P., & Weigl, M. (2017). Virtual reality-based simulators for spine surgery: A systematic review. *The Spine Journal,* 1529–9430. doi:10.1016/j.spinee.2017.05.016

Qin, Z., Tai, Y., Xia, C., Peng, J., Huang, X., Chen, Z., ... Shi, J. (2019). Towards virtual VATS, face, and construct evaluation for peg transfer training of Box, VR, AR, and MR trainer. *Journal of Healthcare Engineering, 2019.* doi:10.1155/2019/6813719

Qualcomm. (2017). *Augmented and virtual reality: The first wave of 5G killer apps.* ©2017 ABI Research. Available at https://www.qualcomm.com/media/documents/files/augmented-and-virtual-reality-the-first-wave-of-5g-killer-apps.pdf

Roy, E., Bakr, M. M., & George, R. (2017). The need for virtual reality simulators in dental education: A review. *The Saudi Dental Journal, 29*(2), 41–47. Published online March 6, 2017. doi:10.1016/j.sdentj.2017.02.001

Sachs, G. (2016). *Virtual reality and augment reality: Understanding the race for next computing platform.* The Goldman Sachs Group, Inc. Available at https://www.goldmansachs.com/insights/pages/technology-driving-innovation-folder/virtual-and-augmented-reality/report.pdf

Sanchez, J. (n.d.). *Augmented reality in healthcare.* Available at https://www.plugandplaytechcenter.com/resources/augmented-reality-healthcare/

Schofield, G., Beale, G., Beale, N., Fell, M., Hadley, D., Hook, J., . . . Thresh, L. (2018, June). Viking VR: Designing a virtual reality experience for a museum. In Proceedings of the 2018 Designing Interactive Systems Conference (pp. 805-815). ACM. https://doi.org/10.1145/3196709.3196714

Seam, A. (2019). *AT&T unlocks the power of edge computing: delivering interactive VR over 5G.* Available at https://about.att.com/innovationblog/2019/02/edge_computing_vr.html

Shah, N. (2019). *The next big thing: Integrating AI into augmented and virtual reality.* Available at https://www.cygnet-infotech.com/blog/integrating-ai-into-augmented-and-virtual-reality

Short, M., & Samar, S. (2017). *Transforming healthcare and saving lives with extended reality (XR).* Available at https://www.accenture.com/us-en/blogs/blogs-extended-reality-for-enterprise-health-care

Sirilak, S., & Muneesawang, P. (2018). *A new procedure for advancing telemedicine using the HoloLens.* IEEE; doi:10.1109/ACCESS.2018.2875558

Smith, T., Nelson, J., & Maul, R. (2018). *Digital reality in life sciences and health care.* Available at https://www2.deloitte.com/content/dam/Deloitte/us/Documents/life-sciences-health-care/us-lshc-tech-trends-digital-reality.pdf

Smithsonian. (2015). *Smithsonian brings historic specimens to life in free "skin and bones" mobile app.* Available at https://www.si.edu/newsdesk/releases/smithsonian-brings-historic-specimens-life-free-skin-and-bones-mobile-app

Solutions, M. (2017, Oct. 26). *Virtual reality and augmented reality in healthcare.* Available at http://moisaka.com/virtual-reality/

Tagaytayan, R., Kelemen, A., & Sik-Lanyi, C. (2018). Augmented reality in neurosurgery. *Archives of Medical Science, 14*(3), 572–578.

The first hybrid neurosurgical simulator based on physical and augmented reality. (n.d.). Available at https://upsim.upsurgeon.com/discover/the-first-hybrid-neurosurgical-simulator-based-on-physical-and-augmented-reality-.kl

The ultimate guide to understanding augmented reality (AR) technology. (n.d). ©RealityTechnologies.com Diversified Internet Holdings LLC. Available at https://www.realitytechnologies.com/augmented-reality/

Virtual Health Clinic. (n.d.). Society of american gastrointestinal and endoscopic surgeons (Sage). Available at https://www.sages.org/virtual-hernia-clinic/

Wang, S., Parsons, M., Stone-McLean, J., Rogers, P., Boyd, S., Hoover, K., ... Smith, A. (2017). Augmented reality as a telemedicine platform for remote procedural training. *Sensors (Basel), 17*(10), 2294. doi:10.339017102294

Weiner, Y. (2018). *39 ways AR can change the world in the next five years.* Available at https://medium.com/thrive-global/39-ways-ar-can-change-the-world-in-the-next-five-years-a7736f8bfaa5

Wright, T., de Ribaupierre, S., & Eagleson, R. (2017). Design and evaluation of an augmented reality simulator using leap motion. *Healthcare Technology Letters, 4*(5), 210–215. doi:10.1049/htl.2017.0070

Zweifach, S. M., & Triola, M. M. (2019). Extended reality in medical education: Driving adoption through provider-centered design. *Digital Biomarkers, 3*(1), 14–21. doi:10.1159/000498923

ADDITIONAL READING

Chen, L., Thomas W Day., Wen Tang., & Nigel W. John. (2017).*"Recent Developments and Future Challenges in Medical Mixed Reality"* IEEE International Symposium on Mixed and Augmented Reality (ISMAR). DOI: 10.1109/ISMAR.2017.29

Gavaghan, K. A., Peterhans, M., Oliveira-Santos, T., & Weber, S. (2011). A portable image overlay projection device for computer-aided open liver surgery. *IEEE Transactions on Biomedical Engineering*, *58*, 1855–1864.

Heather, A. Tudor Chinnah., & Vikram Devara. (2019). *"The Use of Virtual and Augmented Reality in Anatomy Teaching"*. MedEdPublish. DOI: Available from: https://www.mededpublish.org/manuscripts/2195 doi:10.15694/mep.2019.000077.1

Krigsman, M. (2018). *"This medical pioneer trains digital doctors with AR and VR"*. Beyond IT Failure. Available from: https://www.zdnet.com/article/virtual-reality-medical-pioneer-trains-digital-doctors/

Maddox, T. (2018). *"Extending Reality to the Operating Room"*. HEALTH Tech, Tech Trends, VR Tech. Available from: https://techtrends.tech/tech-trends/xr-medical-visualization-tools-reduce-cognitive-load-and-enhance-learning/

Sarah, M. Zweifach & Marc M. Triola. (2019). *"Extended Reality in Medical Education: Driving Adoption through Provider-Centered Design"*. Digit Biomark 2019; 3:14–21, DOI: , © 2019 The Author(s). Published by S. Karger AG, Basel. www.karger.com/dib doi:10.1159/000498923

P. Vávra., J. Roman., P. Zonča., P. Ihnát., M. Němec., J. Kumar., N. Habib., & A. El-Gendi. (2017). *"Recent Development of Augmented Reality in Surgery: A Review"* Hindawi. Journal of Healthcare Engineering Volume 2017, Article ID 4574172, 9 pages https://doi.org/ doi:10.1155/2017/4574172

Workman, S. (2018). *"Mixed Reality: A Revolutionary Breakthrough in Teaching and Learning"*. EDUCASE. Available from: https://er.educause.edu/articles/2018/7/mixed-reality-a-revolutionary-breakthrough-in-teaching-and-learning

KEY TERMS AND DEFINITIONS

Augmented Reality (AR): It is a technology that blends the user's view of real world with digital information on top of it, to provide the user an enhanced version of reality.

Extended Reality (XR): It refers to a continuum, which combines all real and virtual world environments. It encompasses virtual, augmented and mixed reality technologies to provide users a better immersive experience.

Haptics: It refers to the technology that uses tactile (touch) sensation to interact with the computer applications in order to improve user experience.

Head Mounted Display (HMD): It is a computer display system that is mounted on a helmet or a set of goggles.

Immersive Technology: It refers to technology that enables users to interact with simulated environments and objects, blurring the line between the real world and the digital world. It covers a range of technologies such as AR, VR, MR.

Marker Based Augmented Reality: It is a term used to represent an AR application that needs prior knowledge of a user's environment to identify/ locate part of real world that needs to be augmented. This is achieved by placing a marker in the real world where the digital image must overlay.

Markerless Augmented Reality: It is a term used to represent an AR application that does not need prior knowledge of a user's environment to identify/ locate part of real world that needs to be augmented and hold it to a fixed point in space. it is also known as location-based AR. It functions using such technologies as GPS, accelerometer, digital compass and SLAM (simultaneous localization and mapping technology).

Mixed Reality (MR): It brings together real and digital environments that co-exist and interact with each other to produce new environment which allows user to immerse in the world around while interacting with the virtual world.

Virtual Reality (VR): It is a technology that creates a simulated environment that can be similar or completely different from the user's environment. The VR headset gives the user a fully immersive visual experience.

This research was previously published in Virtual and Augmented Reality in Education, Art, and Museums; pages 23-46, copyright year 2020 by Engineering Science Reference (an imprint of IGI Global).

Section 2
Avatars, Virtual Identities, and Virtual Communities

Chapter 17
Pioneering in the Virtual World Frontier

Cynthia Calongne

https://orcid.org/0000-0002-0774-0461

Colorado Technical University, USA

ABSTRACT

Immersion in virtual worlds presented opportunities for simulating the qualities valued in face-to-face classes with the flexibility afforded by online learning. Immersive learning engaged educators, curriculum designers, campuses, conferences, and educational community groups to devise new ways to collaborate and engage learners. Dreaming of opportunities that were not possible in the online classroom, educators saw the potential of building communities in virtual worlds. They gathered to share their and to employ novel approaches to address educational challenges. This chapter explores the phenomenon of selfhood and society integral to the development of a vibrant educational community. At the heart of virtual world education is an ecosystem of institutions, groups, and conferences comprised of the early adopters and pioneers who stimulated their imagination and pooled their resources to encourage and strengthen the community and cast their eye to the future.

INTRODUCTION

With the decline of learner motivation and engagement in the study of science, technology, engineering, and math (STEM), education sought to find novel ways to engage and inspire interest in STEM disciplines. Increases in software capability, social virtual worlds, and high speed internet access made it possible to offer classes set in virtual environments where students studied within 3D spaces.

Similar to any historical record, identifying the beginning of virtual world education is a challenge. Perspectives vary depending on the role, technology used, and the level of immersion experienced during online classes. The narrative offered here is internal and employs an ethnographic lens to report the events and to share how it felt to experience the early discoveries in 3D situated learning.

DOI: 10.4018/978-1-6684-7597-3.ch017

From the fictional roots found in Neal Stephenson's (1993) book Snow Crash, the Metaverse emerged as the 3D Web, a collection of virtual worlds comprised of grids, which are interconnected regions that reside on servers, often within virtual machines (VMs) to optimize their resources and processing requirements. Within the Metaverse resides the technologies that make the worlds come alive, including commercial virtual world servers, and a wealth of software for 3D design, animation design, scripting languages, compilers, interpreters, and libraries, physics engines that simulate the real world behavior, and the people, represented by avatars. The avatars, as educators, came into these worlds, encouraged by institutions and inspired by early adopters and their successes.

What were the forces that drew educational institutions to issue a call to action that stimulated attention from over 150 countries? Highlights from the early work explore how the culture evolved and the people within them formed into communities and support networks. While thousands of groups exist, the ethnographic lens features the major events and group work and shares insights into their early goals, challenges, and discoveries. The summary reflects on the future, and the ongoing work in developing programs that first assess the character strengths that define selfhood and society within a virtual community.

BACKGROUND

The River City project (Dede, 2003) fueled the imagination of educators with a historical multiuser virtual environment (MUVE) created for middle grade science students. Designed within a commercial virtual world called Active Worlds®, the science-oriented learning environment was funded by National Science Foundation grants led by Harvard's Chris Dede (2003) in collaboration with the Virtual Environments Lab at George Mason University, the Smithsonian's National Museum of American history, and research partner Thoughtful Technologies, Inc.

The goal was to help learners discover a love of science. The curriculum mapped to established assessment methods and gave educators tools for studying the *cognitive audit trails*, which served as both a metaphor and a method of assessing when learners were ready for the next level. River City represented the early promise of virtual world education and employed a team-based approach to using scientific methods to analyze and address serious problems while increasing interest and a desire to study science.

The River City simulation featured traveling back in time to address 19th century problems and in particular, three diseases using 21st century tactics. It wove historical, social and geographical content amid the threat of diseases that stemmed from airborne, water-borne, and insect-based sources within the immersive landscape. Harvard University's Graduate School of Education coordinated the design, with pilot tests conducted with Boston public schools and the implementation of the immersive MUVE (Dede & Ketelhut, 2003). The project reflected on scalability issues and how to offer the environment to schools throughout North America. Over 100 teachers and 5,000 students studied in River City across twelve states during the first two years. The River City project inspired the educational community and served as a road map for what might be possible for teaching other subjects. Active Worlds was a popular tool with educators, but a variety of forces, including financial and ownership changes led educators to seek other opportunities.

There®, a virtual landscape that encouraged the public to join the developers' community, encouraged educational use during their beta test that led to a small, but devoted group of educators. The strengths included access to diverse content and technological affordances that supported safe use (dressing rooms appeared when changing the avatar's appearance, classroom animations, vehicle physics, and an education special interest group), but also implemented a content creation and submission system that required review board approval to ensure that the content met community standards, after which, the creator pre-paid for a volume of copies. Mapping the virtual community's goals with the curriculum and school district requirements was for some educators, a challenge.

Philip Rosedale, founder and former CEO at Linden Research (known as Linden Lab), adapted the software tool that they used for haptic interface design and launched it as LindenWorld, and the next year renamed it to Second Life® with 16 regions (Second Life History, 2017, December 29). The sparse user population, known as residents, grew slowly through the first few years.

Major growth in the educational use of Second Life occurred when the New Media Consortium with over 225 universities, schools, and museums invited its members and conference attendees to join their NMC Virtual Worlds group in Second Life.

A CALL TO ACTION

The New Media Consortium (NMC, 2005) and Learning Times, a Web conferencing partner, hosted a conference on educational gaming and invited the attendees to meet in Second Life (SL). The conference attendees were a blend of NMC members, EDUCAUSE members and educational professionals with an interest in online learning, including members of the TCC Worldwide Online Conference. Learning Times provided the hosting service for both the NMC and TCC conferences, and the feeling of community and openness flourished under the TCC Hawai'i Ohana, a Hawaiian word for family, aptly characterizing the TCC close knit community.

NMC's leadership under CEO Larry Johnson and Lev Gonick, former NMC Board Chair and NMC Campus Project partner, envisioned the potential of the virtual landscape as a place for blending the liberal arts and education, for stimulating Renaissance thinking through playful exhibits, gardens, and as a landscape for learning and creativity. The first taste of the promise of this imaginative playground intrigued the attendees, yet frustrated some as the early software tools used to experience the world demanded a steep learning curve and sufficient bandwidth. Despite the initial challenges, the New Media Consortium (NMC, 2006) worked with the creative genius of the Electric Sheep Company to design and launch their virtual NMC Campus (Levine, 2008) for meetings and educators events as seen in Figure 1. The inaugural event attracted campus leaders from their 200 campuses, museums and libraries, who in turn started work on developing an archipelago of educational regions, representing the technology champions from each member institution to realize the NMC's mission of sparking creativity and innovation.

Bryan Alexander (2006), a researcher at the NMC, senior fellow and futurist known for hosting a playful think tank for forecasting predictions called NITLE, the exploration found its roots in shared objects. Engeström (2005, April 13), Alexander (2006), and Da Silva (2015, February 17) noted that what brings people to participate in a social network or an online community is the focus on a shared object that frames the experience, such as photos and images on a photo sharing service. In virtual learning, the shared object serves as a catalyst for connecting social spaces, virtual content, curriculum, and the feeling of presence for the residents within them. Shared objects provide a raison d'etre for community development and participation in virtual spaces. Educational content extends beyond curriculum, rubrics, and 3D designs to feature a sense of place (Bachelard, 1964) that meets certain behavioral expectations and organized by the perceptions of architecture and space (Tuan, 1977). Bachelard noted how objects serve a purpose and fit within their environment while Tuan reflected on the historical view of how communities organize their living spaces within communities, their work environments, and extend that world view from within the community and out to characterize the world around them.

Figure 1. Educators at the NMC Campus

Within these virtual spaces, the terrain, setting, animations, and objects within it presented an environment for learning and are detailed instantiations of the unifying shared objects that define the community's goals. For some educators, learning spaces resembled the physical campus and the familiar look and feel of the classroom. Others envisioned dramatically different learning spaces designed to stimulate the mind and evaluate novel learning techniques.

Amidst the reflections on how to nurture virtual education, external forces were at work that strengthened the call to action and opened the flood gates for educators worldwide.

Community Development

Figure 2 illustrates some of the institutions, communities, conferences, technology, and character strengths (Peterson & Seligman, 2004) that encouraged the virtual pioneers to persevere. The mind map highlights the major groups and events from ten years in virtual world education and the three character strengths most evident in them. The selection of a mind map was intentional as it is order independent, yet suggests the relationships between the groups.

Figure 2. Virtual world communities and conferences

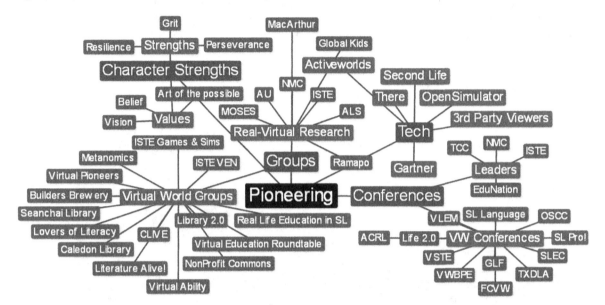

Gartner's Prediction Opens the Floodgates

Gartner Research made a bold pronouncement that generated a flurry of activity and made skeptics wonder if it would be a self-fulfilling prophecy. Long respected for their skillful forecasts on the evolution and maturation of novel technologies, Gartner (2007) made a bold prediction: "By the end of 2011, 80 percent of active Internet users (and Fortune 500 enterprises) will have a "second life", but not necessarily in Second Life, according to Gartner, Inc."

Gartner spoke of collaborative communities and transaction-based commercial opportunities as well as the five laws for business use in virtual worlds. Of interest to educators was the quest for identity and development of selfhood in virtual spaces as represented by the avatar, and to be relevant and add value. Gartner stated the need for cultural development and understanding the (as yet) unwritten rules for behavior, critical for enterprise users and to protect their corporate reputations, equally important for educators and for creating safe learning environments. With regard to relevance, rethinking online education required exploring a shift from asynchronous to synchronous class activities provided a forum for teamwork, for meeting minds and for collaboration.

The fourth law focused on branding and recognizing the threats and affordances within a virtual world. Misconduct and mischievous disruptions were considerations that made educational leaders wonder if a safe learning environment was possible. The fifth law noted the issues with avatar scalability and environment stability as well as the desire to merge virtual worlds and their assets while preserving the rights of content creators while managing the transfer of assets between avatars. These rules stimulated great discussion among the virtual education community.

To understand the power of this prediction, consider for a moment how the Hype Cycle works. The Gartner Hype Cycle reports the inception and evolution of an emerging technology based on practitioner and scholarly interest and use and movement along the Hype Cycle depends on news from the media. The media attention speculates about the technology and suggests the promise of success, yet for the technology to evolve, it needs a history of use, promising test results, and a period of continuous refinement, and a sufficient number of features for the technology to mature into a productive and successful solution.

Gartner tracks the progress of the innovative idea as it moves from the initial Technology Trigger and charts the results on the Gartner Hype Cycle. They track the rise of a technology through the Peak of Inflated Expectations, which by its title suggests that the media promises more than the technology can deliver. After considerable use and criticism from the early adopters and users who try it, only to discover that it does not meet their expectations, Gartner tracks the criticism and shows how it travels down from the Peak to the Trough of Disillusionment, where interest in it declines until the champions of the technology identify successful applications, test their merits and report the results. Some technologies become obsolete before they mature, while others compete with other technological solutions, such as the decline of the Sony Betamax in favor of VHS as an early video recording medium.

The time it takes to move from disillusionment to enlightenment can be slow, and depends on numerous factors, including use cases and a proven record of use, measurement, and success reports followed by papers and studies that study whether the benefits outweigh the risks. The technology moves through the Hype Cycle after achieving certain milestones. The next area in the Hype Cycle is called the Slope of Enlightenment. It offers renewed interest, growth in media attention and the promise of success. It generates keen interest in the technology, which builds momentum and further discoveries as the technology evolves and matures. With growth through continued use, the technology completes the cycle in the Plateau of Productivity, and benefits from widespread acceptance until a new technology trigger challenges it.

When Gartner issued this news release, it magnified virtual world interest among educators and early adopters. The next section reflects on the pioneering efforts and how the communities formed and shared their discoveries.

VIRTUAL WORLD SYMPOSIA AND CONFERENCES

The MacArthur Foundation Digital Media event (Boyd, 2006; NMC, 2006) brought the community together to reflect on the next five years in digital media design and on the current work across different groups. One of the recipients of the MacArthur grants featured Global Kids, whose heart wrenching exhibit on the topic of Child Trafficking awareness and activism was modeled in the virtual world as a maze on the SL Teen Grid. Other attendees included Joyce Bettencourt and Jeroen Frans of the Vesuvius Group, LLC, who also support the Nonprofit Commons, Avacon and the OpenSimulator Community Conference. Peggy Sheehy of the Ramapo project for Suffern Middle School inspired educators to contribute to the project's content. Terry Beaubois of Montana State encouraged collaboration and thoughts on architecture, while Howard Rheingold gave the keynote address on his first day in a virtual world. Boyd (2006) blogged the event and Kanter (2006) shared insights on what it was like to attend a blended reality event in person and online in a virtual world. From the live meeting, Katie Salen and Eric Zimmerman sat with the MacArthur briefing and answered questions from 65 virtual attendees on game development in education during the blended reality question and answer session (Calongne & Hiles, 2007; Kanter, 2006; Levine, 2008).

Technical conferences in these early days included Dr. Dobb's Journal's event, Life 2.0 with more than 1,000 software developers attending either logged in as an avatar in the virtual world or watching the event from a streaming website while sitting in a physical conference room in Silicon Valley. The use of a Chat Bridge allowed virtual and physical conference attendees to ask questions and offer observations during the sessions, and the topics ranged from software engineering issues to security and scalability concerns (AdvertisingAge, 2007, September 10). At one event, the author sat next to an avatar who at the physical conference was sitting next to Bill Gates. Sharing ideas across boundaries, technologies and without regard for ones circle of influence is part of the magic of virtual world events.

EduNation with their emphasis on Language Learning evolved from the early Yahoo Group called Webheads to host meetings and community events as well as the annual SL Languages conference and the Virtual Roundtable. The EduNation region featured a beach-themed build, filled with music videos and conversation nooks to inspire imaginative and relaxing spaces for teaching English as a second language and promote language learning.

The English Village by pioneer Fire Centaur featured language learning games, roleplay and later, the use of Holodecks as conversation nooks. He invited the educational community to participate in their events over the Real Life Education in Second Life group.

Libraries in Second Life

The Community Virtual Library bridges virtual worlds and technologies to offer library services and a virtual world database for education and research use (Community Virtual Library, 2019). For K-12 as well as higher education, the Illinois' Alliance Library System and support from an educational grant led to the design of Info Island, extended into additional regions, including in creating a space for librarians and educators to explore and obtain technology resources on Info Island, and later, HealthInfo Island and additional regions, including the Eduisland regions. The various 3D designs blended the creative efforts of educators and talented designers, including Aaron Griffiths from the Kiwi Educators' group, who wove a picnic rug with animations from the author's designs into a space that appeared on demand, a technology used in later game simulations. The scene appeared when visitors drew near for them to enjoy and disappeared when they left.

The community of librarians from around the world also featured prominently in several conferences, including the Virtual World Library, Education and Museum (VLEM) conference and the Association of College Research Librarians (ACRL) conferences.

The NMC held two virtual world conferences in addition to their summer conference for several years and the topics ranged from digital media and learning or the symposium for the future. After the inaugural campus event in June 2006 (Levine, 2008), they held a fall southwest regional conference in San Antonio and John Lester, known as Pathfinder Linden, gave the keynote address. The presentations ranged from Ruben Puentedura's (2006) session on the Third Place, a social place where everyone knows your name which is vital to life balance and informal learning, to mirror Tuan's (1977), Bachelard's (1964) and Maslow's thoughts (McLeod, 2016; Maslow, 1943) on the needs within the First Place (home) and Second Place (work) as defined and coined by Ray Oldenburg (2002).

Why did these topics matter? The underlying notion of virtual spaces rests in how they sustain individual and social needs. Once selfhood and identity within a virtual world is grounded with a sense of community (Oldenburg, 2002), it is easier to design, evaluate, revise and implement educational programs that blend the playful and social qualities of 3D spaces with curriculum and assessment.

Best Practices in Education and the VWBPE

In 2007, the first Best Practices in Education in Second Life, hosted by Chris Collins (Fleep Tuque) and Beth Ritter-Guth (Desideria Stockton) brought educators together to share their experiences and designs. The BPE in SL conference set the tone for later educational conferences, including the Education Support Faire, and the annual Virtual Worlds Best Practices in Education (VWBPE), hosted by Rockcliffe University under the guidance of Kevin Feenan. In 2009, the SL Education Support Faire under John Lester (Pathfinder) featured 3,785 unique visitors from 93 countries with 50 poster displays and 50 presentations over a five day period (Calongne, 2009).

VWBPE spans several days and supports attendees from up to 150 countries who are passionate about learning. The sessions extend beyond Second Life to embrace other MUVEs, including Unity3D, Blizzard's World of Warcraft®, and Minecraft®. The conference features many sessions, games, social events, tours, and demonstrations of projects and otherworldly educational content.

Virtual Ability and the Nonprofit Commons

Selfhood focuses on how a person's identity emerges and the shared human experience. Virtual worlds attract users from all walks of life and capabilities, and few regions are more welcoming than Virtual Ability (2019a). Gentle Heron at Virtual Ability offers support, acceptance and a warm welcome for all users, and provides particular support and sessions for users who may not be able to walk, hear, or see in the physical world. Virtual world tools are complex to use, yet offer an amazing experience for users. To be able to fly, to run, and to dance when movement is no longer an option is a grand experience. The video called Better Life by Rob Wright (2006), who is well known as SL music and sound pioneer Robbie Dingo, illustrates the opportunity for escapism and transcending physical boundaries in a virtual world.

Virtual Ability hosted conferences on the International Disability Rights Affirmation Conference (IDRAC) (Virtual Ability, 2019b), the Mental Health Symposia (Virtual Ability, 2019c), and strengthen the mentorship and educational programs held weekly at the Nonprofit Commons (2007), a Second Life social good community of the global nonprofit organizations that meets on Friday mornings. Over 150 nonprofit and social good agencies support the Nonprofit Commons in Second Life.

The Military Archipelago

An archipelago of military regions connected The Air University and Squadron Officer College, two centers of learning for the U.S. Air Force, the U.S. Army's Simulation and Training Technology Center with the Team Orlando group, the U.S. Navy, and quite possibly, the U.S. Marines, although they were a lot quieter. Some of these regions were open to the public while others were private.

After publishing an EDUCAUSE Review article in their back-to-school edition on teaching in virtual worlds (Calongne, 2008), The Air University (AU) initiated a collaborative effort that loosely coupled researchers, educators and military enthusiasts across several projects and two events: the Global Learning Forum and bi-weekly lunch and learn meetings. These events welcomed the community and military residents in a wonderfully connectivist fashion, crossing over boundaries and encouraging the use of innovative strategies. The GLF speaker sessions held 2-4 times a year featured Jeremy Bailenson from the Stanford Virtual Human Interaction Lab GLF, the Dean of the Vanderbilt Medical School, Art Langer from Columbia University and Nancy Sherman from Georgetown University, who spoke on moral injury.

From the collaboration came experiments using a custom-designed game simulation kit by Andrew Stricker and Michael McCrocklin called The Hostage Rescue Game: Operation Anaconda with playtesting by community educators and students from Colorado Technical University. Linda Hamons featured the game in her study of shared leadership.

The Mars Expedition Strategy Challenge used a challenge-based method for analyzing a complex problem while flying the learner to Mars. Participants began on a rocket and flew up to the Huffman Prairie Red Lion Deep Space Explorer where they stepped into the role of a science officer en route to Mars. On board, they toured four science stations, reviewed videos, completed a survey and reflected on where the U.S. Congress should direct its budget for the future of the U.S. space program.

The team's innovative design received recognition and the Grand Prize in the first Federal Virtual World Challenge at Defense GameTech. The simulation of a journey to Mars mirrored the self-cleaning behavior and efficiency of a Holodeck from Star Trek (Roddenberry et al., 2007) as it rendered the spacecraft and mining colony when the users drew near and deleted them when they left. They won the $25,000 Grand Prize in the competition. The simulation also rendered space phenomena (a meteor shower, a comet, and a satellite) and different versions of a mining colony on Mars as well as a self-assessment quiz in the form of a trivia game that reminded the participants of the key points from the Mars Expedition Challenge.

One of the advantages of The Air University simulations and games are how the designs focus on identifying the character strengths of the participants and how to leverage them and strengthen other characteristics (Peterson & Seligman, 2004). Strengths-based education reflects on challenging situations and how to call upon the inner strengths in times of crisis and draw upon them to make good decisions. They also center on self-assessment and continuous refinement in addition to formal assessment.

The U.S. Army Simulation and Training Technology Center (STTC) hosted a project called the Military OpenSimulator Enterprise Strategy (MOSES). While the project resided outside of Second Life, two STTC regions offered a site for blended reality conference sessions between the attendees at Defense GameTech in Orlando and the virtual world attendees. The MOSES project designed a custom implementation of the OpenSimulator software and integrated it in a solution called MOSES in a box that simplified the installation and use of custom virtual worlds at educational sites. Volunteers from the MOSES project hosted the Federal Consortium of Virtual Worlds (FCVW) conference, supporting the shift from a physical conference with virtual events to a fully virtual conference in 2015.

During their weekly meetings and in-world activities, the MOSES group researched avatar scalability, open source virtual world stability, physics engine alternatives, avatar realism, and photogrammetry. The MOSES community featured 200 researchers, educators, military personnel, contractors, game designers, businesses, students, and artists collaborating for eight years to advance the state of research in avatar realism, avatar scalability, realism in training, and education in a virtual world. The culture, protocol, and even the avatar names reflect real world practices, and the conference featured tracks in security, modeling and simulation, metacognition and education and training.

One of the differences between MOSES and the AU Metaverse is the perception of education and the community needs. AU focuses on critical thinking, while an important project in MOSES focuses on providing environments and support for military training and familiarization exercises set in realistic landscapes under the leadership of Douglas Maxwell from the STTC. MOSES Community Manager Barbara Truman works closely with the University of Central Florida, while Maxwell coordinates the efforts of simulation experts in the design of a resource fork to the OpenSim software that integrates with Halcyon in its server software and on the development of a custom browser-based viewer.

OpenSimulator Community Conference

Since 2013, the annual OpenSimulator Community Conference bridges open source enthusiasts with the core developers, third party viewer developers, educators, business users, Hypergrid Business, and artists, scripters, musicians, videographers, nonprofits, and entertainers. The conference celebrated the current state of the Metaverse and recommendations for future work. Guest speakers from past conferences featured the CEO from High Fidelity, Steve LaValle, who has two patents for the Oculus Rift, and IBM Fellow Grady Booch, famous for his work on the Unified Modeling Language (UML).

What was amazing was the stable performance of the simulators during the conference, which was designed to support 350-400 users across four main stage regions. Past conferences featured an entire grid for shopping and avatar customization, a sandbox, four expo regions with exhibits and the speaker booths, and four landing points for load distribution and balance.

Virtual reality and its manifestation in virtual worlds changed dramatically over the past 15 years. Rosedale (2015, January 13) in his keynote address from High Fidelity noted the future directions for virtual reality research, including natural gestures, facial expressions, and other techniques designed to strengthen the interaction between avatars.

Table 1. A sample of educational institutions, groups, conferences and meetings

Institution	Mission and Groups	Conferences and Meetings
ISTE	K-12 & Higher Education, ISTE VEN, ISTE Games & Simulations Network, Virtual Pioneers, VSTE affiliate	ISTE annual conference, ISTE NECC, VSTE, Weekly Meetings
EDUCAUSE with the New Media Consortium	Sparking Creativity & Innovation in Higher Education, K-12, Museums, NMC Virtual Worlds Group, NMC Horizon Report with EDUCAUSE eLearning Initiative (ELI)	NMC Educational Gaming, Digital Media & Learning, Symposium for the Future, SL Pro! (with Linden Lab)
Libraries in Second Life	ALS, ACRL Virtual Worlds Interest Group, Seanchai Library, Library 2.0, Caledon Library, Lovers of Literacy, CVL	VLEM, The Future is Now, ALA Annual Conference, SLymposium, Virtual Confs.
EduNation	Language Learning, English as a Second Language, English as a Foreign Language	SL Languages, Virtual Round Table
OpenSimulator	Open source virtual world software development	OpenSimulator Community Conference
Virtual Ability	Research projects, community dances, support for persons with disabilities	MHS, Int'l Disability Rights Affirmation Conference
The Air University	US Air Force education, StudioX, game & simulation design, character strengths, big data analytics	Global Learning Forum, AU Metaverse Lunch & Learn
MOSES	US Army & civilian research, avatar scalability, photogrammetry, realism, military education	Federal Consortium of Virtual Worlds, Defense GameTech (Team Orlando)
State Groups in VWs	Texas, Oregon, North Carolina	TXDLA, CLIVE, SLEC
Dr Dobb's Journal, Sun, IBM	1,000 Software Developers studying development in a virtual world conference	Life 2.0
Virtual Education Roundtable	Virtual Education Roundtable	Weekly educator meetings
Metanomics	Economics in the Metaverse	Weekly Shows & Meetings
Nonprofit Commons	Nonprofits & educators meeting since 2006	Weekly speakers
Rockcliffe University	Virtual Education, K-12, Higher Education	VWBPE
Science Circle	Science archipelago, Science Fridays	Weekly Speakers
Builder's Brewery	Virtual world education in design	Daily classes and events

With over 400 universities and thousands of educators, only highlights appear in this description. Other notable mentions include the Nanotechnology Lab, host of the National Physical Laboratory's launch of nanotechnology innovations during their physics events in Second Life and the Science Circle (2019), an 11-year-old community of scientists and STEM educators from around the world.

See Table 1 for a list of institutions, groups, educational conferences and events.

Notably absent from the list are the early work by 400 universities, including Iowa State University, Boise State University, Ball State University, University of California at San Diego, Princeton University, Stanford University, Wright State University.

Interest in Virtual Worlds and Education

It is hard to characterize all of the major influences on virtual learning due to amount of research and diverse work in the area, but one indicator was the rise in maturity noted on the Gartner (2016) Hype Cycle. The growth in virtual world environments and their capabilities rose steadily. Over 200 virtual world technologies attracted educators due to the need for K-12 friendly environments Calongne, 2009). The most popular worlds offered great content, free student accounts, and a large, diverse community with over 40 daily classes and community events. The various forms of virtual worlds shared elements in common, such as the concept of presence and a unique name for residents. Most important was the concept of an avatar, which served as a representation of self and how other residents observed and interacted with other residents. The avatar modeled real world capabilities and then extended them with flying, elaborately scripted movements, and with the abilities that transcend what is possible in everyday life.

Characteristics in common between virtual worlds include the ability for the avatar to move, animate, gesture and communicate with other avatars within the shared space. Truman's (2013) research elaborated on the importance of these behaviors. What motivates people to feel vested in a virtual community through their group participation and shared presence? She explored two concepts that further define the experience: virtual physioception as an awareness of self, identity and selfhood and virtual-intersubjective presencing which grows from a shared awareness of others that extends out from the individual experience of identity development to shape the avatar's selfhood and emergence as a member of a society. These concepts elaborated on the work of Otto Scharmer (2000) at MIT's Presencing Institute and extended them beyond the interactions between people and the virtual environment.

Early Campus Designs

What did educators do when faced with a barren virtual landscape? They reflected on different strategies for encouraging familiarity, recognition, and preserving the values that matter with the search for motivational alternatives and novel approaches to online education. They examined opportunities to break out of the real-world mold and to reflect on the art of the possible. At a high level of abstraction and not all-inclusive by any means, the early work in the design of virtual learning spaces fell into two categories: 1) emulating the campus to encourage familiarity and recognition for online, hybrid and campus students, often coupled with campus decorum and behavior; and 2) re-imagining the look and feel of the virtual campus as a place to evaluate new strategies and methods.

The institutions that favored emulating the real world campus recognized that they needed support from their champions and to address the concerns of their critics. They saw the virtual world as an extension of the campus traditions and values. To support the classroom emulation model, educators sought out designers or developed their modeling skills to design virtual campuses that resembled the school's physical campus. For tools in class, some featured hand-raising animations consistent with the campus decorum and mirrored the values and classroom behavior best conducive to learning in the classroom designs. The second group reflected on the opportunities presented by the virtual landscape and the virtual reality simulator's potential. Some envisioned unusual, permanent settings or rotating exhibits and buildings for learning spaces, while others preferred an open palette or the use of interchangeable settings packaged as a hologram that appears and disappear upon request, similar to the Holodeck described by Gene Roddenberry and featured on the television series Star trek: The Next Generation (Roddenberry et al., 2007).

Educators fell into three main groups: 1) pioneers as risk takers; 2) settlers who evaluated adapting the real world methods and applying them within the new technology; and 3) the early adopters who reflected on a balanced approach, blending elements from both perspectives. All three of these tactics offered advantages for evaluating the art of the possible while managing risk. In the face of media hype and criticism (Gartner, 2007), each group tested their organizational boundaries and educational opportunities while helping to define social and cultural norms.

Whether the campus was a tribute to the real world environment or an imaginative permanent or interchangeable space, this described only the setting for learning. Educators faced enormous challenges with regard to mapping the curriculum, instructional methods, delivery styles, managing and evaluating student work, performing learning assessments, and reflecting on how to improve the process. The requirements for providing an environment suitable for learning ranged from content creation, delivery styles, ensuring quality instruction, planning for assessment, balancing public versus private access, managing the risks associated with virtual campus misconduct, and concerns over instructional quality as well as compliance with the Family Educational Rights and Privacy Act (FERPA) on the need for privacy and protection of student education records (U.S. Dept. of Ed., n.d.). FERPA compliance includes privacy in the classroom, an affordance that raised concerns over written and spoken communication in virtual world classes. The challenges seemed enormous for some campuses.

CHALLENGES AND STRENGTHS FOR PIONEERS

The cognitive and technological challenges disenfranchised talented educators who saw the appeal, but felt that virtual world technologies were not ideal for certain classrooms. Using the SL or Third Party Viewers required a steep learning curve due to the feature-rich interface. Educators struggled to design 3D tutorial simulations to support the training needed to orient novice learners and educators. The most significant challenge was not resident misconduct (called griefing), inappropriate content, or concerns over safe learning environments, but instead, a major disruption in the economic model for education (Mark, 2014). When Linden Lab announced the end of the educational discount, many schools and educational programs had few options for extending their educational technology budgets in the middle of a school year. A widespread panic, followed by an exodus either to open source virtual worlds or different technologies led to a disruption in the community (Mark, 2014; Young, 2010, October 14). When the furor stabilized, the community remained, but some of them could no longer afford to host educational regions in Second Life and instead, gave up their regions and either moved to Kitely or another open source world, left SL, or used the community and group areas as a social space for attending conferences and connecting with friends and colleagues.

While some wonder what might have happened without this economic pressure, on the positive side, it stimulated growth in open source virtual worlds and challenged educators to find new solutions. In contrast, some abandoned their previous work, noting that the world failed to support them and that the technological hurdles associated with hosting were too steep. Contracting with another service, like Kitely, offered an archipelago of regions devoted to education and like-minded community members.

The changes led to growth, but the timing of the disruption slowed the progress along the Gartner Hype Cycle until the renewed interest in 3D virtual reality (VR) wearable devices and 360 degree video gained media attention.

The Power of Script Creation: Autoscript

During the 2007 NMC Summer Conference, Hilary Mason asked conference attendees to test her design of an automated tool for writing custom scripts for Second Life called Autoscript (Mason, 2007). Hosted on a website, it supports nine main functions and asks 2-3 questions about when the script should execute and how it should behave. Users click three options and then the *Make My Script* button to see their custom script before selecting it, copying it, and pasting it into a new script in Second Life.

The Autoscript tool gave educators, students and virtual world residents the power of creation and taught some basic algorithmic procedures used in software design. Later versions featured the tool in several languages.

Virtual World Technologies

OpenSimulator (2016) was the open source alternative to the Second Life server software, designed by a talented team of volunteers. The content within an OpenSim grid looked similar to SL, but behaved differently. The Third Party Viewers (TPVs) used to access SL also worked in OpenSim with the Open-Sim TPV versions. Most TPVs supported Windows, Mac and Linux users.

Crista Lopes, one of the core developers and a founding member of the Women in Virtual Reality, saw an opportunity for strengthening the need to meet in different virtual worlds and to avoid logging into additional avatar accounts to visit different worlds. To provide greater mobility and connectedness, she introduced features into the OpenSimulator server software to permit users who enabled it on their servers to visit different worlds without needing an account on them. Moving between virtual worlds by entering the address and port number of the destination grid in the world map she called the Hypergrid.

The Hypergrid capability brought the community closer together and the Hypergrid Safari conducted tours of three Hypergrid destinations each week (Lester, 2014; Ember, 2011).

In Pursuit of Selfhood: The Sweet Spot

Think back to that first attempt at riding a bicycle. Teetering, trying to find a sense of balance, the rider struggles and falls, groaning with frustration. Determination and encouragement from others fuels the spirit and causes the would-be rider to get back on the bicycle and try again. For some, the struggle is longer and more arduous, while others slip into balance with a surprising grace.

The magic occurs when that mysterious sweet spot, so elusive before, clicks into place and the rider soars forward, amazed and gratified by the feeling of centeredness and balance. At first, a fragile experience, the rider wavers at the beginning and the end of the ride, and wonders if the feeling of success was accidental, just a moment in time, or whether it can be repeated. With praise and practice, the rider soars, gliding as if flying for the first time.

The feeling of joy that educators shared when they entered the virtual world makes the effort worthwhile. The awareness of others within this magical place transforms them. It is an otherworldly feeling, and like the first bicycle ride, not a simple task nor one that feels natural. Novices often think about the technology, the steep learning curve, and how strange it feels to move, look around and interact with objects, but it is comparable to the early attempts to use the mouse, fumbling and frustrated as the mind wills the hand to respond, yet the cursor goes awry.

Coupled with the technology challenge were the cognitive hurdles. Once the avatar moved, communicated, and manipulated objects, the next decision was what to do and how to translate curriculum and activities into 3D representations that supported education in virtual spaces. In the early days, assessment was one of the challenges, stimulating the need for rubrics and prior planning.

Selfhood, Presence, and the Shared Experience: Community

When asked what the virtual world provides that a well-constructed website cannot, the answer is presence and the intersection and awareness of people and content. It is the connection between people and their shared objects that makes the experience of the world come alive (Alexander, 2006; Truman, 2013). Without other avatars, which are representations of self within these spaces, and their awareness of one another, the experience is lifeless, and the user wanders alone, cut off from the world. Gartner (2007) warned against the use of beautiful, empty spaces, noting that they do not strengthen the brand nor satisfy user expectations.

The awareness of others requires more than bumping into other avatars or seeing them from a distance. It is the shared experience, the interaction of people with the content, and the joyful discoveries as well as those awkward moments when the culture, behavior and social norms within these spaces seem make the users wonder if they are welcome and if they will look or feel foolish. It is the development of a community that struggles together and shares their successes.

The early concerns mirrored life experiences, such as going to school for the first time, meeting new people, teaching those first few classes and having knowledgeable students who exude more confidence than the educator feels. What is it that causes pioneers to overcome these hurdles, master their fears, or to adopt a playful reaction to each stumble, to falter and pull themselves upright, persevering until they feel that connection with the world and others within it?

It is the experience of community, of a society that transforms individuals into a cohesive group, and confirms their connection with the world around them. Extending the analogy, it is the feeling of joining a group, such as a bike-a-thon or a race, and riding with hundreds of other riders, gliding, feeling the shared joy of the ride. It is less about being first, but instead, about feeling the connection with other riders and the beauty of the land around them, the hazards overcome and the feeling of connection.

Pioneers see opportunities and apply the character strengths of perseverance, resilience and grit to study the art of the possible. Educators also include settlers who define pathways for a sustainable practice and document their strategies for mapping the curriculum to a virtual world delivery model.

They are the heroes, transforming minds and encourage motivation and engagement to support lifelong learning. But the individual efforts are even more satisfying when they take shape within the educational community.

FROM CURRENT TO FUTURE WORK

Virtual reality languished for years on the Gartner Hype Cycle for Emerging Technology (Gartner, 2016) in part due to over 20 years of work trying to overcome the technological hurdles and deleterious side effects users experienced when wearing a head-mounted display (HMD) device. In 1995, the General Reality Cyber Eye was comfortable to wear, but suffered from registration issues (objects staying faithful to their location in 3D space), and the fixed focal point of 11' from the user's body. No matter how close a user moved to the content, it rendered 11 feet from the user's body, making it a poor candidate for reading text on screen. In 2016, some users reported feeling dizziness or motion sickness while wearing the Oculus. Aside from wearable technology, the perception of virtual reality resulted in disagreement among members of the community on what defined VR and how VR applications.

In 2016, manufacturers and VR enthusiasts distinguished the technologies and classified them into several categories: 1) VR that used a HMD or smartphone running a 3D VR app, visible using Google Cardboard or a more expensive presentation device; 2) the 3D VR apps featured either 360 degree video with head tracking that allowed users to turn and view content beside or behind them on 3D games; 3) VR simulations for training, research and niche markets.

One of the challenges with 3D games was the need for interaction support and better interfaces. VR games used a controller to interact with objects on screen, such as firing weapons and interacting with non-player characters or other players, and interactive virtual spaces, designed as simulations, museums, learning environments, research, military education, entertainment, or social use. While fine for games, educators needed robust interfaces with additional capabilities to create content, position it, and adjust the environment as well as integrate with external Web resources.

When Mark Zuckerberg, co-founder and CEO of Facebook, acquired Oculus VR in 2014, the virtual reality company that manufactured the Oculus Rift, the world reflected on the implications (Bailenson, 2018). His thoughts mirrored what many educators considered. Will immersive virtual reality require a HMD for full immersion and serve as the next computing platform? If so, how will it work, what will it do, and how can educators and designers contribute and help to shape the future?

Not everyone agreed that the technology was ready for the market, much less ready for widespread use (Sung, 2015). The lack of interfaces to support interaction within the virtual environment as well as support for multiple users coupled with the need to reduce the feeling of motion sickness and nausea led to different perspectives on use in 2016, much less the next few years.

At the 2016 Virtual Worlds Best Practices in Education (VWBPE) conference, educators discussed VR technologies and their implications for virtual worlds, distinguishing the two technologies as if they had little in common. The perception of the differences suggested that VR required a HMD while virtual worlds did not. In this sense, VR represented immersive virtual reality, and for some, focused on 360 degree video with head tracking while 3D VR games used a controller for interaction.

The distinction of virtual worlds as social spaces rather than part of the current definition of virtual reality was surprising. In 2016, virtual worlds like Second Life were hard to use with a HMD, in part due to the wide disparity of content, the user interface and how text appeared on screen. Some of the problems experienced in the past still existed with regard to rendering text, setting a fixed focal point for HMD comfort and to minimize the sense of vertigo when the focus shifted as new objects appeared on screen. Despite these interface limitations, the immersive property of educational virtual worlds made it less dependent on visual representation and more dependent on a sense of avatar involvement and the feeling of engagement and presence.

Driven to third party worlds and open source solutions, educators straddled Second Life compatibility versus the need for new and dramatically different alternatives that appealed to future learners and educators. If not HMDs and 360 video, what was the next viable direction?

With an eye toward the future, Linden Lab designed Project Sansar, a working title for a 3D mesh alternative to Second Life that at this time was not launched. While it may offer better compatibility with VR HMDs, the challenges for use in education may outweigh the high quality graphics and sense of realistic spaces. The desire to stay relevant and current with technology contrasts with the need for content creation tools that allow educators and students to create 3D designs, class objects and projects.

Solutions like High Fidelity by CEO Philip Rosedale (2015) who presented a keynote address at the OpenSimulator Community Conference, integrated community development with high quality strategies for content creation. To handle the processing requirements for use in the future on mobile devices, High Fidelity proposed a distributed peer-to-peer processing architecture with something similar to crypto currencies for compensating users for their off-duty processing support, a concept similar to SETI-at home, only with a modern twist.

What were the implications for educators? As mobile technology use became a vital part of online learning, drawing learners further away from campus classroom into the realm of ubiquitous education, lightweight client tools, such as 3D mobile viewers, may reduce some of the complexity and make it easier and affordable for students and educators to use. Certain challenges remain, particularly for content creation by students and educators as well as hosting class projects that require students to create 3d content that either models their ideas or represents a blended reality example of the problem or the solution.

The power of creation in 3D virtual worlds is breathtaking and a vital component in learning activities that reinforce the concepts through practice by doing activities and projects. If the technology shifts to elegant environments that favor high quality visuals over usability and creation, then the next item on the wish list for the future is the need for easy-to-use tools that demystify how to create mesh content and design 3D environments.

Otherwise, current 3D technologies, like Second Life, OpenSim, Inworldz, Kitely, and other educational grids will continue to flourish until the next technological shift. Once a learner or educator embraces the power of creation, it is hard to step back into cruise control.

CONCLUSION

Ray Oldenburg (2002) observed that community development and time spent in the Third Space contributes to social and psychological health. A lifestyle divided solely between home and work (or school) becomes a routine that does not account for social and psychological needs. A community provides a place for playful banter in contrast to the serious business of work, yet in a fast-paced world, the time spent with a community grows shorter without groups, events, champions and a commitment.

It is with regret that the chapter did not recognize the thousands of amazing educators, librarians, curriculum designers, administrators and technology evangelists who pioneered and shaped virtual world education. Faced with economic pressures, when they closed their educational programs in Second Life, many found alternative paths and developed societies in open source virtual worlds or game worlds as MUVEs.

The rapid growth and large number of groups and communities within Second Life have yet to be rivaled in open source or commercial worlds, but the numbers are steadily growing. Maria Korolov of

Hypergrid Business (2016, November 15) reported record high numbers of regions in open source worlds and steady growth, and noted that the size rivals Second Life.

What will tomorrow bring to shape the future of virtual world education? The successes of the past ten years indicate the promise of a bright future, and this time, driven by technology-enhanced educators, curriculum designers, librarians, administrators, and learners who understand the value of selfhood and society.

REFERENCES

AdvertisingAge. (2007, September 10). Second Life has some firms second guessing [Weblog post]. Retrieved from http://adage.com/article/btob/life-firms-guessing/268564/

Alexander, B. (2006). *NMC 2006 regional* [PowerPoint slides]. Retrieved from http://www.slideshare.net/BryanAlexander/nmc-2006-regional

Bachelard, G. (1964). *The poetics of space*. New York: Orion Press.

Bailenson, J. (2018). *Experience on demand: What virtual reality is, how it works, and what it can do*. New York, NY: W. W. Norton & Company.

Boyd, D. (2006, October 21). Announcing the Macarthur Foundation's digital media and learning initiative [Weblog post]. Retrieved from http://www.zephoria.org/thoughts/archives/2006/10/21/announcing_the.html

Calongne, C. (2008). Educational frontiers: Learning in a virtual world. *EDUCAUSE Review*, *43*(5), 36–48.

Calongne, C. (2009). Virtual worlds: Explorations and implications [PowerPoint slides]. *Association for Information Technology Professionals*. Retrieved from http://www.slideshare.net/lyrlobo/aitp-keynote-on-virtual-worlds

Calongne, C., & Hiles, J. (2007). Blended realities: A virtual tour of education in Second Life. *Proceedings of the 12th Annual Technology, Colleges & Community (TCC) Worldwide Conference*.

Community Virtual Library. (2019). *Real librarianship in virtual worlds*. Retrieved from https://communityvirtuallibrary.org/

Da Silva, M. (2015, February 17). The meaning of social objects [Weblog post]. Retrieved from http://abcofinternetmarketing.co.za/blogging/social-media/meaning-social-objects/

Dede, C. (2003). Multi-user virtual environments. *EDUCAUSE Review*, *38*(3), 60–61.

Dede, C., & Ketelhut, D. J. (2003). Designing for motivation and usability in a museum-based multi-user virtual environment. *American Educational Research Association Conference*, Chicago, IL.

Ember, T. (2011, October 19). HG safari [Weblog post]. Retrieved from https://hgsafari.blogspot.com/2011/

Engeström, J. (2005, April 13). Why some social network services work and others don't -- Or: the case for object-centered sociality [Weblog post]. Retrieved from http://www.zengestrom.com/blog/2005/04/why-some-social-network-services-work-and-others-dont-or-the-case-for-object-centered-sociality.html

Gartner. (2007). *Gartner says 80 percent of active internet users will have a "Second Life" in the virtual world by the end of 2011*. Retrieved from http://www.gartner.com/newsroom/id/503861

Gartner. (2016). *Gartner's 2016 hype cycle for emerging technologies identifies three key trends that organizations must track to gain competitive advantage*. Retrieved from http://www.gartner.com/newsroom/id/3412017

Kanter, B. (2006, October 19). The birth of a field: Digital media and learning [Weblog post]. Retrieved from https://beth.typepad.com/beths_blog/2006/10/the_birth_of_a_.html

Korolov, M. (2016). *November a solid month for opensim growth*. Retrieved from http://www.hypergridbusiness.com/2016/11/november-a-solid-month-for-opensim-growth/

Lester, J. (2014, July 29). Hypergrid safari -- The evolution of exploration across the interconnected Metaverse [Weblog post]. Retrieved from https://becunningandfulloftricks.com/2014/07/29/hypergrid-safari-the-evolution-of-exploration-across-the-interconnected-metaverse/

Levine, A. (2008). The NMC campus. *EDUCAUSE Review, 43*(5).

Mark, C. L. (2014). *Growth and decline of Second Life as an educational platform* (Doctoral dissertation). Available from ProQuest Dissertations & Theses Global. (Order No. 3584527)

Maslow, A. H. (1943). A Theory of Human Motivation. *Psychological Review, 50*(4), 370–396. doi:10.1037/h0054346

Mason, H. (2007). *Script Me!* Retrieved from http://3greeneggs.com/autoscript/

McLeod, S. A. (2016). *Maslow's hierarchy of needs*. Retrieved from www.simplypsychology.org/maslow.html

NMC. (2005, December). Symposium on Games in Education. *Learning Times*.

NMC. (2006). *Symposium on digital media and learning*. MacArthur Foundation.

Nonprofit Commons. (2007, January 30). Welcome to the NPSL blog! [Weblog post]. Retrieved from http://nonprofitcommons.org/node?page=97

Oldenburg, R. (2002). *Celebrating the third place: Inspiring stories about the "great good places" at the heart of our communities*. New York: Marlow & Company.

OpenSimulator. (2016, October 27). *OpenSimulator* [Software]. Retrieved from http://opensimulator.org/

Peterson, C., & Seligman, M. E. P. (2004). *Character strengths and virtues: A handbook and classification*. American Psychological Association.

Puentedura, R. R. (2006). *Game theory revisited: Third places and the new web* [Podcast]. Retrieved from http://hippasus.com/resources/thirdplace/

Roddenberry, G., Hurley, M., Baron, M., Barry, P., Beimler, H., Black, J. D. F., . . . Paramount Pictures Corporation. (2007). *Star trek, the next generation: Season 1*. Paramount Pictures.

Rosedale, P. (2015, January 13). OSCC14 - Philip Rosedale keynote: What is the metaverse? *Second Annual OpenSimulator Community Conference*. Retrieved from https://youtu.be/iR3uUVPyjhU

Scharmer, C. O. (2000). *Presencing: Learning from the future as it emerges.* Presentation at the Conference on Knowledge and Innovation, Helsinki School of Economics, Finland. Retrieved from http://www.ottoscharmer.com/docs/articles/2000_Presencing.pdf

Science Circle. (2019). *Lectures, debates, excursions and symposia.* Retrieved from https://www.sciencecircle.org/lectures-debates-excursions-and-symposia/

Second Life History. (2017, December 29). Retrieved February 20, 2019 from the Second Life Wiki: http://wiki.secondlife.com/wiki/History_of_Second_Life

Stephenson, N. (1993). *Snow crash.* New York: Bantam Books.

Sung, D. (2015, November 13). *Virtual reality realism: Why 2016 might not be VR's big year. Three experts fail to agree on whether 2016 will be the year VR breaks through.* Retrieved from http://www.wareable.com/vr/is-2016-the-year-vr-goes-mainstream

Truman, B. (2013). *Transformative interactions using embodied avatars in collaborative virtual environments: Towards transdisciplinarity* (Doctoral dissertation). Available from ProQuest Dissertations & Theses Global. (Order No. 3628698)

Tuan, Y. (1977). *Space and place: The perspective of experience.* Minneapolis, MN: The University of Minnesota Press.

U.S. Dept. of Ed. (n.d.). *Family educational rights and privacy act (FERPA).* U.S. Department of Education. Retrieved from http://www2.ed.gov/policy/gen/guid/fpco/ferpa/index.html

Virtual Ability. (2019a). *Virtual Ability, Inc.* Retrieved from https://virtualability.org/

Virtual Ability. (2019b). *International disability rights affirmation conference (IDRAC) 2012-2018.* Retrieved from https://virtualability.org/idrac/

Virtual Ability. (2019c). *Mental health symposia 2012-2018.* Retrieved from https://virtualability.org/mental-health-symposia/

Wright, R. (2006). *Better life* [Video file]. Retrieved from https://youtu.be/8_4dW1rZBhI

Young, J. R. (2010, October 14). Academics discuss mass migration from Second Life, The Chronicle of Higher Education [Weblog post]. Retrieved from http://www.chronicle.com/blogs/wiredcampus/academics-discuss-mass-migration-from-second-life/27672

KEY TERMS AND DEFINITIONS

Archipelago: A group of regions that look like islands with a related theme. The NMC hosted an educational archipelago of 110 islands.

AU: The Air University hosts open source virtual worlds for education that feature both practical and playful spaces designed to stimulate thinking and creativity, blending the art of the possible with a passion for excellence. The learning activities to support research in signature character strengths and evaluation of serious games as well as data analytics.

CTU: Colorado Technical University, a for-profit higher education institution that featured doctoral, graduate and undergraduate classes in computer science, emerging media and virtual worlds that met and designed projects in a virtual world from 2006-2016.

Grid: A collection of regions that comprise the virtual landscape. Architecturally, two of Second Life's largest grids featured the Main Grid in which the regions are connected and look like a continent. In the early years, Linden Lab operated a Teen Grid for approximately 6,000 residents ages 13-17.

Hypergrid: Including the ability to move between virtual worlds using the same account.

ISTE: The International Society for Technology in Education offers conferences and year-round support for over 21,000 educators around the world. Each year, ISTE hosts a conference for many of their members, and in the early years, held regional exhibits and a virtual conference simultaneously in Second Life with live speakers presenting from the SL or Virtual Environments Playground.

MUVE: A multiuser virtual environment includes a variety of online shared spaces for large groups of people. Examples include a virtual world, a massive multiplayer online game (MMOG), a massive multiplayer online roleplaying game (MMORPG) like the *World of Warcraft*, or smaller multiplayer games like *Minecraft*, or other shared spaces, like multiuser dungeons (MUDs), chat rooms, and online social spaces.

New Media Consortium (NMC): A consortium of over 200 museums and schools devoted to innovation in technology and education. The NMC and EDUCAUSE published the Horizon Report, a publication that forecasted the next five years for technology in education. Several editions of the Horizon Report are published each year, including Higher Education, K-12, and several international publications.

OpenSimulator: Open source virtual world server software that looks and behaves in a manner similar to Second Life. The code has features that differ from SL, and visitors log into these worlds using a third-party viewer.

OSCC: OpenSimulator Community Conference, held annually to nurture the open source community. The first conference was in 2013.

Region: A virtual world simulator, often installed on a virtual machine that processes and displays the virtual landscape. A single server can host multiple regions.

Second Life: A commercial virtual world operated by Linden Research, which conducts business as Linden Lab.

TCC: The TCC Worldwide Online Conference began in 1995 under the original title Technology in Community Colleges. Over the years, the mission of the TCC conference has evolved, yet continues to foster research and sharing the best practices in online education. The TCC held preconference events in Second Life, and held after hour's events on the Squirrel Island hosted by their conference partner, Learning Times.

Virtual Worlds: A simulated environment where people and 3D content converge. The setting can look like an island, a parcel of land, reside underwater or float high in the air, and the content can vary from realistic objects and buildings to imaginary spaces. The virtual worlds come to life when people interact with one another and the world around them through communication and content sharing.

VWBPE: Virtual Worlds Best Practices in Education, an annual conference since 2008 hosted by the Rockcliffe University Consortium, a virtual world university.

This research was previously published in Recent Advances in Applying Identity and Society Awareness to Virtual Learning; pages 322-342, copyright year 2019 by Information Science Reference (an imprint of IGI Global).

Chapter 18
Participating on More Equal Terms?
Power, Gender, and Participation in a Virtual World Learning Scenario

Mats Deutschmann
Örebro University, Sweden

Anders Steinvall
https://orcid.org/0000-0001-6828-3009
Umeå University, Sweden

Airong Wang
Xi'an Jiaotong-Liverpool University, China

ABSTRACT

This chapter investigates the potential effects of unequal power relations on participation in a group of student teachers and invited professionals in two collaborative workshops in Second Life. The basic research enquiry addresses whether the relative anonymity afforded by virtual world environments has an effect on established power structures, thereby empowering relatively powerless language learners to more active participation than would be the case in more traditional learning set-ups. The data includes recordings, group reflections, and individual questionnaires. Participation was examined from the aspects of floor space, turn length, and utterance functions, and complemented with student reflections. The results show that the differences of floor space and turn length between the invited professionals and the students were small. The invited professionals did more conversational management than the students, while the students performed more supportive speech acts. No major gender differences in participation were found. There was, however, considerable individual variation.

DOI: 10.4018/978-1-6684-7597-3.ch018

INTRODUCTION

The pedagogical potential of virtual worlds for language learning was recognised early in the Computer Assisted Language Learning (CALL) community, and ever since the emergence of these environments in the mid-1990s, there has been a steady stream of studies investigating their potential as language learning environments (Wigham, Panichi, Nocchi & Sadler, 2018). Hew & Cheung's (2010) research review of studies up until 2008 points out that earlier studies were largely descriptive accounts of how environments had been used for learning, and also dealing with the affective domain: participants' likes and dislikes regarding platforms such as Active Worlds and Second Life, for example. Kim, Lee & Thomas' (2012) somewhat later review of 65 studies indicates that, while descriptive research still dominated, there was an increasing interest in experimental research, and also that the use of virtual worlds (VW) as communication spaces had increased drastically. According to Wigham et al. (2018), more recent VW CALL research has been empirical, focusing on the pursuit of finding pedagogic models for how the environments can be used successfully for language learning (see Blin, Nocchi & Fowley, 2013; Panichi & Deutschmann, 2012; Sadler, 2012; Wigham, 2012; Wigham & Chanier, 2013; Zheng & Newgarden, 2012; Panichi, 2014; Wang, 2017).

One feature highlighted as being of considerable significance in the pursuit of understanding and utilizing the full potential of VWs for language learning is that of interaction (Wigham et al., 2018). With reference to the current study, social interaction between the participants is of particular relevance. When studying interaction and participation in VWs, the complexity and the affordances of the environment, and how these in turn may affect participation, is of major interest (Boellstorff, 2015; Gregory, Lee, Dalgarno & Tynan, 2016). With this in mind, Lin, Wang, Grant, Chien & Lan (2014), call for further research into different teaching formats, and methods adapted specifically to VWs. Furthermore, according to Chen (2018, p. 964) a majority research into participation and interaction in VWs to date has been focused on text-based, rather than on voice-based task interaction, an area of research which therefore deserves more research attention according to Chen. The current study can thus be seen as an attempt to fill some of these gaps: we focus primarily on oral interaction between participants and try to evaluate how the learning environment (i.e. Second Life, hereafter SL) impacted the task design and our goals for the particular task at hand.

In spite of Chen's (2018) claims that most VWs studies looking at social interaction have focussed on text-based communication, there are some noteworthy exceptions. Aspects related to designing active and equal oral participation in Second Life language courses are the focus of two studies (Deutschmann, Panichi, & Molka-Danielsen 2009, and Deutschmann & Panichi, 2009b), which analyse variables such as floor space turn length and turn-taking patterns in oral tasks in order to identify how different oral task designs influence learners' participation. The teacher's role in encouraging active participation is also dealt with in Deutschmann & Panichi (2009). Here the authors are able to show how back-channeling and other ways of signaling active listening are important in this type of environment where facial expressions and body language are largely missing. Similar findings are confirmed in Wang (2017). With more specific focus on task design adapted to the affordances of Second Life, Jauregi & Canto (2012) show how a 'networking design' is used to bring native speakers and Dutch second language learners of Spanish together in meaningful interaction. Similarly, Chen (2018) is able to demonstrate how different networking task-designs trigger different types of language output in a mixed (ability and L1-background) group of English as a foreign language learners. Results indicated that more controlled so-called "jigsaw tasks" ("interactional tasks which require that each dyad member contributes equal pieces of information held by him/her in order to reach one single solution" (p. 964) prompted the most complex language output (negotiations and mixed strategy use), whereas freer opinion-exchange based tasks led to less complex interactions.

A key aspect of developing language skills is *usage*, and creating prerequisites for active conversations where learners develop their language skills is accordingly of special significance to task designers. VWs such as SL are open environments that have many tools that support social networking, aspects which make them perfect platforms for assembling participants in collaborative events. VWs thus answer to needs in communicative based language education, where intercultural experiences with more capable native or near native speakers are referred to as key factors of success (Guth & Helm, 2010). It is, however, not necessarily the case that pairing students with capable peers will give the desired result. Research shows that powerful individuals tend to take more space and control the conversation using discursive strategies such as controlling turn-taking, topic control and using elicitation strategies to maximize talking time (Abdullah & Hosseini, 2012). There is thus a risk that less capable students become intimidated by the situation. For example, Toyoda & Harrison (2002) report that native speakers could manipulate the chat communication in Active Worlds freely and elaborately, while the nonnative speakers' lower language proficiency often led to slow responses and confusions in communication.

In this study, we describe and analyse the outcomes of collaborative activities conducted in SL, where a class of student language teachers was joined by professionals working with online language teaching and/or research in order to discuss two pedagogic case studies. These professionals were recruited from all over Europe with the help of networks relating to SL and language learning. The basic research enquiry addresses the question of whether the relative anonymity afforded by virtual world environments has an effect on established power structures, and thereby empowers relatively powerless language learners to more active participation than would otherwise be the case in more traditional learning set-ups. The focus of our study is on quantitative and qualitative aspects of the participation in the activities, and how these can be related to the various power structures within the groups. As the goal of any activity of this sort is to give students an opportunity to learn as much as possible, participatory patterns, and how the environment may affect these, are of special interest.

BACKGROUND

Language Learning, Networking, and Social Software

The affordance of online communication in bringing intercultural learners together to create communities of practice and critical inquiry is particularly valuable in collaborative online language learning (Warschauer, 1997, p. 477). For this purpose, educators are increasingly integrating social software such as blogs, Skype, YouTube, Facebook, Twitter and SL in CALL. The open architectures of such social media support collective online activities, one of the main advantages being that the social networks of the students and the teachers can be integrated into the learning context thus adding to the authenticity of the scenario and increasing engagement (Bowers, Ragas, & Neely, 2009, p. 41; Otto & Pusack, 2009, p. 794). In the context of this study, our ambition was to integrate language teacher students in existing professional networks, a practice which will be discussed further below.

SL as a Learning Space

A recent development in online language learning involves the simulation of real world learning in three-dimensional virtual environments (3D VEs), where one of the most popular sites is SL (Warschauer & Liaw 2010, p. 13). Czepielewski (2012, p. 16) classifies SL as a *Serious Virtual World*, which though initially made for entertainment, cannot be seen as a game. It is rather an open virtual world, where each of the participants can realize his or her own objectives, which may be connected with social life, entertainment business or, indeed, language education. Designed as a place for socialisation, users can communicate in the target language synchronously using voice, chat and instant messaging, asynchronously using the group and private message function as well as note cards and even perform limited human gestures. SL also allows users to create objects and environments, which others can interact with. The 'self' is represented by a so-called avatar, which usually has a human shape (but does not have to). As an open environment with users from all over the world, it has been widely adopted as a learning environment by different educational institutions in the domain of language education, where it provides a contextually relevant language learning space for learners to interact with native speakers of a target language (Wang, Song, Xia, & Yan, 2009, p. 1). In all, SL affords group-based, project-based and student-centred teaching and learning where multiple avatars can engage in an activity simultaneously (Good, Howland, & Thackray, 2008, p. 164).

One of the main advantages of using SL in education, however, is the extensive community of educators that operates within its domains. Panichi (2012) lists a number of educational institutions and projects that operate within SL, and many of these educators are organised in more conventional asynchronous social network sites on the Internet (see also Wigham et al. 2018). In the domain of language learning, there are several forums and online networks such as the SLED List (SL Educators n.d.), the Avalon NING (2012), the Euroversity NING (2012), and the Eurocall/Calico Virtual World SIG NING (2012), where educators can exchange experiences and ideas and connect with others interested in this type of learning design. It is often in such forums that educators find partners for collaborative projects as the one described below, and indeed where we found volunteers in the form of experienced online educators to interact with our teacher trainee students.

However, SL is by no means an easy environment to master and strong technical skills and confidence with the platform are required for teachers and students to take full advantage of its learning potential (Longo, 2012). For this reason, many course designers point to the necessity of technical readiness in SL learning events. Proposed models include so-called technical initiations, where participants are required to attend pre-course session(s) in order to acquaint themselves with the program (Jarmon, Traphagan, Mayrath, & Trivedi, 2009; Mayrath, Traphagan, Heikes, & Trivedi, 2009; Wang, Song, Stone, & Yan, 2009; Blasing, 2010; Molka-Danielsen, Panichi, & Deutschmann, 2010).

The literature on virtual environments for educational purposes has explored some of the potentially important factors affecting participation. These include learner attitudes towards the environment, where some students may find the environment too game-like and inappropriate for serious learning events (Deutschmann & Panichi, 2009a, p. 33). Gender is another variable that has been contemplated as important, but little has been written about how gender may affect language learners' participation or other gender issues in SL (Inman, Wright, & Hartman, 2010, p. 54). Finally, many researchers have pointed to the advantages of computer mediated communication (CMC) in general, and VWs specifically, in reducing so-called Foreign language anxiety (FLA). Gamage, Tretiakov, & Crump (2011), for example, postulate that shy students participate more actively in VWs due to a sense of safety intermediated by the relative anonymity of the avatars. Similarly, Hammick and Lee claim that CMC provides a "sheltering effect" that reduces FLA (2014, p. 303). More systematic studies into FLA and VWs environments do indeed indicate that anxiety is reduced when learners can hide behind avatars (see Reinders & Wattana, 2015; Wehner, Gump & Downey, 2011; Melchor-Couto, 2017; 2018). However, as Melchor-Couto points out other aspects such as lack of facial expressions and lip movements, as well as lack of other non-verbal cues that come into play in VW interaction that may cancel out the presumed positive effects of anonymity (2018, p. 235).

Power in Conversations

The fact that the relational power of participants is an important aspect in conversations came to the fore through the study of gender and conversation. Early research applying a dominance framework (such as O'Barr & Atkins, 1980; West & Zimmerman, 1983) gave a fairly straightforward picture of how power relations and gender combine and affect conversations and the use of language pragmatic features related to conversational control. Later research, adopting a difference approach, identified the application of two conversational styles, collaborative and competitive, correlating with the genders female and male, respectively (see, for example Coates, 2004), as explanation to the imbalance in conversations. Women's collaborative style is supportive, whereas men's competitive style is more adversarial, leading to clashes in mixed-sex interactions and male domination.

Although these observations still hold to a certain degree, the appearance of new theoretical positions, for example a social constructivist perspective of gender as performance and construction, (e.g. Crawford, 1995; Holmes, 2006), and more detailed studies of specific contexts, e.g. workplace management (Ladegaard 2010; Holmes, 2006; Holmes and Schnurr, 2006), have indicated that the picture is quite complex. Holmes (2006, p. 6) points out that the stereotypical characterizations of the difference approach do not take the full complexity of sources of diversity and variation, such as context and power distributions, into account. Explanatory variables for a certain discursive behaviour (power, for example), thereby risk being blurred by gender factors simply because they happen to correlate. For example, Ladegaard (2010), was able to show that both male and female leaders tended to prefer "normatively feminine management styles" (indirect and mitigated directives, interrogatives and modal verbs, for instance). In another study, Hancock & Rubin (2015), were able to show that there were no overall gender differences in the use of such 'gendered' linguistic variables as fillers, hedges, interruptions, and tag-questions among their 40 test subjects.

Research has addressed whether gendered styles would be visible in and affect the climate in online discussions. Herring (2010) could find an effect of gendered styles in a study of floor patterns in asynchronous textual CMC (mailing lists). She concludes that professional recognition and male gender are key factors for gaining the floor in her corpus. Similarly, in a study of synchronous online group-discussion in chats among physics students, Sullivan, Kapur, Madden & Shipe (2015) found that the conversational styles in these chats followed the expected gendered lines. However, they could also identify male use of the stereotypically 'feminine' discourse style and female use of the stereotypically 'masculine' discourse style. More importantly, a careful analysis of contribution showed that, on average, females in male-dominated chats contributed slightly more amount of ideas than could be expected. In contrast, Lin, Dowell, Godfrey, Choi, & Brooks (2019) analysing online synchronous collaboration found no significant differences between men and women in terms of the degree of participation. Their results, however, indicate that women's communication is more likely to be effective and cohesive.

Conversations in some institutions tend to follow particular patterns. Have (1991) observed that certain asymmetries stem from institutional expectations. Although intimately linked to power, institutional conventions greatly dictate roles in most conventional learning contexts making them largely ready-made and expected. For example, Schleef (2008) found that instructors in academia, regardless of gender, tend to use the same speech style and only very seldom draw on wider identity resources. To what extent roles are re-negotiated in a different arena such as SL, and whether an informal role, such as 'expert peer' rather than teacher, affects the power situation has not been addressed previously.

Language proficiency is another variable that will affect the power relation in a conversation. This is especially true in a language learning context and Brislin (1981), for example, lists "language skills" as one of the key skills for opening for a learner's success in a cross-cultural conversation. As pointed out earlier (see Hammick & Lee, 2014, for example) more recent research, however, has shown that language learners tend to feel more comfortable in conversations and less concerned about language deficiencies when communicating online (see also Freiermuth, 2001). In this particular study, we deem language proficiency to be of lesser importance in creating potential power imbalances in the conversations since almost all participants, including the invited educators, could be classified as proficient non-native speakers of English.

Finally, we deem knowledge of the subject matter to be of relevance in deciding the power structures in the present context. This variable occurs in Brislin's (1981) aforementioned list of factors necessary for successful cross-cultural conversations and several studies have shown that non-native speakers communicating with native speakers will dominate conversational contexts where they are perceived as 'experts' in spite of their language difficulties (see Woken & Swales, 1989 and Zuengler, 1989, for example).

Aims

In the task design described below we introduced student teachers to outsiders, professional educators involved in online teaching and/or research, who were relatively more experienced and arguably more knowledgeable in the subject area being studied, namely participation in face-to-face and online educational contexts and pedagogic design to based on the ideas of collaboration and active participation. Given the potentially unequal power relations of the participants in this network design, the aim of this study is to investigate how the different power relations in the discussion groups may have affected participation both in terms of quality and quantity. Here the roles students vs. the invited online educators (so-called 'expert peers' in the context of the project) are of particular interest but we have also included a gender dimension. More specifically, we want to investigate participation in terms of floor space (i.e. the amount of time which different participants contribute to the conversation) and turn length, and examine what roles different individuals play in the conversations in terms of contributing to the task, managing the task at hand and being a supportive peer. In short, we want to find out who controls and 'owns the floor'. A final point of investigation is whether the VW environment had any effect on aspects related to power and participation.

METHOD

Participants and Course Context

The activities described in this article were part of a more extensive project carried out at Umeå University, Sweden, where SL was used in an attempt to explore gender and identity through experiments using gender and voice morphing and discussions with outside agents (for further information see Deutschmann, Steinvall, & Lagerström, 2011). In this chapter, we focus on a group of upper secondary student teachers attending a course on the theme of gender, sociolinguistics and second language education. During the course, two workshops were organised in SL under the project framework, where the purpose was to show how these tools could give access to international networks and contacts for second-language education. Another aim was to introduce the students to the use of Web 2.0 tools in language education and to let them experience the potential challenges and merits of this type of design first-hand.

Before describing the participants and specifics of the course, it is important to clarify the status of English in Swedish higher education, which more or less is that of a second official language. Much of the course literature in most university programs is in English and it is taken for granted that students are reasonably proficient in the language. In programs such as the one our students are partaking, the focus is thus mainly on theoretical content, but given the students' future roles as language teachers, an added ambition is to give students further opportunities to improve their English skills.

Given our course aims, we invited educators working with online language learning to join groups of three-four students as discussion partners in two problem-based case discussions on the subjects of classroom participation and online learning. In the course context, perhaps somewhat misleadingly, we chose to call these invited educators 'expert peers' in order to tone down their status. In the call for volunteers, it was made clear that an 'expert peer' merely had the role of a conversational partner rather than a teacher, coordinator, or facilitator and as such had no explicit responsibilities for the dynamics or outcomes of the discussions.

The 'expert peers' were recruited by sending calls for volunteers to various existing network sites in the domain of SL and language learning including the SLED List (SL Educators n.d.), the Avalon NING (2012), the Euroversity NING (2012), and the Eurocall/Calico Virtual World SIG NING (2012). All in all we recruited 11 volunteers of whom two were males and nine females. Their average age was 40, ranging between 28-54. All of the recruited volunteers were active language postgraduate students, researchers and/or language teachers from various educational institutions throughout Europe including France, Poland, Italy, Spain, Germany, England, Holland, Turkey, Sweden and Finland. Two of these were native English speakers and the rest were deemed to be highly proficient in English.

Participating on the course were 32 third-term students of English within the aforementioned program, English being their first university subject. Of the 32 students, 21 were females and 11 were males. The average age of the students was 24 years with almost all ranging between 20-27 years. There was only one older mature student (a female of 56 years). Their level of proficiency can be described as near fluent.

The invited professionals and the students participated two workshops. Workshop 1 was designed to let students reflect over individual and gender patterns of participation, and also the importance of the quality of attention a pupil gets. To this purpose, the students were given seven statements regarding gender and education from their course literature and were asked to discuss those in relation to participation data from 14 individual pupils in a fictitious second language classroom (very much inspired by Sunderland, 1998, 2000, 2004; the second of which the students later read). The invited professionals were asked to participate in the discussion, in their capacity of experienced teachers with insights from other environments.

The main task of Workshop 2 was to create a lesson or part of a lesson for a group of secondary school pupils in which the use of Computer Mediated Communication was to maximise the activity of the pupils. The participants were encouraged to design the lesson in order to address potential problems of inequality. Here we encouraged students to draw on their own previous experiences (from school, for example) and use the expertise of the invited professionals in order to optimise the design of their fictitious lesson. The invited professionals, on the other hand, had been informed about the tasks and were encouraged to help the students in drawing on their experience and using their expertise.

Collection of Data

The students were organised in groups of 3-4 individuals for the workshops and each group was joined by one so-called 'expert peer'. We had set up sound isolated collaborative spaces in SL where the avatars could sit and the groups could discuss the tasks at hand without disturbances from the other conversations going. The results and reflections on the discussions were later to be presented in a wiki site (*PBworks*) and in a final reflection paper. The two workshops were video recorded using the screen-recording software *Camtasia*. Both students and the invited participants were informed that the group discussions would be recorded and gave informed consent to this. The complete recorded material exceeded 20 hours, but given the practical limitations of a study of this kind, only a selection of this material was transcribed.

Also worth noting here is that participants were instructed to interact using voice primarily. We encouraged participants to limit their text chat conversations to technical issues, as we had two technical facilitators present who were instructed to deal with any technical problems using the chat mode (so as not to interrupt on-going conversations). There was, however, some conversation that went on using the text chat, and the overall distributions are summarised in the results below. Apart from solving technical issues, these contributions mainly consisted of greetings and goodbyes and we have thus not analysed this data qualitatively. Also note that since the students were relatively inexperienced using SL they did not use the 'gestures' tools and our main focus was thus limited to oral communication.

After each workshop, each group presented their group work and group reflections in the wiki. In addition, in order to get a fuller understanding of the students' perspectives, we asked them to fill in individual anonymous questionnaires at the end of the project in which they could react to what had happened in the workshops, and give their personal reflections without being influenced by the group or feel that they may be negatively judged by the teacher. The data from questionnaires plus the group pages from wiki were used as the qualitative part of the results in this study to complement the quantitative data with respect to factors that may have affected participation.

Analysis and Framework

For this analysis, we have limited ourselves to one discussion task only from each workshop. We decided to choose an entire task rather than a random span of time since the former would give a better insight into the group dynamics of how a group tackled the tasks from beginning to end. The discussions generated from the chosen tasks were transcribed, noting the identity and role of the interlocutor, the time of the turn (accurate to the second), utterance content, and utterance function in relation to how it functioned in the conversation.

For this last part, we identified three general pragmatic functions according to which most utterances could be classified: *support*, *management* and *content contribution*. Those that did not fall into these categories were classified in an "other" category. It is important to note that the turns were broken down into these functions, and that it is the time devoted to a particular function which is the main unit for the quantitative analysis. Such a procedure made it possible to relate functions to percentage of floor space and to avoid combined categories as longer turns could contain more than one function. The three categories that we focus on here are related to the macro-discourse marker categories (Starter, Elicitation, Accept, Attitudinal, Meta-statement and Conclusion) discussed by Bellés-Fortuño (2006), but we are considering the function of utterances, and not individual markers. Below a few instances of these categories are presented for illustration. Note here that the letter F represents female students, M, male students and E, 'expert peers'.

Example 1: Support

E4: Yes, yes, we can. (*support*, agreement)
M2: That is a really good question. (*support*, compliment)

As these two examples show, *support* is often given the form of agreements and compliments, thus typically containing an attitudinal discourse marker and markers of acceptance. Acknowledging what is being said through back-channelling is also included in this category.

Example 2: Management

F8: Should we move on to the third one? (*management*, elicitation)
E1: Let's move to statement three then. [To conclude] Women teachers are far more successful than men at giving girls fair share of their attention. (*management*, directions and conclusion)

Management often includes starting the task, suggesting topics for discussion, directing questions to others in order to elicit responses, closing topics, meta-statements, summaries and conclusions.

Example 3: Content Contribution

E1: if someone is raising their hands, and she directs the question to that person, [...] it is quite likely that the most active people, the people who raise their hands most, will get the most questions. (*Content contribution*)
F11: [speaking about a pupil in the case data from, Workshop 1] she almost didn't speak at all. But when she came online, she spoke the most. (*Content contribution*)

As the term *content contribution* suggests the function of such utterances is primarily to add factual substance to the conversation.

We have also included the students' reflections in the analysis, in order to shed more light on how they experienced the conversations, and their roles and we have tried to triangulate these reflections with the observed participation.

RESULTS

Floor Space and Participation

In this first section, we examine the overall tendencies related to floor space that we found in our material. The initial data is based on recordings of discussions of tasks from both workshops, 16 recordings in all. All in all the material constitutes 2 hours and 23 minutes of 'talk time' and the average 'talk time' of each recordings is about 9 minutes, but the lengths vary. Typically, the discussion groups were made up of four individuals: one expert peer (typically female), two female students and one male student, but there is some variation. All in all 43 individuals are represented in the data (32 students and 11 'expert peers').

The average floor space occupied by the different groupings was relatively equal (see Figure 1 below). The 'expert peers' occupied 2.25 minutes per session on average, closely followed by the female students (2.16 minutes) and the male students (2 minutes). It was encouraging to see that the students were not intimidated by the presence of the 'expert peers' and spoke almost as much as these on average. As we shall see in the next section, however, there was great individual variation.

Figure 1. Average floor space – all sessions, in minutes and seconds

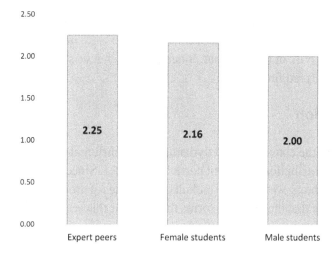

We also examined the average turn length produced by the different groups. Longer turns are often associated with academic discourse of this nature where facts, figures and concepts are discussed, while more everyday conversation is typified by shorter turns (see *elaborated* and *restricted code* – Bernstein, 1971, for example). The turn length thus gives a rough indication of the type of input that was made. The average turn length produced by the 'expert peers' was slightly longer than that of the student groups. There was no difference between the turn length produced by male and female students (see Figure 2 below, turn length in seconds).

Figure 2. Average turn length – all sessions, in seconds

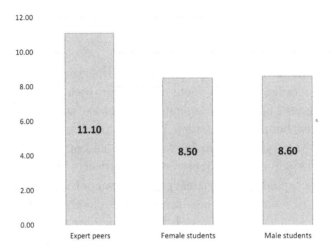

The text chat data for all the recorded material (20 hours) consisted of 2841 words in all, of which 1325 words (47%) were produced by the expert peers and 1516 words (53%) were produced by the students. The average number of words produced in text chat by each expert peer was 74 words and for the students the equivalent figure was 24 words. Note, however, that there was great individual variation here, with a few individuals who had technical problems or who were involved in solving these (mainly expert peers) producing the bulk of the text chat. Since the text chat was mainly used for solving technical issues, it will not be analysed further.

Examining Participation

In this section, we examine the conversational dynamics of the different discussion groups by analyzing the quantity and types of contributions different participants make. Since we want to compare individual performances in both workshops, we have only included recordings of groups that were of similar make-up in both sessions. This means that the data that forms the basis for this section is limited to 10 recordings.

Overall Findings

The analysed data represents spoken material from 22 individuals: six 'expert peers' (all females), and 16 students (11 females and 5 males). The total 'talk time' is 1 hour and 40 minutes and the average 'talk time' of each recording being approximately 10 minutes. The average floor spaces occupied by the different groups were: 'expert peers' 2.38 minutes, female students 2.33 minutes and male students 1.54 minutes. The average turn lengths for the 'expert peers' were 10.4 seconds, female students 6.9 seconds and male students 8.1 seconds. The data, thus, approximately mirrors the overall patterns found in the total recorded material.

The 'expert peers' occupied a slightly larger proportion of the floor space than the students, especially in Workshop 1. The male students were also the ones who were the least active, especially in Workshop 2 (see Figure 3 below).

Figure 3. Average proportion of floor space occupied by the different groups
Note that the percentages above do not add up to 100 since there were generally two female students present in each group.

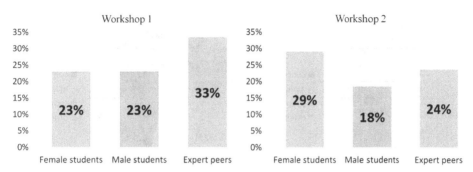

We also looked at the functions of the utterances made in the conversations. The different speech functions of interest here are 'content contributions', 'conversation management' and 'supportive speech acts'. The category 'other' primarily constitutes utterances that could not be classified due to the quality of the recordings. The proportions of these speech functions for the groups 'female students', 'male students' and 'expert peers' in the two workshops are summarised in Figures 4 to 6 below.

Figure 4. Proportion of speech functions, female students

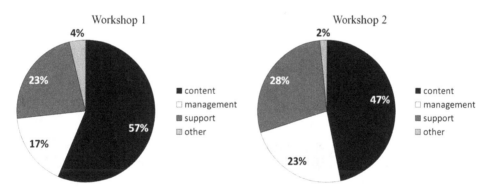

Figure 5. Proportion of speech functions, male students

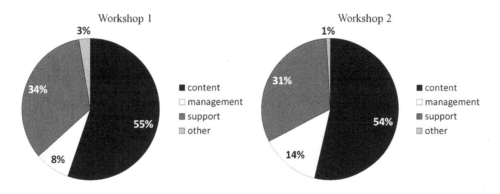

Figure 6. Proportion of speech functions, expert peers.

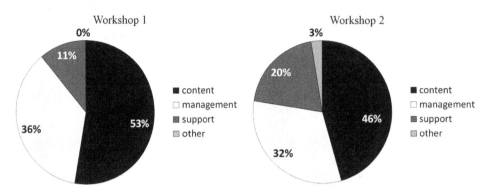

In the material, we find the following general tendencies: There was a slight tendency for students to contribute to the task content more than the 'expert peers'. There was a marked tendency for the 'expert peers' to do more conversational management than the students. On average, the female students also did more conversational management than the male students. Overall, the students performed more supportive speech acts, such as back-channelling and other conversational strategies that indicated active listening, than the 'expert peers'. Contrary to our expectations based on previous research in the field, which indicate that female speakers are more likely to signal active listening through supportive strategies (see Coates, 2004, for example), we found that the male students were particularly active in this respect. Arguably, there were thus some indications (less floor time and more supportive speech acts) that the male students were in a relatively powerless position overall. This could be explained by the fact that they were typically in a 3:1 (female: male) minority in most groups. On the other hand, given the small size of the sample, it could just be individual variation.

Specific Findings From the Workshops

We now turn our attention to a more specific analysis of the individual recordings. The performances of each individual participant in the two workshops are summarised below in Figures 7–11. The data is represented as percentages of the total floor space in each recording so that the individual performances of different sessions can be compared. In each figure we have also included information of the total 'talk time' of each recording, each individual's average turn length, and the percentage of the total floor space taken up by each participant. Note that while the identities of the students are identical in the two workshops (with the exception of F3 who was absent in Workshop 2), some of the 'expert peers' differ.

The results in Figures 7–11 show that the general overall tendencies described above contain great individual variation. For example, there was great variation in the floor space occupied by different individuals. Although the 'expert peers' tended to be among the more active participants in most of the workshops, E4 and E6 were relatively passive in Workshop 2. In many cases, however, individuals tended to show similar behaviours in both workshops. Thus, on the basis of this data F6, F7, M1, M2 and E6 can be described as relatively inactive participants, while F1, F4, F5, F8, F10, M3, M5, E1, E2, E3 and E5 were more active. Others, such as F2, F9, F11, M4, and E4, display varied behaviour, being active in one workshop but less so in the other. One clear tendency that can be seen in almost all the individual data, however, was that active individuals tended to have longer turns on average.

Figure 7. Group 1: Summary of individual participation in Workshops 1 and 2

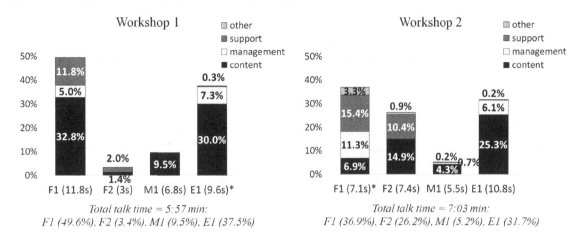

Total talk time = 5:57 min:
F1 (49.6%), F2 (3.4%), M1 (9.5%), E1 (37.5%)

Total talk time = 7:03 min:
F1 (36.9%), F2 (26.2%), M1 (5.2%), E1 (31.7%)

Figure 8. Group 2: Summary of individual participation in Workshops 1 and 2

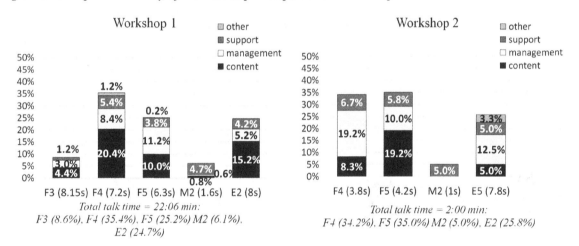

Total talk time = 22:06 min:
F3 (8.6%), F4 (35.4%), F5 (25.2%) M2 (6.1%),
E2 (24.7%)

Total talk time = 2:00 min:
F4 (34.2%), F5 (35.0%) M2 (5.0%), E2 (25.8%)

Figure 9. Group 3: Summary of individual participation in Workshops 1 and 2

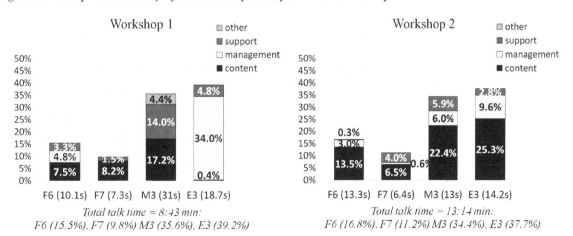

Total talk time = 8:43 min:
F6 (15.5%), F7 (9.8%) M3 (35.6%), E3 (39.2%)

Total talk time = 13:14 min:
F6 (16.8%), F7 (11.2%) M3 (34.4%), E3 (37.7%)

Figure 10. Group 4: Summary of individual participation in Workshops 1 and 2

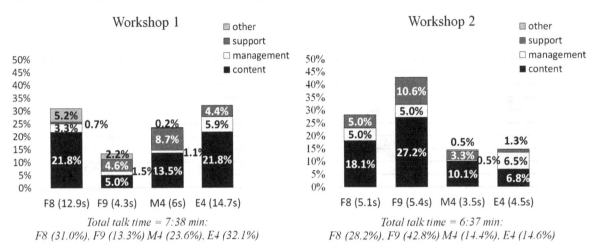

Figure 11. Group 5: Summary of individual participation in Workshops 1 and 2
The numbers in brackets in the figures represent the average turn length for each individual.

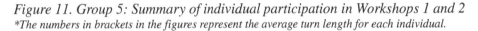

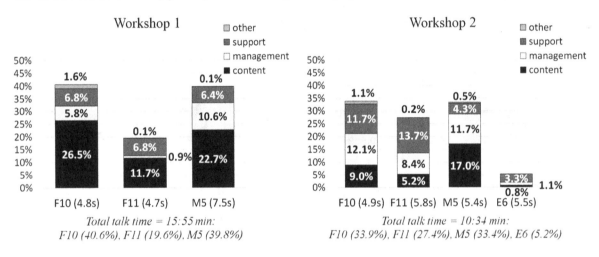

There was also great individual variation as regards the use of speech functions, and from the data above it is clear that individuals had different roles in the conversations, roles that could vary between the two workshops. While most individuals contributed to the task content, some, such as M2 and E3 in Workshop 1, for example, hardly did so at all. While most males tended to do little conversational management, M5 was the most active participant in this respect in both workshops. He was, however, the least active student in displaying support. Some participants, such as F1, F4, contributed relatively little to the actual task content in Workshop 2, but instead spent more time managing the conversation and supporting the others, behaviours that had been less evident in Workshop 1. Other participants, such as F8 and E1, for example, were more focused on contributing to the task content, while M2's contributions almost entirely consisted of displaying support (agreeing with what was being said without coming with any opinions of his own).

Student Reflections

As pointed out in previous research, conversational behaviour cannot be explained by gender, power or relations alone (Kollock, Blumstein, & Schwartz, 1985, p. 44). In this section we employ qualitative data from group reflections and anonymous questionnaires in order to triangulate the quantitative results so as to shed more light on reasons for the observed behaviours.

Overall Reflections

The data in this section was gathered from two sources: the group wikis and anonymous questionnaires. In the former, the students were asked to give general groups reflections on the tasks, and included in the directives students were specifically asked to reflect on the "role of the expert peer". Similarly, in the anonymous questionnaire the students were asked to give an open-ended personal reflection on the project, which could "include anything you think of. For example: [...] the expert peers etc."

The network design, i.e. using external invited professionals as conversational partners, was evaluated as useful and rewarding by nine groups out of ten who discussed this aspect in their group reflections. Similarly, 11 students (10 females and one male) of the 12 students who commented on this aspect in the anonymous personal reflections evaluated the design positively. Inferred from these evaluations, the invited professionals were appreciated since they facilitated group discussions and contributed with their superior knowledge and experiences, and helped with coordinating and supporting the discussions, as the following two quotes from the students' open reflections (answering the question "give your own reflections of the project") indicate:

1. We find that the presence of an expert peer is very useful, and can really help the discussion to move forward, and for the discussion to reach the desired goal. (group reflection)
2. He [the expert peer] was of great help and really facilitated the discussions, and came with good input. (individual reflection, male student)

This is consistent with the quantitative data result in Figure 6 that 'expert peers' spent much time to manage the conversations, but still paid much effort in contributing content and supporting discussions.

One positive finding was that the students contributed to the conversations almost as much as the invited professionals, which seems to suggest that they did not seem to be intimidated by the presence of the latter:

3. Our expert peer contributed with her experience and leadership qualities, and picked up the discussion whenever it was halted [...] and she did a good job not imposing her own opinions on us; on the contrary, she helped us voice our opinions and transfer them into ideas [...] (group reflection)
4. [...] we talked more at ease with our peer since we had no idea who she really was[...] (individual reflection, female student)

Interestingly, according to this female student teacher, the anonymity of the expert peer in their group was mentioned as a factor motivating participation. Other comments indicated that the presence of the invited professional was more problematic:

5. Using expert peers, while a good idea in theory, proved to be a rather unreliable method. (group reflection)

6. [...] our expert peer (though very nice and competent) hadn't really prepared for this. [...] But maybe there can be alternatives to expert peers. (individual reflection, female student)

Specific Reflections

In the results above, we looked at the individual conversational patterns in the different groups, and in this section, we attempt to triangulate the specific findings for groups 1, 2, 3, 4, 5 with the corresponding group reflections and individual comments in the questionnaire. Since the latter data was anonymous and most students did not mention the names of the 'expert peers', it is only when students did so that we can use the data here (limited to comments on E3 and E4).

Group 1

Group 1 only made one comment related to the presence of the expert peer:

7. Although we were technically anonymous to the expert peer, we did not feel like the pseudo-anonymity had much impact on our behavior. (group reflection, Group 1)

This, in contrast with the comment from the female student in (4), implies that the anonymity of invited professionals did not affect their participation (negatively or positively). The participatory patterns of this group were very uneven, with F2 and M1 being very inactive (especially in Workshop 1). From the group reflection we see that Group 1 was quite critical towards using SL as a collaborative tool because technological defects affected their participation negatively. For example, they criticised SL for its lack of visual cues:

8. In our opinion, using SL as a tool for collaborative work is problematic. First of all, there is the issue of not having any body language in the communication. This in turn leads to difficulties when it comes to turn-taking, resulting in interruptions and longer periods of silence where we felt that there was a great deal of uncertainty as to whether or not our messages had reached the other group members. (group reflection, Group 1)

In addition, they were frustrated by the voice quality at times. These negative attitudes towards the tools may explain the passive behaviour of two of its members.

Group 2

Group 2 had two different 'expert peers', E2 and E5, and although both were quite active, occupying approximately 25 per cent of the floor space, E2 did more content contributions while E5 did more conversational management. This data is mirrored in the group reflection:

9. [(E2)...] was very active in our discussions. [(E5)...] wanted us to come up with everything ourselves. [...] To work with expert peers was for us rewarding. They could give us helpful tips and

ideas on how to work with virtual forums [sic. cf. online forums], something we know very little about. (group reflection, Group 2)

There are also some hints that the group thought that the presence of the expert peer helped to make the participation more equal:

10. The role of the expert peers as a moderator would be a suitable tool for making everybody talk and be listened to. (group reflection, Group 2)

It seems that for this group the expert peer(s) seems to have been important in coordinating and motivating participation. In spite of, this M2 was very inactive in both workshops.

Group 3

From the individual evaluations, there were indications that the anonymity of invited professionals had a motivating effect on participation, something which was supported by the reflections of this group:

11. However, we all agreed that the fact that we did not know our expert peer probably made us feel more comfortable talking about our personal feelings and experiences than if E3 would have been one of our teachers, or if we would have known her personally. (group reflection, Group 3)

One interesting finding from the data in 4.2 is that E3 spent much more time to manage the group discussion in Workshop 1 than in Workshop 2, where she mainly contributed to the discussion content. This may be explained by this group reflection:

12. […] when we entered the group discussions with our expert peer, it was hard at times to know who was going to speak, and when. (group reflection, Group 3)

It may be that the students were unfamiliar with SL initially and that E3 with her more advanced technology experience thus took a key role in coordinating the discussion. In addition, the first workshop was more complex in that it involved the discussion of statements in relation to data from classroom observations, which also could explain E3's greater emphasis on management in this session. On the whole, E3's efforts seem to have been appreciated as shown by a female students individual reflection stating that the expert peer "was great!" There were, however, some indications that the presence of the expert peer also may have had an inhibitory effect:

13. […] the expert peer might have caused us to be more cautious and over-polite. (group reflection, Group 3)

This may particularly have been the case for the female students in this group (F6 and F7) who were rather inactive in both sessions.

Group 4

The data in Figure 10 shows that the floor space of E4 was sharply reduced in Workshop 2. Some explanation for this variation is indicated from the questionnaires and Group 4's reflection:

14. Our expert peer (E4) was a good support in answering the questions in the cases. (individual reflection, female student)
15. Our expert peer was professional and did not take that much space in the discussions, which was her intended role. […] our expert peer being quite inactive, however in a good way, since it made our discussions more fluent. […] we felt that the second case worked out better, since that was more focused on our own experiences and discussions rather than looking at graphs. (group reflection, Group 4)

From these comments we may guess that in the more complex Workshop 1, E4 contributed more to the content. In Workshop 2, which was more based on the students' own experiences, E4 took less space and restricted her activities to coordinating the conversation. This illustrates a common dilemma in conversations of this nature, especially when in a position of power: the balance between contributing where necessary but at the same time not taking over the floor.

Group 5

Group 5 is interesting since it did not have an expert peer in the first session but did so in the second session. Two students in particular were active in both sessions: F10 and M5. Of particular interest here is F10, who is a mature student in her fifties and with over thirty years of teaching experience. Listening to the recordings, it is evident that she takes on a leader role in the group, which is also mirrored in the data. Similarly, M5 seems to be active and confident. The inactivity of E6 in Workshop 2 may thus be explained by the fact that the group already had established its roles. In this sense E6 is more of an outsider and in a less powerful position than the students. We may thus be seeing an example of "powerful participants controlling and constraining the contributions of non-powerful participants" (Fairclough, 2001, pp. 38-9). Alternatively, E6 may simply be satisfied with the way students are interacting and she may therefore be standing back intentionally.

In the group reflection, the students claim that the absence of the expert peer did not influence their participation. She was, however, appreciated in the second workshop for "bringing up useful technical suggestions". The results show that formal roles such as that of 'expert peer' do not necessarily mean that one is given a powerful position in a conversation. Other factors such as experience and charisma seem to play an important role too.

DISCUSSION

In our study, we tapped established networks active in SL language education in order to give our student teachers access to far more experienced 'peers' – active professionals in the domain of online language education, researchers and teachers, who could assist and stimulate them in their tasks.

In accordance with studies such as Jauregi & Canto, 2012 and Chen, 2018, this type of networking design turned out to be a good model for our particular purposes. On the one hand, it made it possible to meet the practical demands of the course (the time frame and content), while at the same time introducing an element of the "indeterminate" that so often leads to new meetings and insights. The volunteers also turned out to be engaging discussion partners who contributed with new insights without taking over the conversations. In contrast to Chen's (2018) findings, we found that freer topics (workshop two), where there was room for more personal accounts and opinions, and where students could draw on previous personal experiences, led to the most fruitful interactions. Interestingly, these conversations often became comparative in a cross-cultural sense, where the Swedish students would contrast the Swedish school system and their own school experiences with those of the expert peers', addressing issues such as gender, the role of the teacher, power in the classroom etc. in the different cultures. All in all, our impression was that there was a 'genuine' meeting going on in many groups and that this opened up new dimensions and contacts for our students. Important to note here, however, is that in contrast with Chen's (2018) study, all our participants were advanced learners of English.

One of our concerns was that real or perceived unequal power relations between the students and the invited professionals could have detrimental effects on conversation. There were several risk factors that could have affected the participation of the students negatively: we had an institutionalised situation of a university context where in spite of our efforts to tone down power differences it was likely that participants took on the traditional roles of students and teachers (cf. Have, 1991); we had students being put into a new collaborative arena, and linked to this, technological aspects that had to be overcome. Luckily, our fears were not realised.

Our results show that, on a general level, the division of floor space between participants was reasonably equal. 'Expert peers' occupied slightly more floor space and produced on average slightly longer turns. They also used the text chat more (although these contributions were mainly restricted to technical issues). However, the differences were very small, and the same was true of gender differences among the students. Thus the impact of the institutionalised setting appears to have had little or no negative influence. This may partly have been a result of the learning environment, and that the use of avatars in a VW setting may have blurred traditional power structures. Judging from the reflections, students did not feel inhibited by the formal status of the invited professionals. Here our findings support research claims that the SL technology could be liberating and reduce FLA, for instance by making shy students more active since the (pseudo-) anonymous environment reduced the force of face-threatening situations (c.f. Melchor-Couto, 2017; 2018; Gamage, Tretiakov, & Crump, 2011 above). On the other hand, we specifically instructed the invited professionals not to take on the teacher role, but rather the role of a well-informed conversational partner, so it is difficult, based on our results alone, to claim that it was the relative anonymity afforded by SL environment that alone contributed to the favourable participation patterns.

As far as gender is concerned, there was an unfounded fear that nature of the technology would affect the female students more negatively than the male. We based this erroneous assumption on research, which has shown that girls and women are less involved with virtual world online games (see Hartmann & Klimmt, 2006, for example). Neither the quantitative data nor the reflections suggest that this was the case. Furthermore, contrary to expectations (Coates, 2004; Herring, 2010), male students devoted more speech time to supportive utterances than did the female students. They also occupied slightly less floor space. We have no good explanation for this, but the findings do corroborate other studies that suggest that gender differences in conversational styles may not be as great as once thought (see Holmes, 2006; Ladegaard, 2010, above). More specifically, they support Lin et al.'s (2019) findings from online synchronous collaborations, where no significant gender differences in the degree of participation were found. One could also speculate that this may be the result of the demographics of the group constellations (and the class as a whole), where male students were in a 1:3 minority and may have perceived themselves in a slightly less powerful position. However, other studies have shown that such a configuration of genders does not affect the impact of male contribution (Coates, 2004, p. 116-7). When looking at the dynamics of the individual groups we see a lot of variation, which can be related to individual traits and perhaps preparation for the tasks.

A general view expressed by the students in all the group reflections, however, was their positive experience of collaborating with the invited professionals. Some of the positives mentioned - that the task stimulated the use of the target language, and gave valuable input on how web tools could be used in language education (Workshop 2), and that students gained experience of how to conduct conversational management - were exactly those that we sought after when designing this project. Here it is important to note that it was the engagement of the SL community of language educators that made the design possible, and that the social network sites gave us access to this community. This active network is arguably the greatest asset of SL in language education.

Are there, then, no risks to recruiting peers in this way? After all, we had little control over whom exactly it was that we were inviting into our classrooms. Careful planning and initiation in combination with clear information on expected roles are probably prerequisites for a good result, as expectation on both students and invited participants have to be clear to all parties. Here others, such as Longo (2012), emphasise the importance of netiquette rules in order to reduce the risk of intercultural misunderstandings. However, this does not guarantee a positive result and in the end, it is up to the collaborating participants to maximise the benefits of their meeting. In our study, the results indicate that this was the case on the whole.

FUTURE RESEARCH DIRECTIONS

According to Wigham et al. (2018), VWs potential as learning environments need to be better understood, and in this pursuit the authors call for a "drastic change of approach" (p. 154), which takes the complexity of the environments into account. In addition, we would argue that more systematic empirical research is needed in order to understand the potential benefits and downsides that these environments represent in terms of language learning. In this respect, the research presented above is not without limitations, and we thus take this opportunity to propose a number of potential ways in which we, and others, can contribute to a better understanding of some of the central issues addressed in this study.

Firstly, we would suggest that much more systematic research is needed to address the question of how/whether VWs and other CMC environments can reduce FLA and alter established power structures in interactional language learning contexts. For this research to be robust, we maintain that more controlled research designs that include counter-balanced face-to-face control set-ups are needed. Melchor-Couto's studies (2017; 2018) go some way towards this, but fact remains that her face-to-face and VW learning groups did not interact in identical learning set-ups (only the VW-group interacted with native speakers, for example), and it is thus difficult to elucidate whether the positive outcomes for the VW group as regards FLA were truly the result of the anonymity afforded by SL. The same critique can obviously be made in relation to the current study.

As regards the question of 'power', roles and identity, and how these may affect interaction, we would also argue that more qualitative ethnographic research is needed to establish how interaction through avatars might alter conventional interactional patterns. Does an avatar teacher represent the same role as a face-to-face teacher? To what extent is the physical appearance of the avatar instrumental in establishing roles? What happens to traditional gender roles if participants act through avatars of the opposite sex (note here that voice to can be altered to simulate male or female voices)? These are just some of the issues that can be investigated, and here we would advocate a more qualitative approaches based on interviews, long term observations, careful discourse and conversation analysis.

In this study, we have really only looked at oral participation, but given the complexity of VWs there is obviously great scope to extend the object of investigation to include various modes of participation and interaction. This type of multi-modal research is at its infancy (see Panichi, 2015), and there is much to be done in this field. Here, as pointed out in Wigham et al. (2018), one of the great challenges is establishing research norms of how interaction can be captured, rendered, and interpreted methodologically, and in this field there is great potential for future research.

A final area of research which we think would contribute greatly to the field of language learning using VW environments is a systematic mapping and evaluation of tried learning designs, and how these can cater for different learning goals/learner profiles. As illustrated in this study, where we examined advanced learners of English, the freer task design in Workshop 2 rendered better outcomes in terms of participation than the more question-answer type design in Workshop 1. This result contradicts Chen's (2018) findings, but in the latter case the target learners were beginners and intermediate learners. As illustrated by this example, the suitability of different VW learning designs, depending on aspects such as learner profiles and desired outcomes, are thus an area that needs further mapping and investigation. Here we see great potential in methods involving systematic Action Research designs.

CONCLUSION

The present study provides one model for how online networks can be utilized in order to enrich university language courses and sets up an example of how VWs can be used to offer students opportunities to work with more capable peers from other countries. Our results also suggest that an arena such as SL may well reduce the anxiety associated with set-ups where collaboration is conducted among participants with unequal power relations. The study provides a first step towards further understanding the group dynamics of such meetings and the factors affecting participation – essential knowledge for language educators and practitioners designing more open online learning scenarios.

REFERENCES

Abdullah, F. S., & Hosseini, K. (2012). Discursive enactment of power in Iranian high school EFL classrooms. *GEMA Online Journal of Language Studies*, *12*(2), 375–392.

AVALON Learning NING. (2012). Retrieved June 6, 2012, from http://avalon-project.ning.com/

Bellés-Fortuño, B. (2006). *Discourse markers within the university lecture genre: A contrastive study between Spanish and North-American lectures* (Unpublished doctoral dissertation). Universitat Jaume I, Spain.

Bernstein, B. (1971). *Class, codes and control* (Vol. 1). London: Routledge and Kegan Paul. doi:10.4324/9780203014035

Blasing, M. T. (2010). Second language in Second Life: Exploring interaction, identity and pedagogical practice in a virtual world. *SEEJ, 54*(1), 96–117.

Blin, F., Nocchi, S., & Fowley, C. (2013). Mondes virtuels et apprentissage des langues: Vers un cadre théorique émergent. *Recherches et Applications, 54*, 94–107.

Boellstorff, T. (2015). Three real features for virtual worlds. *Journal of Virtual Worlds Research, 8*(2), 1–5. doi:10.4101/jvwr.v8i2.7167

Bowers, K. W., Ragas, M. W., & Neely, J. C. (2009). Assessing the value of virtual worlds for post-secondary instructors: A survey of innovators, early adopters and the early majority in SL. *International Journal of Humanities and Social Science, 3*(1), 40–50.

Brislin, R. (1981). *Cross-cultural encounters: Face-to-face interactions.* New York, NY: Pergamon Press.

Chen, J. C. (2018). The interplay of tasks, strategies and negotiations in Second Life. *Computer Assisted Language Learning, 31*(8), 960–986. doi:10.1080/09588221.2018.1466810

Coates, J. (2004). *Women, men and language: A sociolinguistic account of gender difference in language* (3rd ed.). Harlow: Pearson Education Limited.

Crawford, M. (1995). *Talking difference: On gender and language.* London: Sage.

Czepielewski, S. (2012). The virtual world of Second Life in foreign language learning. In: S. Czepielewski (Ed.), *Learning a language in virtual worlds: A review of innovation and ICT in language teaching methodology, International conference, Warsaw, 17th November 2011* (pp. 15-24). Warsaw: Warsaw Academy of Computer Science, Management and Administration.

Deutschmann, M., & Panichi, L. (2009a). Instructional design, teacher practice and learner autonomy. In J. Molka-Danielsen & M. Deutschmann (Eds.), Learning and teaching in the virtual world of SL (pp. 27-44). Trondheim: Tapir Academic Press.

Deutschmann, M., & Panichi, L. (2009b). Talking into empty space? Signalling involvement in a virtual language classroom in SL. *Language Awareness, 18*(3-4), 310–328. doi:10.1080/09658410903197306

Deutschmann, M., Panichi, L., & Molka-Danielsen, J. (2009). Designing oral participation in SL – A comparative study of two language proficiency courses. *ReCALL, 21*(2), 206–226. doi:10.1017/S0958344009000196

Deutschmann, M., Steinvall, A., & Lagerström, A. (2011). Gender-bending in virtual space: Using voice-morphing in Second Life to raise sociolinguistic gender awareness. In S. Czepielewski (Ed.), *Learning a language in virtual worlds: A review of innovation and ICT in language teaching methodology, International conference, Warsaw, 17th November 2011* (pp. 54-61). Warsaw: Warsaw Academy of Computer Science, Management and Administration.

Eurocall/Calico Virtual World SIG NING. (2012). Retrieved June 6, 2012, from http://virtualworldssig. ning.com/

Eurocall/Calico Virtual World SIG NING. (2012). Retrieved June 13, 2012, from http://virtualworldssig. ning.com/

Euroversity, N. I. N. G. (2012). Retrieved June 13, 2012, from http://euroversity.ning.com

Fairclough, N. (2001). *Language and power* (2nd ed.). Harlow: Pearson Education Limited.

Fortuño, B. B. (2006). *Discourse markers within the university lecture center: A contrastive study between Spanish and North-American Lectures* (Doctoral Dissertation). Universitat Jaume I.

Freiermuth, M. (2001). Native speakers or non-native speakers: Who has the floor? Online and face-to-face interaction in culturally mixed small groups. *Computer Assisted Language Learning, 14*(2), 169–199. doi:10.1076/call.14.2.169.5780

Gamage, V., Tretiakov, A., & Crump, B. (2011). Teacher perceptions of learning affordances of multi-user virtual environments. *Computers & Education, 57*(4), 2406–2413. doi:10.1016/j.compedu.2011.06.015

Good, J., Howland, K., & Thackray, L. (2008). Problem-based learning spanning real and virtual words: A case study in SL. *Research in Learning Technology, 16*(3), 163–172. doi:10.3402/rlt.v16i3.10895

Gregory, S., Lee, M. J. W., Dalgarno, B., & Tynan, B. (Eds.). (2016). *Learning in virtual worlds: Research and applications (Issues in distance education)*. Edmonton: AU Press. doi:10.15215/au-press/9781771991339.01

Guth, S., & Helm, F. (2010). *Telecollaboration 2.0*. Bern: Peter Lang. doi:10.3726/978-3-0351-0013-6

Hammick, J. K., & Lee, M. J. (2014). Do shy people feel less communication apprehension online? The effects of virtual reality on the relationship between personality characteristics and communication outcomes. *Computers in Human Behavior, 33*, 302–310. doi:10.1016/j.chb.2013.01.046

Hancock, A. B., & Rubin, B. A. (2015). Influence of communication partner's gender on language. *Journal of Language and Social Psychology, 34*(1), 46–64. doi:10.1177/0261927X14533197

Hartmann, T., & Klimmt, C. (2006). Gender and computer games: Exploring females' dislikes. *Journal of Computer-Mediated Communication, 11*(4), 2. doi:10.1111/j.1083-6101.2006.00301.x

Herring, S. C. (2010). Who's got the floor in computer-mediated conversation? Edelsky's gender patterns revisited. *Language@Internet, 7*, article 8. Retrieved April 9, 2013, from http://www.languageatinternet. org/articles/2010/2857

Hew, K. F., & Cheung, W. S. (2010). Use of three-dimensional (3-D) immersive virtual worlds in K-12 and higher education settings: A review of the research. *British Journal of Educational Technology, 41*(1), 33–55. doi:10.1111/j.1467-8535.2008.00900.x

Hirschman, L. (1994). Female-male differences in conversational interaction. *Language in Society, 23*(3), 427–442. doi:10.1017/S0047404500018054

Holmes, J. (2006). *Gendered talk at work: Constructing gender identity through workplace discourse*. Malden, MA: Blackwell. doi:10.1002/9780470754863

Holmes, J., & Schnurr, S. (2006). 'Doing femininity' at work: More than just relational practice. *Journal of Sociolinguistics*, *10*(1), 31–51. doi:10.1111/j.1360-6441.2006.00316.x

Inman, C., Wright, V. H., & Hartman, J. A. (2010). Use of SL in K-12 and higher education: A review of research. *Journal of Interactive Online Learning*, *9*(1), 44–63.

Jarmon, L., Traphagan, T., Mayrath, M., & Trivedi, A. (2009). Virtual world teaching, experiential learning, and assessment: An interdisciplinary communication course in SL. *Computer Education*, *53*(1), 169–182. doi:10.1016/j.compedu.2009.01.010

Jauregi, K., & Canto, S. (2012). Enhancing meaningful oral interaction in Second Life. *Procedia: Social and Behavioral Sciences*, *34*, 111–115. doi:10.1016/j.sbspro.2012.02.023

Kim, S. H., Lee, J., & Thomas, M. K. (2012). Between purpose and method: A review of educational research on 3D virtual worlds. *Journal of Virtual Worlds Research*, *5*(1), 1–18. doi:10.4101/jvwr.v5i1.2151

Kollock, P., Blumstein, P., & Schwartz, P. (1985). Sex and power in interaction: Conversational privileges and duties. *American Sociological Review*, *50*(1), 34–46. doi:10.2307/2095338

Ladegaard, H. (2011). 'Doing power' at work: Responding to male and female management styles in a global business corporation. *Journal of Pragmatics*, *43*(1), 4–19. doi:10.1016/j.pragma.2010.09.006

Lin, T.-J., Wang, S.-Y., Grant, S., Chein, C.-L., & Lan, Y.-J. (2014). Task-based teaching approach of Chinese as a foreign language in Second Life through teachers' perspectives. *Procedia Technology*, *13*, 16–22. doi:10.1016/j.protcy.2014.02.004

Lin, Y., Dowell, N., Godfrey, A., Choi, H., & Brooks, C. (2019). Modeling gender dynamics in intra and interpersonal interactions during online collaborative learning. *LAK19. Proceedings of the 9th International Conference on Learning Analytics & Knowledge*, 431-435. 10.1145/3303772.3303837

Longo, D. (2012). Learning a Second Language in a learning community "Second Life": Critical issues and possible developments. *Conference proceedings international conference ICT for language learning 5th conference edition*. Florence: Pixel.

Mayrath, M. C., Traphagan, T., Heikes, E. J., & Trivedi, A. (2009). Instructional design best practices for SL: A case study from a college-level English course. *Interactive Learning Environments*, *19*(2), 125–142. doi:10.1080/10494820802602568

Melchor-Couto, S. (2017). Foreign language anxiety levels in Second Life oral interaction. *ReCALL*, *29*(1), 99–119. doi:10.1017/S0958344016000185

Melchor-Couto, S. (2018). Virtual World Anonymity and Foreign Language Oral Interaction. *ReCALL*, *30*(02), 232–249. doi:10.1017/S0958344017000398

Molka-Danielsen, J., Panichi, L., & Deutschmann, M. (2010). Reward models for active language learning in 3D virtual worlds. In Y. Peng, G, Kou, F. I. S. Ko, Y. Zeng, & K. D. Kwack (Eds.), *Information sciences and interaction sciences: The 3rd international conference on information sciences and interaction sciences* (pp. 97-109). Chengdu.

O'Barr, W. M., & Atkins, B. K. (1980). "Women's Language" or "Powerless Language"? In S. McConell-Ginet, R. Borker, & N. Furman (Eds.), *Women and language in literature and society* (pp. 93–110). New York: Praeger.

Otto, S. K., & Pusack, J. P. (2009). Computer-assisted language learning authoring issues. *Modern Language Journal*, *93*(1), 784–801. doi:10.1111/j.1540-4781.2009.00973.x

Panichi, L. (2012). Virtual Worlds: An opportunity for thinking about learning. In: S. Czepielewski (Ed.), *Learning a language in virtual worlds: A review of innovation and ICT in language teaching methodology, International conference, Warsaw, 17th November 2011* (pp. 25-32). Warsaw: Warsaw Academy of Computer Science, Management and Administration.

Panichi, L., & Deutschmann, M. (2012). Language learning in virtual worlds: Research issues and methods. In M. Dooly & R. O'Dowd (Eds.), *Researching online foreign language interaction and exchange: Theories, methods and challenges* (pp. 207–234). Bern: Peter Lang.

Panichi, L. J. (2015). *Participation in language learning in virtual worlds: An exploratory case-study of a business English course* (Unpublished PhD thesis). University of Hull. Retrieved from https://hydra.hull.ac.uk/resources/hull:11583

Reinders, H., & Wattana, S. (2015). Affect and willingness to communicate in digital game-based learning. *ReCALL*, *27*(1), 38–57. doi:10.1017/S0958344014000226

Sadler, R. (2012). *Virtual worlds for language learning: From theory to practice*. Bern: Peter Lang.

Scheelf, E. (2008). Gender and academic discourse: Global restrictions and local possibilities. *Language in Society*, *38*(4), 515–538.

SLED list – SL Educators. (n.d.). Retrieved June 6, 2012, from https://lists.secondlife.com/cgi-bin/mailman/listinfo/educators

Sullivan, F. R., Kapur, M., Madden, S., & Shipe, S. (2015). Exploring the Role of 'Gendered' Discourse Styles in Online Science Discussions. *International Journal of Science Education*, *37*(3), 484–504. doi:10.1080/09500693.2014.994113

Sunderland, J. (1998). Girls being quiet: A problem for foreign language classrooms? *Language Teaching Research*, *2*(1), 48–62. doi:10.1177/136216889800200104

Sunderland, J. (2000). New understandings of gender and language classroom research: Texts, teacher talk and student talk. *Language Teaching Research*, *4*(2), 149–173. doi:10.1177/136216880000400204

Sunderland, J. (2004). Classroom interaction, gender, and foreign language learning. In B. Norton & K. Toohey (Eds.), Critical pedagogies and language learning (pp. 222-241). Cambridge. doi:10.1017/CBO9781139524834.012

ten Have, P. (1991). Talk and institution: A reconsideration of the 'asymmetry' of doctor-patient interaction. In D. Boden & D. H. Zimmerman (Eds.), *Talk and social Structure: Studies in ethnomethodology and conversation analysis* (pp. 138–163). Cambridge, UK: Polity Press.

Toyoda, E., & Harrison, R. (2002). Categorization of text chat communication between learners and native speakers of Japanese. *Language Learning & Technology*, *6*(1), 82–99.

Vygotsky, L. S. (1978). *Mind in society: The development of higher psychological process*. Cambridge, MA: Harvard University Press.

Wang, A. (2017). *Learning English in a Multi-User Virtual Environment : Exploring Factors Affecting Participation (PhD dissertation)*. Sundsvall: Mid Sweden University. Retrieved from http://urn.kb.se/resolve?urn=urn:nbn:se:miun:diva-30795

Wang, A. (2017). Using Second Life in an English Course: How does the technology affect participation? *International Journal of Computer-Assisted Language Learning and Teaching*, *7*(1), 66–85. doi:10.4018/IJCALLT.2017010105

Wang, C. X., Song, H., Stone, D. E., & Yan, Q. (2009). Integrating SL into an EFL program in China: Research collaboration across the continents. *TechTrends*, *53*(6), 14–19. doi:10.100711528-009-0337-z

Wang, C. X., Song, H., Xia, F., & Yan, Q. (2009). Integrating SL into an EFL program: Students' perspectives. *Journal of Educational Technology Development and Exchange*, *2*(1), 1–16. doi:10.18785/jetde.0201.01

Warschauer, M. (1997). Computer-mediated collaborative learning: Theory and practice. *Modern Language Journal*, *81*(4), 470–481. doi:10.1111/j.1540-4781.1997.tb05514.x

Warschauer, M., & Liaw, M. L. (2010). *Emerging technologies in adult literacy and language education*. Washington, DC: National Institute for Literacy. doi:10.1037/e529982011-001

Wehner, A. K., Gump, A. W., & Downey, S. (2011). The effects of Second Life on the motivation of undergraduate students learning a foreign language. *Computer Assisted Language Learning*, *24*(3), 277–289. doi:10.1080/09588221.2010.551757

West, C., & Zimmerman, D. H. (1983). Small insults: A study of interruptions in conversations between unacquainted persons. In B. Thorne, & N. Henley (Eds.), Language, Gender, and Society (pp. 102-117). Rowley: Newbury House.

Wigham, C. R. (2012). *The interplay between non-verbal and verbal interaction in synthetic worlds which supports verbal participation and production in a foreign language* (Unpublished PhD thesis). Université Blaise Pascal - Clermont-Ferrand II. Retrieved from https://halshs.archives-ouvertes.fr/tel-01077857/document

Wigham, C. R., & Chanier, T. (2013). A study of verbal and nonverbal communication in Second Life – the ARCHI21 experience. *ReCALL*, *25*(1), 63–84. doi:10.1017/S0958344012000250

Wigham, C. R., Panichi, L., Nocchi, S., & Sadler, R. (2018). Interactions for language learning in and around virtual worlds. *ReCALL*, *30*(2), 153–160. doi:10.1017/S0958344018000022

Woken, M. D., & Swales, J. (1989). Expertise and authority in native-non-native conversations: The need for a variable account. In S. Gass, C. Madden, D. Preston, & L. Selinker (Eds.), *Variation in second language acquisition: Discourse and pragmatics* (pp. 211–227). Clevedon, UK: Multilingual Matters.

Zheng, D., & Newgarden, K. (2012). Rethinking language learning: Virtual worlds as a catalyst for change. *International Journal of Learning and Media*, *3*(2), 13–36. doi:10.1162/ijlm_a_00067

Zuengler, J. (1989). Performance variation in NS-NNS interactions: Ethnolinguistic difference or discourse domain? In S. Gass, C. Madden, D. Preston, & L. Selinker (Eds.), *Variation in second language acquisition: Discourse and pragmatics* (pp. 218–235). Clevedon, UK: Multilingual Matters.

KEY TERMS AND DEFINITIONS

Collaboration: The process of two or more people working together to complete a task or achieve a goal.

Floor Space: Or "floor apportionment" is the proportional amount of time each conversational partner gets in a conversation.

Network: A group with common interests that fosters the exchange of information and ideas. A task using "networking design" taps in on such networks for the purpose of collaborative learning.

Oral Interaction: The use of the target language in its spoken form in meaningful exchanges with conversational partners. It involves language production, but also active listening.

Power: A relative relationship where one person can be seen as having more, less or equal power compared another. Initially often based on formal roles, positions or conventions. A teacher, for example, possesses more power than a student in a conversation due to his/her formal role.

Second Life: A free, open, 3D virtual world where users act and move using avatars, and where they can create, connect, and chat with others using voice and text chat.

Turn Length: The measurable length of a "turn." Turn-taking characterizes the organization in a conversation whereby each participant speaks one at a time in alternating turns.

Utterance Functions: In this study, the functions of utterances in a conversation based on three categories: conversational management, support, and content contributions.

This research was previously published in Emerging Technologies in Virtual Learning Environments; pages 67-94, copyright year 2019 by Information Science Reference (an imprint of IGI Global).

Index

L

M

U

V

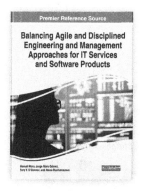

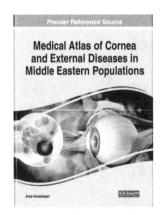
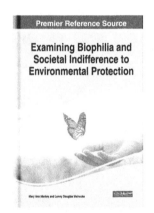
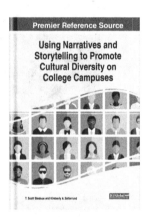

Printed in the United States
by Baker & Taylor Publisher Services